Provenance

Historic Voice Pedagogy Viewed Through a Contemporary Lens

By

Stephen F. Austin

Articles appearing in this book are reprinted from the *Journal of Singing* with the kind permission of the National Association of Teachers of Singing (NATS).

ISBN: 978-0-9905073-7-6

Inside View Press
676 Founders Ridge Drive
Gahanna, OH 43230

www.voxped.com

Contents

Introduction

Originally published in the *Journal of Singing*, volume 60, no. 3, 2004

I like old things. I live in an old house in an old neighborhood. My house is full of old furniture. The house is much better built than the new ones across the highway. The golden oak furniture is sturdy and beautiful. The finish glows like an ember, even after a century of use. The most prized antiques are those that have a story attached to them: the bedspread that belonged to my great-great-grandmother made on a hand loom in the 1860s (with a "psychedelic" geometric pattern that looks like it is from the 1960s), the child's rocker with a woven cane seat that belonged to my wife's great-grand-mother—given to her when she was six years old for her birthday in 1863.There is an old pie safe that came out of a ranch house in east Texas, made with pine that was felled right there on the farm—you can see the crude marks of a horse-powered circular saw on the back. This is provenance—a history, a connection to the past.

I have often commented that voice teachers are among the few professionals who can practice without a thorough knowledge of the history of their craft. Mathematicians cannot contribute anything to mathematics without learning what has already been done in the previous two thousand years or more. Physicists must know the work of ancient great minds in order to build upon previously acquired knowledge. Explaining why the apple falls off the tree has already been done. But how would they know unless they invest themselves in the historical literature that has defined he world they live in?

I trust my point is clear. Do you remember the first voice lesson that you had to give to someone who was a different voice type than your own? Be honest; it was somewhat terrifying! As students, most of us were too busy learning to sing to learn how to teach. The ladies were too busy learning to sing high notes to worry about teaching the male passaggio. We men were too busy ironing out the passaggio to consider how to teach a woman to fill out her hollow middle voice. But we learn. We pick up a few pointers from our colleagues, attend a few workshops, read the Journal of Singing. Some of us may spend sometime in the library reading a few volumes of the dusty pedagogy books that seem to stretch on for miles. But, often because of the antiquated language and a lack of a clear understanding of vocal function, these "historical gems" on voice teaching leave us scratching our heads and wondering why we bothered.

However, I believe that there is much to be gained from looking to our past. It is said that any culture that does not appreciate its own history is doomed to failure. Important lessons may be learned from those who have gone before us, things to remember to do and things that shouldn't be done. It is toward an appreciation of our legacy of pedagogical thought and practice that I hope to make a modest contribution.

Two other columns in my remembrance have appeared in the publication that sought to keep our past in the present. Burton Coffin authored "Vocal Pedagogy Classics," which appeared between 1981 and 1984. In each issue, he reviewed pedagogical texts that he felt were worth remembering. From 1993 to 1997, we enjoyed another wonderful column, *Practica Musicae*, by Craig Timberlake. I treasure these articles and refer to them often.

My goal is to examine ideas about teaching; tenets, if you will, of the traditions of teaching as I have come to know them from my own experience, from reading rather extensively from forgotten old books, and from my perspective as a voice teacher and a voice scientist. I am fascinated to see how good teaching and good science support each other. Truth doesn't change over time. Neither do effective teaching methods. Even as styles have changed, the voice functions as it always has. Methods and ideas that were developed out of successful experience in any age have something to say to us today. The provenance of pedagogical thought is interesting and useful, like that old china cabinet that sat in my grandmother's house when I was a child and now sits in mine. The voices of my ancestors speak to me through my family heirlooms. The voices of great voice teachers from the past speak to me in their own words, and I gain from their experience. Provenance: a connection to our past.

Stephen F. Austin

1. *Chi non lega, non canta.* (He who does not join his notes, cannot sing[1])

Originally published in the *Journal of Singing*, volume 60, no. 3, 2004

Say the word *portamento* and the first thing that may come to mind is a vocal gesture that we hear singers use in Puccini and Verdi and not in Mozart or Rossini, a sort of a sliding between notes (especially after a high one at the end of an aria). Most of us recognize a well-performed *portamento* as an absolute must in order to sing nineteenth-century opera in a stylistically accurate fashion. We also appreciate how difficult it can be to teach our students to perform one in the right way. There is nothing worse than a poorly executed *portamento*.

However, a look back into our pedagogical legacy offers a new appreciation for the *portamento*. As suggested by the Italian phrase quoted above, this vocal gesture has enjoyed special consideration in the past as an essential tool for vocal development. It is clear that many early writers believed that without *portamento* the singer could not learn to sing well. A chronological view of *portamento* as a vocal exercise might begin with Pier Francesco Tosi's *Opinioni de'cantori antiche e moderni* (1723), where he said the following:

> Thereupon he should teach him the art of slurring from one note to another and of dragging the voice smoothly in a pleasant manner on the vowels, while proceeding from high to low. Because these skills, so important to elegance in singing, cannot be taught merely by solmizing,[2] they are often utterly neglected by the inexperienced teacher.[3]

He went on to say that without a good *portamento* in the voice, "all other diligence falls short."[4]

Another great teaching master of the eighteenth century, Giambattista Mancini, agreed that *portamento* was an important skill and defined it thus:

> By this *portamento* of the voice is meant nothing but a passing, tying the voice, from one note to the next with perfect proportion and union, as much in ascending as descending.[5]

Like Tosi, Mancini felt that this was a foundational exercise and should be taught immediately after the full voice has been established.

> ...he ought to have him pass to the study of the *portamento* of the voice, and instruct him well therein, this being one of the principle parts of vocal singing.[6]

Why did these early masters give the *portamento* such emphasis? Manuel Garcia II gave one reason when he suggested that "the *portamento* will help to equalize the registers, the timbres, and the force of the voice."[7] His famous pupil, baritone Julius Stockhausen, said in his own teaching manual: "In the larger intervals the question of registers has to be considered. There is all the more reason not to pass it over, as the *portamento* itself ends to blend the registers."[8] He goes on to say, "it is only by the *portamento* that the singer gets his breathing and voice apparatus under full control."[9]

How is *portamento* performed? Garcia gives very clear instructions when he proposed that the air pressure from the lungs was to remain "equal and continuous" and that there are "gradual changes of tension of the lips of the glottis."[10] Stockhausen cautions that the vowel must remain stable throughout the whole extent, no matter how wide the interval, and that "the *portamento* must not degenerate into an anticipation . . . the pitch of the second note must only be heard at the beginning of the target pitch."[11]

In light of the central position that the establishment of *portamento* enjoyed in the teaching process in ages gone by, it is difficult to understand why many more contemporary sources fail to discuss *portamento* in terms of its importance in a sound pedagogical approach. There are remnants of it in the appreciation of a legato in the voice. However, I agree with Will Crutchfield when he said, "*Portamento*, properly understood, is the basis of legato singing, and as such it is close to the basis of the entire tradition of opera vocalism."[12] In a two part series Crutchfield made the case for *portamento* from several perspectives. He presented clear evidence that it was indeed used in Mozart's time and that the modern abhorrence of *portamento* in Mozart and Rossini is not supportable. He claims it is a part of an attempt to unromanticize Classical Period opera, a movement that developed only since WWII. He also proposed that the decline in singing in this century is due in part to the absence of the benefit that is gained from training voices to sing with a continuous connection between the breath and the voice.

Although it is difficult to find emphasis on the *portamento* in more contemporary writings, it can be found under another name. William Vennard's "yawn sigh" is a close equivalent. He defines it this way: "A vocalise for relaxation, consisting of a *portamento* from quasi-falsetto tone to a lower tone in full voice."[13] His description of the exercise harks back to what Stockhausen said concerning the registration issue:

> What is desired is a light, clear, "heady" voice, the heaviness of which can be increased at will as the pitch descends, in other *words it is an exercise in dynamic registration*.[14]

It is clear in Vennard's discussion of the "yawn-sigh" that it is useful in coordinating the vocal registers. It is helpful to understand the underlying mechanism that explains why certain exercises are helpful. To appreciate the benefit of the *portamento* is quite easy. The ability of a singer to move from pitch to pitch (either adjacent tones in a scale or wider intervals) in a smooth, connected voice is the result of a dynamic exchange of tension between the cricothyroid muscle (the pitch agent) and the vocalis muscle (the register agent).[15] A common model for registration includes the concept of two mechanisms, heavy and light. The goal is to go from low to high, high to low with a smooth, constantly changing balance between these two qualities. The result is an even scale with breadth, freedom, and ring: *chiaroscuro* on every pitch. Without specific work on establishing the *portamento*, singers tend to slightly rearticulate on every pitch. They stop and then start the voice on every note. In my personal experience this is so common that I would say it is the norm. It is rare when I am interviewing a new student that he or she can sing a simple five note scale with fluidity and ease, with an underlying *portamento*. If you listen very carefully, many singers will sing "ha-ha-ha-ha-ha" on a simple five note scale. It may be subtle, but it is there. When singers lack the ability to move smoothly between pitches, they are robbing themselves of the full potential of their instrument. When pitch change happens smoothly without interference to the breath support, the voice has a much better chance of reaching its full potential. This is why *portamento* was considered so crucial to our voice-teaching ancestors and why we should include study of portamento as a part of every lesson.

The good news is that it is quite easy to teach. I usually begin with open fifths in the comfortable part of the range. Most students have to be encouraged to sing "sloppy," literally sliding between the two tones equally with no hint of "stair stepping." It sounds easy to do, but many have difficulty discovering it at first. After the open fifths have been established, add the third for a simple *arpeggio*, slowly at first. A five-note scale then can be attempted, being careful to maintain the *portamento* between each adjacent pitch. With a little patience, *portamento* becomes legato. An old idea becomes useful again!

NOTES

1. William Shakespeare, *The Art of Singing* (Boston: Oliver Ditson Company, 1898), 29.
2. A system of designating scale degrees with syllables.
3. Johann Friedrich Agricola, *Introduction to the Art of Singing*, edited and translated by Julianne C. Baird (Cambridge and New York: Cambridge University Press, 1995), 86. This work is a translation of and commentary on Pierfrancesco Tosi's *Opinioni de' cantori antiche e moderni* (1723), first published in German as *Anleitung zur Singkunst* (Berlin, 1757).
4. Ibid, 223.
5. Giambattista Mancini, *Practical Reflections on the Art of Singing*, translated and edited by Edward Foreman (Champaign, IL: Pro Musica Press, 1967), 40. Originally published as *Pensieri e reflessioni pratiche sopra il canto figurato* (Vienna, 1774; second edition 1777).
6. Ibid, 39.
7. Manuel Garcia, *Complete Treatise On the Art of Singing, Part 1*, translated and edited by Donald Paschke (New York: Da Capo Press, 1984), 55. Originally Published as *Nouveau Traité Sommaire sur l'Art du Chant* (Genève: Minkoff Éditeur, 1847).
8. Julius Stockhausen, *A Method of Singing*, translated by Sophie Löwe (London: Novello, 1884), 43. Originally published as *Julius Stockhausens Gesangs-methode* (Leipzig: Peters, 1884).
9. Ibid, 37.
10. Garcia, 62.
11. Stockhausen, 39.
12. Will Crutchfield, "Crutchfield at Large," *Opera News* 56, no. 5 (November 1991): 66, and *Opera News* 56, no. 7 (December 1991): 54.
13. William Vennard, *Singing: The Mechanism and the Technic* (New York: Carl Fischer, 1967), 261.
14. Ibid, 211.
15. Minoru Hirano ascribed these functions to these two intrinsic laryngeal muscles as a result of a series of electromyographic studies. Minoru Hirano, "Vocal Mechanisms in Singing: Laryngological and Phoniatric Aspects," *Journal of Voice* 2, no. 1 (1988): 51–60.

2. Staccato

Originally published in the *Journal of Singing*, volume 60, no. 4, 2004

I introduced this column in the previous issue by examining the pedagogical importance of *portamento*. Evidence from several historical treatises on voice teaching was presented that suggested the study of *portamento* has been a fundamental building block of voice training in the past. It has been described as the primary means of establishing a true *legato*,[1] and it was considered to be an important tool in coordinating the disparate qualities of the vocal registers into a unified, even scale.[2] *Portamento* and *legato* are only two of several different types of vocalizations that have been described in the literature. In the next several installments of "Provenance," I will call attention to other types of laryngeal articulation as taught by gifted teachers, past and present.

Perhaps the most common vocalization after *legato* and *portamento* is *staccato*. This form of articulation is commonly found in vocal literature for all voices, but especially for the soprano. It is indicated by either a dot or a slash above or below the note. Its proper production is well defined in historical literature, since it was commonly taught as a foundational voice building exercise. Almost any pedagogy treatise from the nineteenth century and early twentieth century will have a section on *staccato*. In his *Complete Treatise on the Art of Singing*, Manuel Garcia described it thus:

> Staccato tones are formed by attacking the tones individually by a stroke of the glottis which detaches them from each other.[3]

The issue of Garcia's "stroke of the glottis" (*coup de la glotte*) will make an interesting subject for a future column, but it is clear that Garcia taught the *staccato* by focusing on the opening gesture of the vocal folds. The glottis is closed and phonation is initiated with a precise opening gesture produced as subglottal pressure exceeds glottal resistance. The famous nineteenth century baritone Julius Stockhausen, a student of Garcia, described it in this way in his practically unknown but brilliant treatise, *A Method of Singing*:

> In this style of vocalisation, the student should concentrate his attention chiefly on the activity of the larynx and the closing muscles.[4]

Contemporary sources offer support to these definitions. In his *Dictionary of Vocal Terminology*, Cornelius Reid combines the opening and the closing gesture in his definition and says that "it is the rapid reiteration of a precise opening and closing movement of the vocal folds."[5] Richard Miller says that "the goal is a clean approximation, and involves the principle of quick alternation between vocal fold adduction and abduction."[6] In *The Structure of Singing*, Miller goes on to quote the physician Friedrich Brodnitz as stating:

> In staccato singing a form of glottal stroke is used to produce the sharp interruptions of sound that characterize it. But in good staccato the glottal stroke which starts each note is well controlled and done with a minimum of pressure . . .[7]

Even with a slightly different focus on the opening or closing gesture or a combination of the two, there is a tremendous amount of agreement among sources that span more than a hundred and fifty years upon how *staccato* is produced. It should not escape our attention that *staccato* is described by all these sources (and many more) as a laryngeal event, requiring the action of the intrinsic laryngeal muscles to open and close the glottis very quickly and with little or no breath allowed to escape between notes. (*Staccato* is not to be confused with *aspiratto,* another vocalization where there is a slight, negligible puff of air emitted with each articulation. The *aspiratto* will be the subject of the next column).

There seems to be an appropriate involvement of the respiratory system for the proper execution of *staccato*. Emil Behnke suggested that a slight inspiration should precede every tone and that this additional element is as beneficial to the respiratory system as the opening and closing action is to the larynx.[8] Stockhausen also spoke of the importance of the support system.

> The action of the diaphragm, which is indispensable for the quick inspirations required for staccato, takes place almost automatically, as nobody can produce short detached notes without moving the muscles of the diaphragm; moreover, we practice them from our earliest childhood, in laughing and sobbing.[9]

It is obvious that *staccato* has been a central element of sound pedagogy for many years. Was this only because composers wrote it in their music and therefore singers needed to be able to sing it, or was there another reason for its prominence in voice building? The benefits of studying *staccato* were described by Garcia.

> Besides the ring which they give to a piece when they are used with taste, they tend to give some elasticity to sluggish throats.[10]

When the vocal folds close completely and suddenly, it results in a very salient, powerful acoustic signal. The energy in the upper harmonics is very high and our ears hear it as brilliant and "ringing." It apparently was used to keep the voice flexible and free as well. The mechanism must be free of unnecessary tension in order for the intrinsic muscles to be able to open and close the glottis so quickly. Others speak directly of the tremendous benefit that awaits the singer as the *staccato* is studied. Stockhausen said:

> Composers therefore generally assign the staccato to soprano voices, who often acquire by the study of this style of vocalisation an unexpected addition to their upper register. The whole technique also gains in precision and facility.[11]

Stockhausen goes on to make a rather compelling statement.

> Female students who have never practiced the staccato have no idea of the capabilities of their voice.[12]

There seems to be some confusion as to its manner of production, even considering the clarity with which the *staccato* is described in these and many other sources. I have often encountered singers (especially sopranos) who are under the impression that *staccato* is produced solely in the support system with no appreciation of the action of the larynx. The contents of the abdominal cavity and/or the thorax cannot be put into motion quickly enough to produce the correct effect due to the resistance (the mass) of the abdominal contents. The system is simply too sluggish to move quickly enough without involving the valving mechanism of the larynx.

I would venture to say that there are teachers who perform *staccato* correctly, but misinterpret what they observe in their own bodies. Each time the glottis closes for *staccato* it interrupts the airflow momentarily. The pressure behind the glottis builds up during this closed phase, and almost immediately a slight bulging may be observed in the abdominal area and/or the thorax. This is similar to the "water hammer effect" that you might have experienced in an old house. (Remember my penchant for old things.) You turn off the water in the kitchen sink and you hear this horrific banging in the walls. The water which was moving through the pipes has been stopped suddenly. Because it has mass and, therefore, momentum, it hits the barrier of the closed faucet and rebounds like a ball off a wall. The pressure wave bounces back and forth between the faucet and some limit at the other end until the energy is dissipated. This may be a part of the bounce at the epigastrium often observed during the correct production of *staccato*. In addition, the brief inhalatory gesture and the action of the diaphragm between each repetition also may result in an obvious "bounce" on the abdominal wall. It seems very complicated for something that is so easy to do correctly!

To teach *staccato* is a simple matter. I usually demonstrate a quick, energetic chuckle on a descending scale pattern, being careful not to sound too much like singing, but just laughing. I have students repeat it until they find the free uninhibited production that is so natural. I call their attention to the involvement of the larynx and make them realize that it is key to the process. I even will have them point to their throats to reinforce the locality of the gesture. (Yes, sometimes I get a little mechanistic.) A descending five-note scale in the midrange follows, but students need to make sure to keep each note very short with little or no aspirated air escaping before each note. When they have mastered this (usually after only a few short minutes), I will have them sing simple arpeggios 1-3-5-8-5-3-1, beginning in the middle voice and taking it higher than they think they can. I find it helpful to remind sopranos that they should tune the vowel as they go up and down the scale, dropping the jaw slightly as they ascend (I suggest that they "drop to the top"). This will help keep the vowel clear as a bell and help them keep the weight out of the sound. The next step is to repeat the pitch on the top, still *staccato*: 1-3-5-8-8-8-5-3-1.

When this is successful, I add a fourth note at the higher octave and sustain it for a couple of seconds, always insisting that the clarity of the attack is not compromised. Dullness may come back into the sustained tone at first, but with practice they can learn to maintain the brilliance that they have achieved from the *staccato* attack. The descending tones must be as short and crisp as they were on the ascent. The books that I have cited offer many wonderful exercises and vocalises for this study.

It is amazing to see what happens over a few weeks and months as singers learn to do this correctly. Stockhausen was right in his observation that a soprano will not have explored her full capacity until this gesture is studied well. The voice takes on new freedom and ring in the tone. The soprano literature really comes to life with this approach. The Queen's aria from *Die Zauberflöte* takes on the right energy and brilliance, as do the Doll's aria and Adele's laughing song— to name only a few.

I continue to gain tremendous insight from our pedagogical ancestors and colleagues. You can learn something about teaching voice by reading about it. *Staccato*, a wonderful tool that I discovered in a pile of old books!

NOTES

1. William Crutchfield, "Crutchfield at Large," *Opera News* 56, no. 5 (Nov. 1991): 66.
2. Julius Stockhausen, *A Method of Singing,* translated by Sophie Löwe (London: Novello, 1884), 43. Originally published as *Julius Stockhausens Gesangs-methode* (Leipzig: Peters, 1884).
3. Manuel Garcia, *Complete Treatise On the Art of Singing, Part 1,* translated and edited by Donald Paschke (New York: Da Capo Press, 1984), 60. Originally published as *Nouveau Traité Sommaire sur l'Art du Chant* (Genéve: Minkoff Éditeur, 1847).
4. Stockhausen, 119.
5. Cornelius Reid, *A Dictionary of Vocal Terminology* (New York: Joseph Patelson Music House, 1983), 352.
6. Richard Miller, *The Structure of Singing* (New York: Schirmer Books, 1986), 12.
7. Ibid.
8. Emil Behnke, and Charles Pierce, *Voice Training Exercises for Soprano* (London: Chappell & Co., 1884), Introduction.
9. Stockhausen, 119.
10. Garcia, 61.
11. Stockhausen, 43.
12. Ibid.

3. *Aspirato*: An Exception to the Rule

Originally published in the *Journal of Singing*, volume 60, no. 5, 2004

In these first few installments of "Provenance," I have been guiding us in a look back into our pedagogical past and examining the practice of training different laryngeal articulations as a part of voice building and as preparation for stylistic performance practice. So far we have looked at *portamento* and *legato*, the *staccato*, and now the *aspirato*. Garcia taught five distinctive articulations and included numerous exercises in his books for each of them (the fifth, *martellato* will be discussed in my next column). Many other authors from the nineteenth century discussed a similar list, although the difference between *aspirato* and *martellato* was not appreciated by all. In this brief discussion we will look at how our predecessors described the proper production of *aspirato* and at the specific musical situations in which this particular mode of articulation was used.

As suggested by the title of this article, the practice of *aspirato* was reserved for a specific musical situation. Garcia called it "an exceptional case, used only in rapid successions of notes repeated 'one time each'."[1] Julius Stockhausen reminded us that "the *legato* is the most important and most beautiful style of vocalisation,"[2] but also said:

> It is a fact, that by this aspirated vocalisation, great flexibility of the larynx, and distinctness of technique can be most surely and quickly acquired.[3]

The proper production of the *aspirato* is rather simple. Garcia described it this way:

> The means of performing these passages consists of a slight aspiration placed before the repetition of each tone. This aspiration emanates from the glottis which allows a small particle of unvoiced air to escape between the repeated tones.[4]

Please recall that this would only occur when a note is repeated only once, and not in any other case. Groups of repeated notes of three, four, or more would require a different articulation. The famous baritone and student of Garcia, Julius Stockhausen, described it succinctly as well:

> . . . the aspirated vocalisation, on the contrary, by the expulsion of a small particle of air, the vocal chink being momentarily opened to an infinitesimal extent, so as to allow the non-sounding air to pass; in a word, by a short 'h', the well-known *spiritus asper*, which forms the required attack for a new note, and necessitates a short interruption.[5]

Apparently this practice was either commonly misunderstood or misapplied, for we see both Garcia and Stockhausen cautioning their readers to avoid too much unused air being allowed to pass through the glottis when it was used appropriately. Stockhausen decried the practice of some teachers of his day who taught all vocalization, including simple scalewise passages, with the overuse of *aspirato* resulting in: ha, ha, ha, he, he, he, hi, hi, hi, etc.[6] Of course, this practice precludes any possibility of creating a legato line.

According to these two nineteenth century masters, the proper application of *aspirato* came in the specific situation of repeated notes, or *note raddoppiate* (doubled notes). Stockhausen said that in the case when two notes of the same pitch have to be distinctly repeated, it can only be achieved by an almost inaudible aspiration.[7] Stockhausen offered many specific musical examples in his book, *A Method of Singing*, including a familiar case of what was then "contemporary" music (Example 1). Stockhausen suggested that the notes marked with the "x" were to be rearticulated with an aspirated attack. He claimed that this was the only means of properly communicating the "joyous animation" of the recitative in Beethoven's Ninth Symphony.[8] He offered another familiar example in one of Donna Anna's arias from *Don Giovanni* (Example 2). Stockhausen suggested that the appropriate sorrowful expression in this aria would be well served with this vocal approach, and that it shouldn't be turned into a *bravura* passage.

Example 1. Beethoven, Symphony No. 9 in D Minor, IV, "Ode to Joy," mm. 1–4; 15–21.

Example 2. Mozart, *Don Giovanni,* "Non mi dir," mm. 68–76.

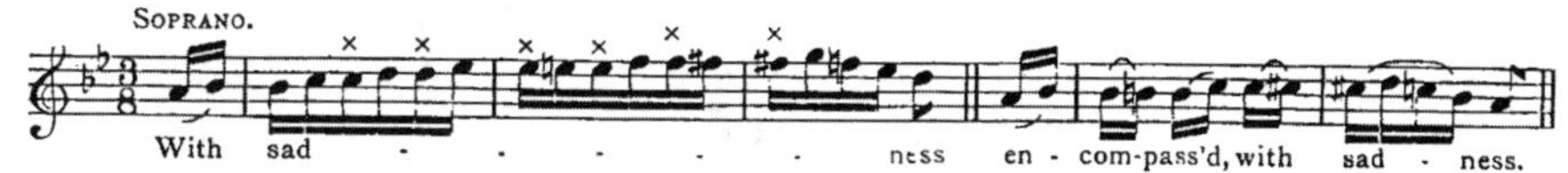

Example 3. Bach, *St. John's Passion,*
"Ich folge dir gleichfalls mit freudigen Schritten," mm. 61–64; 108–110.

There are many more specific musical examples in his book of how the *aspirato* was used to communicate the right emotion or feeling in a song or aria. Stockhausen offers this advice for the soprano in an example from Bach's *St. John's Passion* (Example 3). He suggested that after sounding the marked notes with an *aspirato,* they were to be cut short with a kind of sob. Everything was about expression! I highly recommend his book, *A Method of Singing,* as a valuable resource for performance practice.

The three primary sources that have been utilized for this discussion all include many exercises for practicing the *aspirato* as well as the other types of articulation. This skill was not left to those naturally endowed with flexible voices, but was carefully trained and its appropriate application discussed. Stockhausen included many exercise passages that combined the use of the *legato, staccato,* and the *aspirato* (Example 4).

In this example the *staccato* notes are indicated with a slash. The first note of the exercise would be a *staccato* attack followed by three notes sung *legato.* Since Stockhausen was a part of the Garcia school, the E_4 following the initial C_4 would have been initiated with an appropriately produced *coup de la glotte*. The second C_5, the repeated one at the top of the arpeggio, would be sung *aspirato* and the rest of the descending arpeggio sung *legato*. One can work through the rest of the exercise and apply the rules.

When recently performing the Christmas portion of *Messiah,* I used the occasion to integrate these suggestions in the tenor aria "Every Valley," applying the principles described here. The long melismas contain many repeated notes. As illustrated in Example 5, there is a final eighth note of one group tied to the first sixteenth note of the next group. The pattern repeats in an ascending fashion—a typical Handelian pattern. As a result of rearticulating the repeated note with a slight *aspirato,* rather than losing the impetus of the beginning of the next group by tying it over from the previous note group, the piece took on a new and invigorating crispness. One could argue about the stylistic choice perhaps, but it was interesting to observe the difference in the way my voice took on a more buoyant flexibility.

Later in the aria, the tenor is to leap from G#$_3$ to E_4 on eighth notes on the word "exalted," and then there is a repeated E_4 prior to the tied E_4. It makes sense that the second E_4 would be treated as *note raddoppiate* and rearticulated with an *aspirato*. It does not make musical sense to treat the tied E_4 (the third one) as a separate note, but as the second one carrying over into the downbeat of the second measure of this example. It is clear that Handel meant the strong rhythmic pulse to be felt on the fourth beat, not on the downbeat. Without the *aspirato* on the fourth beat it loses much vitality. I cannot appreciate how else it would be done in this particular situation, but as in all things the application of these principles depends upon taste and judgment (Example 6).

At the same time I was preparing it, I had a student who was singing his first *Messiah,* and he was approaching it with much trepidation. I showed him what I was experimenting with and he was able to utilize with great success. I did not find a specific example of using *aspirato* with *note raddoppiate* that had a tie to the second note, as we find in this particular aria, discussed by any of these authors. However, the musical situation meets all of the "typical" requirements and it did contribute to the feeling of exuberance and hope that the aria is supposed to convey. Of course, pedagogical practice and style are never universally agreed upon. Stockhausen acknowledged that even in his day many singers did not practice or know of the use of *aspirato* for the case of repeated notes. Carlo Bassini described the fact that there was disagreement among singing teachers at the time his book, *Art of Singing,* was first published in 1856. According to Bassini, a teacher named Crivelli warned his students to avoid the aspiration of repeated notes as promoted by Garcia. Bassini made his position clear, however, when he said that in his opinion, Garcia's method of aspirating repeated notes was the only practice worthy of consideration.[9] Most contemporary authors do not mention the practice at all. As a matter of fact, there is a dearth of discussion of laryngeal articulation in most of the methods written in the twentieth century. Perhaps this is one of the reasons that I have been so fascinated to discover the focus that our ancestors directed toward training the various types of articulation. As strange as it sounds, we seem to have forgotten the role of the larynx in singing. Support and resonance occupy so much of our attention. Of course, these are vitally important in any successful pedagogy, but let us not forget to train the larynx. Learning how to support does good only if the vocal folds are capable of dealing with the increased subglottal pressure that we learn to create. We must at the same time train the intrinsic muscles of the larynx to turn that additional pressure and air flow into sound. Specifically training the various types of articulation gives the larynx strength and flexibility: *portamento, legato, staccato,* and now *aspirato*. One very important type of articulation remaining to be discussed, *martellato,* will be the subject of my next opportunity.

Example 4. Stockhausen, *A Method of Singing*, Exercise 1.

Example 5. Handel, *Messiah*, "Every Valley," mm. 47–49.

Example 6. Handel, *Messiah*, "Every Valley," mm. 15–18.

NOTES

1. Manuel Garcia, *Complete Treatise On the Art of Singing, Part 1,* translated and edited by Donald Paschke (New York: Da Capo Press, 1984), 58. Originally published as *Nouveau Traité Sommaire sur l'Art du Chant* (Genève: Minkoff Éditeur, 1847).
2. Julius Stockhausen, *A Method of Singing,* translated by Sophie Löwe (London: Novello, 1884), 46. Originally published as *Julius Stockhausens Gesangs-methode* (Leipzig: Peters, 1884).
3. Stockhausen, 47.
4. Garcia, 142.
5. Stockhausen, 47.
6. Ibid, 46.
7. Ibid.
8. Ibid, 47.
9. Carlo Bassini, *Art of Singing* (Boston: Oliver Ditson & Co. 1884), 116

4. You say '*marcato*,' I say '*martellato*'

Originally published in the *Journal of Singing*, volume 61, number 1, 2004

It is evident from reading pedagogical treatises from the past that a great deal of time and effort was focused upon the acquisition of specific skills that a singer had to possess in order to perform the literature of the day. Garcia stated,

All these means or manners of uttering the passages, namely: *portamentos*; *marcatos*; ties; *staccatos*; while applying to them all the vowels and their timbres: pauses, *forte*, *pianissimo*, *fortissimo*, *piano*, inflections, *mezzoforte*, and their various combinations of these means, form the inexhaustible depth in which the singer finds the brilliant resources which give life to his performance.[1]

Following discussions of *portamento, legato, staccato,* and *aspirato* in previous columns, *marcato* remains. An initial difficulty in its consideration involves the term itself, hence the title of this piece. In his *Complete Treatise on the Art of Singing*, Garcia used the term *agilita martellata* parenthetically in the title of his discussion of "marked vocalization." Paschke used the term *marcato* in his translation of this work, as did Beata Garcia in her translation of Garcia's *Hints on Singing*. Other authors from the nineteenth century, including Garcia's own students, such as Julius Stockhausen, used the term *martellato* when they discussed the types of articulations that were to be mastered. The definition of the term and how and when it was to be applied also differed slightly from one source to the next, but it seems clear that they were talking about the same thing and the two terms are interchangeable.

An early reference to this term is found in Giambattista Mancini's *Practical Reflections on the Figurative Art of Singing*, translated by Pietro Buzzi in 1912.

> One of the most difficult styles is the *martellato* (hammered). This consists of repeating a tone many times, and of the four, the first must be a little higher than the other three, although they are all written upon the same line or space. This is very difficult to render perfectly, as it requires an extraordinarily agile voice, and great assiduity and perseverance to master it.[2]

Mancini also offers an illustration of *martellato* (Example 1).

Example 1. Mancini, from *Practical Reflections on the Figurative Art of Singing*.

The reader will agree that this looks very much like *staccato*, a view that is supported by Mancini's description of the skill necessary to perform it.

> Before undertaking this style, one must have gained perfect breath control, in order that one may break the tone and retake it without effort.[3]

> This sounds very similar to the practice of *staccato* discussed in a previous column. The fact that Mancini does not discuss *staccato* anywhere else in his book leads me to believe that this early use of the term changes as we move into the nineteenth century. He goes on to say that the style is "going out of use"[4] and lists the names of Faustina Haff and Agostino Fontana, both pupils of Antonio Pasi in Milan, as the last practitioners heard in that day (the book was published in 1774).

In the next century, Manuel Garcia defined the production of *agilita martellata.*

> To mark tones is to make them distinct by thrusting them, by supporting each of them separately without detaching them or stopping them. One will succeed in it by supposing that one has repeated the vowel as many times as there are notes in the passage, but without discontinuing the sound for breathing or anything else
> . . . At the same time, one will make a slight pressure with the stomach for each vowel; the pharynx will experience a slight dilation for each tone.[5]

Garcia suggested that the marked tones could help with the "emission of the voice," and help lower voices better define their vocalization. He suggested that it is a primary resource for coloring a passage.6 Garcia said that marked vocalization is indicated by dots and a tie (Example 2).

Example 2. Garcia, from *Complete Treatise on the Art of Singing, Part I.*

Julius Stockhausen seemed to agree that the *martellato* was related to the support mechanism.

> . . . the activity of the larynx has to remain constant both in legato and in martellato singing. It is therefore the respiratory organ which varies in its activities.[7]

He went on to describe that the "muscles of the diaphragm" provide a fresh support for each note, but without discontinuing the sound. It is tempting to believe that he either misunderstood the function of the diaphragm or meant that it would be acted upon by the abdominal musculature. He agreed with Garcia in that he felt that this type of articulation better suited male voices than female and that it would help them with rapid execution, and that it would invest the delivery with a very energetic expression.[8]

Stockhausen gave two different ways that *martellato* is indicated in a score. One is the same that Garcia offered, staccatos and a tie, and the other is with accent marks (>>>>), also with a tie. He gave as an example an excerpt from Mendelssohn's *Elijah* (Example 3). There is no source information or edition listed for the aria in Stockhausen's book. In comparing his excerpt to my own score of *Elijah,* I find that none of the articulation markings appear in the edition published by G. Schirmer, although at the beginning it says, *Allegro con fuoco e marcato*. Stockhausen gave several other illustrations, including one from Rossini's *Il Barbieri di Siviglia,* (Example 4). In comparing this excerpt to the same measures in more modern editions, I find that the G. Schirmer score (1962) and both of the anthologies (mezzo soprano and coloratura) published by G. Schirmer and edited by Robert Larson have only the ties with no *staccato* marks. It is no wonder that we no longer appreciate the difference in various articulations when they are no longer even indicated in the score!

Example 3. Mendelssohn, *Elijah,* "Is Not His Word like a Fire?," mm. 13–21, 57–67.

Example 4. Rossini, *Il barbieri di Siviglia,* "Una voce poco fa, " mm. 30–32.

These and several other sources that I examined from the nineteenth century include many exercises to train the proper execution of the *martellato*. They are often combined with other articulations within the same exercise to clarify the difference between them. Many provide specific examples in the literature as to their common usage.

SUMMARY

Pedagogic treatises in the nineteenth century were primarily focused upon voice building and skill acquisition, and they almost always included specific examples of how these skills were to be applied. Often they included introductory materials that dealt with some anatomy and physiology of the vocal mechanism, but the main focus was upon training specific skills that were required to perform the literature of the day. When thumbing through these books, one sees long series of exercises, often transposed by half-steps and filling many pages. It can be quite overwhelming and seem superfluous until one begins to look closely at the introductory remarks concerning the specifics of articulation and phrasing required for each pattern. This much material was not to have been rushed through in a year or two. The amount of material suggests a lengthy and rigorous training process. At about the turn of the previous century there seems to have been a shift in the way that voices were trained.

Cornelius Reid contends that Garcia and his invention of the laryngeal mirror marked the beginning of the end of a true bel canto tradition in voice training. It is a justifiable position in that interest in the mechanics of the function of the voice seems to have taken over by the turn of the twentieth century. At this time, we see physicians and scientists, and voice teachers under their influence, making theoretical rather than practical contributions to the pedagogical literature: Charles Lunn and Edmund Myers and their theories of inflated ventricles; Dr. Holbrook Curtis and his notions concerning the curative effects of nasal resonance; Ernest White and his "whirling eddies," claiming the voice is produced in the sinuses; Eugene Feuchtinger and the importance of training the strength of the tongue and the importance of the proper "groove"; the list could be considerably expanded.

Among several possible reasons that methods of voice training changed drastically in the last century or so is the fact that many of our young singers now are trained in academic environments. Developing young artists in academia presents certain challenges that were unknown a hundred years ago. In order to assure college and university administrators and colleagues that vocal study is an academically rigorous program, we have established as a measure of that rigor the acquisition of a rather extensive body of vocal literature during the typical degree. As many as sixty songs in at least four languages are to be studied and memorized during the normal undergraduate degree. Constraints of this requirement, especially in the early years of study and for those with serious technical work to do, allow little time to devote to the acquisition of vocal skill when there are six to eight songs and arias to teach every semester for the jury. We have only two years to build a singer who is qualified to be a voice major at the sophomore upper divisional exam— the terms are somewhat different around the country, but we all have this "barrier" exam. When most of the voices that we encounter in our studios have so far to go to even consider a singing career, I would like to think that there is a better way to bring them along in a timely fashion than teaching them songs that they put away and never sing again.

One may ask what there would be to teach during the course of the semester if the majority of the time was not spent coaching the required literature, a question that simply proves my point. We are so far away from the practice of voice building that many of us do not know where to begin. Of course, we can teach a lot about singing through the repertory, but to me this is a somewhat compromised position. We have to do it that way because it is the only way to function within our present system. Perhaps the private voice studio offers a greater potential for perpetuating the bel canto pedagogic paradigm. In comparison, our instrumental colleagues in higher education often have fewer required pieces for their students, particularly in the number of memorized pieces, and spend more time on skill building exercises—etudes, scales, and the like—that may indeed be heard by the jury at the end of the semester and evaluated. Why can we not do likewise?

We in academia have embraced a system that is fundamentally flawed and does not serve the majority of our students. The way we train voices is similar to training professional golfers by handing them a club and a ball, showing them the fairway and sending them out on the course to perfect their skill. After tens of thousands of golf swings, there may a few who are naturally gifted and would rise up out of the crowd and go on the tour. The rest would flounder. The unsuccessful ones are likely to put down the clubs and walk away from the game, forever frustrated at their inability to hit the ball in a straight line. Too many of our students end up in the sand trap and give up singing, frustrated at not being able to do what their gifted friends can do without ever practicing. Singing, like golf, should be a joyous experience. Given the right set of skills and patient, diligent instruction, all of our students should be lifelong musicians who reach their full potential and never forget how satisfying it is to be a singer, whether or not they ever make a single dollar doing so.

NOTES

1. Manuel Garcia, *Complete Treatise On the Art of Singing, Part 1,* translated and edited by Donald Paschke (New York: Da Capo Press, 1984), 111. Originally published as *Nouveau TraitéSommaire sur l'Art du Chant* (Genéve: Minkoff Éditeur), 1847.
2. Giambattista Mancini, *Practical Reflections on the Figurative Art of Singing*, translated by Pietro Buzzi (Boston: Gorham Press, 1912), 155. Originally published as *Pensieri e Riflessioni Pratiche Sopra il Canto Figurato* (Vienna, 1774).
3. Ibid., 156
4. Ibid.
5. Garcia, 58–59
6. Ibid., 59
7. Julius Stockhausen, *A Method of Singing,* translated by Sophie Löwe (London: Novello, 1884), 129. Originally published as *Julius Stockhausens Gesangs-methode* (Leipzig: Peters, 1884).
8. Ibid., 129

5. Register Unification-Give Me a Break!

Originally published in the *Journal of Singing*, volume 61, no. 2, 2004

It commonly has been appreciated by voice teachers and singers throughout the last several hundred years that the untrained voice exhibits several different qualities of sound when the entire extent of the pitch range is considered. Historically, a series of adjacent notes on a scale that have similar qualities has been described as belonging to a particular register. One finds no universal agreement upon how many different registers there are or what to call them, but if there is any consensus it is that the quality of notes in the lowest part of the range is typically different from those of the highest part of the range, at least in the voice of a beginner. Manuel Garcia ascribed the different qualities to a different mechanical action within the larynx itself.

> By the word register we understand a series of consecutive and homogeneous tones going from low to high, produced by the development of the same mechanical principle, and whose nature differs essentially from another series of tones equally consecutive and homogenous produced by another mechanical principle. All the tones belonging to the same register are consequently of the same nature, whatever may be the modification of timbre or of force to which one subjects them.[1]

Even this concise description has not been universally accepted, but it continues to provide a basis for discussion and examination of this rather complex subject.

Premier singers of any age have been noted for their ability to sing with an "even scale," that is, with a uniform timbre throughout the range. Composers of opera and art song expect a singer to be able to use the extremes of the singing range, and to do this, the singer must be able to access notes that span several registers. Therefore, the distinct qualities of the registers must be joined into a two to three octave range that all sound similar. This process has been called register unification.

METHODS OF REGISTER UNIFICATION

Several register unification methods can be found in the literature. In the twentieth century, most of them involve some sort of vowel modification or vowel migration technique. This approach perhaps would be best exemplified by the work of Berton Coffin.[2] Dr. Coffin developed a comprehensive system of vowel modifications as a singer traversed his or her singing range. The procedure is based on the interaction of formants (a resonance of the vocal tract) and partials (sound energy originating at the larynx). The notion is that by tuning formants to partials one can unify the scale by providing the ideal acoustic environment in the vocal tract. Many other proponents of this approach could be named.

Covering is another common register unification device, especially for the male voice. Vowel modification is a part of this method, but covering typically involves specific changes in the vocal tract at particular points in the range. A study by Dr. Ralph Appleman described this process using acoustic analysis and x-ray. Results suggested that in making the transition into the head voice, the larynx would lower and the vestibular space would increase. Results also suggested that the vocal folds would thicken as a part of the change of posture in the lower pharynx.[3] Many practitioners of this method have a particularly noticeable change of quality at the point of transition and many practice a specific pitch on the scale at which the tone must "go over." Covering does provide access to an extended range on the top, but sometimes with a noticeable "ahoogah" quality.

Register building and coordination is a third procedure for unifying registers. It is based upon the notion that the tonal quality associated with a register is the direct result of a particular adjustment of the intrinsic laryngeal muscles. This idea derives from the register definition developed by Garcia. Since each register is the result of a particular muscular adjustment, it should be possible to effect a change in the strength of a register and to coordinate the muscular activity into a unified scale by directed exercise. Proponents of this concept posit that in most voices there is an imbalance of muscular strength and coordination within the intrinsic muscles of the larynx and that this is the cause of the lack of uniformity throughout the scale. The teaching of Cornelius Reid is a well known example of this approach today.[4] When the registers have been sufficiently strengthened they can be coordinated so there is no sudden shift of dominance from one to the other. The result is the even scale.

THE BREAKING POINT

A very curious register unification device is found in many nineteenth century sources, beginning with Garcia. This was the practice of beginning a tone in one register and without stopping the airflow, allowing the tone to "flip" into an adjacent register. Register "breaking" depends upon the fact that the ranges of adjacent registers overlap and a large number of pitches can be sung with one of several laryngeal adjustments, or registers. In Garcia's method these were "first studies." Addressing the female voice, Garcia writes,

> When the chest voice has been well established (which should be done in a few days), the student must immediately work to blend that register with the next. Sometimes nature herself has undertaken that task, but voices thus favored are rare. This necessary study nearly always disheartens the student, but it is up to the teacher to direct capably and to take care of the voice which has been confided to him. One will practice by passing alternately from one register to the other on the tones D_4–F_4 without interruption and without aspirating in that passage between registers. This succession should take place on the same breath; it should be practiced seldom and performed slowly, firmly bringing out the passage, then the speed and the number of repetitions can be increased. At one time the student should begin with the chest register tone, at another with that of the falsetto. One must not be afraid of accentuating the kind of hiccup which occurs in the passage from one register to the other; only continued practice can first alleviate it, then make it disappear.[5]

This is advised for female and tenor voices. Garcia suggests that if the baritone and bass want to blend the two registers, then they should do it too, but a third lower (Example 1).

Example 1. Garcia register breaking exercise.

Charles Battaille shows the influence of his teacher, Garcia, when he prescribed the alternation of registers as well.

> In practice this returns us to the necessity of studying in principle the passage from one register to the other; from F_4 to G_4 for women and tenors, from E_4 to F_4 for baritones, because between these two points the muscular tension is moderated and the falsetto register has gained enough ring for it to be used with advantage. This brings us to the following exercise: the alternating and frequent repetition of the notes F_4 in chest and G_4 in falsetto for tenors and for women, E_4 to F_4 for baritones, producing these two sounds with the aid of a slow and regular expiration. Such movements allow the fascicles of the thryo-arytenoid to become accustomed to being stretched and relaxed with ease, speed, and dexterity.[6]

Here we see the scientist at work. Battaille performed extensive observations using the laryngoscope and posed theories that anticipated the work of Minoru Hirano and associate William Vennard, who in the 1970s described the role of the laryngeal muscles in registration.[7]

Another famous nineteenth century musician, *basso* Luigi LaBlache (1794–1858), described the same exercise in this way:

> The two registers of the male voice frequently afford unequal sounds, which would produce a very disagreeable effect, if the ability to unite them could not be attained by study. The highest tones of the chest are very strong, by the very effort which they require, while the first headtones are very soft and often feeble. Hence it is necessary to apply one's self to strengthening the latter, and softening the former. As our organs permit us to produce the extreme sounds of one register in the next register, the best means of uniting the two kinds of sounds, is to begin by making a single sound pass from the chest-register to the head-register, and vice versa.[8]

Carlo Bassini (1812–1870) was one of America's most popular voice pedagogues in the mid-nineteenth century. He recommended that after the chest and middle voices have been established they need to be united.

> The female voice may begin the task of joining the two registers by using first one and then the other on each of these notes: (C4–G4).Take fresh breath on each sound, until the difference between the two registers is perfectly well heard and understood; afterward, however, sing with the same breath the note twice over; first in the chest and then in the medium register but with great care to make as perceptible as possible the sort of hiccup between the notes, that marks the passage between the two registers when fresh breath is not taken . . . Care must also be taken not to lessen the force or intensity of the chest note, in order to give the medium note all the strength of which it is capable. One of these registers is always the weaker of the two, and the greater strength lies generally in the chest voice: in order to equalize the two, it would seem at first perhaps natural and proper to reduce the power of the stronger to a level with the weaker; but this is wrong; for experience has proved that such a proceeding would weaken the voice.[9]

Bassini includes many exercises for both male and female voices utilizing register breaking for the unification of the registers (Example 2).

Example 2. Bassini register breaking exercise.

I have included a number of extensive quotations here to make the point that this practice was broad and cannot be attributed entirely to the influence of Garcia alone. Many other eighteenth century pedagogues include register breaking in their books. In a fascinating dissertation on this topic, Lyle[10] listed a large number of pedagogues from the nineteenth century who utilized this technique, including the renowned German baritone Julius Stockhausen,[11] Heinrich Panofka,[12] Auguste Panseron,[13] the American George Frederick Root,[14] and the famous Australian Dame Nellie Melba.1[15]

It is difficult to find much twentieth century discussion concerning this practice. One notable exception is found in Richard Miller's *Training Tenor Voices.*

> In the late-teenage tenor voice, it sometimes seems that all attempts to enter upper voice in *voce piena in testa* (full legitimate "head voice") are unrewarding. In such cases, the young tenor should begin with a *falsetto* tone on a pitch that lies a few semitones below the *secondo passaggio,* in the *zona di passaggio,* and then pass from falsetto to legitimate voice on the same pitch.[16]

Miller goes on to say,

> Sometimes the falsetto/full exercises are equally useful above the *secondo passaggio* (G_4 for the lyric), and with some tenors may be extended with comfort up through Bb_4, B_4 and even C_5 (especially with lyric instruments).[17]

Miller cautions that these exercises are not in any way meant to bring the quality of the falsetto into the full voice, but are onset exercises. He states emphatically that the benefit of beginning the tones in falsetto is to "avoid any tendency toward pressed muscular onsets" (Example 3).[18]

Example 3. Miller register breaking exercise.

CONCLUSION

Register switching was a rather common practice for the unification of registers in the nineteenth century, and perhaps earlier.[19] From what is known about the physiology of vocal registers today, there is strong evidence that the register is defined by the state of contraction of the thyroarytenoid muscle (TA), the muscle that makes up the body of the vocal fold. When a tenor begins a tone in falsetto the TA muscle is passive. When he then breaks into the head voice, or the *voce completa*, the TA muscle is engaged, changing the shape of the vocal fold and therefore the quality of the tone. The pedagogical principle is that the TA will engage at a level that is appropriate for the pitch and intensity and will transform the falsetto into the legitimate head voice. This is an alternative to approaching the top always from below, where the tendency is to bring up excess activity of the lower mechanism and delay or prevent the freedom required to attain the operatic head voice. In the female voice the pedagogical notion is that by switching from chest to middle voice, the appropriate activity of the TA will carry over into the middle voice and eventually alleviate the hole in the middle voice.

I have used this process with both male and female voices for a number of years. For women it can be very useful in helping them find and establish their low mechanism. They begin in a very light, breathy mechanism (I call it falsetto) on /ɑ/ at E_4 or F_4 and then they drop a fifth below, letting it "break" into the chest voice. The low voice then can be strengthened and appropriately integrated into the rest of the instrument. This process has been helpful for a number of tenors whose range is too short due to excessive weight in the high voice. I have them sing descending intervals of a fifth or a third beginning at D_4. The initial tone is in falsetto. They then descend with a loud "hiccup" into the coordinated register on the pitch below. Transpose up by half steps so that the lower note is taken through the *passaggio* area. If they keep the vowel quality stable, a transformation of the registration will occur with a little practice and nurturing. I also have them repeat a pitch (perhaps F_4 to B_4) three times, the first two in a strong, supported falsetto. The third time I tell them to sing it in "something that isn't falsetto," but feels a lot like it. I use the term *mezzo falso* (from Anthony Frisell[20]) for this transitional quality. Given a little time and patience, the *mezzo falso* will be able to take on more weight from the low mechanism and bloom into the full operatic head voice. This also can be done without interruption of the tone as recommended by our nineteenth century sources.

The process of register breaking can be a bit disconcerting to the student at first, and might raise the eyebrows of folks walking by your studio door. But I would encourage you to go to some of the original sources identified here and read a little more detail about how to do it, and then try it. This method is "tried and true," a technique with "provenance" for unifying registers and building a beautiful voice that is even from top to bottom.

NOTES

1. Manuel Garcia II, *Memoire on the Human Voice*. Found in Donald V. Paschke, *A Complete Treatise on the Art of Singing: Part One.* (New York: Da Capo Press, 1984), xli.
2. Dr. Coffin's primary works in this area are *Sounds of Singing* (Metuchen, NJ: Scarecrow Press, 1987) and *Overtones of Bel Canto* (Metuchen, NJ: Scarecrow Press, 1980).
3. Ralph Appleman, "Radiological findings in the Study of Vocal Registers," ed. John Large, *Vocal Registers in Singing* (The Hague: Moujton, 1973), 59–92
4. Mr. Reid's singular contribution to this approach is presented in several important texts including: *Bel Canto, The Free Voice* (New York: Coleman Press, 1965), *Psyche and Soma* (New York: Joseph Patelson Music House, 1975), and *An Essay on the Nature of Singing* (Huntsville, TX: Recital Publications, 1992).
5. Manuel Garcia, *Complete Treatise On the Art of Singing, Part 1,* translated and edited by Donald Paschke (New York: Da Capo Press, 1984), 50–51. Originally published as *Nouveau Trait Sommaire sur l'Art du Chant* (Genève: Minkoff diteur, 1847).
6. Charles Battaille, *Physiology as Applied to the Study of the Vocal Mechanism,* in Richard Joiner, tr. and ed., *Pioneer in Vocal Science and the Teaching of Singing* (Lanham, MD: Scarecrow Press, 1998), 178. Originally published as *De la physiologie appliquée á l'étude de la mechanisme vocal* (Paris: Victor Masson and Sons, 1863). Charles Battaille (1822–1872) was a leading bass in France, a physician, and voice researcher.
7. Through the use of laryngeal electromyography, Hirano and his associates suggested that it is the activity of the thyroarytenoid muscle that determines the vocal register. M. Hirano, W. Vennard, and J. Ohala, "Regulation of Register, Pitch and Intensity of Voice," *Folio Phoniatrica* 22 (1970): 1–20.
8. Luigi LaBlache, *LaBlache's Complete Method of Singing* (Cincinnati: John Church Co., n.d.), 6.
9. Carlo Bassini, *Art of Singing* (New York: C. H. Ditson, 1884), 11.
10. John Christopher Lyle, "Register switching as a Pedagogical Device for Register Unification of the Singing Voice: An Historical Analysis" (Unpublished PhD dissertation, University of Oregon, 1995).
11. Julius Stockhausen, *A Method of Singing,* tr. Sophie Löwe (London: Novello, 1884). Originally published as *Julius Stockhausens Gesangs-methode* (Leipzig: Peters, 1884).
12. Heinrich Panofka, *The Art of Singing* (New York: G. Schirmer, 1900).
13. Auguste Panseron, *Method of Vocalization for Soprano and Tenor* (New York: G. Schirmer, 1898).
14. George Frederick Root, *Introductory Lessons in Voice Culture and in the Principles of Execution* (Philadelphia: Theodore Presser, 1901).
15. Nellie Melba, *The Melba Method* (Melbourne: Chappell and Co. Ltd., 1926).
16. Richard Miller, *Training Tenor Voices* (New York: Schirmer Books, 1993), 60–61.
17. Ibid., 63.
18. Ibid.
19. Lyle makes a very interesting case that this practice was common in the nineteenth century among many teachers because it was common practice in the eighteenth century as well.
20. Anthony Frisell, *The Tenor Voice* (Boston: Bruce Humphries, 1964).

6. "Like the squawk of a capon"—the tenor *do di petto*

Originally published in the *Journal of Singing*, volume 61, no. 3, 2005

It was my privilege to moderate a preconvention workshop on training the male high voice this past summer prior to the opening of our national convention in New Orleans. Special guests included Dale Moore of Indiana University and Karen Peeler of The Ohio State University. After some opening remarks by me, each of the three of us worked with two talented young men in front of a wonderful audience of almost two hundred attendees. The purpose of the workshop was to offer different perspectives on training the male high voice. It was a great opportunity to share ideas with the audience and to exchange ideas among those in attendance. There was ample opportunity for questions and comments—a really wonderful learning experience for all of us. I opened the meeting with a brief historical perspective about how the performance of the male high voice as we know it today came to be and a little about the pedagogy that surrounded the development of it. This is a familiar story to many of us, but I got such a positive response from those in attendance, I thought I would include that information here.

In his popular method book of the mid-nineteenth century, *Bassini's Art of Singing* (1856), Carlo Bassini wrote:

> . . . for, if a singer should present himself at the opera in Paris and fail to give the renowned chest C in the "Huguenots" or "William Tell," though singing never so well otherwise he would gain but few admirers and be quite certain of producing but little effect.[1]

By the middle of the nineteenth century, the tenor was expected to produce the top of his voice much like what we know today, sometimes referred to as the "full operatic head voice."

It had not always been so. Just a few years earlier the accepted approach to the male high voice was quite different, at least in some parts of Europe, and Paris in particular. The change in expectation came like a lightning bolt in 1837 with the tenor Gilbert-Louis Duprez (1806–1896) at the Opéra in Paris. It was during a performance of Rossini's *Guillaume Tell* that Duprez was singing the secondary role of Arnoldo. In the fourth act of the opera there is a an extended *stretta* with the chorus following the aria "Asile héréditaire" where the tenor must twice ascend to a high C (Example 1, shown here with Italian text). Duprez sang the high C (C_5) in what was described as the full "chest voice," now known as the *do di petto*, a first for the Parisian audience. It caused quite a reaction by those in attendance, many of whom were thrilled while others were outraged by what they considered to be an uncultured and ghastly scream. Rossini himself found it very disagreeable and said that it "sounded like the squawk of a capon whose throat is being cut"[2] (see Figure 1). This criticism notwithstanding, soon the Parisian audience would have nothing else and life for the tenor since has never been the same.

Example 1. Rossini, *Guillaume Tell,* “Asile héréditaire,” Act IV, scene ii, mm. 188–195.

Figure 1. A contemporary caricature of Gilbert-Louis Duprez.

To fully appreciate the drama of what Duprez did that night, we need to understand what had gone on before. What do we know about the pre-Duprez tenors and how they sang? The English writer and critic Henry Chorley (1808–1872), in his book *Music and Manners in France and Germany* had little good to say of the French singers of the day.

> A gallery of French tenor singers would not be the least edifying chamber in the Pantheon of Art. Few traces would be there found, it is true, of the well-toned and well-cultivated voices, which distinguished the great men of the Italian opera. That they sung through their noses, is as certain as that the Parisian opera songstresses terrified Dr. Burney and Horace Walpole, by their energetic screaming. Many of them, too, were afflicted with that diseased tendency towards a *falsetto*, which, in our own country, has run the inordinate length of pushing innocent, portly, middle-aged gentlemen into warbling (more oddly to the eye than agreeably to the ear) the sublimest songs of Handel's "Messiah."[3]

Chorley displayed a critic's temperament in his comments upon the French style of singing, but it is note-worthy that he suggested that the practice in France was different than what was commonly accepted in Italy. However, Paris was an important operatic center at the time and what was being done there had wide-ranging influence.

Perhaps the best representative of the prevailing vocal technique in Paris during this transitional moment in time was the French tenor Adolphe Nourrit (see Figure 2).[4] Nourrit reigned as the *primo uomo* in Paris for many years (1826–1837), having begun his career as the successor to his father, Louis Nourrit (1780–1831), the leading tenor at the Opéra until 1823. Nourrit was well known and respected as an eloquent singer and an intensely effective actor, very refined in his taste and delivery. He premiered many operas of Meyerbeer and Rossini and created the role of Éléazar in *La Juive* by Halévy. Pleasants states,

> Other tenors may have created more roles, although it is doubtful. No other has created a comparable number of roles so substantial and so enduring. Indeed, until Verdi and Wagner came along, it could be said that Nourrit, virtually singlehanded, had made a repertoire for the dramatic tenor. And singers of so recent memory as Caruso and Martinelli could thank Nourrit for Éléazar, in which each of them found one of his most congenial roles.[5]

It is interesting that Nourrit was recognized as having helped define the genre of the dramatic tenor when it is clear that his vocalization would in no way be characterized as such today.

> Nourrit was an agreeable, strong and expressive voice, capable of a brilliant, though not full-voiced, high C and resourcefully employed in diminuendo, *voix mixte*, *voix de tête* and falsetto.[6]

The characterization of Nourrit as a dramatic tenor must be considered in light of many other factors, not just the weight of the voice at the top. Opera was in transition. It had not been too many years since the castrati dominated the stage. Along with their decline went the training schools that produced singers with incredible skill in the florid style (the names of Farinelli, Pacchierotti, and Caffarelli come to mind). A more dramatic style of singing was emerging with natural voices in the leading roles and the tenor taking a much more dominant position. There was far greater emphasis upon the drama on the stage, demanding a higher level of realism in the acting from the singers.[7] It is for this that Nourrit was so highly acclaimed and that he earned the title of "dramatic tenor."

Figure 2. Adolphe Nourrit (1802–1839).

Duprez was a Frenchman who, after a somewhat mediocre beginning of a career in his homeland, had gone to Italy to study. After several years of considerable success there, it was natural that his countrymen would want to have him back to Paris to sing. This was a great concern to Nourrit, and for good reason. Duprez was hired to replace Nourrit as Arnold in *Guillaume Tell*. Duprez brought something totally different to this opera, a work that was very familiar to the Parisian audience at this time. Duprez's success was remarkable and he soon replaced Nourrit as the tenor making all the news.

Nourrit was despondent over the loss of his position in Paris and determined that he would go to Italy and learn this new technique.

> Possibly in his less gloomy moments, he believed that his day was not yet over; that he had still energy to recompose himself anew; that he would, in short, have a chest voice in place of his own nasal and brilliant *falsetto di testa* and learn that honeyed and long-drawn *cantabile* which his countrymen were beginning to praise as an indispensable treasure.[8]

Indeed, Nourrit did go to Italy and had some success at changing his technique. He had some modest performing success there too, but disliked what he had to give up in order to sing the heavier mechanism in the top. The more physical, less refined approach that was necessary to achieve that goal offended his aesthetics and artistic ideals. In the end it was too much for him, and in 1839 he threw himself from his balcony in Naples.

There is one other singer who must be mentioned. The tenor Dominico Donzelli was described by Pleasants as being the first of the dramatic tenors (see Figure 3). He was well known for the title role Rossini's opera *Otello*.

> He had one of the most mellifluous robust low tenor voices ever heard—a voice which had never by practice been made sufficiently flexible to execute Signor Rossini's operas as they were written, but who, even in this respect, was accomplished and finished if compared with the violent

persons who have succeeded him. . . The volume of Donzelli's rich and sonorous voice was real, not forced.[9]

Figure 3. Domenico Donzelli (1790–1873).

Pleasants also quotes the critic of the *Allgemeine Musikalische Zeitung* as saying this of Donzelli's Otello in 1823:

> He has a beautiful, mellifluous tenor with which he attacks the high A in full chest voice, without once resorting to falsetto, while Signor David rejoices in this higher voice and, on this occasion, once ascended to high F (above high C).

This is a much earlier reference to a tenor singing the high voice in a chest related registration compared to the more typical falsetto of the great tenor David in a performance that took place in Vienna. There can be no doubt about the common practice of using the falsetto in the male high voice in Paris and other major musical centers at the time. However, there were singers like Donzelli and later Duprez who were using a different approach.

> Donzelli was active during the period Duprez was in Italy re-training himself from lyric tenor to heroic tenor, and doubtless Duprez studied his technique closely. . .This is the origin, whether Donzelli or Duprez is responsible, for "covering" the high notes in the male voice.[10]

What was it that Donzelli and Duprez learned to do in Italy that wasn't being taught in France? It is interesting to note that by this time teaching at the Paris Conservatory had been under Italian management for many years. Bernardo Mengozzi (1758–1800) was a well-known singer and composer who taught voice at the conservatory. He along with several other contributors developed a comprehensive voice teaching method, *Méthode de chant du Conservatoire de Musique,* that was initially published in 1803 and served as the basis for all teaching at the conservatory for many years afterward. The method was based upon the teaching of the famous castrato and teacher Antonio Bernacchi with whom Mengozzi studied. Composer and singing teacher Alexis de Garaudé (1779–1852) taught at the conservatory from 1816 until his retirement in 1841. He was a student of another famous castrato, soprano Girolamo Crescintini (1762– 1846). Garaudé reworked Mengozzi's method and published it in 1809 as *Methode complete de chant*. This served as the pedagogical basis for teaching at the conservatory for many years. Another Italian, Luigi Cherubini, was the director of the conservatory from 1822–1842.

It is interesting to realize that even though the conservatory was staffed with Italians who taught the "Italian method," the general practice for the male high voice (at least for the tenor) was to sing in falsetto. It is also interesting to observe that the *Méthode* in both its versions (Mengozzi and Garaudé) relied heavily upon the teaching of two famous castrati. It is difficult to comprehend how this penchant for singing in falsetto came to be favored over a well-integrated registration event leading to the high voice. The castrati apparently did not resort to falsetto for the high voice, although with their altered physiology and in the absence of any contemporary models from which to make evaluations, it is difficult to discuss their practice in some sense. However, if the reader is familiar with Mancini's *Practical Reflections on the Art of Singing,* it is clear that the goal set forth by this singer-turned-teacher was to unify the chest and the falsetto registers to produce the head voice. As the castrati taught "normal" males, the difference in application of those principles could have resulted in the use of a reinforced falsetto, but this is pure speculation.

Needless to say, there must have been another approach practiced and taught in Italy at the time. Donzelli studied in Italy and had a very successful career before going to Paris. He learned to sing his A_4 in the chest register in Italy. Duprez and then Nourrit acquired this new method in Italy as well. In *The Great Singers,* Henry Pleasants describes a conscious effort on the part of Duprez to bring about a change in his singing in order to meet the demands of singing the role of Arnoldo as an emergency replacement for the tenor Pisaroni. He knew that his usual technique would not be satisfactory in this large piece with a big orchestra. Earlier in his career he is said to have had a very modest endowment when it came to the size of his voice. Pleasants says, "one had to be seated in the prompter's box to hear him."[11] He goes on to quote Duprez himself.

> It required the concentration of every resource of will power and physical strength. "So be it," I said to myself, "it may be the end of me, but somehow I'll do it." And so I found even the high C which was later to bring me so much success in Paris.[12]

It is clear that even though this famous story of Duprez's impact singing the *do di petto* for the first time is set in Paris, he had performed it first in Italy. It is perhaps due to the parallel story of poor Nourrit that we are so familiar with this story.

Duprez's new approach to the high voice did not come without a price. It is reported that his career was very short after he began to sing the full voice to the top. Many criticized his brutish vocal approach as well as his dealings with the public and others in the artistic community. Berlioz was not a fan. Pleasants quotes an excerpt from the *Memoirs* of Berlioz.

> "Duprez was very good in any violent scene, but his voice had already ceased to lend itself to soft airs, long-drawn notes, a calm, dreamy music. For instance, in the air 'Sur les monts les plus sauvages,' he could not sustain the high G at the end of the phrase 'Je chanterais gaîment'; and instead of holding the note for three bars as he should have done, held it for only a moment, and thus destroyed the effect."[13]

This performance took place in 1838, only one year after his stunning appearance at the Opéra. However, Pandora's box was now opened and nothing could put things back. Singing for the tenor and high male voice was changed forever.

This is a very interesting story of how singing changed on the operatic stage near the beginning of the nineteenth century. It was a time of transition from one style of music, drama, and singing to something quite different. In my next column I will offer my best understanding of how these events affected pedagogical thought and practice.

NOTES

1. Carlo Bassini, *Art of Singing* (New York: C. H. Ditson, 1884), 1.
2. Henry Pleasants, *The Great Singers* (New York: Simon and Schuster, 1966), 167.
3. Henry Chorley, *Music and Manners in France and Germany* (New York: Da Capo, 1984; originally published in London: Longman, Brown, Green, and Longmans, 1844), 138–9.
4. He was one of the most famous students of Manuel Garcia, father to the well known voice teacher, Manuel Garcia II, and two very famous singers Maria Malibran and Pauline Viardot. Garcia was a famous tenor in his own right and creator of the role of the Count in Rossini's *Il barbieri di Siviglia.*
5. Pleasants, 162.
6. Ibid.
7. Edward Foreman, *Authentic Singing: Being the History and Practice of the Art of Singing and Teaching in Two Volumes*, Vol. 1 (Minneapolis: Pro Musica Press, 2001), 99.
8. Chorley, 74.
9. Ibid.
10. Foreman, 99.
11. Pleasants, 166.
12. Ibid.
13. Ibid.

7. The *voce chiusa*

Originally published in the *Journal of Singing*, volume 61, no. 4, 2005

In my last column, I recounted what is commonly understood to be the story of a change of vocal style that took place in Paris in 1837. The tenor Gilbert Duprez appeared in the role of Arnoldo in the opera *Guillaume Tell* by Rossini and introduced to the Parisian audiences a different approach to the high voice, the *do di petto*, or the high C (C_5) performed in "the chest voice." The reaction of the Parisian audience was mixed at first and was met with shock and disdain by many, but soon it became the only acceptable means of singing above the male *passaggio*. It is difficult to recreate sounds from reading memoirs and criticism, so we will never know for sure what was being done by other tenors at the time before Duprez; but we have criticism by Chorley, Berlioz, and others that describe the *falsetto* dominated tones of other singers in Paris at the time.

I am very grateful for a communique by Evan Walker, who called my attention to his article on Adolphe Nourrit which appears in the *New Grove*. He describes a man who was suffering from severe liver problems as a result of acute alcoholism or hepatitis, and it was his physical condition rather than his disappointment over having been replaced by Duprez as the *primo uomo* at the Paris Opera that led to his suicide in Italy. Walker makes the case that Nourrit's approach was not significantly different from Duprez's, and he sang the high voice much like what we expect to hear today. He bases this opinion upon a review of the roles that were being written for and premiered by Nourrit. He contends that someone who was singing the high voice in *falsetto* would not have been singing the difficult literature that constituted his repertory. I appreciate Dr. Walker's argument, but note that he neglects to include any reports or criticisms of Nourrit's singing by those who heard these performances. Many of those quotes were included in my last article.

One thing is certain: Duprez brought something different to Paris that caused a fundamental shift in performance practice at the Paris Opera. It seems unlikely that Duprez would have generated this kind of response if his approach to the high voice was not substantially different from that which was being done by Nourrit and others. Since there are not many options for the male voice on a high C, I am drawn to the conclusion that Nourrit was a *falsettist* and Duprez introduced to the Parisians a full "operatic head voice" that is much more akin to what we expect today than that to which the Paris audience was accustomed.

Soon after Duprez's debut in June of 1840, a report was made to the French Académie des Sciences by two French biologists, Diday and Petrequin. They described the new timbre and the laryngeal posture as practiced by Duprez, which they called the *voix sombrée ou couverte* (dark and covered voice). The fact that the singing of the new tenor at the opera house warranted a scientific report before a government agency gives credence to the notion that his approach was something quite new and remarkable. A few months later a new teacher at the Paris Conservatory by the name of Manuel Garcia II made his own report to the Académie describing the same phenomenon, and claimed that he had been teaching this new technique since 1832. Garcia went on to describe in much greater detail the effect of laryngeal posture, the vocal registers, and the two vocal timbres he called the *voix sombrée* and the *voix claire*. These and other concepts were included in Garcia's *Complete Treatise on the Art of Singing* first published in 1847.[1] Garcia is the first source that specifically teaches the low larynx and *voix sombrée*. He was also the first teacher to separate the contribution of registers and timbre. He proposed that the fundamental registers of the voice were the "chest" and the "falsetto-head" and that the singer had two fundamental qualities or timbres, the *voix claire* (also known as the *voce aperta* or open voice) and the *voix sombrée* (the *voce chiusa* or closed voice). The timbres and the registers could be combined in several ways. One could sing any register in either the open or the closed quality, but Garcia recommended the closed quality as the primary timbre to be used and, most importantly, that it was the result of maintaining the lowered laryngeal posture.

The pedagogy of the low larynx and the vocal timbres became common themes in pedagogical treatises from the nineteenth century, as we will see from some of the important literature from the past.

Julius Stockhausen (1826–1906) was one of the most celebrated baritones in the middle of the nineteenth century. He was a renowned operatic baritone as well as a respected oratorio and recital singer. He did a great deal to popularize the music of Schubert and Schumann in much of Europe. Johannes Brahms wrote his *Magelone Lieder* for him as well as the baritone solos in his *Requiem*. He was also a conductor and teacher. On the subject of the laryngeal posture, Stockhausen was unequivocal in his *Gesangsmethode*.

> The dangerous tendency of the larynx to rise to the position it takes in speaking must be carefully avoided.[2]

He further states,

> . . . it is only with a fixed position of the larynx, and with the right use of the two chief qualities of sound, that a beautiful, well-rounded whole can be produced.[3]

The Italian baritone Enrico Delle Sedie (1822–1907) was known for having sung Germont, Renato, and Figaro at Covent Garden and La Scala. He taught at the Paris Conservatory beginning in 1867 and was the author of seven volumes on training the voice, including his four-volume *Esthetics of the Art of Singing*. He held views similar to those of Stockhausen and Garcia concerning the position of the larynx.

> The soft palate rises in a direction opposite to that of the larynx, following the same regular order of gradations; viz.: it rises with the height of sound, whilst the larynx, for giving to the voice a homogenous and easy tone should descend in the same order.[4]

He described what happens when this advice is not heeded.

> When the larynx is so raised we may emit high sounds, but thin and shrill. It is true that we are disposed to raise the larynx when we want to emit high sounds, but if we would closely observe the timbre, we would recognize that they are thin, contracted and shrill.[5]

Apparently, like today, many must have disagreed with this thinking and Delle Sedie showed signs of weariness over the arguments.

> I will not extend myself too much on a subject so often disputed, but will limit myself to expose the practical use of my theory.[6]

Charles Amable Battaille (1822– 1872) was a French *basso profundo* and a student of Garcia who also taught at the Paris Conservatory and conducted extensive experiments on phonation using the laryngeal mirror. He reported his findings in *Nouvelles recherches sur la phonation* (1861), the first of a planned multivolume work. On the subject of laryngeal posture he posed,

> Moderate lowering of the larynx has the certain result of giving the voice suppleness and power, thereby encouraging the enlargement of its natural limits.[7]

He also offered a historical perspective.

> This procedure, familiar to the great Italian School, has been given the term *somber voice*, and it has been associated with vocal emission. Duprez "naturalized" this term in France during his operatic debuts, but the expression had already been in use in Italy for some time.[8]

Stockhausen and Battaille were both students of Garcia, so some agreement in philosophy shouldn't be surprising. However, other authors without such close connections to Garcia's legacy promoted similar ideas. Edmund Meyer (1846–1934) was a well-known teacher and a prolific author. In his book *The Renaissance of Vocal Art*, he said,

> For artistic tone, the soft palate must be high, the larynx must be low, and the throat and mouth allowed to form, not made or compelled . . . The larynx must be low in adjustment for the production of beautiful tone, but it must never be locally adjusted.[9]

Meyer identified a common point of contention. Many teachers then, as now, were opposed to any sort of localized effort or to directing the attention to the function of a part of the mechanism. This is evidenced in the fact that there arose two opposing schools, the "local effort school" and the "no effort school." The latter arose as a direct reaction against the mechanistic methods of Garcia. The goal seemed to be the same, but the methods differed considerably. No better example of this can be found than the sentiments expressed by D.A. Clippinger (1860–1938) who decried the "lowered larynx" as an abomination but gave as his first exercises to develop the male head voice descending scale passages using /o/ and /u/; both vowels defined by the larynx in a low position when pronounced properly.[10]

The famous teacher G. B. Lamperti (1830–1910) was the son of Francesco Lamperti, a famous teacher in his own right. William Earl Brown, a longtime student and protégé, recorded Lamperti's thoughts in his book *Vocal Wisdom*. Here are some of Lamperti's dictums and sayings as recorded by Mr. Brown:

> "Covered tone" is a misleading term. "Closed tone" should take its place.[11]

> In their inception all tones are dark to be opened or closed at will.[12]

> All tones are closed until opened.[13]

> Although you may acquire a wide range of voice, you cannot modulate the sounds until the resonance of your tones becomes round and rich, *chiaroscuro*.[14]

The guiding principle expressed by Lamperti was that there was a balance of color or timbre that was to be established and maintained. The closed quality of the vowel was at the center of the ideal. The source of the closed quality was defined by Lamperti to Brown during one of his own lessons with the master.

> One must sing all exercises with an open throat—then the voice develops by itself. If you sing exercises with a dark (covered) tone, the voice cannot develop as it should. Later on, one can sing all tones (dark and light) with an open throat. If you begin studying the voice with dark tones only, it will be difficult to sing clear (light) ones.[15]

Lamperti is expressing the legitimate caution that the open throat and closed timbre are not to be misunderstood. Note his caution in the use of the word "covered" as opposed to "closed." The *chiaroscuro* is a balance of color, and the balancing quality of the brightness should not be neglected.

Many more contemporary sources may be cited in support of this pedagogical practice, but Richard Miller put it succinctly.

> There can be little doubt that in desirable "closed voice" (*voce chiusa*), a timbre that should prevail throughout the singing voice regardless of range, as opposed to "open voice" (*voce aperta*), there is a stabilized laryngeal position—relatively low—and a somewhat widened pharynx. These conditions together with proper vowel modification (*aggiustamento*) produce the so-called "covered sound" of the upper range.[16]

Summary and Application

The practice of maintaining a lower than neutral laryngeal posture provided the means for taking the qualities of the low mechanism above the natural limits of the "chest voice." This practice apparently began in Italy in the early nineteenth century and was introduced to Paris by the tenor Gilbert Duprez in 1837 with his historic performance in Rossini's *Guillaume Tell*. The impact was remarkable and prompted a report by the biologists Diday and Petrequin before the Académie des Sciences in 1840. Within a few months the new teacher at the Paris Conservatory, Manuel Garcia, appeared before the same group and presented his ideas concerning vocal registers and the two timbres of the voice, the *voix sombrée* (sombre timbre or *voce chiusa*) and the *voix blanche* (clear timbre or *voce aperta*), with the former being the preferred tonal quality. It is clear from the descriptions offered by both Diday and Petrequin and Garcia that the source of the desired timbre is the lowered laryngeal posture, known as the "open throat." A proper balance of the open throat with appropriate vowel color has been described as *chiaroscuro*.

The practice of the open throat has been promoted by many voice teachers during the nineteenth and twentieth centuries, as evidenced by selected pedagogical writings that have been presented. Even when there were objections or concerns about focusing directly on the lowered laryngeal posture, similar results were sought via indirect methods including timbral goals and specific vowel suggestions that encourage the lowered laryngeal posture.

From my own teaching experience, it would be difficult to name a single technical issue that has been the source of so much vocal difficulty as a habitually high larynx. I have encountered many students who have had years of vocal study but who are faltering in their ability to take the next step in their vocal journey, due in large part to limitations imposed by the fact that they have adopted a laryngeal posture that does not provide the proper environment for optimal singing. Difficulties can arise on several fronts. One of the most common is a misclassification of voice type. A young man whose "natural" vocal timbre is bright and light might be identified as a young tenor. As his study continues the high voice never comes in and he is not able to sing above F#$_4$ or G$_4$ and those pitches are open (*voce aperta*) and "yell-like." There may be an extended range at the bottom (with solid tones down to G$_2$ or A$_2$, beyond the typical tenor range), but the timbre belies the range. This young man (not hypothetical at all, as I have encountered this exact situation numerous times) is probably singing with a high laryngeal posture. Because the vocal tract is relatively short, the formant frequencies are high and the timbre takes on a characteristic tenor-like quality. The range of the voice is that of a baritone, but the habitual quality convinces the teacher that he must be a tenor with a short top. With retraining, the larynx can be taught to remain comfortably low and stable throughout the range. One of two things will happen. The true baritone quality of the voice will have a chance to come in with the establishment of the *voce chiusa*. The voice will take on the breadth and depth that were laying fallow with the inappropriate laryngeal posture. The chest voice can be integrated into the whole range and the yell at the top will be replaced by the appropriate high voice quality for the male voice with the appropriate "turn" at the top. The second possibility is that the voice is indeed a tenor. With the comfortably low larynx the young man would be able to access the top that has eluded him because the mechanism was not able to gain the high voice due to the instability of the mechanism. In either case, a positive step will have been achieved.

I also have worked with sopranos who struggle with the same issue. I recently began teaching a soprano who was experiencing great difficulty with her high voice. It is a sizeable instrument with a rich timbre, but she experienced great difficulty ascending into her high voice beginning at about F_5. Her voice would sometimes shut down above the top of the staff. We began our work by focusing on laryngeal posture and building her chest register. We retrained her laryngeal posture by working slow scales with /o/ and /u/ vowels, first in the low voice and gradually working our way up while carefully monitoring the timbre (which was intentionally exaggerated at first—very dark or "covered"). We used the "yawn-sigh" technique as described by Vennard, utilizing the body's natural reflex of lowering the larynx at the beginning of a yawn. After a breath is taken in through the mouth and the feeling of the inception of a yawn has taken place, the singer lets the air out (generously) on an audible sigh. Gradually more adduction can be engaged while the singer constantly monitors the laryngeal posture until a descending five note scale can be successfully executed in full voice. Descending is always easier than ascending and the descending scales should be well established before ascending scale work begins. I am not hesitant at all to have the singer monitor laryngeal position directly by observing it in the mirror or with palpation (light contact with the fingers). Sometimes there is no substitute for letting the student feel what the larynx is doing. When the timbre of the voice is changing due to the change of laryngeal position (sometimes quite drastically), singers may feel like they have difficulty in making judgments about their progress, or even to know if they are doing the right thing. With light contact of the fingertips they can gain valuable biofeedback and be sure that what they are doing is the right thing, or not. I know that many will react negatively to being that direct, but I am comfortable in guiding them through this so that they feel at ease with it. The question of how to teach someone to keep the larynx from rising with pitch is answered by "Any way you can"! To return to my soprano, after a few months (this work is often slow and painstaking) the top began to open up as the tension began to disappear. After two years, it is so much better, but still requires diligence. This habit dies hard and the work can be very frustrating to both teacher and student. Persistence pays off. After teaching the same lesson for a few months, it is tempting to begin to accept as passable that which is not; a desensitization to the issue can take place. This is where a dependence upon function rather than quality can serve both the student and teacher. It is important to listen carefully and understand the timbral result of less-than-optimal function. For this young lady, the problem didn't begin at F_5. Her entire range was produced with the *Knödel* (the high larynx), but caused no difficulty until she needed to sing above the top of the staff. At this point the larynx was under tremendous stress from being pulled up in the neck at the same time the demands of increasing the tension along the vocal folds for the high notes resulted in a collapse of the mechanism. No amount of resonance work or discussion of support methods would fix this problem.

Once you have identified the timbre of the *voce chiusa*, you will hear it in almost every elite singer; it is that quality that separates amateurs from professionals. Listen to Joan Sutherland, Nicolai Gedda, Richard Lewis, Martina Arroyo (insert your favorite singer here). It is that slightly darkened, burnished quality that is there all the time irrespective of changing pitch and vowel. It is absent in some very successful voices, particularly the character tenor. We need character tenors in the world, but I for one do not want to allow one of my students to do something that is inherently limiting in hopes that they could have a *comprimario* career unless they do so by choice, not because they have no options.

Scientific Support for the Comfortably Low Larynx

There is some fascinating new scientific work that seems to support the pedagogy of the low laryngeal posture. Dr. Ingo Titze showed us at our national convention this past summer how lowering the larynx increases the length of the epilaryngeal tube (the small air space defined by the aryepiglottic folds often called the "collar" of the larynx) and can increase something called "inertive reactance" in the vocal tract. He would say that doing so increases the maximum flow declination rate of the airflow pulse, and as a result we can gain significant energy in the upper partials, which contributes to the "ring" and brightness of the tone. Years ago we all learned from Johan Sundberg that the singer's formant is produced in the lower pharynx when the larynx is below resting level and the epilaryngeal tube becomes acoustically isolated from the pharyngeal space to give the voice a tremendous advantage in the acoustic environment of the orchestra hall. In yet another fine session at our national convention this summer, Dr. Ron Scherer shared the results of a study that he undertook with a voice teacher colleague in which they strove to identify what really accounted for significant improvements in the quality of voice when specific pedagogical ideas were incorporated. The teacher had little or no formal understanding of the anatomy or physiology of the singing voice. Videoendoscopy revealed that when he felt like he was singing with his optimum voice (a beautiful full baritone) the larynx had acquired a lower position in the neck, which was plainly seen in the video image. The particular pedagogical method practiced by this teacher never discussed the lowered laryngeal posture during singing, but focused on lower abdominal support and a feeling of placement in the cranium.

In Conclusion

This is a complex issue. There is room in the vocal world for voices that are brighter and darker all falling within a range of what we would describe as beautiful. However, in my opinion this is an issue that needs to be better understood. The habitually high larynx can be the source of a great deal of difficulty for a singer. It is not just about timbre or quality of sound: it is about freedom and being able to use all the assets of the instrument. The comfortably low larynx and the *voce chiusa* are a part of our historical legacy for the performance of art song and opera in the Western tradition. Confirmation of these techniques is coming from the voice science community, and when this happens it gets my attention. However, let us not lose sight of which came first. Singers have been doing it right for many years, and teachers have been leading their students to optimal function and beautiful singing for a long time. Many of them have left us a wonderful written legacy of their experience. I say again: we can learn something about teaching voice by reading a good book!

NOTES

1. Manuel Garcia, *Complete Treatise On the Art of Singing, Part 1*, translated and edited by Donald Paschke (New York: Da Capo Press, 1984), 50–51. Originally published as *Nouveau Traité Sommaire sur l' Art du Chant* (Genéve: Minkoff Éditeur, 1847).
2. Julius Stockhausen, *A Method of Singing*, translated by Sophie Löwe (London: Novello, 1884), 44. Originally published as *Julius Stockhausens Gesangsmethode* (Leipzig: Peters, 1884).
3. Ibid., 43
4. Enrico Delle Sedie, *Esthetics of the Art of Singing, Vol. II* (New York: G. Schirmer, 1885), 25.
5. Ibid., 22.
6. Ibid.
7. Charles Battaille, *Physiology as Applied to the Study of the Vocal Mechanism*, in Richard Joiner (trans., ed.), *Pioneer in Vocal Science and the Teaching of Singing* (Lanham, MD: Scarecrow Press, 1998), 174. Originally published as *De la physiologie appliquée á l'étude de la mechanisme vocal* (Paris: Victor Masson and Sons, 1863).
8. Ibid., 174.
9. Edmund Meyer, *The Renaissance of Vocal Art* (Boston: The Boston Music Company, G. Schirmer, 1902), 87.
10. D. A. Clippinger, *The Head Voice and Other Problems* (Boston: Oliver Ditson Company, 1922), 19.
11. William Brown, *Vocal Wisdom, Maxims of Giovanni Battista Lamperti* (New York: Taplinger Publishing Co., 1957), 37.
12. Ibid.
13. Ibid., 53.
14. Ibid., 38.
15. Ibid., 129.
16. Richard Miller, *The Structure of Singing* (New York: Schirmer Books, 1986), 151.

8. The Attack on the Coup de la Glotte

Originally published in the *Journal of Singing*, volume 61, no. 5, 2005

I don't recall exactly when I became a proponent of the "well-coordinated onset," but it must have been early in my undergraduate training. Perhaps it was in my voice pedagogy class while studying William Vennard's *Singing: the Mechanism and the Technic.*[1] Vennard promoted the idea of "imaginary h" as the ideal way to initiate a tone and warned against the dangers of the glottal plosive. He suggested that the *coup de la glotte* or "stroke of the glottis" as defined by nineteenth century voice teacher Manuel Garcia had been misinterpreted and fallen out of favor over the years.[2] He made a very convincing argument citing the benefits of airflow-induced glottal closure with the help of an aerodynamic principle called the Bernoulli Effect. As a result, I always have taught the well-coordinated onset as the ideal way to initiate a tone, starting with a real aspirate and working gradually to eliminate the excessive airflow until proper coordination was achieved.

I suppose changing one's mind about a pedagogical issue is similar to what happens when a child grows up in a family that supports a particular political party. As a youngster, you declare your allegiance to those same precepts, trusting your parents to have examined the issues and to have made the correct judgment. Perhaps later in life you reach a place far enough removed from familial influence that you examine those principles for yourself. Maybe you encounter someone who presents such a cogent argument for the other side that you are forced to consider your choice for the first time. That is exactly what happened to me when I read James Stark's book *Bel Canto: A History of Vocal Pedagogy*.[3] For the first time I was presented with the other side of the *coup de la glotte* issue. I was challenged to examine my prejudices about it and as a result of the evidence that he presented, I switched parties.

It is difficult not to simply restate Stark's arguments here. His chapter is much more thorough than I can be in these few paragraphs, but having acknowledged my appreciation for his contribution, I will present part of the other side of the argument using the words of those that have taught before us.

No one prior to Garcia wrote very specifically about how to initiate a tone. As in so many areas concerning voice production, Garcia was the first to try to describe in detail this aspect of voice production.

> Hold the body straight, quiet, upright on the two legs, removed from any point of support; open the mouth, not in the form of the oval 0, but by letting the lower jaw fall away from the upper by its own weight, the corners of the mouth drawn back slightly. This movement, which holds the lips softly pressed against the teeth, opens the mouth in the correct proportion and finds it an agreeable form. Hold the tongue relaxed and immobile (without lifting it either by its root or by its tip); finally, separate the base of the pillars and soften the entire throat. In this position, inhale slowly and for a long time. After you are thus prepared, and when the lungs are full of air, without stiffening either the phonator or any part of the body, but calmly and easily, attack the tones very distinctly with a light stroke of the glottis on a very clear [a] vowel. That [a] will be taken well at the bottom of the throat in order that no obstacle may be opposed to the emission of the sound. In these conditions the tone should come out with ring and with roundness.[4]

This was the beginning of a lifelong controversy for Garcia. For the next sixty years, he would defend this tenet of his method. Perhaps he could foretell the difficulties to come when he warned,

> One must guard against confusing the stroke of the glottis with the stroke of the chest (*coup de poitrine*), which resembles a cough, or the effort of expelling something which is obstructing the throat.[5]

By the last third of the nineteenth century, Garcia's critics were vehemently opposed to the technique. Many understood the *coup de la glotte* to be an excessively violent release of air from tightly adducted vocal folds that if practiced regularly would result in the ruination of the voice. In Garcia's last written work, *Hints on Singing*, he answered once again the question that had plagued him for so many years.

> Q. What do you mean by the stroke of the glottis?
> A. The neat articulation of the glottis that gives a precise and clean start to a sound.[6]

Apparently there was genuine cause for concern if the technique were abused. Critics spoke of ruined voices. However, according to Hermann Klein (a longtime student of Garcia and a well-known music critic), none of Garcia's own students ever had difficulty as a result of the *coup de la glotte*.[7] This is restated in a footnote written for the second edition of *Hints on Singing* by Klein.

> It is of the utmost importance that these observations should be studied and correctly understood. The meaning of the term "stroke of the glottis," which was invented by the author, has been seriously misrepresented, and its misuse has done a great deal of harm.[8]

The controversy played out in public forums and newspapers in a fashion that must have been similar to what we have observed in recent years over the low-carb diet craze. Author and critic George Bernard Shaw took many opportunities to lambaste Garcia.[9] Stark discussed several examples of public forums where Garcia's methods were criticized.[10] At one particular event, the popular artist and personality Victor Maurel offered exaggerated examples of the onset to a crowd and harshly criticized Garcia with him in the audience. Dr. Henry Holbrook Curtis, the famous New York physician and friend of tenor Jean de Reszke, decried the *coup de la glotte* as harmful and led a movement against its use.

> The shock, or *coup de glotte*, is death to the voice; it is born of ignorance, and to teach or allow its continuance is a crime.[11]

Having been personally attacked by Dr. Curtis and his disciples, Blanche Marchesi, famous singer and student of Garcia who was a highly respected teacher wrote,

> They could not distinguish between the hitting and closing of the glottis, and at once decided to condemn every method that allowed singers to make their vocal cords meet when emitting sounds.[12]

In one of his last attempts to answer the criticism, Garcia wrote to British voice teacher Charles Lunn who published this statement in his book, *Philosophy of Singing*.

> I do insist on the attack; but it must be the delicate, precise action of the glottis, not the brutal pushing of the breath that goes by that name, fit only to tear the glottis, not to rectify and regu-

> late its movements . . . (My merit or demerit consists in having noticed it and given it a name.) No one who starts the voice properly can eschew it.[13]

Mr. Lunn was in total agreement with Garcia as to the value of the *coup de la glotte*,[14] as is evident in this quote from his book, *Philosophy of Voice*:

> Now this, small though it be, is the one important principle of training that has been successful in results; by it great singers have been made; without it, many possessing all other requirements have failed, and it served its purpose before the introduction of the laryngoscope.[15]

What is there to gain?

Why did Garcia insist upon this point over his long career in the midst of so much virulent controversy? His position was that the brilliance of the vocal tone resulted from firm glottal closure.

> Various simultaneous causes can modify the timbres of the voice . . . according as the glottis narrows or partially opens, it produces ringing or lusterless tones.[16]

It was all about the quality of the sound. Remember that Garcia was the first to describe tone quality separate from timbre. The timbre of the tone was the result of the contribution of the vocal tract, but the basic quality came from the larynx. The way that the vocal folds approximated and specifically the way the vocal processes of the arytenoids came together during phonation determined the quality of the tone. After describing the dull quality of the breathy voice, he said,

> Consequently, it is necessary to conclude that the brilliance of the voice results from the firm closure of the glottis after each pulsation.[17]

Garcia taught for many years after his definition of the *coup de la glotte* first appeared. Scores of pedagogy books were written after his *Complete Treatise on the Art of Singing* was first published in 1847; many agreed with Garcia, including the great father and son Francesco and Giovanni Lamperti. In *The Art of Singing*, Francesco Lamperti wrote the following in his discussion of acquiring agility:

> Agility should be studied slowly. The example should be executed so that the intervals are clearly distinguishable. The breath should be held steady in the passage from one note to the other, and the notes should be produced clearly with a *shock of the glottis* [italics are mine]. By this means the pupil will acquire the power of taking the exact note without sliding up to it, a fault which a beginner is very likely to confound with legato.[18]

In the tradition of the Socratic style of question and answer format as we saw in Garcia's *Hints on Singing*, Lamperti further commented:

> Q. What is meant by the just emission of the voice?
> A. It means attacking a note, with the greatest possible clearness, with a pure and correct intonation, and sustaining it to the full extent of the breath.[19]

The words of the younger Lamperti were recorded by William Earle Brown in his book *Vocal Wisdom: Maxims of Giovanni Battista Lamperti*. Here are a couple of quotes concerning this issue:

> The vocal cords, in separating, start the glottis to pulsating on the desired pitch.[20]

> The energy to start a tone must come from the action of the vocal cords themselves, as they separate, not from the impact of the breath pushed against them.[21]

> Release the compressed breath to start your tone, do not push nor pull muscularly.[22]

The agreement among these giants of voice teaching in the nineteenth century on this issue is quite compelling. Austrian singer and teacher Ferdinand Sieber (and the composer of almost 700 *solfeggi*) put it this way:

> The singer should hold the breath at the moment when he intends to strike a tone, and close the glottis. By this means he will avoid a too voluminous exhalation (as the air is accumulated below the vocal chords [sic] and will flow out in smaller quantities) and, at the same time, gain a good attack of tone.[23]

What does "is" really mean?

Opposition to the *coup de la glotte* came from those who witnessed its misuse by practitioners (other than Garcia and his disciples) who exaggerated the gesture and abused voices with it. Equally unfair to Garcia are those that have redefined what he meant by it. This is apparent in a contemporary quote from Meribeth Bunch.

> The attack involves a precise coordination of the onset of sound, the oscillating movement and the opening and closing of the folds. The ideal attack is one in which the breath begins to flow gently and is followed by a precise momentary closure of the vocal folds which meets this stream of air. When correctly done, this attack is crisp, clear and without tension. The exact terminology relating to the attack is confusing. Garcia (1897) called it the "*coup de glotte*"; Vennard (1967) has called it the "imaginary aspirate."[24]

In no way can the *coup de la glotte* and the imaginary aspirate be the same thing. Bunch does not carry the blame for this; she is merely reiterating an error put forth by the physician/voice teacher team of Lennox Brown and Emile Behnke in 1904. After describing two alternate ways to begin the tone, they state:

> The vocal ligaments meet just at the very moment when the air strikes against them; they are, moreover, not pressed together more tightly than is necessary. No preliminary escape takes place . . . and no obstacle has to be overcome . . . but the attack is clear and decisive, and the tone consequently gets a proper start. The mechanism by which this is done is the "*coup de glotte*" or "shock of the glottis.[25]

Of course, what they described is exactly what Vennard defined as the "coordinated onset," not the *coup de la glotte*. One cannot read Garcia's own words and understand that he meant anything other than the fact that the vocal folds must be in full contact and momentarily resist the pressure built up in the trachea prior to the gentle plosive from the vocal folds as they release the pressure cleanly and neatly. How could this error in understanding what Garcia described and many others promoted have happened? Perhaps there has been felt a need to come to terms with Garcia's position, so these authors have redefined his argument rather than have to deal with the possibility that contemporary thinking on the matter is incorrect. Barbara Doscher puts it plainly: "The glottal plosive is destructive, however, and may lead to vocal nodules."[26]

This is a common position among voice professionals today. How could Garcia have really meant what he said? Since Garcia was by most accounts a successful and respected teacher, what he said cannot have been what he meant. But here it is in his own words:

> As a matter of fact, the two little lips which, in the larynx, form between them a passage for the breath (the glottis), adhere to each other and cause a certain accumulation of air. That air by virtue of the elasticity which it acquires due to the pressure exerted upon it, separates the lips of the glottis, and, expanding, exits with a burst. But, at the same instant, relieved of the pressure from below and pulled by their own elasticity, the lips meet again to give rise to a new explosion. From this series of successive and regular contractions and expansions or explosions is born the emission of the voice.[27]

The influence of those who misrepresented or misunderstood Garcia's intent still guides popular opinion today. Authors Frederick Hustler and Yvonne Rodd-Marling bring an interesting perspective.

> In general physiologists are against the *coup de la glotte* . . . Yet great singers and teachers often hold the opposite view: Garcia, Carulli, Duprez, Viardot-Garcia, Fauré, Lablache . . . [28]

In addition to that list we could add those that I have quoted here plus Julius Stockhausen, Carlo Bassini, Charles Bataille, Edmund Myer, William Shakespeare, and Matilda Marchesi.

Not only is it difficult to find a physiologist who supports the use of the *coup de la glotte* today, it is equally difficult to find a contemporary published voice pedagogue who acknowledges anything but the "well-coordinated onset" as the *sine qua non* of initiating the tone. Stark states that the last book of any note to be published in support of the *coup de la glotte* was *The Foundations of Singing* by Franklyn Kelsey in 1950.[29] Stark quotes Kelsey:

> The establishment and maintenance of a perfect approximation of the vocal cords is the key problem in singing . . . he who cannot teach it cannot teach true singing, for it is the sole means which the singer has at his disposal for launching a tone which has not an undesirable content of unphonated air.[30]

Summary

In light of the tremendous weight of support for the use of the *coup de la glotte* from highly respected teachers from the nineteenth century, I believe that this issue is worth reconsideration. After reading Stark's arguments and then reading extensively on my own, I am convinced that I had been misinformed by well-meaning teachers who were convinced that the use of the glottal plosive was always abusive. I do not believe that it is. While I acknowledge the necessity for prudence in this matter, as there are dangers that can result from exaggerated application, it is simply impossible for me to imagine those elite teachers such as Garcia, the Lampertis, and all the rest in a long list of successful teachers were wrong and spent their careers ruining voices. Instead, I have come to wonder what my students have missed by my having ignored it.

A compelling argument also may be made using voice science in support of the *coup de la glotte*. Stark does a wonderful job of bringing these issues to the fore; I refer the interested reader to his book. My purpose for this column is to explore historical pedagogy literature in search of forgotten truth. Suffice it to say that it is common knowledge that when the vocal folds close firmly and are completely adducted during each glottal cycle the air flow cuts off suddenly and the energy in the source spectrum is much higher than when a "loose glottis" is allowed. I have understood that principle for many years, but when I saw for myself the support for the use of the *coup de la glotte* and really understood its "provenance," I was compelled to reconsider my long-standing position on this issue and change my pedagogical approach with my students.

I am reminded of something that William Vennard said to a student during one of the lessons that he taught on the collection of recordings called *Developing Voices*.[31] He posited that there was a dangerous moment in the life of a student singer when he or she begins the transition toward singing with a professional quality. He said that he always waited until there was a fundamental freedom in the technique before he introduced the aggressive quality that is necessary to take the step into the professional world. This is a profound observation. The *coup de la glotte* must be used within the structure of a technique that is free from extraneous tensions. It must also be understood to be what it is, not what we are afraid that it is.

NOTES

1. William Vennard, *Singing: The Mechanism and the Technic* (New York: Carl Fischer, 1967).
2. Ibid., 44–45.
3. James Stark, *Bel Canto: The History of Vocal Pedagogy* (Toronto: University of Toronto Press, 1999).
4. Manuel Garcia, *Complete Treatise On the Art of Singing, Part 1,* translated and edited by Donald Paschke (New York: Da Capo Press, 1984), 41-42. Originally published as *Nouveau Traité Sommaire sur l'Art du Chant* (Genève: Minkoff Èditeur, 1847).
5. Ibid., 42.
6. Manuel Garcia, *Hints on Singing*, translated from the French by Beata Garcia; new and revised edition by Hermann Klein (London: E. Ascherberg, 1984), 13.
7. Hermann Klein, *Thirty Years of Musical Life in London, 1870–1900* (London: Heinemann, 1903), 37.
8. Garcia, *Hints on Singing*, 13.
9. George Bernard Shaw, *Music in London* (London: Constable and Company, 1932).
10. Stark, 15.
11. Henry Holbrook Curtis, *Voice Building and Tone Placing* (New York: D. Appleton and Company, 1901), 159.
12. Blanche Marchesi, *Singer's Pilgrimage* (New York: Arno Press, 1977; originally published in London: G. Richards, 1923), 91–93.
13. Charles Lunn, *The Voice: Its Downfall, Its Training, and Its Use. A Manual for Teachers, Singers, and Students* (London: Reynolds & Co., 1904), 21.
14. Lunn is remembered for the promotion of a theory developed by his student Orlando Steed concerning the importance of inflating the ventricles for proper phonation. This theory was continued in the writings of British teacher and author Edmund Meyer.
15. Charles Lunn, *The Philosophy of Voice: Showing the Right and Wrong Action of Voice in Speech and Song, with Laws for Self-Culture* (Huntsville, TX: Recital Publications, 1984; originally published in London: Baillière, Tindall and Cox, 1886), 5–6.
16. Garcia, *Complete Treatise on the Art of Singing*, 28.

17. Ibid., 27.
18. Francesco Lamperti, *The Art of Singing*, translated by J. C. Griffith (New York: G. Schirmer, 1916), 15.
19. Ibid., 12.
20. William Earle Brown, *Vocal Wisdom: Maxims of Giovanni Battista Lamperti* (New York: Taplinger Publishing Co., 1957), 45.
21. Ibid., 45–46.
22. Ibid., 46.
23. Ferdinand. Sieber, *The Art of Singing and Vocal Culture*, translated and adapted from *Kataechismus der Gesangs Kunst*, 1862 by A. W. Dohn (New York: Oliver Ditson Company, 1880), 20.
24. Meribeth Bunch, *Dynamics of the Singing Voice* (New York: SpringerVerlag, 1995), 70.
25. Lennox Brown and Emile Behnke, *Voice, Speech, and Song* (New York:
1. G. P. Putnams' Sons, 1904), 162.
26. Barbara Doscher, *The Functional Unity of the Singing Voice* (Metuchen, NJ: Scarecrow Press Inc.), 61.
27. Manuel Garcia, *Complete Treatise on the Art of Singing*, 23.
28. Frederick Hustler and Yvonne RoddMarling, *Singing: The Physical Nature*
2. *of the Organ* (London: Faber & Faber, 1965), 75.
29. Stark, 24.
30. Franklyn Kelsey, *The Foundations of Singing* (London: Williams and Northgate, 1950), 14.
31. William Vennard, *Developing Voices* (New York: Carl Fischer, 1970).

9. Two-headed Llamas and the *lutte vocale*

Originally published in the *Journal of Singing*, volume 62, no. 1, 2005

We all remember that fanciful creature from Dr. Doolittle, the one with a head at each end of his body called the Pushme-Pullyou. The image of this creature has served as a metaphor for all kinds of things that we experience in our lives. It describes the way that we can see things from different perspectives, which lead to difficult choices. It can also represent the fact that we have qualities in our own personalities that seem diametrically opposed; they pull us in one direction and push us in another.

Singing can be described as the result of opposing forces in the body; the pull of the cricothyroid against the thryoarytenoid to produce pitch and determine the register, or the pull of the suprahyoids against the infrahyoids to position the larynx in the neck would be two examples. An examination of the physiology of breathing and support also provides us with an example of muscles that work in opposition to create a desired balance of force.

The anatomy and basic function of human respiration has been understood for a very long time. While a complete review of these principles is beyond the scope of this column, a brief summary in outline form might be useful.

- The lungs are the reservoir for the air supply.
- Compressed air drives the vocal folds.
- The lungs are housed in a flexible "strong-box" called the thorax.
- The diaphragm is a muscular sheet that divides the thorax from the abdomen and is described as the primary muscle of inspiration.
- The lungs are "tied" to the thorax and diaphragm via a principle called "pleural linkage"; if the thorax or the diaphragm moves it affects the volume of the lungs.
- Air moving in and out of the lungs is driven by pressure changes which are the result of volume changes.
- Volume changes are created by muscular forces acting on the thorax.

Early pedagogical writings offer surprisingly little instruction in how to breathe and support. A well-known early source is Tosi's *Opinioni de cantori* of 1757. No specific information is offered on how to take the breath. The main concern for Tosi was where to take the breath so as not to harm the musical phrase and that the taking of the breath should not be obtrusive.

> Let him show in all sorts of compositions the proper place to take breath without fatigue; because there are singers who give pain to the hearer as if they had an asthma, taking breath every moment, with difficulty, as if they were breathing their last.[1]

In her presentation of Agricola's translation of Tosi, Julianne Beard said:

> Perhaps the most valuable service that Agricola provides in the chapter on divisions is to explain when and how to take the breath; for few treatises of this period even mention breathing, much less provide the useful directions afforded by Agricola.[2]

Even Agricola's lengthy commentary on Tosi's words deals primarily with "when and where" rather than "how." However, a brief comment, which is easily overlooked, introduces us to the topic at hand: "One must pay careful attention to saving the breath immediately after inhalation."

This notion of "saving the breath" is a recurrent idea throughout the history of voice pedagogy. As a way to begin, let me remind us of a few additional principles of respiratory action:

- Inspiration occurs when the volume of the thorax is increased.
- The lungs are made of very elastic material.
- When the lungs are full there is a "restoring force" that will cause them to deflate just as a balloon does when it is filled and then released.
- When the thorax is expanded (for inhalation), it too has elastic properties that will compel it to go back to its "at rest" posture.
- Other forces act upon the thorax to return it back to its "at rest" posture, such as gravity and torque acting on the ribs.

This notion of saving the breath can be illustrated in the principle of "checking action." Figure 1 is based upon Agostoni and Mead's relaxation pressure curve.[4] The elongated s-shaped curve in the middle of the top figure represents the passive pressures generated in the lung solely by elasticity, torque, and gravity. If one were to take a full breath (100% vital capacity), close the glottis (using a "valsalva maneuver"), and then totally relax all muscles of the thorax and abdomen, we could measure approximately 40 cm H_2O of pressure in the lungs.[5] If we were then to go down the full range of vital capacity and measure the pressure in this way from 100% to 0%, we could generate a similar curve. The three vertical lines on the right side of the figure represent the average pressure that it takes to sustain an utterance at three dynamic levels: soft, medium, and loud. For the loud utterance, we can see by dropping down to the x axis at the bottom of the figure that we need approximately 20 cm H_2O to sustain it. Were one to take a full breath, prior to the vocal gesture, the passive forces are generating an excess of 20 cm H_2O over what is needed. What do we do? We have to "check" these passive forces with active ones. We have to apply enough inspiratory force to take the excess pressure off of the vocal folds, so we use inspiratory muscles during exhalation (support) to balance the pressure. If we could add the element of time to this figure, it would start at the top of the vertical line and go to the bottom of the figure. As we sustained the vocal gesture, we would gradually move from the place where the passive forces exceed what is required into the area where passive forces were no long sufficient (at about 70% of the vital capacity). At that point our expiratory drive would have to turn on and begin to actively generate enough pressure to maintain the 20 cm H_2O that is required. This is typically what we call "support"; using muscular action to generate enough pressure in the lungs to drive the vocal folds to meet the pitch and intensity requirements. It is a dynamic situation in that the requirements are constantly changing, and this is for a simple vocal task. It should be understood that 20 cm H_2O is typical for loud speech, but the pressure required for loud singing can greatly exceed this number.

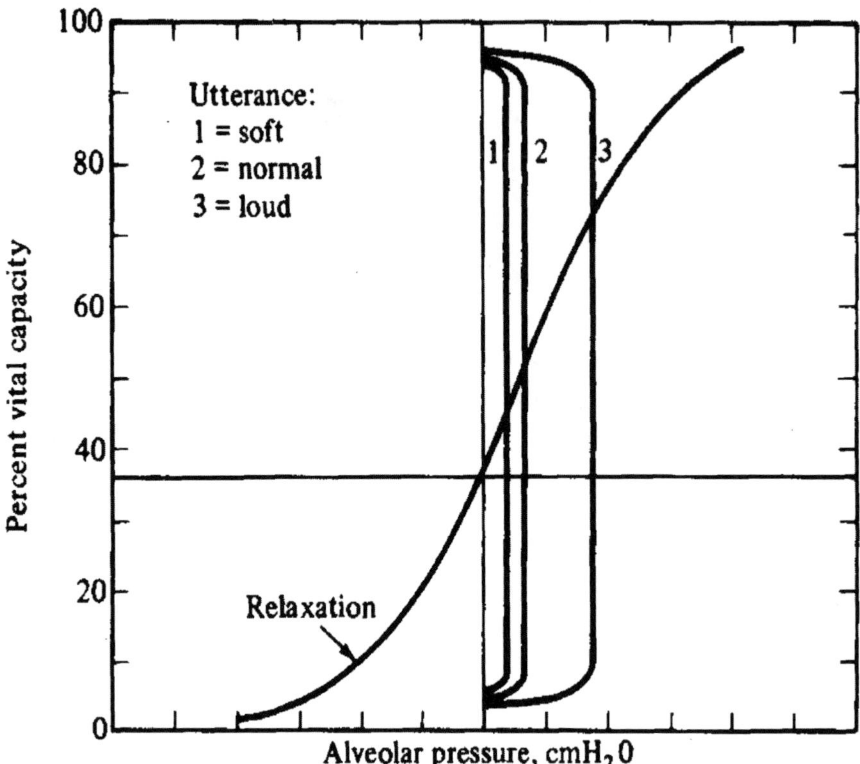

Figure 1. Passive expiratory forces expressed as pressure in the lungs generated by elasticity of the lungs and thorax, torque and gravity as a function of vital capacity. Vertical lines represent lung pressures required for a sustained vowel at different dynamic levels.

Thus, at least one explanation of saving the breath as Tosi suggested at the beginning of a phrase may be a matter of checking excess passive expiratory forces with an active inhalatory gesture. A similar notion is found quoted by James Stark, who cites Jean Paul Egide Martini.

> When upon respiration, the lungs are filled with air, it is necessary to hold back the air with greatest care and not let anything be expelled other than the portion required to make the vocal chords [*sic*] vibrate.[6]

This concept is restated years later in Leo Kofler's *The Art of Breathing*.

> The elasticity of the lungs not only makes their expansion or inflation possible, but also expels the air in their endeavor to return to a condition of repose . . . But in singing and speaking this return action of the lungs must be retarded; the slower this is done, the slower will the air escape from the lungs and the more control will be gained over the tone.[7]

The act of retaining some of the air, especially at the beginning of a phrase, can be seen to be an old concept. This principle is evident in an exercise offered by Manuel Garcia in his discussion of breathing.

1. First one inhales slowly and during the space of several seconds as much breath as the chest can contain.

2. One exhales that air with the same slowness as with which it was inhaled.
3. One fills the lungs and keeps them filled for the largest time possible.
4. One exhales completely and leaves the chest empty as long as the physical powers will conveniently allow.[8]

Without delving too far in the musculature involved in these respiratory efforts, it is clear that this series of exercises targets those muscles that are involved in taking in breath and in holding the thorax and the abdomen still at points in the respiratory cycle that are not typical in normal speech, but critical for singing. Holding the lungs full in step three (while the glottis is open) trains the inspiratory muscles—diaphragm and external intercostals. I invite you to try this gesture for yourself. It is important that you keep the larynx open so that air *could* move in and out of the lungs, but doesn't because you are maintaining a steady volume in the thorax. After several seconds you will begin to feel the effort of the muscles of the chest wall and perhaps the pressure of the descended diaphragm. It can be fatiguing at first. Brown and Behnke in their monumental work *Voice, Speech, and Song* disagree with Garcia in how long the breath should be held, or at least offered this advice to the beginner:

> The time of holding the breath is not, at the outset, to exceed four seconds, and the student must never, on any account, fatigue himself with these exercises; they may, however, be frequently repeated at intervals.[9]

Holding a steady posture at the end of the expiratory cycle as described in step four will also result in a slight fatigue after a few seconds. I would assume that these are the internal intercostals and certainly the muscles of the abdominal wall that are holding in a contracted state. These are the two opposing muscle groups of respiratory drive. This is a great exercise for building strength and control in these important muscle groups.

It is interesting to note that in Donald Paschke's translation of Garcia's treatise, only three pages of well over two hundred in volume one are dedicated to breathing. However, lest we misunderstand Garcia's cursory treatment of the subject, he stated:

> The breath, which holds the entire instrument under its subjection, exerts the greatest influence on the character of the performance and can make it calm or trembling, connected or detached, energetic or lifeless, expressive or devoid of expression.[10]

THE LUTTE VOCALE

Giovanni and Francesco Lamperti contributed greatly to pedagogical thought and practice, especially to the role of breathing and support. Their development and use of the concept of *appoggio* and the popularization of the term *lutte vocale* were firmly established in their writings. In his description of *appoggiata*, Francesco Lamperti includes a now familiar concept.

> By singing *appoggiata*, is meant that all notes, from the lowest to the highest, are produced by a column of air over which the singer has perfect command, by holding back the breath, and not permitting more air than is absolutely necessary for the formation of the note to escape from the lungs.[11]

This concept of "holding back the breath" is central to the idea of *appoggio*. The first use of the term *lutte vocale* is credited to Dr. Louis Mandl of Paris. Francesco Lamperti quotes from Mandl's *Hygiène de la voix,* 1876.

> To sustain a given note the air should be expelled slowly; to attain this end, the respiratory muscles, by continuing their action, strive to retain the air in the lungs, and oppose their action to that of the expiratory muscles, which, at the same time, drive it out for the production of the note. There is established a balance of power between these two agents, which is called the *"lutte vocale"* or vocal struggle. On the retention of this equilibrium depends the just emission of the voice, and by means of it alone can true expression by given to the sound produced.[12]

Mandl's work was very influential and often quoted in many sources of the time. Like so many important works from this period, it is not readily available and a modern translation and edition would be a worthy subject for a masters or doctoral thesis.

At the risk of quoting one too many sources on this topic, I offer William Shakespeare's contribution to the definition of the *lutte vocale*.

> We have then at our control the powerful breath pressure necessary to loud singing, for we can regulate this by balancing the upward and downward action of the muscles of the ribs . . . There can be inside the body, therefore, an opposition between the muscles which send out the breath and the muscles which draw in the breath. The latter restrain and regulate its outrush, economizing it.[13]

CONCLUSION

The concept of holding back the breath has been with us since at least the early eighteenth century. A possible explanation has been offered in the particular situation when the passive forces supersede those required for a particular vocal gesture. At soft dynamic levels and at high lung volumes, pressure within the lungs can exceed that required for a particular phonatory task, and in that case a checking action is required to counterbalance the passive forces with an active inspiratory force. This does not apply to full-voiced singing when the required subglottal pressures often exceed the passive forces.

The real problem in this matter arises when we consider that the vocal folds are subjected to the pressures that the expiratory muscles produce directly and instantaneously. Can the vocal folds manage 90 cm H_2O all at once when a singer supports a tone and still remain free to oscillate? Or is there somewhere in the respiratory system a way of balancing these forces to protect the larynx and the vocal folds? As I am writing this column, I am sitting no more than a couple of hundred yards from one of the greatest rivers in the world, the mighty Mississippi. People throughout the flood plain of this awesome body of water have taken control over nature's regular invasion of flood waters by building a complex system of levees to protect cities and farm lands from sudden incursions of high water from melting snows up north and spring rains in the midwest and south. Is there a levee system in the body to protect the vocal folds? Several noted voice teachers over the past two hundred years have insisted that there was, but voice scientists have not uniformly supported the source of it. The "vocal struggle" of the *lutte vocale* has been difficult to identify.

One common pedagogical notion has been that the diaphragm acts as an intermediary between the strength of the abdominal musculature and the vocal folds, acting like a levee system to take sudden increases of pressure and then releasing it slowly in a controlled fashion. That is to say, that after the diaphragm descends for the inhalatory gesture it does not immediately go passive when the expiratory effort begins. However, voice scientists do not uniformly agree that the diaphragm acts in this manner. Another possibility is that the muscles of the rib cage control the volume of the thorax in such a way that it acts as a flexible reservoir that is capable of responding to changes in pressure produced by the abdominal muscles. When the abdominals contract to generate a positive pressure in the abdominal cavity, the diaphragm is pushed back up toward its rest position. This infringement, if you will, into the volume of the thorax by the diaphragm results in a change in pressure in the thorax, which is necessary to drive the air flow for phonation. The intercostal muscles are considered to be capable of responding quickly enough that they are able to react to this sudden decrease of volume from the floor of the thorax by raising the ribs slightly and counteracting the sudden increase in pressure by slightly enlarging the thorax in the lateral and anteroposterior dimension. Of course, you will recognize my bias as to the source of support in this discussion. There is also the possibility that the muscles of the thorax are the source of support in that they are in control of the volume of the thorax through lifting and lowering the rib cage with some contribution from the abdominal wall. Chances are that practice differs among singers and no uniform definition is possible.

One thing is certain: it has been a common experience among singers that there seem to be opposing forces involved in elite singing. Voice teachers have described it for many years. Garcia and others offered specific exercises to isolate the muscles of inspiration and exhalation in order to train singers to be strong and coordinated in their ability to manage breath pressure. Our experience tells us that two-headed llamas are real, and not just a figment of our imagination.

NOTES

1. Pier Francesco Tosi, *Observations on the Florid Song*, trans. Mr. Galliard, ed. Michael Pilkington (London: Stainer & Bell, 1987), 24.
2. Johann Friedrich Agricola, *Introduction to the Art of Singing*, trans. Julianne Baird (Cambridge and New York: Cambridge University Press). [This work is a translation of and commentary on Pier Francesco Tosi's *Opinioni de cantori* of 1757, published as *Anleitung zur Singkunst* (Berlin, 1757).]
3. Ibid., 166.
4. Thomas Hixon, "Respiratory Function in Speech," in Fred Minifie, Thomas Hixon, and Frederick Williams, eds., *Normal Aspects of Speech, Hearing, and Language* (Englewood Cliffs: Prentice-Hall, Inc., 1973), 105. [The relaxation curve after E. Agostoni and J. Mead, "Statics of the Respiratory System," in W. Fenn and H. Rahn, eds., *Handbook of Physiology* (Washington, D.C.: American Physiology Society, 1964).]
5. Pressure in voice production is often reported in terms of how high a column of water would be displaced when exposed to it. This is determined by the use of a U-tube manometer, a common laboratory tool. It is not technically a measurement of pressure, but has been commonly used.
6. James Stark, *Bel Canto: The History of Vocal Pedagogy* (Toronto: University of Toronto Press Inc., 1999), 96.
7. Leo Kofler, *The Art of Breathing as the Basis of Tone Production* (New York: Edgar S. Werner, 1893), 66.
8. Manuel Garcia, *Complete Treatise On the Art of Singing, Part 1,* trans. and ed. by Donald Paschke (New York: Da Capo Press, 1984), 41-42. Originally published as *Nouveau Traite Sommaire sur l'Art du Chant* (Genève: Minkoff Editeur, 1847).
9. Lennox Brown and Emil Behnke, *Voice, Speech, and Song* (London: Sampson Low, Marston, Searle, and Rivington, 1884), 187.
10. Garcia, 35.
11. Francesco Lamperti, *The Art of Singing*, trans. J. C. Griffith (New York: G. Schirmer, Inc., 1890), 22.
12. Ibid., 25.
13. William Shakespeare, *The Art of Singing* (Boston: Oliver Ditson Company, 1910),
14.

10. "There's a hole in the middle, the middle, the middle." In Defense of Garcia's Placement of the Falsetto in the Middle of the Singing Range in Both Men and Women.

Originally published in the *Journal of Singing*, volume 62, no. 3, 2006

As this column is submitted, this author is participating in the sixth Pan European Voice Conference held in London at the Royal Academy of Music. The gathering has been titled "Mirroring Voices" and is in celebration of 150 years of multidisciplinary voice care which began with the historic contribution by Manuel Garcia II, who brought the laryngeal mirror into common use in 1855 and changed voice care and voice teaching forever. Garcia taught at the Royal Academy from 1848 to 1895 when he retired at age 90. He continued to teach in London for the rest of his life, which came to an end in 1906. He was 101 years old.

While attending a meeting such as this, it seemed appropriate for me to document my appreciation of Garcia's continuing influence by discussing some aspect of his contributions to voice pedagogy. Voice scientists and physicians often acknowledge Garcia as the individual responsible for illuminating the larynx with reflected light from a series of mirrors. Many of them, however, along with a number of voice teachers, really do not understand the huge impact that he had on the art of voice teaching. Anyone who has read this column before knows that Garcia's work is often discussed here. I have learned a great deal about being an effective teacher from his important treatises, including *A Complete Treatise on the Art of Singing* and *Hints on Singing*.

One aspect of Garcia's pedagogical thought that has puzzled me for many years is his use of the term *falsetto*. I took this occasion to try to come to terms with what to me always has been a confusing aspect of Garcia's teaching. Figure 1 is a table of the vocal registers according to Garcia as presented in his first work, *Mémoire sur la voix humaine,* presented to the French Academy of Sciences in 1840.[1] In this figure one notes that he has placed the falsetto register in the middle of the voice range between the chest voice and the head voice. Garcia applied this same scheme to all voices, including men, women, and children.

A more common placement of the falsetto can be seen in Figure 2, a registration scheme for a tenor from Richard Miller's *Training Tenor Voices*. There are a number of subdivisions for each major registration event with the falsetto at the top, above the head voice.[2]

Most descriptions that one would find in any twentieth-century source would look more like Miller's description than Garcia's. An examination of these two figures would cause one to scratch one's head and wonder how these two respected pedagogues could be talking about the same thing. Falsetto in the middle? Falsetto in the female voice? It is tempting to discard Garcia's register scheme altogether and attribute his "mistake" to the fact that it was a less sophisticated time and that he simply did not understand the voice very well. I think this would be dismissive of a fine artist and teacher. Recall that this is the same man who gave us the definition for vocal registers that is still used today in its entirety or some form of it:

> By the word register we understand a series of consecutive and homogenous tones going from low to high, produced by the development of the same mechanical principle, and whose nature differs essentially from another series of tones equally consecutive and homogenous produced by another mechanical principle.[3]

Garcia was an eminent voice teacher and one of the first voice scientists whose contributions are still "ringing in our ears." There must have been some rationale that remains for me undiscovered.

HISTORICAL PRECEDENCE

In his *Mémoire* Garcia stated,

> . . . one can establish that the human voice, in the largest sense, is composed of the different registers; Chest Falsetto-head[4]

Garcia described the falsetto-head as belonging to the same mechanism. This defines a two-register theory and, apparently, this practice follows the convention of the time. James Stark defends Garcia's position by saying that:

> The old Italian concept of two registers was still widely accepted, and Garcia was well acquainted with the works of Tosi, Mancini, Herbst, and Agricola, all of which he cited in his *Traité*. He was familiar with the treatise of J. P. E. Martini, as well as the tutors by Mengozzi and Garaudé, his mentors at the Paris Conservatoire. All these authors supported a three-register theory for female voices and a two-register theory for male voices.[5]

Confusion over what these authors believed concerning the number and names of the vocal registers persists. Stark seems to suggest that there were either two or three registers, depending on whether you were talking about male or female singers. However, Mancini stated plainly that there are only two: "The voice ordinarily divides itself into two registers, one called chest register and the other head register, or falsetto."[6]

Additionally, Mancini said: "It is a rare case when the two registers are both united into a chest register in one person. This total union is generally produced only by study and the help of art."[7]

So, which is it, two or three? Garcia explained that "to these two registers is added the third, or the head voice, which is nothing but the continuation of the falsetto voice."[8]

Garcia clarified this by saying that he falsetto-head register was often perceived as two distinct mechanisms, but that they were actually the same. He proposed that the difference in the qualities of the two mechanisms was due to the fact that in the falsetto register the space between the arytenoids was loosely engaged in phonation and allowed a posterior gap. This was the source of the breathiness and the "veiled quality" of the falsetto. When the falsetto voice reached about $C^{\#}_5$ the space between the arytenoids closed and vibration was limited to the margin of the vocal folds, providing the clear, ringing quality. With this important exception the mechanism of vibration on the vocal folds was the same, so he considered them to be the same register. It is important to remember that the theories presented in the *Mémoire* were written more than a decade prior to his visual observation of these events using the laryngoscope. It is noteworthy that his theory about the function of vocal registers was for the most part confirmed after he was able to see the larynx at work in his own throat and those of his students.

Garcia applied the two-register scheme for men, women, and children. Some of Garcia's observations about the registers of the voice included the following (refer to Figure 1):

1. The notes on the staff represent the full compass of the range of both men and women. Any individual voice will fall within it.

2. There is a range of pitches (from A_3 to $C^{\#}_5$) that can be produced in either the chest or falsetto (in both men and women, although this full range would not be found in a typical individual).
3. The head voice extends above the range of the falsetto, and the chest voice extends below it.
4. The quality of the chest register is the same in men, women, and children. It is described as "brilliant" and "penetrating." The range of the chest register exceeds the falsetto at the low end but parallels it at the high end.
5. The falsetto belongs particularly to women and children. The register is weak, covered, and rather resembles the low tones of a flute.
6. According to Garcia, women and children speak in the falsetto voice.
7. The head voice is not a different register, but is merely a continuation of the falsetto that begins at about $C^{\#}_5$. It is described as "distinctive and brilliant" in the woman's voice, beginning at the point where the falsetto ceases.
8. Me[5]n lose the head voice at puberty; some, however, maintain perhaps a major third of the range of the head voice.

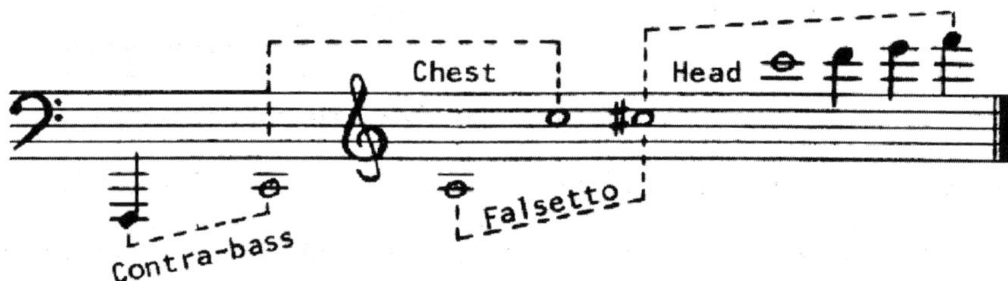

Figure 1. Table of the registers for the human voice from Manuel Garcia's *Mémoire sur la voix humaine* of 1840.

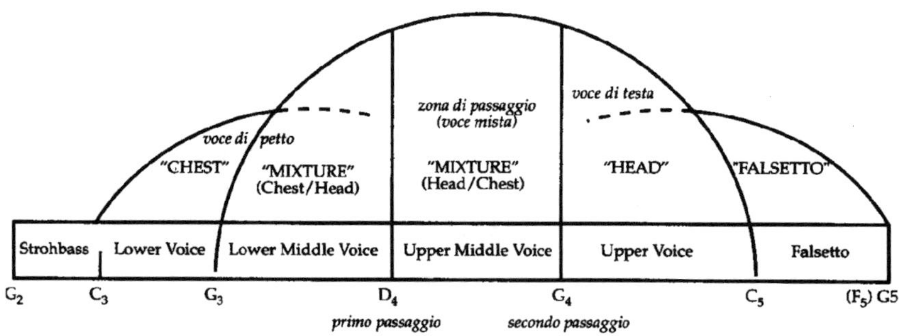

Figure 2. Table of the registers for a tenor from Richard Miller's *Training Tenor Voices*.

According to Garcia, there are two things at work that produce the transition from the falsetto to the head voice. First, adductory forces resulting from the elongation of the vocal folds assist in closing the gap between the arytenoid cartilages. The second influence in the transition is the use of the somber timbre.

> The sombre timbre modifies them in a more striking manner, and people have thought they saw a new action where there was only an extension of the same action.[9]

FEMALE VOICE

In the female voice Garcia suggested the outside ranges of the falsetto were typically weak. In the low part of the falsetto (B_3 to F_4 for the soprano):

> [i]t is absolutely necessary . . . to substitute for them the corresponding tones in the chest register, which, although they do not have much power, do not lack bite.[10]
>
> In the upper range of the falsetto the notes are also weak ($C^{\#}_5$ and D_5), while the tones E^b_5 –F_5 which are the first in the head register are round and pure.
>
> Since this roundness and this purity proceed only from the position of the pharynx and the contraction of the glottis, one will impart them to the preceding tones by arching the velum and by avoiding all loss of unused air. It is thus by the position which the pharynx adopts in the sombre timber[11] and by the pinching of the glottis that these two registers are equalized.[12]

The weak outer margins of the falsetto are made useful by substitution on the low end and by bringing down the qualities of the head voice to modify the function of the mechanism through the use of the *voix sombrée* and a descending portamento. For the middle of the falsetto Garcia prescribes that the tones be "emitted in pure falsetto and that one attack them by the stoke of the glottis."[13]

It is obvious that this mechanism is the "middle register" in today's parlance. Later in his *Hints on Singing*, Garcia himself changed his terminology and used the terms chest, medium, and head, although he stated immediately that in his opinion "these names are incorrect, but accepted."[14] Later in the same discussion we find this clarification:

> The *medium* or *falsetto* is the result of similar actions, save that the lips come into contact, not through their depth but merely at their edges. In both registers the glottis has its length diminished from the back, by the arytenoids, which advance their contact till their adhesion is complete. As soon as this takes place, the *falsetto* ceases, and the glottis, consisting of the vocal cords alone, produces the *head* register, and the feebler opposition presented by the edges produces the *falsetto*.[15]

In a footnote, long-time student of Garcia and music critic Herman Klein explained that the term *falsetto* was no longer in use as a name for the medium register in the female voice, but that it was used by Garcia's contemporaries due to the fact that the mechanism was similar to the falsetto as demonstrated in the male voice. There is evidence, however, that common usage of these terms was not so far removed from the time that Garcia wrote his *Hints on Singing*. Emil Behnke was a well-known teacher and advocate of the laryngoscope. He worked closely with physician Dr. Lennox Browne on a number of projects including a very popular book, *Voice, Song and Speech,* which went through many printings and editions. At a meeting of the Musical Association in London in 1886 Behnke stated,

> When I went beyond the "thick" register, commonly called the "chest" register, the moment I put away that mechanism and sang in the "thin" register, or, as it is commonly called, the "falsetto," we saw quite a different picture.[16]

Behnke agreed with Garcia in saying that there was a third register which he called the "small" register (Garcia's *head voice)* in the voices of women and children and that this register was not accessible to men.

MALE VOICE

For male voices the falsetto is not so universally important, according to Garcia. He said that basses can use the chest voice exclusively and suggests that they have difficulty attacking the falsetto notes at all. The head tones are completely absent. In this context Garcia also complained that the bass voice was disappearing from the stage, being replaced by the baritone. He stated that the range of the falsetto for the baritone voice extends from B_3 to B_4 but that few of them would use it successfully. However:

> The falsetto united with the chest register is, for the tenors more than for the baritones, a successful and natural resource. The much too elevated *tessitura* of the music composed today for tenors does not permit them to do without the falsetto register. But the use of that resource, however, should be determined by the ability of the organ to blend together the metals [timbres] of the two registers; otherwise, however well-conceived the transition between the registers may be, the disparity of the sounds would shock the ear and destroy the unity of the effect; one would think one was hearing two different individuals singing alternately in the same phrase.[17]

I believe that this view of Garcia falls into a generally accepted principle for the tenor that a lighter registration is needed for the high voice. Most teachers today would call this the "head voice," although it is clear that this was not Garcia's terminology. Remember, according to Garcia the head voice is lost to the male singer at puberty, except for a few rare voices who could access the interval of a third above C_5. So, what did Garcia call the "extension" at the top for the tenor? He clarifies this in a footnote in Part 2 of the *Complete Treatise*:

> Whatever the character of these tones may be, they belong to the chest register, but with a modification of volume with which we are going to concern ourselves. The designations of *voix mixte* and *mezzo petto* are equally improper, for they would make us suppose that these clear and high pitched tones are produced by the two mechanisms of the chest and falsetto registers at the same time. Now, physiologically, the simultaneous conjunction of two different mechanisms servicing to produce the same note, or two notes in unison, is an unacceptable idea.[18]

Garcia rejects the notion that registers can be "mixed" to form the head voice because they have different mechanisms and cannot coexist. So, what is he saying, especially in light of the previous quote where he talked about "blending the metals" of the two registers? I believe that he suggests that it is necessary for the chest voice to maintain its fundamental identity even as the male singer ascends to the top. In the same footnote he said:

> Moreover, it is demonstrated that the glottis, by the gradual tension of its lips and the successive reduction of its dimensions, produces the entire series of chest tones; but the vibrations generated in the glottis acquire all their power only provided that they are extended into the ventricles, then into the pharynx.[19]

Garcia is stating that as the tenor (for instance) ascends the scale, the tension along the vibrating margin increases (due to the elongation produced by the cricothyroid muscle), but the shape of the vocal folds must change gradually. However, they must maintain their depth (rounded under belly) to a degree in order to maintain the quality of the chest voice.[20] Garcia is also stating the importance of the resonance of the lower vocal tract to the ability of the tenor to maintain the chest voice quality.

> It is in fact this result that a capable singer knows how to obtain, when on one side he completely relaxes all the muscles of the pharynx, and on the other he narrows more and more the column of air. In these circumstances, the glottis, endowed with a complete liberty, can reach the final limits of its action. One is astonished to see a tenor give, without any apparent effort, the notes A_4, B_4, C_5, $C^{\#}_5$, D_5 .[2]

The narrowing of the air column is what I believe Ingo Titze has brought to our attention recently in his discussion of the importance of inertive reactance of the air column; that is, the ability of the air space to store energy that comes from the larynx under certain circumstances and to increase the amount of energy in the upper partials. This can occur when the air column is narrowed directly above the vocal folds and the epilaryngeal tube is elongated by a slight lowering of the larynx.[22]

CONCLUSION

The name and placement of the falsetto register in the middle of the singing range for both men and women can be explained as follows. First, it was the historical tradition to do so at the time that Garcia offered his first written essay, *Mémoire sur la voix humaine*. The two-register theory that Garcia supported was well documented in the important treatises of the previous age, and he was very familiar with what authors such as Tosi and Mancini had to say on the subject. Secondly, he predicted a similar mechanism in that part of the range in the voices of men, women, and children. Of course, this was prior to his "invention" of the laryngeal mirror, so he had not actually seen what he predicted to be true. He theorized that in the range of A_3 to $C^{\#}_4$ only the margins of the vocal folds were involved in phonation and that in this range the space between the arytenoids was not closed. This differed drastically from the chest register where the full body of the vocal folds was engaged in the cyclic opening and closing action and from the natural extension of the falsetto, the head voice. In the head voice the space between the arytenoids closed and the clarity of the mechanism emerged due to the use of the somber timbre at the top part of the falsetto. This action was primarily accessible to the female and child larynx. In a male singer, the falsetto voice does exist in the range where Garcia placed it. It is not limited to the range above the E_4 as it might occur in a novice male singer. The falsetto has no performance value in the male voice, and Garcia cautioned that it must be avoided, except for particular circumstances. Nonetheless, its functional value is acknowledged by Garcia for the male singer, especially for the tenor. He states clearly however, that only the chest voice is acceptable for performance for the male singer and that this range when properly developed and utilized will support the full range up to C_5 and above.

When carefully considered, the schematic of the registers presented in his *Mémoire* does make sense after all. The two-register theory is a justifiable position from a pedagogic perspective, and our current understanding of the physiology of the vocal registers supports this approach.23 It is a part of a well integrated and quite thorough pedagogic theory that is worth our consideration. I think we can change the names, even if Garcia thought it was wrong to do so.

NOTES

1. Manuel Garcia II, "*Mémoire sur la voix humaine*," in *A Complete Treatise on the Art of Singing, Part 1*, translated and edited by Donald V. Paschke (New York: Da Capo Press,1982), xlix. Originally published as *Nouveau Traité Sommaire sur l'Art du Chant* (Genève: Minkoff Éditeur, 1847).
2. Richard Miller, *Training Tenor Voices* (New York: Schirmer Books, 1993), 7.
3. Garcia, xli.
4. Ibid., xl.
5. James Stark, *Bel Canto: The History of Vocal Pedagogy* (Toronto: University of Toronto Press, 1999), 67–68.
6. Giambattista Mancini, *Practical Reflections on Figured Singing*, translated and edited by Edward V. Foreman (Minneapolis: Pro Musica Press, 1967), 39.
7. Stark, loc. cit.
8. Garcia, xliii.
9. Ibid., liii.
10. Manuel Garcia, *Complete Treatise On the Art of Singing, Part 1*, translated and edited by Donald Paschke (New York: Da Capo Press, 1984), 18. Originally published as *Nouveau Traité Sommaire sur l'Art du Chant* (Genève: Minkoff Éditeur, 1847).
11. Stephen Austin, "The *voce chiusa*" in *Journal of Singing* 61, no. 4 (March/April 2005): 421–426.
12. Garcia, *Treatise, Part 1*, 45.
13. Stephen Austin, "The Attack on the *coup de la glotte*," in Journal of Singing 61, no. 5 (May/June 2005): 525–529. Garcia, Treatise, Part 1, 45.
14. Manuel Garcia, *Hints on Singing*, translated by Beata Garcia (London: Ascherberg, Hopwood and Crew, Limited, 1894), 7.
15. Ibid., 8.
16. Emil Behnke, "The Registers of the Voice," *Proceedings of the Musical Association*, 13th Session (Oxford University Press, 1886–1887), 5.
17. Garcia, *Treatise, Part 1*, 20.
18. Manuel Garcia, *Complete Treatise On the Art of Singing, Part* 2, translated and edited by Donald Paschke (New York: Da Capo Press, 1984), 161. Originally published as *Nouveau Traité Sommaire sur l'Art du Chant* (Genève: Minkoff Éditeur, 1847).
19. Ibid., 162.
20. I refer the reader to a full discussion of the importance of the shape of the vocal fold and the quality of the sound that they produce in Stephen Austin, "'Treasure chest'—A Physiological and Pedagogical Review of the Low Mechanism," *Journal of Singing* 61, no. 3 (January/February 2005): 241–251.
21. Garcia, *Treatise, Part 2*, 162.
22. Ingo Titze, "A Theoretical Study of F0-F1 Interaction with Application to Resonant Speaking and Singing Voice," *Journal of Voice* 18, no. 3 (September 2004): 292–8.
23. Stephen Austin, "Scientific Support for the Two-Register Theory," in *The Modern Singing Master: Essays in Honor of Cornelius Reid* (New York: Scarecrow Press, 2002), 62.

11. Just for the "Trill" of It!

Originally published in the *Journal of Singing*, volume 62, no. 4, 2006

In previous "Provenance" columns I have written about several vocal gestures that have served historically as important exercises for voice building and that have provided the basis for specific articulations found in the vocal literature: *staccato, martellato, aspirato*, etc. Another important vocal gesture is the trill or *trillo*. The *trillo*, of course, has been used for many centuries. A comprehensive study of the history and appropriate application of the *trillo* (also called the shake) and its many different forms through the centuries would be far beyond the scope of this brief review. The trill and many other vocal embellishments are best understood perhaps by our early music practitioners, and since I claim no expertise in early music performance practice, I leave that discussion to those who are qualified to undertake it. My purpose in this article is to examine what teachers have said about how to teach the trill, and not the wondrous complexity of its proper application, even if something significant is lost in separating the two.

One theme occurs over and over again in the literature: for some singers the trill comes quite naturally, but if a singer is not gifted in this way, it is difficult to teach.

> We meet with two most powerful obstacles informing the shake. The first embarrasses the master for, to this hour, there is no infallible rule found to teach it; and the second affects the scholar, because nature imparts the shake but to few. The impatience of the master joins with the despair of the learner, so that they decline further trouble about it. But in this the master is blameable in not doing his duty, by leaving the scholar in ignorance. One must strive against difficulties with patience to overcome them.[1]

These words from Pier Francesco Tosi come from a time when the trill was the hallmark of fine singing and its appropriate use was the definition of skill and good taste. Tosi dedicated a whole chapter to the shake and its many forms, but offers no specific instructions as to how to teach it. He says only:

The shake then being of such consequence, let the master, by the means of verbal instructions and examples vocal and instrumental, strive that the scholar may attain one that is equal, distinctly marked, easy, and moderately quick, which are its most beautiful qualifications.[2]

Giambattista Mancini also dedicated a chapter of his well-known *Riflessioni pratiche sopra il canto figurato* to the trill and described the importance of acquiring it.

> In the times past, it was believed that if the trill was not given by Nature, it could not be acquired by art. I do not deny this, but may I be permitted to say that our ancient masters did not allow voices with natural agility to sing imperfectly, as we observe today. Moreover, it has been seen in many cases that a pupil (even in the face of the most rigid obstacles met with earnest work) aided by the industry, ingenuity and indefatigable patience of his teacher, succeeded in developing and mastering the trill.[3]

Although no specific instructions for teaching the trill were offered, Mancini offered hope that it could be accomplished, even though he failed to tell us how!

In the nineteenth century we find some specific suggestions about how to teach that which was still in the opinion of many unteachable. A common approach was a movement between two adjacent notes (whole step or half step) which is practiced slowly at first and gradually sped up until the trill spontaneously "takes over." It is often presented as a dotted rhythm with stress being given initially to the first pitch or main note of the trill and then to the auxiliary note (Example 1). The great basso Luigi LaBlache suggested this in his treatise:

> The most efficacious means for attaining it, is to practice it in strict time, counting the number of alternations to be made in the time of a given note. This practice should be done at first slowly, without moving the tongue or the chin, regarding with care the intonation of each of the two notes which form the trill, and avoiding a certain roughness in falling upon the lower note. This fault, to which a person is unfortunately too much inclined, is absolutely opposed to the lightness which the trill ought to have.[4]

Example 1. LaBlache trill.

There are many similar examples of this process throughout the last two hundred years. On the other hand, Manuel Garcia stated that this is not at all the way the trill is acquired.

> The trill does not result from two notes struck one after the other and accelerated to the greatest rapidity, as for example [Example 2] . . . This passage will never be anything but an agility passage which can precede or follow the trill . . . [5]

In lieu of this approach, Garcia described the following mechanism as the source:

> It is necessary to impart to the larynx a regular oscillatory up and down movement, similar to that of the piston working in the body of a pump, taking place in the pharynx. One would not know how to make the pharynx too supple in order that the shortening and lengthening of the depressor and elevator muscles may take place with ease and rapidity. One will have an approximate idea of this operation if one suddenly and rapidly, while holding the mouth open, makes movements of swallowing; in this case the base of the tongue fills the principal function. In the trill the point of action is placed elsewhere, and the tongue yields to the agitation which is transmitted to it. These movements, appreciable to the touch, are more or less visible on the exterior in proportion to the fleshiness of the neck.[6]

Example 2. Garcia trill.

Garcia recommended practicing this oscillation on intervals from the second to as wide as a fifth. He also stated that the traditional method of using alternate notes as described by LaBlache and others is "radically bad" and urged students to seek the trill through the spontaneous trembling of the throat, and not through progressive movement of two adjacent notes.[7]

The physician and basso Charles Battaille provided more detail concerning the physiological function of the trill as he understood it. Even though he studied with Garcia briefly, his description of acquiring the trill sounds more like LaBlache than Garcia.

> The trill is produced mostly by the rapid and repetitive contraction and release of the tensor muscle, the vocal ligaments, and the cricothyroid muscle. It may be inherent to a particular voice, and, if so, it manifests itself in two ways: completely, in which case it can be used at will to embrace all the intervals comprising a whole tone. In this case the teacher can add very little assistance. In other cases, due to natural laryngeal inability, the trill is limited to the interval of a semitone or even a quartertone or eighthtone.
>
> . . .
>
> I begin by seeking absolute flexibility, first in the student's lower jaw, then in the suprahyoid muscles, and finally in the laryngeal muscles themselves. Next I have the student slowly then rapidly execute on a single breath the intervals of a second, a third, and even a fourth on the scale degree where the larynx seems stiff.[8]

Carlo Bassini held the opinion that "the trill is effected by a quick oscillatory motion of the larynx"[9] and gave an exercise beginning with the interval of a third, gradually narrowing to the second (Example 3).

Bassini agreed with Garcia and stated that "the mechanism of the trill consists of a regular up and down movement, or oscillation of the larynx, which causes the larynx to play in the pharynx in the same manner as a piston in a cylinder."[10]

Example 3. Bassini trill.

Noted baritone and teacher Julius Stockhausen stated in his *Method of Singing*:

> The method which the old Italian masters employed to teach their pupils the shake was to make them practise early all the *manieras* (graces or ornaments) which have any resemblance to it. We follow the same method, and introduced the exercises for the shake after those for the ornaments. We shall see how the motion of the larynx, which is indispensable for the shake, can best be acquired.[11]

Stockhausen made a recommendation that I did not find anywhere else in the literature that I reviewed. He suggested the use of a repeated tone.

> Repeating one note with the help of the *spiritus asper*12 is an exercise which will render even the stiffest larynx movable. . . For the execution of a correct trill, with increasing rapidity, we require the movement of the larynx which we observe in a nightingale's throat, and can also feel in our own throat if we put our finger on the shield-cartilage (commonly called the Adam's apple), and sing repeated aspirated notes. It will then be observed that the aspiration seems gradually to produce a second note of a slightly lower pitch, which, if the throat be at all flexible, soon produces a minor shake. It is therefore advisable to practise this until the movements of the larynx have grown rapid and easy. Once this is achieved it will only be a question of time and patience till the major shake can also be produced. It is therefore quite unnecessary to practise the oscillations of the larynx in thirds and fourths as is now the fashion, exercises which have no practical value, and often produce an incorrect shake. They are dangerous experiments for the acquirement of an ornament which demands such a very delicate execution of tone and semitone.
>
> I maintain therefore that the movement of the larynx necessary for the execution of the shake is to be acquired by the repetition of one note with the help of the aspirated vocalisation.[13]

With or without the use of wide interval exercises, the idea of a laryngeal oscillation appears over and over again, often likening the motion of the larynx to the throat of a nightingale or a mechanical device. Twentieth-century sources reflect similar thinking. William Shakespeare proposed:

> Towards the acquirement of the trill little more can be suggested than that which has been the ground work of our scale practice; e.g., the rapid reiteration of the "lah" on two notes, faster and faster, until the rapidity prevents the pronunciation of the "l" and it becomes the trill, or the rapid succession of staccato "ahs," until the staccato becomes impossible, and a true rapid legato ensues, forming a trill.

. . .

> But in practicing it may be suggested that it is advisable, in order to gain a feeling of even oscillation, to begin with a larger interval, e.g., of a fourth, then reducing it to a third and lastly to the trill itself [Example 4].[14]

Example 4. Shakespeare trill.

Twentieth-century sources are like earlier sources. Often they describe the trill, but do not offer specific instructions as to how to teach it. Herbert–Caesari stated:

> It is produced by a peculiar mechanism in that it consists of a sustained basic note, produced in the usual way, and a second note superimposed—generally a tone higher. This superimposed note is not actually or, say, deliberately made by the singer but is the result of a piston-like action of the entire larynx, lightly and almost imperceptibly bobbing up and down in the throat automatically with extraordinary rapidity.[15]

Ida Franca described it this way:

> It is done by moving the larynx regularly up and down, and the more regular and freer these throbbing movements are, the more birdlike will sound the trill. These throbbing movements can be learned through imitation only and never through explanation. Two factors are most essential: the teacher must have a perfect trill; the student must have a free throat.[16]

Douglas Stanley offered a different opinion concerning the freedom involved. He stated unequivocally that "it is impossible for the singer to trill properly if his throat is relaxed."[17] Stanley separated the study of the "shake" (the up and down oscillatory motion) from the trill.

> The first stage in this phase of the technical training is the study of the shake. At the start, the pupil should be instructed to shake slowly and great pains must be taken to make the movement at the larynx as definite as possible, even if it has to be somewhat jerky. A small, narrow movement or a "slurry" shake is worthless. When this broad movement has been properly sensed, the pupil may be instructed to increase its speed. Let it be clearly understood that the shake is a consciously controlled action. When this "trick" has been mastered, it should be practiced at various speeds, within certain limits, until it is under perfect control.

> When the shake has been thoroughly mastered, the trill may be attempted. The student should first shake a few times very vigorously at high speed and then attempt to convert this shake into a trill. The trill is a semi-controlled action, since its speed cannot be consciously regulated. As with the shake, the movement must be broad since, if it is too narrow, the result will be a mere tremolo. The maximum possible movement must be sought and the trill should, at first, be sung vigorously. Later the intensity may be varied. Further suggestions are impractical, since the trill is, in a sense, merely a trick with the larynx which must be learned under the direct guidance of the teacher. Of course the ability to trill is sometimes natural.[18]

It is interesting to note that in most modern sources that I consulted for this review (i.e., those written within the last twenty-five years), the trill was not even mentioned. Richard Miller supported the idea of the laryngeal oscillation as the source of the trill and the idea that the trill is the result of vocal freedom, although no specific exercises for developing the trill were offered.

> When trilling is first attempted, the oscillatory motion of the larynx may feel somewhat wild and uncontrolled. It is exactly therein that its advantage as a freedom-inducing device lies! Although it is not the case that "unless you can trill you cannot sing freely" (a maxim in some quarters of voice teaching), letting the larynx suddenly engage in such loose movement can free the instrument.[19]

The neglect of the trill in many modern sources may be related to a statement by Victor Fuchs in his book, *The Art of Singing*.

> The trill went out of vogue in the US for a very simple reason. In a successful career of more than twenty years, Lilly Pons has hardly ever used a trill, so that multitudes of young coloraturas think it is unnecessary and do not study it. To make up for it, they insert too many runs, staccato passages and other embellishments into their cadenzas.[20]

SUMMARY

There is no doubt that some voices come to the trill more easily than others. That has been a common position for several centuries. It would be a justifiable position to say that all singers would benefit from studying and acquiring the trill order to perform the literature for their voice types; however, even many coloratura sopranos have neglected to undertake a serious study of the trill. I reviewed scores of treatises for this review and in only a small percentage was there specific discussion about how the trill is produced and how to teach or acquire it. A few more authors gave musical examples and discussed the proper application of the trill with no instruction as to how it was produced or how to teach it, and as already mentioned most did not address it all. Surely this reflects the reality of it. For some singers, all that is needed is a few exercises and a good example from their teacher and they are on their way. For others, it is not so easy, and it is for these folks that a method is helpful.

The idea of establishing freedom in the laryngeal mechanism by first developing the "shake"—getting the larynx to bounce up and down as described by Garcia and many others (like the throat of a nightingale)—is somehow appealing. There can be little doubt that a good trill taps into a reflex of some sort that we can see in other parts of the body. For instance, when you hold your open hand up and wave it back and forth, there is a certain frequency beyond which you can no longer do it voluntarily, but a reflexive action takes over and it just goes into a sustained oscillation that does not need our conscious effort. Another example would be the leg bouncing up and down when the weight of the leg has been put onto the front of the foot and you give a little kick start. It will bounce up and down all by itself (a favorite annoyance to teachers in the classroom). The idea of the larynx bouncing up and down in the neck must be related to the same physiological response to opposing muscles in the right balance of tension. I am sure this must be well understood by physiologists. It is a matter of finding the trigger in the suspensory muscles of the extrinsic laryngeal muscles. The implementation of this approach would be strictly experimental on my part, but I am going to put it to the test.

Is that not what we as voice teachers do? We have an idea about how something works, we make a suggestion to a student, encourage their dedication to it, and observe the results. Each lesson is a little scientific experiment. If the same suggestion works with many people, we have a method! We have to maintain some objectivity for this process to really work. Part of the job of a scientist is to accept the results of the experiment, even when they do not support a theory to which he or she may have dedicated years of work.

A significant complication in our experimental work is the response of the subjects. Our students do not all react to the same conditions or suggestions in the same way; that is part of the wonder of human nature. Our knowledge of the structure and function of the vocal mechanism can be vital to our ability to derive principles of application and execution that are meaningful to as many of our charges as possible.

Untold thousands of those experiments have already been done and reported in the literature over several hundred years. As you know by now, it is my belief that we miss a great deal of wisdom if we do not read and try to understand what has been done before.

NOTES

1. Pier Francesco Tosi, *Observations on the Florid Song*, translated by Mr. Galliard, edited by Michael Pilkington (London: Stainer & Bell, 1987), 14.
2. Ibid.
3. Giambattista Mancini, *Practical Reflections on the Figurative Art of Singing*, translated by Pietro Buzzi (Boston: Gorham Press, 1912), 126. Originally published as *Pensieri e riflessioni pratiche sopra il canto figurato* (Vienna, 1774).
4. Luigi LaBlache, *LaBlache's Complete Method of Singing*, translated from the original French (Cincinnati: John Church Co., nd), 59.
5. Manuel Garcia. *Complete Treatise On the Art of Singing, Part 2*, translated and edited by Donald Paschke (New York: Da Capo Press, 1984), 161. Originally published as *Nouveau Traité Sommaire sur l'Art du Chant* (Genève: Minkoff Éditeur, 1847).
6. Ibid.
7. Ibid., 163.
8. Charles Battaille,. *Physiology as Applied to the Study of the Vocal Mechanism,* in Richard Joiner, ed., *Pioneer in Vocal Science and the Teaching of Singing* (Lanham, MD: Scarecrow Press, 1998), 183. Originally published as *De la physiologie appliquée á l'étude de la mechanisme vocal* (Paris: Victor Masson and Sons, 1863).
9. Carlo Bassini, *Art of Singing* (New York: C. H. Ditson, 1884), 129.
10. Ibid.
11. Julius Stockhausen, *A Method of Singing,* translated by Sophie Löwe (London: Novello, 1884), 75. Originally published as *Julius Stockhausens Gesangs-methode* (Leipzig: Peters, 1884).
12. The *spiritus asper* was another name for aspirated vocalization being careful not to allow enough air to pass that it was audible.
13. Stockhausen, 75.
14. William Shakespeare, *The Art of Singing* (Boston: Oliver Ditson Co., 1898), 119.
15. Edgar Herbert-Caesari, *The Voice of the Mind* (Boston: Crescendo, 1963), 245.

16. Ida France, *Manual of Bel Canto* (New York: Coward-McCann, Inc., 1959), 57.
17. Douglas Stanley, *The Science of Voice* (New York: Carl Fischer, 1929), 160.
18. Ibid., 159.
19. Richard Miller, *The Structure of Singing* (New York: Schirmer Books, 1986), 196.
20. Victor Fuchs, *The Art of Singing* (London: John Calder Ltd., 1985), 123.

12. Suoni Filati: The Messa di Voce

Originally published in the *Journal of Singing*, volume 62, no. 5, 2006

The artistic execution of the *messa di voce* has been a hallmark of refined singing for several centuries. The perfect delivery of this vocal gesture has served as a standard against which singers have been judged, especially in earlier times. Giambattista Mancini stated, "If this is perfectly executed, by uniting the trill to it, it makes the cadenza and the singer perfect.[1] Mancini offered this definition:

> *Messa di voce* is that art in which the singer gives to any sustained note its graduation, starting it with almost a thread of voice and then reinforcing it proportionately to the greatest power in which it can be developed, and then takes it back with the same graduation that has been used in going from soft to loud.[2]

At the time Mancini wrote his book *Practical Reflections on the Art of Singing* (1774), vocal performance practice was quite different than that of today or even 100 years ago. The training of young singers was intense and would usually begin at a very young age. Daily study was thorough and included vocal training, keyboard, theory, and ear training. Musicianship and vocal skills were extraordinary compared to the typical experience of singers of today. The *messa di voce* was an important part of their training and was perfected over years of study and artistry. William Shakespeare in his book *The Art of Singing* (1921) bemoaned a vanishing practice.

> Having accomplished this change from *f* to *p*, accompanied if necessary by an imperceptible change of register, the singer may now proceed to the more difficult transition involved in passing from *pp* to *forte*; a change so difficult that it is rarely attempted by the modern artist, though once the great resource of the singer of a past generation.[3]

Even so, the *messa di voce* remains a part of our performance practice and we still thrill at a well-executed display of this deceptively difficult expression.

Through the ages there have been differences of opinion as to when in the training of a singer the *messa di voce* should be taught. In the middle of the nineteenth century, Carlo Bassini wrote in his very popular method book *The Art of Singing* (1856):

> A perfectly incomprehensible thing to me is the practice with singing book makers of commencing their studies with swelling the tones!—How illogical—how absurd—how perfectly impracticable.
>
> To swell a tone correctly is to be a perfect singer. For consider—this involves the following things:—complete mastery of the action of the lungs and the diaphragm, of the glottis-stroke, of the different positions to be assumed by the pharynx, of the blending of the two registers, chest and falsetto: (for it would be impossible smoothly to swell a sound without having first, by practice, perfectly united these two registers, so that the necessary passage from one register to the other during the progress of the swell may be quite imperceptible) and finally

> a mastery of the two timbres, clear and sombre—as we already have demonstrated in speaking of the different timbres.
>
> Let me repeat, then, elegantly to swell a sound is to be a perfect singer. How absurd would it be for a painter to demand of a pupil that he should elegantly finish a head at the first lesson. And yet the swell is the crowning task and glory of the singer.[4]

Bassini was a disciple of Manuel Garcia II and many of his ideas reflect Garcia's method. Garcia taught the *messa di voce* late in the training of a pupil and many authors agreed with the practice. We find another caution against the practice of early study of the *messa di voce* from the physician/voice teacher team of Lennox Brown and Emil Behnke in the book *Voice, Song & Speech* (1884).

> We may say in passing that we hold the very general practice of commencing the education of a vocalist by teaching him the *messa di voce* to be wrong. This ornament is far too difficult for a beginner, and the earliest moment for attempting it is when the student has fully mastered his respiration.[5]

G. B. Lamperti also cautioned in his *Technics of Bel Canto* (1905),

> Not until the voice has gained decided agility and facility should the pupil begin to practice sustained tones, together with the *messa di voce* (the long, even crescendo and decrescendo).[6]

As only one example from a contemporary source, Richard Miller stated,

> Attempts to achieve the highly controlled *messa di voce* must wait for general technical stability.[7]

Miller went on to say that once a certain level of proficiency is gained it should become an essential part of the daily regimen.

> The maturing young artist and the seasoned professional should regard the *messa di voce* vocalise as an essential part of each day's technical work. Younger singers should not attempt that skill until they have acquired a thorough grounding in vocal technique.[8]

Even though our artistic understanding of the *messa di voce* is clear, there is not unanimous agreement upon the means of producing it. Garcia described a very complex coordination involving a change of registers (from *falsetto* to the chest voice evidenced by a change from breathy to firm phonation) and with the larynx changing positions in the neck resulting in a change from the *voix claire* to the *voix sombrée*. Here is how Garcia described it in his *A Complete Treatise on the Art of Singing* (1847):

> The student will begin the tone softly in the falsetto and in sombre timbre. As we have seen, this procedure makes the larynx firm and contracts the pharynx. Then, without varying the position, and, as a result, the timbre, one will pass into the chest register, fixing the larynx more and more firmly in order to prevent making the abrupt movement which produces the hiccough at the moment of the separation of the two registers. Once established in the chest

register, one will raise the larynx again and will dilate the pharynx to clarify the timbre in such a way that toward the middle of the duration of the tone it will have all its brilliance and all its force. In order to soften the tone, the student will do the reverse; that-is-to-say, that before passing into the falsetto register, at the moment the voice is diminished he will darken the chest tone, again fastening the larynx low and contracting the pharynx in order to support it and to avoid the jerk of the change of registers. Then he will pass slowly from the chest register to the falsetto; after which he will relax the pharynx and extinguish the tone. I deduce this rule from the physiological fact that the larynx, being held low by the sombre timbre, can produce the two registers without being displaced. Now, the displacement produces the hiccough which so disagreeably separates the one register from the other.[9]

Not everyone has agreed with this means of producing it. Francesco Lamperti in *The Art of Singing* (1884) stated,

Given a phrase, it is indispensable that the same energy of vocal emission should be employed in singing it *piano*, as in singing it *forte*, or, to express it better, the same intensity of internal effort. The volume and sonorousness of the voice are qualities entirely independent of what I call internal effort. If, in emitting a small quantity of voice, the tension of the diaphragm be diminished, the result will be that the *piano* will have less life, less colour than the *forte*, whereas it often requires more. There must therefore be no relaxation of tension in the abdominal muscles . . .[10]

James Stark offered an in-depth discussion of this difference in his book *Bel Canto: A History of Vocal Pedagogy* (1999).[11] Stark defined the two schools of thought on this matter as the Garcia method and the Lamperti method. Stark identified the source of the latter method to be that of Alexis Garaudé who taught at the Paris Conservatory before Garcia. Stark provided this discussion which included his own translation from Garaudè's book, *Méthode complète de chant* (1830).

'Each tone of the scale is made on the vowel [a], and it must be *filé*; it is said that it must begin very sweetly, and be gradually increased until halfway through the note (where it reaches its greatest force), then diminished insensibly to the end of the note. This manner of spinning the tone [*filer les sons*] is called *mise de voix* or *messa di voce*.' He continued by saying that the *messa di voce* must be done 'with purity and without effort. In reinforcing the weak tones, it must be done without altering the organ or disfiguring its sound. The quality of the timbre (*metallo*) of the voice must be natural.' He maintained that 'one must not change the timbre. The registers should remain the same regardless of the force of the voice, and one should not use the *voce di testa*.'[12]

The most obvious difference between the two methods has to do with vocal fold adduction. Garcia's method began with loose adduction at the beginning and increased toward firm phonation as a part of the crescendo. The effect of this would be a constantly changing source spectrum. We know that the acoustic energy in a breathy tone (Garcia would have called it *falsetto*) is very modest compared to the spectrum of fully adducted vocal folds with high subglottal pressure. In the Garcia method there would have also been a change of timbre associated with the change of laryngeal height, going back and forth between the somber and clear timbre. The Lamperti school would have displayed a less drastic change in timbre of the sound due to the fact the glottal adduction was firm from the beginning to the end and did not apparently include the change of laryngeal posture. Both methods would require a great deal of skill on the part the singer and require a complex interaction between the respiratory system and the muscles of the larynx.

There is an inverse relationship between subglottal pressure and tension along the margin of the vocal fold when you consider the pitch of the voice. Given a particular state of contraction of the cricothyroid, an increase in subglottal pressure (support) would drive the vocal folds further apart during each phonatory cycle. The increase in amplitude of vibration is in itself a pitch raising maneuver since the vocal folds are traveling further apart during each cycle, stretching the vocal ligament. Since the pitch is determined by the amount of tension in the ligament the frequency would rise. To maintain the same frequency the cricothyroid muscle must relax and release some of the tension. If you have ever asked an amateur choir to crescendo on a sustained chord you may have experienced that the pitch tends to rise. They have not learned to compensate for the change of breath pressure with less pull of the cricothyroid. Mancini noted a similar tendency when the control of the breath was lacking.

> When one starts a tone with so much impetus of breath, the voice goes sharp at the beginning of the tone, and flattens at the end of it, producing the most disagreeable effect upon the listener.[13]

The complexity of these interactions speaks directly to the caution that the *messa di voce* should be studied only after significant skill has been acquired.

The *messa di voce* has not only served as an important musical embellishment, but also as a tool for training the singing voice. This is especially true for register unification. William Vennard noted:

> The great teachers have always recognized the overlapping of registers and the possibility of going from one to another on the same pitch, while making a *crescendo* or *descrescendo*. This is the essence of the *messa di voce*. Garcia recognized that a woman's chest voice overlaps her middle voice (which in his early writing he called "falsetto," which is rather confusing because "head" was still higher) and he proposed that she change on different notes for different artistic purposes. He also noted an overlap in men's voices and pointed out that tenors, especially, benefit from passing from one register to another while singing certain single tones in the area of the overlap. He said, "It is very difficult, but once mastered, of great use."[14]

Of course, one can hardly mention the concept of register unification without referencing one of my valued mentors, Cornelius Reid. He has written so extensively on this subject that any brief quote hardly does him justice, but among many excerpts that I could offer the reader is a brief note from his first important work, *Bel Canto* (1950).

> The joining of the registers, therefore, begins by building up "the extremity of that which happens to be weakest" which, almost without exception, will be the lower portion of the falsetto. The device invented to secure the unification of the *voce di testa* with the *voce di petto* was the messa di voce, or swell tone.[15]

Summary

Suffice it to say that the *messa di voce* has served the singing community for several hundred years as both an expressive tool and as a pedagogic means of developing the proper coordination between the respiratory and phonatory systems. It has also been used in the process of uniting the registers of the instrument. There seems to remain two distinct schools of thought on the proper execution which reflect fundamental differences in concept. The Garcia method is one thing, the Lamperti method another. I believe that both are used by great singers depending upon the tradition of their training. Perhaps the same singer utilizes both methods depending upon the artistic need. Differences notwithstanding, both approaches challenge the mechanism and should be a part of our own study and our teaching if we care about fully exploring the potential of our students and practicing our craft as a part of the tradition that has been handed down to us.

This my twelfth article in this column. Each of them has dealt with some pedagogic concept or idea that is found in our long tradition of voice training. What a challenge it is to take a young promising talent and walk him or her through several years of guided study and help him or her become an artist. My focus here has been on the technical aspects. Of course, this is but a small part of artistry. I tell my students that a good technique is good for only one thing: to give your voice the freedom to express what your heart is telling it to do. But a good technique is hard to achieve. In my own studio, I equally divide the hour lesson with technical work and repertory study. The first half of the hour is spent voice building—no matter what the pressure of an upcoming performance. I never skip it. I do not have any students who do not need it. That leaves only the second part of the hour and the weekly studio class to work on all the other equally important aspects of becoming a singing artist. There is adequate time for neither. I really would really like to know how we arrived at the practice that a vocal performance major at a college or university is given only one hour with their teacher per week in which to accomplish the unrealistic goal (for most) of going from novice to artist in four short years. We all have run the numbers. Each semester consists of about fourteen hours of individual study. I need not remind you that they spend three or four times that singing in choirs. In an entire undergraduate degree, our students will have spent less than 120 hours in our presence. Is it any wonder that so few of our undergraduates go on to compete at the next level? Is it any wonder that our graduate programs are stocked with young people who do not yet sing well enough to gain professional experience? How is it that we have lived with this system for so many years? Is it time to take another look? I met a teacher who taught in an academic program in Germany a couple of years ago and was pleasantly surprised to hear that they had two one-hour lessons with their students each week. Why not for us? I know that at some point it must boil down to tuition dollars and cents and faculty loads (our administrations hate our contact hour numbers already), but I want to state for the record that I believe that it is a broken system and "needs fixin'" as we say in the South. What better source for a move to a better system than through our own professional organization. I would love to hear from you if you have ideas about this.

In the meantime, I will, like you, do the best that I can to offer the best training that one hour a week will allow.

NOTES

1. Giambattista Mancini, *Practical Reflections on the Figurative Art of Singing*, translated by Pietro Buzzi (Boston: Gorham Press, 1912), 118. Originally published as *Pensieri e Riflessioni Pratiche Sopra il Canto Figurato* (Vienna, 1774).
2. Ibid., 117.
3. William Shakespeare, *The Art of Singing* (Boston: Oliver Ditson Company, 1921), 126.
4. Carlo Bassini, *Art of Singing* (New York: C. H. Ditson, 1884), 17.
5. Lennox Brown and Emil Behnke, *Voice, Song & Speech* (London: Sampson Low, Marston, Searle, and Rivington, 1884), 186.
6. G. B. Lamperti, *The Technics of Bel Canto* (New York: G. Schirmer, 1905), 21.
7. Richard Miller, *The Structure of Singing* (New York: Schirmer Books, 1986), 175.
8. Ibid., 181.
9. Manuel Garcia, *A Complete Treatise On the Art of Singing, Part 1,* translated and edited by Donald Paschke (New York: Da Capo Press, 1984), 135–6. Originally published as *Nouveau Traité Sommaire sur l'Art du Chant* (Genève: Minkoff Éditeur, 1847).
10. F. Lamperti, *The Art of Singing According to Ancient Tradition and Personal Experience*, translated by W. Jekyll (London: G. Ricordi, 1884), 52. Originally published as *L'arte del canto in ordine all tradizione classiche ed particolare experienze* (Milano: G. Ricordi, 1883).
11. James Stark, *Bel Canto: The History of Vocal Pedagogy* (Toronto: University of Toronto Press, 1999), 246.
12. Ibid., 97.
13. Mancini, 120.
14. William Vennard, *Singing: The Mechanism and the Technic* (New York, G. Schirmer, 1967), 77.
15. Cornelius Reid, *Bel Canto* (New York: Coleman-Ross Company, Inc., 1950), 98.

13. Words from William Shakespeare

Originally published in the *Journal of Singing*, volume 63, no. 1, 2006

It has been my purpose in this column to present pedagogic theory and practice gleaned from treatises and books written over the past 250 years and to provide, when appropriate, some scientific support for particular theories that seem apropos for the studio teacher of today. My usual practice has been to present a review of a particular topic from many sources with the purpose of suggesting some uniformity or agreement amongst voice professionals spanning many years of practice. Of course, there has been and always will be a certain diversity of opinion on matters of taste and preference. In this column, however, I present in full a report of a lecture made to the Musical Association of London November 15, 1904 by William Shakespeare (not the Bard, 1849–1931). Shakespeare was a composer, a pianist, and a tenor who at one time studied with Lamperti in Milan. His book The Art of Singing,1 first published in 1899, was rewritten and published again in 1921. It is commonly available in music libraries as it was a popular contribution to the pedagogic treatises of the time. A second book, Plain Words on Singing,[2] repeated several chapters from his first book and included some discussion of the "old masters" along with some essays on the singers of the day.[3]

I think that you will find that Mr. Shakespeare's comments are as appropriate for today as yesterday. I can imagine this same address being given by a respected colleague at our own national conference today. It is worthy of careful review, not because it offers anything particularly new to our present age, but because it summarizes succinctly issues that were and continue to be of concern as we train singers for the twenty-first century. We see that the world of singing has not changed too much in the one hundred years since Mr. Shakespeare's address, reproduced here exactly as it appeared in the Proceedings of the Musical Association.[4]

SINGING AS AN ART

By William Shakespeare

The limited time at my disposal this afternoon compels me to be brief in my remarks on "Singing as an Art."

I must preface what I have to say with a few words on the historical development of the art, recalling to your memories the names of some of the most eminent of the writers for a single voice.

We know that Henry Lawes, b. 1595, wrote capital songs, demanding some sustaining power, and that Purcell, b. 1658, composed his touching and sustained air, "Dido's Lament," as well as songs demanding the execution of scale passages, such as "Let the mighty engines."

Alessandro Scarlatti, b. 1659, wrote such airs as "Toglietemi la vita ancor" and "O cessate di piagarmi."

Lotti, b. 1667, who used modern harmonies with freedom and grace, composed "Pur dicesti," and Caldara (1678) wrote the air, "Selve amiche," which is a splendid specimen of the *sostenuto* or sustained style. These and many other composers wrote splendidly for the voice. All goes to prove that at this period there existed already a school of singing.

Bernacchi, b. 1690, was equally celebrated both as a singer and as a singing-master. He received instruction from Pistocchi, then the first singing-master in Italy, where, we read, there were not a few of such at that time. Bernacchi was engaged by Handel in 1717 to sing in his opera "Rinaldo."

Porpora, a pupil of Scarlatti, teacher of singing and composer, was born at Naples in 1686. He wrote many operas and established a school for singing, whence issued those wonderful pupils who made his name so famous. He was the greatest singing master who ever lived, and from his pupils have been handed down to us the relics of a grand style.

William Shakespeare (1849–1931)

Porpora has left us no written account of his manner of teaching, and his solfeggi, or vocalises, differ from others of his time only in being more exclusively directed to the development of flexibility of the voice.

To a profound knowledge of the human voice and an intuitive sympathy with singers, Porpora must have united the genius of imposing his will on others. It is said of him that he kept his pupil Caffarelli to a sheet of exercises for five years, and on the pupil asking if he might not be allowed to sing an aria, the Master replied, "Go, my son, I have nothing more to teach you, you are the greatest singer in Europe." Caffarelli excelled in slow and pathetic airs as well as in the bravura style, and was unapproachable in beauty of voice and in the execution of the trill.

Porpora's pupil, Farinelli, when the Emperor Charles the Sixth expressed his regret that so consummate an artist should devote himself entirely to exhibitions of skill and bravura, struck by the truth of the criticism, resolved to appeal more to emotion, and proved adequate by becoming the most pathetic as he had been the most brilliant of singers.

Farinelli had an inimitable power of swelling a note by minute degrees to an amazing volume and afterwards diminishing in the same manner to a mere point. This singer excited such enthusiasm in his audiences that one lady ejaculated the phrase (perpetuated by the painter Hogarth in "The Rake's Progress") "One God and one Farinelli." It was Farinelli who sang a cadence in a song with a trumpet obbligato, and after finishing a long note so that the trumpeter had to give up out of breath, extended the cadence with a further vocal passage in the same breath.

Farinelli, however, was not so fortunate when singing with a great rival, the already-mentioned Bernacchi, for on their meeting in public, after Farinelli had sung an air with great effect, Bernacchi repeated this with the same trills, roulades and cadenza *in such a manner* that Farinelli, who possessed the sweetest and most modest disposition, owned his defeat and entreated his conqueror to give him further instruction, which Bernacchi generously did. Farinelli thus perfected his style, and became the most remarkable singer, perhaps, who ever lived.

Pacchiorotti who, with a defective voice, possessed high intelligence and made himself a consummate artist, was followed by many great singers. Among them were Gizziello and later on Crescentini.

In the time of Mozart the singer Faustina was credited with such extraordinary powers of respiration that it was supposed she could sing while taking in as well as sending out the breath.

The roll of famous artists in modern times includes among others Catalani, Malibran, Grisi, Rubini, Tamburini, Lablache, Guiglini, Mario, down to Adelina Patti, Santley and Jenny Lind. The last-mentioned genius I myself heard sing Mozart's air from his opera "Il Re Pastore," and in this she sang a trill with violin obbligato in the most perfect *legato* style, so that every note agreed with the trill of the violin—a marvelous achievement, but in addition, the feeling of the song was expressed in the most touching way.

Now what are the technical terms which can convey the qualities of this grand vocal art?

Surely they are the unerring attack of the note in the very centre of the sound: the *sostenuto*, or sustaining all notes and joining them to others with a perfect *legato* without either jerkiness or slurring, and with the quality of expression intended; the *messa di voce*, or swelling from *piano* to *forte* and back to the softest sound without loss of quality; command over execution; expression and pathos; breadth of phrasing which is only possible to those who have command of a long breath; and intensity or carrying power sufficient for the largest halls or theatres.

Handel, Bach, and Mozart, and, among the moderns, more especially Rossini, Bellini, Donizetti and Verdi, knew how to bring into play all the resources of their singers in respect to the points I have just mentioned. They gave them time to breathe and collect themselves between the phrases by a bar or two of the orchestra, in a manner quite different from later composers who often give little or no time for the singer to breathe.

Bach and Handel, both born in 1685, were two of the greatest musicians who ever lived. Handel in 1706 traveled all over Italy, met the well-known singers of the day and composed operas for them, and for many years was connected with the King's Theatre, London. In the numberless masterpieces of this great composer we meet with every device favourable to the singer's art. Matchless recitative—loveliest airs—slow, sustained notes fostering *messa di voce*—many spaces for the singer to recover *breath* and calm—trills and passages—invocations and triumphant phrases. For recitative, "Deeper and deeper still," and for sustained notes, "Waft her, angels" and "Comfort ye"; for vigorous passages, "Ev'ry valley" and "Love sounds the alarm"; for prayerful utterance, "Pious orgies"; for invocation, "O sleep," "Father of Heaven," and "O liberty," also "Heart, thou source of pure delight" ("Acis and Galatea"). How many of these commence with the voice unaccompanied! Note the phrasing of Handel, where he interrupts the musical phrase, sometimes more than once, on a single word, in the air "Where'er you walk" from "Semele."

Sebastian Bach, who was neither a traveler nor a writer of operas like Handel, at times gives to the singer uncouth and awkward passages, difficult chromatic intervals—words recited on the highest notes—a voice-part perhaps treated too much like a solo stop on the organ— disregarding the compass or most favourable parts pertaining to the different voices.

Yet in spite of all this, what effects! In recitative and *sostenuto*, "Ah, Golgotha"; and the following air, in religious fervour and slow passage singing, "With Jesus will I watch and pray"; for quicker passage singing, "Haste, ye shepherds"; for holy devotion, "Into Thy hands my spirit I commend," etc.

Glück, a German composer, born 1714, studied in Milan, and his first operas met with some success. Handel, however, declared his music at this period to be detestable, and asserted that he knew no more about counterpoint than his (Handel's) cook. Glück went on persevering. He entirely reformed the style of writing for the stage, and in 1762 brought out his opera "Orfeo ed Euridice." He was not satisfied until he introduced what he considered a still more truthful kind of declamation, and banished all false and useless ornaments from operatic music. Note the profoundly dramatic accents of *Orfeo* in the recitative and lovely air "Che faro." In the air, he uses the *legato* effects of the voice in often giving more than one note to a word. What a stirring climax there is at the end of the piece!

Now unfortunately little is known of the methods adopted by the old masters of singing. They were not in the habit of printing their secrets as nowadays.

According to precepts handed down to us, we may gather that singing "as an art" consists in freedom of the throat and command over the breath. That is to say, by breathing out slowly on an imaginary object with perfect command so that the breath goes out as one wills and, furthermore, by loosening the throat—a much more difficult matter—so that all the notes sound to this controlled breathing, the result is "perfect production." The voice can now be produced with greater force—a force proportioned to the increased command of breath and to the perseverance of the singer in developing his vocal range.

The interesting question now arises: What would a singer of the old school find if he were to appear today? He would ask himself, "Is singing still an art?" and how could he use his masterly effects, so necessary in a past age? He might inquire "What is there to sing to in modern vocal works?" Could he make use of his *sostenuto*, his *legato*, the *messa di voce*, the *fioritura* execution and trills? I fear he would find that modern music affords no scope for these effects. Modern music has generally a separate syllable for every note—only forte singing is required, by reason of the presence of elaborate and powerful accompaniments.

A voice that has always to be produced at high pressure will, in the end, of necessity fail to produce a pure sound. We constantly hear singing out of tune. The artist can scarcely avoid fatigue in making the strenuous efforts which are demanded under modern conditions, and one result is that audiences become gradually indifferent to perfect singing in tune, and to steadiness of voice, and are no longer sensitive to delicate effects.

How then is an artist to touch his audience when they have become accustomed to notes that are not commenced in the centre of the sound, and to a forcing of voice and sentiment alike? There is only one possible way of attaining the desired result. He must do what Verdi had asserted to be essential, namely, *ritornare all' antico, i.e.*, return to the old Masters, and he must begin afresh to educate his audience to a higher appreciation of the art of singing.

If the artist only perseveres he is bound to succeed in this, and we shall see a restoration of the true art of singing.

It is time now to give a short sketch of the technique of singing as practiced by a past age.

Singing is a *prolonged* talking, and must be higher and louder than the voice we use in ordinary conversation, and more especially is this the case when the voice has to be used in a large hall.

Some people say "*breathe naturally*." One may as well tell the gymnast to perform naturally. His wonderful feats may appear natural, but they are result of a vast extension of that which is natural to us.

If when we draw in the breath we feel expansion about the soft place under the breast bone, we have done so by using the diaphragm.

Another mode of drawing in the breath is to expand the ribs. Now the ribs, when we raise them, move outwards and the cavity inside is made larger than before.

A singer must use *both* these methods; he must feel an expansion of the body at the soft place, and he must also feel an expansion of the sides by lifting the ribs.

Perhaps the greatest fault that we can make is to raise the ribs by the muscles which are fixed to the points of the shoulders on front.

We should avoid this error by the use of very *powerful* muscles *which are felt at the back* under the shoulder-blades and under the arms, and so expand enormously the sides of the body.

The muscles by which we drive out the breath are principally situated in the abdomen. They perform a double duty: one is to pull down the ribs, and the other is, by their pressure inwards, to cause the diaphragm to ascend again.

By the control of the breath we mean that we can regulate the action of the muscles *which draw in the breath, at the same time* that our expiratory muscles are *sending it out*. There is then a struggle between these two forces, the one force causing a continuous pressure while the other regulates, controls and economises this same pressure, which if not regulated would let the breath escape altogether and the phrase sung would come to a premature end.

We see the result of a clumsy way of breathing in the unpleasant gaspings and noisy breathing produced by those who rely on the raising of the chest and shoulders. The poet puts this correctly when he says, "My bosom heaved with many a sigh."

On the other hand, the result of a right method of drawing in the breath is noiseless and imperceptible respiration. It should be so imperceptible that the audience is unaware of the breath being taken.

The old Masters knew nothing of anatomy, yet science only proves how right they were in their ideas of breathing. In accordance with the accepted axiom, "Summa ars celare artem" (the highest art lies in its concealment), they insisted that the goal of the singer should be "imperceptible and inaudible breathing." The celebrated master Lamperti was never tired of insisting that the points of the shoulders must be free, and that the breathing of a singer should resemble that of a swimmer.

The great tenor Rubini was once closely watched for several minutes by the equally celebrated bass Lablache, and although the latter was holding Rubini's hand while singing a duet, he declared that he was unable to observe when or how he breathed, so noiseless and imperceptible was his method of respiration. An oft-repeated anecdote of Rubini, however, describes that, later in his career, being desirous of bringing out the high B flat he used so much force as to break his collar-bone! First, I do not believe this story, but, if it were true, either the artist's collar-bone had become very brittle, or else he was not singing with that schooled respiration described on the occasion of his duet with Lablache.

A friend of mine tells me that his father knew Lablache intimately, and that this artist one day for fun sang a long note from *piano* to *forte* and back to *piano*, then drank a glass of wine, and without having breathed, finished by singing a chromatic scale in trills up the octave all in the same breath and finally blew out a candle with his mouth open!

There were giants in those days!

A word on voice-production: When we sing, the delicate edges of the vocal chords [*sic*] are brought together so that the pressure of the breath sets them into vibration, and prolonged sound is the result. The muscles connected with the vocal chords [*sic*] enable us to tune them to the notes of the scale, and melody ensues.

Whilst many earnest scientists have endeavoured to determine the exact action of the most delicate muscles in the larynx, nothing of so simple a character has yet been discovered as to make the study of singing any easier.

We shall learn more by observing what happens to the muscles which form the floor of the mouth.

They assist in holding the larynx in its proper position, and become tenser as we ascend the scale in the different register. The muscles, however, connected with different movements of the tongue *lie just above these*; indeed, they also help to form the floor of the mouth.

The least rigidity of the floor of the mouth involves the muscles of the tongue, and the tone as well as the pronunciation is distorted through the awkwardness of the singer. The term "placing the voice" is so commonly used that I do not hesitate to employ it here.

But when the voice is rightly produced the placing muscles do not interfere with the muscles above them which move the tongue, and so pronunciation and tone are now unimpeded, for they act independently.

By whispering a sentence and then suddenly singing it we can observe how the placing muscles come into play, and how they are quite different from those we employed in whispering only.

Thus we see that the difficulty lies not in the pronunciation itself, but in singing in such a manner that unconscious pronunciation is a result.

In bad singing the jaw is always fixed; indeed, a triple combination for evil is coincident in the fixedness of the tongue, throat and jaw. When one is rigid all are rigid, and this could be easily explained scientifically.

The old masters of singing, without any knowledge of anatomy, held it to be of the greatest importance that during the singing of scale passages the jaw was not to move.

Their maxim was "He who moves the mouth cannot sing."

Pacchiorotti held that "He who knows how to breathe and how to pronounce" knows how to sing. Crescentini averred that "Looseness about neck and the voice on the breath" is the art of singing. If we do not produce the voice rightly, either the throat contracts in a manner which we recognize as throaty, or the nasal cavities are rigidly held and we say the sound is nasal; or we hear a hooting, lugubrious sound, terribly monotonous and sepulchral; or silly sounds are produced which have been called in Italian *Voce bianca, Voix blanche* by the French, or white, blatant, colourless voice, like that produced by the half-witted.

Awkward rigidity about the floor of the mouth is also fatal to the freedom of the muscles which tune the larynx. So when a note starts exactly on the pitch intended, it is the most important sign of perfect voice-production.

Many of us at times have sung a note which seemed to roll out in unconscious freedom and with great sonority. The art of singing is to find out how this excellence may be attained in all the notes of the voice.

There are placing muscles and tuning muscles. When length, breadth and thickness of the vocal chords [*sic*] are rightly adjusted, the intrinsic muscles of the larynx can tune the different notes in unconscious ease. Moreover such notes respond to the right breath control.

We learn from the old Masters that they arrived at placing the voice, poising the larynx on the breath, by the very simple method of endeavouring to sing a note while they measured the breath by breathing on a mirror or against a lighted taper held opposite the mouth. They could thus judge whether the note sounded fully without disturbing the breath. Supposing the note was not placed, the singer was compelled to press more than he could do without upsetting the breath control. This caused a puff, which was considered a disaster. Under this system it was found that that was the right note which produced the most sound with the least breath. Scientifically they were right, for they produced a greater result with less means.

The student, in trying to sing a note, frequently forgets his breath control, and this will bring home to him the truth of the old saying, "The art of singing is the school of respiration."

The looseness of the neck and unconscious feeling about the throat during singing caused the old singers to boast that the Italian singer has no throat. They might have added no jaw and no tongue.

Then a note may be described as *placed* if it speaks to the breath we are able to control, if it can be produced in the very centre of the sound intended, if it leaves in freedom the pronunciation and the expression.

The essence of the teaching of the old Masters is contained in the axiom: "Every note of the voice should be produced by a column of air over which the singer should have perfect control."

The attack of the note (that is to say, the art of starting a sound with frankness in the very centre of the pitch intended) has always been regarded as a great test of good singing. The many scoopings up to, or "seeking or feeling for the note," are of course a sign of bad production.

The accomplishment of what is known as *"legato singing,"* namely, *that joining of the notes* which yet must at the same time all be "clean cut out," was looked upon by the old Masters as another of the great signs of good singing. They said, "He who cannot join cannot sing." All the notes of a passage on the same vowel should be "like pearls on a string," and the string supporting them is the right control of the breath. Those who have mastered breath control and freedom of the throat and tongue are now in a position to add tone to the voice through the loose, unrestrained condition of the space behind the tongue and the nasal cavities.

The throat in its normal state and when we are asleep is wide open, and only bad singing interferes with this. For some vowels the throat space undoubtedly has temporarily to be somewhat contracted, and possibly as we sing higher there may be a corresponding modification of the throat space. But all these changes are unconscious, and the contortions of the bad singer render these natural conditions impossible, just as the unconstrained throat of the good singer leaves nature free to utter her loveliest tones.

With the throat wide open, the vowel sound which is emitted is *Ah*. This pure *Ah* was the goal towards which the Italian singers never ceased to advance, as affording the greatest test of tone and facility of pronunciation.

As an aid to the freedom necessary to this perfect vowel the student was wont to practice a rapid tongue movement before the Ah, and the consonant *l* was generally adopted on account of its demanding a free movement of the whole of the tongue. On singing *lah* rapidly the inclination to stiffen the instrument was overcome. This sudden tongue movement, when done *with entire absence of hesitation* and in conjunction with a proper breath control, became the foundation for the attack of the note, and the freedom and richness of the *Ah* was found to depend on its daring and spontaneity. The value of *lah* as a foundation study cannot be over-estimated by the student, who through it will discover freedom of throat. The sudden, rapid movement of the tongue in reiterated *lahs* was the device used by the old Masters for bringing about the freedom of the tongue and jaw which invariably accompanies good singing.

Sing with frank and fearless attack *lah, lah, lah, lah, lah* on the same note. Was the tune commenced in the very centre of the sound intended? Was there no hesitation at the commencement? Was the jaw in repose and independent of the movement of the tongue?

Another mode of finding the perfect *Ah* is to repeat it in a slow, staccato manner on the same note in the same breath. If we tune with absolute accuracy, and if we open the throat so as to emit a *pure Ah*, we shall be compelled to control the breath rightly. These exercises each produce in the end precisely the same result, viz., the fullest natural tone.

Let us now take a step forward and vary the vowel sounds used in the exercise, while strictly regarding the rules just laid down for naturalness of tone. We will sing, *Lah, leh, lee, Ah, eh, ee*. Can we change the position of the tongue (which rises somewhat in the centre for *eh*, and still more for *ee*), *without moving the jaw*, or allowing the breath to slip and the throat to close?

We have now arrived at the *last test* of good singing, which I must insist upon. When we sing two or more notes on the same syllable do they join in the *legato* style? Dare we sing with unerring tuning?

Really, *we have arrived very nearly at the goal of voice production* if we can do this on consecutive notes on all the intervals.

Lastly, if we can sing in the *legato* style we have arrived at a state of freedom which will permit, with practice, the execution of the most rapid passages.

A Word about Registers.

In the Italian language, the steps of the organ are called the *registers*. Now because of this, the three different characteristic series of tones which exist in every voice have been named the three registers. One might say these three stops are the *grand* stop, the *brilliant* stop, the *flute* stop.

We have all heard of the *chest* voice. This simply means that the lowest notes of the voice when produced naturally in a certain way cause a *remarkable sensation of vibration in the chest* which can be physically felt by the hand of the performer, as well as heard by the audience! Such notes are manly and grand in character.

In the middle of the voice immediately above the chest register is another series of notes usually termed the *medium register*. In these notes *the most characteristic sign of singing rightly is the extraordinary sense of vibration of the air in the mouth*, which seems to strike the upper teeth.

The notes of this series of sounds are distinguished by their brilliant and silvery quality.

The third register is known as the *head voice*, by reason of the sensation felt by the singer, and recognized likewise by the listener, that the sound reverberates in the skull beyond the last upper teeth. All the teeth that are shown when we smile must be shown when we sing the head register. These head notes are characterized by *a fluty and bird-like character* and a womanly quality of surpassing loveliness.

The first notes of all the registers are weak and a source of trouble to the student, for the breath slips out until some experience is gained. For this reason, instead of strengthening the lower, weak notes of the medium register, the inclination of all voices is to *hurry on their studies by forcing up the chest notes when they ought to sing medium*, with the result that the men are said to shout or bawl, or yell like the men in the streets, and the contraltos and sopranos force up the chest notes and emit sounds more like boys shouting to each other.

Mezzo-sopranos and sopranos, moreover, are very prone to *avoid* the cultivation of the head-notes altogether, and to force up the medium register, with a sad result. It is no longer singing in a high sense, it is not expressive of lovely feelings, pronunciation is impossible, and the characteristic sound of the voice is described as screaming, screeching; whereas nothing in nature is more lovely and truly womanly than the sound of the head voice.

The registers so dovetail one into the other, or overlap one another, that we can sing softly some notes in one register and repeat the same notes loudly in another register. We can also commence a note *pp* and swell it out to *ff* and return to the softest *pp*, but probably not always with the same throat mechanism; indeed the achievement of this was formerly considered the culminating effort of the singer, and was termed the *messa di voce*. It is, however, as necessary to sing with loose throat to do this as it is to join the notes in the *legato* style.

The trill was another of the accomplishments highly thought of as proving the mastery of the vocal art. It is perhaps the most delightful of all the embellishments of music.

The trill is still written in pianoforte and violin pieces, where it is still regarded as a worthy aid to expression. Singers, however, finding its accomplishment beyond their powers, are wont to assume that it, together with scales and passages, is unworthy and meretricious and, as an ornament, is but an empty and stale device for showing off the voice.

The trills have not yet been cut out of Beethoven's Sonatas, so we may not deem them unworthy of a word here. As the performance of this delightful ornament is a sure sign of the greatest freedom of the instrument, the two notes must be perfectly produced by one or both of the devices already mentioned. That is to say, we must sing the two notes on *Lah, la la la*, faster and faster until an even trill is the result, or we must do staccato notes more rapidly until the notes join and trill of themselves. In practicing this, never sing faster than you can sing exactly in tune, exactly in time (that is, not jerking), with the perfect pronunciation of *Ah*, and with a smiling tone which must reveal absolute ease of manner.

The *portamento* is another graceful effect.

Pronunciation.

The vowels of the English language are thirteen in number, and as we have conquered the pronunciation of the typical *Ah*, we must sustain the other twelve sounds with similar freedom. Starting with *Ah*, we find such sounds as *a*t, *a* (and *air*), *e*t, *i*t, and *ee*, which are different upward tongue positions; then come changes of lips and throat, such as *oo*, h*oo*d, *aw*, *o*, *o*t, *e*r, and *u*t.

As singing words at first takes out attention from the unerring tuning which we should associate with our studies, beware of commencing too soon to attempt singing with words. The old Masters insisted on solfeggi and vocalises or songs without words of a considerable time before permitting an aria.

Intensity and Expression.

By intensity the good singer means the intense pressure of the breath on the voice which gives effect to any and every emotion he chooses, because he has power over the breath that intensifies, and has acquired the freedom of the instrument. By means of this he can make the loudest sounds possible *expressive*, and he can also cause the *softest* sounds to be carried to the farthest end of the theatre or concert hall.

The artist when he intensifies a *pianissimo* note can make this travel to the end of the room and touch his hearers, and arouse emotions as of distance brought near to us, or of memories of the past recalled. The bad singer has to rely on his loud notes, which become monotonous; he dare not sing softly, he would most likely become inaudible.

Let us never cease striving to bring out all the force and intensity with which nature has endowed us; but, at the same time, let us endeavour *never* to give out more force than that with which we are able to express. The real amount of fervour we can produce depends on our instinct and individuality, and the result is the depth and intensity of expression of which we are capable.

The sacred warmth of expressive melody is the gift of the gods, and without it there will be little emotion.

The play of the face varies the expression of the voice. How could the inanimate face produce sounds other than monotonous? *It is impossible* to smile with the face and express sorrow with the voice.

Every emotion has its appropriate facial expression. So if we insist on expressing with the face the sentiment we sing, and at the same time control the breath, we shall certainly succeed in our art.

Phrasing.

Let us study the words and music we have to sing until both are mastered mentally, the picture of the words and the phrasing of the music; the *crescendo* of the ascending notes of the melody and the *diminuendo* of the falling cadence; the accents necessary to the words, the sensitive loveliness of the accents which belong to the melody.

The effect of diminishing the power of the voice on nearing the end of a phrase is sometimes magical.

Let us avoid dragging and hurrying. The greater the artist the less he tampers with the time of the music, without due consideration.

The old Masters prided themselves on their phrasing, on the calmness of the tempo, on the just accent, and on the *crescendo* and *diminuendo*.

The singers were so sensitive to lovely phrasing that the clarinetist, Lazarus, whom I knew intimately, on being asked "Where did you learn your exquisite phrasing?" said, "I learnt it from the singers at the Opera, some fifty years ago." On the other hand, a great tenor, on being asked, "From whom did you learn your phrasing?" said, "I fancy I learnt more from hearing Lazarus play the clarinet than from anyone else."

Nowadays the *instrumentalists* are certainly ahead of the singers in loveliness of phrasing, but formerly the contrary was the case.

The development of the orchestra has of course been carried to its highest pitch by Wagner. But, unfortunately, while he has increased the volume, the richness and complexity of the *orchestra* to an unprecedented degree, he has been unable to add *anything whatever to the volume of the human voice.*

There still live composers who have written music full of deep feeling, true loveliness and dramatic character, yet not nearly so well-fitted for the voice, and indeed sometimes almost incapable of successful performance.

As a public singer I have had to sing cantatas and other works which, though written for a tenor, were quite unsuitable, and I have heard many times artists singing music too low, or painfully laden with words on the highest notes, parts almost impossible to render with any true vocal effect.

Vocalists have asked the composer, "For what voice is this written?" He answers, "Well, I do not mean exactly any particular kind of voice; it is for a kind of baritone or mezzo-soprano." What a confused idea of the capabilities of the different voices!

Some two years before his death, I begged the great Brahms to write some songs specially for a tenor voice. I told him I found his lovely songs too low. He said, "Transpose them higher, for I like them to be transposed according to the voice." "But," I said, "If I put them up, then there are notes which will be too high, for the tenor voice is only good between the two A flats. Your songs are too extensive in compass." "Ja, ja," he said, "that is what my friend Walther, the tenor, tells me." What a loss to singers it is, then, that the beautiful songs of Brahms, as well as those of other great men, were not written for some particular voice, like the music of the Italian composers.

The question suggests itself, why do not composers study singing before writing for the voice, just as they must study the pianoforte or the violin before writing a concerto for these instruments?

It is well-known how much Mendelssohn was indebted to his friend David for the excellence of his violin part in the Concerto, one of the most grateful works ever written for any instrument. Brahms, too, sought the assistance of Joachim when engaged in composing his violin Concerto.

In the olden times, singers were frequently composers and composers were singing-masters. Furthermore, Handel and Mozart both went to Italy and studied singing, and associated with singers.

I believe the time is fast coming when there shall spring up composers who will study singing and singers, and find the *legato* style of singing—the long, expressive notes, the invocation—and all the charms of a classic school as worthy of their attention as the pianoforte, violin, and other instruments.

There exist the same splendid voices now as ever, and the same poetic imagination. There are already signs everywhere that an inquiry is being made relative to singing and singers, which augurs well for the art.

The more the subject is discussed the better. Such discussions cannot fail to be the means of bringing together the composer, the singer, and the singing-master, and it is only by the constant association of these three elements that we shall realize the great object on which the hopes of all of us are set, namely, great works of art that shall open to us new fields of beauty through the medium of the only instrument that is at once human and divine.

DISCUSSION

The Chairman: Our first duty is to thank Mr. Shakespeare for the paper he has given us to-day. It is so full of points of interest and touches such a variety of subjects that we might go on talking not only for an hour, but for very many hours, without exhausting it. I will confine my remarks to two heads: (1) the historical portion, (2) the technical portion. With regard to the history, I would remind him and you that in taking records of those who lived long ago we have no means of knowing what their standard was. We can only judge from what they wrote about it. But I may tell you that in looking over old music prepared for students by men who descended from the Italian professors, one does not form a high idea of their judgment. One of the most celebrated of these, Domenico Carri, who lived in this country—part of the time in Edinburgh, and part in London—has published three or four volumes of songs with directions for phrasing and breathing; and all I can say is that the standard of this work would never be accepted to-day. The violation of the sense of the words is dreadful, and the phrasing, particularly in respect of the marks for breathing, is absolutely bad. Again, I think of another man who succeeded in his day; he was the teacher of Miss Stephens, afterwards Countess of Essex—Thomas Welsh. I have some music which he prepared for Miss Stephens. This is not a mere MS.; it was printed and published by the Harmonic Institution, with full directions for phrasing and breathing, and I am bound to say they are absolutely detestable. So I would prefer to come down to what we know. With many points brought forward by my friend Mr. Shakespeare I fully agree; in particular with what he says about Jenny Lind's vocalization—it was perfect. But when we talk about the people of old times, though I read of them with great interest I do not know what their standard was, and therefore am not prepared to join in all the admiration that is expressed by those who have written about them. With regard to the technical portion of his paper I think he has given us some very valuable hints. It is quite true in these days singing is rather giving place to shouting. It is a great pity. There are many causes. One is that we have such large audiences and consequently have to sing in such large buildings that people think they must strain their voices to make themselves heard. But they never think of that in the case of instrumental solos. A flute or an oboe is perfectly well heard; so why should not the human voice be heard if it is properly used? It is not at all necessary for a singer to shout. I hear sometimes that the Albert Hall is very trying to singers. May I give you a personal anecdote? I trust you will forgive me if it appears somewhat egotistical, because it is really a very good exemplification of what I have just said. I remember the late Queen ordered a State concert at the Albert Hall when the Emperor of Russia came to London, and Sir Michael Costa had to furnish the programme. I was one of the fortunate ones engaged to sing on that occasion. He asked me what I would sing. I daresay you all suppose I would have chosen "Sound an alarm" or "The death of Nelson," or something with some fine high A's in it. Instead of this I decided to sing a little song of Felicien David's, "O ma maîtresse." "But," said he, "you know that is so very soft; are you sure you will be heard?" I said, "I shall be heard all right." Well, I sang that song, and it was the only song re-demanded that evening. I quite agree that the voice should be the first thing. Like opening a pianoforte warehouse, it is no use to open it unless you have something to sell; and a singer has no business to try to sing until he has thoroughly qualified himself by making the voice such as God meant it to be—the very best. So far as words are concerned, that point also needs attention; but it should be taken separately and cultivated apart from the voice. The voice should be the first consideration before anything is taken with words. But I must not go into technicalities now. I have been delighted to be here and to listen to all that Mr. Shakespeare has said, and if time permitted I would like to say a great deal more about it. Just one word about Gluck. Handel did say that Gluck knew no more about counterpoint than his cook; but his cook happened to be Waltz, who was a very good musician, and who sometimes performed on the stage. He played the violoncello in Handel's orchestra and assisted in the scoring of his works. Gluck at the time was playing the musical glasses at the Haymarket Theatre.

(A vote of thanks was passed unanimously.)

Mr. Shakespeare—I thank you most sincerely for the very kindly reception you have given me. I am very glad to have had this opportunity of coming before you.

NOTES

1. William Shakespeare, *The Art of Singing* (London: Netzler & Co., 1899. Revised edition entirely rewritten, New York: C.H. Ditson & Co., 1921).
2. William Shakespeare, *Plain Words on Singing* (London: G.P. Putnam's Sons, 1924).
3. Brent Jeffery Monahan, *The Art of Singing: A Compendium of Thoughts on Singing Published Between 1777 and 1927* (Metuchen, NJ: Scarecrow Press, Inc.), 285.
4. William Shakespeare, "Singing as an Art," *Proceedings of the Musical Association*, 31st Sess. (1904-1905), 1-16.

14. Flapping Jaws and Acoustic Laws

Originally published in the *Journal of Singing*, volume 63, no. 2, 2006

Professional journals often include a *"letters to the editor"* section in order to give readership a chance to reply, rebut, or perhaps supplement what someone else has written. Occasionally a single topic can occupy the attention of readers for several issues, giving interested parties a chance to iron out their differences in a public forum. One such exchange took place in the The Musical Times in 1937. Here is a part of it that will introduce the topic at hand.

A pupil of Garcia's on his teaching

Sir: Twice a week for three years I sat in Manuel Garcia's drawing room at Cricklewood from 10:30 a.m. till the time of my own lesson, 1:30, and listened to his teaching. May I be considered qualified to reply to your correspondent 'J.M.L.' on one or two trifling points?

He says 'the mouth was only opened sufficiently to admit to the tip of one finger between the teeth.' Señor Garcia insisted on the width of *two* fingers as the proper opening for *Ah* (all our exercises were sung on *Ah*). For words of course, one had to adjust the aperture, but he never told us to make it as narrow as possible. One of his favourite cures for a stiff jaw was to make the student hold a little piece of wood between the teeth while singing exercises (on *Ah*). 'While you are biting upwards,' he would say, 'you cannot push the jaw downwards.' He would cut a little post for this purpose, with an old knife from a stick of firewood, and it was always quite one and a half inches high. The 'tip' of nobody's finger is that width.

To forestall misapprehension I add that he never intended this appliance to be used much. It was merely to convince students that they could sing without a rigid jaw. They were then expected to reproduce the sensation in their own practice.[1]

The following response appeared in the next issue:

Opening the Mouth in Singing

Sir: Mrs. Rees-Pedlar's recollections of Manuel Garcia's teaching caused her to reply in an interesting letter to some representations of mine as to the opening and shape of the mouth according to the Porpora tradition received through Garcia. May I quote Garcia's words from his 'Art of Singing'?

> "It is generally believed that the more we open the mouth, the more easily and powerfully can sounds be emitted; but this is quite a mistake. Too large a separation of the jaws tightens the pharynx and consequently stops all vibration of the voice, depriving the pharynx of its vault-like, resonant form. Besides, if the teeth be too nearly closed, the voice will assume a grating character, somewhat like the effect produced by singing through a comb. By projecting the lips in a funnel shape, the notes become heavy. When the mouth assumes an oval shape, like that of a fish, the voice is rendered dull and gloomy; the vowels are imperfectly articulated, and all but indistinguishable; besides which, the face has a hard, cold, and most unpleasing expression. To open the mouth, the lower jaw should be allowed to fall by its own weight, while the corners of the lips retire slightly. This movement, which keeps the lips gently pressed against the teeth, opens the mouth in just proportions and gives it an agreeable form."

Sir Charles Santley, who was for two years a pupil of Nava in Milan, and on his return to England had some lessons from Garcia, writes in his 'Art of Singing' (Macmillan):

> "The mouth ought not to open more than sufficient to introduce the tip of a finger; if the under-jaw is lowered beyond what is necessary for this it is impossible to pronounce the consonants promptly and firmly, as the tongue, teeth, and lips will be too far apart to fulfil their office . . . The most advantageous, and at the same time the most pleasing and elegant position of the mouth is the approach to a smile."

Tosi (b. 1683) says in his 'Observations on the Florid Song' (1723): "The mouth ought to be composed in a manner (if the sense of the words permit it) rather inclined to a smile, than too much gravity."

Isaac Nathan (for five years a pupil of Domenico Corri, who was for seven years a pupil of Porpora) has, in his 'Musurgia Vocalis' (1823), pages on the opening of the mouth. He begins: "Opening the mouth to the fullest extent is by many persons considered the very acmé of perfection," and later says: "Exclusive of external appearances, it is extremely disadvantageous to the voice to keep the mouth in so open a position; for the fleshy substance of the cheek must thus necessarily press against the teeth and deaden the sound . . . It is when the mouth is in a smiling form, that the sweetest tones are produced . . . It is advisable to form the mouth in an easy manner, so as to give due articulation to every word in singing as in speaking."

Gustavo Carulli (b. 1801) in a 'Méthode de chant' (1838), dedicated to and approved by the celebrated and accomplished French tenor Duprez, prints a charming illustration of a mouth in the proper form for singing the first Italian vowel. The teeth are moderately separated and the lips smiling: the author, in the text gives the space of separation as some six or eight music lines, a little less or more than half an inch, and draws attention to the extension of the mouth at the sides and the resting of the lips on the teeth according to the conformation of the mouth, so that the teeth can be seen.[2]

Finally, this response from E. Herbert-Caesari finished the exchange:

Opening the Mouth in Singing

...Procedures (as quoted by 'J. M. L.') such as employing "wooden posts," "showing six teeth," "the lips smiling," "a smiling form of mouth," mean absolutely nothing to the student seeking the truth; indeed, they mislead because they teach nothing. The fact of "smiling with the lips" is assuredly not the keystone to vocal mechanics. It is worthy of note that not one of the quotations given by 'J. M. L.' from works of the distinguished departed mentions the factor of pitch. Did anybody ever see a great singer produce a high note forte with a "smile" on his lips, or with his mouth open no more than "sufficient to introduce the tip of a finger" as advocated by Santley? Now Santley was a fine singer; but like so many great artists (and teachers), he omitted to amplify or complete his ideas, and just revealed one aspect of a many-sided procedure.[3]

To Drop or Not to Drop

This exchange provides some interesting historical perspective on a matter of important consideration: What should we do concerning the position of the jaw for singing? What are the implications of a wide or narrow space between the teeth? Is there any logic behind the various positions that teachers and singers take on the subject?

Unlike the writers quoted above, many of our membership are engaged in teaching different vocal styles. One of the first things that deserves consideration on this subject is the fact that different vocal styles may have different requirements. Does an operatic soprano follow the same practice as a pop singer? Acknowledging that "a picture is worth a thousand words" may be helpful to conjure up a few mental images of well-known individuals that most people would recognize as representatives of a few of the vocal styles we may deal with. First, consider the the great operatic soprano Leontyne Price singing at the top of her range with the mouth gaping wide, but who used much less space in the middle and low range. There is Lyle Lovett, the country and western singer with a guitar in hand who sings in a relatively limited pitch range and hardly opens his mouth at all. Luciano Pavarotti, the great operatic tenor who sang throughout his range with minimal space between the teeth (even at the top of his range), especially compared to the prima donna standing next to him. Finally, there are iconic entertainers from the past such as Cab Calloway from the big band era who sang with a huge gaping maw throughout his limited range, or the inimitable Ethel Merman from the historical American Theater tradition, belting throughout her range with mouth wide open! Here we have several different vocal styles, each requiring a different sound quality. The question is, does the mouth opening have anything to do with acquiring these unique vocal qualities? A brief tutorial in acoustics and how the vocal instrument works may be of assistance.

Back to Basics

The vocal folds within the larynx are driven into vibration by an air stream produced by the respiratory system. The phonatory cycle consists of the vocal folds opening and then closing, interrupting and then emitting airflow. The vocal folds are literally blown apart due to air pressure coming up from the lungs, and they close due to the elastic properties of the vocal folds themselves (and some additional help from negative air pressures in the glottis). It is the interruption of the airflow that produces the sound of the voice. The tone produced by the larynx is a mere buzz before it is shaped by the vocal tract. A comparable tone can be produced by vibrating the two lips as if you were blowing into a trumpet mouthpiece, but without the mouthpiece. The vocal folds produce a complex tone, that is, it has acoustic energy at the fundamental frequency or F0 (usually the "pitch" that we hear) and a series of partials or overtones above it. The partials above the F0 are spaced regularly at frequencies that are integer multiples of the F0. If the F0 is 100 Hertz (Hz), partials occur at 200 Hz, 300 Hz, 400 Hz, and so on. A complex tone is the result of many simple tones (similar to the sound produced by a tuning fork) all added together. Light is a good metaphor for understanding the nature of the complex tone. We know that "white" light actually is made up of many colors by observing what happens when it is passed through a prism. A complex tone is similar; when we pass it through an "acoustic prism" (a Fourrier transform), we see that a complex tone is many simple tones occurring at once. We do not usually perceive the individual sounds or partials, but instead our ears merge them together. We perceive this complexity as *timbre*.

The manner in which the airflow comes to a halt has important implications for the quality of sound. If the vocal folds shut off the airflow suddenly and then remain closed for a significant portion of the whole cycle (over fifty percent), there will be a lot of acoustic energy in the high partials. We would characterize this sound as ringing and bright (characteristic of the belt voice or the operatic sound). If, on the other hand, the airflow is less suddenly interrupted, or some minimal airflow remains throughout the whole cycle, then we have a tone where the energy in the upper partials is much weaker than the first case. The quality of this tone is likely to be soft, muffled, and much less brilliant. It is appropriate for many vocal styles (the breathy voice of Nora Jones comes to mind), but not for the operatic performer unless used for special effect.

The source is only the beginning. The sound produced at the vocal folds is a very unattractive buzz when it leaves the larynx. The vocal tract (the pharynx, oral cavity, and sometimes the nasal cavity) has a profound effect upon the sound produced by the vocal folds. The vocal tract has been described as a selective filter which shapes the sound by favoring some frequencies more than others.

To begin to understand the filtering process, we often model the air space of the vocal tract as a simple tube of uniform diameter, open at one end and closed at the other. I use a mailing tube from the post office as a teaching tool for this purpose. To demonstrate the selectivity of the filter, I put one end of the tube up to my mouth and seal it as best I can. This is the closed end of the tube. I then sing a long glissando from low to high and ask the group to see if there is a particular frequency that becomes louder as I go up and down the pitch range. There are indeed several points along the way where the sound emitted out of the open end of the tube is suddenly much louder than the frequencies above or below that particular pitch. The air space in the tube is "tuned" to that particular frequency and not to others. This is the selective effect of a resonator. A complete explanation of this is beyond the scope of this brief review, but suffice it to say that if there is acoustic energy (a partial or harmonic) near the frequency of the resonator, the air space will amplify it and will make it louder.

The air space in the vocal tract is not exactly like a mailing tube, but it does behave in a similar fashion. The movement of the tongue, lips, jaw, larynx, and soft palate all have an effect upon the shape of the air space and, as a result, the tuning of the resonances (formants). The shape of the vocal tract determines the specific frequencies of the resonances. The frequencies of the first two formants identify the vowels. For [ə] the first formant (F1) is about 500 Hz and the second formant (F2) is about 1500. For [i] F1 is about 350 Hz and F2 is about 2100 Hz, and for [a] they are about 850 Hz and 1200 Hz. The tongue moves and the resonance frequencies are changed because the airspace has a different shape. I teach this concept with the notion of making "vowel cookies." The larynx produces the raw material, the "vowel dough." Each vowel has a specific resonance shape and it imposes its shape upon the raw material, and the result is a unique and distinct acoustic form that we identify as easily as we can perceive the difference between a star shaped cookie and a moon shaped one.

It is hoped that this brief review of old concepts will reinforce some basic principles that have been studied in more depth before. There is one more very important new component to this before we can really answer the question at hand: How wide do we need to drop the jaw for singing?

Something Called Inertive Reactance

Ingo Titze enlightened those in attendance at the 2004 NATS conference in New Orleans about something called inertive reactance. He took over an hour to explain this in some detail. For a more complete review and some helpful graphs and visual aids, I refer you to his Power Point presentation that can be viewed on the website of The National Center for Voice and Speech at NCVS.org.

According to Titze, the vocal tract actually can store energy and help the vocal folds function under certain conditions. When levels of inertive reactance are high, the airflow cuts off more suddenly when the vocal folds close. This produces greater energy in the upper partials, a sound that we would describe as bright and rich in timbre. Dr. Titze described two ways that singers can take advantage of inertive reactance. The primary means of increasing levels of inertive reactance are to elongate and narrow the small air space directly above the vocal folds, called the epilaryngeal tube. This is accomplished by lowering the larynx below its resting level or speech level. (The gesture of lowering the larynx is related to the concepts of *chiaroscuro* and *voce chiusa* that I have discussed in previous columns.) To narrow the entrance into the epilarynx we learn to "squeeze" the entrance into the epilaryngeal tube by contracting the muscles of the aryepiglottic folds and lowering the epiglottis. These gestures are commonly observed in classically trained singers and have been described in the literature since the time of Garcia's observations with the laryngeal mirror.

The second means of utilizing inertive reactance in the vocal tract is through formant tuning. Titze proposed that the level of inertive reactance is highest just below the frequency of a formant. Years ago, we learned from Johan Sundberg that a soprano can gain as much as 30 decibels (dB) of intensity by tuning F1close to (just above) the frequency of F0. A doubling of intensity is a 3dB increase, so this is a huge advantage! This is the influence of the resonator adding gain to the partial. It is crucial to appreciate that the frequency of F1 is influenced tremendously by the position of the jaw (mouth opening). If you lower the jaw you raise the frequency of F1, and, conversely, it goes down when the mouth opening is made smaller. This principle is practically applied when the pitch that a soprano is singing is higher than the first vowel formant, which is a common experience for her. Recall that the range of F1 is from about 300 Hz for [i] to 850 Hz for [a] with all the other vowels falling in between. We can see that this is within the common pitch range of the soprano voice, so the option of formant tuning is almost always there when she sings above E_5. She drops her jaw to raise F1 as the F0 goes up. Formant tuning is an important principle for two reasons: gain from the resonator and high levels of inertive reactance.

Dénouement

Titze went on to explain another very important principle that applies to all styles of singing. It has to do with maintaining certain relationships between the F1 and the lowest two partials of the source spectrum. The quality that we recognize as an operatic soprano singing above the staff is due to the fact that only the F0 is below the frequency of the first vowel formant, an event that occurs only in the high part of her range. When an operatic (or classically trained) soprano sings above the staff and drops her jaw, she raises F1 slightly above the pitch of the F0. She takes advantage of the boost from the resonator and she takes advantage of the inertive reactance that helps her vocal folds close firmly and suddenly giving as much energy as possible into the sound from the source. That is a specialized gesture in her high voice for a particular vocal quality.

A totally different quality of tone results when there is more than one partial below the level of F1. When a contemporary commercial music (CCM) singer carries the belt voice (or belt mix) up toward the top of the staff, he or she will drop the jaw while ascending as well. But remember we are talking about maybe an octave lower than the situation for the operatic soprano that was just discussed. They also drop the jaw to raise the F1 so that at least the first two partials remain below it (F0 and the second partial). If the second partial goes above the first formant, the belt quality goes away and there is a switch in register qualities. This is a partial explanation for the limited range of this voice. It can go no higher than the relationship between F1 and the second partial can be maintained. Recall that the second partial is twice the frequency of the F0. The F1 for [a] has the highest frequency for all the vowels at about 850 Hz. For an F0 that has a second partial no higher than 850 Hz we are talking about a sung pitch at about 425 Hz—about the frequency of A^{b4}. This is a common limit to the trained belt voice. Of course, some singers who do this style learn to raise that by a considerable amount; but the important message is that it is not just that they train the chest register (the vocalis muscle) to be strong enough to do this, they also learn to modify the vocal tract so that they raise F1 far above its normal boundaries.

A totally different quality exists when the F0 and all the partials are above the frequency of F1. Titze described this as "mixed quality." Two examples of this are the tenor who is singing what we might call the "head voice" at or above his *passaggio* (about F_4) and female "middle" voice. Many fine singers will use very little mouth opening in this situation. If you watch Pavarotti sing through this part of his voice and above, he uses surprisingly little mouth opening. The [a] is more open than the other vowels, which is the case even in the speech literature for "normals" (singers are not "normals"), but he never utilizes the kind of space that the soprano does at the top of her range. There would be no advantage to do so. A tenor cannot achieve the tuning relationship between F0 and F1 that the soprano can because of the difference in the frequency range of men and women. The closed vowels [i], [e], and [u] are so good for training the male voice above the staff because they have low F1 frequencies and it is relatively easy to keep the F0 and all the partials above F1. By keeping the mouth opening small a male voice can lower F1 and keep this arrangement over his whole top and achieve the head voice quality. The same gesture works for the female voice in the middle and low part of her range. This is what we often observe when we see a female singing in her middle range. Keeping her mouth opening relatively closed allows her to maintain the middle voice or Titze's mixed register quality that helps her unify the registration with the low mechanism and maintain a real presence in the middle range.

To be sure, all singers do not do the same thing. An obvious example in the operatic tenor voice was Giuseppe Di Stefano who tended to use a wide mouth opening at and above his *passaggio*. The sound was very exciting, partly because it sounded so raw and even dangerous— it was rather "belty" in quality. As a young singer Pavarotti became enamored of Di Stefano's sound. His father (also a fine singer) cautioned him not to use this technique because it would be dangerous for him to do so. The danger was that the top was too open and would stress the instrument too much. It has been said that Di Stefano paid a price for his approach, but who can argue with his success? We can see another example in old films of the great heldentenor Lauritz Melchior. We see him opening at the top much in the same fashion as Di Stefano. The *passaggio* is open and the turn that we expect at the *passaggio* is extended higher than normal or never really happens. For Melchior we can say that his practice worked for the repertoire he sang—and who did it better? The vocal demands are simply different according to the range, style, and timbral expectations.

CONCLUSION

One of the first things we can do to organize our thinking and observations on this matter is to realize that singers who sing in styles that typically use amplification systems are likely to use different strategies than those who have to sing over large numbers of instruments and other voices. These would include folk singers, country and western, and other intimate vocal styles. For them an exaggerated mouth opening serves no purpose. They do not need to take advantage of the acoustic principles discussed above. What they need most is to sound natural, and that does not include the kind of gestures that are necessary for the singer of classical music and other highly energized vocal styles.

On the other hand, for the young operatic and classical voice in training there are certain articulatory practices that allow them to optimize the output of both the source and the filter. One often observes young women who have not learned to drop their jaw as they approach their top. The most common flaw that I observe is that they do exactly the opposite! They may tip their head down, *close* the mouth and smile and wonder why they have no high notes.

Consider the young men who have not learned to access the high voice. As they approach the *secondo passaggio* at about E_4 or F_4, they may try to increase their mouth opening to a point where it fails. The tone is white and sounds too open to our ears. Singing the closed vowels [i], [e], or [u] through the *passaggio* is helpful because the first formant is low; we produce those vowels with a relatively small mouth opening, keeping the formant as low as possible so that the F0 and all the partials are above it. If the young male singer would learn to maintain his larynx in a comfortably low posture and keep his mouth relatively closed at the top, the head voice could be there waiting to be discovered.

The CCM singer may need to learn to increase jaw opening starting at a much lower pitch than the classically trained counterpart. These performers may not always want the mixed quality in the middle voice, and instead need to keep the belt quality as they ascend to the top of their range. This information may be especially helpful to singers who are attempting to be crossover artists; each style has a distinct *timbre* that is the result of different articulatory gestures.

The fact that we are now coming to a scientific understanding of long-standing practice should help us define techniques that are taught to everybody who is studying a particular vocal style. There is plenty of room for individuality after certain principles that are "tried and true" are established in our student singers.

NOTES

1. Jean Hunter Rees-Pedlar, *The Musical Times* 78, no. 1130 (April 1937): 358.
2. J. M. L., *The Musical Times* 78, no. 1131 (May 1937): 450-451.
3. E. Herbert-Ceasari, *The Musical Times* 78, no. 1132 (June 1937): 551.

15. Buried Treasure

Originally published in the *Journal of Singing*, volume 63, no. 3, 2007

I recently became aware of a very unique journal that was published in the United States during the late nineteenth century. Edgar S. Werner (1850–1919) published his magazine on voice culture under three different titles, *The Voice* 1–10 (1879–1888), *Werner's Voice* Magazine 11–14 (1889–1892), and *Werner's Magazine* 15–30 (1893–1902).[1] Werner was a voice teacher in New York City and dedicated his journal to all aspects of voice production, vocal training, physiology, vocal defects, and voice care.

Each issue contained reviews of vocal performances from around the country as well as featured articles by guest contributors, including familiar pedagogues of the day, such as Carlo Bassini, Emil Behnke, Edmund J. Myer, Julius Stockhausen, and the subject of this column, Frederic W. Root. Root was a member of a well-known American family of musicians. He trained both in the United States and Europe and wrote a popular multivolume treatise, *Technic and Art of Singing* (1901).

What follows is a report of an address by Mr. Root to the national conference of the Music Teacher's National Association that appeared in the magazine. I found his treatment of the problems encountered in the "voice-culture" profession very interesting and relevant today. After the text of the address there follows a brief biographical sketch of Mr. Root that also was published in *Werner's Voice Magazine*, presumably written by Mr. Werner, the editor.

The Voice Teacher's Problems

By Frederick W. Root

[Read before the Music Teacher's National Association, Cleveland, Ohio, July 6, 1892]

A lady once visited the studio of a singing-teacher, and after listening for a time to what was going on she remarked: "What a delightful existence it must be to be sung through life in this way"—taking a beautifully sentimental view of the profession which I represent. Now this profession, like any other honorable and useful one, has its rewards; but it has its knotty problems and its hard trying places as do others.

To one who is conscientious and feels his responsibilities keenly, these problems are often of a very disquieting character. Possibly there are some teachers who do not mind them: the irresponsible creatures who skip about upon the surface of things, including the surface of the earth—for they are not likely to stay long in one place—content with the gold of the sunbeams which fall upon all, and constitutionally indisposed to dig below the surface for what gold may be hidden there. I once entered the studio of one of these butterflies of the profession, and surprised teacher and pupil in the midst of a piano lesson. The pupil was busily fumbling away at a study with such fingering as came to her upon the inspiration of the moment, and such notes as she chose to substitute for those printed upon the page before her, while the teacher, at a window at the opposite side of the room, was seated in a chair with his feet on another, amusing himself with his reflections, which did not seem to be in any way connected with the performance going on under his auspices; in fact, I think he had been dozing. Another one told a pupil of mine that it was no use to bother your head with rudiments; why not begin with opera at once? They do not bother their heads with the needs of the pupil nor the researches of thinkers.

There is a class among musicians who enter the profession for reasons alluded to by Rubinstein in his autobiography. He says that a lady once brought her son to the conservatory over which he presided, remarking that she had already put him to various things, but as he did not seem to have much brains she would let him try music. Perhaps an author might be guilty of inventing an incident like this in order to enliven his pages, but to me it does not seem a very improbable case when I reflect how universally people seem to regard music and music study as a matter of peculiar inspiration, outside the pale of logical thought and scientific method. We never hear of a "wonderful" method of teaching mathematics, for that is scientifically established and the process is generally understood; but we do hear the words wonderful and magical applied to the process of music-teaching, especially in the department of voice-training, showing the credulous and unscientific attitude toward this study held by the majority of those who contemplate it.

Before describing some of the problems of the voice-teacher as they appear to me, permit me to make the positive statement that these problems should be met with just as much rational consideration, logical thought, observance of minute facts, and painstaking arrangement of the smallest details as are the problems of mathematics or any other study, and that there is just as much use for the brain and the reasoning faculties in our profession as in any other.

A very large contingent of the teachers of voice-culture assume the same relationship to the problems of their profession as do people in general toward those of theology, or politics, or anything requiring concentrated study and thought—they accept certain formulae upon the authority of others. One says that his conscience and his creed are in the keeping of his church, and he does not care to discuss the religious questions which are agitating people about him. Another says: "I believe that Mr. So-and-So knows what he is talking about, and I shall vote as he says." A teacher of voice-culture has been told by some professor of wide reputation that the management of the breath is all there is in singing; that to breathe well is to sing well, and with diaphragmatic effort every element of vocalization can be set right and developed. Another feels the same way about placing, and another is all for registers.

These are the one-formula teachers who are, upon the authority of some one else . . . dogmatically sure that they are completely and unquestionably right . . . They are certain that anyone who entertains different ideas is a dangerous and subversive character, whom it is righteous to defame and oppose, assuming the attitude of a ward politician toward one of another party. These one-formula teachers, too, despise problems, and look with suspicion upon anyone who occupies his mind with them.

Some of the voice-teacher's work is very comfortable, presenting no problems that he does not at once see the solution of. We all of us have a few pupils—enough to restrain us from suicide in trying times—who come regularly to their lessons, and make steady progress in all departments of the study; who are amiable and contented, and who do not expect more from your teaching than you think they can attain. In the department of musicianship you see them becoming fairly good readers of music, respectably familiar with the literature of vocal composition and with musical theory and definition, while their voices gain steadily in quality, power and compass, and their style of singing becomes more and more refined and effective.

On the other hand, there are plenty of pupils who give you all the problems you can stagger under; some expect you to make bricks without straw. There is the pupil who has never had strict government at home, and has never learned the lesson of application to anything. The problem of the voice-teacher is to see how much he can do without qualities which are usually considered indispensable in any other study. These pupils who cannot do efficient work according to any method which you can devise are usually the ones who inquire most. The case is similar to what one observes among students of languages abroad. One learning German, for instance, who is never likely to attain even to the grammar of a peasant, or get the accent as good as the lowest Platt-Deutsch, is very particular to go to Hannover because they have so much better accent than in Berlin. The affected nonsense which fills the heads of such pupils in singing affords the teacher problems indeed.

Such a case as this suggests a very comprehensive heading under which to range a voice-teacher's problems, viz., pupils' mistaken estimate of their needs and possibilities. There is the familiar type of a pupil who, with unformed voice and underdeveloped musicianship, expects to get a position to sing for pay in two or three months. It is the bane of vocal education that nearly all pupils expect to make it pay in dollars and cents, sooner or later; and pupils paying out considerable money for their training in singing expect, unlike the mass of pianoforte pupils, for instance, to reap a golden harvest from the results. The problem, then, lies in the discrepancy between the pupil's expectations and the teacher's belief regarding the ultimate possibilities. You know that this pupil will not be able to earn money by singing in the time which she allots for the purpose, and you doubt if she ever will; still you believe that for purposes of general education she ought to learn music, and that, as an amateur singer, she can do fairly well.

I confess that this is the problem which I endeavor to avoid as much as possible. If a pupil of only average ability asks me, "Will my singing have a money value?" I make it a practice to discourage him. I shape my teaching, as far as possible, in the line which is naturally taken by most pianoforte instructors, who are not eternally bothered by being expected to put most of their pupils, from the very beginning of their studies, in the line of making money; who are not continually tempted to neglect fundamental work and occupy themselves with glittering devices to catch public favor for financial ends; they teach with solid education in view.

But the worst obstacle we encounter in trying to make vocal pupils do their work on well arranged educational lines, is not the pupil's own eagerness to make money and to shine in public so much as the influences that are brought to bear upon them by outside advisers and critics. Voice-culture is the most indefinite item in the whole range of educational matters. People in general have no standards except the most superficial ones by which to measure progress in this department, or by which to compare the value of the various things which enter into vocal education. A pupil may be pursuing the very best course possible, one that will surely bring out all her possibilities; and yet, because she does not meet the views of some officious adviser—one who knows nothing about elementary stages; one who has not knowledge enough of the subject to see progress of the solid kind; the shallow "know it all" adviser, with whom tinsel and glitter are the net result of music study, and yet whose airy assumption seems to impress music students—because such a one's irresponsible notions are not met during the earlier stages of a pupil's education, she is continually assured that she is going wrong, and the heart is entirely taken out of her study.

These intermeddlers are sometimes teachers, who expect to profit by the change; but more often they are of the dilettanti class, creatures of the hour, devotees of fashion, who have heard and seen a great deal, and have, in their dainty manner, dipped into so many reservoirs of art, literature and science, and have talked so much and given so many glib opinions upon these subjects, that they have come to assume that their standpoint commands the entire range of human achievements. They are to me the most painful people I come in contact with.

The nervous, unsettled, over-impatient pupil affords a teacher an opportunity for positive heroism at times. It is no easy problem to decide what to do in the case of one who would be better satisfied if you omitted much of the work which you are convinced ought to be done, and confined yourself to a few showy items of instruction, and outraged your conscience by assuring such a one that the work was going on splendidly. Perhaps luck would bear you out and the pupil would go through life without finding out that her education had amounted to nothing. But there is always the disquieting possibility that a turn of fortune may bring the pupil face to face with actual facts, and that she will anathematize you as a charlatan when she finds that you did not give her the adequate preparation which you assured her she was getting.

On the other hand, with some pupils it is of no use to set a standard high and be comprehensive, for they have no capacity to receive anything but elementary and partial training. I think teachers as often make the mistake of trying to do too much for their pupils as of actually doing too little. I once had a call from a lady who had gone forth from some rigidly classical alma mater to teach in an out of the way district, where musical appreciation was at a low ebb. She was inspired by the loftiest purposes, and was going to make those people play and sing the classics or know the reason why. Well, she had had a pretty hard time of it, and she came to me with her troubles. She had been told never to lower her standard, and accordingly she had held it up beyond the reach of her constituency until her soul was weary. She had been making a martyr of herself, and did not enjoy it. I told her to put her own standard away out of sight somewhere, and take up that of her pupils to begin with; commencing the ascent of Parnassus from a real and not an imaginary starting point. Then she heaved a sigh of relief, and said she was glad to think that was the right way to do.

Sometimes a pupil comes to you who has had a long-continued and expensive education, but who has been badly taught and should begin at the very beginning. Her voice is about ready to give way under the strain which false method has put upon it, and yet she thinks that she simply needs a little finishing work. Another has some fine tones in her voice, and she has given pleasure by her singing so long that she wishes just a little coaching in order to enter the profession. The difficulty in this case is that she does not know one key from another, cannot read the simplest thing, or sing anything with certainly of getting all the notes right. To know absolutely what is best to do in these cases, the teacher should be little short of omniscient. He should explore the past and foresee the future, and then, with superhuman wisdom, patch and prop up the pupils' acquirements to just that point which shall enable them to get along. Some of us have not this amount of wisdom, and will lie awake nights trying to determine what we ought to do for such pupils.

Innocently happy is your one-formula teacher under these circumstances. He has his patent medicine warranted to cure everybody and everything under all possible circumstances. If his treatment does not work it is the pupil's fault, and—happy provision of nature—the pupil will believe almost anything you say if you assume a positive tone. I have heard of teachers who disposed of all their difficult problems very successfully, by laying the blame of bad results upon the pupils. I have tried to do this in some minor cases, but found I had not the cheek to carry it through successfully.

But I will bring my catalogue of difficulties to a close, although there still arise before my mind visions of what the surgeons would call "interesting cases." There are the opera aspirants. There is the man with a big voice and no imagination or sentiment. There is the beauty who is always posing, and whose attention to anything but herself is hard to get. There is the society lady with so much vivacity of manner that one feels as if he were trying to teach a squirrel. There is the very intellectual person, who proposes to master all branches of study, including music, but has not a particle of music in his nature. There is the pupil whom you ought to scold, but who is so amiable that you haven't the heart to; also the one who breaks down and weeps whenever you are somewhat firm in your exactions, and so on.

It would be a great comfort for me to talk about these to a company of people, many of whom know how it is themselves. We always like to pour out our woes into a sympathetic ear. But feeling that I shall never get a chance to pour out any more before this association if I talk too long, I will desist, and shall listen with much interest to whatever discussion these remarks of mine may be favored with, hoping for many suggestions looking to the satisfactory solution of "The Voice-Teacher's Problems."[2]

Frederic Woodman Root

The world admires those who uphold the dignity and add to the luster of an honorable family name. Such an one is Mr. Frederic W. Root, of Chicago, whose relatives and ancestors, maternal as well as paternal, have been for generations, prominent players, singers and choir leaders. His mother was a semi-professional vocalist of wide popularity, while his father, Dr. George F. Root, is known wherever song finds expression in the English tongue.

Frederic Woodman Root was born in Boston, Mass., June 13, 1846. When but five years old his father gave him his first musical instruction, writing out the exercises for him; and at intervals his musical relatives took their turn at the work of making him an efficient musician. But not until he was placed under the charge of Mr. B. C. Blodgett, then a talented young pianist newly graduated from the Leipsic Conservatory, did our young musician really begin to strike root in the field of music. He was then about 14 years of age. Mr. Blodgett took the profoundest interest in his pupil, and used to spend one afternoon each week in playing the classics for him. By this course he became very familiar with the works of the masters, and the profit he derived from this advantage cannot be over-estimated.

His subsequent teachers were Dr. William Mason, in New York, and Mr. Robert Goldbeck, in Chicago. He studied the organ principally under Mr. James Flint, then of the Madison Square Church, New York, and at one of the evening services of that church made his debut as organist.

In 1863, Dr. Root removed to Chicago, and for several years the son, Frederic Root, did considerable solo playing both upon the piano and organ in that city and throughout the Northwest, though his tastes and gifts had no striking bent in that direction. In 1867, he made a very extensive convention tour with his father, assisting him as pianist and conductor. In the intervals he took voice lessons with Carlo Bassini, in New York, having previously made himself acquainted with the rudiments of voice-culture through his father's instructions.

In 1869, Mr. Frederic Root went to Europe and spent several years in study and travel, visiting all points of interest from the north of Scotland to the south of Italy. He studied piano in Germany and voice in Italy, under the celebrated Vannuccini. Upon his return home, he resumed his professional occupation at a session of the National Normal Musical Institute, where he taught voice, piano, organ and harmony, at the same time continuing his studies under Dr. Mason and Bassini, who were of the faculty. Since then he has been steadily at work in Chicago.

Mr. Root's method of teaching voice is intended to be comprehensive, including and classifying many things rather than emphasizing some specialties. For instance, instead of maintaining that breathing for singing must be done in one way, he develops all the breathing actions and assigns to each the resources of expression or technique which belong to it; or, rather than teach that the voice should be drilled in clear timbre mainly, with open and forward tone, or, on the contrary, in deep, covered, somber tone, he holds that both are equally necessary in training, being complementary halves of voice-production. Instead of condemning this or that course in voice training as ruinous to voices, he is in the habit of assorting all reputable methods that come under his notice as good for certain states and conditions of pupils, and determining in his own mind their relative values and special uses. He has an omnivorous way of assimilating everything that is going on.

Mr. Root's plan of instruction comprises three distinct planes: The lowest, or most material; the middle, or more subtle; and the highest or most interior. In the first, attention is called to certain mechanical actions, as the position of mouth, throat, etc.; in the second, to certain sensations of tone, as high placing, bringing forward, etc.; in the third plane, the thought of emotional effects, as gayety or sadness, is depended upon for the desired vocal result. With the highest grade of pupils there is little use for any but the higher planes of instruction; but the majority of students are better off for being approached in all three directions.

In teaching Mr. Root is at his best before the large companies of people that he instructs in classes. There it is that all the magnetism, logic, humor and illustrative and executive ability with which he is charged come to the front. Several years ago he introduced his system of class-teaching in Chicago, and has succeeded in making it quite a factor in the musical life of that city. His work in this respect has been so fruitful, that he was invited to read an essay on the subject before the National Educational Association, at its recent meeting in Chicago, a report of which was published in *The Voice* for September, 1887. Still he is principally known as a private teacher, many of his pupils occupying prominent positions in church choirs and on the concert and operatic stage. Some of them are Miss Hope Glenn, Mrs. Jessie Bartlett-Davis, Miss Mae St. John, Mr. W. H. Clark (of the Boston Ideals), and Mr. John McWade.

Mr. Root is a busy man, having more applications from pupils than he can accept. His music rooms are pleasantly situated and he has an assistant who receives visitors, attends to a large part of his correspondence, and gives some lessons. For many years he devoted considerable time to musical composition and chorus-conducting, and was for several years the editor of a musical journal; but now the demands of voice culture are such that he has no time for anything not immediately connected with the welfare of his class and private pupils in singing, of whom he has about 400 a year.

While many of our best musicians are so imbued with European ideas that they cannot adapt themselves and their methods to American customs and needs, it is a pleasure to know that Mr. Root's position in the musical world is decidedly an American one. He is no musical aristocrat. Although educated in the higher things of the art, he has great sympathy with the musical aspirations of the masses, and always inclines toward methods and movements that tend to popularize, practically, real musical progress, and to disseminate as widely as possible the benefits of the art. While he has a bent in the direction of harmony and counterpoint, and has an original system for their study, which he hopes some day to elaborate and publish, his chief work lies in the direction of making voice culture as clear and as correctly systematized as piano playing, harmony, or any other department of musical study. A formulation of his ideas on this subject was given last year at the Boston meeting of the M.T.N.A., when he, as one of the committee appointed at the preceding meeting, made his report on vocal terminology, a very able treatise. From the first meeting of the Music Teachers' National Association, at which was read his essay, "Intellectuality among Musicians," to the present time, he has been a principal member of the Association, doing what he could to make it a success. He has persistently refused to accept office in it, saying that he could do greater service in the ranks, and his counsels have always tended toward the building up of the Association and to the progress and welfare of the musical fraternity. This year he is on the program committee of the M.T.N.A. When *The Voice* was begun, in 1879, he became a subscriber, and has ever since given the journal a warm support, and has contributed to it a number of valuable articles. We are, therefore, glad of this opportunity of paying a tribute to him. He is in the prime of life, is active and energetic, a thinker ever speculative and searching, an intelligent laborer, and the musical profession may expect a great deal from him if his life and health are spared.[3]

NOTES

1. Iris S. Levine, "Werner's Magazine: An Annotated Bibliography on Articles Pertaining to the Singing Voice" (DMA treatise, University of Southern California, May, 1990), 1.
2. Frederick W. Root, "The Voice Teacher's Problems," *Werner's Voice Magazin*e 14, no. 9 (1902): 254–255.
3. Edgar S. Werner, "Frederick Woodman Root," *The Voi*ce 10, no. 10 (October, 1887): 149–150.

16. Herman Klein; A "Contemporary" Link to Mozart (I)

Originally published in the *Journal of Singing*, volume 63, no. 4, 2007

During my study of the work of Manuel Garcia II, I became aware of the name of Herman Klein. Klein was a well-known music critic and voice teacher in London who also spent several years in New York City. Among many other literary accomplishments, he provided critical reviews of newly released recordings for the English journal *The Gramophone* from 1924 until his death in 1934. He was the first to offer critical analysis of recordings (mainly singers) made during the infancy of the recording industry and during its transition from the original acoustic method to the birth of the electrical age of sound recording.[1]

One of the life experiences that qualified Herman Klein for his role as a critic of singing was his long association with Manuel Garcia. Klein's family hosted Garcia in their home in London for several years beginning in 1874. Garcia's studio was on the first floor of their home in Manchester Square. Klein studied with him for a period of about four years while he was a young man still living in his parents' home. Klein always showed promise in literary pursuits, and Garcia advised him that a professional singing career was probably not in the cards. So, he dedicated himself to writing and the study and teaching of singing. He became a highly respected teacher in his own right and continued his friendship with Garcia. He helped the old man write his last work, *Hints on Singing*, published in 1894.

In 1923 Klein published a modest book entitled simply *The Bel Canto*.[2] In this book he sought to describe the technical foundations that he felt were important for singing the music of Mozart. Klein's expertise in this area came from the fact that he had worked so closely with a man who had a very close association with first and second generation Mozart singers and whose father was Rossini's favorite tenor (Manuel Garcia *pere*).

I hope that you find this as interesting as I have. Here is the first part of an extended excerpt from *The Bel Canto* in which Klein discusses his understanding of *bel canto* and the difficulties of singing the music of Mozart.

THE VOCAL DEMANDS OF MOZART'S MUSIC

A distinguished authority, Mr. Edward J. Dent, has recently stated that what the London opera-goers and critics of the seventies 'like best were Mozart's most obvious tunes'; and that this 'naturally led to the notion that Mozart's operas were nothing more than a string of pretty tunes, tunes so pretty that no one but Patti could ever be allowed to sing them.'

Nothing could be farther from the facts. Whatever our elders may have misunderstood concerning the growing complexities of modern music, they knew their Mozart well and listened to him with a degree of appreciation which their greater familiarity with the vocal art of their era made wholly trustworthy. To realize this it is only necessary to turn up the files of the old newspapers and read the operatic criticisms—often prosy, sometimes prejudiced, but always independent, fearless, and authoritative—of writers like Davison and Chorley.

Moreover, it is unfair to the memory of the other great singers of the mid-nineteenth century to suppose that Adelina Patti, because she was called the *diva*, enjoyed any sort of monopoly of the 'Mozart tunes.' In all her career she sang but one Mozart role, namely, Zerlina; whereas Tietjens was equally good, in the public estimation, in the three parts of Donna Anna, the Countess, and Pamina. Patti in later years essayed 'Voi che sapete'; but she had not studied it as she did Zerlina with Maurice Strakosch (her brother-in-law and 'coach,' who had acted as accompanist for Pasta when the latter was teaching); and here Patti missed the right rendering. On the other hand, both Pauline Lucca and Trebelli were exquisite Cherubinos, and their delivery of the immortal air was absolutely without flaw.

Most of the traditional Mozart singers whom it was my good fortune to hear received their training from teachers whose memories, if not their actual instruction, dated back to those surviving artists who were actively working upon the stage either in Mozart's lifetime or during the years that immediately followed. They were thus the third generation of his interpreters. It may therefore reasonably be assumed that they did exactly what he intended, and I cannot but think that he would have approved their treatment of his music as surely as he would have admired their voices and their pure Italian method.

This method was the one then being taught by such Mozartians of the second generation as Garcia, Lamperti, Sangiovanni, and Nava (the teacher of Santley). It was the method which Wagner openly proclaimed to be indispensable for the satisfactory rendering of the trying declamatory music of his opera and music-dramas. Indeed, practically the whole of the experienced German artists who created the heroes and heroines of *Der Ring des Nibelungen* and *Parsifal* were trained in the Italian school.

So long as the notable singers of that generation lived and flourished the Tradition held its own. All so far was well; but when they began to retire from the stage in the final decades of the past century, it quickly became apparent that they had no worthy imitators. So gradually the succession of the Mozart tradition weakened, until lately it has broken completely, though an occasional demonstration may still be heard.

To re-discover the art of these old singers, it is necessary to know what demands were made on them by Mozart's music. Mozart was surrounded by such consummate vocalists that apparently he could never write anything too difficult or too brilliant for them. Anyhow, he was too wise to write beyond his artists' powers. But the difficulty of his vocal music did not lie solely in its *bravura*, its daring *fiorituri*, its flights into *altissimo*. It lay even more, perhaps, in its extreme simplicity.

For Mozart was one of the greatest tune makers that ever lived; and there is nothing harder to sing beautifully than a simple tune. Other composers before him also wrote wonderful tunes—Purcell, Bach, Handel, Lully, Gluck, Haydn. But as a composer for the stage this tune-maker transcended them all. Mozart may have reeled off his tunes by the hundred; but if he fitted the simplest of them to words, it never failed to embody in every accent and every phrase the full emotional content of the poet's lines. Alike as a piece of vocal music and as a vehicle for the expression of human feeling, it was complete, perfect in itself. The consequence is that it demands from the singer, besides a simplicity equal with its own, a purity of *legato*, a charm of style, a certain warmth of expression, a depth of sentiment and even of passion, which the music of Mozart's contemporaries and his predecessors (with the exception perhaps of Gluck) had never required. He was a man of strong temperament, and every bar he wrote for the voice overflowed with the essence of his own nature.

Many singers today fail, if for no other reason, to do justice to Mozart because they approach his music without the necessary warmth and intensity of feeling. They think that it suffices to sing him calmly and prettily. They could make no greater mistake, unless it be perhaps to treat him sentimentally and warble his 'pretty tunes' as though there were nothing beneath their surface. In reality there is so much that every bar needs to be deeply studied and thoroughly understood. Above all, to do Mozart justice you must love him.

It is often said nowadays that beauty of vocal tone does not matter as much as musical knowledge, rhythmical accuracy, and clear diction. That may apply to liturgical Tudor music or the secular writings of the old English composers. Somehow loveliness of vocal quality and temperamental curves have not invariably been associated with these things. A tradition here is not directly to be traced at all. The right reading can, however, be sufficiently gathered from the printed page, and 'sound common sense' may be trusted to supply the rest.

But of what avail would scholarship, historical erudition, or the cold process of reasoning be to the artist in the achievement of the right singing of Mozart? He may hate the so-called shackles of tradition as much as he pleases; he may treat it with contempt, dispense with it, deny its authority or its very existence. But he will probably live long enough to see the operas of Mozart in even worse plight, for lack of adequate vocal skill and traditional handling, than they are even now.

To no other cause can be attributed the unquestionable deterioration that has already come about. It is certainly not that today human beings are not born with equally beautiful voices. It can only be because—here in England at least—modern conditions do not provide or insist upon the essential training, the essential technique, the essential knowledge of what Mozart really demands.

Mozart demands everything. To begin with, a beautiful voice controlled and directed by correct scientific breathing; ample resonance; and equal scale achieved by the perfect blending (or if you like it better, the obliteration) of registers; a clean attack; a steady *sostenuto*; a smooth, pure *legato*; an elegant use of the *portamento*; a well-graduated *messa di voce* or management of *crescendo* and *diminuendos*; flexibility, agility, and brilliancy of execution; and, not least of all, the capacity to sing absolutely in tune.

With vocalization of this kind the obstacles of language should give no trouble. The right principles of articulation, diction, and accent, the distinct enunciation of every consonant, are more important than the question of the language in which Mozart is sung. My personal choice is for the language in which he composed his music. But naturally the texts of his operas, to be comprehensible to an English audience, are best sung in English.

In the rare but necessary combination above described are to be found the chief material and technique of the singer's art. One voice may, of course, be less beautiful, less flexible, less extended in range than another; but those are merely individual limitations, . . . and Mozart has written for voices of every type and size. Apart from physical and technical considerations, there still remain the important questions of musical intelligence and culture, rhythmical sense, dramatic feeling, and the instinctive gift for interpretation. I will first deal, as briefly as I can, with the technical.

THE TECHNIQUE OF THE 'BEL CANTO'

I do not propose to attempt here more than a bare description of the principal features of the so-called 'Bel Canto,' or old Italian method of singing. A closer analysis, if required by the reader, must be sought for in pages specially devoted to the method itself, without reference to the interpretation of any particular composer.

Many people imagine that there is involved in the teaching of the Italian method something in the nature of a great secret. As a matter of fact, there is nothing more secret about it than there is about the characteristics of the tradition of Mozart.

In a recent review of a book of musical recollections, the complaint was made that it contained no suggestions for remedying certain vocal abuses and malpractices denounced by the author; the reason given for the omission was that probably the latter had thought it unadvisable to give away the 'stock-in-trade' of the teacher's art. The true answer to that suggestion is that if trade secrets of the kind ever existed they were divulged by Manuel Garcia years ago.

It is not easy, of course, to grasp and co-ordinate the various factors that make up the true art of singing from the printed page alone, nor can they effectively be put into practice save under skillful and experienced guidance. Art is a thing of imitation, and in the study of singing you require the aid of the living model and critic as absolutely as in the study of painting or dancing. Nevertheless, a clear record or statement of facts is essential, and the printed page may therefore be regarded as a valuable accessory to the work of the teacher.

Garcia recognized this when he published in this country an English translation of his famous *Traité complet de l'Art du Chant*, which first appeared in Paris in 1840; and again when he supplemented it fifty-four years later with his *Hints on Singing*, which embodied all the subsequent experience garnered during a lifetime of successful teaching.

The main essentials of the Italian system are the mastery of—

(A) Breathing
(B) Resonance
(C) Vowel-formation and Attack
(D) The Sostenuto (Sustained Tone)
(E) The Legato (Slow Scale, Registers)
(F) The Portamento
(G) The Messa Di Voce
(H) Agility (Coloratura, Ornaments, etc.)

This order of progression is natural but by no means invariable. For example, the formation of a vowel shape must necessarily precede the attack of a sound, but the study of its manifold variations would have to come later. So the slow scale will naturally proceed simultaneously with the *legato*; whilst the quick scales form part of the acquisition of *agility*.

(A) Breathing

Although scientific breathing stands both at the base and the apex of the whole vocal structure, it is, nevertheless, the thing most neglected and most misunderstood in the average modern practice of this art. Correct instruction in respiration is, I think, the feature which chiefly differentiates the good teacher from the bad, the efficient master from the charlatan who misleads, cheats, and defrauds the innocent and unwary pupil. We cannot too frequently repeat the familiar saying of Maria Celloni:

Chi sa respirare sa cantare[3]

But commonly the novice is told, if told anything at all about respiration, to take a 'deep breath'; to fill the lungs with air as though crowding the chest with ozone or inhaling the perfume of flowers; to breathe in or out 'from the waist' (wherever that may be), or even to expand the abdomen with a vigorous outward push of that obscure muscle, the diaphragm.

Obedience to these familiar rules must inevitably tend to guide the student in the wrong direction and lead to bad habits which, once acquired, are exceedingly hard to eradicate. The breathing taught by the old Italian masters entirely reverses the order and changes even the physical character of the usual processes of inhalation and exhalation which form part of our daily life. Singers proceed differently; hold their bodies differently; train their muscles and organs to act differently. And yet from first to last the whole procedure is normal, beneficial to the health, unfailing in its accomplishment of the right result.

One seldom hears talk of abdominal breathing. It is this filling of the lowest part of the lungs by the expansion of the stomach which not only flattens (and therewith locates) the hidden diaphragm, but prepares for its contraction when the stomach is drawn in and the ribs are raised, thus giving the necessary impetus for the expulsion of the breath by muscular pressure from below the middle of the body, not from the regions of the chest.

This mode of inhalation is doubly beneficial: (1) because we are only able completely to inflate the lower part of the lungs by slowly introducing the air there first and filling the upper part during the same inhalation afterwards; (2) because, where we feel the breath go, thence shall we expel it; and, inasmuch as steadiness and purity of tone are only to be obtained by this upward pressure from between the lower ribs, just above the stomach, we thereby learn how to avoid all superfluous or ill-directed pressure; we learn how to control our breathing action from the region of the diaphragm; and how, finally, to keep the chest high and firm, utilizing it as a receptacle for air not inhaled directly into it from without, but pressed into it from the lung spaces underneath.

Thus concentrated, the breath virtually becomes 'compressed air,' that is, air possessing an inherent force of its own. Hence its greater power, moving always by muscular contraction in the upward (the necessary) direction, and so doing its work of creating tone in all degrees of loudness with the minimum of physical action or effort, and with a total absence of strain.

This I believe to be the old Italian system of breathing, as it was taught by Manuel Garcia, and as I have taught it myself for many years. The secret of its success lies primarily in the controlling power of the abdominal support and action. Much depends, however, upon a correct attitude of the body, the capacity for retention and expulsion of the breath in any required volume or degree, and the ability to perform the mechanical functions of the breathing apparatus either slowly or quickly, as may be needed, with the same subconscious, automatic accuracy, smoothness, and noiselessness of operation.

(B) Resonance

The old Italian teachers had no trouble in obtaining a bright, ringing tone. 'Resonance,' therefore, may not have entered largely into their theory, but was far from being ignored in the practice. Thanks chiefly to their 'open' vowels an easy 'forward' tone came naturally to the majority of their students, especially the native ones. If it did not, the masters opened their pupils' throats (temporarily at least) until the sound-waves had learnt to find their way to every facial cavity or space (besides the mouth) that was capable of 'reflecting' a vocal tone. The idea seems simple enough. The voice, in order to acquire its full vibrant power must have the aid of a 'reflector,' just as surely as the light burning in a lighthouse. The singer can no more dispense with its aid than the performer on the piano or the violin could dispense with that of a sounding-board.

As the act of singing is a natural organic function, common to the majority of civilized people, there is no need to discuss here the physiology of tone production. The point is, rather, whereabouts is that tone situated or sounding when it has left the larynx? The answer is that a clear note is, at the moment of its utterance, instantly ringing clear and true in its ultimate position, projected and maintained there by steady diaphragmatic breath-pressure, and enhanced in strength and colour by shape and other influences. To the singer the resulting sensation is that the tone is coming not from the throat at all, but existing ready made in the area to which it is reflected.

Free, unobstructed access to these 'forward' cavities can alone enable the voice to obtain all the advantages of complete resonance. Properly directed and well supported by the breath, it can entirely escape the danger of a nasal quality and attain increased beauty of timbre, diversity of colour, and penetrative power.

(C) Vowel-formation and Attack

The formation of some vowel shape must necessarily precede the attack of a vocal sound—an act which involves the opening of the mouth. If we sing with the mouth shut we hum, but the act of humming is not without its use as a means for indicating where the vibration of the sound-waves may be felt re-echoing in the facial resonators when unable to make their exit by the ordinary route.

When we open the mouth to sing a note, it must be done by dropping the lower jaw, and without moving the head, which remains erect and still. The tongue flattens as the jaw descends, whilst the pharyngeal space at the back of the throat enlarges as the soft palate rises and forms the roof of the mouth into a dome or arch. The shape thus created gives us, without further preliminary action, the natural mold for the formation of the universal vowel sound 'ah'—that is, the first vowel of the Italian alphabet.

The formation of all other vowels, no matter what the language, is simply a variation on this fundamental process, although the sense of their location seems to the singer to be different with different vowels. In reality vowels sounds should all *feel* alike, to the extent that they feel so when we speak them. Only, some vowels create a more naturally 'forward' position than others, and those that do not must, by correct treatment, be made to acquire an actual degree of resonance.

The outcome of this assimilation is that the singer finds both tone and vowel impinging upon the same identical facial area, that is to say, in the 'mask'; and there alone, will their union be made perfect. In no other fashion and by no other mechanical means can 'speech and song' be resolved into a single function.

Garcia says (*Hints on Singing*, p. 12) that 'the Pharynx ought to be considered the real mouth of a singer.' The idea is not an easy one to convey in words, but I understand it to mean that, just as the mouth contains the organs of speech (with especial reference to consonants), so the right place for forming vowel shapes and originating tonal character is the passage leading from the throat to the mouth and the nasal cavities. I also believe the idea in question to have been an essential feature of the old Italian method.

Another idea was that the utterance of 'open' sonorous vowels in a natural manner ensured a free, elastic movement of the jaw, without the least muscular stiffness, leaving the tongue 'limp and motionless,' yet not entailing an excessively wide opening of the mouth, which 'favours neither low nor high notes.' This, the true singing position, is a matter of the utmost importance and it is peculiarly associated with the teaching of Manuel Garcia.

The assuming of the singing position as a mental and physical attitude corresponds to the spontaneous gesture of the speaker. It coincides with the inhalation of the breath, and is immediately followed by the act of phonation or attack of the sound. The old Italians were right in their location of the true source of attack when they said *respirare, e poi appoggiare*: inhale, and then support with the breath. An inflated air-cushion, once the screw is tightened, affords a firm and resilient support for the whole weight of the body. Similarly, the voice must rest easily and comfortably upon the solid column of air that holds it in position.

And it must do this from the outset. From the moment that the singing position is assumed and the vowel shape formed, the diaphragm takes control; the breath is impelled upwards into the chest, towards the throat, where it becomes tone, and towards the resonators, where it becomes a voice. The whole process is comprised in a single physical movement, in a smooth, even exhalation. Therewith, not in the throat nor with any perceptible action of the glottis, but in the ultimate 'forward' area to which it has been projected, does the attack of the vocal tone actually begin.

I scarcely need add that the misuse of Garcia's scientific definition, *coup de la glotte*, is no longer tolerated by the best teachers.

In vocal attack the intensity of the glottic action may vary according to circumstances. It depends largely upon the nature of the utterance or the emotion to be expressed. A perceptible glottic impetus is not in certain cases inadvisable. For the singer there must be but one aim—that the tone, whatever its character, is to be so prepared, mentally and physically, that it shall sound perfect from the start.

NOTES

1. William R. Moran, *Herman Klein and The Gramophone* (Portland: Amadeus Press, 1990).
2. Herman Klein, *The Bel Canto* (London: Oxford University Press, 1923).
3. He who knows how to breathe knows how to sing.

17. Herman Klein; A "Contemporary" Link to Mozart (Part II)

Originally published in the *Journal of Singing*, volume 63, no. 5, 2007

The March/April and current installments of "Provenance" present *in toto* chapter five of Herman Klein's rather modest (in size only) text, *The Bel Canto*. It is tempting to reprint the entire book over the next several issues, but instead I encourage you to search your music libraries for the chance to peruse the whole volume. It is worth the effort! In other chapters he addresses the "traditional" approach to interpretation, the proper delivery of the recitative, the correct production of the appoggiatura, and numerous other important facets of what many would describe as the "lost art" of bel canto. William R. Moran's book *Herman Klein and The Gramophone* (Portland, OR: Amadeus Press, 1990) reprints the entire book along with Klein's critical reviews published in the magazine *The Gramophone*. This book might be much more likely to be found in your library.

(D) The Sostenuto (Sustained Tone)

In the old Italian school of singing nothing used to be more admired and cultivated than an absolutely steady tone. To-day even in Italy a strong vibrato or a quivering *tremolo* is generally preferred. Consequently, the modern Milanese 'maestro' encourages it.

Whether a trembling tone can ever furnish a satisfactory medium for the singing of Mozart is another question. We have evidence, both internal and external, that the voices for which Mozart wrote did not suffer from this particular drawback. The sin did not become common until some years after it had started at the Paris Opéra in the midway of the last century. Meyerbeer, Auber, and Gounod openly expressed their detestation of it. In alliance either with a strain of pure melody on a declamatory passage, a trembling voice, no matter how pleasing its quality *per se* has always sounded disagreeable to the ears of an English audience.

Intelligent use of the method of breathing described above practically obviates all danger of an unsteady tone. Instinct for the exactly right amount of breath-pressure should be natural to the good singer and made reliable by practice and experience. It contributes, moreover, to the liquid purity and clearness of timbre resulting from an undisturbed adjustment of the vocal cords.

This economy of breath and this adjustment are interdependent, since the muscles of the throat respond and resist automatically in exact proportion to the varying degrees of pressure from the lungs. Yet the need for care does not end there. The singer intent upon the tone must not think of the throat, but of where and how the tone itself is being reflected or placed: that is the true *point d'appui.*

It follows that a perfect *sostenuto* can only be obtained when the singer has the sensation of direct and uninterrupted breath support extending from the region of the diaphragm to the area of resonance.

The gradations of strength and varieties of tone colour, like the cultivation of the *mezza voce*, are things that cannot be wholly explained or taught in books. They are best acquired by careful listening and clever imitation.

The value of a beautiful *mezza voce* ('half voice' never seems to convey the same idea) cannot be overestimated. Every singer ought to possess it; but, like the old *falsetto*, now happily discarded by most singers, it comes more easily to some voices than others. Learning the *mezza voce* is not unlike acquiring the knack of a stroke at golf or lawn-tennis; and the ear must be kept upon the tone as the eye upon the ball.

The art of skillfully graduating a *crescendo* or *diminuendo* (dealt with later under the head of 'Messa di

Voce') should be associated with a constant endeavour to purify the tone. It is the pure sound that travels farthest, not the merely loud one. The delicate *mezza voce* of a soprano or a tenor can provide an instantaneous contrast not less delightful than that of the most exquisite variation in nuances of colour. These are things that must be studied and worked at, for years if necessary, until they're definitely gained.

(E) The Legato (Slow Scale, Registers)

It is one thing to sing a single note well. To sing a group of notes all equally well, with a clean, direct transition from the middle of one to the middle of the next involves a good deal more than appears upon the surface.

It means, to begin with, command of the pure *legato*, a term more readily understood on an instrument than in the human voice. The singing of the scale in the legato manner has often been compared to the stringing of a row of pearls. When they are perfectly matched they form the perfect necklace. The act of uniting notes identical in quality and colour with unbroken smoothness constitutes the perfect legato.

The first step is the management of the breath. Every note must be supported from the region of the diaphragm with the degree of pressure that it demands, not for itself alone, but in its relation to its neighbors and the true gradation of the entire series. The higher that pitch of the note the greater the degree of pressure required, and vice versa; the ear and the sense of volume must combine to secure and preserve the even gradation of the scale up or down. The great point is to make sure of the identity of the tone.

It is not necessary to begin either at the top or the bottom of a scale. The old Italians were wise enough not to enforce an arbitrary rule on this point. Their plan (adopted also in Paris by the great singer and teacher, Fauré) was to find the best note in the middle of the voice and use it as the pivot on which to balance the two halves of the scale lying above and below it. In this way they had less difficulty in obtaining an even scale and a smooth legato.

This device is so effective that many years ago I invented for the study of it a form of rhythmical slow scale in three sections, each commencing on the dominant. The key must be varied so that the dominant in every case may afford the safest model for the succeeding notes:

This slow scale must be sung with the dark or 'closed' tone (*voix sombre*), whereas quick scales and runs are best executed in the bright or 'open' tone (*voix claire*), which lends itself more readily to passages requiring flexibility.

Just as the dominant or initial note supplies the model for the others, so must the breathing of the descending scale be imitated in the ascending scale (not the reverse). The legato is always easier, neater, and to be employed with better gradation on the down scale— certainly at first.

The point is that, whether the voice be mounting or descending the scale, the same note shall always be sung in the same manner; the scale, the same note shall always be sung in passing, shall invariably sound quite the same.

The ability, however, to manage this depends also upon the correct blending of the registers, an important matter upon which I can only touch briefly here. Unless the differences of sensation and changes of mechanism which characterize what are known as the 'registers' of the human voice have so merged into each other as to create a harmonious whole, smoothness of scale or legato singing is out of the question.

The provision of registers, with their three different mechanical actions, enables the same vocal cords to produce a succession of sounds of extensive range. They thus add to what might otherwise be a relatively limited compass and provide for an infinitely greater variety of timbres. Until Manuel Garcia discovered and invented the laryngoscope, the nature of these different mechanisms was not understood; the effect was known, but not the cause. From close observation, however, one fact appears—that we must not alter our manner of singing because we feel the mechanism to be in some subtle way altering its automatic procedure. Interference is bound to entail disaster.

The solution of the problem lies in uniformity—uniformity of breathing, of 'singing position,' of resonance—the last is perhaps the most important. So long as the voice is securely reflected in its ultimate forward position and is sustained there by the breath, supported from the diaphragm, the vocal cords will enjoy the elasticity and freedom essential for modifying their action, without that sudden change or 'break' which is commonly heard. Otherwise the modification cannot be made imperceptibly, and the abrupt transition from one register to another will become audible. The blending tone, if properly graduated, extends over three or at most four notes, to which the French give the name of *voix mixte*.*

With the aid of this *voix mixte*, the union of the 'chest' and 'medium,' of 'medium' and 'head' tones, proceeding either up or down the scale, the voice can be brought into line throughout its whole compass. Once the uniformity is achieved the secret of the legato, elusive as it may appear, becomes comparatively clear. The eclectic ear of the singer must do the rest.

(F) The Portamento

The portamento resembles the legato, only in its execution the carrying of the voice is made audible over the interval separating the two notes.

The mastery of the portamento is not more elusive than that of the legato; but its application to a musical phrase, the choice of a right mode of executing it, and various other considerations which musical feeling and experience alone can satisfy, combine to make it the more subtle and difficult device of the two. In the singing of Mozart both play an exceedingly important part.

The English word 'slur' is capable of too many interpretations, and has not the same precise significance as the Italian *portamento* or the French *port de voix*. These imply a mode of carrying the voice which, if employed gracefully and in the right place, always adds character, elegance, force, or intensity of expression, to the delivery of a phrase. Without one of these purposes in view it had better not be used. But, correctly to fulfil the traditions of the Italian school, it cannot be dispensed with.

To enhance the elegance of a phrase, the portamento should as a rule be lightly sung. Merely pushing the voice up or dropping it down from note to note deprives the device of all charm. The tone must be delicately poised and supported by the breath; it must likewise be carried without jerk or interruption over the whole of the interval, attaining its goal with perfect intonation and quality. Correct breath-pressure and intelligent anticipation of resonance will alone make this possible.

To impart declamatory force or vigour of sentiment, the portamento should be employed with an energy and directness that leaves no doubt as to its object, yet always with the greatest discretion. The in-

---

* The finest exercise I know for obtaining clearness and uniformity of tone in the medium register is that which Garcia gave to Jenny Lind when she went to him in Paris in 1841 to 'mend her worn and uneven voice.' It will be found on p. 16 of Hints on Singing. It is not to be used merely as a remedy, but as a study for maintaining a ringing quality of tone on the descending scales, and at the same time preparing the way for a natural pure legato.

tention of the composer must be carefully studied, and this in the case of Mozart will scarcely leave room for mistaken zeal or choice of the wrong place. The portamento is not invariably indicated, but where it is not, tradition and taste enable us to mark the spot.

As an ordinary device for adding sentiment to the music, the portamento has been exaggerated and overdone to an extent that has created a prejudice against its use at any point. That, of course, is absurd, like most objections that go to an extreme. Sixty years ago the excessive use of the portamento was unknown. The great singers used it in just the right measure and no more; they made it rare enough for the ear to be grateful for its charm, never 'slurring' two or three intervals in succession or spreading the tone up and down with sickly heaviness. I remember the period when the exaggeration gradually set in. The song-writers of the eighties were as much responsible for it as the singers, one of the most popular of them, Grieg, suffering from an inordinate love of portamento, as his songs show.

Then began a reaction. The more cultivated English audiences became familiar with the Passion-music and cantatas of Bach, and learned to appreciate the proper reticence in this matter. They began to enjoy a final cadence without the customary upward or downward *glissande* to the concluding note. Musicians perceived that the artistic singers were imitating the grace, perception, and restraint of players of the violin or the violoncello like Joachim, Sarasate, Ysaye, Lady Hallé, Hollman, Hausmann, and Piatti, who were the right models from whom to acquire them.

(G) The 'Messa di Voce'

The English meaning of the curious term is naively but accurately defined by Garcia in *Hints on Singing*. The *messa di voce*, he says, stands for the process of singing 'swelled sounds,' which should 'begin pianissimo and by degrees acquire increasing force till they arrive at their loudest, which should happen at half their length; then the process should be reversed.'

The apparently simple act of swelling and diminishing tone, not alone on single notes but on sentences or phrases, is the central characteristic of the old Italian school. The mastery of the 'straight line' must come first, as it would precede that of the 'curve' in drawing. But one does not suffice without the other—above all in the singing of Mozart, who demanded the *messa di voce* at nearly every turn of every piece that he wrote for the voice.

Here, once more, it is diaphragmatic breathing that enables the singer to accomplish the well-directed support of a steady tone while swelling or diminishing the strength and volume with perfect evenness and regularity of gradation.

The action of the *messa di voce* becomes, with practice, mechanical and subconscious. The utmost care is therefore needed in the exercise of a dynamic force that is liable to overassertion and to produce a certain monotony of style. It may be constantly used, but only if guided by ease and economy of breath-pressure, coupled with musical intelligence.

A Mozart singer who does not possess this gift would, in my judgement, be an anomaly.

(H) Agility (Coloratura, Ornaments, Etc.)

It is a common belief that only light voices are fitted by nature for the execution of florid or *coloratura* music. That is a misapprehension which has only grown up in recent times, and did not prevail among the old teachers, because their pupils, even those with the heaviest organs, were continually demonstrating the opposite. Bach, Handel, Mozart, and Rossini, wrote many passages that are *tours de force*, it is true; but, generally speaking, the former did not write their runs and 'divisions,' or the last-named his brilliant passages and cadenzas, for what they would have called exceptional voices. They wrote them indiscriminately for singers of every calibre—and for basses and contraltos as much as for sopranos and tenors.

The basis of all flexibility is the pure vocalization of the quick scale upon the bright tone, or *voix claire*. In order to be able to sing clearly, evenly, and rapidly an octave or more notes, one must be able to do the same thing on two, three, or five notes. That means careful and constant practice with correct breathing and mechanism, adequate resonance, a true ear, freedom from muscular rigidity of the throat or larynx, and the natural impulse which imparts ease and abandonment to the steady, effortless flow of tone.

The free oscillation of the tone from note to note necessary for the preparation of the quick scale is also the right beginning for the practice of the shake or trill. But when more than two notes are attempted the larynx does not oscillate; the voice glides smoothly over the group with a slight accent upon each note, so that, no matter how rapid the movement, the singing of the scale becomes clear, definite, flexible, and of even strength throughout.

The main factor in the attainment of this lightness, elasticity, and accuracy is the supreme controlling action of the breath, working in complete accord with mind and ear. To sing scales crisply and clearly we must be able to *think* them in perfection.

Similar rules apply to the practice of runs (or 'divisions'), which form perhaps the most characteristic and persistent feature of Italian music of the seventeenth and eighteenth centuries. The mastery of these is the key to every branch of florid singing. They provide the groundwork for all vocal agility, for the ease and brilliancy of rendering which alone justifies the survival of this class of music.

Apart from smoothness and beauty of tone, a clear accentuation of the various rhythms is extremely important. Usually the accent falls upon the first note of a group of four, six, or eight notes, but the singer must be able to place it anywhere without interfering with the rhythm and clarity of the run. Nothing can be worse than triplets sung with a slurred and indistinct middle note, except perhaps a jumbled 'turn' of which the final note is not audible.

In the singing of Mozart, correctly-marked rhythms— he has such an extraordinary variety of them— constitute a vital feature, notably in the concerted music of the operas and in the play between solo voice and orchestra. The ability to observe peculiar or divergent rhythms, in addition, is frequently essential in passages where agility is also called for. The study of one should therefore go hand in hand with the other; though naturally the scales and runs have to be mastered first.

With Mozart's special *ornamentations*, the point is that he treats the various types of ornaments, not as mere embellishments, but as integral parts of the composition. He thus enhances their dignity and makes their faultless execution of equal importance with that of the main melody.

The master had his favourite 'ornaments.' Grace notes simply abound in his music: turns (*gruppetti*), *appoggiature*, repeated and staccato sounds, shakes, slurred notes (*notes coulée*) constantly arrest the attention of the student. One and all demand the utmost purity and flexibility of voice and delicacy and finish of execution.

Mozart was especially fond of *notes coulée*, which are very difficult to sing really well. They belonged rather to the technique of the violin or the 'cello than of the voice. Two gliding notes to a single 'up or down bow' are comparatively easy to play (compare the semiquaver passages in the *Tannhäuser* overture); but two notes to a syllable for a few bars in succession present a greater difficulty to the singer because of the certainty, smoothness, and grace that are demanded of the executant, who should here closely imitate the violin.

At the root of the matter lies the command of agility, and every student of this art who works diligently enough can be trained to become a more or less accomplished singer of florid music.

18. First Things First

Originally published in the *Journal of Singing*, volume 64, no. 1, 2007

Many vocal methods begin with perhaps the simplest of all vocal gestures, the sustained tone. The practice is too common to be accidental and can be found in treatises from the eighteenth century to the present day. As is frequently true, the apparent simplicity belies the complexity of the effort and the enormous benefit to be gained from its use.

There are many examples of sustained tone pedagogy to be found in the historical literature. Sometimes we find these first efforts accompanied by an explanation of how and why it should be done, sometimes without. One of the commonly expressed goals of studying the sustained tone is to build strength in the voice, sometimes with the specific goal of strengthening a particular register. In speaking of how to "draw out" the voice, that is, to make the weak or underdeveloped voice "robust," Mancini (1774) suggested:

> It will prove to be of great help to a pupil who has a weak and limited voice, whether it be soprano or contralto. He must exercise with a solfeggio with sustained notes in his daily study. The result will be further assured if such solfeggio is kept within the limit which the voice permits at that time. It must be suggested to those who are confronted by these conditions, to increase the volume of their voices each day little by little, directing them thus, with the aid of art and continuous exercise, until they become vigorous and sonorous.[1]

The physiologic basis for this claim is well understood and has been thoroughly explored in another article by this author, called "Treasure Chest."[2]

Madame Cinti-Damoreau was a famous soprano at the Paris Opera who taught at the Paris Conservatory in the 1830s. She wrote her own method, which was officially adopted by the conservatory. Her use of the sustained tone was indeed the first element in her method, but she also included the use of the *messa di voce*. As has been discussed in a previous column, "Suoni Filati*: The Messa di Voce*,"[3] some teachers delayed the use of the *messa di voce* until much later in the training process (Garcia among them). Example 1 shows Cinti-Damoreau's first exercise.[4]

Crivelli, whose method was published in this country sometime in the first half of the nineteenth century by Oliver Ditson, included the sustained tone as his first rule.

Example 1. **Sustained tone with messa di voce** ***from Cinti-Damoreau's Method of Singing***

> Rule 1st. The chief attention of the student ought to be directed to the manner of forming and sustaining the voice. The best means of attaining this object is by constantly practicing the scales arranged in semibreves; taking care to begin each note in a tone firm and distinct, yet not too loud; afterwards swelling it out, though not to excess, and then gradually diminishing it to the softest piano.[5]

If the reader were to undertake the process of singing through an octave or more by ascending and then descending in a scale-wise manner, one would certainly appreciate that this is no trivial matter. The work load is significant and demanding!

The great baritone Julius Stockhausen often has been quoted in this column. He brings to the discussion the goal of developing a beautiful tone through the use of the *tenuto di voce*. As is so typical of the progressive nature of much of the pedagogy practiced by our ancestors, he cautioned in his *Method of Singing* (1884) that we should take first things first.

> The old Italian and German masters, whose schools produced such excellent singers of both sexes, show by their writings that their first endeavour was to teach their pupils how to form a beautiful tone and to render their voices flexible and of a telling quality. There was no question of exercise in a large compass, nor of say, in the *solfeggio*—our ancestors began by teaching how to establish and sustain the voice.[6]

He went on to call attention to some of the detail of the beginning of the tone, considered to be so important.

> It is the well known *tenuto di voce*, sustained notes of equal and medium power. This is the chief condition of musical phrases for a perfect delivery . . . The pupil must first attack the note according to the nature of the consonant, which may be hard or soft or sonant, or according to the character of the vowel, but, as Andreas Herbst expresses it, "on the right note," and I may add with precision and fixed larynx.[7]

Stockhausen alluded to a fault among singers of his day and of ours: the habit of beginning a tone below the center of the pitch with some sort of a slide or "hitch" into the note.

Part of the usefulness of the sustained tone exercise is that it frees the mind of the student to consider the complexity of the gesture. No better exposition of this benefit can be found than one by Frederick W. Root. Perhaps you will recall a reprint of an article by Mr. Root in a previous column, "The Voice Teacher's Problem."[8]

> Many habituate themselves to a distorted position so thoroughly, that it seems natural, possibly easy, to them.
>
> If the face is not perfectly at repose, if the forehead is wrinkled, the nostrils dilated, or the mouth drawn into a position not used in speaking, it is an unerring indication that there is distortion in the throat. To rid yourself of wrong habits in this respect, or to prove that there are none, try this:
>
> Fill the lungs; let the countenance assume an expression of repose; relax the muscles of the throat; open the mouth well; place the tongue as above directed; then exhale slowly and steadily, at first without producing a tone, but after two or three seconds allow the vocal cords to vibrate, watching carefully to see that there be no change of position. Repeat this process several times, at first making the tone very soft; then, if successful in retaining the right position of all the members, exhale a little faster, making a louder tone. It is often of assistance to watch this process with a looking-glass.[9]

Example 2. **Table of first exercises from Frederick W. Root's School of Singing (1873).**

Root's book, *School of Singing* (1873) is a treasure of sound, logical, no-nonsense advice, and would be widely appreciated by thoughtful teachers today. The insight of this teacher is especially clear in the following advice:

> Try to overcome all tendency to tremulous tones, by striving for a steady and regular pressure of breath from the lungs. Certain tones, those in the neighborhood of E, will be, in most voices, more tremulous than the others, and the learner is sometimes surprised to find that in ascending the scale the quality of the tone suddenly changes at a certain pitch. But remember that nothing must interfere with the prescribed rules for producing a tone. Accept without question the tone that comes when you have assumed a natural position. Attack each tone with precision, and so avoid the bad but very common habit, of commencing below the proper pitch and sliding to place.[10]

Root's caution not to judge the outcome of the exercise but to commit to the right process is in line with the teaching of Cornelius Reid and many others whose first purpose is to build upon the natural response of the voice, and not to train the singer to produce a sound of a particular quality. Note here again the caution concerning the precise attack of the tone. Root's book is not only a valuable resource for a voice teacher; it is also a beautiful book, released by a publishing house owned and operated by his own family, founded by his well-known father, George F. Root. Example 2 is the first of several tables included in the book to aid the student.

Edmund Myer was a prolific author on vocal matters. In one of his many books, *Vocal Reinforcement* (1891), he included a chapter entitled "A Study of Level Movements." He described the benefits of singing sustained tones in that it provided the opportunity of proper mental and "moral" focus.

> This study is founded upon a balancing of the forces, the motive power and resisting force, or equal pressure and resistance. This is the only way in which it is possible to secure true conditions at the organ of sound . . .[11]

Here we arrive at the heart of the matter. There are two primary opposing forces that must coordinate their actions in order to create a stable and beautiful tone: the breath and the resistance offered by the vocal folds. How many different ways has this principle been described: *lutte vocale, appoggio,* and now *tenuto di voce*. Of course, this balance can be disrupted at almost any point in the body—and it is this point that makes the simplicity of the sustained tone so useful to a great extent.

Like Root, Myer went on to advise caution when judging the success of these efforts.

> Study the way and manner of doing, more than the result; the way of doing, at first, is of far more importance than the result. Be assured that when the effort is right the result will surely be right, or will come right. The tendency on the part of beginners is to study the result at once; the tone must be made to sound something near right, it matters not what the effort may be.[12]

In a very popular class voice method published in 1932, D. A. Clippinger cautioned that first things should not be mastered and forgotten.

> The following simple exercises are for the practice of *legato* and *sostenuto*—the connected and sustained style. These two principles are so fundamental and necessary to good singing that they should be practiced persistently and with great care. Like all other exercises necessary to gaining control of the voice, they should be practiced until long after the student feels he has mastered them.[13]

Example 3. **Exercises for sostenuto from D. A. Clippinger's Class Method for Voice (1932).**

In Example 3 Clippinger led the singer to the broader application of the principle of *sostenuto* to more than one tone—in fact, to a whole phrase. The ability to sustain the intensity and beauty of the tone throughout the whole range with a true *legato* line is, of course, a characteristic of fine singing. As a final example we go once again to Richard Miller's *The Structure of Singing*.

> The ultimate test of technical ability lies in sustained singing. Energy and power are frequently required, but these attributes of the good singer must be balanced by freedom. The problem in sustained singing is that primitive sphincter action, which ordinarily prevails in such heavy activities as lifting and pulling, is often carried over into energized singing.[14]

It can be challenging to make our students understand the importance of doing simple things in their own practice time; to make them really seek perfection of action and clarity of function in something as simple as sustaining a vowel sound. We must find ways to challenge them to spend the time to do the first exercises so that they lay a roadbed for more complex gestures and exercises leading to skillful performance. Mr. Miller put it very well:

> Where voice technique is founded on systematically acquired skills, sostenuto fills its role as a builder of the instrument. Sustaining power will increase vocal stamina and ensure vocal health.[15]

Notes

1. Giambattista Mancini, *Practical Reflections on the Figurative Art of Singing,* translated by Pietro Buzzi (Boston: The Gorham Press, 1912), 102. Originally published as *Pensieri e Riflessioni Pratiche Sopra il Canto Figurato* (Vienna, 1774).
2. Stephen F. Austin, "'Treasure Chest'—A Physiological and Pedagogical Review of the Low Mechanism," *Journal of Singing* 61, no. 3 (January/February 2005): 241.
3. Stephen F. Austin, "Suoni Filati: *The Messa di Voce*," *Journal of Singing* 62, no. 5 (May/June 2006): 573.
4. Laure Cinti-Damoreau, *Method of Singing* (Philadelphia: A. H. Rosewig, n. d.), 9.
5. D. Crivelli, *Instructions and Progressive Exercises in the Art of Singing* (Boston: Oliver Ditson, n.d.), 7.
6. Julius Stockhausen, *Method of Singing* (New York: Novello, Ewer and Co., 1884), 15.
7. Ibid., 18.
8. Stephen F. Austin, "Buried Treasure: *The Voice Teacher's Problems* by Frederick W. Root," *Journal of Singing* 63, no. 3 (January/February 2007): 335.
9. F. W. Root, *School of Singing* (Chicago: Geo. F. Root & Sons, 1873), 4.
10. Ibid., 5.
11. Edmund Myer, *Vocal Re-inforcement* (New York: American Publishing Co., 1891), 235.
12. Ibid., 236.
13. D. A. Clippinger, *The Clippinger Class Method of Voice Production* (Philadelphia: Oliver Ditson, 1932), 36.
14. Richard Miller, *The Structure of Singing* (New York: Schirmer Books, 1986), 108.
15. Ibid., 109.

19. Eye Witness Views

Originally published in the *Journal of Singing*, volume 64, no. 2, 2007

In my exploration of old dusty books and musty music journals, I always am thrilled to find an account of a witness to the art of a venerated professor of voice teaching from the past. It is one thing to read the official record written by masters in order to set down their fundamental truths for posterity, most typically in a formal "method"; it can be quite a different experience to read of a master teacher's work from someone who sat in the studio and observed his ideas at work. These are rare!

What follows is the first part of a series of articles that appeared in *Werner's Magazine* (published from 1879–1902 under various titles, including *The Voice*). Each of three articles was a report of the author's personal observations of several important European voice teachers of the day; Manuel Garcia II, Emile Behnke, William Shakespeare, all teaching in England at the time and, finally, Antonio Sangiovanni in Italy. This first article in the series appeared in the January, 1886 edition. So, here is an "eye witness report" of the teaching of Signor Manuel Garcia. Nothing of the author, Mr. Tubbs, is known to me, other than the fact that he was a regular contributor to *Werner's Magazine* over a period of many years.

As you will recall, Garcia gave us the first concise definition of voice registers in his first book, *The Compete Treatise on the Art of Singing*. In light of that early work in his life, the discussion by Mr. Tubbs on Garcia's approach to voice registers almost fifty years later is most interesting!

European Voice Teachers[1]

By Frank H. Tubbs
New York

I.

Manuel Garcia

In America, thousands of miles away from home, the name of Signor Manuel Garcia is known to every educated singer, and is familiarly known by the last name. I called at the publishing house of Novello, Ewer & Co., in London, and asked the clerk: "Can you tell me the address of Signor Garcia?"

"*What* Signor Garcia?"

(This gave a shock! Could there be any but *the* Signor Garcia?) Suppressing my indignation, I answered: "Signor Manuel Garcia."

The address was Manchester Square, which, being near, I sought at once. I found that he had abandoned his office and gave lessons only at his house. At first, no one was found who knew where the house was; after a while, the manservant appeared who had assisted in moving, and he had the new address: "Cricklewood, Kilburn." Being a stranger, my next application was to a policeman, who pointed out the 'bus to Kilburn, "but as for Cricklewood, he knew nothing about it."

I was going to find Garcia, if possible. On the bus I learned that Cricklewood was a village in the parish of Kilburn, and fully a half-mile beyond the end of the bus route. When I had walked about the half mile, I began inquiring for Signor Garcia. Each time came the information:

"Yes, this is Cricklewood, but we know no one named Garcia."

Call after call was made in street after street, and no one was found who could give the desired information, until the sun was declining in the west, making that mellow, golden light never seen outside of England. The postman, making his round, was observed, and from him the location of Signor Garcia's house was found. Strange to say, it was next door to where inquiry had been made! Could it be possible! The next neighbor did not know Signor Manuel Garcia! Of what avail is greatness?

Walking up the nicely-kept garden, and ringing the bell, brought the servant who, after showing me into the drawing-room, summoned "the master." He entered, drawing off heavy gloves as he came, for he had been pruning his fruit-trees in the orchard.

It was with a feeling of greatest veneration that I stood in the presence of this man. He it was who first saw the vocal cords in their work, by means of the newly-discovered laryngoscope. There before me stood the man whose vocal cords were first seen, and I was to hear their tone. He it was who taught Jenny Lind and Bataille. Were I in the presence of a king, I could not feel more like bowing my head, than I did as I came before this man. He is small, compact and wiry, then (1882) 78½ years old. The snow-white hair and moustache, and the piercing dark eye distinctively mark positiveness of mind, and the life and animation entering every word and action impress the visitor, even at first sight. In spite of the white hair, Garcia appears much younger than his years indicate.

Signor Garcia condenses his voice-cultivation into five distinct subjects: (1) "Sure intonation"; (2) "same strength of tone"; (3) "same quality throughout voice"; (4) "meaning of text apparent"; (5) "perfect enunciation." The importance of these headings he impresses upon the pupil over and over. Upon examination, it will be seen that much is condensed therein.

"Why do you sing so stiffly?" he would ask; "do you not realize that stiff singing indicates a rigid throat, and a rigid throat interferes with sure intonation and good pronunciation?" Or: "Do you not observe that continual explosive tone, the loud voice softened so suddenly, is because you have so little control of the respiratory muscles? Keep the same strength of tone."

So it would seem that all the subjects and principles discussed and employed by teachers are condensed into but five by Signor Garcia. That to which he refers most often is quality of tone, asserting that if the quality of tone is not good to our ear (providing our ear is cultivated), the voice is faulty in one or more of these great principles.

The voice, according to Signor Garcia, is "bright" or "dark"; or, to apply other terms, "clear" or "veiled." The "clear" quality is produced by lowering the soft-palate and raising the larynx; placing the throat in much the same position as when swallowing. The "veiled" quality is produced by reversing these positions—that is, by raising the soft-palate so that the back of the throat and roof of the mouth form an arched reflector; the larynx held low. These positions allow the extreme differences in the quality of tone. Between are the various gradations of tone-quality, and it is a principle of the method that the palate, pharynx and throat shall be so drilled that all may take, in response to instinctive command, that position which will produce the best and most appropriate quality which the meaning of the words demands. To this end, it is the custom of this master to exercise the voice with the Italian vowel [a]; first slowly and softly; and, as the muscles and membranes become more pliable and under control, more rapidly and with more fullness of tone. This fullness must never be allowed to become great in exercise-practice, and under no circumstance should a tone be allowed to sound harshly.

The reason assigned by Signor Garcia for using [a] in all exercise-practice, is because the tongue and throat are, while using this vowel, nearer their normal position (as in quiet breathing) than when using any other vowel. As strength and confidence come to the pupil he adds other vowel practice. He uses, however, the vowel sounds [o] and [I] for specific purposes; namely: the [o] for drilling the larynx to hold a low position, producing the "veiled" quality, and the [I] for producing the "clear" quality by raising the larynx.

The subject of registers is avoided by Signor Garcia. "There are no registers; or, if so, they should be drilled out of sight. There is but one voice; make it of the same quality throughout and you see no registers; therefore, you have none." When, however, the certain changes which one discovers constantly in untrained voices are referred to, the master readily explains the mechanism which produces such changes of quality, but adds in a tone which ends all questioning:

"Practice! Practice! Time will make the quality alike throughout the voice."

To illustrate: The question was asked: "What makes the 'bad note' at E or F of the tenor voice?"

"The tones below the bad note are produced by the vibration of the whole glottis; those above, by the thin inner lips. Where the inner lips join the thicker portion is a little fatty substance, and it requires much practice to bring this into perfect vibration. But don't think anything about it. Practice will remove all difficulty."

The mechanical effort of respiration receives more attention from Signor Garcia, and yet he refers continually to the *tone* and advises one to observe *that*, to see if the breathing is correctly performed. How to breathe, according to the master's method, can be given almost in his own words:

"Some people think, when they commence to inhale, that they must expand greatly the abdomen. Not so. The portion at the end of the breast-bone must push out a little when the breath is first drawn; but after the beginning of inhalation, the portion below the ribs should not expand much. The ribs at the sides should spread all they can, and the chest must expand fully. Then the lungs have all the air they can hold. While singing, be careful not to allow the air to *rush* out, but use it economically. Keep the quality of tone smooth. Don't allow the tones to begin loudly and suddenly die away. That shows loss of breath on them. Watch the tones the violinist produces. Hear how smooth all of them are. Hear how evenly the phrase of tones is made. Imitate that. While singing, select a good place for taking a breath, and take all that is possible. Do not raise the shoulders in inhaling, for that crowds the throat muscles, and this will not permit tones of good quality to be made. While singing, let the tones be peaceful and beautiful and the breathing will be good."

Of course, when asked to describe fully the mechanical action required for the act of respiration, Signor Garcia is ready to give in detail the desired scientific information. It will be seen from the above brief summary, that strictest attention is to be given to producing a good quality of tone; that this good quality depends upon certain specified positions of the vocal apparatus, so drilled as to instinctively adjust themselves to express the meaning of the words employed, as fully as the intellect of the performer comprehends the meaning.

Additional to such drill as has been mentioned, Signor Garcia uses practice in producing distinct word-sounding, and also, over and again, in studying an aria, appeals to the intelligence of the pupil, that he may better comprehend and render clearly the meaning.

"Of what avail are good tones if you say nothing? Why should we merely vocalize before our audience? Give the meaning clearly and intelligently, or don't sing at all. What were we singing? Oh, yes! Now let us tell the story as if our hearers never heard it before and it is full of interest to them."

He claims that if our tones have been delivered with a good quality before words are attempted in song, that our chief attention (while song-singing) may be given to consonant formation. "Do you realize," says he, "how badly we would discover the meaning of a sentence were we to omit the consonants? So it is in singing. Here, if I write the vowels of this sentence, can you make out what it means? I will space them, too, as they belong in the sentence:"

e ee i y a e a e o i u oo.

After puzzling a moment and not discovering the meaning, he handed me another paper with the consonants of the sentence, similarly arranged:

Th tr s n m g rd n r n t n fll bl m.

It took little more than a glance to read:

The trees in my garden are not in full bloom.

"The consonants," says Signor Garcia, "present the obstacles to sound, and they are produced by five arrangements of tongue, lips and teeth:—

1. Lips together, as for *pa, ba, ma*.
2. Lips and teeth together, as for *fa, va*.
3. Teeth and tip of tongue together, as for *da, tha, ta*.
4. Tip of tongue and palate together; as for *la, na, sir*.
5. Root of tongue and arcade together, as for *ka, ga*.

"Practice such exercises as will drill these parts to produce instinctively the right consonant sounds, without interfering with the quality of tone produced. Now our mechanical work is out of the way, let us study our arias."

And the eyes of the grand old man would glisten as he turned to a loved opera or oratorio. The pleasure of writing of those pleasant memories must be deferred, for it is the purpose of this article to refer more to methods of mechanical drill than to the artistic portion of the teacher's work. One enjoys heartily the enthusiasm which Signor Garcia uses while teaching an aria.

NOTES

1. Frank H. Tubbs, "European Voice Teachers," *The Voice* 8, no. 1 (January 1886): 10–11.

20. "Lean on Me!"; The Art of the Appoggiatura

Originally published in the *Journal of Singing*, volume 64, no. 3, 2008

I believe that it has been demonstrated in this column that building the voice historically has been accomplished with the use of a progressive method that usually included a study of the vocal registers (including the chest voice and falsetto), specific articulations (*legato, staccato, aspirato, marcato*), breath support (*appoggio*), resonance (the study of the "pure vowel," formant tuning), and other postural gestures (jaw opening and laryngeal position). Equally important was the training of appropriate stylistic performance practice. It was up to the voice teacher to instill a sense of style and musical tradition and interpretation. Many authors such as Garcia, Stockhausen, Lablache, Delle Sedie, and others gave equal or greater amount of emphasis to this goal.

One of the most important interpretive skills was the use of the *appoggiatura*. Mancini stated:

> The appoggiatura, trillo and mordente in reality are nothing but embellishments of the melody, yet they are so necessary that without them singing would be monotonous and imperfect, while with these embellishments singing acquires its greatest splendor.[1]

It is very helpful to know that in the method of Manuel Garcia and many others we have very clear guidelines set forth to inform us how it was being done in the middle of the nineteenth century. These resources serve as a performance guide to opera, art song, and oratorio being performed at the time—much of which is still in the repertory today.

Rather than try to summarize what a few writers have said about the proper use of the *appoggiatura*, extended excerpts from Manuel Garcia's important early treatises will be presented. After all, it has been one of the primary goals of this column to include extended quotations from original sources. Since most of these books are not known to many of us, it is hoped that this practice has stimulated some interest on the part of readers to go and search out for themselves some of these important resources.

The first excerpt is taken from my personal copy of an English version of Part 1 of Manual Garcia's complete treatise published under the title *Garcia's Singing School* in the United States by Oliver Ditson in the mid-nineteenth century (undated):

Example 1.

Example 2.

The Appoggiatura and Small Notes

Of all the ornaments of singing, the appoggiatura is the easiest to perform, and at the same time the most frequent and most necessary.

The appoggiatura, as expressed by its Italian name, is a note on which to support the voice. This note is mostly foreign to harmony; it precedes and serves to attain one of the notes really in accord. It may be superior or inferior; if it be superior, it is taken as the scale gives it, either at the distance of one tone (1), or of a semitone (2); if it be inferior, it is almost invariably taken at a semitone (3) [see Example 1].

Sometimes a note of the harmony performs the office of the appoggiatura, and then the latter may be separated from the note to which it belongs, by any of the intervals which occur in the chord (4).

The appoggiatura may also be given by the simple delay of a real note of the harmony (6). It is the only case in which the appoggiatura should be prepared, which was not the case in the preceding hypotheses. Although usually indicated by a note of a small character, the appoggiatura always lasts longer than the note to which it belongs [see Example 2].

The passage from the appoggiatura to the following note is affected smoothly, by connecting the voice without dragging it.

We annex a few examples which combine the different appoggiaturas of which we have just spoken.
The duration of the appoggiatura is extremely variable. If the measure is even, the appoggiatura takes half the value of the note which it is destined to embellish. Example [2]A.

If the principal note is pointed, or if the measure is uneven, the appoggiatura borrows two-thirds of its value from the principle note. Example [2]B.

The appoggiatura absorbs the entire value of the principal note when the duration of the latter is prolonged by a tie. Example [2]C.

Finally, the appoggiatura can be excessively rapid. Example 4
[see (4) in Example 1].

The wants and nature of the melody will determine the choice of these different applications more safely than can be done by precept.

Among the appoggiaturas, the acciaccatura must be distinguished. The latter is a little, brisk, note, which precedes a second note as short as itself, at the distance of a whole tone or a semitone. The voice urges forward, so to speak, these two notes, and halts only on the third.[2]

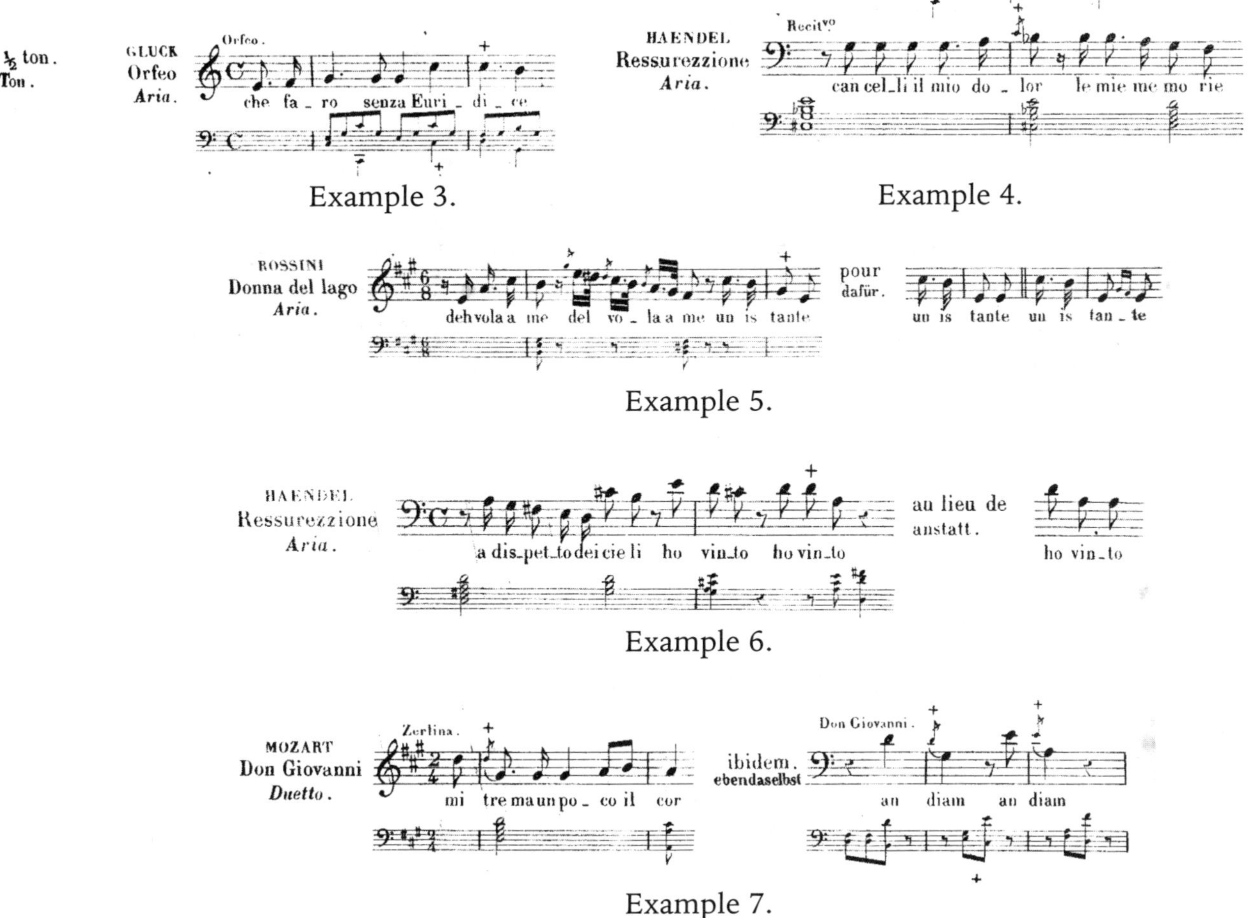

Example 3.

Example 4.

Example 5.

Example 6.

Example 7.

Garcia's Singing School included only Part 1 of his *Complete Treatise on the Art of Singing*. In Part 2 Garcia elaborated further upon the specific use of the *appoggiatura* with copious examples taken from the vocal literature.

The source of the text quoted here comes from Donald Paschke's edition and translation published in 1975 by Da Capo Press. The second part of Garcia's work is less well known than the first and an even greater misfortune that both volumes are now out of print. Prior to 1975 this important work was practically unknown to modern teachers and singers. The musical examples that are provided are taken from an undated publication *École de Garcia Traité Complet de L'art du Chant*, an early version of Garcia's work published in side-by-side columns of French and German by B. Schott.

APPOGGIATURAS

The appoggiatura, as its name indicates, is a note on which the voice marks a stress. This note is almost always non-harmonic and should be resolved to a harmonic note. The harmonists consider only non-harmonic major and minor seconds attacked by conjunct intervals as appoggiaturas; but singers should, I believe, besides these seconds, regard all the intervals which fulfill the same functions, such as the delayed notes and the disjunct intervals, as appoggiaturas and subject them to the same rules.[3]

Garcia offered a number of examples for this without further comment.

(1) Minor second (Example 3).
(2) Major second (Example 4).
(3) Third (Example 5).

(4) Fourth (Example 6).
(5) Fifth (Example 7).
(6) Sixth (Example 8).
(7) Seventh (Example 9).
(8) Octave (Example 10).

Garcia also offers examples of ascending *appoggiaturas* including the following for an ascending third (Example 11) and for the ascending fourth (Example 12). The *Don Pasquale* excerpt includes examples of *appoggiaturas* for a descending fifth, descending fourth, descending second, as well the ascending fourth.

Example 8.

Example 9.

Example 10.

Example 11.

Example 12.

Example 13.

Continuing:

When the two first notes of the measure end a member of the phrase, the first always carries the prosodic accent, and for this reason it must be changed into an appoggiatura (Example A); the effect of the two equal notes (C) would not be tolerable. One should exempt from this rule the cases where the two notes make the essential part of the motive (B) [See Example 13].[4]

Garcia included tables of various ways to vary the final two notes when it was followed by a rest (Examples 14, 15).

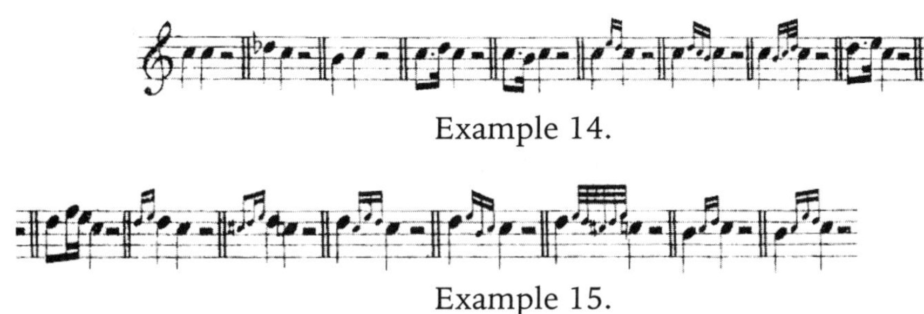

Example 14.

Example 15.

In his book *Method of Singing,* Julius Stockhausen presented a similar list of rules for the proper application of the appoggiatura, saying that the practice as defined by Tosi still were applicable in that day. In the introduction to the subject he includes the following footnote from Agricola, an early translator of Tosi's book (1723) into German (1757):

> Why is the use of the *appoggiaturas* such a difficulty to many? Why do they not follow the simple rules of the old masters? Probably the way in which the *appoggiaturas* are marked has something to do with it. Before Tosi's time they were never written, a fact which is evident from his own words. In Scarlatti and Lotti's cantatas, for instance (a good many of which I am acquainted with), there are none. Tosi, in his *Anleitung zur Singkunst,* is therefore very severe upon the "fashionable *virtuoso*," who in his day invented a new mode of writing them. "Poor Italy!" he exclaims. "Do singers nowa-days not know where to put in *appoggiaturas* unless they are marked by sign posts! Oh! The weakness of him who condescends to follow precedents! What a disgrace it is to you modern singers to accept instruction which is only necessary for children!" and so on. Now-a-days it is just the same. The *appoggiatura* is often omitted altogether, and replaced by an ordinary full note.[5]

Many modern music editions of the eighteenth and nineteenth centuries have "filled in the blanks" by providing some of the *appoggiaturas,* but certainly not all. A perfect example of the absence of any indication of the *appoggiatura* is in G. Schirmer's score of *Le nozze di Figaro*. A well-known place to look is Susanna's recitative and aria "Guinse alfin il momento" and "Deh vieni non tardar." There are none of the *appoggiaturas* indicated. Of course, it is required that they be inserted, so our students need to learn this simple art of "decorating" the line. William Shakespeare in his *Art of Singing* (1898) included the entire recitative and aria (just the melodic line with the text) to show how it appeared and how it was to be performed, including the *appoggiaturas*.[6] Example 16 is only the recitative.

Example 16.

With a little understanding of performance practice guidelines as described by Garcia and others, the modern performer will be able to approach this subject armed with the experience of those who have gone before us.

NOTES

1. Giambattista Mancini, *Practical Reflections on the Figurative Art of Singing*, translated by Pietro Buzzi (Boston: Gorham Press, 1912), 115; originally published as *Pensieri e Riflessioni Pratiche Sopra il Canto Figurato* (Vienna, 1774).
2. Manuel Garcia, *Garcia's Complete School of Singing*, translator unknown (Boston: Oliver Ditson, no date), 63.
3. Manuel Garcia, *Complete Treatise On the Art of Singing, Part 2*, translated and edited by Donald Paschke (New York: Da Capo Press, 1984), 117; originally published as *Nouveau Traité Sommaire sur l'Art du Chant* (Genève: Minkoff Éditeur, 1847).
4. Ibid., 122.
5. Julius Stockhausen, *A Method of Singing*, translated by Sophie Löwe (London: Novello, 1884), 65; originally published as *Julius Stockhausens Gesangs-Methode* (Leipzig: Peters, 1884).
6. William Shakespeare, *The Art of Singing* (Boston: Oliver Ditson Company, 1898), 115.

21. Plugging in the Holes

Originally published in the *Journal of Singing*, volume 64, no. 4, 2008

I often find myself browsing through old books and magazines in used book stores and antique shops. It is not unusual to find occasionally an old *The Etude* Magazine. Theodore Presser founded the musical copy of journal in 1883 in Lynchburg, Virginia, and later moved the business to Philadelphia, where it continued to be published until 1957. It was begun primarily as a magazine to promote excellence in piano teaching; however, it included sections of broad appeal for professional and student musicians and had edited sections for organ/choir, strings, and voice.

I have found several interesting articles from the 1930s by a man by the name of Homer Henley. I know nothing of Mr. Henley other than the fact that he contributed regularly during those years, writing on many topics of interest to singers. I especially appreciate his awareness of the work of Garcia and other important teachers of the turn of the century. Here are two articles by Mr. Henley on topics that are still *a propos* for our conversations today. In the first he discusses the importance of eliminating the leakage of air through the glottis for classical singing and suggests a useful exercise to do so. In the second he discusses another type of leakage, that of sound into the nasal cavities. He could be accused of being a bit opinionated in the second article, but I hope it will stimulate some discussion around the water fountain.

Garcia's Second Discovery[1]

by Homer Henley

Manuel Garcia discovered the laryngoscope in 1840, winning immortality for himself thereby and conferring a boon in perpetuity on mankind. Another discovery Garcia made, one scarcely less far-reaching in its benefits to singers, but, amazing to relate, [is] quite unknown except for the few singers and teachers of singing who have read his book on the voice, and apparently almost overlooked even by them.

This discovery relates to that large class of voices marked by a leakage of breath with the tone. That is to say, the tone is surrounded by a fuzzy aura of breath which escapes with the sound and engenders a slight but distinctly audible or whistling sound with it. It is due to the imperfect approximation of the glottis, and is caused, it may be, by a faint congestion of the vocal cords themselves and a consequent relaxation of their normal tension. This causes the glottis chink to be a bit "bow-legged," as it were, instead of functioning in normal parallels.

Garcia found the cure for this condition—a cure by singing without the adventitious aid of medical treatment of any sort. The treatment according to his method was to sing chromatic scales of groups of five semitones in the middle of the voice—about from f, first space, to c, third space—in sharply struck staccato. Although Garcia merely sets down the cure without explanation, a moment's reflection will disclose the principle underlying this device. The vocal cords, being in a relaxed condition in the cases of those who have the breath-leakage, require a certain massaging or exercising of an active nature to restore them to their normal habit of attrition. That massaging or active exercising they do not receive when singing scales, solfeggio, or songs in the usual manner. Because when the vocal cords are not in use, they lie back in circular repose against the circular walls of their tiny home. When speech or song directs, they leap together and the edges or lips of these two delicate membranes vibrate to the breath stream which presses against them. When the phrase of the singer is ended the cords fly back again to their circular repose against the circular walls of their home only to leap together once more on the new phrase. But it will be noted that the vocal cords, for the duration of the entire phrase, have leaped together and retired again but *once*. What is needed for the restoration of their tension and attrition is the active leap done countless times. This is done by means of the staccato, because the cords make their full leap and return on *every staccato note*.

Here is an illustration. If a scale of the ninth is sung in groups of four notes, in even time, and that scale is sung twice on the same breath, thirty-two actual notes will have been sounded, but if there is no break in the sound the vocal cords will have come together and returned only *once*. If the same scale were done staccato, however, the vocal cords would have leaped together and returned *thirty-two* times on one breath. It will, therefore, readily be seen what a tremendous exercising of the actual vocal cords goes on if much staccato work be done daily. And of course it is this tremendous amount of healthy exercise which brings relaxed vocal cords up to their normal tension again, and, by the closure of the "bow-legged" orifice, excludes the breath and restores the voice to its rightful clear and incisive tone.

In cases of a bad breath-leakage it has sometimes taken a year to cure the escape, but perseverance in the exercise will cure the worst leak. It may be added that Garcia recommended the vowels E and A for this exercise as being of a more sharp and ringing character in themselves and therefore the more helpful in bringing back the ring to the whole voice.

The Truth About "Nasal" Tone[2]

by Homer Henley

If, by the phrase, "nasal tone," we mean that rasping, whanging sound made familiar by down-East comedians, then such sound is anathema in the legitimate singing voice. If we mean the sound taught in the average studio of America, and having for its avowed objective an intentional crowding of the voice into a geographical center variously designated as "In the bridge of the nose"; "Over-and-forward between the eyes"; or even "In the mask of the face" (quite a different thing, by the way, from that *dans le masque*, by which is characterized certain sounds in the French language), then the inadequacy of such misdirected efforts to attain the lovely head resonance of the great singers, becomes the more pathetically tragic as one reflects upon the almost national prevalence of their well meant, but disastrous blundering, as Horace has it, "on the dubious waves of error tost."

The late William Shakespeare, one of my European teachers, said, when asked about "nasal" singing, "If a sound be 'nasal,' that sound never can be singing—it is only an ugly, misdirected vocal sound. So called 'nasal singing' seems to be peculiar to America; we have little or none of it in Europe. That lovely, singing tone, which is distributed throughout the head spaces of all great singers, is quite another affair; but it cannot be acquired by aiming the voice at the nose."

Giovanni Sbriglia, another of my teachers, said: "Crazy, crazy! Nasal sound belongs to a horse when he screams. The nose is not for beauty in singing. But if breathing is right, and throat free, the 'bell' sounds itself." Very many of the great singers of today, of both sexes, have told me personally that they believe the "nasal" tone, taught in studios of this country, is a national blight on the progress of our young singers. "You will not hear this taught or sung in Europe," they say. "It seems to be something originated by Americans. No doubt what they are trying to teach, is the wonderful resonance of the head spaces which every really fine singer employs. But the nose sound, that is terrible!"

The Other Side

In rebuttal of this testimony, it may be adduced that the great Jean de Reske once said, "Singing becomes more and more a matter of the nose." But even so, it must be remembered, first, that while Jean de Reske was one of the finest interpretative singers, and one of the finest teachers of singing style, he was, after all, a singing coach and not a voice pedagogue.

Secondly, it is well not to lose sight of the age old fact that the great singing virtuosi of the world not only afford the most surprising examples of how little a singer may reliably know of his own vocal processes, and also that the ranks of great singing teachers have had almost no recruits from the immemorial company of great singing artists. The elder Lamperti was an indifferent singer. So was Manuel Garcia; and Sbriglia and William Shakespeare were tenors of small repute. The old masters of *bel canto* were not great singers. Porpora was a composer, as was Caccini. Tosi sang well, but his pupils sang better. Agricola, Frederici and De Bacily were choirmasters with but little personal vocal gift.

It is perhaps, not amiss in this connection, to repeat what Shakespeare once told me: "It seems incredible as a fact, and a great pity to have to say it, but I am convinced that there are not, on the face of the globe, more than ten persons who really understand the human singing voice." And the writer of this article says "amen" to that, especially in relation to the widespread prevalence of misconception regarding the quality, character and location of that ineffable tone of vocal resonance which all the great singers of the world hold in common possession, but which appears persistently to elude the pursuit of voice teacher and voice students alike.

Where is the Vocal Highway?

If we are to attach to these unequivocal pronouncements from authorities so exalted in the musical firmament the importance they deserve, then we must admit that something is very wrong with the popular conception of the location and quality of the "great tone" so successfully employed by all the preeminent singers of the world. Let us grant that the great singers are born with that tone; but, granting it, must we also conclude that the great singers alone are born with it? And must we also assume that the great singers, possessing it, enjoyed this rare and perfect tone without having had to develop it in the first place? The answer to both questions is a decided "No!"

There have been very few of the great singers of our own time, or in the annals of the past, but have had to develop the great gifts of their natural endowment through prolonged and intensive study. It is a matter for belief that countless numbers of great voices have been born into this world and passed on into a better world without ever having been developed at all. And it is a matter for credibility that there exist at this moment thousands, perhaps, of great voices which will never be heard, as such, for lack of teachers great enough to hear and free their potentialities.

All voices do not possess that heavenly rapture of haunting seduction we call the "great tone." Yet how many teachers there are who would be glad to admit that they have heard from time to time, in the singing of one or more of their students, isolated tones or phrases which undoubtedly did possess that "seldom rapture" of perfect tonal beauty—transiently, perhaps; only a single note, perhaps; but still the "great tone." From that premise, does it not rather inferentially and pointedly suggest itself to us that if one phrase or even one note can be great, why not, then, every phrase and every note? There can be but one answer to such a question; if one tone be produced perfectly, then all the others can be so produced likewise—*provided* there be at hand a teacher who understands, and who can impart to a pupil's understanding, the difference between the so-called "nasal" tone of the average studios, and the sublimated beauties of that tone which circulates in joyous iridescence throughout all the nacreous cavities of the head, and which goes by the name of the "great tone."

Tonal Release

Technically, the difference lies in the physiological location of the sound. The "nasal" tone is crowded either into the cavity of the forehead or into the immediate forward wall of the corridor of the head cavities, generally called the mask of the face. The "great tone" is crowded nowhere at all, but roams freely through all the chambers of the cavities of the head. It flows as much in the region just above the soft palate as it does in the cavern just above the middle of the mouth. And indeed, it streams quite as much into the mask of the face as it does in the other regions enumerated. But it does so automatically and as a result of its initial free-flowing in the regions farther back (as a free-flowing tide would wash all the shores of a landlocked bay) and not by reason of its being directed arbitrarily into a limited segment of the whole. The "great tone" sets into active vibration the bony plates of the whole skull and not merely the restricted bony area known in studios as the "mask of the face." The proper tone resounds and vibrates quite as much in the top and in the back of the head as it does in the face and nasal region. And it has, moreover, the supreme advantage of thereby releasing, into colored, electric motion, the "great tone."

In those last three sentences may be found the answer to a vexed problem which has spelled disaster for so many thousands of vocal aspirants. They have failed because they have tried to force their voices into the frontal bones of the face, over an intentionally lowered soft palate. The result has been a constricted sound, semi-strangled into a wiry, cutting resonance of disagreeable nasal quality, generally suggesting a whine, and often accompanied by a compression of the openings of the nostrils.

But how shall they succeed, who have failed? Most probably by relinquishing all attempts whatsoever to "place" the tone in the "mask of the face," "in the bridge of the nose," or "over and forward between the eyes." After that, the resonance of the whole head may be tried for—the Italians call it "singing in the bell" (meaning that the rightly produced tone causes the bones of the skull to ring like a bell). The first step must be a comprehensive freeing of the throat, the jaw, and the tongue; and this can be compassed only by right breathing. Now this right breathing can be almost instantaneously brought about by a correct standing position. Here it is, in brief: if the chest be expanded and held high; if the shoulders be held down and back; if the abdomen be slightly flattened; and if this position be not suffered to change whilst singing, the breathing will be right. With right breathing, the throat is naturally opened, offering a free progress of the voice into the full spaces of the head.

After that there are contributory devices for amplifying freedom and doing away with obstructions. Giovanni Sbriglia said, "The secret of singing consists in keeping the entire voice (high, low and middle) singing in the chest; only so are the head cavities unlocked." (This is one proved road to the goal.) William Shakespeare taught, "Tune the voice in the very exact center of the note. This 'tuning' starts the tone correctly in the head spaces." (Another proved road to the goal.) Lesser devices, useful in themselves, are a curling upper lip, dilated nostrils, and a gently smiling position of the mouth.

But after the laws of *bel canto* are read, and all the rules laid down in print, there remains the necessity of finding *the teacher whose ear knows the "great tone" when he hears it* and who, later, knows how to open one of the several roads leading to it. This is not by any means impossible. Such teachers exist in America, though they are but few; and they can be found by those determined enough to unearth them. And they may be recognized by the seeker of the truths laid down in this article. Let our students avoid, by every power in them, the teacher of the "national blight on the progress of our young singers," the "nasal" tone. But let them cling, with all their might, to the man who can open his ear and his understanding to that intense but effortless sound of soaring ravishment which fills every branching corridor of the resonating spaces of the head with what is so happily and rightly known as the "great tone."

NOTES

1. Homer Henley, "Garcia's Second Discovery," *The Etude* 49, no. 5 (May 1931): 360.
2. Homer Henley, "The Truth About 'Nasal' Tone," *The Etude* 54, no. 7 (July 1936): 448.

22. Filling the Gap with Guiseppe Aprili

Originally published in the *Journal of Singing* volume 65, no. 2, 2008

The serious student of historical voice pedagogy will be familiar with several important treatises on the art of singing that date back to the eighteenth century. The earliest commonly known source (not to slight Caccini's *Le nuove musiche*, 1602) probably would be Tosi's *Opinioni de' cantori antiche e moderni* published in 1723. A few years later came Mancini's *Pensieri e riflessioni pratiche sul canto figurato* which appeared in 1774. The next treatise that most of us would be able to identify in a chronological order would be the monumental *Traité complet sur l'art du chant*, by Manuel Garcia II. Part One appeared in 1841, followed by the second volume in 1847. Seventy years separated Mancini and Garcia. What was happening in voice pedagogy during the intervening seventy years?

Jeffrey Monahan in his book *The Art of Singing* (1978) offers a review of pedagogic thought gleaned from sources published between 1777 and 1927.[1] He includes a chronological listing of treatises published in this time period. Between 1777 and the publication of Garcia's first volume in 1841, he lists fewer than one hundred treatises published in all languages. Although I consider myself fairly well read in this area, only a handful of them were familiar to me at all. The reason might be that few have been made available to modern readers and even fewer in an English translation. Some of those treatises that may be familiar include: Johann Hiller's *Anweisung zum musikalischzierlichen Gesange* of 1780 (a modern translation was published in 2001 by Suzanne J. Beichen), Crivelli's *Art of Singing* (publication date is not known for certain, but available in English published by Oliver Ditson), Mengozzi's *Méthode de chant du Conservatoire du Musique* (1807; not available in English, I believe), Garaudé's *Nouvelle Méthode de chant et de vocalization* (1809, not available in English), and finally a method by the famous basso at the Paris Opera, Luigi Lablache's *A complete method of singing for the bass voice* (early 1800's; I own a copy of a somewhat later treatise by Lablache published by Root & Sons in America in 1860).

All this is to say that I was very excited to meet, via the internet, Simon Fleming of Great Britain who has in his possession an original copy of *The Italian Method of Singing*, a treatise first published in 1791 by Guideppe Aprili. Simon contributed the following brief introduction to Aprili.

Aprili and The Italian Method of Singing

Simon D. I. Fleming

Giuseppe Aprili (1732–1813), although a fairly minor name in music from the eighteenth century, was an important Italian soprano castrato and composer during his lifetime. At the time of its publication, and in the centuries that followed, he was best known for his work *The Italian Method of Singing*, which appeared in editions in both Paris and London.

Aprili was born in Naples in 1732, and received his early musical tuition from his father, Fortunato, before studying under Gregorio Sciroli (1722–c.1781) at the Conservatorio della Pietà. He made his operatic début in Sciroli's *Il barone deluso* in 1752, but also sang in the royal chapel in Naples, as well as in Turin and Rome. He also visited other important cities, including Venice, Madrid, and Stuttgart, where he, for the most part, remained from 1762–69, and appeared in several operas by Niccolò Jomelli (1714–74). He subsequently returned to Naples where he continued his collaboration with Jomelli, and in 1783 became the first castrato of the royal chapel. Burney, who met Aprili in 1770 during his "musical tour" to collect material for his seminal *A General History of Music* (1776), did not think highly of his abilities, recording that he "has a weak and uneven voice, but is constantly steady, as to intonation. He has a good person, a good shake, and much taste and expression." However, Mozart also heard him in Italy, and in contrast thought that "Aprili, first man, sings well and has a beautiful, even voice." Between 1774–80 his operatic appearances were primarily in Florence, Turin, and Rome, with his last known performance being at Naples in 1785, where he was pensioned in 1798.

Aprili was well known as a teacher. His students included the important Italian musician Domenico Cimarosa (1749–1801) and the Irish tenor, and friend of Mozart, Michael Kelly (1762–1826). Kelly, who met Aprili in Naples around 1779, referred to him as "the greatest singer and musician of the day," and also recorded that the Italians referred to him as "Il padre di tutti i cantanti," the father of all singers. After hearing Kelly sing, Aprili thought he showed significant potential, so much so that he, most unusually for him, offered to give him free lessons. During his time with Aprili, Kelly accompanied him to several important engagements, including Gaeta, where Aprili was conducting a music festival, as well as other private occasions in the homes of local aristocracy. Upon completion of his lessons, Aprili went so far as to arrange a post for Kelly at Florence; he also provided means of getting there and some additional financial assistance. Kelly, feeling grateful for the help he had received, gave Aprili the piano that he had brought from Ireland.

Aprili wrote numerous pieces, many of which were published during his lifetime, and most of these, understandably, are written for voice. His *Solfeggi* was without doubt his most well-known publication, having been published first in Italy in 1790, and the complete set of thirty-six was attached to his 1791 London edition of *The Italian Method of Singing*. Solfeggi are a type of textless vocal exercise, and Aprili's own include a bass part with figures to enable accompaniment with the keyboard. Along with the solfeggi, the 1791 publication included an introduction that is comprised of twenty-one rules "for Students and Dilettanti," as well as a series of "progressive examples." Despite being published in Aprili's name (or, as in this case, Aprili), these rules were taken from Giusto Tenducci's (c. 1735–90) *Instruction of Mr Tenducci to his Scholars*, which was published in London in 1782. Aprili's edition appears to have been highly successful, and appeared in at least three British editions.

Select Bibliography

Monson, D. "Aprili, Guiseppe." *Grove Music Online*, ed. L. Macy (accessed 24 May 2008), http://www.grovemusic.com.

Fiske, R. and D. Monson. "Tenducci, Giusto." *Grove Music Online*, ed. L. Macy (accessed 24 May 2008), http://www.grovemusic.com.

Kelly, M. *Reminiscences* (London: Oxford University Press, 1975).

Scholes, P., ed. *Dr. Burney's Musical Tours in Europe* (London: Oxford University Press, 1959).

Burney, C. *A General History of Music* (London, 1776–1789).

Simon was gracious enough to provide photographs of the first several pages of the book for publication here. The book is very fragile, and therefore taking electronic scans was not feasible due to potential harm to the document. All the images are fairly easy to read except the title page and parts of the front page which include the "rules for singing." I considered it important to present these in their original form, even if they are not the best images. Editor Sjoerdsma tells me that this may be the first time *Journal of Singing* has published facsimile representations of an ancient document.

Following is a transcription of the title page and the rules, followed by a facsimile of the exercises included in the book.

The Modern
Italian Method
of Singing
with a Variety of Progressive Examples and
THIRTY SIX SOLFEGGI

by SIGR. D. G. APRILI.

NECESSARY RULES
For Students and Dilettanti of
VOCAL MUSIC

I. The first and most necessary Rule on Singing, is to keep the voice steady.
II. To form the voice in as pleasing a Tone as is in the Power of the Scholar.
III. To be exactly in Tune, as without a perfect Intonation, it is needless to attempt singing.
IV. To vocalize correctly, that is, to give as open and clear a sound to the Vowel, as the Nature of the Language in which the Student sings, will admit.
V. To articulate perfectly each Syllable.
VI. To sing the Scale, or Gamut frequently, allowing to each sound one BREVE or two SEMIBREVES, which must be sung in the same Breath, and this must be done, in both. A MEZZA DI VOCE, that is by swelling the Voice, beginning Pianissimo and encreasing [*sic*] gradually to Forte, in the first part of the Time and so diminishing gradually to the end of each Note, which will be expressed in this way.

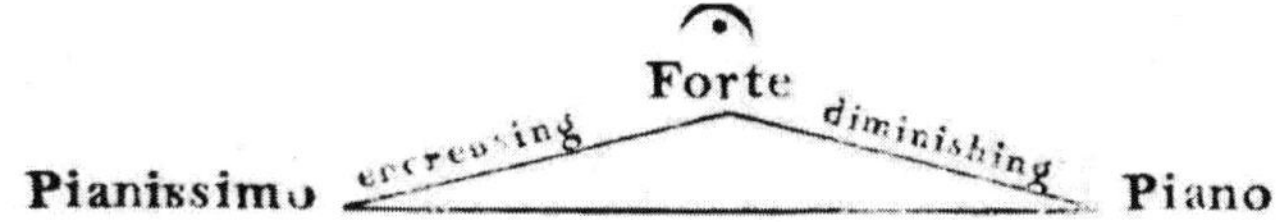

VII. To exercise the Voice in SOLFEGGIO every Day; with the Monosyllables Do, Re, Me, &c.
VIII. To copy a little Music every Day, in order to accustom the Eye to divide the Time into all its Proportions.
IX. Never to force the Voice, in order to extend its Compass in the Voce DI PETTO upwards, but rather to cultivate the Voce DI TESTA in what is called FALSETTO, in order to join it well, in imperceptibly to the VOCE DI PETTO, for fear of incurring the disagreeable Habit of singing in the Throat or through the Nose; unpardonable Faults in a Singer.
X. In the Exercise of Singing, never to discover any Pain or [dif]ficulty by distortion of the Mouth, or Grimace of any kind, which will be best avoided by examining the Countenance in a Looking glass during the most difficult Passages.
XI. It is recommended to Sing a little at a Time, and often, and, if standing so much the better for the Chest.
XII. That Scholars should appear at the Harpsichord and to their Friends with a calm and cheerful Countenance.
XIII. To rest or take breath between the Passages, and in proper Time, that is to say, to take it only when the Periods, or members of the Melody are ended: which Periods or Portions of the Air, generally terminate on the accented parts of a Bar. And this Rule is the more necessary, as by dwelling too long upon the last Note of a musical Period the Singer loses the Opportunity it affords of taking Breath, without breaking the Passages, or even being perceived by the Audience.

XIV. That without the most urgent necessity, of either a long Passage, or of an affecting Expression, Words must never be broken, or divided.

XV. That a good MEZZA DI VOCE or Swell of the Voice must always precede the AD LIBITUM Pause U and CADENZA.

XVI. That in pronouncing the Words care must be taken to accord with the sentiment that was intended by the Poet.

XVII. That the acute, and super-acute sounds must never be so forced as to render them similar to shrieks.

XVIII. That in Singing, the Tones of the Voice must be united, except in the case of Staccato Notes.

XIX. That in pronouncing the words, double Consonants in the Italian Language must be particularly enforced, and Care must be taken not to make those that are single seem double.

XX. To practice the Shake with the greatest Care and Attention, which must generally commence with the highest of the two Notes and finish with the lowest.

XXI. That the Ornaments and Embellishments of Songs should be derived from the Character of the Air, and Passion of the words.

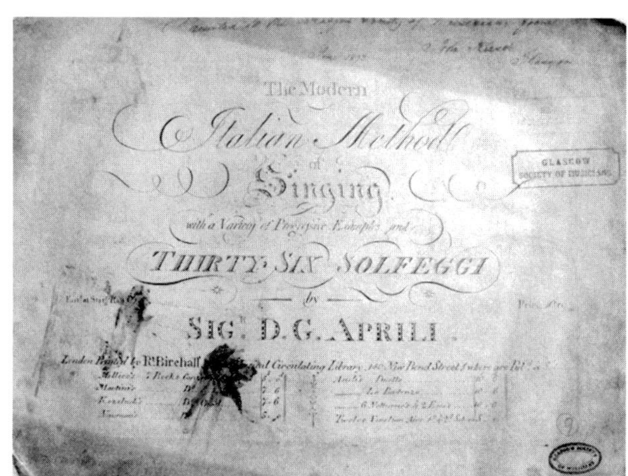

NECESSARY RULES
For Students and Dilettanti of
VOCAL MUSIC

I. The first and most necessary Rule in Singing, is to keep the voice steady.

II. To form the voice in as pleasing a Tone as is in the Power of the Scholar.

III. To be exactly in Tune, as without a perfect Intonation, it is needless to attempt singing.

IV. To vocalize correctly, that is, to give as open and clear a sound to the Vowel, as the Nature of the Language in which the Student sings, will admit.

V. To articulate perfectly each Syllable.

VI. To sing the Scale, or Gamut frequently, allowing to each sound one BREVE or two SEMIBREVES, which must be sung in the same Breath, and this must be done, in both A MEZZA DI VOCE, that is, by swelling the Voice, beginning Pianissimo, and encreasing gradually to Forte, in the first part of the Time and so diminishing gradually to the end of each Note, which will be expressed in this way.

Forte
Pianissimo encreasing diminishing Piano

VII. To exercise the Voice in SOLFEGGIO every Day, with the Monosyllables Do, Re, Mi, &c.

VIII. To copy a little Music every Day, in order to accustom the Eye to divide the Time into all its Proportions.

IX. Never to force the Voice, in order to extend its Compass in the VOCE DI PETTO upwards, but rather to cultivate the Voce DI TESTA [illegible] called FALSETTO, in order to join it well, and imperceptibly to the VOCE DI PETTO, for fear of incurring the disagreeable Habit [illegible] singing in the Throat or through the Nose; [illegible] unpardonable faults in a Singer.

X. In the Exercise of Singing, never to discover any Pain or [illegible] by distortion of the Mouth, or Grimace of any Kind, which will be best avoided by examining the Countenance in a Looking glass during the most difficult Passages.

XI. It is recomended to Sing a little at a Time, and often, and, if standing so much the better for the Chest.

XII. That Scholars should appear at the Harpsichord and to their Friends with a calm and chearful Countenance.

XIII. To rest or take breath between the Passages, and in proper Time, that is to say, to take it only when the Periods, or members of the Melody, are ended: which Periods or Portions of the Air, generally terminate on the accented parts of a Bar. And this Rule is the more necessary, as by dwelling too long upon the last Note of a musical Period the Singer loses the Opportunity it affords of taking Breath, without breaking the Passages, or even being perceived by the Audience.

XIV. That without the most urgent necessity, of either a long Passage, or of an affecting Expression, Words must never be broken, or divided.

XV. That a good MEZZA DI VOCE or Swell of the Voice must always precede the AD LIBITUM Pause 𝄐 and CADENZA.

XVI. That in pronouncing the Words care must be taken to accord with the sentiment that was intended by the Poet.

XVII. That the acute, and super-acute sounds must never be so forced as to render them similar to shrieks.

XVIII. That in Singing, the Tones of the Voice must be united, except in the case of Staccato Notes.

XIX. That in pronouncing the words, double Consonants in the Italian Language must be particularly enforced, and Care must be taken not to make those that are single seem double.

XX. To practice the Shake with the greatest Care and Attention which must generally commence with the highest of the two Notes and finish with the lowest.

XXI. That the Ornaments and Embellishments of Song [illegible] from the Character of the Air, and Passion of the [illegible]

SHORT AND EASY LESSONS FOR THE EXERCISE OF THE VOICE.

LESSON for ascending and descending by the interval of a 3d. with and without the intermediate note or guide

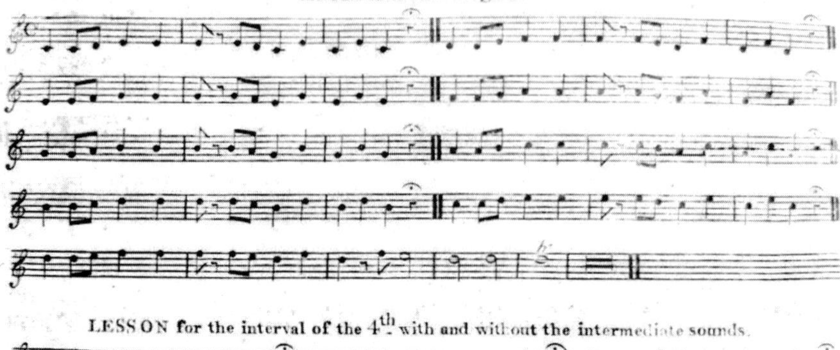

LESSON for the interval of the 4th. with and without the intermediate sounds.

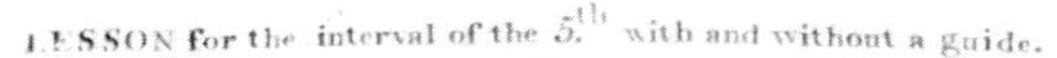

LESSON for the interval of the 5th. with and without a guide.

LESSON for the 6th.

LESSON for the 7th
LESSON for the Octave or 8th.
Exercise of all the intervals in the diatonic genus or Scale

Exercise in little divisions or flights in ascending and descending eight notes
Division or volata of 8 notes ascending and desending successively in the same breath
Exercise of the 9th in gradual ascent and of the 8th descending
Exercise of the 10th in the diatonic Scale ascending

The well-read pedagogue will recognize that these rules represent the mainstream of pedagogic advice gleaned from the common sources from this period. They are simple, direct and *very important*. I am convinced that if we concerned ourselves with some of the wisdom contained therein our students would benefit greatly. Just to highlight a few of those points, allow me to exegete them in this way:

III. "To be exactly in tune…" As a rule, we no longer train intonation as used to be done. Most progressive studies from our historical record include interval studies, not only to train one of the basic building blocks leading to knowledge of music theory, but also to train the acuity of the ear to perceive precise intonation. We use the piano too much to "support" the student when vocalizing, and therefore many tuning errors pass unnoticed. Tosi cautioned about always playing for the scholar while vocalizing. There is a difference here between tuning problems due to a lack of ear training and due to a technical issue; both can result in intervals and—especially—passages that are not accurate. Technical deficiencies must be corrected, but the ear has to be trained as well. I believed that our colleagues in jazz studies and other commercial music idioms do a much better job on this matter than the rest of the voice profession; at least their expectations tend to be much higher.

VI. "To sing the Scale, or Gamut frequently . . ." Most historical progressive methods began with long-held sustained tones. This fundamental exercise will strengthen the instrument and provide the opportunity to establish a solid technique. The simplicity of the task gives the student the opportunity to focus on breath management and support, posture, and purity of the vowel. It teaches the breath and the larynx to engage one another and provides the opportunity to train the steadiness in the voice, as mentioned in Rule I. Whether studied early or late in technical training, the *messa di voce* is an important musical element and a profound technical feat when correctly learned. This exercise serves as a basis for a high level of coordination between the intrinsic muscles of the larynx and the muscles of the respiratory system. It is a very complex gesture that represents the highest level of artistry and ability now, as then. For a more complete discussion of this important pedagogic tool, I refer the reader to my earlier column.[2]

IX. "Never to force the Voice, in order to extend its Compass in the Voce DI PETTO upwards . . ." In order for the full range of the voice to be established, most singers will have to learn to let go of the weight of the voice as they ascend the scale. It was common in the eighteenth and nineteenth centuries (and since) to make use of the various register adjustments that our voices are capable of in order to establish the ability to coordinate the activity of the intrinsic muscles so that the chest voice is not carried too high. Some teachers will utilize the falsetto, as Aprili suggests. This concept has fallen out of favor in a lot of teaching because the work takes time and a thorough understanding of how the registers work. This process was better understood in earlier times than is common today. I have written on this subject in this column before, and I refer the reader to those articles for a more complete discussion.[3]

XI. "It is recommended to Sing a little at a Time, and often . . ." I know that I am usually more concerned about my students spending enough time in the practice room, rather than too much! However, it has been the wisest of counsel for scores of years not to overdo it in sessions that are too long. We only now are beginning to understand the limits of voice use that a singer can experience before short and long-term effects are inflicted upon the voice. Overuse can lead to significant problems, which can lead to nodules, hemorrhage, and other forms of tissue fatigue. How much is too much? Garcia recommended multiple 15 to 20 minute sessions with rest in between.

This is an ideal which few of us could realize, but how common is it for us to hear the speaking voices of our students raspy and rough after rehearsals or intense practice sessions? Youth is often on their side in providing a quick recovery from these events, but make no mistake about it, if you can hear it in their speaking voices, they have inflicted some change in the lamina propria of the vocal folds themselves. The quality of the voice should not deteriorate due to the amount of time that they use their voices. Much more on this subject will appear in our journal and elsewhere as we understand more about the real health risks involved in being a musician.

XVIII. "That in Singing, the Tones of the Voice must be united, except in the case of Staccato Notes." The ability to sing a true legato line is a very important gesture and has been a hallmark of good singing for hundreds of years. However, I continue to meet singers with several years of training who have never been taught to do so. It has to be specifically trained in the same way that the *staccato* and other articulations must be trained. It does not come naturally to most of us, and many of us have experiences early in our musical training that tell us to do quite the opposite: to separate the tones from one another for the sake of clarity in an ensemble, for instance. Then as now, it was understood that the overall growth of the instrument and the artist depended upon the ability to connect tones and stay "on the breath" without little signs of interruption to the tone or the air.

The exercises that follow the Rules are progressive in nature and not unlike hundreds of other methods published since. They intend to offer the scholar opportunities to incorporate the ideas offered at the beginning of the book. They begin with long-held sustained tones and include the use of the *messa di voce* at the same time. Exercises for the trill follow with examples of how they would be used. The next few exercises focus on interval training, divisions (scale passages), common rhythmic alterations, and finally opportunity to practice common forms of passages found in theatrical, operatic, and dramatic music. As mentioned earlier, the attribution of the rules and even the exercises to Aprili has been questioned. However, Edward Foreman states that "they are the most concise statement of the principles of the period known to this author."[4]

Foreman also observes that there are many similarities between Aprili's rules and those offered by Garcia in his *Traité complet sur l'Art du Chant*. This is significant because it points out that Garcia's ideas were indeed a continuation of what had been taught for many generations and represents a connection back to the methods of the eighteenth century. Foreman quotes the famous Viennese musicologist Franz Habock, author of a very important book on the castrati, *Die Kastraten und ihre Gesangskunst*, who states that the young Manuel Garcia II was taken to Naples by his father and there received lessons from Aprili.[5] Of course, Garcia's scientific contributions to the understanding of the voice and how it worked would significantly change the nature of the vocal method forever. Garcia provided the enlightenment of the age to what had been a rather simple but effective tradition.

I think it is tempting to read through Aprili's list of rules and dismiss them as too simplistic, too much lacking in explanations of how things work to be useful to the modern singer. I think this is a mistake. Simple principles learned through generations of teaching and singing experience that were then taught and practiced to perfection provided singers of this age with the technical foundation to sing very difficult repertory very well.

NOTES

1. Brent Jeffrey Monahan, *The Art of Singing: A Compendium of Thoughts on Singing Published Between 1777 and 1927* (Metuchen, NJ: Scarecrow Press, Inc., 1978).
2. Stephen F. Austin, "*Suoni Filati*: The *Messa di Voce*," *Journal of Singing* 62, no. 5 (May/June 2006): 573.
3. Stephen F. Austin, "Register Unification—'Give Me a Break!'" *Journal of Singing* 61, no. 2 (November/December 2004): 199; Stephen F. Austin, "Treasure 'Chest': a Physiological and Pedagogical Review of the Low Mechanism," *Journal of Singing* 61, no. 3 (January/February 2005): 241.
4. Edward Foreman, "A Comparison of Selected Italian Vocal Tutors of the Period Circa 1550 to 1800" (PhD dissertation, University of Illinois, 1969), 69.
5. Ibid., 66.

23. Julius Stockhausen's Method of Singing

Originally published in the *Journal of Singing*, volume 65, no. 3, 2009

The great nineteenth century baritone Julius Stockhausen (1826–1906) is no stranger to readers of this column. He has been quoted often as an important resource in an effort to present historical traditions of voice teaching. As a singer he is best remembered as a champion for the presentation of lieder in the concert halls of Austria. During the first thirty years of the nineteenth century it was rare to hear even a single song presented as part of a concert. Even the great songs of Schubert were considered to be appropriate only for the parlor. Julius Stockhausen took it upon himself to introduce the great songs of the early nineteenth century to the public. In 1856 he announced that he would sing the entire *Die schöne Müllerin* in its first complete performance in the concert hall in Vienna. He was also the first singer to present complete performances of *Winterreise* and *Dichterliebe*. His dedication to presenting the lied on the concert stage helped change a long-standing bias against the practice.

Stockhausen studied with Garcia in Paris in the 1840s and followed him to London. He later became highly regarded as a choral conductor and as a teacher of singing in his own right. In 1884 he published his *Gesangsmethode* in German, and at the same time *A Method of Singing*, its translation by Sophie Löwe, appeared. It is a valuable guide to the teaching of elite singing. In 1888 *A Method of Singing* appeared in serial form—one chapter per issue—in Edgar S. Werner's magazine, *The Voice*, published in the United States from 1879 until 1902.

A Method of Singing is not easily located in the United States. I found a copy on interlibrary loan a few years ago. Since it likely is unknown to most of us, a few of the most important chapters will be presented here—in serial form—like it first appeared to singers and teachers in the United States over one hundred years ago.

A Method of Singing

by Julius Stockhausen

III.

The vowel attack is produced by the lips of the glottis being closed, and then a moderate explosion or expulsion of air taking place through the vocal chink. It must be distinct and decided, but free from harshness. The degree of firmness depends on the expression intended.† By the study of the elements of speech we not only lay the basis for a distinct pronunciation and good quality of tone, but we also learn to distinguish the "mediate" consonant attack and the immediate vowel attack. In the same way that the out-rushing air meeting an obstruction in the cavity of the mouth produces a consonant, so the breath escaping through the narrowed aperture in the vocal chink produces a vowel sound. Compare, for instance, *pa* and *a*, *ba* and *a*, *ma* and *a*, while imitating with the vowel attack the relaxation of the tensions on the lips. It will then be found that, in order to sing with expression, the vowel attack has to be quite as varied as the consonant attack. The latter being visible serves to explain the former, which is invisible.

For the production of speech-sound three agents are always required: (1) An escaping current of air, whose varying force and duration are regulated by the muscles governing the breath; (2) An obstruction of

---

† Garcia's "Shock of the glottis" (*spiritus lenis*) can only be described as a kind of attack. The celebrated maestro himself writes: "The energy of the attack should be proportional to the degree of force that you wish to communicate to the tone." Experience teaches that the shock of the glottis, unaccompanied by a lowering of the larynx, is never favorable to the attack. It makes the notes poor and thin, and in the middle register often throaty and nonresonant.

this current which produces sound, and varies according to its place, degree, duration and energy. The energy of the obstruction depends on that of the expiration, and does not therefore require further consideration; (3) A resonance-cavity which gives the sound produced by the cooperation of 1 and 2 its special quality.

The position of the mouth depends in general on the required expression of the face; the stereotyped smile of the old Italians is, therefore, to be considered a thing of the past. The mobility of the jaw is of much greater importance than this antiquated rule, as the proper position of the tongue and correct vocalization often depend on it. The following is worthy of notice: We can, contrary to the natural method, produce [o], [u], [ø] and [y] with the corners of the mouth drawn back; [i] and [e] with the lips pushed forward; from this we conclude that the epiglottis plays an important part in the formation of vowels.[1] Otherwise it would be impossible to produce these vowels equally distinctly with a cheerful or sad expression of the face. In order to produce a free and well-developed tone of a telling quality, as well as to acquire a correct and distinct pronunciation, one should at first practice with a moderate expenditure of breath; that is, with *mezza voce*; and by degrees more voice may be used. In the first exercises the syllables of the solfeggio will be of more use than vowels alone; as, when the organs of voice and speech act together, the voice of the beginner issues with greater ease and purity.

One should therefore, sol-fa first and only vocalize when the emission of voice has become quite unimpeded by the use of the syllables. The vowel attacks will, after a short time, have neither throaty nor nasal quality. One degree of power will be found in every voice in which the tone can be emitted pure and free; this will be ascertained by holding back the breath—that is, moderating the amplitude of the vibrations—and, if necessary, by having recourse to the extremest *pianissimo*. The throaty quality can, it is true, be combated by practicing on the nasal consonants [m] [n] [ŋ]; and the nasal quality can be cured by raising the soft-palate on the open vowels [ɛ] and [ɔ], but *piano* sol-faing is the best exercise for acquiring an unimpeded tone.

The first exercises must be easily within the compass of the voice. Our modern scale is too extended and too difficult for the first steps in the art of singing. Few beginners have eight notes of equal power in their voice. The hexachord of the middle ages, *ut re mi fa sol la,* "the home of the voice," as Fr. Chrysander calls it, is quite extensive enough for developing voice and technique, and has the advantage that it does not include the tritone (the augmented fourth), which is too complicated for the beginner.

The best accompaniment for the voice in the progress of training is a second, or a second and third voice, not an instrument like a piano, the notes of which are tuned in intervals that are only approximately correct. In practicing with the piano neither pupil nor teacher can hear the singing quite distinctly. The louder the accompaniment is, the more difficult it is to judge of the purity of intonation. The first exercises should be sung without any accompaniment. Learn first to distinguish the three tetrachords which the hexachord contains: tone, tone, semitone; tone, semitone, tone; semitone tone, tone. A tuning-fork, a violin, or a note struck on the piano are sufficient to indicate the first sound, or to test the purity of intonation. The pupil should then make himself acquainted with the difference between tones and semitones.

The speaking level, that is, that natural position of the larynx, is not good for artistic singing; it produces, especially in the middle register, thin and poor notes. The high or low position of the tongue, the lip-modifications, the shortening or elongation of the cavity of articulation, and the great resulting variety of vibrations, giving corresponding shades of vowel tone, require a lower and quieter position of the larynx in singing than in speaking. It should, therefore, be put in the right position before beginning to sing. The singer must not confound the position of the larynx, and the firm tension of the vocal cords, with the veiling or cover of the tone by means of the epiglottis.

For the repose of the larynx, diaphragm and rib-breathing is indispensable. Clavicular breathing (which raises the collar-bone) draws the larynx rapidly down and lets it rise with equal suddenness when the voice is emitted. The restless state in which the larynx is thus kept is fatal to the development of the voice and to technique in general. Diaphragm-breathing is sufficient for the quick or half breath (*mezzo-respiro*), but for the full breath (*respire pleno*) rib-breathing is indispensable. Breathing through the nose is very favorable to the repose of the larynx, and it furthers, at the same time, the activity of the diaphragm. The respiration must be noiseless except, perhaps, occasionally to express great emotion.

A succession of vocal sounds produced by the same mechanism is called register. The human voice has three kinds of registers, called chest-voice, falsetto or middle-voice, and head-voice. I quite agree with Battaille, who proves that for the chest-voice the whole width of the vocal cords is required, for the falsetto only two-thirds. It is much to be regretted that in physiological works, as a rule, only chest and head-voice are spoken of. The register between these two (for this reason perhaps, called sometimes the middle register) is surely the most important for the development of the voice; but until now it has not been sufficiently examined by physiologists. I do not venture to express an opinion about the origin of the head-voice, which both Battaille and Garcia regard as a continuation of the falsetto, as even the physiologists and laryngoscopists cannot agree as to its mechanism; but experience shows daily that it is different from that of the falsetto. Whether it is due to the vibration of the thin edges of the true vocal cords only, or whether the false cords help in any way, or whether, finally, as some thing, it is produced by nodes of vibration, in a way similar to the flageolet tones of the violin, I do not know. But I know, from long experience, that this register is quite indispensable for all female voices, and that the lowest notes of the head-register a^1 g^1 f^1 e^1, like those of the falsetto e^1 d^1 c^1 b sound very weak, but that an octave higher both can acquire great power by contracting the vocal chink and using more breath.[3] Our mouth-whistle also has similar notes—for instance f^4 g^4 a^4 B^4 flat. It seems therefore that they depend on the density of the breath, as in the formation of the before-mentioned lip-sounds [p] [b] [m].

Male voices use two registers only, the chest and falsetto. Quite exceptionally tenors may use head-voice. Male choruses whose first tenors sing with head-voice are badly trained. The effect often resembles a child's or woman's voice, if a tenor has not learned to sing the high notes in falsetto.

Generally, female voices use three registers, the only exception being very high sopranos, which sometimes use only falsetto and head-voice, and not the chest-register. The principal register of female voices is the falsetto, of male voices the chest-register. The notes common to all are b c^1 d^1 e^1.
The same notes are common to two registers in every voice. They may be B flat, C D E flat, B C D E, or C D E F; it depends on the nature of the four voices. The extent of the registers is not the same in every voice.

The registers naturally overlap each other. The two chief registers of every voice have many notes in common, which can easily be equalized with a fixed position of the larynx. The blending of the chest and falsetto registers can be achieved in ascending by using the somber quality, in descending by using a clear quality of tone. In this instance, the working of the epiglottis is unmistakable. For the deep vowels, [o] [ø] [u] [y], it seems to cover the larynx like a damper. It acts almost like the hand of a player of the French horn when he produces closed notes.

The perfect evenness of the registers on a single tone produces the *messa di voce*. This consists in the art of sustaining a note in one breath with a varying degree of power, and without altering the pitch. The note is first produced *piano*, then *mezzo-forte* and *forte*, and then decreases gradually to *pianissimo*. As a rule, the *messa di voce* can only be executed with the help of two registers, especially in the middle of the voice. Beyond f^2 the head-register suffices for high soprano, below b for bass voices, the chest-register. We learn to equalize the registers by means of the *messa di voce* in the same way in which we learned to form sounding soft and hard consonants on the lips, for instance, [m] [p] [b]. Just as the lips contract more tightly for [b] than for [m] for [p] than for [b], and by increasing in thickness get more power to resist the rush of air, so do the vocal cords increase their resistance when the column of air increases, by passing gradually from a membranous to a thicker tension. This is the only means by which a sustained note, especially in the middle of the voice, can be sung with a varying degree of power without losing its purity or tiring the voice.[3]

NOTES

1. Stockhausen did not have the benefit of the International Phonetic Alphabet. I have taken his original vowel designations and transcribed them into IPA using a table that he included in Chapter 1 of his method.
2. The notation used by Stockhausen was that developed by Helmholtz in his book *Die Lehre von den Tonempfindungen als physiologische Grundlage für die Theorie der Musik* which was first published in 1863 and translated into English in 1875. Middle C (C_4 in modern scientific notation) was notated by c^1 the next octave was c^2 (C_5), etc. Below C_4 was the "small octave" and notated by a small letter with no number; C_3 would be simply c. The lower octave (C_2) would have been called the "great octave" and represented by a capital C.
3. Julius Stockhausen, "A Method of Singing, Part III," *The Voice* 10, no. 3 (March 1888): 44–45.

24. Stockhausen's Method of Singing (Continued—part II)

Originally published in the *Journal of Singing*, volume 65, no. 4, 2009

The following article is the second of a series of excerpts from Julies Stockhausen's *A Method of Singing*. Stockhausen issued what seems to be a condensed version of his book (published in 1884) serially in Edgar S. Werner's *The Voice*, a journal published in the United States between 1879 and 1902. This was the fourth article in the series and was published in April, 1888.[1]

A Method of Singing

by Julius Stockhausen

IV.

Attack and Emission of the Voice—
Sustaining the Voice and Messa di Voce

The old Italian and German masters, whose schools produced such excellent singers of both sexes, show by their writings that their first endeavor was to teach their pupils how to form a beautiful tone and to render their voices flexible and of a telling quality. There was no question of exercises in a large compass, nor of developing a powerful tone on one vowel, as is now the fashion. In the elementary instruction—that is to say, in the solfeggio[‡]— our ancestors began by teaching how to establish and sustain the voice. They next proceeded to exercises in a small compass, such as are provided by ornaments (appoggiaturas, turns, mordents, etc.), and then let their pupils practice on the five elementary vowels and without accompaniment. We have to proceed in the same way if we wish our pupils to acquire not only a powerful, but also a beautiful and expressive tone, a flexible voice, and good pronunciation.

The laws for the management of the voice always remain the same; it is only necessary to know them and to observe them conscientiously. In Agricola's translation of Tosi, one of the most important works on the art of singing, after the "remarks for the use of singing-masters," the appoggiatura follows as second heading, and the trill as third.

In Herbst's "Musica moderna prattica," 1653, we find by way of first exercises the appoggiatura. Formerly the attack was always accomplished with an appoggiatura, now we use it only as a means of expression, or as an ornament. The Italians call this kind of attack *cercar la nota*—to feel for the note. This must be combated from the commencement, by a careful and precise pronunciation of the consonants, and a decided attack of the vowels.

Giulio Caccini, singer and composer, one of the first to introduce solo singing in the early part of the seventeenth century, subjects the "feeling for the note" to a severe criticism. He writes in the "Nuove Musiche" (1601): "Some attack the note by first sounding the lower third, others attack it firmly and allow it to swell gradually. This style is recognized as the best. As regards the first, one cannot lay it down as a universal rule, for it seldom suits the harmony; even where it might be used it has become commonplace through the fault of the singers, who, instead of merely indicating it, generally remain on the lower third. Far from being graceful, it, on the contrary, hurts the ear." Caccini then quotes a third kind of attack. He calls this *esclamazione*. It consists in striking the note vigorously, and then allowing it to decrease rapidly. The *esclamazione* is, as it were, the second half of the *messa di voce* (swelling and diminishing the voice upon a sus-

[‡] Solfeggio means exercises in which the notes are called by their several names—Ut (Do), Re, Mi, Fa, Sol, La, Si (English Sol-faing).

tained note). It is easier for the pupil to execute than the entire *messa di voce,* for he is able, after having just taken breath, to attack the note powerfully, and then to allow the breath to subside naturally, causing the power to diminish of itself; for the whole *messa di voce* he must, on the contrary, laboriously hold back his breath. Therefore, I divide this exercise, and let my pupils practice at first only half of it, the *esclamazione.* The combined *crescere e scemare della voce* will always remain the basis of voice-culture, and at the same time the highest attainment in the modulation of the voice. The teachers of the old Italian and German school were never tired of insisting that their pupils should acquire absolute correctness of intonation and elasticity of tone, both in *piano* and *forte* passages. That this art could only be acquired by two different kinds of mechanism of the vocal muscles, especially on the transition notes, every teacher felt, and therefore tried to teach by example.

Nothing was then known of the laryngoscope, and but little of the anatomy of the larynx. But Caccini and his contemporaries knew that open vowels have more sound than closed ones and therefore favored the stronger register. They were also well acquainted with the action of the primary vowels. Caccini says, that "*i* [ee] is a favorable vowel for tenors, and *u* [oo] for sopranos." That was sufficient. The deepest vowel gave high voices more roundness, and the highest gave the tenor voices brilliancy in their upper notes. Contraltos and basses were little required for solo singing.

By singing on a sequence of the primary vowels to *a* [ah], the vowel *par excellence,* a natural *messa di voce* was produced on the transition notes, as was seen in the introduction. This fact the singing-masters used as the basis of their theories for voice-culture. The object was to equalize this natural swelled note, and to execute on one vowel a pure and telling *piano, crescendo, forte* and *diminuendo*; to invent a safe gymnastic exercise for the vocal cords in which great care was at the same time to be bestowed on the beauty of tone. Many will therefore be surprised that Garcia, in his "Nouveau traité sommaire," does not describe the sustained notes before page 60, instead of commencing his treatise with them. It is still more surprising that he does not make his theory of the lowered position of the larynx the basis of voice-culture and technique in general, and the *condition sine qua non* for rhythmical *coloratura.*

Was the great maestro afraid that by a moderately low position of the larynx voices would not acquire the flexibility necessary for the execution of Rossini's fine works? It almost seems to me that, when I reflect that in France everybody is trained for some specialty, and that the different branches of an art are quite separate from one another, and especially when I examine his own and his father's variations for airs of the old and modern Italian School, Garcia's explanation is to be considered the basis of voice-culture, and I will quote his own words:

"Great difficulty is evinced in drawing the tones in two registers at once, which occurs for females and tenors. The pupil must commence the note *piano* in falsetto, and in the somber quality. As has been seen, this process fixes the larynx and contracts the pharynx. Afterward, without varying the position, and consequently the quality, he must pass to the register of the chest, by fixing the larynx more and more, in order to prevent it making the abrupt motion which produces the hiccough at the moment of the separation of the two registers. Once entered upon the register of the chest, he must raise the larynx and dilate the pharynx in order to clear the quality, so that toward the middle of the duration of the note it has acquired its whole brilliancy and power. In order to extinguish the sound, the pupil must practice the reverse; that is to say, before passing to the register of the falsetto, when the voice is diminished, he must deaden the sound from the chest, still fixing the larynx below and contracting the pharynx, in order to support it and avoid the jerk on the change of the register. He must then proceed slowly from the register of the chest to the falsetto, after which the pharynx should be rendered supple and the sound ended. I deduce this rule from the physiological fact that the larynx, being lowered by the somber quality, can produce the two registers without displacing itself. Besides, the displacing brings on the hiccough, which so disagreeably separates one from the other."

A fixed and moderately low position of the larynx is necessary for single notes as well as for scales and runs, and even beauty of tone and clearness of execution are equally dependent on it.

Besides the *messa di voce* and *esclamazione*, a simpler kind of tone production must be pointed out as indispensable. It is the well-known *tenuta di voce*, sustained notes of equal and medium power. This is the chief condition of musical phrases for a perfect delivery. The old rule, that each note even of moderate duration had to be enlivened by a *messa di voce*, does not apply to our animated modern music. On the contrary, by sustaining the voice quietly and evenly, the effect of accentuations, *esclamazione*, and other dynamic signatures is heightened. Compare, for instance, Beethoven's "Adelaïde" with a *messa di voce* on each note of the *larghetto* and without it.

The pupil must first attack the note according to the nature of the consonant, which may be hard or soft or sonant, etc., or according to the character of the vowel, but as Herbst expresses it, "on the right note," and I may add with precision and fixed larynx. This is the only means by which to equalize the effect of the vowels on the vocal cords and that of the cavity of articulation on the phonator. The notes are to be called by their several names first, and to be practiced on long and short vowels as well.

The exercises in most methods of singing are written in C major and in the compass of an octave. This is, however, too tiring for young voices and presents certain musical difficulties. The first exercises can hardly be too simple for beginners, whose sole talent sometimes consists in the power of imitation. It is well known that in the middle ages the semitone was always called *mi-fa* in the solfeggio. This of course, occurs only once in the scale of six notes which is a great advantage for master and pupil, as the difference between major and minor seconds proves often such a difficulty to beginners that one might here quote the words used for false relation: "Mi contra fa est diabolus in musica." The hexachord is also the contrapuntal theme *par excellence*, and, therefore, valuable for exercises for two or more voices.

NOTE

1. Julius Stockhausen, "A Method of Singing, Part IV," *The Voice* 10, no. 4 (April 1888):87-89.

25. Stockhausen's Method of Singing (continued—part III)

Originally published in the *Journal of Singing*, volume 65, no. 5, 2009

The following article is the third in a series of excerpts from Julius Stockhausen's *A Method of Singing*. Stockhausen issued what seems to be a condensed version of his book (published in 1884) serially in Edgar S. Werner's *The Voice*, a journal published in the United States between 1879 and 1902. This was the fifth article in the series and was published in May, 1888.[1]

A Method of Singing

by Julius Stockhausen
V.

The old practice of calling the notes by their names (sol-fa), a great help in singing intervals, ought to be re-introduced into our schools. The vowel, which is only a sound, acquires a meaning when combined with a consonant. In the same way, sol-faing explains the interval to a beginner. When the singer practices on his mysterious hidden instrument, the syllables *do re mi fa sol la si* form, as it were, little levers which help to bring out the sound, like the keys of the piano and organ, or the valves in wind-instruments. The obstruction which the air experiences in the articulating-cavity seems to increase the tension and to favor the contraction of the glottis, which is required for the formation of sound. The variety in the formation of the elements of speech, by momentarily relieving the vocal cords of the constant expulsion of air, forms short moments of rest for the voice. The emission of consonants acts on the vocal cords almost like blinking does on the eye. If, however, the pupil endeavors to sing passages on one vowel, and in proper time, he will be sure to execute them indistinctly. With the syllables they will appear correctly; separated and yet united, they will resemble a string of beads. Every passage must therefore be sol-faed first, and only vocalized when the muscles of the larynx, guided by the ear, can execute the necessary tensions correctly.

It is needless to add that sol-faing also forms the basis of a good pronunciation, and of sustained singing in general, if the teacher takes care that each vowel is distinctly articulated, and that the consonants *d, r, m, f, l* are correctly employed, according to their length and character. The habit of pronouncing well in sol-faing transfers itself, later on, to the words of the text. Technically, it is much the same thing whether the melody is practiced with the names of the notes or with the words, but the former is easier and therefore slow vocalises sol-faed are better for beginners than songs, which distract their attention from the actual tone-production. It also seems much more logical, in default of good exercises, to sol-fa beautiful songs and airs, instead of adapting words to inferior vocalises as has been done of late.

It is a notable fact that the Italians, who pronounce and accentuate their language most distinctly, and articulate single and double consonants rapidly and clearly, make the best singers. Those who have heard Lablache, the greatest singer of modern times, will agree with me that the combination of word and tone in such perfection can only be achieved by those, who, from their youth upward, have learned to pronounce vowels and consonants distinctly and beautifully by means of the solfeggio.

If the voice be accompanied by another melodious part, the pupil will acquire more independence than by the ordinary harmonized piano accompaniment. This is a fact of great importance to operatic singers. When an *a* occurs, prevent the larynx from rising, which would produce a meager note, and carefully observe the action of the articulating-cavity. The pupil should from the commencement make himself acquainted with the diphthongs *ei (ài), eu (eü), au (aaù)*. In changing from one vowel to another great care must be taken to prevent any alteration in the tension of the vocal cords, which would otherwise produce a change of registers. In a diphthong the first vowel, on which vocalization always takes place, should be long, the second quite short. The organs of pronunciation should also be independent of the vocal organs. The alterations in the position of the mouth required for the production of the different vowels should interfere as little as possible with the tensions in the larynx. The vocal chink should be firmly closed. The vowels *oe, ue, o–u* should be practiced also with the corners of the mouth drawn back. The upper teeth will touch the lower lip instead of the lips being pushed forward as usual.

The Carrying of the Voice (Portamento).

There is an intimate connection between the portamento and the art of sustaining and increasing the tone, the *messa di voce*. It is only by the portamento that the singer gets his breathing and voice-apparatus under full control. To carry the voice from one note to another, means to let it glide in ascending through all the narrowings of the glottis, and in descending through all its expansions, so as to touch all the differences of pitch produced by these tensions before reaching the final note. This kind of execution can best be acquired by the help of the *messa di voce*, which can unite two different registers on one note, provided the position of the larynx remains fixed. The portamento may become one of the most expressive kinds of vocalization. But the singer must be careful not to look upon every slur in our modern music as representing a portamento. This must be used very sparingly, since it is as dangerous to a beautiful and natural delivery as the "feeling for the note," the *cercar la nota* of the Italians mentioned already. The portamento can be executed either with equal power or crescendo and diminuendo. In describing this kind of vocalization I quote Tosi:

"An equally necessary practice is the pleasant exercise of carrying the voice, without which all other diligence is useless. Those who want to perfect themselves in this must listen more to the dictates of the heart than to the laws of art."

Then follows a perfect laudation of the human heart. It deserves to be quoted here, as Tosi's work[§] has become a rarity. The teacher must translate the word "heart" by "imagination," whose wings often make the heart beat more loudly, and he will surely be able to appreciate Tosi's panegyric. In Agricola's German translation the passage reads:

"What a great master the heart is! Say yourselves, dearest singers, and say it out of due gratitude, that you would not have become the greatest in your art if you were not its pupils. Say that in a few lessons it has taught you the most beautiful expression, the best taste, the noblest action, and the most ingenious art. Say, even if it may sound incredible, that it mends the shortcomings of nature in softening rough voices, in improving inferior ones, and in rendering good ones perfect. Say that when the heart itself sings (*sic*) you cannot possibly dissemble, and that the truth never possesses greater persuasiveness than at that time. Make it known, finally (for I cannot teach it), that from the heart alone you have learned a certain indescribable charm which runs softly through all the veins and finally reaches the seat of the soul. Although the way to touch the heart (let us say to excite the imagination) is long and troublesome, and only known to a few, the difficulties which oppose us are, nevertheless, not insurmountable for him who does not tire of studying. The greatest singer in the world must go on studying quite as much to preserve his reputation as he did to gain it. In order to reach this laudable end, there is, as everyone knows, no other means but study. But his is not enough in itself, one must know from whom to learn."

The answer seems to me simple enough, learn to sing from him who can teach you a beautiful tone, and has the finest delivery. It does, indeed, require mental life, feeling and imagination to learn to judge when this most expressive kind of vocalization, portamento, is to be used, and how to execute it; for composers

[§] A copy of this book may be had for $6. Address, Edgar S. Werner, 48 University Place, New York.

do not always mark it, where it is capable of increasing the effect.

Many passages can only acquire their full meaning by the portamento. The teacher can explain how they are to be rendered, and he can also show, by his example, how to execute them; but those who do not possess the feeling, the "heart" for such passages, will only imitate mechanically and without expression. One of the principal rules is that the vowel must remain the same during the whole duration of the portamento. Another important rule is that the portamento must not degenerate into an anticipation. The narrowings and extensions must be gradual and slow. The pitch of the second note must only be heard at the beginning of the third beat. Practice at first without crescendo or decrescendo, but always with fixed larynx.

The study of the mute vowel, the final (German) *e* must be begun early. This mute vowel is of great importance to English singers, for each of the five vowels sometimes has this sound, e.g., *a* as in *cellar, e* in *err, ea* in *earn, i* in *fir, o* in *oven, u* in *up.* Most beginners form this vowel incorrectly. Some sing "Rosèn," others "Rosön," or "Rosòn," or even "Rosan," and emphasize the unaccented final syllable in a disagreeable manner. They are seldom able to produce the colorless final *e* in its real shape. Sievers, in his "Phonetik," calls the position of the tongue in the formation of the medium *a* the passive position. This expression is even more applicable for the position of the tongue in the formation of the vowel *e*. If the singer succeeds in mastering this passive position he will avoid the pressure of the root of the tongue on the epiglottis, which, as is well known, produces the disagreeable guttural tone, especially in the vowel *a*. The antidote is to practice much on the primary vowels *i* and *u* (*ee* and *oo*, English), and also on the mute *e*.

In large intervals the question of registers has to be considered. There is all the more reason not to pass it over, as the portamento itself tends essentially to blend the registers.

I. The register of the chest is the characteristic of the whole compass of male voices, the falsetto (or medium) that of female voices. High sopranos and tenors (contraltinos) are exceptions.

II. In all the different voices it is always easy to unite two of the three registers; chest-voice and falsetto in male, falsetto and head-voice in female voices—the reason for this is that they have many notes in common. This fact, proved by experience, is not only important for the blending of two registers on one note, but also for the use of registers in diatonic and chromatic scales. But there are also notes for which both registers can be used, and which all the different kinds of voice have in common—for instance, $b\ c^1\ c^{\#1}\ d^1\ d^{\#1}\ e^1$. Bass, tenor, contralto and soprano voices meet on these notes. They are accessible to the bass and soprano voices in the chest and the falsetto register, in piano and forte, although they represent the lower limit for the soprano and the highest for the bass voices. In contraltos and tenors they occur in the middle of their compass, and are, consequently, almost the same in quality. It is well known that high tenor voices sound like low contraltos, and vice versa. Composers, therefore, in their choral works often strengthen the contraltos with tenors, or soften the tenors with contraltos. Why should it, therefore, not be easy to blend the registers when soprano and tenor voices, for instance, have at least twelve semitones each for two registers in common? We, therefore, teach that the registers cross each other in a much larger degree in one voice than they do in the different kinds of voices compared to each other, but it is only with a fixed position of the larynx, and with the right use of the two chief qualities of sound, that a beautiful, well-molded whole can be produced.

III. The blending of registers is achieved by the two chief qualities of sound, the clear and the somber—in ascending by gradually lowering, and in descending by raising the epiglottis. The simplest way, therefore, for uniting the registers is to use the corresponding qualities of vowels; closed ones in ascending with chest-voice, open ones in descending in falsetto, until the vocal apparatus, guided by the ear can give the necessary covering to the short vowels also. The blending of the registers depends as much on the ear as on the dexterity of the epiglottis. The principal rule for portamento, which is never to stop on the intermediate notes, facilitates, especially in larger intervals, the uniting of registers. Female voices may therefore, in passing, touch higher notes in chest-voice and lower ones in falsetto. The tendency of the larynx to rise to the position it takes in speaking must be carefully avoided.

NOTE

1. Julius Stockhausen, "A Method of Singing, Part V," *The Voice* 10, no. 5 (May 1888): 72-73.

26. Stockhausen's Method of Singing (concluded—part IV)

Originally published in the *Journal of Singing*, volume 66, no.1, 2009

The following is the fourth and final excerpt from Julius Stockhausen's A Method of Singing that will be offered here. Stockhausen issued what seems to be a condensed version of his book (published in 1884) serially in Edgar S. Werner's The Voice, a journal published in the United States between 1879 and 1902. This was the sixth article in the series and was published in June, 1888.

A Method of Singing

by Julius Stockhausen

IV. Legato Singing—Aspirated Vocalization—Ornaments ("Grace" Notes or Passages)

The most important and most beautiful style of vocalization is the legato. It forms the basis of vocal technique, embracing, as it does, all diatonic, chromatic and broken runs, arpeggios and ornaments, and must be studied both with and without words.

Triplets, groups of four notes, and all kind of runs are much more difficult to execute evenly when broken by syllables than when sung on one vowel alone. They require special study, and peculiar dexterity of the articulating muscles. In words like *volpa soprafina*, the hard consonant *p* on the unaccented part of the bar can hardly be formed quickly enough. It generally destroys the distinctness of the four successive notes. In this kind of vocalization the object should be to produce on one vowel the sudden contractions and expansions of the vocal chink from note to note in ascending and descending sequences with increasing or decreasing power, sometimes in strict time, sometimes *ad libitum*, but always firmly and clearly. In order to achieve this, the pupil must first of all learn to control his breath, and especially to hold it back, in order not to impede by too great a gush of air the action of the ring-shield muscle, which, in this instance, plays a most important part. The lungs must work without jerking and without the aid of the diaphragm, and must at first give forth only a small quantity of air.

The greatest activity is therefore required from the larynx. It is advisable at the beginning to make use of a decrescendo, especially in the ascending scale. The pupil will, by this means, succeed in avoiding a "synergy," or simultaneous action of two different groups of muscles of the larynx, which might prove fatal to the voice and to a perfect delivery. Finally, the vowel must keep its characteristic form through the whole duration of a passage. The legato style, therefore, requires, in runs which are to be performed on a single vowel only, a quiet action of the lungs, great activity of the muscles of the vocal cords, and a uniform position of the articulating-cavity.

If a sustained melody is to be sung with words, the chief condition is that each note and each syllable shall receive its full value. The effect of legato delivery is totally destroyed by detaching the notes, by unduly prolonging a consonant, or doubling it when single. As regards the pitch, the working of the larynx is exactly the same as in vocalizing and solfeggio.

The well-known fact that for beginners the production of a note is easier with the help of the *spiritus asper (h)* than without, has induced many masters to prescribe this aspiration (that is, a slight escape of air between each note) even for legato passages, and to teach a style of vocalization resembling solfeggio. Instead of practicing on a vowel the pupils have to sing *ha, ha, ha, hé, hé, hé, hi, hi, hi*. This is not only ugly, but quite wrong, for it destroys all legato. It is quite a different thing to employ the *spiritus asper* for aspirated vocalization. In this case, two notes of the same pitch have to be distinctly repeated, and this can be only achieved by an almost inaudible aspiration. Of course, the intonation must not be endangered by the insertion of the aspirate in repeating the note; many allow it to fall too much.

To most of our modern singers this kind of vocalization is unknown. They try, as a rule, to get over the difficulty by a syncopation, or by marking, or by emphasizing the second note. Even modern musicians seem to ignore it, which I gather from the fact that in a new edition of old music, marks for taking breath are put between repeated notes. When, for instance, in an *Adoramus* of Palestrina, in the word *tibi* G and F are twice repeated on the same syllable, this expressive kind of vocalization must not be interrupted by taking breath. If the singer feels short of breath, he can take a new one before the first F. In methods of singing of the 17th century, we find repeated notes designated as a *trillo*.

This kind of vocalization, viewed as a technical study, forms the transition from the solfeggio to vocalization, to a more instrumental style of singing, if I may so express myself. It is a fact that by this aspirated vocalization great flexibility of the larynx and distinctness of technique can be most surely and quickly acquired. I therefore describe it at the same time as the legato, and recommend it to teachers, especially for heavy bass voices, and those whose technical studies have remained unfinished.

In modern methods of singing we find the expressions *vocalisatione aspirate* (aspirated vocalization), or *note raddoppiate* (doubled notes). It is thus that Hauptner calls it, and he adds in parenthesis *martellato*. This however, is incorrect. The *martellato* is produced by a movement of the diaphragm for each note, without discontinuing the sound; the aspirated vocalization, on the contrary, by the expulsion of a small particle of air, the vocal chink being momentarily opened to an infinitesimal extent, so as to allow the non-sounding air to pass; in a word, by a short *h*, the well-known *spiritus asper*, which forms the required attack for a new note, and necessitates a short interruption. Hauptner describes the execution of this by the expressive phrase "inaudible aspiration," but prescribes the *spiritus lenis,* that is, a brief shock of the glottis. The "inaudible aspiration," however, suffices for correct execution without discontinuing the notes in the way he indicates by rests. This discontinuance, indeed, would not be possible without the shock of the glottis, which is incompatible with inaudible aspiration. The execution of aspirated notes resembles a note on the piano struck several times with a different finger, or several notes of the same pitch produced by a violinist with one stroke of the bow. This is called in French *ondulation de l'archet*.

Legato and Portamento.

Beginners will find great difficulty in executing portamento, runs and passages of various kinds, to get the tones and semitones accurately without using the *spiritus asper*—that is, the consonant *h*—for the attack. I therefore subdivide the hexachord into three tetrachords (or succession of four notes) in order to secure purity of intonation. In the C major exercises the semitone will always be *mi-fa*, but it will occur sometimes in the beginning, sometimes in the middle and sometimes at the end of the tetrachord. The pupil must endeavor to get the correct tensions in the larynx without the help of the aspirated vocalization, and to produce a distinct legato. The position of the larynx must not be altered after the vowel *u* when followed by *a*. The jumping up of the larynx at once produces a thin, meager note.

Tosi writes: "Short notes which follow a dot (especially semi-quavers and demi-semiquavers, or quavers in all breve time) should be rapidly executed, not accented, and their duration curtailed." This holds good whether there be one or several notes, and the tempo be slow or fast. The note which precedes the dot should be accented and its duration increased. If a short note comes first and the second is dotted, the duration of the first note should be curtailed, and that of the dotted note increased proportionately. In such cases, however, the first short note should be slurred to the dotted note, the former accented and the latter taken softly at first, held to its full value, and, if time permits, gradually increased in force.

Ornaments

It is unnecessary to give here a minute description of ornaments in general; it will be enough to show how a correct and animated execution may be acquired by following the rules given by Tosi. These rules are recognized to this day, and are still applied to the compositions of the old style which adorn our operatic and concert programs.

"The object of appoggiaturas is either to make the melody more flowing, to fill up what may appear to be gaps in the movement, to make the harmony more rich and complex, or, lastly, to invest the melody with greater animation and brilliancy. All appoggiaturas belong to the time of the note which follows them, not of that which precedes. The syllable which belongs to the principal note must be pronounced on the appoggiatura."

There are two kinds of appoggiaturas, the "short" and the "long." Some are quite short, and remain the same regardless of tempo, or of the value of the note they precede. They take as little as possible of the time which belongs to the principal note, but are usually found to be short notes. Before triplets the appoggiatura is always short. It is sometimes called the *acciaccatura*.

Some appoggiaturas are longer than those just mentioned, but they are not always of the same duration, as they depend on the value of the note they precede. Long experience and a refined taste are necessary for the graceful rendering of such ornaments. As a rule, the long appoggiatura takes half of the principal note. It the principal note is dotted, the appoggiatura takes the value of the whole tone, and this is only sounded in the place of the dot. All appoggiaturas must be joined to the principal note by a graceful portamento. Every appoggiatura, whether long or short, must be more accented than the principal note. Before two consecutive descending leaps of thirds the appoggiaturas are short; if a third follows, it is long. Naturally, the variable appoggiatura (sometimes long and sometimes short) can only precede notes which, according to their own value, or the movement of the piece, are rather long, and allow the use of a discord. Therefore, the variable appoggiatura only precedes notes which occur on the accented part of the bar; occasionally, also, in slow movements, each beat may have one. The appoggiatura which occurs before unaccented or passing notes, and before all short notes, is always short or invariable.

All after-turns must be very short, and, as in the case of the short appoggiatura, must take as little as possible from the value of the note to which they are attached. The turn should be closely joined to the preceding note. The turn from below is often attached to trills. With descending chains of trills the turn is seldom used, the notes of the trill itself forming the after-turn. The double appoggiatura is only an appoggiatura from below, with an after-turn.

The slide or slurred note moves only by consecutive notes; the double appoggiatura, on the contrary, can only consist of notes separated by an interval. It takes some of the value of the principal note, and forms part of an ascending scale. The slur of three notes is almost identical with the unprepared double turn, only the lower auxiliary note is not accented. "The execution of this slow slur of three notes is always soft, gentle, dragging and languid," says Tosi.

The double turn consists of a short appoggiatura, the principal note and an after-turn joined together. In its execution the same rules apply as in that of the appoggiatura and after-turn, i.e., the former gets the chief accent, the principal note then follows smoothly after it, and the turn after the principal note. The first and second notes must always follow each other rapidly, the last two, which form the after-turn, can be executed with a variable degree of rapidity. Three different kinds of double turns thus result: commencing with the principal note; commencing with the lower note, which then becomes an appoggiatura; commencing with the middle or principal note.

27. Frederic W Root's "Systemizing Voice Culture"

Originally published in the *Journal of Singing*, volume 66, no. 2, 2009

I am grateful to David Grogan for providing me with the following article that appeared in The Musical Visitor, a magazine of music literature and music published in the United States from 1883 to 1897. David is a DMA candidate at the University of North Texas and is completing his thesis on the life and teaching of American educator Frederic W. Root.

Regular readers of this column might remember an earlier article by Root called "The Voice Teacher's Problems."[1] *Root was a well-known voice teacher in this country as well as a very prolific author and regular guest lecturer. The following is a lecture that he presented at a meeting of the Canadian Society of Professional Musicians, December 31, 1890. My purpose of presenting these comments is as an introduction to the principles of pedagogy as he expressed in his popular method books, including School of Singing (1873), Root's New Course in Voice Culture and Singing (1891), and the monumental Technic and Art of Singing (1901) that was published in eight volumes. It makes sense to follow the address offered below with his solution to what he perceived to be a common problem: the absence of a consistent method that is universally trusted and taught. While some of his remarks might be considered a bit inflammatory, I believe that it is a good thing to consider how far we have come in the last one hundred years.*

I wonder if teachers generally ever stop to consider how poorly our science compares with others in the matter of Pedagogics; how imperfectly its professors have as yet approached the standard of the professors of other branches of instruction, as regards analysis, scientific statement, careful gradation and systematic instruction. Do we ever reflect that, while a parent wishing to have his child taught science, literature or languages, can find on all sides schools in which he justly has perfect confidence, if he wishes to have him taught voice culture, and is highly ambitious as to the result, he searches long and anxiously for some teacher or institution, where he may experience a comfortable certainty as to the result?—a certainty not so much that the finest educational work will be done, as that the voice shall not be ruined and the mind filled with affectation and nonsense.

Our public schools afford an example of what scientific pedagogy may be. Notice the accuracy of statements made in their textbooks; observe the copiousness of illustration of every point, and the well-considered gradations of all difficulties; observe how foundations are laid first, and how, as the subject is developed, one step prepares for another in logical sequence. Notice the methods by which the pupils are examined at intervals to ascertain if every step has been correctly taken; and lastly, appreciate the fact that graduation from one of our higher educational institutions, which carry the public school course to conclusions, means real mastery of certain subjects of study. As further proof that education in such lines of study is broadly established upon a sound pedagogic basis, and is scientifically administered through civilized countries, we perceive that graduates of reputable institutions everywhere compare similarly; that they are similarly equipped, and are not in serious conflict as to definitions and results. We shall find each to revere his Alma mater, and all to respect each other's attainment. Indeed, the same thing is true of music-study in all its departments except Voice Culture.

It is possible that some would claim that such was the case with Voice Culture as well; that its principles are established, and generally understood. You might say that a singer's education is well and thoroughly provided for in such important and sufficient considerations as placing or locating the tone in the head rather than in the throat; changing registers at proper places so that there shall be no forcing of the voice; breathing abdominally, and hence deeply and effectively; purifying vowel sounds, articulating forcibly and elegantly, executing clearly and rapidly, etc. supposing I concede your claim that vocal education is completely provided for to this extent that all departments of such education are generally recognized among the profession; but have you justified a belief that there is, therefore, a pedagogic system for vocal education? For instance, let me ask how you cause a pupil to place the tone in the head? Has the tongue any part in the process, or the palate? Does the position of the larynx in the throat affect the process, and if so, how? What vowel sound is best to begin with? What compass is most available for the first step? How do you describe the succeeding steps? How long does it take to go from one to another? May tones be equally well placed, yet sound very differently? What are the sensations of placing, as how do they differ under different circumstance? What is the relation of breathing and placing? What that of registers? What that of covered tones? Is placing the first thing to teach a pupil, and if not, where does it come in a system of voice culture? Are there any dangers attendant upon continuous effort to place the voice?

What should be done with the pupil who, during the effort to place the voice in the head, has contracted the habit of sharping, and has acquired the fault of breathiness? Shall such an one go right on with the effort to place the voice higher in the head, or is there any principle which supplements and corrects this, which should be explained and practiced at this point?

Now a pedagogic system should take many such points into account. Let me make myself plainly understood as admitting that there are many individual teachers who do this as well as can be done, considering that it has never been the custom of our professors to write out their systems and so perfect them; but in spite of this admission, can we truly say that teachers in general have carefully considered these details and have established systems embodying them? That there was no individual or college to which one could go, confidently expecting that they would be well and thoroughly taught, impressed Rubinstein in his survey of the field twenty years ago. He says in his recently published autobiography, that even the best teachers of singing will ruin some voices.

The topics, departments and subjects may be commonly understood, but has there been effective analysis in which are carefully considered grades and combinations, resulting in a method which begins at the beginning and proceeds with logical, educational steps to the end of the subject?

Let us look at teachers as they appear to use today, for surely the teachers must be the repositories of pedagogy in any science.

We find prominent professors advocating all sorts of diverging theories, sometimes giving them the coloring of science, sometimes founding them upon imagination and inspiration, sometimes pinning their faith entirely upon sensation and sound, some claiming a more or less scientific, mysterious discovery by which they produce marvelous results. We find one class of instructors making a particular point of physiology, advertising courses of lectures on this subject, and claiming as credentials for the work of voice training, in some cases, to have been the pupils of noted physiologists; while other teachers, equally eminent and successful, condemn physiology as a waste of time. Others pursue special parts of vocalization, as if they were the entire foundation of the subject; "Register," for instance, of "freedom in emitting the tone." Now, emitting the tone is the mechanical part of singing. I recollect instances of pupils taught on this specialty, where this freedom of delivery of tone had completely extinguished the human element in the voices, and they sounded like some newly invented instrument. Breathing is often represented to be the all of voice culture; and a certain maestro is often quoted as saying: "To breathe well is to sing well." Some guide pupils entirely by sound and sensation, contradicting physical facts by asserting that the throat has nothing to do with the singing, and that the tones are produced anywhere from the pit of the stomach to the crown of the head, excepting in the throat.

Others seem to make special use of modern discoveries in acoustics, and we hear much of the overtones of the voice, the different vowel shades in which the voice is resonated, and about an imaginary focus of tone upon the palate, against the teeth, or even against the opposite wall of the room; theories which are often absurdly unscientific and generally wrong from the pedagogic standpoint, because of dealing with effects rather than with causes. Other prominent professors, either from disinclination, lack of knowledge, or from reaction from the absurdities practiced in the name of science, deal with subjects of vocal culture wholly in an inspirational or imaginative fashion. One takes pride in presenting to the mind all sorts of peculiar images by which to guide tone formation; others depend largely on general excitement, and often try excessive force to drive the voice into a correct method. "You won't get hold of my method," says one of these; "It's all in me,"—a sort of claim that is listened to with awe by students of singing, but which would be laughed at by students of anything else.

Opposite to this we have teachers who advertise to impart the principles of voice culture by a simple and natural method. If vocal culture were on a pedagogic basis, it would seem very simple and natural in theory, doubtless; but the professors who make this claim nowadays, when called upon, are generally found to beg the question, and proving that their simple and natural method is simply to steer clear of all difficulties, and leave faults to correct themselves. Besides these classes there is the rather numerous class of professors who adopt the "laissez aller" principle; they give their pupils no instruction worthy of the name, but merely shout and pound the piano during the lesson, allowing the pupil to come tumbling after. One such pupil told me that he had sung through the operas of "Trovatore," "Martha," and "Faust," before he discovered that he was not learning anything. A young lady once brought me three operas when she came to take her first lesson, doubtless expecting me to take a similar course with her.

The clouded state of comprehension with which the subject is regarded both by the professors and the public is further exhibited in the startling claims in which some teachers make, as for instance, that they have studied with all the great masters of the world, and now in teaching they adopt the best features of the method of each, rejecting the poorer ones; which modest claim, when translated into plain English is: "I am a better teacher than all the masters of Europe put together." Nearly all these classes march under the same banner; and "Italian method" is the legend which most frequently adorns their professional card. However much they invent, experiment, lecture on physiology, or make use of the modern scientific discoveries, or however widely they differ among themselves, and denounce each other as humbugs, they all continue to assure the public that they teach the pure "Italian method," or, as the very *ne plus ultra* of hypothetical excellence, the "Pure Old Italian method."

Perhaps we can best illustrate the standing of voice culture among pedagogic systems by imagining arithmetic to be no better understood than is voice culture today. We will suppose that there is no established school of mathematics, but that there is much discussion of the comparative worth of German, Italian, French and other schools where the science is taught; we will suppose that each has enthusiastic disciples and each equally confident detractors, who talk with hysterical eagerness of the wonders which are done here in the teaching of mathematics, the ruin which is wrought there among students of the same; that in one place the whole subject from addition to the conic sections can be taught in one term of lessons, by a mysterious method known only to some one individual; and that in certain other schools pupils are deceived and misled as to the result of two plus two, in order to keep them longer in the state of pupilage, with the consequent financial gain to the teacher. We will suppose that pupils are constantly urged to leave one teacher or school of mathematics and go to another, on the ground that one is radically wrong, and another supernaturally right. Then we must further suppose that long ago there lived people who, according to tradition, were marvelous mathematicians and astronomers and engineers; that among these was one Euclid, who was supposed to have been the chosen instrument of something little short of a divine revelation to man upon the subject of mathematics. We must be very particular, also, to suppose that neither Euclid nor any other of the prophets of the "Golden Age" of mathematics left any records; they were supposed to have taught mathematics by an incredibly scientific system, but that they never made an intelligible explanation of that system; notwithstanding which, teachers, to recommend their own capabilities, generally endeavor to put themselves before the public as especially endowed apostles of these mysterious prophets of a former age. This places mathematics in the position of voice culture today. Now let us see how such a system of mathematics would apply in a community to which it was administered, and we shall probably throw some light upon the pedagogic standing of voice culture as it has been so largely administered in the past, and so far as I am able to judge, is still administered, though with unmistakable signs of better things in the near future.

A young man, knowing nothing of arithmetic and having no special bent in that direction, comes into possession of large property. His friends tell him he will have to learn mathematics in order to manage his estate; so he begins to consider the subject of a teacher and school where he may learn the science. He finds many advertising to teach the science, most of them with glittering promises of brilliant and speedy results. But he observes that they do not agree among themselves as to the method by which mathematics is to be taught, and each one of them privately assures him that all the other are humbugs. In the light of present knowledge upon the subject we see plainly what this young man should do. But to make our parallel correct we must imagine that our young man in search of mathematics has no more certain refuge than has one in search of Voice Culture today.

The first teacher he chooses is one who relies principally upon imagination in the method of instruction, and he draws glowing pictures of a landed estate with fanciful sketches of converting the same into stocks, bonds and mortgages interspersing this with rhapsodies upon the subject of interest and coupons. But he scorns primary details. We will suppose our young man to handle his estate according to such instructions until he loses enough to bring him to his senses, whereupon he concludes to change teachers, and goes to another whose advertisement states that he teaches mathematics by a plain, natural method. This he finds to consist in letting him do about as he likes in a matter of study, the lessons being to contemplate great mathematical problems without analyzing them, the teacher keeping up a running commentary upon the beauties of mathematics in general, and the pupil's remarkable talents in particular. The results of this treatment being no better than in the former case, he makes another change.

He has heard of Euclid as a great scientific mathematician of former times, and the supposed founder of a school of instruction, so perfect that all the efforts of modern times have resulted in nothing but degeneracy. So the next teacher he employs is one who advertises to teach the pure, old Euclidian method. The teacher now regales the pupil with discourses upon the glory of that former epoch, and intimates to him that all other teachers except himself have wandered far from the magical perfections of this method, into sloughs and jungles of modern thought. In spite of all this the pupil strongly suspects that the instructions he receives, given with so much pomp and circumstance, are, after all, nothing but the teacher's own notions, unaided by any revelations whatever. At all events he fails to see anything remarkable in the pure, old Euclidian instruction he is receiving and in the meantime his estate evidently needs the application of a little homely common sense, and a few fundamental facts of arithmetic to save it to its owner.

He is, therefore attracted by still another advertisement, that of a teacher who claims remarkable scientific simplicity for his method. This method proves to be founded on one undoubted fact of mathematics, addition for example, and as this suffices in some small transaction to do with the management of his estate the pupil thinks with relief that he has at last gotten at the truth of the subject, until some day, in a complicated transaction, he realizes that other principles than addition are necessary to his purpose.

One other teacher whom he tries relies entirely upon imitation for his purpose. And the pupil finds that while at lessons he can copy the teacher's figures, and so do prodigies in mathematical calculation, when he is left to himself he does not know how to proceed.

We need not carry the parallel farther, except to say that if natural mathematicians were as common as natural musicians and singers, each one of these teachers would be able to point to successful mathematicians, claiming them as their pupils and pointing to them in triumphant vindication of their method of instruction.

Cases of those who know music intuitively and of those who can sing with correct method without instruction are to be found on all sides. Moreover, singing is not a rudimentary necessity to human life. For whatever reasons, the department of education known as Voice Culture has never engaged the best scientific thought of man, but, with honorable exceptions here and there, it has always been the prey of ignorance and charlatantry.

Except in a comparatively few instances, its systems are unsatisfactory, its methods conflict. We rarely find its professors to rank with those of other departments of education, and have no textbooks nor schools universally admitted to be standard.

Need this be so? Can not the fundamentals of voice culture be made as plain as those to arithmetic? Why is it possible to state the truths of long division any more correctly than those of breath support? And can not a teacher of voice culture arrange the course of study as systematically as a teacher of anything else? Perhaps some are doing this—writing out details and perfecting grades.

I, for one, endeavor to practice what I preach, although I might never have done this had not chance thrown it in my way to teach the subject to pupils in large classes.

Aiming to teach each pupil in a class what I would teach the same individual in private and secure the best results, I soon found that it would not do to treat my subject superficially or imaginatively, or conventionally, or to rely upon imitation, or to omit details here and there as one may do with private pupils, or to begin anywhere but at the beginning of my subject. I could find no text-book which marked out a course of study. There were many so-called methods to be had, such as they were. Some of these gave anatomical pictures and definitions which were neither interesting nor profitable to the average student. Many gave the limits of soprano, contralto, and other compasses of voice, limits referring not the natural state of the voice where pupils begin, but the final development of the voice, and therefore calculated to confuse rather than aid the beginner. Most of them defined the registers of a voice, some in one way and some in another, none showing the different stages the registers pass through in different manifestations and development, but regarding them as though they were stops on an organ, fixed and rigid. All of these methods were full of runs and scale passages, which from the outset included the extremest compass of voice and were likely to develop more faults of vocalization than graces. Where directions were given they were generally mere platitudes and invariably regarded the finished tone, never the crude, introductory stage through which all pupils, except great geniuses, must pass.

So I determined to strike out for myself, and began by stating the principles of voice culture as I then understood them, suggesting analytical exercises for practice which I thought would answer my purpose. I am afraid nowadays to look those statements in the face; they must have been very questionable, to say the least. At all events, the experience from year to year showed huge gaps in the method, by which pupils went astray. But profiting by these experiences, and with continuous study of the subject, the statements were improved year by year and the exercises remodeled to greater efficacy. In Chicago, my classes at first were composed of teachers in the public schools; and the fact of having pupils who could appreciate a well-arranged system gave a renewed impetus to my effort to make one. I began, therefore, printing a list of exercises, together with memorandums of the principles which they embodied; and for the last eight years have changed this every year to conform with the experiences obtained through the instruction of about three hundred pupils a year, until at last a plan crystalized which seems to me to cover the ground successfully. It may be of interest to some for me to specify a few things which give my point of view.

(Mr. Root then spoke without notes, giving the association a synopsis of his system of voice culture, as embodied in his new work, "Root's New Course in Voice Culture and Singing.")

NOTE

1. Stephen Austin, "Buried Treasure," *Journal of Singing* 63, no. 3 (January/February 2007): 335-340.

28. Carlo Bassini's *The Art of Singing,* Part 1

Originally published in the *Journal of Singing,* volume 66, no. 5, 2010

This article appeared as the introduction to a facsimile reproduction of Bassini's book published by Plural Press in 2007.[1] *While much of the information herein has appeared in previous columns, it is hoped that presenting it in context of Bassini's method will be of interest to the reader.*

If we were able to travel back in time and peruse the bookshelf of a singer or voice teacher in the United States during the last half of the nineteenth century, it is likely that you would find a copy of Carlo Bassini's *The Art of Singing,* first published in 1857. This book was perhaps the most popular text on the art of singing published in America during this period.

Little is known today about Bassini. Born in Cuneo, Piedmont Italy in 1812 of parents who were both musicians, he received intensive training on the violin as a youngster. He began his adult life as a professional violinist. One source suggested that he first came to South Americas as a part of an opera orchestra from Genoese. From there he went to New York to seek fame and fortune as a solo artist. This effort failed, and soon thereafter he was building a reputation as a voice teacher. A somewhat different story was related in a letter to the editor of *The Boston Home Journal* (later reprinted in *Dwight's Journal of Music* in 1878). Ship captain James Madison Hill reminisced about his long-time friend, Carlo Bassini, who had died in Irvington, New Jersey in 1870. He said that he met Bassini in southern France while there on a merchant venture. He reported that he gave Bassini and his whole family free passage from the Gulf of Lyon to New York on his ship in order to flee the terror of Napoleon III. According to Captain Hill, Bassini and his wife Pauline along with five children boarded his ship with nine other passengers for the long journey. At least part of this romantic tale does not stand up under scrutiny. Census records of the United States in 1870 show that the Bassini household included Carlo, his wife and three children, who were all born in the United States!

Even though there is some confusion about how Bassini arrived in the United States, there is no doubt about the reputation he enjoyed as a voice teacher and the success of his method books. He was a prolific author. He published six method books,[2] and was a frequent contributor to the music journals of his day, such as *The New York Music World* where he offered two extended series of articles on voice teaching. Richard Storrs Willis, editor of this particular journal, served as editor for *The Art of Singing,* Bassini's first book.

BASSINI'S PEDAGOGIC ROOTS

There is little doubt about Bassini's pedagogic heritage. His method reflected that of Manuel Garcia II (1805– 1906), the preeminent teacher in the West during the nineteenth century. Garcia had a clear influence over Bassini's pedagogic thought and practice. His ideas concerning the centrality of vocal registers to the process of voice building, the proper onset—including the controversial *coupe de la glotte,* the timbres—*voix claire* and the *voix sombrée* (a result of the lower laryngeal posture)—all come from Garcia, whom Bassini mentioned repeatedly in his books. His approach was methodic and progressive. This was the tradition of the *bel canto* method that can be traced through the experience of Garcia from his famous tenor father, Manuel Garcia *pére.* The elder Garcia was a student of Ansani, who was a student of Porpora.

Bassini's method is not just a historically interesting document; it is the method of *bel canto*, containing the wisdom of the eighteenth and nineteenth centuries. Principles illuminated in the book were those used to train the great singers who were the first to sing the operas of Donizetti, Bellini, Rossini, and early Verdi. Voice training of the period included specific study of the different types of articulation: *portamento, legato, martellato,* and *staccato*. The timbres of the voice— "closed" and "open"—were specifically studied, and development and coordination of the registers of the voice were central to the method. Bassini promoted register "breaking"—going back and forth between the chest and head voice in an intentional break or yodel— in order to strengthen the registers and ultimately to eliminate the break between them. As was traditional at the time, Bassini offered specific directions pertaining to the appropriate performance of the *appoggiatura*, the *acciacatura*, and the like.

There are a few inaccuracies in Bassini's writings concerning certain vocal and respiratory functions.[3] The value of Bassini's book lies in its pedagogic value as well as its heritage. Even though it is obviously based on the monumental work of Garcia, it is not known whether Bassini ever studied directly with Garcia—possibly in Paris before Garcia went to London and before Bassini came to the United States. Garcia's monumental text *The Complete Treatise on the Art of Singing* would certainly have been available to Bassini.[4] It very well may be that Bassini was teaching fundamental principles that he learned from Garcia's book—a concept that is often rejected by teachers today: that one can learn anything about teaching voice from reading a book!

Central to most methods of the nineteenth century was the concept that vocal exercises were the means for training the ear and developing the necessary coordination between breath, voice, and articulatory structures. Specific exercises were also used to acquire or restore proper muscular strength in the intrinsic muscles of the larynx and their ability to coordination appropriately. Through careful evaluation of the tone of the voice, the teacher would determine the deficiencies of the instrument and proceed with appropriate remediation. Targeted exercises strengthened the registers and, as a consequence, the voice would take on size and ring, brightness and flexibility.

Bassini's method can best be appreciated by putting some of the major concepts found therein in context of pedagogic thought of the nineteenth century. It is not that *The Art of Singing* is difficult to read; quite the contrary. But any historical document is best understood when it evaluated in light of the culture from which it arose.

VOCAL REGISTERS—A LARYNGEAL EVENT

The registers of the voice have been the subject of intense scientific investigation over the last several decades, yet agreement in the voice community as to how many registers there are or what to call them remains elusive. Science has taken most of the mystery out of the subject, and our understanding of the physiology of the vocal registers is at this point well defined. It is interesting that even though the physiology of the registers has been defined by voice scientists only in the last fifty years, we see practical application of that knowledge practiced in previous centuries, long before teachers really understood why. Careful observation in the studio over many decades revealed these truths to those who taught. It really should be no surprise that this is the case, since optimum voice use would naturally be narrowly defined and guided by the potential and limitations of the human voice. Art follows nature.

Anatomic structures concerned with voice production had been clearly described for many years by the time Bassini wrote his book; however, a statement concerning the nature of the registers of the voice awaited Manuel Garcia's first edition of *The Complete Treatise on the Art of Singing* in 1841.

> By the word register we understand a series of consecutive and homogeneous tones going from low to high, produced by the development of the same mechanical principle, and whose nature differs essentially from another series of tones equally consecutive and homogeneous produced by another mechanical principle. All the tones belonging to the same register are consequently of the same nature, whatever may be the modification of timbre or of force to which one subjects them.[5]

This observation came ten years before he was to visualize the larynx with the laryngeal mirror. The definition seems almost too simplistic to be true in today's tangled web of terms and ideas about the registers, but Garcia's idea reflected the thinking of the time. The teachers of the eighteenth and nineteenth centuries had a much simpler approach to registers than might be found today. There were usually only two or three that had been defined. There was the chest voice—everyone agreed on that. Giambattista Mancini (1714–1800) described a second register that he called falsetto *or* head voice in his well-known book of 1774, *Pensieri, e riflessioni pratiche sopra il canto figurato*.[6] Mancini said that there were only two fundamental registers of the voice. The chest voice or *voce di petto* was the full, bright, ringing quality of the lower range in most singers. Mancini stated that if the voice were big and powerful, it is so because the chest voice was strong and well developed. If a voice were weak and light in quality, it was because the chest register was undeveloped. He went on to say that if a "feeble" voice was to sing only in the chest voice for a while, then it would grow and become more robust! Some voices were by nature big and bright, but if it were not so endowed, it could be acquired by "study and art."

The falsetto was not considered to be a viable option for performance, but useful nonetheless because of its positive influence upon the upper part of the chest voice. Our modern understanding of falsetto is usually the sound produced by most countertenors. It is doubtful that was what these early masters had in mind. A few years ago a scientific investigation by Rubin and Hirt identified two distinct qualities of tone in the human larynx, both called falsetto; the "open" and "closed chink" falsetto.[7] In the closed chink falsetto the vocal folds made contact at the midline during each phonatory cycle, producing a brief moment when airflow was completely (or nearly) cut off. This adjustment produces the imitative soprano sound in the male singer. The open chink falsetto was characterized by a constantly open glottis with the vocal folds oscillating, but not touching. This of course produces a very breathy quality—Garcia likened the sound of falsetto to "the low tones of a flute."

The practical use of falsetto was to introduce ease and to modify the overpowering strength of the chest voice when it occurred. It is useful to remediate excessive tension in the larynx.

Bassini said "in theory, all are falsetto tones, which are not produced from the chest," affirming the traditional view of his day, that there were only two registers for the male voice.[8] He went on to say:

> But men have nothing to do with the head register. It is feminine and, in them, effeminate. Mario has occasionally struck a high note with the head tone; but this great tenor only thereby lost musical caste and respect, with all persons of culture and good taste.[9]

This idea has been confirmed by the work of Minoru Hirano and William Vennard (1907–1971) in a series of studies using electromyography that identified the vocalis muscle as the primary "register agent."[10] They showed that the chest voice was always characterized by high levels of contraction in the vocalis muscle. When the vocalis muscle was passive the register was falsetto.

One recalls the story of the tenor Duprez who returned to France to sing at the Paris Opera after a successful career in Italy. While there he acquired a new way to sing the high voice. He returned to Paris in the role of Arnoldo in Rossini's *Guillaume Tell* and amazed the audience with a full-bodied tone all the way up to the tenor high C—reportedly the first time that it had ever been heard in Paris. They called it the "do di petto," the C_5 in the chest register. Because of the reaction that it received it is reasonable to conclude that there was another type of sound that was being used in Paris before Duprez. The great tenor Nourrit who was the reigning *primo uomo* before Duprez apparently approached his high voice in a lighter mechanism that we might call today *voix mixte* or perhaps an intensified *falsetto*—what Bassini would have called "head voice." Of course, it is difficult to know for sure.

Bassini suggested that men, women, and children all have the chest voice. He also described the medium register in men and women, although particularly to women's voices. He suggested that the medium register goes to about C_5 (the octave above middle C, or C_4) in both men and women and that the head voice goes up to D_6 or higher in the female voice, but not in the male.

Although the nomenclature and the theory may be a little different than the way the registers are discussed today, the pedagogic process is clear:

> In training the voice, the teacher should commence with the chest register: and this from the fact, that where the chest and medium registers play into each other (in the manner shown) the voice is weak and uncertain, and it is an extremely difficult matter to strengthen and equalize it. But this equalization is just the important task to be accomplished. The method to be pursued is this:—the tones which are common to both the chest and medium registers must be practiced alternately with each. For, just as the skilful workman, who would join two pieces of wood and make the strength at the points of adjustment equal to the rest, will dove-tail the two, by extending the end of one sufficiently far in upon the end of the other to prevent any weakness at the extremities; so the skilful teacher will extend the limit of one register into the middle of the next, until the weak tones of both are blended and become equally sound and strong—the point of contact being smoothed and obliterated altogether.[11]

The idea that the medium register is an entity in itself and therefore can be strengthened by exercising the tones associated with the medium register is not supported historically. However, it is common to find teachers who strive to fix the problem of the weak middle voice by drilling the middle voice. The singer often resorts to altering the vowel—usually toward a darkened or covered vowel quality. They may also use pressed phonation that impedes the free access into the high voice.

REGISTER SHIFTING

Register shifting was a common unification device found in many sources in the nineteenth century, beginning with Garcia. It was the practice of beginning a tone in one register and, without stopping the air flow, allowing the tone to "flip" into the adjacent register. Register shifting, or "breaking" as it is sometimes called, depends upon the fact that the range of adjacent registers overlap and a number of pitches can be sung with one of several laryngeal adjustments, or registers. In Garcia's method these were "first studies." Speaking of the female voice:

> When the chest voice has been well established (which should be done in a few days), the student must immediately work to blend that register with the next. Sometimes nature herself has undertaken that task, but voices thus favored are rare. This necessary study nearly always disheartens the student, but it is up to the teacher to direct capably and to take care of the voice which has been confided to him. One will practice by passing alternately from one register to the other on the tones D_4-F_4 without interruption and without aspirating in that passage between registers. This succession should take place on the same breath; it should be practiced seldom and performed slowly, firmly bringing out the passage, then the speed and the number of repetitions can be increased. At one time the student should begin with the chest register tone, at another with that of the falsetto. One must not be afraid of accentuating the kind of hiccup which occurs in the passage from one register to the other; only continued practice can first alleviate it, then make it disappear.[12]

This advice applied to female and tenor voices. Garcia suggested that if the baritone and bass want to blend the two registers, they should do it too, but a third lower.

The great basso of the Paris opera (who was also a physician) Charles Battaille (1822–1872) prescribed the alternation of registers as well.

> In practice this returns us to the necessity of studying in principle the passage from one register to the other; from F_4 to G_4 for women and tenors, from E_4 to F_4 for baritones, because between these two points the muscular tension is moderated and the falsetto register has gained enough ring for it to be used with advantage. This brings us to the following exercise: the alternating and frequent repetition of the notes F_4 in chest and G_4 in falsetto for tenors and for women, E_4 to F_4 for baritones, producing these two sounds with the aid of a slow and regular expiration. Such movements allow the fascicles of the thyro-arytenoid to become accustomed to being stretched and relaxed with ease, speed, and dexterity.[13]

Battaille performed extensive observations using the laryngoscope and posed theories that were confirmed by the work of Hirano and Vennard one hundred years later.

Another famous nineteenth century *basso,* Luigi LaBlache (1794–1858), described the same exercise in this way:

> The two registers of the male voice frequently afford unequal sounds, which would produce a very disagreeable effect, if the ability to unite them could not be attained by study. The highest tones of the chest are very strong, by the very effort which they require, while the first head-tones are very soft and often feeble. Hence it is necessary to apply one's self to strengthening the latter, and softening the former. As our organs permit us to produce the extreme sounds of one regis-

> ter in the next register, the best means of uniting the two kinds of sounds, is to begin by making a single sound pass from the chest-register to the head-register, and vice versa.[14]

It should be no surprise then, that Carlo Bassini also utilized this method for unifying the registers. He recommended that after the chest and medium voices have been established they need to be united.

> The female voice may begin the task of joining the two registers by using first one and then the other on each of these notes: [C_4-G_4].Take fresh breath on each sound, until the difference between the two registers is perfectly well heard and understood; afterward, however, sing with the same breath the note twice over; first in the chest and then in the medium register but with great care to make as perceptible as possible the sort of hiccup between the notes, that marks the passage between the two registers when fresh breath is not taken . . . Care must also be taken not to lessen the force or intensity of the chest note, in order to give the medium note all the strength of which it is capable. One of these registers is always the weaker of the two, and the greater strength lies generally in the chest voice: in order to equalize the two, it would seem at first perhaps natural and proper to reduce the power of the stronger to a level with the weaker; but this is wrong; for experience has proved that such a proceeding would weaken the voice.[15]

Bassini included many exercises for both male and female voices utilizing register shifting for the unification of the registers. In his method one will note that over each note he placed a "C" for the chest voice, an "M" for the medium voice, and an "H" for head voice.

I have included a number of extensive quotations here to make the point that this practice was broad and cannot all be attributed to the influence of Garcia alone. Many other eighteenth-century pedagogues included register breaking in their books. In a dissertation on register switching, Lyle[16] listed many other pedagogues from the nineteenth century who utilized this technique including the renowned German baritone Julius Stockhausen,[17] Heinrich Panofka,[18] Auguste Panseron,[19] the American George Frederick Root,[20] and the renowned Australian Dame Nellie Melba.[21]

The voix sombrée and the voix claire

Soon after Duprez's debut in June of 1837, a report was made to the French Académie des Sciences by two French biologists, Diday and Petrequin. They described the new timbre and the laryngeal posture as practiced by Duprez, which they called the *voix sombrée ou couverte* (dark or covered voice). The fact that the singing of the new tenor at the opera house warranted a scientific report before a government agency lends *gravitas* to the notion that his approach was something quite new and remarkable. A few months later a new teacher at the Paris Conservatory by the name of Manuel Garcia made his own report to the Académie where he described the same phenomenon and claimed that he had been teaching this new technique since 1832. Garcia went on to describe in much greater detail the effect of laryngeal posture, the vocal registers, and the two vocal timbres he called the *voix sombrée* and the *voix claire*. Garcia was the first writer who specifically taught the low larynx and *voix sombrée*; he was also the first teacher to separate the contributions of register and timbre. He proposed that the fundamental registers of the voice were the "chest" and the "falsetto-head," and that the singer had two fundamental qualities or timbres, the *voix claire* (also known as the *voce apperta* or "open voice") and the *voix sombrée* (the *voce chiusa* or "closed voice"). The timbres and the registers could be combined in several ways. One could sing any register in either open or closed quality, but Garcia insisted that closed voice be thoroughly taught. The use of open timbre was probably more frequently heard in his day than now. Garcia talked about using open timbre to portray specific emotional content, even above the *passaggio* for the male voice.

The pedagogy of low larynx and vocal timbres became common themes in pedagogic treatises in the nineteenth century, including Carlo Bassini's. The importance of this concept is supported by the regularity of its description by other noted authorities.

Julius Stockhausen (1826–1906) was one of the most celebrated baritones in the middle of the nineteenth century. He was a renowned opera singer as well as a respected oratorio and recital performer, and he did a great deal to popularize the music of Schubert and Schumann in much of Europe. Johannes Brahms wrote his *Magelone* lieder for him, as well as the baritone solo in his *Requiem*. He was also a conductor and teacher. On the subject of the laryngeal posture, Stockhausen was unequivocal in his *Gesangsmethode*.

> The dangerous tendency of the larynx to rise to the position it takes in speaking must be carefully avoided.[22]

And further:

> . . . it is only with a fixed position of the larynx, and with the right use of the two chief qualities of sound, that a beautiful, well-rounded whole can be produced.[23]

Italian baritone Enrico Delle Sedie (1822–1907) was known for having sung Germont, Renato, and Figaro at Covent Garden and La Scala. He taught at the Paris Conservatory beginning in 1867 and was the author of seven volumes on training the voice, including his four volume *Esthetics of the Art of Singing*. He held similar views as Stockhausen and Garcia concerning the position of the larynx.

> The soft palate rises in a direction opposite to that of the larynx, following the same regular order of gradations; viz.: it rises with the height of sound, whilst the larynx, for giving to the voice a homogeneous and easy tone should descend in the same order.[24]

He described what happens when this advice is not heeded.

> When the larynx is so raised we may emit high sounds, but thin and shrill. It is true that we are disposed to raise the larynx when we want to emit high sounds, but if we would closely observe the timbre, we would recognize that they are thin, contracted and shrill.[25]

Apparently, like today, many must have disagreed with this thinking and Delle Sedie showed signs of weariness over the arguments.

> I will not extend myself too much on a subject so often disputed, but will limit myself to expose the practical use of my theory.[26]

Bataille reported his findings on the subject of laryngeal posture.

> Moderate lowering of the larynx has the certain result of giving the voice suppleness and power, thereby encouraging the enlargement of its natural limits.[27]

He offered an historical perspective.

> This procedure, familiar to the great Italian School, has been given the term *somber voice*, and it has been associated with vocal emission. Duprez "naturalized" this term in France during his operatic debuts, but the expression had already been in use in Italy for some time.[28]

Stockhausen and Battaille were both students of Garcia, so some agreement in philosophy shouldn't be surprising. However, other authors without such close connections to Garcia's legacy promote similar ideas. Edmund Myer (1846–1934) was a well-known teacher and a prolific author. In his book *The Renaissance of Vocal Art*, he said:

> For artistic tone, the soft palate must be high, the larynx must be low, and the throat and mouth allowed to form, not made or compelled . . . The larynx must be low in adjustment for the production of beautiful tone, but it must never be locally adjusted.[29]

Myer identified a common point of contention. Many teachers then, as now, were opposed to any sort of localized effort or to directing the attention to the function of a part of the mechanism. This is evidenced by the fact that there arose two opposing schools: the "local effort school" and the "no effort school." The latter arose as a direct reaction against the mechanistic methods of Garcia. The goal was the same, but the methods differed considerably. No better example of this can be found than the sentiments expressed by D. A. Clippinger (1860– 1938) who decried the "lowered larynx" as an abomination, but gave as his first exercises to develop the male head voice descending scale passages using [o] and [u]; both vowels are properly produced with the larynx in a low position.[30]

The famous teacher G. B. Lamperti (1830–1910) was opposed to many of Garcia's teachings, particularly his description of the onset, the *coupe de la glotte*. William Earl Brown (1863–1940), a longtime student and protégée, recorded Lamperti's thoughts in his book *Vocal Wisdom*. Here are some of Lamperti's dictums and sayings as recorded by Mr. Brown:

> "Covered tone" is a misleading term. "Closed tone" should take its place.[31]
>
> In their inception all tones are dark to be opened or closed at will.[32]
>
> All tones are closed until opened.[33]
>
> Although you may acquire a wide range of voice, you cannot modulate the sounds until the resonance of your tones becomes round and rich, *chiaroscuro*.[34]

The guiding principle expressed by Lamperti was that there was a balance of color or timbre that was to be established and maintained. The closed quality of the vowel was at the center of the ideal. The source of the closed quality was defined by Lamperti to Brown during one of his own lessons with the master.

> One must sing all exercises with an open throat—then the voice develops by itself. If you sing exercises with a dark (covered) tone, the voice cannot develop as it should. Later on, one can sing all tones (dark and light) with an open throat. If you begin studying the voice with dark tones only, it will be difficult to sing clear (light) ones.[35]

Lamperti expressed the legitimate caution that open throat and closed timbre are not to be misunderstood. Note his caution in the use of the word "covered" as opposed to "closed." The timbre identified as *chiaroscuro* is a balance of color, and brightness should not be neglected.

Many more contemporary sources may be cited in support of this pedagogic practice, but Richard Miller (1926–2009) put it succinctly.

> There can be little doubt that in desirable "closed voice" (*voce chiusa*), a timbre that should prevail throughout the singing voice regardless of range, as opposed to "open voice" (*voce apperta*), there is a stabilized laryngeal position—relatively low—and a somewhat widened pharynx. These conditions together with proper vowel modification (*aggiustamento*) produce the so-called "covered sound" of the upper range.[36]

The practice of maintaining a lower than neutral laryngeal posture provided the means for giving access of the qualities of the low mechanism all the way to the top in the male singer. This practice apparently began in Italy in the early nineteenth century and, as was already noted, introduced to Paris by the tenor Gilbert Duprez in 1837.

Bassini offered specific instructions on how to produce the clear and the somber timbre. Like Garcia before him, he promoted a more liberal use of the open timbre than would be acceptable today.

NOTES

1. Carlo Bassini, *Bassini's Art of Singing*, ed. by Richard Storr, with introduction by Stephen F. Austin (San Diego: Plural Pub., 2007; originally published by C.H. Ditson, 1857).
2. *The Art of Singing* (1857), *Melodic Exercises* (1865), *Education of Young Voices* (1865), *Method for the Tenor* (1866), *Method for the Baritone* (1868), and *New Method* (1869).
3. Bassini ascribes to the diaphragm the important function of moving air out of the body, rather than its only true function moving air into the body as the primary muscle of inhalation, not exhalation. This was and remains a very common misconception among voice teachers and singers.
4. Manuel Garcia, *Complete Treatise On the Art of Singing, Part 1*, trans. and ed. by Donald Paschke (New York: Da Capo Press, 1984), 50–51; originally published as *Nouveau Traité Sommaire sur l'Art du Chant* (Genève: Minkoff Éditeur, 1847).
5. Manuel Garcia II, "Memoire on the Human Voice," in *A Complete Treatise on the Art of Singing, Part 1*, xli.
6. Giambattista Mancini, *Practical Reflections on Figured Singing*; editions of 1774 and 1776, compared, trans., and ed. by Edward V. Foreman (Minneapolis: Pro Music Press, 1967).
7. H. J. Rubin and C. C. Hirt, "The Falsetto. A High Speed Cinematographic Study," *Laryngoscope* 70 (1960): 1305-1324.

8. Bassini, 6.
9. Ibid.
10. Minoru Hirano, William Vennard, John Ohala, and Bjorn Fritzell, "A Series of Four Electromyographic Studies" (Jacksonville, FL: NATS, 1971).
11. Bassini, 7.
12. Garcia, *Complete Treatise On the Art of Singing, Part 1.*
13. Charles Battaille, *Physiology as Applied to the Study of the Vocal Mechanism,* found in *Pioneer in Vocal Science and the Teaching of Singing,* trans. and ed. by Richard Joiner (Lanham, MD: Scarecrow Press, 1998), 178; originally published as *De la physiologie appliquée á l'étude de la mechanisme vocal* (Paris: Victor Masson and Sons, 1863).
14. Luigi LaBlache, *LaBlache's Complete Method of Singing,* translated from the original French (Cincinnati: John Church Co., n.d.), 6.
15. Bassini, 11.
16. John Christopher Lyle, "Register-switching as a pedagogical device for register unification of the singing voice: an historical analysis" (PhD dissertation, University of Oregon, 1995).
17. Julius Stockhausen, *A Method of Singing,* translated by Sophie Löwe (London: Novello, 1884); originally published as *Julius Stockhausen's Gesanges-Methode* (Leipzig: Peters, 1884).
18. Heinrich Panofka, *The Art of Singing* (New York: G. Schirmer, 1900).
19. Auguste Panseron, *Method of Vocalization for Soprano and Tenor* (New York: G. Schirmer, 1898).
20. George Frederick Root, *Introductory Lessons in Voice Culture and in the Principles of Execution* (Philadelphia: Theodore Presser, 1901).
21. Nellie Melba, *The Melba Method* (Melbourne: Chappell and Co. Ltd., 1926).
22. Stockhausen, 44.
23. Ibid., 43.
24. Enrico Delle Sedie, *Esthetics of the Art of Singing,* Vol. II (New York: G. Schirmer, 1885), 25.
25. Ibid., 22.
26. Ibid.
27. Bataille, 174.
28. Ibid.
29. Edmund Myer, *The Renaissance of Vocal Art* (Boston: The Boston Music Company, G. Schirmer, 1902), 87.
30. D. A. Clippinger, *The Head Voice and Other Problems* (Boston: Oliver Ditson Company, 1922), 19.
31. William Brown, *Vocal Wisdom, Maxims of Giovanni Battista Lamperti* (New York: Taplinger Publishing Co., 1957), 37.
32. Ibid.
33. Ibid., 53.
34. Ibid., 38.
35. Ibid., 129.
36. Richard Miller, *The Structure of Singing* (New York: Schirmer Books, 1986), 151.

29. Carlo Bassini's *The Art of Singing*, Part 2

Originally published in the *Journal of Singing*, volume 67, no. 1, 2010

THE "COUP DE LA GLOTTE"

No one prior to Garcia gave specific instructions on how to initiate a tone. As in so many areas concerning voice production, Garcia was the first to try to describe in detail this aspect of voice production.

> Hold the body straight, quiet, upright on the two legs, removed from any point of support; open the mouth, not in the form of the oval 0, but by letting the lower jaw fall away from the upper by its own weight, the corners of the mouth drawn back slightly. This movement, which holds the lips softly pressed against the teeth, opens the mouth in the correct proportion and finds it an agreeable form. Hold the tongue relaxed and immobile (without lifting it either by its root or by its tip); finally, separate the base of the pillars and soften the entire throat. In this position, inhale slowly and for a long time. After you are thus prepared, and when the lungs are full of air, without stiffening either the phonator or any part of the body, but calmly and easily, attack the tones very distinctly with a light stroke of the glottis on a very clear [a] vowel. That [a] will be taken well at the bottom of the throat in order that no obstacle may be opposed to the emission of the sound. In these conditions the tone should come out with ring and with roundness.[1]

This was the beginning of a lifelong controversy for Garcia. For the next sixty years he would defend this tenet of his method. Perhaps he could foretell the difficulties to come when he warned:

> One must guard against confusing the stroke of the glottis with the stroke of the chest (*coup de poitrine*), which resembles a cough, or the effort of expelling something which is obstructing the throat.[2]

By the later third of the nineteenth century, Garcia's critics were vehemently opposed to the technique. Many misunderstood the *coup de la glotte* to be an excessively violent release of air from tightly adducted vocal folds that if practiced regularly would result in the ruination of the voice. In Garcia's last written work, *Hints on Singing*, he answered once again the question that had plagued him for so many years.

> Q. What do you mean by the stroke of the glottis?
> A. The neat articulation of the glottis that gives a precise and clean start to a sound.[3]

Apparently there was genuine cause for concern if the technique were abused. Critics spoke of ruined voices. However, according to Hermann Klein (1856–1934), a longtime student of Garcia and a well-known music critic, none of Garcia's own students ever had difficulty as a result of the *coup de la glotte*.[4] This is restated in a footnote written for the second edition of *Hints on Singing* by Klein.

> It is of the utmost importance that these observations should be studied and correctly understood. The meaning of the term "stroke of the glottis," which was invented by the author, has been seriously misrepresented, and its misuse has done a great deal of harm.[5]

The controversy played out in public forums and newspapers in a fashion that must have been similar to what we have observed in recent years over the low-carb diet craze. Author and critic George Bernard Shaw took many opportunities to lambast Garcia.[6] Stark discussed several examples of public forums where Garcia's methods were criticized.[7] At one particular event, the popular artist and personality Victor Maurel offered exaggerated examples of the onset to a crowd and harshly criticized Garcia, who was in the audience. Dr. Henry Holbrook Curtis (1856–1920), the famous New York physician and friend of tenor Jean de Reszke decried the *coup de la glotte* as harmful and led a movement against its use.

> The shock, or *coup de glotte*, is death to the voice; it is born of ignorance, and to teach or allow its continuance is a crime.[8]

Having been personally attacked by Dr. Curtis and his disciples, Blanche Marchesi (1863–1940), famous singer and student of Garcia who was a highly respected teacher wrote:

> They could not distinguish between the hitting and closing of the glottis, and at once decided to condemn every method that allowed singers to make their vocal cords meet when emitting sounds.[9]

In one of his last attempts to answer the criticism, Garcia wrote to British voice teacher Charles Lunn (1838– 1906), who published this statement in his book, *Philosophy of Singing*:

> I do insist on the attack; but it must be the delicate, precise action of the glottis, not the brutal pushing of the breath that goes by that name, fit only to tear the glottis, not to rectify and regulate its movements . . . (My merit or demerit consists in having noticed it and given it a name). No one who starts the voice properly can eschew it.[10]

Mr. Lunn was in total agreement with Garcia as to the value of the *coup de la glotte*,[11] as is evident in this quote from his book, *Philosophy of Voice*:

> Now this, small though it be, is the one important principle of training that has been successful in results; by it great singers have been made; without it, many possessing all other requirements have failed, and it served its purpose before the introduction of the laryngoscope.[12]

Why did Garcia insist upon this point over his long career in the midst of so much virulent controversy? His position was that the brilliance of the vocal tone was the result of firm glottal closure.

> Various simultaneous causes can modify the timbres of the voice . . . according as the glottis narrows or partially opens, it produces ringing or lustreless tones.[13]

It was all about the quality of the sound. Remember that Garcia was the first to describe tone quality separate from timbre. The timbre of the tone was the result of the contribution of the vocal tract, but the basic quality came from the larynx. The way that the vocal folds approximated and specifically the way the vocal processes of the arytenoids came together during phonation determined the quality of the tone. After describing the dull quality of the breathy voice, he said:

> Consequently, it is necessary to conclude that the brilliance of the voice results from the firm

closure of the glottis after each pulsation.[14]

Garcia taught for many years after his definition of the *coup de la glotte* first appeared. There were scores of books on voice culture written after his *Complete Treatise on the Art of Singing*. Many agreed with Garcia, including the great father and son Francesco and Giovanni Lamperti. In his book *The Art of Singing* Francesco Lamperti (1813–1892) wrote the following in his discussion of acquiring agility:

> Agility should be studied slowly. The example should be executed so that the intervals are clearly distinguishable. The breath should be held steady in the passage from one note to the other, and the notes should be produced clearly with a *shock of the glottis* [italics are mine]. By this means the pupil will acquire the power of taking the exact note without sliding up to it, a fault which a beginner is very likely to confound with legato.[15]

In the tradition of the Socratic style of question and answer format as we saw in Garcia's *Hints on Singing*, Lamperti further commented:

> Q. What is meant by the just emission of the voice?
> A. It means attacking a note, with the greatest possible clearness, with a pure and correct intonation, and sustaining it to the full extent of the breath.[16]

William Earle Brown records the younger Lamperti on this subject:

> The vocal cords, in separating, start the glottis to pulsating on the desired pitch.[17]

> The energy to start a tone must come from the action of the vocal cords themselves, as they separate, not from the impact of the breath pushed against them.[18]

> Release the compressed breath to start your tone, do not push nor pull muscularly.[19]

The agreement between these giants of voice teaching in the nineteenth century on this issue is quite compelling. Austrian singer and teacher Ferdinand Sieber (1822– 1895) who composed almost 700 *solfeggi* put it this way:

> The singer should hold the breath at the moment when he intends to strike a tone, and close the glottis. By this means he will avoid a too voluminous exhalation (as the air is accumulated below the vocal chords [*sic*] and will flow out in smaller quantities) and, at the same time, gain a good attack of tone.[20]

Opposition to the *coup de la glotte* came from those who witnessed its abuse by practitioners (other than Garcia and his disciples) who exaggerated the gesture and abused voices with it. Equally unfair to Garcia are those that have redefined what he meant by it. This is apparent in a contemporary quote from Meribeth Bunch:

> The attack involves a precise coordination of the onset of sound, the oscillating movement and the opening and closing of the folds. The ideal attack is one in which the breath begins to flow gently and is followed by a precise momentary closure of the vocal folds which meets this stream of air. When correctly done, this attack is crisp, clear and without tension. The exact terminology re-

lating to the attack is confusing. Garcia (1897) called it the *coup de glotte*; Vennard (1967) has called it the "imaginary aspirate."[21]

In no way can the *coup de la glotte* and the imaginary aspirate be the same thing. Bunch does not carry the blame for this misstatement, but is merely reiterating an error put forth by the physician/voice teacher team of Lennox Brown (1841–1892) and Emile Behnke (1836– 1892) in 1904. After describing two alternate ways to begin the tone, they stated:

> The vocal ligaments meet just at the very moment when the air strikes against them; they are, moreover, not pressed together more tightly than is necessary. No preliminary escape takes place as in #1, and no obstacle has to be overcome as in #2: but the attack is clear and decisive, and the tone consequently gets a proper start. The mechanism by which this is done is the "*coup de glotte*" or "shock of the glottis."[22]

They described exactly what Vennard (1909–1971) defined as the "coordinated onset," not the *coup de la glotte*. One cannot read Garcia's own words and understand that he meant anything other than the fact that the vocal folds must be in full contact and momentarily resist the pressure built up in the trachea prior to the gentle plosive from the vocal folds as they release the pressure cleanly and neatly.

How could this error in understanding what Garcia described and many others promoted have happened? Perhaps there has been felt a need to come to terms with Garcia's position, so these authors have redefined his argument rather than have to deal with the possibility that contemporary thinking on the matter is incorrect. Barbara Doscher (1922–1996) puts it plainly:

> The glottal plosive is destructive, however, and may lead to vocal nodules.[23]

This is a common position among voice professionals today. How could Garcia have really meant what he said? Since Garcia was by most accounts, a successful and respected teacher, what he said cannot have been what he meant.

> As a matter of fact, the two little lips which, in the larynx, form between them a passage for the breath (the glottis), adhere to each other and cause a certain accumulation of air. That air by virtue of the elasticity which it acquires due to the pressure exerted upon it, separates the lips of the glottis, and, expanding, exits with a burst. But, at the same instant, relieved of the pressure from below and pulled by their own elasticity, the lips meet again to give rise to a new explosion. From this series of successive and regular contractions and expansions or explosions is born the emission of the voice.[24]

The influence of those who misrepresented or misunderstood Garcia's intent still controls popular opinion today. Authors Frederick Hustler (1889–1969) and Yvonne Rodd-Marling (??-1982) bring an interesting perspective:

> In general physiologists are against the *coup de la glotte* . . .Yet great singers and teachers often hold the opposite view: Garcia, Carulli, Duprez, Viardot-Garcia, Faure, Lablache . . .[25]

In addition to this list we could add those that I have quoted here, plus Julius Stockhausen, Carlo Bassini, Charles Bataille, Edmund Myer, William Shakespeare, and Matilda Marchesi.

> Not only is it difficult to find a physiologist who supports the use of the *coup de la glotte* today, it is equally difficult to find a contemporary published voice pedagogue who acknowledges anything but the "well-coordinated onset" as the *sine qua non* of initiating the tone. Stark stated that *The Foundations of Singing* (1950) by Franklyn Kelsey (1892–1959) was the last book of any note to be published in support of the *coup de la glotte*.[26]

> The establishment and maintenance of a perfect approximation of the vocal cords is the key problem in singing . . . he who cannot teach it cannot teach true singing, for it is the sole means which the singer has at his disposal for launching a tone which has not an undesirable content of unphonated air.[27]

In light of the tremendous weight of support for the use of the *coup de la glotte* from highly respected teachers from the nineteenth century, including Carlo Bassini, I believe that this issue is worth consideration. After reading James Stark's arguments and then reading extensively on my own, I am convinced that I had been misinformed by well-meaning teachers who were convinced that the use of the glottal plosive was always abusive. I do not believe that it is. While I acknowledge the necessity for prudence in this matter, as there are dangers if exaggerated, it is simply impossible for me to imagine those elite teachers such as Garcia, the Lampertis, and all the rest in a veritable pantheon of successful teachers were wrong and spent their careers ruining voices. Instead, I have come to wonder what my earlier students have missed by not learning it.

Vennard commented in his *Developing Voices* that there was a dangerous moment in the life of a student singer when they begin the transition toward singing with a professional quality.[28] He said that he always waited until there was a fundamental freedom in the technique before he introduced the aggressive quality that is necessary to take the step into the professional world. This is a profound observation. The *coup de la glotte* must be used within the structure of a technique that is free from extraneous tensions. It must also be understood to be what it is, not what we are afraid that it is.

SUMMARY

Carlo Bassini's *The Art of Singing* is a valuable historical document in that it was a very popular teaching method in the United States during the second half of the nineteenth century. Historical significance notwithstanding, *The Art of Singing* is most of all a useful teaching method. Its pedagogic pedigree is traced directly to Manuel Garcia II, the eminent voice teacher who was the first to attempt to bring together the science and art of voice teaching. The techniques presented in this book are valid, "tried and true." It is hoped that now that this book is available to a modern audience of voice teachers and singers it might have a real impact upon the reinstatement of effective tradition methods of voice building that have for the most part been long forgotten.

NOTES

1. Manuel Garcia, *Complete Treatise On the Art of Singing, Part 1,* translated and edited by Donald Paschke (New York: Da Capo Press, 1984), 50–51. Originally published as *Nouveau Traité Sommaire sur l'Art du Chant* (Genève: Minkoff Éditeur, 1847), 41-42.
2. Ibid., 42.
3. Manuel Garcia, *Hints on Singing*, translated from the French by Beata Garcia, new and revised edition by Hermann Klein (London: E. Ascherberg, 1984), 13.
4. Hermann Klein, *Thirty Years of Musical Life in London, 1870– 1900* (London: Heinemann, 1903), 37.
5. Garcia, *Hints on Singing*, 13.
6. George Bernard Shaw, *Music in London* (London: Constable and Company, 1932).
7. James Stark, *Bel Canto: The History of Vocal Pedagogy* (Toronto: University of Toronto Press, 1999), 15.
8. Henry Holbrook Curtis, *Voice Building and Tone Placing* (New York: D. Appleton and Company, 1901), 159.
9. Blanche Marchesi, *Singer's Pilgrimage* (Reprint: New York: Arno Press, 1977; originally published: London: G. Richards, 1923), 91-93.
10. Charles Lunn, *The Voice: Its Downfall, Its Training, and Its Use. A Manual for Teachers, Singers, and Students* (London: Reynolds & Co., 1904), 21.
11. Lunn is remembered for the promotion of a theory developed by his student Orlando Steed concerning the importance of inflating the ventricles for proper phonation. This theory was continued in the writings of British teacher and author Edmund Myer.
12. Charles Lunn, *The Philosophy of Voice: Showing the Right and Wrong Action of Voice in Speech and Song, with Laws for Self-Culture* (Reprint: Huntsville, Texas: Recital Publications, 1984; originally published: London: Baillière, Tindall and Cox, 1886), 5–6.
13. Garcia, *Complete Treatise on the Art of Singing*, 28.
14. Ibid., 27.
15. Francesco Lamperti, *The Art of Singing*, translated by J. C. Griffith (New York: G. Schirmer, 1916), 15.
16. Ibid., 12.
17. William Earle Brown, *Vocal Wisdom: Maxims of Giovanni Battista Lamperti* (New York: Taplinger Publishing Co., 1957), 45.
18. Ibid., 45-46.
19. Ibid., 46.
20. Ferdinand Sieber, *The Art of Singing and Vocal Culture,* translated and adapted from *Kataechismus der Gesangs Kunst* [1862] by A. W. Dohn (New York: Oliver Ditson Company, 1880), 20.
21. Meribeth Bunch, *Dynamics of the Singing Voice* (New York: Springer-Verlag, 1995), 70.
22. Lennox Brown and Emile Behnke, *Voice, Speech, and Song* (New York: G. P. Putnams Sons, 1904), 162.
23. Barbara Doscher, *The Functional Unity of the Singing Voice* (Metuchen, NJ: Scarecrow Press Inc., 1994), 61.
24. Manuel Garcia, *A Complete Treatise on the Art of Singing*, 23.
25. Frederick Hustler and Yvonne Rodd-Marling, *Singing: The Physical Nature of the Vocal Organ* (London: Faber & Faber, 1965), 75.
26. Stark, 24.
27. Franklyn Kelsey, *The Foundations of Singing* (London: Williams and Northgate, 1950), 14.
28. William Vennard, *Developing Voices* (New York: Carl Fisher, 1970).

30. "On Time" with Manuel Garcia

Originally published in the *Journal of Singing*, volume 67, no. 2, 2010

Several articles have appeared in this column on the work of Manuel Garcia, eminent teacher from the past. His *Complete Treatise on the Art of Singing* in two volumes is still a valuable resource, even though it is difficult to obtain at the present time. The first volume of the *Complete Treatise* was originally published in 1841 during the time that Garcia was teaching at the Paris Conservatory. It was a progressive vocal method that included descriptions of the vocal instrument and how it worked—most of the ideas therein are still valid today. The *Complete Treatise* contained the pedagogic thought of the day, but included several new concepts that reflected a change in the common practice of the time: the importance of the low larynx, Garcia's definition of vocal timbres, his famous definition of a vocal register, and the controversial *coup de la glotte* (all of which have been discussed in this column). His method included many exercises designed to train the musician (interval studies, scale work, and how to interpret the musical score correctly) and to build the voice (register building, register unification, *messa di voce,* velocity, etc.). Volume two was originally published in 1847 and is much less known to the modern reader. It taught the interpretation of song (and arias) and offered practical applications of the techniques learned in the first volume. It was full of examples from the operatic literature performed at the time—much of which is still in the active repertory today. It is an invaluable resource for understanding performance practice of the period.

One of the subjects addressed by Garcia in volume two is the appropriate management of time. In the introduction to the topic titled "On Time," he offered this quote: "Il tempo é l'anima della musica".[1] Garcia goes on to say that "time gives regularity, firmness, and ensemble to music, while irregularities add interest and variety to its execution."[2] It is to the concept of intentional irregularities that the following extended excerpt is given. The source of the text is from *Garcia's New Treatise on the Art of Singing,* published in the United States by Oliver Ditson. It is undated but probably appeared in the 1870s or 1880s. Music examples are taken from an undated but early publication, *Traité complet de L'art du Chant,* with parallel French and German texts published by B. Schott in Leipzig.[3]

Example 1.

Example 2.

TEMPO RUBATO.

By *tempo rubato* is meant the momentary increase of value, which is given to one or several sounds, to the detriment of the rest, while the total length of the bar remains unaltered. This distribution of notes into long and short, breaks the monotony of regular movements, and gives greater vehemence to bursts of passion [Example 1].

To make *tempo rubato* perceptible in singing, the accents and time of an accompaniment should be strictly maintained; upon this monotonous ground, all alterations introduced by a singer will stand out in relief, and change the character of certain phrases. *Accelerando* and *rallentando* movements require the voice and accompaniment to proceed in concert; whereas, *tempo rubato* allows liberty to the voice only. A serious error is therefore committed, when a singer, in order to give spirit to the final cadences of a piece, uses a *ritardando* at the last bar but one, instead of the *tempo rubato*; as while aiming at spirit and enthusiasm, he only becomes awkward and dull.

This prolongation is usually conceded to appoggiaturas, to notes placed on long syllables, and those which are naturally salient in the harmony. In all such cases, the time lost must be regained by accelerating other notes. This is a good method for giving colour and variety to melodies [Example 2].[4]

Two artists of a very different class—Garcia [the author's father] and Pagannini—excelled in the use of the *tempo rubato*. While the time was regularly maintained by an orchestra, they would abandon themselves to their inspiration, till the instant a chord changed, or else to the very end of the phrase.

Example 3.

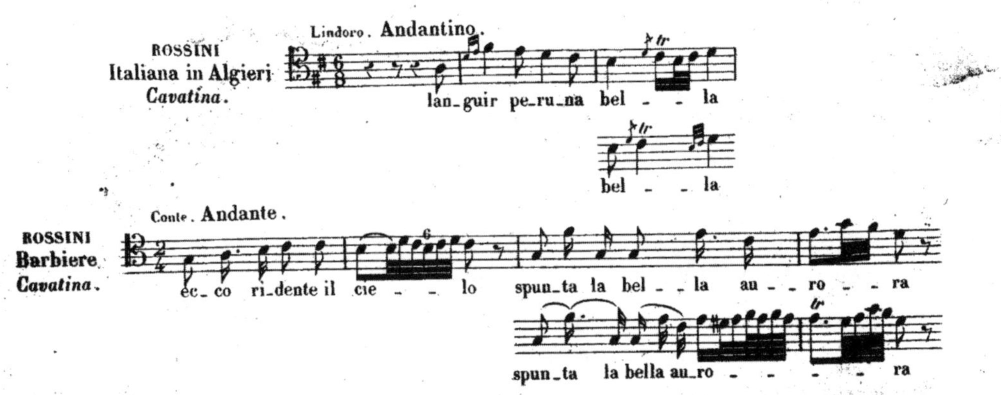

Example 4.

An excellent perception of rhythm, and great self-possession on the part of a musician, however, are requisite for the adoption of this method, which should be resorted to only in passages where the harmony is stable, or only slightly varied—in any other case, it would appear singularly difficult, and give immense trouble to an executant. The annexed example illustrates our meaning [Example 3].

The *tempo rubato*, again, is useful in preparing a shake, by permitting this preparation to take place on the preceding notes; thus: [Example 4]

The *tempo rubato*, if used affectedly, or without discretion, destroys all balance, and so tortures the melody.

* * *

Other sources contemporary to Garcia offer similar instructions in the use of *tempo rubato*. Carlo Bassini said:

> The *tempo rubato* is an effect much employed—it is much used but also much abused. Indeed, the correct application of the *rubati* is extremely difficult. When a passage is thus treated, the measure of the accompaniment should be maintained with great precision, while the singer is free to accelerate or retard, giving thus to passages an entirely new character.[5]

Bassini offered Example 5 as illustration.[6]

CONCLUSION

Both Garcia and Bassini warned that proper use of the *tempo rubato* was a difficult matter and that it should be guided by discernment and good taste. Tastes change over time, especially in matters of music and how it is to be performed. In my roles as college voice teacher and a choir director of amateur singers, I often find myself having to convince singers to let go of their rigid concepts of what musicality means so that the words they sing and the musical phrases they are trying to bring to life have a chance to have *anima*.

Example 5.

It was heartening for me to see venerated teachers trying to guide singers into letting go of always reading the score literally when beautiful expression could be found by slightly altering the notes as they appear. I know this is not now as commonly practiced as it was in Garcia's day, when it is clear from reading these and other historical writings of the period that absolute obedience to the written score was not necessarily the goal. Perhaps it is because we do not take the time to teach *tempo rubato* adequately so that "good taste" is established. We have placed the musical score "on the altar" in ways that the composers of the nineteenth century never intended. We all know the famous story of how Rossini was so fed up with singers who took too many liberties with his music that he began writing out all embellishments and ornaments. Apparently this did not mean that all freedom was gone for the artist to breathe life into the music by slight alterations of rhythm and even of the notes in the score. Composers often made changes to the score to fit the particular talents (and limitations) of particular singers who were singing their leading parts.

Some of the best examples of *tempo rubato* that I know today are found in popular music styles. When I want a good demonstration of this principle I break out my recording of Willie Nelson singing "Moonlight in Vermont." There is a steady beat from the ensemble, and of course the harmonic rhythm is maintained, but the words are sung in a rhythm that to Mr. Nelson represented the correct sentiment behind them—with extremely good taste earned over many years of his own brand of artistry! It seems to me to be exactly what Garcia was describing . . . being "on time" sometimes meant being a little "out of time."

NOTES

1. Manuel Garcia II, *Garcia's New Treatise on the Art of Singing* (Boston: Oliver Ditson & Company, n.d.), 52. ("Time is the soul of music," quoting Anna Maria Cellini from her *Grammar of Song*.)
2. Ibid.
3. Manuel Garcia, fils, *École de Garcia: Traité complet de l'Art du Chant* (Leipzig: B. Schott, n.d.).
4. From Garcia's *Traité complete L'Art du Chant.* Excerpts from *Lucia di Lamermoor* and *Anna Bolena*. The aria "Perche non ho del vento" was sometimes used as a substitute for "Regnava nel silenzio." It is more commonly known to be from *Rosmonda d'Inghilterra.*
5. Carlo Bassini, *Art of Singing* (historical reprint; introduction by Stephen F. Austin) (San Diego: Plural Publishing, 2008; originally published in NY: Oliver Ditson, 1852), 16.
6. From Bassini's *Art of Singing.* This excerpt is from the aria "Non v'ha squardo" from *Anna Bolena*, indicating correct use of *tempo rubato.*

31. Pedagogy from the Archives

Originally published in the *Journal of Singing*, volume 67, no. 3, 2011

It has been my purpose in the "Provenance" column to bring to the attention of our readership important pedagogic writings from the past. This article, "Pathways to Vocal Pedagogy," is taken from the archives of our own journal.[1] It appeared originally in 1955 in what was then known as *The Bulletin*. I think the words of Mr. Gerry are as appropriate today as they were then.

Pathways to Vocal Pedagogy

Arthur Gerry

For some reason, whenever referring to the art of vocal teaching, I find myself concerned with the fundamental element upon which the art of singing depends. The acquisition of a sound vocal technique is never come by in a short time, but now, as always in the past, takes years of persistent effort.

The present-day argument that there is not sufficient time available in the prevailing scheme of things musical to permit the thorough procedure advocated in these words will prove to be something of a myth if the vocal teachers will square themselves to the situation in a courageous stand for that which they know, within themselves, is right and sane.

Perhaps it would not be out of order to call attention to the widely known fact that competent and interested scholars have done a great deal of research into the history of the development of the vocal art. They have found that from the latter half of the 17th century (and perhaps even earlier) to well into the 19th century, many of the best musical minds of Italy were occupied in developing the technique of singing and in establishing sound rules and laws for the development of the singer, based entirely upon the empirical approach. As a result, the art of the singer rose to heights never before attained. This school of singing has been called by many names, but can correctly be termed the Italian School, inasmuch as most of those concerned in that development were Italian.

Let us consider for a moment a little bit of what might be termed the genealogy of vocal teaching. One of the earliest and most noted of these musicians was Alessandro Scarlatti. Although today we think of him as a composer, the truth is that during his lifetime he was very famous as a singer and a teacher of singing. In his declining years he had as a pupil Niccolo Porpora. They must have been his declining years, for he was twenty-seven years older than his pupil. Porpora lived to be nearly eighty years old, and became perhaps the most famous teacher of singing of all time. As he died in 1766, it is reasonable to suppose that some of his students were themselves teachers of singing in the early days of the 19th century, and passed on his principles of vocal training to others who were teaching within the past hundred years, and who were undoubtedly responsible for the so-called "Golden Age" of singing which we enjoyed at the turn of this century.

The truth is that the "Golden Age" extended far back before that time. How do we know? It is true that most of the evidence is hearsay, but there is one undeniable fact. The music that the singers of one hundred years ago and more were able to negotiate with comparative ease offers difficulties that very few singers of today can surmount. Whether they should be able to do so, or not, must remain a matter of opinion.

Unquestionably, one of the main factors that led to the supremacy of this Italian School of singing was unanimity. Another was language. Throughout this period of about two hundred years, all recognized and legitimate teachers taught in the same manner. Their ideas were woven into approximately the same pattern, in seeking to develop the voice. The student need not be dismayed if his teacher moved away, or if he was obliged to move away from this teacher, because the next maestro found would, with minor variations, follow the same general procedure. The language of song was their native tongue, the cleanest and purest and simplest in its vowel sounds. There was practically absolute agreement as to the best method of producing an even scale and a well-schooled, fully developed technique. We are creditably informed that the scales and exercises used by Niccolo Porpora were substantially the same as those used later by the great Caruso in the development of his own voice. We will venture to say that the teaching procedure was largely oral. Undoubtedly, at first, it was to a certain extent imitative, for, rest assured, these teachers were also *singers*. By means of freely emitted natural vowels, colored to suit the pitch, a perfectly focused tone was produced on every note in the scale, from the bottom to the top. Very briefly, the "ah" of the low voice was gradually darkened to a perfectly focused "ah" at the middle of the voice, permitted to close to an "oo" on approaching the head voice, and became again "ah" at the top. Other vowels were employed from time to time, particularly the "ee" which was developed from the closed lips' hum, but basically the scale was as described, and was worked upon in such fashion.

Scales, exercises, and vocali[s]es on the vowels just quoted were the order of the day, until the proper vowel color became a subconscious reaction to pitch. Patience and perseverance were an absolute necessity to these early teachers, and students did not know the meaning of the word "hurry." They were working to develop technical proficiency and ease of production. Happily, these vocali[s]es have been preserved and are now available to all in volume publication.

It was no unusual thing for a student to work several years before being taught any repertoire. He was not required to study the anatomy of the human head, nor was he required to think about or to know the names of muscles over which he really had no conscious control. He was taught only to listen for and to note the sensation of beautiful tone.

So it must be realized that in those early days—(shall we call them the "Golden Age of Vocal Teaching"?)— the supreme effort was directed toward the development and perfection of the instrument itself, as such. Without the perfected instrument, fine singing is not possible. We would certainly have no Heifitz today if violins had never developed beyond the cigar box stage.

In looking over the field of vocal pedagogy today, we are impressed by the state of confusion that seems to exist as to what constitutes the correct manner or method of teaching singing. There seems to be no general agreement as to how to get results. This confusion does not exist in vocal teaching alone. It seems to exist in the field of art in general. We have the so-called modernism in musical composition, which some of us try in vain to understand. Our composers seem to be falling over backward in an effort to be different, and one could breathe a sigh of relief when some young composer is spoken of as another Puccini, a new Verdi, or a reincarnation of Wagner. It would appear that our painters are in no better position, for they too seem to be trying very hard to be different from the great examples of painting of previous years. We cannot speak for the composer or the painter, for we are neither. But the confusion that exists in the field of vocal teaching is difficult to understand to one who has been through the rigorous training of the old school. There is no need for this confusion. The exact laws of vocal technique and the approach required to perfect it, although generations old, are the same, for the human throat is still the same identical mechanism that it was two hundred years ago.

There is nothing mysterious about this old-time technique. The path to its acquisition is narrow, but exceedingly well defined. The more it is pursued, the more sure and definite it becomes. There is one absolute requirement—time. In addition, there must be patience and persistency and a willingness to let all else slide until that technical mastery is attained. Let us consider for a moment the beauty of motion and posture that we find in the classic ballet, and realize that all of that ability rests upon between eight and twelve fundamental exercises persistently employed daily for from six to eight years in order to acquire a sufficiently secure technique and coordination to be able to appear in public. Singing is also a matter of perfect coordination in the physiological production of tone to the point where the singer takes no thought of the act itself, but only of the interpretation of the text.

It is not difficult to make students see the sense of this. They soon get to the point where they genuinely enjoy their scales, exercises, and vocali[s]es. Very much as a golfer practices persistently to reduce his score, they will work diligently to acquire greater ease or production, a smoother scale, a more dependable breath support. If they will not, there is very little use in wasting our time as teachers, and theirs. They may learn to parrot a few songs, but they will never be able to stand on their own feet, artistically. On the other hand, the student who takes the time to acquire the proper fundamental technique will ultimately become an artist in his own right, and will continue to improve, vocally, for many years to come. As has been said before, a rash of different methods has been developing over the country, and the world. We could not begin to name them all. But they have unquestionably produced the picture we have today of singing artists being given all credit for fine interpretation, excellent diction, deep artistic insight into their songs, and, in a separate paragraph, being castigated for bad vocal production even to the extent of bad pitch. Such artists are hard-working, sincere, earnest students as well. They sing as they have been taught to sing.

Those who are teaching in colleges and universities have a priceless opportunity. In the four years, and sometimes five, there can be laid a sound and dependable technical foundation, if at least two lessons a week are required, and an hour of daily practice on technique alone. Less than that will not do. From a disciplinary standpoint, the institution has great advantages. The private teacher finds it more difficult, for he has not the same control over the student, nor does he issue grades to denote the quality of the work done. He can only acquire a reputation for demanding the wholehearted cooperation of the student if the latter is to remain in his class.

The operatic, concert, and radio fields offer one thing in common—hard, grueling work. It is not unusual, except while on concert tour, to sing six or more hours a day. The concert artist must be in top-notch condition three or four times a week. Not many stand the pace for very long, and none do who do not have absolutely secure vocal technique. The singer of today who can look back on twenty five years or more of successful performance found this technique. The many thousands who fell by the wayside did not. And it is trite to say that unless their teachers had themselves successfully acquired this fundamental technique of the art of singing, they could not possibly have taught it. Therein lies the difficulty in the pathway leading to vocal pedagogy.

NOTE

1. Arthur Gerry, "Pathways to Vocal Pedagogy," *The Bulletin* 11, no. 4 (May/June, 1955): 7.

32. "Auch kleine Dinge"

Originally published in the *Journal of Singing*, volume 67, no. 4, 2011

"Auch kleine Dinge können uns entzücken" (Even little thing can delight us).[1] Hugo Wolf, inspired by poetry translated by Paul Heyse, brought to us the *Italienisches Liederbuch,* a collection of songs that begins with the sentiment that good things come in small packages.[2] When it comes to building a voice and establishing an elite singing technique, no part of the production of beautiful tone is too small to consider. Every detail of what we teach should be guided by specificity as a part of comprehensive pedagogic method. The more we leave things to chance the less likely our students will be successful in their attempts to go on to the next step in their progression to artistry.

In 2005 I wrote about vocal onset in "The Attack on the *coup de la glotte*."[3] In that article I discussed the importance of the initiation of tone and the historical controversy over Garcia's *coup de la glotte*. Another detail of the proper onset deserves consideration: the vocal scoop!

Voice teachers have been decrying the scoop as a vocal fault for generations. According to many venerable teachers from the past, a preparatory slide on the way to the intended pitch should be considered a vocal fault. Garcia stated,

> One will take care not to slur the tones before arriving at the correct intonation, which, furthermore, one should never seek with the voice, but always approach boldly.[4]

As clearly as this is stated from the eminent Garcia, one of his contemporaries put it even more plainly.

> Everything being favorably disposed, then, for tone, the point is, to attack a given sound, previously in the mind, with precision and confidence. This must be done without the slightest audible preparation or circumlocution. By circumlocution, I mean *feeling* for the tone, as in a gliding through other tones up to it, or down upon it, from above, or again by any *aspiration* whatever; as, for instance, the vowel *a* (pronounced *ah*) as though an *h* were before it; like *h'a*. *The attack must be direct and instantaneous*.[5]

Sliding into a tone could give the impression that the singer is searching for the right pitch.

> Each tone must be started exactly on the pitch. Slipping up to the pitch give one's singing a feeling of uncertainty and destroys the good effect of the song.[6]

Many readers recognize the name of Herbert Witherspoon, a well-known American bass who performed at the Metropolitan Opera from 1908 to 1914. He retired from singing and focused on teaching and arts administration, and served a brief assignment as general manager of the Met before his untimely death in 1935. In his wonderful pedagogy book called *Singing,* Witherspoon put it clearly: "The voice should be attacked cleanly and instantaneously without scooping . . ."[7] Even the controversial Douglas Stanley spoke directly on this point.

> The good singer attacks a tone right in the center of the pitch and holds a constant intensity throughout the duration of the tone.[8]

Stanley went on to explain a part of his thinking concerning why the scoop was detrimental to singing.

> Suppose the pupil slurs up to a high tone: he will be holding the throat adjustment which is, at best, correct for the lower tone. Thus the upper tone will inevitably be improperly resonated. Such slurring may in many cases cut out from five tones to an octave from the top of a given voice.[9]

While I believe Stanley was correct in his proposition that a student could "hold the throat" in a posture that would not properly resonate the following pitch, I think there is a more important issue. I believe that a student who initiates a tone below the intended tone can carry up the weight of the tone below. This can significantly limit access to the high voice, not exclusively due to resonance issues, but because tension in the intrinsic muscles is maintained at the level of the lower pitch and not allowed to give a little to achieve the proper balance for the high note. This is especially troublesome to young high voices who are learning to sing the top of their range with freedom.

Training singers to be precise with the pitch that they intend to sing can be transformative. Scooping is so common that it may not be perceived, even by many experienced teachers. I encounter too many graduate students and "long-studied" singers who do it constantly and are unaware of it to believe otherwise. This issue is complicated by the fact that a preparatory slide into the target pitch is often a desirable part of musical expression. I recently was told by a student of mine that a coach at a summer program in Europe complained that they didn't scoop and asked them to be more musical!

As an element of musical expression the scoop certainly has a place, but it must be accomplished after the singer is properly prepared. A precocious young singer who emulates his/her favorite singer's every nuance can unwittingly create vocal stumbling blocks by doing that which is for an accomplished singer not necessarily a problem.

It can often take extended "sensitivity training" to make singers aware of what they are doing. As with everything else in training a singer, we must be patient but persistent and diligent. I have seen remarkable things take place when singers learn not to "lean into the tone" and they learn to clean up their act! This insipid little habit has been long practiced and has long been decried as a vocal fault. I offer just a few references from our historical pedagogic literature on this subject in an attempt to keep this brief, in keeping with the introductory words: short is sweet!

NOTES

1. Paul Heyse (1830–1914) translated the texts from anonymous Italian folk and traditional poetry.
2. Hugo Wolf set a total of 46 poems published in two volumes by primarily anonymous poets. Volume 1 was published in 1890 and Volume 2 in 1896.
3. Stephen Austin, "The Attack on the *coup de la glotte*," *Journal of Singing* 61, no. 5 (May/June 2005): 525–529.
4. Manuel Garcia, *Complete Treatise On the Art of Singing, Part 1,* translated and edited by Donald Paschke (New York: Da Capo Press, 1984), 42; originally published as *Nouveau Traité Sommaire sur l'Art du Chant* (Genève: Minkoff Éditeur, 1847).
5. Carlo Bassini, *Art of Singing* (New York: C. H. Ditson, 1884), 10.
6. D. A. Clippinger, *The Clippinger Class-Method of Voice Culture* (Philadelphia: Oliver Ditson, 1932), 6.
7. Herbert Witherspoon, *Singing* (New York: G. Schirmer, 1925), 116.
8. Douglas Stanley, *The Science of Voice* (New York: Carl Fischer, 1939), 405.
9. Ibid. 92.

33. Singers on Singing

Originally published in the *Journal of Singing*, volume 67, no. 5, 2011

While pursuing a website that sells music memorabilia, I ran across an old 78 RPM recording from about 1911 of a tenor named Evan Williams. Having never heard of Mr. Williams I moved on to the next item. Within the hour, I was reading a newly acquired old book, *Great Singers on the Art of Singing* by James Francis Cooke published in 1921.[1] The very last chapter was contributed by none other than Evan Williams! As I read the introduction to Cooke's book, I noted that he singled out Mr. Williams's views on teaching and singing as being particularly well informed and insightful. I learned that Evan Williams was a very successful American singer of Welsh descent, having grown up in a mining community in Ohio. He became a recording artist with Victor Red Seal (78 RPM records) and was the Victor Company's third most popular recording artist after Caruso and John McCormack. Though successful as a singer—primarily in oratorio— Williams had consistency issues with his singing that he found quite perplexing. He determined to understand his voice more completely and retired from singing for a period of three years while he undertook an intensive self-study. He resumed his singing career but died prematurely in 1918.

This coincidence was more than I could ignore. Here is the chapter by Mr. Williams *in toto*. I hope you find his thoughts interesting and challenging. Many of his ideas reflect historical pedagogic thought as reviewed in this column, although he describes no pedagogic lineage. His ideas on the importance of establishing the dark quality in the tone and then adding brightness are especially relevant for us today. There are many examples of Mr. Williams's recordings on YouTube.

How I Regained a Lost Voice
Evan Williams

There is nothing so disquieting to the singer as the feeling that his voice, upon which his artistic hopes, to say nothing of his livelihood, depend, is not a reliable organ, but a fickle thing which to-day may be in splendid condition but to-morrow may be gone. Time and again I have been driven to the verge of desperation by my own voice. While I am grateful to all of my excellent teachers for the many valuable things they taught me, I had a strong feeling that there was something which I must know and which only I myself could find out for myself. After a very wide experience here and in England I found myself with so little confidence in my ability to produce uniformly excellent results when upon the concert stage, that I retired to Akron, Ohio, resolving to spend the rest of my life in teaching. There I remained for four years, thinking out the great problem that confronted me. It is only during the last year that I have become convinced that I have solved it. My musical work has made me well-to-do and I want now to give my ideas to the world so that others may profit if they find them valuable. I have nothing to sell—but I trust that I can put into words, without inventing a new and bewildering nomenclature, something that will prove of practical assistance to young singers as it has been to me.

AN INDISPUTABLE RECORD

In 1908 I left Akron and resolved to try to reinstate myself in New York as a singer. I also made talking machine records, only to find that seldom could I make a record at the first attempt that was up to the very high standard maintained by the company in the case of all records placed upon the market for sale. This meant a great waste of my time and the company's material and services. It naturally set me thinking. If I could do it one time— why couldn't I do it all the time? There was no contradicting the talking machine record. The machine records the slightest blemish as well as the most perfect tone. There was no getting away from the fact that sometimes my singing was far from what I wished it to be.

The strange thing about it all was that my singing did not seem to depend upon the physical condition or feeling of my throat. Some days when my throat felt at its very best the records would come back in a way that I was ashamed of. It is a strange feeling to hear one's own voice from the talking machine. It sounds quite differently from the impression one gets while singing. I began to ponder, why were some of my records poor and others good?

After deep thought for a very long period of time, I commenced to make certain postulates which I believe I have since proved (to my own satisfaction at least) to be reasonable and true. They not only resulted in an improvement in my voice, but they enabled me to do at command what I had previously been able to do only occasionally. They are:

1. Tone creates its own support.
2. Much of the time spent in elaborate breathing exercises (while excellent for the health and valuable to the singer, in a way) do not produce the results that are expected.
3. The singer's first studies should be with his brain and ear, rather than through an attempt at muscular control of the breathing muscles.
4. Vocal resonance can be developed through a proper understanding of tone color (vocal timbre), so that uniformly excellent production of tones will result.

TONE CREATES ITS OWN SUPPORT

The first two postulates can be discussed as one. Tone creates its own support. How does a bird learn to sing? How does the animal learn to cry? How does the lion learn to roar? Or the donkey learn to bray? By practicing breathing exercises? Most certainly not. I have known many, many singers with splendid voices who have never heard of breathing exercises. Go out into the Welsh mining districts and listen to the voices. They learn to breathe by learning how to sing, and by singing. These men have lungs that the average vocal student would give a fortune to possess. By singing correctly they acquire all the lung control that any vocal composition could demand.

As a matter of fact, one does not need such a huge amount of breath to sing. The average singer uses entirely too much. A goose has lungs ten times as large as a nightingale but that doesn't make the goose's song lovely to listen to. I have known men with lungs big enough to work a blast furnace who yet had little bits of voices, so small that they were ridiculous. It would be better for most vocal students to emit the breath for five seconds before attacking the tone. One of the reasons for much vocal forcing is too much breath. Maybe I haven't thought about these things! I have spent hours in silence making up my mind. It is my firm conviction that the average person (entirely without instruction in breathing of a special kind) has enough breath to sing any phrase one might be called upon to sing. I think, without question, that teachers and singers have all been working their heads off to develop strength in the wrong direction. Mind you—this is not a sermon against breathing. I believe in plenty of breathing exercises for the sake of one's health.

A GOOD POSITION

Singers study breathing as though they were trying to learn how to push out the voice or pull it out by suction. By standing in a sensible position with the chest high (but not forced up) the lung capacity of the average individual is quite surprising. A good position can be secured through the old Delsarte exercise which is as follows:

I. Stand on the balls of your feet, heels just touching the floor.
II. Hold your arms at your side in a relaxed condition.

III. Move your arms forward until they form an angle of forty-five degrees with the body. Press the palms down until the chest is up comfortably.

IV. Now let your arms drop back without letting your chest fall. Feel a sense of ease and freedom over the whole body. Breathe naturally and deeply.

In other words, to "poise" the breath, stand erect, at attention. Most people when called to this "attention" posture stiffen themselves so that they are in a position of resistance. When I say *attention,*—I mean the position in which you have alertness but at the same time complete freedom,—when you can freely smile, sigh, scowl and sneer,—the attention that will permit expansion of the chest with every change of mood. Then, open the mouth without inhaling. Let the breath out for five seconds, close the mouth and inhale through the nostrils. I keep the fact that I breathe into the lungs through the nostrils before me all the time. Again open the mouth without allowing the air to pass in. Practice this until a comfortable stretch is felt in the flesh of the face, the top of the head, the back, the chest and the abdomen. If you stretch violently you will not experience this feeling.

SENSATIONS

I fully realize that much of what I have said will not be in accord with what is preached, practiced and taught by many vocal teachers and I cannot attempt to reply to any critics. I merely know what sensations and experiences I have had after a lifetime of practical work in a profession which has brought me a fortune. Furthermore I know that anything anyone might say on the subject of the human voice would be at variance with the opinions of others. There is probably no subject in human ken in which there is such a marked difference of opinion. I can merely try to describe my own sensations and vocal experiences. In trying to represent the course of the sensation I experience in producing a good tone, I have employed the following illustration. Imagine two pieces of whip cord. Tie the ends together. Place the knot immediately under the upper lip directly beneath the center bone of the nose, run the strings straight back an inch, then up over the cheek bones, then down around the uvula, thence down the large cords inside the neck. At a point in the center between the shoulders the cords would split in order to let one set go down the back and the other toward the chest, meeting again under the arm-pits, thence down the short ribs, thence down and joining in another knot slightly back of the pelvic bone. Laugh, if you will, but this is actually the sensation I have repeatedly felt in producing what the talking machine has shown to be a good tone. Remember that there were plenty to laugh at Columbus, Gallileo and even Darius Green of the Flying Machine.

Stand in "attention" as directed, with the body responsive and the mind sensitive to physical impressions. When opening the mouth without taking in air a slight stretch will be experienced along the whole track I have described. The poise felt in this position is what permitted Bob Fitzsimmons to strike a deadly blow with a two-inch stroke. It is the responsive poise with which I sing both loud and soft tones. Furthermore, I do not believe in an absolutely relaxed lower jaw as though it had been broken. Who could sing with a broken jaw?— and a broken jaw would represent ideal relaxation. The jaw should be slightly stretched but never strained. I think that the word relaxation, as used by most teachers and as understood by most students, is responsible for more ruined voices than all other terms used in vocal teaching. I have talked this matter over with numberless great singers who are constantly before the public, and their very singing is the best contradiction of this. When you hold your hand out freely before you what is it that keeps it from falling at your side? That same condition controls the jaw. Find it: it is not relaxation. If you would be a perfect singer find the juggler who is balancing a feather. Imagine yourself poised on the top of that feather, and sing without falling off.

CONTRASTING TIMBRES THAT LEAD TO A BEAUTIFUL TONE WHEN COMBINED

We shall now seek to illustrate two contrasting qualities of tones, between which lies that quality which I sought for so long. The desired quality is not a compromise, but seems to be located half way between two extremes, and may best be brought to the attention of the reader by describing the extremes.

The first is a dark quality of tone. To get this, place the tips of the second fingers on the sides of the voice box (Adam's apple) and make a dark almost breathy sound, using "u" as in the word hum. Do this without any signs of strain. Allow the sound to float up into the mouth and nose. To many there will also be a sensation as though the sound were also floating down into the lungs (into both lungs). Do not make any conscious effort to force the sound or place it in any particular location. The sound will do it of its own accord if you do not strain. While the sound is being made, there will be a slight upward pulling of the voice box, a slight tugging at the voice box. This, if course, occurs automatically, and there should be no attempt to control it or promote it. It is nature at work. The tongue, while making this sound, should be limp, with the tip resting on the lower front teeth. All along it is necessary to caution the singer not to strive to do artificial things. Therefore do not poke or stick the tip of your tongue against the front teeth. If your tongue is not strained it will rest there naturally. Work at this exercise until you can fill the mouth and nose (and also seemingly the chest) with a rich, smooth, well-controlled, well-modulated dark sound and do it easily,—with slight effort. Do not try to hold the sound in the throat.

The second sound we shall experiment with is the extreme antithesis of the first sound. Its resonance is high and it is bright in every sense. Place the fingers on the joints just in front and above holes in the ears. Open the mouth without inhaling and make the sound of "e" as in when. As the dark sound described before cannot be made too dark this sound cannot be made too strident. It is the extreme from the rumble of the drum to the piercing rasp of the file. I have called it the animal sound, and in calling it strident, please do not infer that the nose, or any part of the mouth or soft palate, should be pinched to make it nasal, in the restricted sense of that term. When I sing this tone it is accompanied with a sensation as though the tone were being reflected downward from the voice box over to each side of the chest just in front of the arm-pits and then downward into the abdomen. Here the great danger arises that the unskilled student will try to produce this sensation, whereas the fact of the matter is that the sensation is the accompaniment of the properly produced tone and cannot be made artificially. Don't work for the sensation, work for the tone that produces such a sensation of upward reflection, as though it arose at the back of the voice box and separated there, passed up behind the jaws to the points where your fingers are resting, entering the mouth from above, as it were from a point just between the hard and soft palates, and becoming one sound in the mouth.

The uvula and part of the soft palate should be associated with the dark sound. The hard palate and part of the soft palate should be associated with the strident tone.

THE TONGUE POSITION

In making the strident sound the tongue should rest in the same position as for the dark sound. The dark tone never changes and is the basic sound which gives fullness, foundation, depth to the ultimate tone. Without it all voices are thin and unsubstantial. The nearer the singer gets to this the nearer he approaches the great vibrating base upon which the world is founded.

Remember that the dark tone never changes. It is the background, the canvas upon which the singer paints his infinite moods by means of different vowels, emotions, and the tone colors which are derived in numberless modifications from the strident tone. Another simile may bring the subject nearer to the reader student. Imagine the dark tone and all the sensations in different parts of the body as a kind of atmosphere or gas which requires to be set on fire by the electric spark of the strident tone. The dark tone is all necessary, but it is useless unless it is properly electrified by the strident tone.

A PRACTICAL STEP

How shall we utilize what we have learned, so that the student may convince himself that herein lies the truth which, properly understood and sensibly applied, will lead to a means of improving his tone? If the foregoing has been carefully read and understood, the following exercise to get the tone which results from a combination of the dark and the strident is simple.

1. Stand erect as directed.
2. Open the mouth *without inhaling.*
3. Produce the dark tone ("u" as in hum).
4. Close the mouth and allow the air to pass in and out of the nostrils for a few seconds.
5. Open the mouth without inhaling.
6. Make the strident sound ("e" as in when).
7. Close the mouth and let the air pass in and out of nostrils a few seconds.
8. Open the mouth without inhaling.
9. Sing the vowel "Ah" as in *father* in such a manner that it is a combination of the dark tone and the strident tone.
10. Do this is such a way that all of the breathy disagreeable features of the dark tone disappear but its foundation features remain to give it fullness and roundness, while all of the disagreeable features of the strident tone disappear although its color-giving, light-giving, life-giving characteristics are retained to give the combination-tone richness and sweetness. A beautiful result is inevitable, if the principle is properly understood. I have tried this with many people who have sung but little before in their lives and who were not conscious of having interesting voices. Without a long course of vocal lessons or anything of the sort they have been able to produce in a short time—a very few minutes—a tone that would be admired by any critic.

A COMFORTABLE PITCH

It is to be assumed that the student will, in these experiments, take the pitch in his voice which is most comfortable. Having mastered the combination tone on "Ah" at any pitch, it will be easy to try other pitches and other vowels. "Ah" is the natural vowel, but having secured the "know how" through a correct production of "Ah" the same results may be attained with any other vowel produced in a similar way. "E" as in *see* has of course more of the strident quality, the high, bright quality and "OO" as in moon more of the dark, but even these extreme tones may be so placed that they become enriched through the employment of resonance of all those parts of the mouth, nose and body which may be brought naturally to reinforce them.

"PING"

I have never met a singer who was not looking for "ping" or what is called brightness. Most voices are hopelessly dead, and therefore lack sweetness. The voices are filled with night—black hollow gloomy night or else they are as strident as the caterwauling of a Tom Cat. The happy mean between the extremes is the area in which the singer's greatest results are attained.

Think of your tone, always. The breath will then take care of itself. If the tone has a tremulo, or sounds stuffy or sounds weak, you have not apportioned the right amount of breath to it, but you are not going to gain this information by thinking of the breath but by thinking of the tone.

LET YOUR OWN EARS CONVINCE YOU

Now, that is all there is to it. I am not striving to found a method or anything of the sort; but I have seen students waste years on what is called "voice placing" and not come to anything like the same result that will come after the accomplishment of this simple matter. Try it out with your own voice. You will see in a short time what it will do. Your own ears will convince you, to say nothing of the ears of your friends. All I know is that after I discovered this, it was possible for me to employ it and make records with so small a percentage of discard that I have been surprised.

It remains for the intelligent teachers to apply such knowledge to a systematic vocal course of exercises, studies and songs, which will help the pupil to progress most rapidly. Don't think that I am pretending to tell all that there is to vocal culture in an hour. It is a great and important study upon which I have spent a lifetime. However, as I said before, I have nothing to sell and I am only too happy to give this information which has cost me so many hours of thought to crystallize.

NOTE

1. James Francis Cooke, *Great Singers on the Art of Singing* (Philadelphia: Theo. Presser, 1921), 291.

34. Canaries in the Coal Mine: The Pure Vowel

Originally published in the *Journal of Singing*, volume 68, no. 1, 2011

I understand that miners used to take birds along with them when working underground. Canaries are particularly sensitive to poisonous gasses, which are often not detectable by human noses. As long as the birds were singing, everything was fine. If the singing stopped and the bird was not healthy, it was a warning that the miners had better get to the surface immediately!

This is not going to be an article on the singing of birds (although there is a huge literature on this topic). The thesis of this little article is that a distorted vowel is like a "dead canary in the mine" to the observant teacher. It is a warning that the voice is in a compromised condition. Addressing the vowel quality is therefore a critical step in the process of putting the voice right and should not be ignored.

I will avoid here a discussion of the acoustics of the vocal tract; I do not believe that another explanation of formants and partials is necessary in this discussion. Neither is this going to be discourse on the adjustment of vowels that an artist may utilize: vowel modification, *aggiustamento*, vowel migration, etc. This is a critically important skill that singers must learn to do, although there are the purists who claim that no change in vowel quality is ever needed or allowed. I appreciate how useful this position can be pedagogically, even if the truth of it in absolute terms is not supportable. Most of us realize that some shift of vowel quality is helpful if we are to optimize the resonance characteristics of the vocal tract as we sing throughout the full range of the voice. This idea was codified in the work of Berton Coffin. Dr. Coffin's systematic approach might be a bit bewildering upon first exposure to his famous vowel chart, but the acoustic science behind it is absolutely valid. In summary, slight adjustments to the formants (a formant is a resonance of the vocal tract) are made to maintain an optimal tuning between them and the partials or overtones emitted from the larynx during phonation. Since the partials are constantly changing frequency (because they move every time the pitch changes) the relationship between formants and partials is a constantly changing scenario. The result is a slight modification of the absolute quality of the vowel— call it what you want!

I hear so many singers who do not have a clear concept of vowel quality and who sing distorted vowels even in the range where no systematic adjustment should be necessary. If a singer cannot sing an Italianate [a] vowel anywhere in his range, the technique is fundamentally flawed and he will be in a constant state of excessive tension and compromised vocal production. Vowel distortion is a symptom of a poor concept of tonal quality and/or excessive tension in the tongue. This idea is the heart of the concept of the "pure vowel" which was addressed by Tosi in 1723.

> Let the scholar be obliged to pronounce the vowels distinctly, that they may be heard for such as they are. Some singers think to pronounce the first, and you hear the second; if the fault is not the master's, it is of those singers who are scarce got out of their first lessons. They study to sing with affectation, as if ashamed to open their mouths. Others, on the contrary stretching theirs too much, confound these two vowels with the fourth, making it impossible to comprehend whether they have said "balla" or "bella," "sesso" or "sasso," "mare" or "more."[1]

What does it mean to pronounce a vowel "distinctly"? Only part of the issue is intelligibility, as Tosi suggested at the end of the quote above. There is much more to it than this. There is an aural definition of vowel quality in the collective consciousness of good teachers and singers everywhere. If it were not so there would be no agreement on what constitutes beautiful singing at all. The existence of a universal defined vowel quality may be "pie in the sky," but is fundamental to what we do as voice teachers. Of course this assumes keen discernment in the ear of a voice teacher. We should all be able to agree upon what [a] should sound like in any voice, whether male or female, low or high. If this is so, then we should be able to recognize when it is distorted. This realization should motivate us to help the singer—at any level, correct the distortion. Cornelius Reid said:

> The full import of Tosi's advice becomes more forceful when considered in its practical implications. As the direction concerning vowel purity is more specifically given to include the degree of loudness, posture, and exact shading of the vowel, a student has been given an idea, i.e., the creation of a pure, undistorted *vowel quality*. Fixing his attention upon this idea of quality expressed in terms of vowel, he will, instead of producing a "made" quality artificial to his voice, create a genuine phase of tone color, unaffected and not in any way "put on." This is the initial and most important concept in voice training.[2]

There have been several theories over the years concerning the origin of vowels. You can find sources that say that vowels are formed by the vocal folds. We now know that this is not the case. The vowel is formed primarily by the position of the tongue, although all the articulators (lips, jaw, soft palate) can influence the vowel color. The position of the tongue in the oral cavity defines the frequencies of the formants of the vocal tract. The frequency of the two lowest formants defines the vowel quality. The [a] vowel is produced with the tongue literally pulled back in the throat. We have the idea that [a] is a relaxed vowel with a big open space in the back of the oral cavity. In reality there is a narrow constriction between the back of the tongue and the posterior pharyngeal wall. If there is not, then it no longer sounds like [a]. It requires a certain amount of tension in the tongue to pronounce [a] distinctly. For [i] the tongue is tensed in the front and the primary constriction is between the blade of the tongue and the alveolar ridge—right behind the front teeth. It is classified phonetically as a tense vowel because it takes a lot of effort by the muscles of the tongue to put itself into the right position to produce [i]. All the other vowels—the pure ones and the distorted ones are produced by appropriate tension in the tongue. That is what makes this such a difficulty. It is not that tension distorts the vowel, excessive tension distorts the vowel. How do you know if there is excessive tension? The vowel is distorted. It is as simple and as complex as that!

This is the reason that the identity of our target "pure" vowels is so important. It is like putting just the right amount of salt in a recipe. If there is too much you taste the salt, not enough and it loses something that it needs. Just the right amount of salt is required. If vowels do not have just the right color, just the right timbre then there is probably excessive tension in the tongue that is going to be a problem.

Head posture can also influence the quality of a vowel. If the head is tilted (chin against the sternum) the vowel is going to be distorted because the shape of the air space in the vocal tract has been distorted. This particular position usually darkens the vowel and gives the impression of more color or weight in the tone. I often see singers with heads lowered. This is to be avoided, even if we see our favorite professional singers doing it. If the head is habitually turned to one side or the other, the vowels will all be distorted. I call this "choir folder syndrome." The posture of the head relative to the body is turned—usually to the left—because we all have spent so many hours holding a folder in the left hand. The head can be too elevated as well—this tends to bring an open, yell-like quality to the vowel. Trying to correct these postural concerns can be a real difficulty, but it must be done if we are to help the singer to a better place.

It is common to find singers who are trying to impose a quality that they believe should be there but isn't by nature. Not to pick on mezzo sopranos, but it is verycommon to hear them darkening their vowels to make the voice "rich" or "dark" or "big" enough. (Do I need mention that baritones, sopranos, and tenors do this as well?) This is an artificial means of adding weight or color to the voice and there is always a price to pay for it. The distorted vowel is almost always produced by excessive tension in the tongue and it can absolutely take over the whole mechanism and leave it so tied up that it cannot do anything successfully. Flexibility can be compromised, pitch can be affected, and access to the low voice and the high voice is also inhibited. How many times have I personally encountered a soprano who did not have access to her high voice whose head remained tilted down (chin toward sternum) as she tried to sing above the staff. If I can get her to simply lift her head, sing a bright vowel and drop her jaw the voice easily goes through F5. All this could have been avoided if their ears had been trained to sing pure vowel qualities.

If a vowel is distorted it is the result of unnecessary tension somewhere in the vocal tract, most typically tension in the tongue. We can eliminate the excessive tension through specific exercises designed to get the tongue into motion and by focusing on the quality of the vowel. Both of these are legitimate approaches to purifying the vowel. Simply things like repeating [la] quickly on a scale or arpeggio can help free up the front of the tongue. Likewise, [ka] or [ga] addresses the back of the tongue. I say that if a muscle is tense, give it something to do! I also use [mnja]—an exaggerated "hummy" glide performed very slowly, relishing every moment of the tongue in motion to release tension in the tongue. Of course, at the same time we must create the correct vowel identity in the imagination of the student. If students cannot imagine it, they cannot sing it clearly. They cannot imagine it if they have no concept of what it should sound like.

I have always loved the sound of happy canaries!

NOTES

1. Pier Francesco Tosi, *Observations on the Florid Song,* trans. Mr. Galliard, ed. Michael Pilkington (London: Stainer & Bell, 1987), 6-7.
2. Cornelius Reid, *Bel Canto: Principles and Practice* (New York: Coleman-Ross Co., 1950), 58.

35. A Footnote to History

Originally published in the *Journal of Singing*, volume 68, no. 2, 2011

In volume two of *The Complete Treatise on the Art of Singing*, Manuel Garcia discussed the current principles guiding performance practice and how to effectively interpret the score. He elaborated extensively upon how the emotional motive behind the words should lead an artist to make choices concerning color, timbre, and dynamic level, including copious musical examples with very specific instructions or recommendations. It reminds me of how Boris Goldovsky would work with people on how to move across the stage; everything is motivated by the text and your relationship with the other characters. Some of us have read volume one of Garcia's important work, but volume two remains practically unknown to most of us. Of course, the purpose of the technical work described in volume one was so that one could execute the concepts in volume two.

In the second volume Garcia was careful not to discuss technical issues extensively; however, in a couple of places it seems that he could not resist the temptation to elaborate on the technical implications of his discussion. I find these footnotes very illuminating to Garcia's thinking, and they also shed some light on the thinking of the day. Following are two of those footnotes with comments by this author in asterisked footnotes.

In Chapter IV entitled "Expression," Garcia discussed timbres of the voice and how they communicate emotion. He reminded the reader that in volume one he pointed out that the sombre timbre was produced with the low larynx, and the clear timbre with the larynx in a slightly elevated posture. He said in this chapter that this understanding was simply not precise enough for the particular discussion of expressing specific emotions and that the "lips of the glottis" also play an important role in determining the timbre of the tone.

> When one very vigorously pinches the arytenoids together, the glottis is represented only by a narrow or elliptical slit, through which the air driven out by the lungs must escape. Here each molecule of air is subjected to the laws of vibrations, and the voice takes on a very pronounced brilliance. If, on the contrary, the arytenoids are separated, the glottis assumes the shape of an isosceles triangle,** the little side of which is formed between the arytenoids. One can then produce only extremely dull notes, and, in spite of the weakness of the resulting sounds, the air escapes in such abundance that the lungs are exhausted in a few moments. This enormous expenditure of air, which coincides with the production of veiled tones, indicates, according to us, that the glottis assumes the triangular form. One understands in fact that the air does not encounter any resistance toward the base of the triangle, and that it passes freely through the glottis almost without receiving any vibrations from it. It is only at the summit of the angle which parts from the thyroid cartilage that the condensations and rarefactions of the air are formed in a complete manner. Likewise, but in the opposite way, the brilliance of the sound and the fourfold or fivefold duration of the breath indicate that the organ is offering no more than a linear or elliptical slit. Let us add that when we pinch the glottis strongly, we synergistically bring about a

---

**The reader is reminded that this volume was written in 1847, and Garcia did not invent the laryngoscope until 1854. His theory concerning the triangular shape of the space between the arytenoids was not confirmed when he visualized the larynx with his own eyes. The effect of incomplete closure on the timbre of the voice is not in question.

> certain contraction, a kind of condensation of the tissues of the pharynx, most favorable states for the vitality [*nerf*] and the brilliance of the voice. On the contrary, the separation of the arytenoids brings about the softness of these same tissues, as a result of which, the sonorous waves, absorbed or poorly reflected, lose nearly all their brilliance. One sees, according to what precedes, that the timbre depends not only upon the modifications which the tube imparts to the sonorous waves, but also upon the place where these vibrations are born; that is to say that the voice receives its first character in the glottis, then from the numerous modifications of the pharyngeal and buccal cavities. One can summarize what proceeds in this principle: that each modification in the mode of production of the vibrations develops a different timbre, and each modification which the tube through which it passes undergoes modifies the original timbre.[1]

Garcia differentiated between the contributions of the larynx and the vocal tract to the resultant tone for the first time. Its implications are profound; they have withstood the test of time and are a part of contemporary understanding.

Later in the same chapter Garcia discussed specific timbre choices for particular purposes. He said a tone that lacks brilliance should be used to express feelings that are "disturbing to the soul": tenderness, timidity, fear, embarrassment, terror, etc. On the other hand, full brilliance is used to express vivid joy, anger, rage, and arrogance. In a footnote he said:

> The character of these timbres is necessarily related to the age and to the nature of the organ of each individual; let us even say that in young singer's extreme freshness should be the dominant quality: it indicates an organ which is in all its virginity. When a voice has been experienced by the emotions, age and work, it is modified; the freshness and the brilliance of the timbre make way for solidity and volume. Some young people make the error of wanting to imitate the organs of artists matured by the stage and by years, and by means of obstinacy, they succeed in aging their voices before their time. Sometimes, by a contrary error, some singers, already aged, borrow, in order to rejuvenate themselves, a childish timbre. The voice, like everything else, should follow the progress of time.[2]

Garcia offered sound advice to all generations of singers and teachers who are impatient concerning the critical decision of when to take on mature repertory!

In the next paragraph Garcia discussed the "language of the soul," which included the use of tears, interjections, cries, sighs, etc., and suggested that every dramatic singer should be familiar with them, as they "will become the principal source of his success." At the very end of the chapter on expression he included the longest footnote in the treatise. In it, Garcia argued that it is impossible for two vibratory mechanisms on the vocal folds to coexist and form a third. The end of the footnote will challenge your brain, as it did mine, but it's worth digging a little on this one.

We will terminate this chapter on the timbres by some important observations on the kind of voice incorrectly named the mixed voice, or mezzo petto; their rather technical nature advises us to put them into the form of a footnote.

In France, the highest part of the chest voice, including from f^1 to c^2, is given the name of mixed voice [*voix mixte*], whether the voice presents in this range the characters of the somber timbre, or, on the contrary, the tones are excessively clear and sharp [*diliées*]. In Italy this same range is called, in the first case, voce di petto, and the second, voce di mezzo petto. Whatever the character of these tones may be, they belong to the chest register,* but with a modification of volume with which we are going to concern ourselves. The designations of voix mixte and mezzo petto are equally improper, for they would make us suppose that these clear and high pitched tones are produced by the two mechanisms of the chest and falsetto registers at the same time. Now, physiologically, the simultaneous conjunction of two different mechanisms serving to produce the same note, or two notes in unison, is an unacceptable idea. In fact, the production of any one sound places the organ into entirely different and irreconcilable conditions, according as it is formed by the mechanism of the chest voice or that of the falsetto. The conformity of position could be encountered only in the simultaneous emission of two notes of different pitch. But then one would have to ask oneself if it is possible for the larynx to simultaneously produce two distinct tones. This possibility would be admissible by supposing a larynx shaped in such a manner that the different registers remain independent of each other in their mechanism. The history of music furnishes several examples of this phenomenon (see Part One). The thin character of the high tones of the so-called [*prétendue*] mixed voice results only, according to us, from the vibrations of the vocal cords, without the cooperation of the pharynx to reinforce them. One knows in fact that the intensity of a tone depends in general upon the number of partials which vibrate concurrently to form it, and upon the amplitude [*étendue*] of the vibrations which these partials execute; as a consequence, by reducing the number of vibrating partials, one decreases the sound. Moreover, it is demonstrated that the glottis, by the gradual tension of its lips and the successive reduction of its dimensions, produces the entire series of the chest tones; but the vibrations generated in the glottis acquire all their power only provided that they are extended into the ventricles, then into the pharynx.* According to that, one understands that if it were possible to limit the vibrations to the glottis by reducing the ventricles and the pharynx to a purely passive role, one would have the thinnest tones possible. It is in fact this result that a capable singer knows how to obtain, when on one side he completely relaxes all the muscles of the pharynx, and on the other he narrows more and more the column of air.** In these circumstances, the glottis, endowed with a complete liberty, can reach the final limits of its action. One is astonished to see tenors give, without any apparent effort, the notes a^1, b^1, c^2, $c^{\#2}$,

---

* Garcia stated that the male high voice is all chest register. This was a common understanding of registration for the day. Garcia's table of the registers gives the range of the chest voice up to C_5. We are so accustomed to thinking in terms of head voice starting at the *passaggio* around E_4 or F_4. Garcia would agree with Don Miller who has made the case that our perception of head voice is when the first vowel formant is lower in frequency than the second partial—often with the third harmonic in the second vowel formant. Scott McCoy and others report high closed quotients of .7 and .8 in operatic tenors singing all the way up to the top of the range. This suggests a laryngeal configuration that is indeed in chest mode. Our perception of the timbre changes when partials and formants interact, but it does not necessarily change the way the vocal folds are oscillating, and that is the point to which Garcia is addressing his comments.

* This is an early statement of what we now call the source-filter theory of vowel production. Garcia was the first to describe the powerful influence of the vocal tract acting as a resonating body upon the partials produced by the vocal folds. This theory of tone production is largely accepted today. The exact role of the ventricles in all this is still under examination, but scientists such as Johan Sundberg have suggested an important role.

** Perhaps readers are familiar with Ingo Titze's discussion of the influence of long, narrow tubes in terms of "inertive reactance" in the vocal tract and its influence upon the vibration of the vocal folds. The idea is that by elongating the epilaryngeal tube (by lowering the larynx), and by narrowing the opening of the additus (by "tuning" the position of the epiglottis), it literally feeds energy into the oscillation of the vocal folds by increasing the maximum flow declination rate—how suddenly the vocal folds close during each cycle. This creates increased energy into the high partials of the spectrum. This was an incredible insight on Garcia's part.

d^2. For women, and especially for children, in whom the glottis is very narrow at the same time as the arytenoideous muscles are very delicate, one does not know how high the series of tones might rise: we presume, a priori, that it would go at least to the g^2. We always advise that it is well if these notes are replaced in practice by the falsetto tones, preferable in all respects. If, while the glottis alone vibrates and all other parts of the instrument are relaxed, one moderately increases the pressure of the air, one obtains an increase of brilliance and intensity, but never an increase of volume. One can conceive the immense advantage which the male voice can draw from these observations, completely new in theory, and too rarely applied instinctively by some artists. They serve to clarify the relatively high notes ordinarily so thick in basses, baritones, and tenors. They indicate to these latter the mechanism to practice [*suivre*] to increase the range of the chest register; they permit the piano and mezzo voce use of this register in the high tones and thus the dispensation of the excessive use of the falsetto tones;[††] finally, they facilitate the union of the registers, etc.

The list of facts which we have just enumerated is completely modified when the contraction of the pharyngeal muscles is added to that of the glottis.

> The instrument then forms a single whole which the excessively held column can no longer make vibrate, but which was sufficient to set the glottis alone into motion. A vigorous thrust here becomes indispensable to put the entire mass into action. The voice in this case has all its amplitude and power, but can no longer reach the extraordinary notes which concern us. The bflat^1, b^1, and the c^2 require energetic efforts which in the preceding hypothesis would not be appropriate. The glottis is pinched as much as the tone which one wants to produce requires, but the column of air, too powerful for its muscular strength, obliges it to enlarge and to lower the pitch. I am fully aware of it, a very strong thrust raises the pitch without the need of new contractions; but this procedure does not entirely remedy the weakness of the vocal cords. The reduction of size is already a fact in the clear timbre, where no infrahyoideous muscles came into action to counteract the action of the arytenoideous muscles; but it is especially striking, if we produce the sounds in the somber timbre [*voix sombrée*]; the lips of the glottis must then, by their own contractive force, resist not only the column of air, but also the opposed and considerable force of the depressor muscles, which tend to open the thyroid cartilage and to separate these same lips. Some extraordinary efforts can momentarily overcome this resistance; but exhaustion and paralysis of the organ are the inevitable and unfortunately too frequent result of the use of the procedure.[3]

NOTES

1. Manuel Garcia, *Complete Treatise on the Art of Singing, Part 2*, translated and edited by Donald Paschke (New York: Da Capo Press, 1984), 152–153; originally published as *Nouveau Trait Sommaire sur l'Art du Chant* (Mayence: B. Schott's and Sons), 1847.
2. Ibid., 160.
3. Ibid., 161–162.

[††] This is the criticism that we read of the tenor Adolphe Nourrit—that his high voice was sung in falsetto and quite nasal, according to the English critic Henry Chorley, *Music and Manners in France and Germany* (1844). Duprez replaced Nourrit in *William Tell*, and in that role premiered the *do di petto*, the high C in the chest voice for the Parisian audience.

36. Bobble-heads

Originally published in the *Journal of Singing*, volume 68, no. 4, 2012

I recently had the pleasure of traveling to Columbia, South Carolina, where I met with wonderful NATS colleagues for their state-wide conference. I gave two lectures on historical pedagogic principles, and in the afternoon I worked with some talented young singers in a master class. While I was in the neighborhood, I visited Winthrop College and then Coastal Carolina University, where I did master classes for their students as well. Other recent travels included Luther College and Simpson College in Iowa. What an amazing experience to hear and work with such talented singers from the south and the heartland!

I am always honored by the opportunity to share ideas with fellow pedagogues and then to have the opportunity to apply those principles in a master class. After all, "the proof of the pudding is in the tasting!" I am happy to say that the concepts and ideas that I have shared over the years in this column actually work. I always see results, even within the parameters of a 15 or 20-minute session that one usually has within the context of a master class. I am quick not to take credit for this. These concepts are not original, they can be found in our own literature and are "tried and true."

Young precocious singers often discover that if they tilt their head down when they sing they can produce tones that simulate those of someone more mature. One of my students told me that she was even taught to do this. Making this type of postural adjustment sometimes results from exploring the physicality that characterizes singing in the *bel canto* style. A singer can learn to create a tone that is more complex, darker, and bigger by lowering the head and engaging the suspensory muscles that are associated with the larynx. There is often a big price to pay. It can prevent access to the high voice and often leads to premature fatigue. Taken to excess the vibrato can become uneven and slow. These singers often have difficulty moving their voices freely.

One does not have to read far in most of our legacy pedagogy texts to run across some discussion of posture. Typically, it focuses on the proper placement of the feet, posture of the chest or thorax—related to the breathing method that is being promoted, position of the arms and shoulders, etc. Tosi explained,

> 1.25 Let him take care, whilst he sings, that he gets a graceful posture and makes an agreeable appearance.
>
> 1.26 Let him rigorously correct all grimaces and tricks of the head, the body, and particularly the mouth...[1]

The importance of appearance has been a concern since the beginning. We as performers need to be free from poor habits that interfere with our ability to communicate ideas and emotions. Unwanted physical gestures related to poor singing habits distract from honest communication. Victor Fields quotes Cimini: "Keep the natural vertical position of the head, the neck free and loose."[2] A short sentence but it contains powerful advice. He summarizes then recent (1947) contributions of authors concerning posture.

> Because many common faults of phonation are attributed to faulty posture, authors of singing texts continually stress the importance of head position, chest position, tongue position, etc., as technical elements in maintaining a correct over-all posture of the body for artistic singing. Freedom and flexibility of the neck, shoulders, spine, ribs and chest are therefore contributing fac-

> tors in phonation. Artist singers caution beginners against assuming backward tilting head positions, flat chest or drooping shoulders. Such postural deformities impose abnormal strains upon the neck muscles which in in turn, might set up chronic laryngeal tensions and result in injuries to the vocal apparatus under the exertion of sustained singing.[3]

I met several young singers recently who immediately after taking their breath tilted their heads low with the chin tucked down (toward the sternum) before beginning singing. Their voices were in my judgment overly compressed and muscular, although the tone was attractive and sounded in some ways more mature than their age. One young soprano was amazed at how much easier her singing was when I insisted that she keep her head up when she sang "level with the horizon," as I put it. Her impression was that it whitened the voice and was "too easy to be right." My impression was that the voice found its more optimal freedom, resonance, and power. More amazing to her and her teacher was how this simple gesture gave her immediate access to her high voice. She had (like so many sopranos) experienced difficulty singing through the top of the staff, E_5–G_5. They tend to darken the vowel, tuck the chin, over-sing, and wonder why $F^{\#}_5$ is so hard! It is hard because they make it so by imposing too much constriction upon their singing through an otherwise innocuous gesture: tilting their heads down like they see some professional singers do. Keeping the head in a high, proud posture releases the grip on the larynx and allows it to do what it needs to do. I have seen this over and over again with singers of all ages and levels of experience, not just the precocious youngsters and not just the women!

Figure 1.

To share a little of my personal journey through the mine field of voice study, I can tell you that when I completed my own masters work in vocal performance years ago, I was in exactly the same boat. I studied as a baritone throughout my school years. I was told by several people that I would probably be a tenor one day, but no one knew how to help me make that happen. So, I had good ears, knew what I was supposed to sound like, and went about all the manipulations that my coordinated mechanism was capable, and produced fairly convincing sounds. Like the young soprano mentioned above, the sound was mature and impressive for about an aria and a half! After that, fatigue usually took over and took the bloom off of the end of the second aria due to excessive medial compression, excessive subglottal pressure, and distorted vowels. Several well-known, highly regarded teachers allowed me to continue that practice until I met Dr. Don Maxwell who teaches at Midwestern State University in Wichita Falls, Texas. Five minutes after I sang for Don he lifted my head off of my sternum and "took all my toys away." He immediately found my true voice (a light tenor) because the false one that I had created was not possible to produce without lowering my head. I was completely devastated and confused at what had just happened, and that is exactly what needed to happen. He showed me how to strengthen my weak chest register so that my voice had color and ring naturally and not artificially. He showed me how to sing freely, and that made all the difference.

I often suggest to singers that they should be able to imitate the action of their favorite celebrity bobblehead doll: able to move in all directions in small discreet motions and in all directions like it was mounted on their shoulders on a spring. This helps assure that their voice is appropriate for them at this point in their development and not imposed on a mechanism that is not ready to make sounds that their ears tell them they should make. It will also help assure that their voices will grow into their potential. Many of our revered artists, especially those with big voices sang with very open postures. My favorite example of this is Birgit Nilsson, one of the biggest, freest voices in memory (Figure 1).

Remember: you *can* learn something about voice teaching by reading a book!

NOTES

1. Pier Francesco Tosi, *Observations on the Florid Song,* trans. Mr. Galliard, ed. Michael Pilkington (London: Stainer & Bell, 1987), 7.
2. Victor Alexander Fields, *Training the Singing Voice* (New York: King's Crown Press, 1947), 82.
3. Ibid., 127.

37. Awesome Voices!

Originally published in the *Journal of Singing*, volume 68, no. 5, 2012

I listened recently to scores of recordings that were submitted to the university where I teach as a part of our required screening process. A successful screening leads to an invitation to do a live audition for admittance. Sadly, many of the voices that I heard suffered from leaky glottis! So many breathy voices! It is impossible to evaluate talent in the sound of rushing air.

Breathiness in young voices is common. It is the result of incomplete closure between the vocal folds in the posterior part of the glottis. There are two specific muscles that are responsible for closing the glottis firmly, the lateral cricoarytenoids and the interarytenoids. These muscles contract to bring the vocal folds together at the midline of the glottis, create medial compression between the vocal folds, and when functioning optimally close the small gap or "chink" that can occur between the arytenoid cartilages in the posterior part of the glottis.

Some voices never really deal with this issue and seem to be just naturally clear and bright. Others, however, can require specific attention that must be addressed in the studio. I think the issue is not always recognized for what it is; inexperienced ears do not always alert to breathiness. It can be so commonplace in our studios (if you work a lot of young singers) that we may come to accept it as normal! Or, if it is recognized, it may be that the teacher has been told that breathiness is just a normal part of the adolescent and teenage voice and they will simply out grow it. They may have been taught that it is better not to focus on this issue because to do so could lead to an unhealthy result.

The solution to the first case is to learn listen critically. Pay attention! All young voices are not breathy—learn to hear the difference. Young voices are capable of making clear ringing sounds. The young singers who are precocious and successful early on—in high school and middle school—are typically those with natural clarity or those who have been taught to sing a clear tone. This is the most defining characteristic that separates them from their less than remarkable colleagues. All breathy voices sound the same; the individual character of a voice does not show itself until the tone is clear. This is the reason that we can help a choir blend by adding a bit of breathiness (I call it "cushion" with my church choir). If you do it intentionally, great! If it is the only sound a singer is capable of doing then it is a primary limitation.

Our expectation for the teenager needs to be quite high. Young singers are capable of doing great things given the right developmental tools. Unfortunately, many voice teachers take the position of "do no harm" and pass the work to the next teacher, believing that they do not possess the requisite technical skills to address breathiness. This is not what we are being paid to do. It is our responsibility to recognize the issue and then to know how to lead the student to optimal vocal function. Once you recognize it, the cure is pretty simple and can be found in foundational developmental exercises from our historical legacy of training in the *bel canto* style.

The first point of attack is at the onset of the tone (pun intended). If the onset is breathy, the tone will remain breathy! If the onset is "neat and clean" as I call it, the tone is off on the right foot and has a better chance of remaining clear. The "firm onset" was described first by Garcia who called it the *coupe de la glotte*. As I described in an earlier column, this important concept has been misunderstood for many years and supplanted with the intentional use of airflow prior to the onset.[1] It is what William Vennard described as "well-coordinated" onset. It is interesting to listen to Vennard demonstrate onset in recordings of his teaching. It is clear that he is utilizing the correctly executed *coupe de la glotte*, and not what he describes.

"Neat and clean" gives the voice ring. A simple, failsafe method of teaching the "neat and clean" onset is to have your student speak the word "awesome" with enthusiasm. In the normal speaking voice this provides the correct model for the singing voice onset. The word is so commonly used today by young and old, it provides a great way to introduce this idea to the singer. Speak it— sing it: *come si parla, si canta!* This does not have to lead to a crude, harsh onset, as it has been so misconstrued over the generations. Neat and clean is not to be feared. There is no harm in beginning the tone with tone, not airflow. I would be so bold as to suggest that you should not be afraid to overdo it on the way to finding the right balance. If you hear a harsh click, it's too much, but if you hear an audible aspirate, it is not acceptable. Like any pedagogic process, we must be diligent in correcting every incorrect attempt. You have to train yourself to listen carefully: hear it and then correct it every time. I guarantee when the right balance is found, you will hear the difference in the tone quality instantaneously.

Our good friends and neighbors who are trained as speech pathologists are typically taught that the "glottal stroke" is harmful and to be avoided at all costs. A habitually harsh onset in the speaking voice can certainly lead to a harmful result. They often work with young voices whose energetic personalities and loquacious natures lead to harmful speech pattern, including constant harsh glottal onsets. This type of speech can lead to vocal nodules. A softer onset is helpful for them, especially if they are recovering from nodules or polyps. But the notion that a breathy onset and intimate voice quality is sufficient for artistic voice use is totally absurd. Remember, they most often deal with injured voices and work to rehabilitate them. We work with normal voices to make them extraordinary.

My typical approach to this is to have a young singer speak the word "awesome" on a low tone—in the range of the chest voice. For a young female voice, I would cue her with a C_4 from the piano and ask her speak it on pitch. Care must be taken to make sure that she is not offering a sung tone, which will probably not be like her speaking voice. Demonstrate in a spoken tone quality on C_4 the word "awesome," and then ask them to do the same. Once this has been successfully executed, go up and down the scale by half tones, but not higher than they can speak in the chest voice (speaking voice quality). Go as low as they can speak . . . you might be surprised at how low it will go. This can be easily accomplished within a minute or two. The next step is to follow the spoken word with a sung tone that has every characteristic of the spoken example using [a]. So, it would be a spoken "awesome" followed immediately by a sustained tone at the same pitch on an [a] vowel. Insist that they maintain the same quality for the total duration of the tone. Do this through the range of the chest voice. You might have to remind them that vibrato is a normal part of the singing voice and probably the only difference in the two tones. After the work in the chest voice, go to the middle range. This is much more difficult to accomplish here, but, with a little time and conscious effort, the middle voice will begin to take on the same clarity as the chest voice.

Another important exercise for ridding the voice of breathiness and establishing clarity in the voice is the staccato. Use simple arpeggios 1-3-5-8-5-3-1 on an [a] vowel using the "neat and clean" onset on every pitch. Most young singers and a lot of more mature singers use a slight aspirate for staccato, but this is not correct. As I discussed in another column, this exercise is very important for voice building, and to great extent it is because it trains the muscles that are responsible for closing the glottis.[2] Begin this simple arpeggio at B_3 for a young soprano. Make sure that the first tone is produced "neat and clean" and that it is in the chest voice. It doesn't last very long, but it must be clearly in the low mechanism. The other tones of the arpeggio will not be in the chest voice but must be articulated correctly. This will profoundly influence the quality of the B_4 if properly executed. Execute this exercise through the entire range of the chest voice on the low tone. The next progression of this work is to sustain both the initial and the top tones, that is, a sustained 1 followed by staccato 3–5 and a sustained 8, all on [a]. All the onsets must be "neat and clean." I guarantee remarkable results very quickly with this. After the bridge across the *passaggio,* start in the middle range and take it above the staff. Just pay close attention to details of the execution, the rest will take care of itself.

As a new tonal concept emerges, you must guide them to use it all the time. Giving a few minutes of intentional focus on this issue at the beginning of each lesson and then insisting that the singer is striving for clarity will lead to a difference that you will both soon appreciate. Inform then insist!

This is an important issue for young voices of all types. The process described above will work for young male voices as well. Simply adjust for the pitch differences. Many of the young singers that I listened to during the recent screening process were not recommended for a live audition because the voice was so breathy I could not properly adjudicate the potential in the instrument. College auditions are competitive, and we need to help our young singers have a successful experience. Many famous singers made professional operatic debuts in their teens. They did not achieve that goal by running a vacuum cleaner in their throats! That wasted air must be turned into beautiful tone. We can help turn their average voices into awesome voices!

NOTES

1. Stephen Austin, "The Attack on the *Coupe de la Glotte*," *Journal of Singing* 61, no. 5 (May/June 2005): 525–529.
2. Stephen Austin, "Staccato," *Journal of Singing* 60, no. 4 (March/April 2004): 405–407.

38. The Greatest Generation...

Originally published in the *Journal of Singing*, volume 69, no. 1, 2012

The most recent acquisition to my library of old pedagogy books is a copy of Mathilde Marchesi's *L'Art du Chant*, published in 1890[1]. It is in beautiful condition and in an excellent binding, published in parallel German, French, and English. I purchased the book online, and when I examined it for the first time, I found the following inscription on the front page:

S/Sgt. Otto R. Kundert
1 September-1945
Wiesbaden, Germany

A quick inquiry on the Internet reminded me that the war in Europe ended in May of that year. Sgt. Kundert must have been a soldier stationed overseas when he acquired this book on singing in war-torn Germany. In 1945 this book was almost sixty years old. After another quick trip to the Internet I found out that Wiesbaden was largely spared the destruction experienced by so many German cities, so it made a little more sense how a book like this might have been acquired in such trying times.

I entered Sgt. Kundert's name into my favorite search engine on the Internet (the modern source of all knowledge!) and found an audio recording of this same man in the Veterans History Project (Library of Congress, American Folklife Center).[2] I went to the Library of Congress website and listened to Mr. Kundert interviewed for almost two hours—a part of a large collection of interviews with men and women who had served our country in WWII. He talked about his youth in South Dakota where he grew up living with his grandmother and speaking only German with her. He talked about his early study of music and singing as a young man in Chicago, about his time in the war in Germany where he served as a translator, using the German that he learned while growing up. Interestingly, Mr. Kundert talked a lot about his singing and voice study in the interview. He mentioned at least a dozen different voice teachers throughout his life, including Marshall Bartholomew, the long-time director of the University Glee Club in New York City. He discussed at length his voice study while stationed in Wiesbaden with a Russian teacher who called himself Alexander Revala. He said that he had two lessons a day and learned to sing his high C under his tutelage. He said that when he finally achieved that goal he "buried his face in his teacher's lap and cried."

Staff Sergeant Kundert was in charge of a War Crimes Branch translation section for the Nuremburg war crimes trials. He also interrogated many German soldiers who were returning from the Russian front. After the war he spent almost thirty years working for the CIA as a German and Russian translator and economic analyst. He retired in 1976. I also found his obituary online. He died in December, 2008 at the age of 88. He was a life-long singer and music educator, along with his other work for our country. What an unexpected and incredible story. In case you're not sure about the title of this column, this is *provenance* at its best! The story behind this book makes it priceless to me.

L'Art du Chant was written by Mathilde Marchesi (nee Graumann, 1826–1913). Marchesi was a highly respected voice teacher of women. After her early studies with composer Carl Otto Nicolai (1810–1849) in Vienna, she studied with Garcia in Paris, beginning in 1845. In 1849 she moved to London, presumably following her teacher, Garcia, who fled Paris because of the revolution. She enjoyed great success as a concert singer in Europe and married the Italian baritone Salvatore Marchesi in 1852. Her teaching career began with an appointment at the Vienna Conservatory in 1854 and later at the Cologne Conservatory in 1865. She ultimately returned to Paris and taught there for the reminder of her life. Among her most eminent students were Dame Nellie Melba, Emma Calvé, and the American soprano, Emma Eames. Marchesi was highly decorated by the royal courts of Europe. She published twenty-four books on singing, including *L'Art du Chant* (opus 21).

L'Art du Chant was written in the nineteenth century tradition of a progressive method. The book has an extensive preface and then three parts. In Part I are elementary exercises, Part II has thirty vocalises, and Part III has twelve vocalises for two voices. This book is still available in many forms and is a tremendous resource, particularly for women's voices. In the preface Marchesi sets down the fundamental tenets of her teaching. Here is her opening section as it appears in the English column of Otto Kundert's book.

Preface

The present, the second edition of my "Art of singing," which I have revised and enlarged in accordance with the experience of the last twelve years of my teaching, comprises the theoretical-practical part of my system. It includes exercises and elementary and progressive Vocalises for the development of the mechanism of the voice; a series of two-part Vocalises, for practice in singing a second part, and lastly, melodies with words, to combine articulation with vocalization.

I take this occasion of once more calling attention to the fact which I have laid down in various prefaces to my other works, namely that in order to achieve speedy and successful results, it is necessary to set difficulties before the pupil one by one, and to assist him in overcoming them, by presenting them in their natural and progressive sequence.

Teachers and students cannot be too strongly urged to spend as much time as possible over the elementary vocal studies, and to pass on to singing with words only when the pupil's voice is perfectly placed throughout its entire compass, when the three registers are completely blended, and when the vocal organ has acquired a sufficient degree of ease and flexibility.

I assume that each teacher before undertaking the difficult task of the formation of the voice, and the heavy responsibility of the artistic future of his pupils, has studied anatomy, physiology and acoustics to the extent requisite for laying down and carrying out the following precepts.

1. Position of the Pupil

The position of the body, while singing, should be as natural and unconstrained as possible. The pupil should stand straight, the head erect, shoulders drawn back without effort, and the chest expanded. All stiffness in the body must be avoided in order to secure the greatest possible freedom of action to the organs concerned in voice production.

2. Position of the Mouth

The smiling mouth recommended by so many old and modern masters is entirely contrary to the laws of the formation of sound. The pupil should open the mouth quite naturally, lowering the chin, as though to pronounce the vowel A slightly darkened, and should keep it unmoved during the continuance of the emission of the sound.

It is necessary to remind the student, that the lower part of the mouth alone opens, the upper part remaining fixed; hence the necessity of lowering the chin.

3. Respiration

Normal respiration, characteristic of a healthy person, is diaphragmatic or abdominal. In the two other ways, which we reject, viz: clavicular and lateral respiration, the lungs are but partially filled, hence the necessity of breathing more frequently and the impossibility of singing long phrases in one breath.

4. The attack of a note (Stroke of the glottis)

The mechanical action which constitutes the attack or placing of the voice, is produced by preparing the glottis and the mouth to form some particular vowel sound.

The type of vowel preferable for the formation and development of the voice is however the Italian A, slightly darkened as indicated in #2.

The pupil should understand clearly that the stroke of the glottis is a normal function of the vocal organ, and that he has simply to subordinate to his will the spontaneous action which was developed at his first attempt to cry as an infant. It is in point of fact, by means of this innate aptitude that we form all vowels in speaking.

5. The three registers of the female voice

Female voices are classed thus:

Contralto, Mezzo-Soprano, dramatic Soprano and high, light Soprano (sfogato).

The upper limit of the chest register in all female voices varies between these notes: E4, F4, and F#4.

Contralto and Mezzo-Soprano voices have usually a chest register of much greater compass than Soprano voices, which extend more or less into the lower notes.

In order to equalize and unite the chest register with the middle register, the pupil must darken slightly the last two chest notes in ascending and open them in descending the scale. Every strain made on the upper notes of a lower register not only increases the difficulty of developing the strength of the first notes of the following register, but at length renders the union of the two registers completely impossible.

When the limits of the registers are not clearly defined, there will always be a series of uncertain weak and false tones in singing scales with full voice, or in sustained passages.

According to the modern pitch, the highest chest note of almost all Contralto and Mezzo-Soprano voices will vary between E4 and F4.

There are some which, on account of an unusual position of the larynx, never succeed in developing the head-voices. These voices of short compass, which use only the chest and middle registers, are however, rare exceptions, and can only aspire to a concert career.

The limit of the middle register for all female voices may vary between the following notes: F5-F#5. The general rule however places G5 as the last note.

6. Method of Practicing

Rational and progressive study is capable of developing a great elasticity as well as considerable suppleness in the muscles of the sound-producing organs without ever fatiguing them; whereas, the least excess of practice produces exhaustion.

At the commencement of his studies, the pupil should therefore not sing too long at a time, and during the first few days, he should not practice more than five or ten consecutive minutes. Practice thus limited may be repeated three or four times a day at long intervals. The time devoted to exercising the voice may be increased five minutes at a time up to half an hour.

If, as happens frequently, the pupil, not being imbued with these precepts, practices at home longer than the teacher has sanctioned, the sad result, fatigue of the voice (of the vocal chords [*sic*]) will rapidly ensue.

7. Analyses

The majority of pupils, who study singing are not very musical. Consequently they begin to sing the exercises and scales mechanically, guided solely by ear, without paying any attention to the length of each bar and to rhythmical division, and thus without appreciating the respective value of each note. This habit of allowing oneself to be guided by ear is very harmful and causes an incalculable waste of time to the pupils. Furthermore, by thus always feeling for the note, the pupil is obliged to repeat the same passage incessantly, which, instead of assisting progress, ends by fatiguing the vocal organs. From the first lesson therefore, the student should accustom himself to analyse, that is to say, to reflect on what he has to do: in a word, it is necessary that the material work should be preceeded by mental study.

If this analytic system of study is adopted by the pupil from the beginning, it will prove very useful to him throughout the different progressive stages of his studies, and also the practice of his profession in studying new characters.

8. Style

With the exception of national songs which have an entirely popular and local character, peculiar to each nationality, in point of styles, there are in the world but two, a good and a bad style, just as there are but a good and a bad method of singing. It is utterly wrong therefore, to talk of a German, French, English or Italian style or method of singing in the strict sense of the word. In all ages, we have had in fact hundreds of examples to show that great singers of both sexes, belonging to diverse nationalities have been received with the same enthusiasm in Rome, Paris, London, Vienna, St. Petersburg, etc.

Many teachers of singing maintain that in modern vocal music, where sustained and declamatory phrases have replaced rapid runs and graceful turns, singers do not require to develop the mechanism of the voice, thus only fatiguing the vocal organs and robbing the pupil of valuable time.

As regards fatigue of the voice from study, its avoidance depends entirely on the skill of the teacher and the intelligent receptivity of the pupil.

As to the technical requirements of the sustained and declamatory phrases, the statements are erroneous.

A singer who has learned to breathe properly, equalized her voice and blended the registers, and who has systematically developed the flexibility of the larynx, the elasticity of glottis and resonant cavities, so as to be able to produce all possible shades of timbre, intensity and expression, can unquestionably sing sustained and declamatory phrases perfectly well without fatigue or effort, that is to say without exaggeration or screaming. Whereas another singer, who is struggling with her breathing and the mechanism of her voice, and who consequently exaggerates and disfigures the modern musical phrase by screaming, very soon ends by fatiguing her voice.

Every art consists of a technical and an aesthetic part; he who is insufficiently prepared to overcome the difficulties of the former, will never attain perfection in the latter, be he even a genius.

January 1890.

Mathilde Marchesi

Summary

In 1988 Tom Brokaw wrote a popular book describing the generation of Americans who grew up during the depression and who then went on to defend the United States and Europe during the Second World War.[3] He suggested that it was the tempering of that generation, through the hardships of the first part of the twentieth century that led those same people to create the greatest nation on earth in the second half. Staff Sergeant Otto Kundert was a member of what Brokaw calls "the greatest generation." Mathilde Marchesi was only a voice teacher, and in no way am I equating the two, but she was a part of another great generation who had a clear vision of how to train the human voice to accomplish the things that Otto Kundert pursued his whole life—even while he was doing the work of the United States government in Europe. That these two lives crossed in any way is fascinating to me. That they "met" in Germany and that we know anything about this story is incredible! Say what you will, the Internet is an amazing thing.

Notes

1. Mathilde Marchesi, *L'Art du Chant* (Leipzig: Aug. Cranz, 1890).
2. http://lcweb2.loc.gov/diglib/vhp/story/loc.natlib.afc2001001.04797/transcript?ID=sr0001.
3. Tom Brokaw, *The Greatest Generation* (New York: Random House, Inc., 2008).

39. Hints on Singing... Hints Indeed!

Originally published in the *Journal of Singing*, volume 69, no. 2, 2012

Manuel Garcia II was only thirty years old when he was appointed to the faculty of the Paris Conservatory in 1835. It was quite an honor for such a young teacher. His training and experience with his famous father and the family troupe of singers (including sisters Pauline Viardot and Maria Malibran) were excellent preparation for a career of teaching.

Garcia published *The Complete Treatise on the Art of Singing* in two volumes, 1840 and 1854. Volume one was a description of the vocal mechanism and a complete method for training the voice; volume two was a detailed summary of performance practice in the mid-nineteenth century. Garcia did not invent anything new, but recorded the traditions of voice teaching that he learned from his father. Garcia stated in volume one:

> It is his method which I have wanted to reproduce by trying to reduce it to a more theoretical form and by attaching the results to the causes.[1]

Garcia's method is important because it is a description of the common practice of training singers during the time when the art form reached its pinnacle. It took Garcia over 500 pages to deliver his understanding of the art of *bel canto*.

Forty years later Garcia restated his thinking in his last book, *Hints on Singing* published in 1894.[2] After forty years of teaching some of the greatest singers of the age it took him only seventy-five pages to say what he thought we should know. *Hints on Singing* was written in a question/answer format, that is, a Socratic method of teaching. It is an easy read and widely available (it can be downloaded from the Internet at no charge), unlike *The Complete Treatise*, which unfortunately is difficult to find.

Below is an extended excerpt from *Hints on Singing*. Garcia is discussing where a singer is to take a breath. (Garcia is nothing if not practical!) I encourage you to study the music examples closely; many remain well known to us today. This excerpt begins on page 54 of the text. In the footnote, H. K. refers to Herman Klein, who helped Garcia with the editing.

38. Breathing Places

Q. Where is a singer to breathe?

A. Mere common sense forbids breathing in the middle of a word or between words intimately united by grammatical sense. So, obviously, the singer must breathe where the punctuation of words and music agrees.

Q. What if the melody, offering no rests, overtasks the breathing power of the singer?

A. The knowledge of the extent of phrases, their sections, and figures will assist to find places where to introduce rests [Example 1], and even, if necessary, to make those places by the interpolation of words [Example 2].

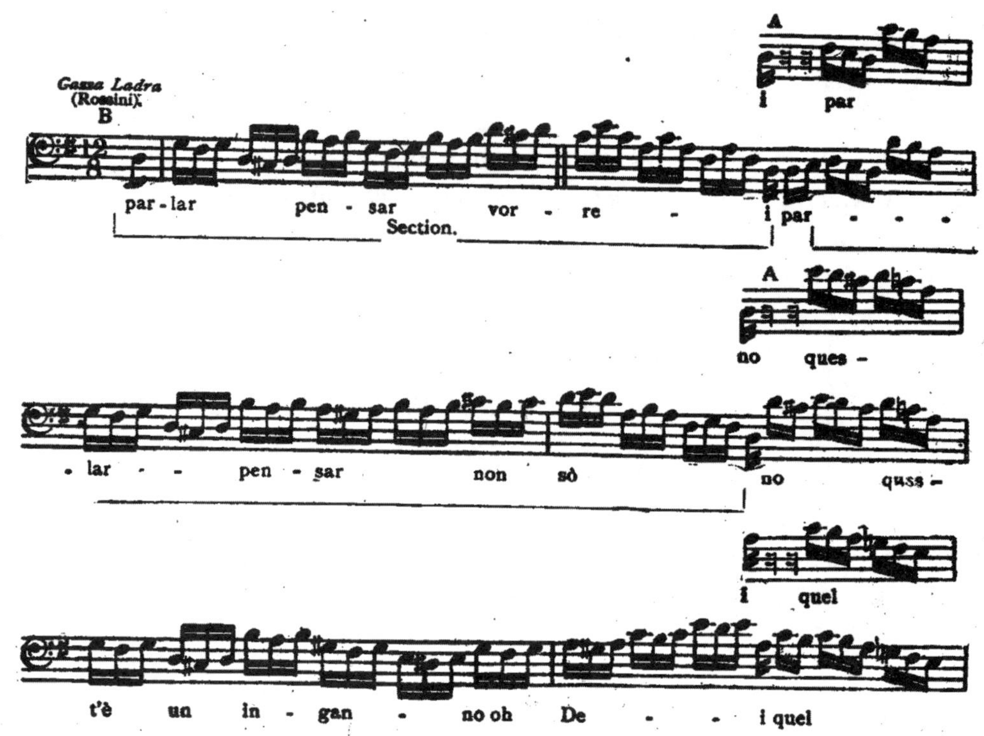

Example1.

Q. Is it always possible to introduce words?

A. In cases where this device is not convenient, if it be absolutely necessary to divide a word by breathing, the singer must then dissimulate the action with such art that the audience ignores it absolutely. To betray the necessity by the slightest noise, pause, or movement, would be a great fault. The preceding examples show the importance of being in full possession of breath before a difficult point. As it is not always possible to breathe deeply at the last moment, this must be done at the nearest preceding long rest, while the partial expenditure needed in the interval is recovered by half-breaths. As thus: [Example 3]

Q. Have you any particular case to mention?

A. In the following example it is easy to conceal the inspiration if taken through the nose while preparing the explosive *t*, for example: [Example 4]

When a cadenza occurs after a long holding note, the singer, if necessary, may take advantage of the orchestral accompaniment to breathe: [Examples 5 and 6]

When two notes are united by a portamento and breath must be taken between the two, this must be done after the portamento. [Example 7]

In some particular cases the effect is enhanced by suppressing the rests which separate the two phrases. [Example 8]

Example 2, page 1.

Example 2, page 2.

Example 3.

Example 4.

Example 5.

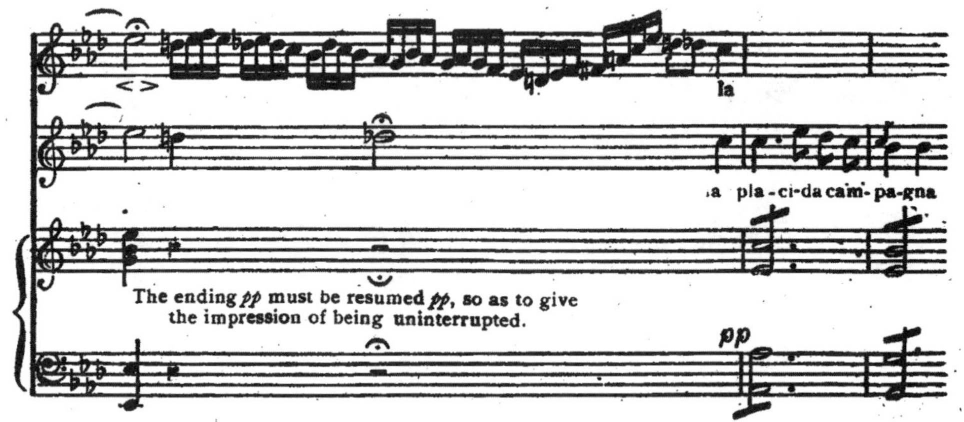

Example 6.

Example 7.

Example 8.

SUMMARY

There is good reason that Garcia is still acknowledged as one of the greatest teachers who ever lived. He was exceptionally insightful and knowledgeable about the anatomy and function of the vocal mechanism and thoroughly trained in the tenets of *bel canto*. He recorded for posterity the common practice of teachers who trained generations of singers who premiered great operatic, oratorio, and song repertory of the eighteenth and nineteenth centuries. His methods are applicable for singers in this age as they have been in the past. You can learn something about teaching voice from reading a *good* book.

NOTES

1. Manuel Garcia, *Complete Treatise On the Art of Singing, Part 1,* translated and edited by Donald Paschke (New York: Da Capo Press, 1984), 41–42; originally published as *Nouveau Traité Sommaire sur l'Art du Chant* (Genève: Minkoff Éditeur, 1847), XIX.
2. Manuel Garcia, *Hints on Singing* (London: Ascherbert, Hopwood and Crew, Limited, 1894).

40. Building Strong Voices—Twelve Different Ways[1] Part 1

Originally published in the *Journal of Singing*, volume 69, no. 3, 2013

If you examine pedagogic sources from the eighteenth and nineteenth centuries, you find concepts and forms of exercises that were commonly practiced. Historical methods were progressive in nature, like a traditional instrumental method, an approach that is not commonly practiced today in voice training. I have written about many of these over the last several years in this column. In this piece, however, I want to present a list of a dozen exercises that will result in vocal growth and development when properly and consistently applied in the studio and practice room.

Here are a few assumptions that I believe will help us identify a number of tools for building strong voices:

Premise 1: Teachers have been successfully building voices for several centuries and many have recorded their ideas for posterity.
Premise 2: Voice science has helped us understand the way the voice works and therefore has given us a means of judging the effectiveness of a particular method. This is particularly helpful if we are considering methodology that is outside our own personal experience.
Premise 3: Most eighteenth and nineteenth century historical methods focused on training the larynx as the primary component of the vocal instrument.
Premise 4: The concept of the "pure vowel" has always been a primary tenet of the study of elite singing. A vowel is formed by the position of the articulators: tongue, jaw, larynx, soft palate, and lips. A well-produced vowel requires a certain amount of tension to produce it correctly, but excessive tension distorts the quality of the vowel. A distorted vowel quality indicates excessive tension that will interfere with optimal vocal production.
Premise 5: The concept of *voce chiusa* represents to singing what *chiaroscuro* represents to all art: a balance of darkness and brightness. Many important historical methods state that *voce chiusa* should be established right away and that it will facilitate the other studies, particularly those concerning equalization of registers. Most modern methods do not even mention this important concept in favor of "forward placement," "frontal or nasal resonance," and other timbral directives.

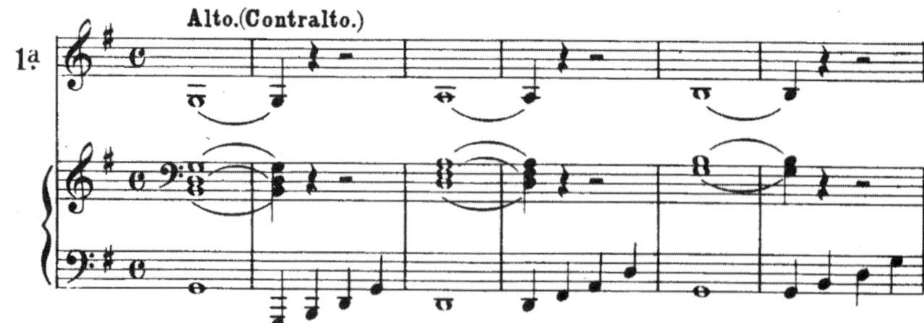

Example 1. ***Sostenuto*** **exercises from Franz Abt,** ***Practical Singing Tutor for All Voices.***

The exercises below are commonly found in eighteenth and nineteenth century methods. Music examples are taken from original sources. The exercises are presented in the order in which they were typically studied; the implication is that the order makes a difference.

1. *Sostenuto* or Sustained tones.[2] Historical progressive methods typically begin with sustained tones. It is the most fundamental vocal expression, and yet requires an extraordinary combination of effort from the phonatory, respiratory, and articulatory systems. *Sostenuto* requires that the singer maintain a tone at the same pitch and intensity for the duration of the exercise, typically over several seconds. These exercises always begin in the low range because of the long held belief that all voices gain from developing the low mechanism (chest register). Strength in the low mechanism can be likened to the concept of "core strength" in exercise physiology: a strong core (primarily abdominal, thoracic, and back muscles) provides the foundation that the body needs to do everything else well. A strong chest voice provides the strength for the entire instrument for all voice types. I will address this further in one of the later points.

Sostenuto exercises are to be sung at the maximum intensity level that the voice can produce freely and without distortion. The voice will grow through the daily practice of *sostenuto*. In most historical methods the exercise is accompanied in order to encourage a sense of musical expression. The vowel varied somewhat, but most sources began with [a]. Example 1 is the first exercise in a well-known method by Franz Abt that is still available today.[3] It is taken from the book for alto voice. Notice that the initial pitch is G_3; no doubt that Franz Abt expected this exercise to be executed in the chest register.

Sustaining a tone strengthens the intrinsic musculature of the larynx. It is an isometric exercise for the thyroarytenoid and the cricothyroid muscles, the two muscles that control pitch and register. The relative simplicity of the gesture provides the opportunity to address a number of other technical concerns, including onset (discussed in detail below), proper breath management and support, vowel purity, posture, and facial repose. The benefit is belied by its simplicity. Most methods include a full octave ascending and descending by whole or half steps. It is not a trivial task to execute—you really feel like you have done some work at the completion of this task. One of my doctoral students commented to me that "there is no place to hide" in this exercise! Indeed. No detail is small enough *not* to be addressed along the way.

2. *Portamento*.[4] Most historical methods introduce *portamento* immediately following *sostenuto*. It was considered to be a vitally important tool in voice building, not just a musical device. *Portamento* is to the voice what *t'ai chi ch'uan* is to the body: a controlled, fluid exchange of dominance between opposing muscles. A *portamento* is a change from one pitch to another that is evenly distributed along the way: a continuity of tone from the first to the second note.

Imagine a practitioner of *t'ai chi* going through his or her exercises: no discrete movements, but smooth motion from one position to the next. We should have a similar goal when singing *portamento*. When I ask a singer to sing a *portamento* on the interval of a fifth, there is typically some underlying scale-wise movement. The ability to do it smoothly requires great skill and usually has to be carefully studied. In the beginning, a singer may be resistant to the sound when it is correctly produced, because it just feels sloppy to them. I sometimes liken the correct execution of *portamento* to the sweeping of the second hand of certain types of clocks: smooth and continuous. When poorly executed we hear discrete movements like the ticking of a different kind of clock.

Example 2. **Portamento exercises by Manuel Garcia from *The Complete Treatise on the Art of Singing* (1847).**

Manuel Garcia's monumental work *The Complete Treatise on the Art of Singing* is typical of nineteenth century methods in that it includes specific exercises for *portamento*.[5] He begins with small intervals and progresses to larger ones. I find it much easier to begin with larger intervals and narrow them as skill develops over time (Example 2).

The practice of *portamento* trains a smooth coordination between the thyroarytenoid and the cricothyroid muscles of the larynx.

Example 3. **Legato exercises by Luigi Lablache, Complete Method of Singing.**

As these muscles are strengthened through the use of *sostenuto, portamento* trains them to work together along the way, keeping the voice free. *Portamento* requires a stable and constant breath flow, or support. Any intentional change in pressure from the respiratory system will be evidenced by unevenness in the loudness and quality of the vowel. This is a good time to address the support mechanism and a chance as well to discuss the application of subglottal pressure smoothly and continuously.

Portamento was also considered to be a primary register unification device. The underlying principles of register study will be addressed more fully later, but suffice it to say that there are innate qualities of the chest voice that are desirable throughout the whole range: clarity, breath efficiency, and a certain robust quality. The chest register is limited to a particular range and should not be used where it does not belong, but some of the desirable qualities of the chest voice can be transported beyond its pitch boundaries through the use of specific exercises, including the *portamento.* A good example of this would be to have a soprano or alto sing [a] energetically on B_3 (once the chest voice has been firmly established) and then quickly ascend to the upper octave without disengaging the voice—using a quick but distinct *portamento* to B_4. This exercise can help bridge the *passaggio* (usually around E_4 or F_4) and helps to equalize the registration event. *Portamento* can assist middle tones to take on the clarity of lower ones.

Portamento is also one of the traditional solutions to the breathy middle voice, so commonly found in young singers. The more contemporary notion of exercising the notes in the middle range to strengthen them and to thereby eliminate these problems is very common, but not as effective as the historical method. Exercising the middle register as a way to strengthen the middle register usually results in vowel distortion and hyper adduction. Addressing it from the historical concept that it is the "meeting place" of the low mechanism and the high mechanism can more effectively result in a middle voice that has strength and clarity. Like *sostenuto, portamento* provides the opportunity to focus on a number of other technical issues, including vowel quality, posture, support, and facial repose.

3. *Legato.*[6] *Portamento* provides the technical foundation for connecting the tones without discrete motion or sliding—a true *legato*. These exercises can take many forms. Example 3 is from a method by the famous nineteenth century basso Luigi Lablache (1794–1858).[7]

Example 4. **Legato interval studies from Cinti-Damoreau's *Method of Singing* (n.d.).**

I always ask new students to sing a five-note scale, usually starting on C (C_3 or C_4 depending upon the gender of the student). I inevitably hear discrete sounds on all or most tones, rather than a *legato* scale. Between each adjacent pitch they introduce a discontinuity of the tone, involving a change in the glottis. It can either be a separation of the vocal folds that creates an ever-so-slight aspirate between each note, like "ha-ha," or little glottal stop-starts. Between these two extremes (or accompanying them) might be a slight modulation of the tone from the breath. Building legato in the voice will absolutely promote growth of the voice. Legato is the default articulation and is to be used unless there are articulations marked in the score or there are other specific circumstances where another articulation is understood, as in *aspirato,* to be discussed at a later time. This is stated specifically in multiple sources.

4. Other legato interval studies. Traditional method books from the past typically included many varied forms of interval studies. The two exercises in Example 4 are taken from a method book written by Madame Cinti-Damoreau, a famous soprano with the Paris Opera in the 1820s and 1830s.[8] She went on to teach at the Paris Conservatory of Music, and her method was adopted by the school for use by the entire student body. Although there is no date in my original copy of this book, the best publication date that I can determine from secondary sources places it in 1849.

Singing increasingly wide intervals while maintaining a *legato* line supports the building of the voice in many ways. As already mentioned in the discussion of *portamento,* interval studies help to unify the disparate registers of the singing voice by giving the voice the experience of singing through the breaks, or *passaggi,* often enough that the boundaries begin to disappear. I liken this to what happens when you walk repeatedly through a field along the same route. Eventually a path begins to form, and what was once rough and uneven becomes smooth and easily traversed.

Studies like those found in Example 4 can also help singers desensitize themselves to unnecessary concerns of the high notes in their own voices. Singers should be encouraged to sense that all the notes emanate from the same place, eliminating any sense that there is high or low. I suggest to them that they feel all the notes on one level or plane so that they do not reach up for the high notes or down for the low notes. In Example 4b, for instance, the singer should sense all notes emanating from the first tone—the C_4 (middle C). The singer supports the first tone and then sings E_4 without any evidence of disconnecting the tone or changing the vowel.

Example 5. **The great "Rossini Scale" as found in Cinti-Damoreau's *Method of Singing* (n.d.).**

Each interval proceeds in the same way with the lowest tone serving as the anchor to all the rest. The singer should be cautioned not to provide intentional extra effort to the higher tones, but to let the body respond naturally to the extra physical demands of singing the higher pitches. He should monitor himself in a mirror to assure that the repose of the body remains calm and that no facial or articulatory distortions occur as he goes through the exercise.

Another exercise, also from Cinti-Damoreau's method, is attributed to Rossini (Example 5). It should be sung *legato*. In the male voice this exercise is great for training through the *passaggio* using [o] or [u] at the top to keep the throat open (larynx down). The male voice should approach the top with limited change in the mouth space; in other words, without dropping the jaw. Any change of the natural repose of the singer should be avoided. After [o] and [u] have been established the singer should use [a], but allowing the work from the previous two vowels to inform the throat they will avoid an open yell at the top.

This is also a good exercise for training the soprano and mezzo-soprano to drop the jaw as they go above the top of the treble staff. This is called formant tuning, and it allows the high voices to gain in intensity by tuning the lowest vowel formant close to the fundamental frequency. This will be taken up in greater detail in a later discussion, but suffice it to say that this is a critical issue for the female singer and it should be specifically trained. It is so common to see a young woman struggling with her high notes when the solution is so simple: "Drop to the top"! I have experienced so many times an instantaneous release of the tensions in singing high notes resulting in guaranteed smiles of amazement from a young singer who first experiences this in her singing.

5. Onset.[9] The onset must be addressed at the very beginning of the work. It is a part of the proper execution of *sostenuto, portamento,* and *legato*. The proper way to begin a tone has been a controversial issue at least since Manuel Garcia first described what he observed singers doing in the professional marketplace of his day. Garcia coined the term *coupe de la glotte,* or "shock of the glottis," as the ideal onset of tone.

EXERCISES TO SECURE THE RIGHT ACTION OF THE GLOTTIS.

In commencing these exercises I stated that the word *sca* would be used on account of certain advantages its structure secured, as to a pleasant and natural position of the mouth, and the proper stroke of the glottis.

I need not here dilate upon the difficulty of obtaining from a beginner in the study of music a correct emission of the vowel *a:* it is sufficient that this is the fact. and it was to avoid the loss of time that the word *sca* was used. But we have now arrived at a point where we can dispense with it, and use the proper vowel *a.*

In singing, if you wish to alight upon the tone with neatness, with true intonation, and will not have the tone preceded by some undesirable aspiration, like *h'a* ; or, if you wish to avoid wasting a particle of your breath, the proper action of the glottis must be employed.

The following four exercises are written with a view to this end, and will prove a valuable study, not only on account of this glottis-stroke, but as a means of learning how to command the motions of the diaphragm. Baritone voices will find these exercises of special use.

Let there be a short interval, or rest, between every note, apply neatly to the first note the syllable *sca,* and then, without taking breath or changing the position of the pharynx, pronounce *a* to the other notes, precisely as you did in its connection with *sca.* The principal agent in this exercise is the diaphragm. Let every note be given with an outward impulsion of the diaphragm. It can easily be felt by holding your hand on the lower part of your chest. Begin very slowly and take the *a* from the bottom of the throat. Recollect that the *a* has the Italian sound, like *ah.*

Example 6. **Exercises for training the "right action" of the glottis, from Carlo Bassini, *Art of Singing* (1884). In the exercise he explains his understanding of how the onset should be produced.**

Immediately much of the voice community reacted negatively to it; however, many nineteenth century sources promoted Garcia's definition of the *coupe de la glotte*. The proper application of the term promotes a clean, precise onset where the vocal folds are in full contact just prior to phonation. The singer develops just enough subglottal pressure to begin the tone without any airflow preceding it. This is analogous to what one can observe on the lips when pronouncing [pa]. If it is pronounced in a natural way, the pressure behind the lips builds until an emission of voice occurs. Detractors have claimed that practitioners have ruined voices due to the aggressive, overly muscular nature of the gesture, but the examples that they offer are typically grossly exaggerated and do not reflect the gentle approach that was described by Garcia.

Proponents claim that the correct balance of medial compression or closing effort and breath pressure provides a clear, ringing quality that cannot be accomplished with other concepts such as the "coordinated onset" or "balanced onset." We know that firm glottal closure produces greater energy in the higher partials. Depending upon the desired timbre and dynamic level that is called for, this approach creates the fullest, richest sounds of which a singer is capable without undue effort.

Of course, one does not always want the full-voiced richness of firm glottal adduction. An intentional "cushioning" of the tone with a little air slipping by unrealized by the vocal folds can sometimes be just what is artistically desired and can provide a softer, "loftier" sound. My point on this issue is that singers should be able to do both, but that a habitual easy onset robs the voice of maturity, fullness, and richness of tone. New York voice teacher David Jones promotes the idea that training the clean onset can be easily accomplished by having the singers say "uh-oh" like a young child who has just dropped something. This is brilliant and very simple! It is a light, yet clean onset of tone: not "huh-hoh." Example 6 is from Carlo Bassini's method, the most popular book on singing printed in the United States in the second half of the nineteenth century.[10] I am pleased to say that it is available again in an historic reprint with an introduction provided by this author.[11]

The *coupe de la glotte* trains the intrinsic laryngeal muscles that are responsible for opening and closing the glottis. These muscles are critical for firm closure, the source for ring in the voice. As I indicated in a previous column, my opinion and practice on this issue has changed completely in the last ten years.[12] I was taught the "well-coordinated onset" as described by William Vennard in his writings. I was presented with unjustified bias against the *coupe de la glotte* in every pedagogy class I had in graduate school, so I thought I was doing the right thing. A few years ago I read Stark's excellent history of voice pedagogy and was convinced by his persuasive argument that I had been unintentionally misled.[13] Upon reading Garcia's actual words for the first time and the clear directions that he offered (as presented in Stark's book), I began to experiment with my students and in my own singing. There is no doubt remaining in my mind that Garcia's onset, which I simply call "neat and clean" is the only way to fully develop the full potential in a singer. I have noted that when you listen to Vennard himself demonstrate the beginning of the tone in his *Developing Voices* recordings, he actually demonstrates the historic *coupe de la glotte* and not his own "well-coordinated" one![14] He describes an onset that seems less harsh than his misunderstanding of the original idea, but clearly uses Garcia's onset—because it is the only way to optimize the quality of the tone. This argument plays itself out in academic circles. Professional singers use the "neat and clean" onset because it is the only way they can keep their voices fresh and "in the house." Many of our problems arise from misuse of terminology and the misunderstanding of the words we use.

NOTES

1. A similar paper under the same title appeared in *The Choral Journal* 48, no. 7 (December 2007).
2. Stephen F. Austin, "First Things First," *Journal of Singing* 64, no. 1 (September/October 2007): 89.
3. Franz Abt, *Practical Singing Tutor* (New York: G. Schirmer, 1921), 2.
4. Stephen F. Austin, "Chi non lega, non canta," *Journal of Singing* 60, no. 3 (January/February 2004): 301.
5. Manuel Garcia, *Complete Treatise On the Art of Singing, Part 1*, transl. and ed. by Donald Paschke (New York: Da Capo Press, 1984): 63, 65; originally published as *Nouveau Traité Sommaire sur l'Art du Chant* (Genève: Minkoff Éditeur, 1847).
6. Austin, "First Things First."
7. Luigi Lablache, *Lablache's Complete Method of Singing* (Cincinnati: John Church Co., n.d.), 10.
8. Laure Cinti-Damoreau, *Method of Singing* (Philadelphia: A. H. Rosewig, n.d.).
9. Stephen F. Austin, "The Attack on the *coupe de la glotte*," *Journal of Singing* 61, no. 5 (May/June 2005): 521.
10. Carlo Bassini, *Art of Singing* (Boston: Oliver Ditson & Co., 1884), 116.
11. Carlo Bassini, *Art of Singing*, with an introduction by Stephen F. Austin (San Diego: Plural Pub., 2008).
12. Austin, "The Attack on the *coupe de la glotte*."
13. James Stark, *Bel Canto: A History of Vocal Pedagogy* (Toronto: University of Toronto Press, 1999).
14. *William Vennard, Developing Voices* (New York: Carl Fischer, 1973).

41. Building Strong Voices—Twelve Different Ways, Part 2

Originally published in the *Journal of Singing*, volume 69, no. 4, 2013

Historical methods were progressive in nature, like a traditional instrumental method, an approach that is not commonly practiced today in voice training. I have written about many of these over the last several years in this column. Having begun in the previous issue of *Journal of Singing*, I continue here to present a dozen pedagogic principles that are based on the historical tradition of a progressive method and will result in vocal growth and development when properly and consistently applied in the studio and practice room.

6. Register Studies. No area of study concerned with vocal development carries with it more confusion than the registers of the singing voice. Rather than try to refute, correct, redirect, or otherwise dispel the mythology in this area, I will present some practical information that is both historically and scientifically supported. It is not possible to cover every nuance of this issue in a few short paragraphs. For a more thorough exploration I would refer you to two articles that will be helpful: "Treasure Chest"[1] and "Register Unification: Give Me a Break!"[2]
We should begin with a definition:

> By the word register we understand a series of consecutive and homogeneous tones going from low to high, produced by the development of the same mechanical principle, and whose nature differs essentially from another series of tones equally consecutive and homogenous produced by another mechanical principle. All the tones belonging to the same register are consequently of the same nature, whatever may be the modification of timbre or of force to which one subjects them.[3]

These words were written by Manuel Garcia in 1840 in his first formal treatise, *Memoire sur la voix humaine*.[4] He stated that there are different qualities of sound associated with different parts of the singing range and that those different qualities are produced by different adjustments at the vocal folds. The length, tension, position, and shape of the vocal folds are determined by the actions of the intrinsic laryngeal muscles. Traditional voice building techniques targeted these muscles in specific exercises in order to build strength, train sophisticated coordination, and shape the vocal folds for optimal sound generation.

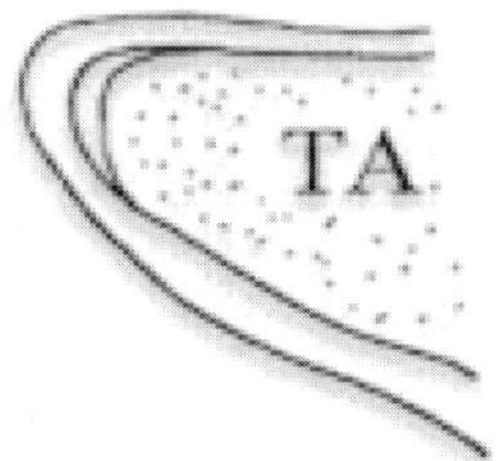

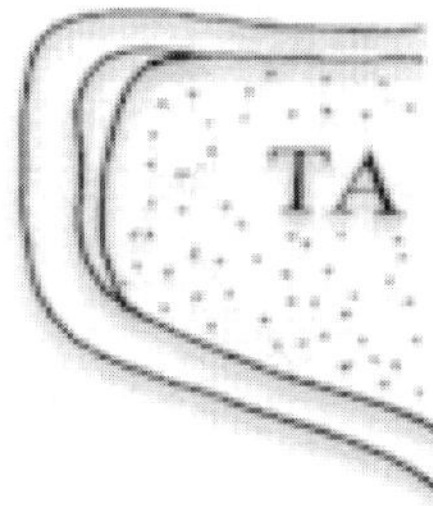

Figure1. Cross section of the vocal folds. The thick square folds on the right are associated with robust voices. The slight folds on the left suggest a weak or feeble voice. (Ingo Titze, *Principles of Voice Production* [Englewood Cliffs, NJ: Prentice Hall, 1994]

Voice building through the development of the vocal registers preceded Garcia's definition. Tosi, and

Mancini before him, talked at great lengths about the importance of building and balancing the registers. Fundamental to the process was the understanding that great voices always had a strong chest register (low mechanism, modal voice, Register 1, whatever you want to call it). It was common knowledge even in the eighteenth century that if a voice were weak and frail you could make it stronger by exercising the chest voice. Today we understand the mechanism behind this long observed truth. Laboratory studies conducted on singers show that chest voice is produced by contraction of the thyroarytenoid muscles (TA). The TA makes up the body of the vocal fold and runs parallel to the vibrating margin from the vocal process of the arytenoid cartilage to the anterior attachment at the commissure of the thyroid cartilage. When the TA muscle is strong and bulky, the vocal folds are rounded and thick from bottom to top and vibrate in a way that produces a complex tone that has a lot of energy in the upper partials, giving fullness and ring to the voice. When the TA is weak and underdeveloped the tone is less robust and even frail. Figure 1 illustrates two vocal folds: the right one would produce a robust tone, the left one a feebler tone. Some singers naturally have vocal folds that resemble the shape of the square folds. Those are the gifted singers who seem to be able to produce interesting sounds from the very beginning of voice study, assuming willingness to do so. Others begin their journey with folds shaped more like the slim ones. The good news is that this can change with exercise and over time; the process of changing one to the other is the heart of voice building.

The process of building a robust voice is similar to building big biceps. If you go to the gym and lift weights regularly, muscles respond by building more muscle tissue. Muscles become stronger and the mass of muscle is increased. The upper arm, for example, becomes thicker and bulkier with a fullness or roundness. The same effect is achieved when we exercise the TA—the muscle literally grows and the vocal folds become thicker and more rounded. As a result of its new shape, they go into oscillation with less subglottal pressure and produce sound much more efficiently. When the vocal folds close (the source of the acoustic excitation) they do so more suddenly and completely.

Through exercise the shape of the bicep is changed permanently, not just while it is being exercised. As the muscle grows, the shape of the arm is different even at rest. For this same reason the quality of the voice is changed throughout its range, not just for the occasional low tones that a singer might sing (in the case of a soprano or alto). The tones that are produced in the higher range are richer and more interesting because the vocal folds have been reshaped and oscillate in a different way. This is why building the chest register does not make the voice weighty. The tone is different because the vocal folds are a different shape, not because the singer is necessarily adding more chest register to singing throughout the range. This is a critical difference.

Historical treatises promote exercise for the chest register in all voices. Like Tosi, Mancini, and Garcia, I consider it to be the foundation of the entire voice, and I always begin each lesson with exercises that target the TA, using long held sustained tones and small scale work in the range of the chest register. They must be sung with enough energy in the tone that it speaks out clearly; a clean onset is critical. Garcia stated that a woman should be comfortable singing in the chest register from perhaps as low as F_3 and as high as E_4 or F_4. Please note: this does not mean that women would or should sing notes that high in full chest! That decision is based upon the artistic intention—the meaning of the words, the musical style, the timbre choice for balancing the ensemble—all these things guide the artistic choice for a performance. But the register should be exercised daily through its full range. I recently attended a wonderful performance of *Aida* at our local opera house, and I guarantee you chest voice was used by all women on the stage, and the floating high voice from Aida would not be possible without a strong chest voice and vocal folds that are effective oscillators!

Many voice teachers choose not to train the chest voice because the quality of the tone does not fit into their aesthetic model or preference. This is unfortunate. If the full potential of the instrument is to be realized the chest register must be exercised and integrated. Too many of us limit what we do in the studio guided by our own limitations or experience. I have a colleague who is fond of saying that you can't learn anything about teaching from reading a book. I beg to differ. If training the chest voice is outside of your own personal experience, you can and should learn to do so, and that you can learn from reading about it.

A young man can be limited by an underdeveloped chest voice as well, leaving his tone light and somewhat breathy. When the chest voice is engaged and strengthened it will help his voice grow and develop the fullness of tone that is within his potential. It is counterintuitive, but absolutely true that many young men and women have unsuccessful high voices until they build the chest voice. I have seen it in my own studio and I have had many people report this to me as I talk about this subject around the country.

This is not complicated work. With regular exercise the tone quality changes gradually over time due to the effects of exercising the TA. We do not even have to be very clever about how to coordinate the chest voice with the rest of the instrument. If the work is being done correctly, changes will happen quite naturally because the vocal folds are being changed. There are exercises that can help encourage a new function outside of the range of the chest register that can be considered. Example 1 is a suggested vocalise for that work. Once the full chest voice is established the singer should execute the low tone in the full chest voice and ascend suddenly to the octave *without* separating the tones. Use a quickly executed portamento to assure that there is no discontinuity of the tone. Sing it at a tempo of the half note equals 40 bps and repeat it several times in a row before moving on the next pitch, ascending by half steps. If the singer is capable of the upper octave in the full chest, start at a pitch where he/she can not, but where it is going to go into the upper register. Guided to take the same energy but not the register to the upper octave, the vocal folds will maintain the more optimum shape and offer a fuller more interesting tone with time. As always, a clean onset will assure the proper execution and optimum quality. Establishing the chest register may be done in the open or clear timbre; however, working to integrate the good qualities of the chest voice should be done with the help of the somber or the *voce chiusa* timbre. This will produce a tone quality that is optimal for operatic singing. The *voce chiusa* will be discussed later in this article.

Some voices are dominated by the chest voice and cannot seem to do anything else. Occasionally, a woman can extend her chest voice well beyond its normal limits, maybe C_5 or higher. This is not unusual if she sings some types of commercial music. However, when she has to exceed the range of the chest voice, the tone can suddenly become weaker, very breathy, and usually exhibit a noticeable break. If her goal is to learn to sing higher successfully, the use of the chest voice needs to be rebalanced. Part of the solution would be for her to restrict use of chest voice for a time and sing only in the lighter mechanism until it becomes stronger. This can be a very difficult problem to manage and can take a significant period of time to put right.

Of course, also a man's voice can be limited when the TA is too dominant. Tone quality can be quite satisfying up to C_4 or D_4, but then it stops or goes through an unsatisfying adjustment (just like the belter described above). I am working with a young bass baritone who came to my studio at 18 years old with a robust quality, but a limited range.

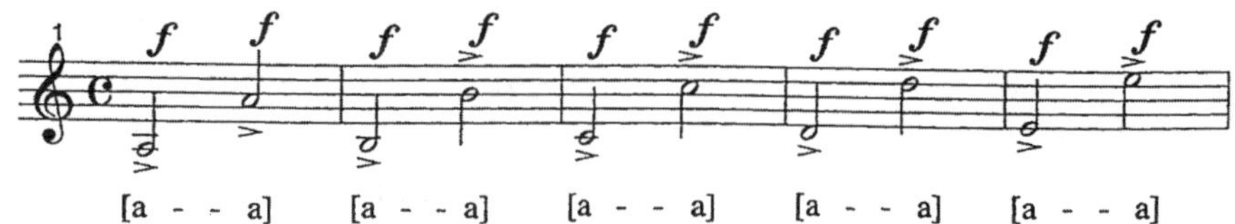

Example 2. Exercise for expanding the benefit of the heavy mechanism above the range of the chest voice.

When we began our work almost two years ago, he could sing only up to about C_4. Beyond that it was strained and unpleasant. The larynx would rise and often the voice would break into falsetto. We have faithfully exercised the chest register; always beginning in the low range, and progressively worked to stretch the range of the chest voice—all the while insisting that the laryngeal posture remain stable. At the same time, we worked the falsetto, or breathy voice to help release constriction in his tone. You can hear William Vennard use his "yawn-sigh" exercise on a series of recordings of his teaching found on *Developing Voices* that I have mentioned earlier.[5] The tone begins high and somewhat breathy, and as the singer descends on a spoken sigh he brings in the full voice, usually with a break at first, but that will go away with practice. When he has learned successfully to coordinate the contraction of the TA with the adductors, the break disappears. The result of developing both registers and then coordinating them is that he is now singing up to F_4 and occasionally higher with a committed tone that matches his beautiful low and middle voice. He recently performed a credible Friar Laurent in our university production of *Romeo et Juliette*. The sound that is associated with squeezing or grunting is almost gone.

My own work with Don Maxwell and Cornelius Reid convinced me that all voices benefit from developing the chest voice and the falsetto, and then coordinating them to create a full bodied seamless range. This is the historical model. The falsetto is breathy and hooty. Garcia described it as one of the two primary registers: chest and falsetto, common to all voices. He placed it in the middle range from about A_3 to C_5, overlapping the range of the chest voice. This is why it is useful to help balance the weight of the chest. Falsetto is not an artistic sound, but functionally it can be very useful.

The quality of the falsetto can be improved with practice. Daily vocalizing in the falsetto can clarify it in the same way that the chest voice will benefit from regular work. The pure falsetto quality in the male voice has the capacity to be either hooty and breathy without any tone color, or it can be clear and soprano-like. Both can be beneficial. The latter is called "closed chink falsetto" and is probably what some men utilize to develop their countertenor voice. All men are not equally able to make a beautiful clear falsetto, but can train it. The clarity is a symptom of a certain level of freedom and balance at the level of the vocal folds and should be sought.

Historically some pedagogues would teach both men and women to intentionally break yodel as a means of establishing an optimal balance of the two registers. You can ask a young tenor to sing F_4 in falsetto and then descend to B_3 (with a continuous tone), but ask him to let the voice "break" into chest voice on the lower tone. The break is to be encouraged at first. Eventually you make the interval pattern smaller until he is able to break from falsetto into chest voice without changing pitch. This process will help him find a tone quality that is not too heavy but is still considered viable. Depending on the strength of the chest voice he should be able to produce a break up to around G_4 or $A^b{}_4$. Above that the chest voice may not be strong enough to produce an obvious break, but the quality will still change as the singer literally turns on the TA and activates the chest voice.[6] The resulting tone will be a better balance of weight from the chest than if it were simply approached from below.

This same procedure can be used to help female singers establish the chest voice and then create the "blended" tones of the middle voice. This was the primary method of fixing the weakness of the middle register found in the nineteenth century. Garcia's first exercise for the female voice was alternating between chest and head voice on a sustained tone as seen in Example 2. The singer was encouraged to welcome the break at first and gradually the break would begin to disappear with repetition. In its place the full middle register would arise. I would refer you to my article in the reference list on register breaking.

Every female is capable of singing in the "flute voice" (sometimes called the whistle or flageolet register). I always follow chest voice with flute voice exercises with my female students. Physiologically the TA is turned off and is in a passive state. The cricothyroid (CT) is free to elongate the vocal folds without opposition. Vocalizing in the whistle register is a great stretching exercise. It reminds me of a gymnast touching the floor with the palms of the hands while keeping the knees perfectly relaxed and straight. To be able to do that tells us something about the condition of the body. A female voice should be able to sing in flute register at least up to E_6 and maybe as high as C_7!

Example 3. Register breaking exercise from Garcia's *Complete Treatise*, intended to create a smooth transition out of the heavy mechanism.

It is simple to guide singers to this voice if they do not know how to access it. They must follow one simple rule: sing [u] high and light. The production of this register depends upon a unique acoustic coupling between the vocal tract and the fundamental frequency. The [u] has a low first formant and so the first harmonic (H1) can be locked with the lowest resonance and this produces the flute voice. It can easily be accomplished with lips extremely rounded and mouth opening very small. The suggestion that I offer is they must keep their lips so small that the opening is no bigger than a pencil. I have them sing an ascending interval of C_5–G_5 going from [a] to [u] with a portamento, and then a descending five-note scale. If they can keep from opening the lips too wide, it will go into whistle voice. With relaxation and a small lip opening they can learn to vocalize freely to the extreme top.

I personally do not attempt to blend or coordinate this sound down into the high voice, though there are teachers that do. I use it as an element in the voice building process only because I believe that we are isolating and exercising the cricothyroid (CT) or the pitch muscle, while at the same time teaching the TA to relax sometimes when opposed.

There are many ways in which the development of the registers of the voice can be helpful. It is right to think of a register as the result of a muscular function. We want our singers to be strong vocal athletes with elite muscular coordination. Building chest register is building TA muscle. It provides the foundation for the basic timbre of the voice. Building chest voice can be very helpful in building size and improving over-all quality of the voice.

Exercising the lighter mechanism helps train proper balance of weight in the voice. It is common for voices of all types to try to take too much weight up as they seek to stretch their range. The practice of register breaking or yodeling can be helpful in finding a good balance of weight and effort in all voices.

I realize that I have covered some information here that may be unfamiliar. I guarantee that everything here is found in historical sources and supported by the science of the singing voice. I believe that if one were to undertake some of the suggested activities and simply observe the results over a period of time, one would gain some skills that would be helpful to singers. These are complex issues to write about. I have written more about these matters in other articles referenced above. It is very interesting that simply by doing these exercises the voice improves. We do not even need to know what the outcome should look like for this work to be effective. Our studios are our laboratories and much can be gained from a little guided experimentation.

7. The Stable Larynx. I recently served as a judge for a session of senior men at our regional NATS conference. Of the twelve young men I heard in the preliminary round, only three of them knew how to sing their top. The timbre of the others was white, open, and shrill; it was a yell rather than a beautifully balanced timbre. This is simply unacceptable and tragic. It is not that difficult to teach this important function. The larynx is capable of a wide excursion up and down in the neck. For swallowing it ascends as a part of the protective mechanism against aspiration of food or fluid into the lungs. When we yawn the larynx descends to open the airway for optimal air intake. Unfortunately, it is the natural response of the larynx to rise when we ascend in pitch. We swallow thousands of times a day, so this reflex is quick to respond to the physical stresses of singing. It is fortunate that the yawn reflex puts the larynx in the right place (not the full-blown yawn, but the beginning of the gesture).

The quality of the tone associated with a high larynx in a man is unmistakable. We all know the "Kermit the Frog" sound, sometimes called the "necktie tenor." When the larynx rises, the length of the vocal tract is shortened and alters the resonance characteristics; that is why the timbre changes. Perhaps more importantly, when the larynx is pulled up while we are phonating, normal free function of the vocal folds is not possible. When I am teaching these principles I use the example of a tennis player with a belt around his arms, tying them to his side. Sure, he can still play and someone who is really an expert could still beat me, but their optimal function is seriously compromised. The range of the high voice is limited by this action and the vocal folds are put under great tension.

The habitually high larynx can lead to a misclassification of the voice. With a shorter vocal tract, the timbre of the voice may take on a tenor-like quality. If the voice is actually a lower placed instrument, the timbre belies its true character. The singer can be considered to be a "short tenor" with the range stopping at F_4 or G_4. Years of struggle can ensue as singer and teacher hope that one day the A_5 or $B^b{}_5$ will appear. I have worked with full-grown adult men who have never been taught the concept of the open throat and have struggled with this issue their whole lives. Taken on directly this habit can be retrained and sometimes within a few short minutes they can experience what it feels like to successfully sing through the *passaggio*. Once the larynx is trained to remain low, access to the high notes may appear for the first time and with the appropriate darker timbre that characterizes the operatic tenor. It could be that the voice is a lower range voice, misidentified because of the timbre. Opening the throat will provide the natural timbre, and because the larynx is no longer under excessive stress access to the low voice may suddenly appear. They are reassigned to their rightful place among the baritones. I had a student a number of years ago who was confused when it can to his vocal identity. He sang tenor in the choir and baritone solo literature for his applied study. Once he learned to keep his larynx from rising the depth and fullness of the voice came out and he is now having an international career as an operatic baritone!

An elevated larynx can be equally devastating for women. I have worked with many women whose high voice changed quality at the top of the staff and who did not have access to the full range. At F_5 or G_5 the timbre shifts from an opulent sound to one that becomes somewhat thin and sometimes strangled. Their effort level increases as they struggle against the tension. Their previous attempts at addressing the problem focused on their support, the placement of the voice, everything except the real issue, because the high larynx was not identified. Sometimes this situation is described as tongue tension. The tongue may indeed be too involved, but relaxing the tongue will not likely provide the correction. With proper training of the laryngeal posture, the top can "bloom" in the upper range and effort level in singing the high voice will be significantly reduced. Tension in the neck and face visibly disappear when they get this right.

The traditional training technique to achieve this postural goal is the acquisition of what is called the *voce chiusa* timbre.[7] This term literally means "closed voice," but we are more familiar with referring to it as "open throat." The goal is to train the larynx to remain low and still. In order to achieve that the singer will probably have to make some sounds that are not very beautiful for a period of time. The singer should be instructed to vocalize on closed [o] and [u] in the low range of the voice—for men and women it is the same. If done properly the timbre of the voice is closed—very dark and hooty, some might call it pharyngeal. It may be a sound only a teacher could love, at least at the beginning. You will visually recognize the proper pronunciation of the vowel sounds by lips that are extremely rounded and extended. The jaw opening should be minimal. The singer should be aware of a distinct sense of fullness in the throat—the sensation associated with the yawn—that sensation is the larynx lowering in the neck.

Unfortunately, the low larynx may feel much like the high larynx. The singer may report just a feeling of pressure in the throat. You have to rely upon the timbre to verify that the larynx is low and not being pulled up.

Teacher and the student need to be patient with this work. It can take weeks or months to retrain the muscle memory associated with the high larynx. Vocalizing should be done in a range where it can be accomplished, usually low in the range and then gradually explore higher notes while maintaining the dark timbre. Over a period of time the singer should be able to maintain the comfortably low laryngeal posture throughout the singing range. Eventually, the more open vowels can be tried. I describe the [a] vowel as being just the same as the [o], but with the lip rounding relaxed. This maintains the dark quality (*chiaroscuro*) while singing a bright vowel too. My suggestion to both men and women is that you keep [o] in the throat and sing a bright vowel on top of it.

A very successful gesture that I use to communicate this idea is easy to do, but hard to describe. I will first demonstrate a very closed quality [o] in my speaking voice on a small descending glide: around my speaking pitch B_3. I'll then ask them to make a sound like that and we continue until that is successfully accomplished. I will then give them a triad in the low range and ask them to "speak" on an ascending and then descending glide—not singing, but speaking on pitch. I describe the shape of the gesture like a bell-shaped curve: start low and ascend to the peak of the curve and then let it fall back down to the beginning pitch range. It needs to be done like a true glide with no discrete pitches. Once established I have them "speak" this gesture as high as they can go, all the while maintaining the right closed quality. If the exercise is properly produced, singers will be able to ascend through any previously experienced bottlenecks in their range. Once established the next step is to maintain the same posture and sing a more formal five-note scale ascending and descending executed quickly.

Another traditional exercise for this is an arpeggio built on 1-3-5-8-5-3-1 on the words "*bella signora*" with the [o] at the top note. This is especially helpful to the young men at the *passaggio*. At first the [o] must remain very closed. If the tone opens up it may sound like a Broadway belt. In that case the laryngeal posture and the *voce chiusa* have been compromised and you must repeat it until it is successful.

The proper laryngeal posture and vowel color will lead young men to true head voice quality. The great tenor Jussi Bjoerling would "place his voice" by singing a simple ascending then descending five-note scale on the vowel series [u-o-a-e-i]. The [u] at the beginning of the exercise would put the throat right and then all of the other vowels were made to followed right in line.

I have spent a good deal of my teaching career training singers to maintain a laryngeal posture that would allow their voices to work in an optimum fashion. If this issue were addressed early on in one's vocal experience it would benefit the singer immensely.

Many teachers are squeamish about a direct approach to this issue. It has often been said that to call the singer's attention to something so physical as the position of the larynx would only confuse the singer and interfere with the natural voice. My answer to that objection is that there is little about great singing that is natural. It is no more natural to sing well than it is to compete on the parallel bars at the Olympics. It is in fact *super*natural and must be studied carefully and trained specifically. If teachers are sure about the goal, they will be able to achieve the desired result—whether or not they ever mention the position of the larynx, the desired result can be accomplished utilizing vowel color and other suggestions.

The comfortably low laryngeal posture puts the vocal mechanism in its ideal posture for singing. Unnecessary tensions upon the larynx are avoided and therefore it is free to do what it needs to do; make sound freely from the bottom to the top of the range. The natural size and timbre of the voice is made evident and misclassifications are less likely to occur. Of course, it is understood that the realization of voice type may not happen until the singer is in his or her middle twenties and sometimes beyond. My pedagogic rule is that the open throat must be accomplished no matter what it takes. We must remember that the characteristic timbre *chiaroscuro* is the result of optimal function. As the art form of operatic singing developed and singers needed to be able to sing at such elevated dynamics and pitch, they found that the best way to accomplish it was to open the throat. Aesthetics followed function.

NOTES

1. Stephen F. Austin, "Treasure 'Chest': A Physiological and Pedagogical Review of the Low Mechanism," *Journal of Singing* 61, no. 3 (January/February 2005): 241-251.
2. Stephen F. Austin, "Register Unification: Give Me a Break!" *Journal of Singing* 61, no. 2 (November/December 2004): 199-203.
3. Manuel Garcia II, *A Complete Treatise on the Art of Singing: Part 1,* translated and edited by Donald V. Paschke (New York: Da Capo Press, 1984), xli, originally published as *Nouveau Trait Sommaire sur l'Art du Chant* (Genève: Minkoff Diteur, 1847).
4. Published as a part of the *Complete Treatise on the Art of Singing, Part 1.*
5. William Vennard, *Developing Voices* (New York: Carl Fischer, 1973).
6. Austin, "Register Unification."
7. Stephen F. Austin, "The *voce chiusa,*" *Journal of Singing* 61, no. 4 (March, 2005): 421.

42. Building Strong Voice—Twelve Different Ways, Part 3

Originally published in the *Journal of Singing*, volume 69, no. 4, 2013

8. Jaw Opening.[1] I remember visiting a local high school to judge a regional competition for high school singers. I was placed in the choral rehearsal room where on the board was written "Ten Rules for Singing" that students were to observe. The number one rule was that there should always be at least three fingers of space in the front of the mouth. At best, I believe that this is a gross simplification of a rather complex issue.

As with many of the other points that I have made in this article, I believe that correct practice depends upon the goal. The amount of jaw opening that a singer uses has very specific implications for the timbre of the voice. If you observe a range of vocal expression and common practice on this matter across musical genres, you will see somewhat different behaviors. Take Mick Jagger (or your favorite rock star), for instance. When he is singing high and loud, his mouth is famously wide open. There are certainly more than three fingers of space in the front—most of us would be able to stick our whole fist in his gaping maw! His vocal goal often is to sing with a powerful chest-belt throughout his range, but especially all the way to his limit at the top. His mouth opening is a crucial part of achieving that goal—he absolutely would not be able to do what he wants to do with his mouth closed.

Female belters (Broadway or pop) follow a similar approach to the full-throated high voice. Consider the iconic Barbra Streisand. You can go on YouTube and watch her sing "My Man," for instance. She sings in a chest-related belt up to E_5, and when she does, her mouth is wide open (and her head is tilted back). I know there are lots of different ideas about what to call the register up there, but the point is that it is a powerful source function with an open quality that she achieves by dropping her jaw. If she closed her mouth it would not work.

A quite different approach is taken by those who sing in a more intimate vocal style. Observe your favorite country and western or folk singer (mine is Willie Nelson). As a general rule their goal is to present the text in a very available way that closely mimics natural speech. If you pay attention to what they do with their jaw opening, it looks as if they were speaking. It would be absurd for them to use the same exaggerated space that Jagger or Streisand use. It would not achieve their artistic goals.

It gets complicated when we look at common practice among opera singers. First, it differs between men and women, and sometimes among men and women. My usual place to start this discussion is to observe the practice of the great soprano Leontyne Price. In my estimation there has been no finer singer in my lifetime. If you observe carefully, the opening of the mouth is quite variable depending upon where she is in her singing range, the dynamic level, and her artistic goals. You will see that in the low and middle of her singing voice her mouth opening is usually quite moderate. The combination of her open throat (lowered laryngeal posture) and her relatively closed mouth opening gives her what some would call the "middle voice" or "mixed voice." There is a strong acoustic signal originating at the larynx providing a rich harmonic spectrum. The timbre is not identified as the chest voice, however. The closed mouth posture has kept the first vowel formant low in frequency so that particular partials from the source are above it in frequency, and, according to Ingo Titze, this is what accounts for the particular quality of sound associated with that articulatory scheme. This is in part what gives us the acoustic impression of "middle register." There are acoustic rules for why this is the case, and for a more complete discussion of the importance of partial formant interaction and "inertive reactance" in the vocal tract, I refer you to the article that I referenced at the beginning of this section, "Flapping Jaws and Acoustic Laws," which appeared in this column.

As Ms. Price ascends into her high voice, we see her jaw opening behave more like Mick Jagger's. Beginning at about the top of the staff she opens her mouth progressively wider with each ascending tone—especially when she is singing in her full voice. The top is free, opulent, and magnificent. Like Mick, she could not possibly make those sounds with her mouth closed. When she wants to decrescendo or color the high voice, she uses the mouth opening with the same skill as a soaring raptor—using subtle changes in its wing feathers to trim and control its flight. It is a wondrous thing to behold! I should complete the description of her practice to say that when she is artistically motivated in the low range and she goes into the chest voice, she again opens her mouth wide and the chest voice speaks with firmness and clarity—in all honesty similar to what a Broadway belter would do. It is very exciting!

Luciano Pavarotti, in my estimation, was one of the great voices and technicians of our time. He never opened his mouth in Mick Jagger style. His high voice was produced with a very modest mouth opening all the way to his C_5. The result is the same kind of "mixed" sound that Ms. Price achieved in her low and middle voice. This practice helped create a tonal quality that is a central tenet of the Italianate ideal. With the throat open and mouth closed the voice "goes over" at the *passaggio* and is ringing and bright at the same time that it is dark, a quality known as *chiaroscuro*. Other singers behave differently, but there is always a timbral consequence. The great Wagnerian tenor Loritz Melchior approached his high voice in a very different way. At the *passaggio* you could see that his mouth opening was quite wide, but the tone was more open than we would ever hear Pavarotti sing. Of course they didn't sing the same literature! The Wagnerian tenor rarely sings to the extreme top, the tenor high C, but he sings at and above the *passaggio* in a tone quality that often can be more open. Lower male voices can do the same thing since many of them do not have to traverse the *passaggio*. They can maintain an open mouth posture up to the E_4, F_4 or even G_4, and even though the tone maybe in an open timbre the chest voice is strong enough to hold up to it in small doses. It is not unusual to see bass voices sing with wide-open mouths all the way to the extreme high voice for them. You will notice that many of them never "go over"; they do not have to. Practice among operatic baritones varies. There are many who do not overtly open their mouths, following the same practice as many tenors.

It is on the one hand an aesthetic choice if the voice is innately strong and robust. But if it is not, over opening the mouth can be a primary limitation to the progress of the singer. The proper acoustic environment can help the vocal folds close more suddenly. When the timbre is "closed" the tone can have a much richer harmonic content, especially in the high frequencies. For most voices in training, learning to sing with the mouth opening less-than-more can be a tremendous aid in establishing the full voice.

The point to all this is that the amount of jaw opening is not the same for everyone in all parts of the range. Women must learn to "drop to the top" at about E_5 or F_5, as they must open their mouths to produce tones that are full, free, and opulent. This is called "formant tuning," and she is indeed tuning the first resonance of the vocal tract to just above the frequency of the fundamental or the pitch being sung. This provides her with a significant boost in intensity and allows for much greater ease. If a soprano needs to sing softly above the staff, she can close her mouth and achieve her artistic goals.

So many young women do not understand this very important principle and are hindered by it unless someone teaches them to do it. I am always meeting young women in high school who have studied voice for many years who do not know that, to successfully sing above the staff, they have to drop the jaw as they go up. Instead, they learn, or have been taught, to tuck their chin and close their mouths! Disaster! In five minutes you can have them soaring past the F_5 that has been this huge issue in their singing, simply by learning to lift their heads and drop the jaw position. This is what all professional singers do, but like so many obvious things in singing, it does not necessarily become a part of our pedagogic practice.

The young men that we teach cannot be treated similarly. If they open their mouths wide as they ascend toward the top, the resulting tone will always be too open and yell-like. A wide open mouth can encourage the larynx to rise and they will not be able to achieve the "head voice" quality that will make their lives so much easier when singing above their *passaggio*.

Mouth opening is an important control mechanism that a singer can utilize to optimize vocal function and to take advantage of very specific acoustic principles that apply to the vocal tract.
If you want your singers to be able to make a variety of timbres for different styles of music, then we must all be aware of the tremendous implications of the size of jaw opening. Being informed will allow your singers to be flexible without being confused and trying to apply articulatory gestures that will work in one style but not another.

9. Velocity. Voice building has historically included exercises designed to train the voice to move with ease and accuracy throughout the full singing range. Exercises took many forms, but usually included both diatonic and chromatic scale patterns, arpeggios, and patterned passages. They were typically accompanied and progressive in difficulty, intended to be transposed throughout the appropriate range for a particular voice. Patterns were usually offered in ascending and descending form, because they were acutely aware that tuning descending passages was of particular concern. Examples 1 and 2 are excerpted from Garcia's *Complete Treatise on the Art of Singing*.[2] Here you see a very typical presentation of pattern exercises that increase in complexity. Garcia included patterns using up to thirty-two notes per grouping in this section of his book.

It is rare to find such disciplined focus in the experience of most voice students today, and, as a result, it is considered to be the rare singer who is capable of singing the music of Rossini effectively. Only those for whom it seems to come naturally ever attempt it.

Students are introduced to the need for this skill more often in the choral rehearsal than in the voice studio. In the absence of specific training to establish the ability to sing melismas freely and with legato, they often learn to separate each note or a group of notes with a slight aspirate "ha." Every source that I can find from the eighteenth and nineteenth centuries specifically says that legato is the default articulation in the absence of specific markings and that melismas are to be sung legato. I realize that there are lots of different opinions about this, but I believe that they are reactionary to the inability of most singers to do it correctly.

Melodic patterns (like those found in Examples 1 and 2) should be practiced enough so that the singer can execute them without conscious thought. Once the pattern of the notes has been learned thoroughly, it can be helpful to select a tempo that is slightly faster than they can do it with conscious control. At first they will not believe that they are actually doing the exercise, but eventually they build trust in their ability to do it based upon the natural reflex of the voice.

All voices should be flexible. Some come to it more naturally than others, but all can achieve it to some level. A flexible voice is a free voice. Velocity should be a part of the vocalises and literature selected for a singer. I think there is a widely held belief that beginners should not be assigned literature that requires the voice to move. I see it all the time at my university in the music assigned by our graduate teaching fellows. Their students will come to their juries with nothing in their repertory that requires them to sing even the simplest melismatic passage. This is unfortunate and should be avoided. The ability to move the voice quickly, accurately is a skill that must be acquired. Like all fine motor skills, it takes time and an ably directed course of study to achieve. Historical methods provide useful patterns and a progressive approach that will lead to success.

Example 1. **Velocity exercise taken from Manuel Garcia's *The Complete Treatise on the Art of Singing*, first published in 1845**

10. Other Articulations. There are three other laryngeal articulations that have been an important part of the pedagogic process for over two hundred years: *staccato*,[3] *marcato*,[4] and *aspirato*.[5]
According to nineteenth century sources, *staccato* is correctly produced at the larynx while the breath flow remains constant. It is produced by opening and closing of the glottis. There is a great deal of confusion on this point. I have taught any number of students—particularly sopranos whose literature most often calls for the gesture—who have been taught that the *staccato* is produced from the abdominal wall. This is incorrect. The best explanation that I have for the confusion is that a slight pulsing of the abdominal wall can be observed when the *staccato* is being produced correctly. When the breath is in motion and the vocal folds come together to close the glottis, the airflow is suddenly interrupted by the vocal folds. Since air has mass and, therefore, momentum, there is a reflected pressure wave that travels back down the vocal tract. This can result in an observable bounce from the pressure pulse that is visible on the abdominal wall. Singers who perform the *staccato* correctly may observe this in their own body and misinterpret it as the source of the *staccato* rather than a result of an action elsewhere. The *staccato* will always be sluggish when the singer attempts to produce it from the support mechanism and will never be satisfactory. One noted author, the great baritone Julius Stockhausen, insisted that if a soprano had not thoroughly studied the *staccato* in her own singing that she did not even know her own voice!

Example 2. ***Velocity exercise taken from Manuel Garcia's*** **The Complete Treatise on the Art of Singing, *first published in 1845.***

Example 3. **Exercises on staccato tones taken from Carlo Bassini's book *The Art of Singing* published in 1884.**

I teach the *staccato* on a simple 1-3-5-8-5-3-1 pattern insisting upon lightness and clarity of tone with minimal or no breath flow between tones—some aspiration may be allowed at first, but the goal is to eliminate any perceptible aspiration on each tone. I also use this pattern to reinforce the principle of jaw opening in the female voices as described earlier in point #8. Beginning about F_4, the ladies should drop the jaw gradually as they ascend to the top of the pattern, so that by the time they sing the high note the mouth is more open than at the bottom. With each ascending half step the jaw is dropped incrementally all the way to the highest tones. Each singer must learn to judge how much space is necessary—there is no exact formula for this, but the principle must be applied.

Example 3 is a typical example of an exercise for *staccato* taken from Carlo Bassini's method.[6] Historical sources often used melodic passages with accompaniment for practicing specific exercises. There are several articulations in this passage that should be applied when indicated.

BASSINI'S ART OF SINGING. 117

EXERCISES ON REPEATED NOTES.

No. 79.

Example 4. **Exercises on repeated tones taken from Carlo Bassini's book *The Art of Singing* published in 1884.**

Example 5. **From Julius Stockhausen's *A Method of Singing*. This is an example of how to execute repeated tones found in the soprano aria, "Ich folge dir gleichfalls mit freudigen Schritten," from Bach's *St. John's Passion*.**

Staccato is always indicated with a mark; either a dot or a slash above or below the note. If there is no marking it is to be sung legato. If there is a slur over dots or slashes it is not *staccato*, but *marcato*; a different articulation altogether.

Marcato can be thought of as almost the opposite of *staccato*. *Staccato* is produced by opening and closing the glottis with the tone interrupted, but with a steady support gesture. *Marcato* is produced with the glottis constantly closed and continuous tone with a pulsed support gesture from the muscles of the chest wall and/or the muscles of the abdomen. The vocal folds do not open and close, but remain in constant contact during its execution. The result is a series of tones that are fundamentally connected but accented with a slight pulse of air pressure. The change must come from the respiratory system, not the larynx.

A third type of articulation that was always included in a progressive method was the special case of repeated tones. Example 4 is an exercise taken from Bassini's method. This musical situation was considered by all great singing masters as a unique situation. When a note was repeated without a tie or slur and without a change of syllable or vowel, it required a special articulation, it was either sung with a clean *staccato* or an aspiration. Garcia and Stockhausen insisted it was to be aspirated, so this is the way that I teach it. In Example 4, exercise #1 illustrates that between the repeated E_4 the singer is to release the tone of the first E_4 and attack the repeated one with a slightly aspirated onset. The amount of aspiration was to be developed to a minimum so that it was not heard. Garcia said that this articulation gave great suppleness to the voice. Beginning in exercise #6, the repeated tones are combined with patterns that are to be sung legato. The first repeated tone occurs in measure #3 after the first C_5 quarter note. It is important to note that in this exercise he provided a repeated vowel underneath the repeated tone. In the musical context of singing a score that would not be the case; the note would be repeated without a change of vowel.

Example 5 is from the soprano aria No. 9 from Bach's *St. John's Passion*, "Ich folge dir gleichfalls mit freudigen Schritten." This is an example found in Julius Stockhausen's *A Method of Singing* used an English translation (mm. 61–64 to the double bar, and mm. 108–110 after the double bar).[7] He suggested that after sounding the marked notes with an *aspirato*, they were to be cut short with a kind of sob. Everything was about expression! I highly recommend his book as a valuable resource for performance practice.

These articulations are found in the vocal literature and so the singer must understand the correct musical execution. However, they are also very important tools for voice building and were indispensable for developing strength and coordination in the vocal instrument.

11. Breath Management. The voice requires a positive pressure in the lungs in order to drive the vocal folds into oscillation and to keep them moving freely. This is what we call "support." The amount of support varies in absolute terms depending upon pitch, intensity, register, etc. Singers learn to vary this important element with experience and proper guidance.

Though there are a number of quite elaborate, exquisitely complex ideas about how a singer should breathe and support, the basic organization of breathing for singing can be quite simple if we rely upon what we know about respiratory physiology. The diaphragm is the primary muscle that we use for inhalation. It is located at the base of the chest wall and divides the abdominal cavity from the thorax—literally separating the two spaces with a flexible muscular wall. The diaphragm at rest is domed, and when it contracts (this is all a muscle is capable of doing) it flattens and descends. As it does, it pulls the floor of the lungs down, increasing the volume in the thorax. The increase of volume in the thorax produces a partial vacuum or a low-pressure zone in the lungs, and if the vocal folds are apart and the mouth is open, air will rush in to equalize the pressure to the ambient pressure outside the body—we have just taken a breath. A relatively high, somewhat stable chest can free the diaphragm from having to lift the weight of the thorax while it lowers into the abdominal cavity. The space below the diaphragm is not empty; in fact, it sits directly above the contents of the abdomen: the liver, stomach, etc. When the diaphragm descends it pushes down against the internal organs of the abdominal cavity. Since our tissue is mainly water and therefore non-compressible, the result of a descending diaphragm would be an expansion of the abdominal wall. The diaphragm displaces the abdominal organs outward against the soft pliable wall of the abdomen, much like squeezing a water balloon between your hands. It bulges out around the sides because that is where the wall is flexible.

The expansion of the abdominal wall presupposes that the singer has relaxed the abdominal muscles enough to allow expansion to happen. If he carries too much tension in the abdominal muscles (rectus abdominus, internal and external obliques, and the transverse abdominus), then the descent of the diaphragm will actually be limited and a deep breath is not possible without resorting to a rising ribcage. In this case one might observe the chest wall rising and falling instead. Some ideas about breathing for singing allow for a certain movement in the chest wall if there is also a movement of the abdominal wall. The main idea is that there should be freedom in both places.

The support part of the respiratory cycle comes when the singer uses the muscles of the abdominal wall and/ or the chest wall to gradually decrease the volume of the thorax and lungs. This can be accomplished by squeezing the contents of the abdominal cavity back where they came from, using the muscles of the abdominal wall. This action pushes the diaphragm back up into the thoracic cavity, increasing the pressure in the lungs beneath the glottis. The alternative is to compress the thorax directly with the internal intercostal muscles found between the ribs. Either way will work—or a combination of the two.

Now we have the required positive pressure in the airway necessary to drive the vocal folds into vibration. We do not support with the diaphragm! The diaphragm is a muscle of inhalation, not exhalation, and since "support" is an exhalatory gesture, it does not have a primary role—even though many think of it as having a balancing function to the abdominal muscles in the support process. I will not argue that point; it may very well be true.

The basics are pretty simple. I believe that you can teach principles that I have outlined above in fifteen minutes. However, developing a singer who does consistently what he/she knows he/she is supposed to do takes time. Reinforcing the concepts on a daily basis will eventually bring the student around to free and efficient respiratory function.

As I mentioned, there are more exotic ideas about breathing and support, which may include parts of the anatomy whose respiratory role is difficult for me to imagine. (The psoaz muscle is my favorite! Look that one up and explain to me how one is supposed to support with it.) Other methods of "back breathing," "expanding the wings," "squeezing the dime," "using the pelvic diaphragm," and many others, all have validity in the minds of those who practice them, but they certainly can obfuscate the elegant simplicity of our anatomic structures and the physiology of respiration. My opinion is that too many teachers talk about support and ignore many of the other elements that are required for building a voice.

12. Posture. Some elements of this issue have been part of other points of consideration that I have covered, but there are at least two things that I feel are worthy of a few final words.

The posture of the head and the neck has tremendous implications for what a singer is able to do. For hundreds of years teachers have insisted that the head sit naturally on the top of the spine. It is, however, very common for singers to do otherwise. I believe the most common fault is to habitually lower the head in the front, "tucking the chin." This action always leads to excessive tension in the tongue and the throat; it tends to constrict the airway and inevitably distorts the vowel, particularly the [a]. You can at least appreciate the reality of this by simply sustaining a vowel and then lower and raise your head. It is impossible for the change of position not to affect the vowel quality.

An elevated head position is often associated with a high laryngeal posture. One may observe this in beginners who have not been taught to maintain the larynx in the comfortably low position. These two things do not necessarily go hand in hand, however! Once the larynx has been trained to remain still throughout the range the slightly elevated head posture can be an important part of a great technique. Many great singers, especially the big voices, tend to sing with their heads elevated above rest level. Observe Birgit Nilsson, or the wonderful young soprano Latonia Moore, for instance. When they sing in their most opulent tone, the head is held high, the throat is free, and the sound is thrilling. You can find many examples of this among our favorite singing artists.

Lifting the head as a pedagogic tool can be extremely helpful. Having singers lift the head when they sing can help them "let go" of improper tensions that they carry in the tongue, jaw, and throat. I have mentioned my own work with my great friend and colleague Don Maxwell years ago when I was in big trouble as a young singer. I will never forget our first lesson. I had acquired every possible wrong action as evidenced by what happened when he insisted that I lift my head to vocalize . . . I could not make a sound! In this one simple action he took away all my crutches and began to help me build a voice based on freedom and proper function. I will always be in his debt for this simple but profound action. I have seen the same thing work in my own studio over the years. If you do this, you had better be prepared to offer something in its place, and this has been the subject of this column for over six years now. I have never found it helpful even as a transitory action to ask a student to intentionally lower his head while singing.

Finally, I want to say a word about those who sing in choirs, and that includes most of our students. Most singers hold their choir folders in the left hand, typically read from a folder that is beneath their natural eye level, and tend to habituate a posture where the head is lowered and turned slightly to the left. If you put a folder into the hands of choristers and then ask them to freeze while you remove it from their hands, you will likely observe what I mean: they are literally singing toward the floor with their heads pointed to the left. I find this to be a very difficult habit for many student singers to break, but I consider it to be very important in terms of their future vocal development. I encourage "eyes level with the horizon," or "sing to the balcony." That usually helps to accomplish a free voice.

Good posture is important for one reason when it comes to singing: it allows us to sing better. Alignment of the body is crucial for proper coordination and strength of all the muscles that are involved. Tensions in the head, neck, torso, arms, shoulders, and legs, are all observable by a critical eye. Any habituated tension in any of these places can be holding the key to any number of vocal problems and limitations. It is not to be taken for granted. Sometimes when I have students read our earliest pedagogy texts they are disappointed by the lack of specific vocal exercises to be found. Instead, the authors spent a great deal of time talking about posture, alignment, and the repose of the face and the head, vowels, articulations, and registers.

CONCLUSION

There are at least 12 (or 112) additional points that could be made about building strong voices in the studio. I have attempted to discuss briefly several components of an historical method that are "tried and true," in that they are described in the heirloom pedagogy literature and are supported by our understanding of the vocal mechanism.

It is usually in the absence of clear and specific concepts and goals that bad habits and poor singing techniques are acquired. It is not that most singers are taught to do it wrong, but that they have not been taught to do it right.

It is a highly competitive environment out in the world. Even high school seniors who will be auditioning for ever-decreasing scholarship dollars at their music school of choice are facing tough competition. Unless those young singers show that they have already begun to develop their vocal potential, the chance of receiving support or even admittance is not guaranteed. It is our responsibility to prepare them musically and vocally. That is my operational assumption. It is a wonderful opportunity to do good work.

My hope is that you will benefit, as I have, from the accumulated wisdom of folks who taught successfully and took the time to record for posterity the means for building strong voices. I know of at least 12 different ways to do so! You do not have to know the outcome of applying these principles. The result will be obvious.

NOTES

1. Stephen F. Austin, "Flapping Jaws and Acoustic Laws" *Journal of Singing* 63, no. 2 (November/December 2006): 211.
2. Manuel Garcia, *Treatise on the Art of Singing*, ed. Albert Garcia (London: Leonard & Co., 1924), 15.
3. Stephen F. Austin, "Staccato," *Journal of Singing* 60, no. 4 (March/April 2004): 405.
4. Stephen F. Austin, "You say *marcato*, I say *martellato*," *Journal of Singing* 61, no. 1 (September/October 2004): 89.
5. Stephen F. Austin, "*Aspirato*: An Exception to the Rule," *Journal of Singing* 60, no. 5 (May/June 2004): 33.
6. Carlo Bassini, *Art of Singing* (New York: Oliver Ditson & Co., 1884), 122.
7. Julius Stockhausen, *A Method of Singing*, translated by Sophie Loewe (London: Novello, 1884), 46; originally published as *Julius Stockhausen's Gesangs-Methode* (Leipzig: Peters, 1884).

43. Timeless Advice from the *Etude*

Originally published in the *Journal of Singing*, volume 70, no. 1, 2013

My personal introduction to *The Etude* magazine happened years ago as a teenager. My younger brother discovered several copies in an old abandoned farmhouse in Brown County, Texas where we grew up, issues from 1910–1912. I have held on to them these many years—I have a penchant for old things, you might have realized by now!

Some very interesting articles appeared in this music magazine over the many years of its publication. It was published by Theodore Presser from 1883 to 1957. A tremendous lifetime! The present article from January, 1912 was written by Dr. J. Herbert Sanders, who was a student of the voice teacher William Shakespeare. There were several articles by Dr. Sanders in *The Etude* during these years which appeared in the "Department For Singers" column.

I found the content of this particular article especially gratifying. I have the great privilege of doing workshops and master classes around this country and often in Australia, and everywhere I go the most common limitation for the singers that I encounter is that they do not sing with their "throats open." Apparently, some things have not changed much in the last 110 years, as you will see in the following article.

THE LARYNX, ITS POSITION AND MOVEMENTS IN SINGING[1]

by Dr. Herbert Sanders.

Probably every student of vocal science has difficulty, at some time or other, in ascertaining the significance of the movements of the larynx. Perhaps it would be unreasonable to expect it otherwise when authors, singers and teachers—the pillars of the art—cannot agree among themselves as to whether the larynx should be fixed, or whether its control should be conscious or unconscious. The time has come, however, when the correct visible movements of the larynx would be generally known and this knowledge practically applied in vocal training. The outcome of this would undoubtedly be beneficial in assisting the development of the voice, and especially in extending and adding resonance to the upper register. In the following observations all points open to dispute have been carefully avoided, so that the reader can here regard himself as being on perfectly safe ground. The principles here stated he can therefore incorporate into his teaching without fear of any but the most desirable and often astonishing results.

ITS MECHANISM.

It is unnecessary for any practical purpose for the singer to understand the mechanism of the larynx in detail. This would be interesting, but it is outside the scope of the present article. It must suffice to state that the larynx or voice-box (which is higher in women than in men) is formed of numerous cartilages connected by fibrous bands or ligaments. It is situated on the top of the windpipe and is open above and below for the breath to flow through in order to set into vibration the vocal cords. In shape it is triangular above and cylindrical below. It is the apex of the triangle that causes the prominence in the front of the neck which is known as "Adam's Apple"—so called because of the tradition which says that when Adam ate of the forbidden fruit it stuck in his throat and made it bulge out. *It is important to remember that the larynx is attached by ligaments to the tongue-bone, and that the tongue-bone is connected with the root of the tongue.*

ITS MOVEMENTS.

Let us for a moment study the visible movements of the larynx. Open the mouth as if to sing and while doing so let the fingers rest lightly on the larynx. During this operation the larynx is felt to move to a lower position. Still keeping the fingers in position, breathe through the mouth—it will be felt that the larynx moves lower still. This low larynx is found to be largely the correct position for singing, as it induces a tone at once resonant and pure and easy to produce. In the act of swallowing the larynx is at its highest point, while in the various whispered vowel sounds it ascends in the order of oo, ah, ai, ee.

"FIXED" LARYNX.

The discovery of this advantageous low position has given rise to some false theories, the most erroneous of which is that known as the "fixed" larynx. There is, of course, a distinction between a "low" larynx and a "fixed" larynx. The former has proved its desirability by its accompanied improved tone; the latter is unscientific, for, as the larynx is tied to the root of the tongue, it must move in correspondence with every movement of the tongue whether in singing or speaking. It is not to be wondered at, then, that teachers and singers have attributed any ugly and unpleasant tones to the "fixed" larynx. With tongue and larynx at variance no other result could be expected. As the "fixed" larynx must of necessity constrict the movements of the tongue, the tone must inevitably suffer, for how, without perfect freedom and correspondence of tongue and larynx are we to articulate?

It is possible that the low larynx has been blamed for many vocal defects which have been the direct result of a high larynx. Certainly it is that when the larynx is allowed to rise with the tone the muscles governing the vocal cords have difficulty in acting, and only do so under undue strain.

Not a few masters state that the movements of the larynx are automatic, and when the singer attempts to bring it under conscious control it loses its automatic response to the demands of the musical sense. It gets, so to speak, out of gear, with the result that the voice loses in quality. The only truth here lies in the generally accepted fact that in order to obtain a supple vocal mechanism the mind must be fixed intently not on the *means* (*i.e.*, the mechanism) but the *end* (*i.e.*, the tone). Therefore attention to the larynx may be harmful, and would be, if the mind were fixed on it unduly, but it is possible to control it without the mind being on it at all, as will be proved later.

REASONS FOR HOLDING THE LARYNX LOW.

1. It is generally understood that every musical instrument requires some enclosed space near the seat of vibrations, so that the enclosed air can vibrate in sympathy with the original vibrations, or, as we say, "give it resonance." This enclosed space (or partly enclosed—as in the violin which has the *f* holes) is called a "resonator." One of our chief vocal resonators is the chest. When the larynx is low and the upper chest arched and raised the instrument of vibration and the cavity of resonance assumes that near relation occupied by other instruments the tones of which would be ruined were the resonator placed far from the vibrating element.
2. The resonators of the voice, other than the chest, are above the vocal cords. The space above the cords must be enlarged as much as possible so as to give ample room for the sound waves to vibrate. This vibrating space is what is often called the "open throat," without which all tone is defective. It is in the higher register that the "open throat" is difficult to obtain. And why? Simply because the larynx is allowed to ascend and *close the throat*. The greatest enemy of the "open throat" is the high larynx. It is the function of the soft palate to alter the shape of the mouth for the production of the higher notes—and not of the larynx. This can be verified by observing the extended condition and lower position of the soft palate in singing in the head voice than in the lower registers.

HOW TO CONTROL THE LARYNX.

As the larynx moves a little for each vowel, consonant, pitch and intensity, this is no valid reason why it should be left alone. Without being "fixed" it can be steadied. In fact, this must be done to resist the flow of breath from the lungs. An uncontrolled larynx means an uncontrolled tone. Browne and Behnke, in *Voice, Song and Speech,* state that the larynx possesses what are known as the "extrinsic laryngeal muscles," best described as the "depressors" and "elevators," which as their names imply, have the power of lowering or raising the larynx. But whether it is possible to control the larynx independently of the movements of jaw and tongue is possibly of little importance to the singer. Few seem to have this power anyway. But the preceding observations put into actual practice will prove how imperative it is that the mouth should be well opened in singing so that the larynx can assume its most favorable position and the throat its most "open" condition for the attainment of the fullest development and largest compass of the voice. Many singers (and other voice-trainers will support my contention) have been unable to gain their full vocal compass simply because they will not open their mouth sufficiently wide. Some believe that on high notes it is necessary to "shade" the vowels by partly closing the mouth, but the intensity of a note can be determined by the force and direction of the breath blast. Others, in their anxiety to keep the jaw muscles supple, are afraid to open their mouths enough. The common danger, I believe, is not in that direction, for the nearly closed mouth is in singing, often an indication of muscular tension, and the mouth, on being more opened, will often cause the muscles to relax. A mouth well open during the singing of head notes will often do *more* to give muscular suppleness and ease of production than any other artifice. If in doubt observe the best singers, and especially note their suppleness of jaw movement even in the production of their highest notes, when the mouth is open to its widest extent. Dr. Fillibrown, in *Resonance in Singing and Speaking,* authoritatively sums up the matter: "The larynx and tongue should not rise with the pitch of the voice, but drop naturally with the lower jaw as the mouth opens in ascending the scale. *The proper position of the tongue will ensure a proper position for the larynx."*

FUNCTION OF THE LOWER JAW IN SINGING.

The lower jaw should be active neither in song nor speech. Its function is merely to open the mouth or vowel chamber. This is not done by a downward pressure of the jaw, but simply by the relaxation of the muscles which govern its movements. The single exception to this rule is in the initial and consonant form of y, as in "ya," "yes," "yacht," etc. This incessant closing and opening of the mouth is wisely condemned by Shakespeare in *Hamlet*:

> "Speak the speech, I pray you, as I pronounced it to you, trippingly on the tongue: but if you mouth it, as many of your players do, I had lief the town crier spoke my lines."

This "mouthing" as it is now called, is wrong, for it shows the want of muscular suppleness (the jaw trying to do the work of the organs of articulation). The free vibration of air in the vowel chamber is rendered impossible and every closure of the mouth is accompanied by the high larynx. Dora Duty Jones, in *The Technique of Speech,* says " . . . the student of diction, whether singer or speaker, whether studying to acquire foreign languages or to perfect his own, must, first of all, correct this fault *by learning to open the mouth properly."*

TWO DIFFICULT VOWELS.

The two vowels generally found to be somewhat difficult to produce with the lower jaw well depressed are oo and ee. The closure of the lips necessary for oo should not be aided by allowing the jaw to rise, but simply by allowing the tongue and lips by concerted action to form the vowel. The raised jaw and larynx will not rob the vowel of its resonance, and, as it is, it is the least resonant of all the vowels. The vowel ee is usually the weakest spot in a singer's enunciation, since it is generally sung through the teeth. In order to secure the correct resonance for this vowel, practice on lah, leh and lee on one continuous tone with the lower jaw still and depressed. The consonant l must be the result of tongue movement only.

Anyone can test for himself the principles here laid down, and it is safe to assert that with diligent application they will carry with them the conviction of their truth and will result in a marked improvement in both the singing and speaking voice. This practical application must be the test of their truth.

NOTE

J. Herbert Sanders, "The Larynx, its Position and Movements in Singing," *The Etude* XXX, 1 (January 1912): 56–57.

44. Adolphe Nourrit—The Rest of the Story

Originally published in the *Journal of Singing*, volume 70, no. 2, 2013

The legendary rivalry between Gilbert Duprez and Adolphe Nourrit at the Paris Opera during the 1830s has always fascinated me. I first heard a version of the story from my teacher John Large in one of the pedagogy classes that I took from him many years ago. The basic storyline is familiar: Duprez introduced the Paris audience to the *do di petto*, the tenor high C in the chest voice, and in doing so supplanted Nourrit and his falsetto dominated high voice in his role as the leading tenor at the Paris Opera. I have often included parts of the story (as I have understood it) in my own lectures and writings over the years. I recently found a brief account of Nourrit published in 1839 in an American journal published in 1839 from a wonderful resource called American Periodicals Series Online (a produce of a company called ProQuest). The following article was so informative to me in understanding some of the details of that story that I wanted to share it with you.[1]

Biographical Memoir of Adolphe Nourrit[2]

The name of this celebrated singer is inseparably connected with the history of the French opera, which underwent a marked revolution during the sixteen years of Nourrit's successive engagements. In the above interval Rossini adapted to French texts his two masterly productions, *Guillaume Tell* and *Moïse*, and they were performed at the French Opera with triumphant success.

Adolphe Nourrit was born in Paris on the 31st of March, 1802. His father, who as a singer of some reputation in the old French school, destined his son for mercantile pursuits, and young Nourrit was successively employed in commercial houses in Lyons and Paris. Though this occupation was not in accordance with the bent of this inclination, yet he discharged the duties it imposed upon him with the utmost diligence and punctuality. His passion for music led him to study that art as a source of recreation and amusement; and, possessing a fine voice, he was induced to take lessons in singing from Garcia, the father of Madame Malibran.

The proficiency which young Nourrit attained under the tuition of his able master, tended to increase his distaste for the career which his father had marked out for him; and, by degrees, he wholly devoted himself to that calling which his genius irresistibly prompted him to adopt. On the 10th of September, 1821, Adolphe Nourrit made his *debut* at the Academie Royale de Musique, in the character of *Pylade*, in Gluck's *Iphigenie en Tauride*.

An agreeable person, a fine clear tenor voice, refined taste, and correct execution, could not fail to ensure his success. He speedily became an established favorite, an unrivalled representative of many of the principal characters of the French opera. By dint of unwearied efforts, and unabated study and practice, Nourrit succeeded in attaining conjointly the highest power of expression in singing and in musical declamation.

From 1821 to 1826 Nourrit appeared in most of the operas forming the old *repertoire* of the Academie Royale, and likewise in two operas composed by his master, Garcia, viz., *Florestan*, and *La Mort de Tasso*. In 1826 Rossini determined to employ his talents in the service of the French opera, and, in consequence, Madame Cinti Damoreau and Levasseur, previously members of the Italian company, were engaged for the Academy. In the *Siege de Corinthe*, a translation from *Maometto Secondo*, Adolphe Nourrit performed the part of Niocles. He was especially successful in the pathetic air in the third act, which Rossini added to the score, having composed it expressly for Nourrit. The *Siege de Corinthe* was succeeded by the translation of *Mosé*. In that superb opera the talents of Madame Damoreau, Nourrit, and Levasseur, were for the first time united.

But the character which secured to Nourrit his greatest triumph both as a singer and as an actor was *Masaniello*. In this part his talents were developed quite in a new light, and his reputation as an able comedian took its date from the production of Auber's *Muette de Portici*. Nourrit's versatility of talent as an actor was indeed truly remarkable. What a powerful contrast was exhibited by his personation of the simple, clownish peasant in the *Philtre*, and the chivalric dignity of *Robert le Diable*.

How much is it to be regretted that a man possessed of talents so superior should have been wanting in strength of mind—that the very many eminent qualities with which he was endowed did not preserve him from an excessive susceptibility of feeling, which caused him to dread all rivalry, all professional competition. He was unfortunately spoiled by sixteen years of uncontested public favor. The operatic stage was to him a throne, not an arena, and he could not endure to share with another, honors which had previously been all his own.

Whilst Nourrit reigned triumphantly at the Acadamie Royale de Musique, a young French singer, named Duprez, made his appearance at the Italian Opera. In 1825 he had performed in obscure characters at the Odeon, and he subsequently appeared at the Feydeau. He was a pupil of Choron and had acquired all the impassioned style of his master; in short, Duprez solved the problem of the possibility of singing well with an indifferent voice. But though his talents were duly appreciated in amateur circles they did not please the public. Duprez had been tolerated at the Odeon, but he completely failed at the Feydeau, and a few days after his unsuccessful *debut*, he set out for Italy. There, by dint of unremitting labour, he formed his voice—became a great singer and a great musician, and the reputation which he earned in Italy found its way to Paris.

In no country in the world are public singers subjected to such a routine of laborious exertion as in Italy. There, under pain of imprisonment, they are compelled to sing, whether they be ill or well, hoarse or not hoarse. Unless they can produce a certificate signed by two well-known physicians, to prove that they are confined to their beds by a fever, or suffering under a total extinction of voice, they *must* appear—they must perform every night (Fridays excepted) and rehearse every day. Lablache has been heard to say that when he was first engaged in Paris he felt as though he was picking the manager's pocket. He used to declare that an operatic engagement in Italy is an affair of life or death, and that of several singers who commenced their career with him at San Carlos, in Naples, he alone survives. Two *prima donnas* died during the first season, and the tenor was obliged to retire, to save himself from a similar fate. In short, Lablache has often remarked that a young singer possessing talent in Italy, must either die or rise to eminence.

In this sort of deadly conflict Duprez had been victorious, and in 1837 he left Italy for Paris, whither his reputation had preceded him. Dupouchel, the manager of the French opera, engaged him, never suspecting that by securing Duprez, he should lose Adolphe Nourrit. The Italian opera had presented many examples of the amicable exercise of rival talents—harmonious conflicts, in which both parties had been victorious, and both crowned with equal glory. The brilliant *duos* of Pasta and Fodor, of Sontag and Malilbran, were still fresh in the memory of the Parisians. When Dupouchel mentioned to Nourrit his intention of engaging Duprez, it met with his perfect accordance, and for the space of a fortnight the two rivals maintained an unbroken interchange of friendly sentiments. However, they were not on an equal footing. The one had been enervated by long triumphs, by sixteen years of uninterrupted victory and undisputed favor. The other had been brought up in the school of ill fortune, and had passed through the ordeal of public disapprobation. He had won success only by dint of persevering efforts, and undaunted courage.

Thus, whilst Duprez, the man of adventurous chances and dearly purchased triumphs, was confidently preparing himself for his last perilous trial, the courage of his rival was sinking. One evening Nourrit performed in the *Muette*; (by this time every preliminary was arranged for the *debut* of Duprez.) Suddenly

Masaniello perceived his rival in the pit attentively listening to him. Nourrit became agitated. He left the stage, and was unable to proceed with his part.

Next day, in an interview with M. Dupouchel, he said, "I give it up. I cannot enter upon a conflict, the idea of which intimidates me. I have been too long the first of all; I cannot now consent to be the first *of two*. We must part"—Dupouchel was astonished. He would have made any sacrifice rather than lose Nourrit. He made the most liberal pecuniary offers; proposed to accede to any arrangement that would be satisfactory to him; but all in vain! Nourrit was inexorable, and he performed for the last time in Paris on the 1st of April, 1837. On the 17th of April, Duprez made his *debut* in *Guillaume Tell*, and his success was the more triumph [. . .] inasmuch as he had to contend against the recollections of Nourrit in the same part, and the universal regret inspired by his departure.

Nourrit, after visiting Brussels and several towns in the south of France, proceeded to Italy. There he had to encounter chagrin and disappointment of various kinds. Some circumstances which occurred during his recent visit to Naples produced a marked effect on his mind and spirits. He had himself, with very considerable talent, arranged an opera, from one of Racine's tragedies. Donizetti had composed the music, and Nourrit hoped that this piece would afford him an opportunity of developing to the Neapolitans, all the peculiarities of his talent. The censorship prohibited the performance of the Opera. The vexation caused by this affair, the particulars of which have already been laid before the public, is supposed to have led to the melancholy termination of Nourrit's life.

He had for several years previously to his death, betrayed marked indications of a nervous susceptibility, accompanied by a want of due confidence in his own talent. During his visit to London in 1832, the lukewarm reception given to *Robert le Diable*, caused him to sink into a state of gloomy despondency. At a benefit concert in Italy, he sang with Granchi the famous duo from *Norma*. At its conclusion a single hiss was heard amidst a torrent of approbation. That hiss went to Nourrit's heart like a poignard. He did not reflect that Rossini and Malibran had in their turns endured a similar outrage.

At the commencement of his career, Nourrit possessed a voice of unparalleled sweetness and purity. He gradually lost this juvenile freshness, but it was more than atoned for by the energy which succeeded, and the deep and true feeling which characterized his singing.

NOTES

1. For additional information on Nourrit, including historical context and vocal production, see Evan Walker, "The Fable of Adolphe Nourrit," *Journal of Sing*ing 64, no. 4 (March/April 2008): 411–416.
2. Author unknown. "Biographical Memoire of Adolphe Nourrit," *Spirit of the Times; A Chronicle of the Turf, Agriculture, Field Sports, Lite* (May 25, 1839): 9, 12.

45. Herman Klein: A "Contemporary" Link to Mozart (III)

Originally published in the *Journal of Singing*, volume 70, no.3, 2014

In 2007, I presented in two subsequent columns[1] excerpts from Herman Klein's book *The Bel Canto*.[2] Klein was a former student of Garcia and became a well-respected critic and voice teacher. I was reminded of Klein and his work through Daniel Shigo's blog called Voicetalk[3] and an article he wrote concerning his work on Klein's all-but-forgotten manual, *The Phono-Vocal Method*. Here is the introduction to that original column from 2007 followed by additional chapters from *The BelCanto*.

During my study of the work of Manuel Garcia II, I became aware of the name of Herman Klein. Klein was a well-known music critic and voice teacher in London who also spent several years in New York City. Among many other literary accomplishments, he provided critical reviews of newly released recordings for the English journal *The Gramophone* from 1924 until his death in 1934. He was the first to offer critical analysis of recordings (mainly singers) made during the infancy of the recording industry and during its transition from the original acoustic method to the birth of the electrical age of sound recording.

One of the life experiences that qualified Herman Klein for his role as a critic of singing was his long association with Manuel Garcia. Klein's family hosted Manuel Garcia in their home in London for several years beginning in 1874. Garcia's studio was on the first floor of their home in Manchester Square. Klein studied with him for a period of about four years while he was a young man still living in his parents' home. Klein always showed promise in literary pursuits, and Garcia advised him that a professional singing career was probably not in the cards. So, he dedicated himself to writing and the study and teaching of singing. He became a highly respected teacher in his own right and continued his friendship with Garcia. He helped the old man write his last work, *Hints on Singing*, published in 1894.

In 1923 Klein published a modest book entitled simply *The Bel Canto*. In this book he sought to describe the technical foundations that he felt were important for singing the music of Mozart. Klein's expertise in this area came from the fact that he had worked so closely with a man who had very close to association to first and second generation Mozart singers and whose father was Rossini's favorite tenor (Manuel Garcia *pere*).

VI. Language and Diction

To the code of laws that governs the Italian school of singing there need only be added a few words on the subject of enunciation and diction. Here the laws are again almost universal; but the rules for their application should be modified according to the language employed by the singer.

'Music,' as Garcia has said, 'though the language of the emotions, can only arouse them in a vague and general manner. To express any feeling or idea we must make use of words. Hence the importance for the singer of delivering these with the utmost distinctness, correctness, and meaning, under the penalty of losing the attention of the audience' (*Hints on Singing*, p. 45).

The mechanism of verbal utterance is the same in singing and in speaking. So far as the pronunciation of consonants is concerned, it must not be altered or varied, unless greater distinctness of articulation can be so obtained. For instance, what might be regarded as exaggeration in ordinary speech or drawing-room conversation seems perfectly natural in singing or stage elocution. I have generally found that, granted the vocal gift, the person who speaks well stands a better chance of making a good singer than the person who speaks badly.

The disparity between English and Italian as singing languages is greatly over-estimated and can always be overcome, although it seldom is. The advantage of the Italian lies chiefly in the more 'open' vowels—an advantage not to be despised, seeing that 'intonation, sustaining of the voice, expression or quality of timbre, tonic accent, and vocalization are all entrusted to the care of the vowel.'
But when the openness, the amplitude, the freedom of the Italian vowels are reproduced in the formation of the equivalent English sounds, together with a similar forward projection of the resultant tone, the disparity should almost entirely disappear.

The true explanation why this does not always happen lies in the fundamental obstacles presented by English consonants, as they are pronounced with half-closed mouth and tightened jaw by the vast majority of people to whom the English language is the mother-tongue. With their fixed 'singing position,' their rigid facial muscles, their inelastic joints, and their rebellious tongues, their common habit is to allow syllable after syllable to slither out half articulated. Thus vowels which might otherwise be admirable for singing are badly shaped, inadequately, and impure.

I have tested and proved this in hundreds of instances, on both sides of the Atlantic, proving it most decisively by the facility with which foreigners can be taught to surmount the difficulties of English pronunciation. With their superior method of vowel formation and enunciation, they invariably learn to make themselves better understood in singing than their English-speaking colleagues.

As a medium for beauty of speech and vocal sound, the language of Shakespeare is not less favourable than any other tongue spoken upon the earth. Patti could sing with equally irresistible charm in English, French, Spanish, Russian, German and Welsh.

My preference for Italian in the singing of Mozart is where he himself employed an Italian text for his compositions; and he employed it for most of his operas. He loved the language. Its softness, its sweetness, its poetic grace, its graphic force appealed to him; and he knew how to set it to music with the maximum of racial flavor and rhythmic feeling. The least the singer can strive to accomplish is to do Mozart justice by a clear, refined utterance of the words to which he allied his ineffable melodies.

Singers with beautiful voices and moderate executive ability do not sufficiently recognize the tremendous influence of diction on their art. As a rule they think too much about their tone. On the other hand, those possessing only fair voices often do wonders by delivering the poet's lines with some peculiar charm of style, with distinctness, intelligence, refinement, and the requisite sense of contrast. But the proper combination is rare.

The mechanism for clear, emphatic, or rapid articulation is granted by nature to 90 percent of well-bred people; yet probably not one-twentieth of that number is so trained as to display their valuable faculty to advantage in either speech or song. The neglect of the former in childhood, crudities of dialect, and a slipshod mode of speaking that have not been corrected soon enough, are common obstacles to the would-be vocalist, and are exceedingly hard to overcome.

The old Italian singers were adepts in the art of 'patter.' They could rattle off their words at a rate that was simply astounding, and so distinctly that the audience could understand every syllable, which was perhaps the sole excuse for treating dialogue in opera, as Mozart did, in the form of *recitativo secco*, which I confess to finding extremely dull, with its eternal accompaniment of chords scraped by the principal 'cello and double-bass. But the art of the *recitativo secco* made it easy for the singers to pronounce the words of their airs with ease and clarity. The one was regarded as a preparatory study for the other.

A most remarkable illustration of this was the famous baritone, Cotogni, who used to sing Figaro to Patti's Rosina at Covent Garden in Rossini's *Barbiere.* His delivery of the 'Largo al factotum' was as quick and lively as that of the present-day Titta Ruffo, and certainly more distinct; and in the recitative of the Figaro of *Le Nozze* his clear utterance was beyond reproach. Yet it is a fact of which all his friends were aware that Cotogni suffered from an impediment in his speech which in ordinary conversation was painfully evident. He did not stammer—people who stammer badly but do not hesitate when singing or reciting are not uncommon. He made a whistling sound with the sides of his tongue against his teeth that was worse than a lisp. The moment he began to sing it entirely disappeared.

In Mozart we find the need for a quality additional to good diction—the quality of drama. Other composers before him made, indeed, a similar demand; but Mozart in some manner asked for a greater union of rare gifts than any of them.

The all-round development of the many rare talents here referred to constitutes what we now regard as the *sine qua non* for the interpretation of the classical Lied and the higher type of modern song, wherein poem and music are supposed to be brought absolutely into line with each other. Mozart was among the earliest of the great musicians to equalize the importance of both elements.

It was not as a writer of Lieder that Mozart displayed this gift. None of his songs is worthy of discussion here except that masterpiece 'Das Veilchen,' the model of the felicitous treatment of a simple theme that was followed by so many illustrious song-writers. I mention it not in order to show how it should be sung; the song itself shows that; but because it stands apart from everything else that Mozart wrote. Otto Jahn, his biographer, says of it:

> 'The crown of all the songs, by virtue of its touching expression of emotion and its charming perfection of form, is unquestionably Goethe's "Veilchen."
>
> 'In other songs we discern musical genius divining and bringing to light the poetic germ which lies hidden in the words; here we have the impression made upon Mozart by true poetry. It may seem remarkable that so simple a lyrical poem should have been treated by Mozart as a romance, giving a certain amount of dramatic detail to the little story; and yet it must not be overlooked that the masterly touch which repeats the closing words: "das arme Veilchen! es war ein herzigs Veilchen!" fully reasserts a genuine lyric element. Goethe's clear and plastic presentation of a simple image, true in every feature, could not fail to impress him deeply.'

The singer who can do justice to 'Das Veilchen' probably owns most of the qualities required for the interpretation of the Lieder of Schubert, Schumann, Brahms, and even Wolf and Strauss.

VII. Traditional Interpretation

Mozart wrote easily and rapidly but never carelessly. His tireless industry for thirty years resulted in a prodigious output, which prematurely sapped his vitality. But he never put on paper a note or a sign that he did not want to be observed. Grace and symmetry were as natural to him as to a Greek sculptor; and he was one of the greatest masters of musical form that ever lived.

We can scarcely realize how marvelously original he was. At the time he lived and wrote a large proportion of his melodies, his peculiar rhythms, his turns of phraseology and expression, his cadences—his individual mannerisms—were things that must have sounded absolutely new.

When I was studying an air from *Don Giovanni,* I once asked my master how I could best improve my phrasing of Mozart's music and my rendering of his ornaments.

'Go to the "Pops" every week,' said Garcia. 'Go to St. James's Hall and listen to Joachim and Piatti and Norman-Néruda. Make a turn or a shake or an *appoggiatura* as they do; make your *portamenti* as lightly, as delicately, and with as much reticence. The great violinists and 'cellists have preserved that art much better than the singers. You can learn from them everything that you want to know about it, and you may imitate them without fear.'

This was said over forty years ago, and it stands good to-day, even though the vocalist has always something to add to the instrumentalist's clarity.

A close study of Mozart's operas shows his amazing aptitude for colour, for an individual quality of dramatic expression, peculiar not only to each character, but to every thought or feeling of that character. This aptitude is the more astonishing because it is obviously spontaneous, not the result of long reflection or laborious effort.

Observe, for instance, how in the two airs of the Countess in *Le Nozze di Figaro* 'Porgi amor' introduces the proud but neglected lady in a prayer for help to the god of love; while the first part of 'Dove sono' is rather an outpouring of vain regrets over a happy past that shows little promise of renewal. The music of each differs in character from the other; yet both are generally sung in the same monotonous key of misery and boredom, and with exactly the same vocal colouring.

The gramophone, had it been invented thirty years earlier, would provide evidence of Theresa Tietjen's reading of these two pieces, and prove how a great dramatic singer could infuse into each its full and individual qualities. Description cannot replace such evidence; but it may at least be said that, apart from her eloquent colouring of each utterance, Tietjens achieved not a little of her triumph by the purity and simplicity of her phrasing and the natural, unforced tragic grandeur of her style. To her the instinct for variation or contrast came without being sought, and it enabled her to realize Mozart's exact intention.

The same may be said of Patti's delicate differentiation between the two airs of Zerlina in *Don Giovanni*, which she made partly by instinct and partly because she had been trained in the right tradition.[‡‡] Her singing of 'Batti, batti' was always marked by a mixture of coquetry and flattery obviously meant to coax Masetto into forgiving her for her flirtation with the amorous Don. Zerlina knows, of course, that her simple sweetheart would never raise a finger to hurt her, but she offers to submit to corporal punishment all the same. On the other hand, in 'Vedrai, carino' one could instantly perceive, when Patti sang it, the tone of unaffected regret and anxious sympathy aroused by Masetto's physical suffering, even with the undercurrent of humour that accompanies the air.

Apart from tradition, however, the composer's intention was clearly conveyed by the nature of the vocal treatment revealed in these two airs. In 'Batti, batti,' the repeated downward trend of the quavers plainly suggests a sort of caressing, insinuating motion, which the singer must render with an unbroken surface of legato, yet with scarcely a shade of portamento anywhere. This restraint imparts the greater effect to the delicate gliding of the *notes coulées* on the phrase 'E le care tue manine.'

In 'Vedrai, carino' there is more scope for an expressive portamento, very lightly graded on the slurred quavers; and no less important is a neat execution of the mordent on the word *carino*, which gives

---

[‡‡] Adelina Patti is often belittled because of certain breaches of artistic taste that occasionally disfigured her concert career after she had left the stage. The younger generation who never heard her in opera could only judge her by what she did on her periodical appearances at the Albert Hall for twenty years with the *beaux restes* of a marvelously-preserved voice. At Covent Garden between 1861 and 1885 she had, at any rate as Zerlina, done something more than warble Mozart's tunes; she had established her fame as a genuine Mozart singer. One reason for this was, that she had studied the role with her brother-in-law, impresario, and 'coach,' Maurice Strakosch, who previously acted for some time as accompanist for the great Pasta when she was teaching at Como. There Strakosch learned the tradition of the part of Zerlina from one who had sung Mozart in London less than twenty-five years after the composer's death. The tradition was therefore direct and (in the opinion of Garcia) correct.

the cue, as it were, for Zerlina's attitude of real solicitude this time. As a musical indication of her *certo balsam,* that runs of three notes is a stroke of genius; and so, too, are the three taps when she places her hand upon her heart and slyly says, *Sentilo battere.*

Although portamenti as a rule are to be lightly sung, that is, when uttering 'moderate or tender sentiments,' they must, when 'applied to expression of powerful feelings, be strong and rapid' (*Hints on Singing,* p. 63). Examples of the latter are frequently to be met with in Mozart, especially in *Don Giovanni,* where he uses the portamento again and again as a means for dramatic expression and indicates it (as in the opening phrase of the Don's serenade) in a manner that cannot be mistaken. The mastery of this vocal grace is essential and of the highest value to the dramatic singer.

The music of Donna Anna and Don Ottavio contains many similar instances—the former in 'Non mi dir,' the latter in both his solo airs, notwithstanding the extraordinary contrast that they otherwise present. In 'Dalla sua pace' the word *morte,* sung without a strong portamento from the D to the G, would be ineffective; while in 'Il mio tesoro,' which is as florid and declamatory as the other air is lyrical, there are similar points to be observed.

So again, in the part of Donna Elvira, Mozart has employed the same mode of heightening emotional fervor in music that is otherwise quite different in cast, like, for example, the opening of the trio 'Ah, chi me dice mai' and the very difficult aria 'Mi tradi alma ingrata.' The explanation of the disparity in Donna Elvira's case is, curiously enough, identical with that in Don Ottavio's, namely, that the two pieces were not written for the same artists. 'Dalla sua pace' was composed for a Viennese tenor, Signor Morello, who found 'Il mio tesoro' too much for him; whilst 'Mi tradi' was introduced into the opera for the famous Madame Cavalieri because there was not a show-piece brilliant enough for her liking.

Yet 'Mi tradi' is not difficult on account of its brilliancy. It has nothing in common with the vengeful outbursts of the Queen of Night. The strange mixture of contradictory feelings that besets Donna Elvira finds expression here in one long series of *notes coulées,* extremely difficult to sing with neatness and at the same time the right dramatic accent. The question has been asked why Mozart set the air in this manner. It was either because he wished to illustrate Donna Elvira's unbalanced, hesitant condition of mind (she was supposed to be a *ci-devant* nun, whose troubles had upset her mentally), or because Mme Cavalieri was an uncommonly good executant of Mozart's favourite *notes coulées.*

I once heard Christine Nilsson in this role (Tietjens being the Donna Anna and Trebelli the Zerlina); and although I saw many good Elviras subsequently, I never again experienced the same realization of the unfortunate lady's state of mental distraction or the same rare beauty of voice and method in performing the 'ups and downs' of 'Mi tradi.' It reminded me of the exquisite bowing of Sarasate. Even if the gift came to her by intuition, how hard she must have practiced at first!

NOTES

1. Stephen F. Austin, "Herman Klein, A 'Contemporary' Link to Mozart (I)," *Journal of Singing* 63, no. 4 (March/April 2007): 469; Stephen F. Austin, "Herman Klein, A 'Contemporary' Link to Mozart (II)," *Journal of Singing* 63, no. 5 (May/June 2007):577.
2. Herman Klein, *The Bel Canto* (London: Oxford University Press, 1923).
3. http://www.voice-talk.net/.

46. Herman Klein: A "Contemporary" Link to Mozart (IV)

Originally published in the *Journal of Singing*, volume 70, no. 4, 2014

This is the final installment of a guide to singing written by Herman Klein call *The Bel Canto: With Particular Reference to the Singing of Mozart*, published in 1923.[1] Klein, a well-known music critic in the early 20th century, studied singing with Manuel Garcia II as a young man and maintained a close relationship with him until Garcia's death in 1906. I believe that there is much to be gained from Klein's perspective on singing. It is more important than just a historical relic (that is practically unknown to us); this modest little book outlines Garcia's understanding as it relates to the singing of Mozart's music. Garcia began teaching in the early 1830s. He had the opportunity to learn the style of Mozart's music from listening to and working with singers who had learned from Mozart himself. Garcia lived long enough to bring that experience into the 20th century, and it is passed on to us through his student Herman Klein. Personally, I have found Klein's (perhaps outspoken) caution concerning the application of appoggiaturas and cadenzas in Mozart's operatic works very enlightening. The text is reproduced exactly as it originally appeared.

IX. THE APPOGGIATURA

The appoggiatura has been much discussed and at times has led to more heated argument than it demanded. The rules pertaining to it were laid down (or gradually laid themselves down) on perfectly clear lines, and have only to be understood for mistakes or misinterpretations to be avoided. For these rules I have, where possible, found it better to consult tradition rather than text-books—excepting of course in the case of Garcia, who put the one into the other.

The *appoggiatura* dates back to the now remote period when composers left the choice of ornaments and graces to the artists who sang their music. It was a stupid fashion, but doubtless there were good reasons for it, until, over a century ago, Rossini gave it up on the sensible ground that he found himself better served by supplying his own ornaments.

But in music of a date earlier than Rossini's one has still to deal with the old custom that gives a loophole for wrong treatment to the ignorant, the ill-informed, or the bigoted; or to those who imagine that every note written by the old masters, in recitative or elsewhere, should be literally sung as it appears on the printed page; who imagine that because Bach does not require—nor should he indeed receive—the usual Italian interpretation of the appoggiatura, the same strict law must perforce apply to Mozart.

The master's obvious conclusion, according to Garcia, was that the appoggiatura 'must be introduced.' That is to say, 'when a sentence ends with two equal notes, in the Italian style, we raise the first a tone or a half-tone, according to the degree of the scale.' And he adds, 'the exception to this rule is when the two notes are both an essential part of an idea, when they belong to concerted voices, or when the harmony does not permit the alteration' (*Hints on Singing*, p. 67).

These exceptions have to be very carefully considered; but in the majority of cases their treatment has been made familiar by tradition. They rarely occur in recitative, where the intention is generally too plain to leave room for misconstruction. The need for the heightened accent afforded by raising the first note seems unmistakable. In the three sentences with which Susanna begins the recitative 'Giunse alfin,' preceding 'Deh vieni,' a literal rendering of the same notes on the penultimate syllables of *momento, affanno,* and *mio* would sound bald, ugly, unlike Mozart, although he wrote them so. In the aria greater latitude is possible; but it should not be left to the teacher or singer of no special knowledge to decide where the two notes are or are not 'essential part of an idea,' or where the appoggiatura is calculated to spoil the harmony. There is another point—the *length* of the raised note. Should it be permissible to alter it? In my opinion, certainly not. When Mozart wrote a crotchet he did not mean it to be sung as a quaver. Susannas like Marimon and Sembrich did not depart from tradition in one regard, nor did they willfully disobey it in another. Thus, in 'Deh vieni' they naturally sang the appoggiatura where it does and should occur, namely, on the last two notes of the first and fourth phrases, on *bella* and *tace*; also again on *l'aura* and *adesca*. But I never heard them convert the crotchet-quaver of these two syllables into two quavers, as the late Mr. Randegger gave them in his Novello edition of the arias of Susanna and Cherubino.

In concerted music the appoggiatura must *not* be introduced, above all where the voices are singing together. It brings in a note foreign to the chord and creates an effect that the composer did not intend. If Mozart wished for an appoggiatura in one of the themes of an ensemble he never failed to indicate it in the orthodox way by a small note (to be accorded the same value as a large one). Examples of this occur in the duet 'La ci darem' (*Don Giovanni)* where Zerlina has twice to glide down a whole fifth on *Mi trema un poco il cor*. But it would not justify her in raising the last note but one, as many a Zerlina has done, on the subsequent word *Masetto*.

Similarly with the two duets in *Le Nozze*: Susanna must sing the word *boschetto* in 'Sull' aria' without the appoggiatura, although the countess sings it with one; the text of the music clearly indicates this in each case. In 'Crudel, perchè' the Count should never alter the C sharp on *verrai* and *mancherai,* since obviously the composer has never asked or meant him to do so. But I admit that every famous singer I have heard in the part has sinned by transgressing this rule, probably because it sounds rather prettier.

Here, for once, authoritative tradition exemplifies the fact that recognized laws may be broken by the people who as a rule accord them the most implicit obedience. But on the whole I prefer a sound, definite law to a doubtful tradition, however widely accepted.

MARKS OF EXPRESSION

Breathing-Places, etc.

In teaching I have found it convenient to make use of modern editions of Mozart's operatic airs because they are well printed and have fewer misprints than the old sheet-music copies published years ago. Many of the indications and substituted notes are correct and some of the marks of expression permissible; those which are not one can always change.

But therin lies the danger. These 'edited' versions are too untrustworthy to be followed without question. The student should carefully think out the doubtful points and reject without hesitation all changes or embellishments which seem out of keeping with the true characteristics of the Mozart style of which I have endeavoured to indicate the salient features. For his own marks of expression—*p* or *f*; *cres.* or *dim.;* the acceleration or slackening of *tempo*; pauses, and so forth—it is necessary to look to the accompaniment even more than the voice part, for there they are mostly to be found.

It was not the custom of the day to indicate *breathing-places* otherwise than by rests, and then only in the rarest cases, except in recitative, where the natural accentuation and rounding-off of the phrase, as in ordinary spoken declamation, provided obvious opportunities. The latter were intended not so much to indicate silence as to serve the purpose of punctuation.

In the solos and concerted pieces the musical phrase dictates the best place for taking breath as well if not better than the text. The charm and symmetry of the musical effect needs to be the first consideration in the rendering of all Mozart's melodies, and the singer may, in this particular matter of phrasing, be as accurately guided by good taste and right feeling as by the most reliable tradition. On the other hand, I do not agree, where faulty English translations are the cause, with new breathing places that upset the melody for the sake of badly-fitting sentences. The words are important, but in Mozart it must be the music, first and last.

Beyond a doubt Mozart wrote for singers who had a prodigious breathing capacity, as did Bach and Handel before him; but only now and then did he call upon them to sing passages which we should to-day find impossible of execution in a single breath. There is no virtue in accomplishing these *tours de force* when the passage can be so much better sung with the aid of an extra breath, taken imperceptibly at the right moment and in the right way.

It is a serious question whether many of the trying passages, based upon a single syllable, that are so familiar to Mozart students, were invariably sung a hundred years go in a single respiration. Manuel Garcia never expected it, for example, in the extended run that occurs in 'Il mio tesoro,' but at once marked the conventional breaths—the same that I heard Caruso take on the solitary occasion when he sang Don Ottavio at Covent Garden. Nor did the old teacher act differently in other cases, such as the long runs in 'Gli angui d'inferno,' 'Ah, lo so,' 'Non mi dir,' 'Zeffiretti lusinghieri,' &c.

XI. UNION OF GRACE AND SKILL

Grace of execution must distinguish the rendering of Mozart's *ornaments*. These *gruppetti* or turns, these quick *appoggiature* and *acciaccature* ('two rapid descending notes ornamenting a third note'), these repeated or staccato sounds, and, perhaps most important of all, the perfect shake or trill, must be at the command of the thoroughly-trained vocalist.

But to mechanical accuracy must also be added two things—entire ease of manner and constant unfailing obedience to the rhythmical accent of the bar.

In Mozart there is never occasion either to hurry or to drag the 'grace' notes. The ornament, whatever it may be, always has its precise place in the theme or phrase, and, if properly executed, there is always abundant time for singing it with smoothness, clarity, and distinction. Yet how seldom do we hear this done, especially where the *turn* is concerned. A violinist will take pains to make you hear the last note of the turn; a singer will trouble less about it. Above all, every note of every ornament must be as perfectly in tune as the theme which it embellishes.

It is almost a crime to add to or take away from the literal text of Mozart's ornaments. They suffice as they stand. The great Italian singers used occasionally to insert a turn or a mordent after a pause on a long ending note. Mario did so in 'Il mio tesoro' on the words *a vendicar io vado;* Patti sometimes on the *dove mi stà* in 'Vedrai, carino.' But these were among the later traditions not so strictly to be imitated. Mozart is best left alone.

Pasta invented more changes and additional ornaments than any other *coloratura* soprano of her time. But she reserved them exclusively for Bellini, who wrote *Norma* and *Sonnambula* for her; for Donizetti, who adored her Anna Bolena; and for Rossini, who thought her the ideal Semiramide. She never altered or added a note to Mozart. There the singer declared herself 'on holy ground.'

The *cadenza*, again, was a growth of the nineteenth century. It is out of place in Mozart's vocal compositions because the scheme of his design is complete without it; besides, when he wishes, they contain quite sufficient elaborate passages for display to serve the ambition of any average good singer. The cadenza belongs, properly speaking, to the school of the Italian composers above name, and to Verdi or Meyerbeer.

I have now, I think, enumerated all the principal points involved in the application of Italian singing to the music of Mozart. The perfect union of the two is the goal that the student should have in mind from the start; and the conscientious labour required for its accomplishment can hardly fail to be rewarded, since the key to the 'Bel Canto' unlocks in Mozart the richest storehouse of vocal treasures that musician ever gave to the world.

NOTE

1. Herman Klein, *The Bel Canto* (London: Oxford University Press, 1923).

47. Is It Time for a Change?

Originally published in the *Journal of Singing*, volume 70, no. 5, 2014

As I am preparing this article, the New Year has just begun. For many it is a time of reflection on the past and pondering the future, and I guess I am not immune. It is difficult for me to believe that I began this column in 2004, a decade ago. Ten years is a long time. When I have been doing anything for such a period it is typical for me to think about a change: to do something novel, something different. I also just celebrated my 60th birthday, so I am at that point in life when some of us wonder what we are going to do when we grow up. I thought long and hard (again) about buying a big Harley motorcycle. We are the guys you see riding those things, after all: Baby Boomers who are 60 plus with full leathers and a headband! But something about the cliché of it was more than I could take. So, instead of a Harley I took over the chairmanship of our division of vocal studies where I teach, something I swore I would never do! But, I was feeling a need for something different to do professionally, and it seemed to make more sense than abandoning my academic career and selling real estate or killing myself on a bike. Much to my surprise, I am finding it quite satisfying.

Another aspect of this need for change is to consider this column and its place in my life and in the life of the journal. It should not go on forever, but how long is long enough? Writing a column for this publication was on my "bucket list," and I have gotten so much out of doing it. Does it need a new title? A new focus? Does it need an updated headshot? After ten years, shouldn't it be something different?

Change is so glorified in our culture: new houses, new cars, New Year's resolutions. In academia a new dean brings new ideas even when the old ways of doing things were very successful. A new university president has to change things so that it looks like he or she is really worth that multimillion dollar contract. Even successful corporate businesses change operational models every so often, sometimes with disastrous results—JC Penney comes to mind. How many different strategic plans have I seen in my academic career? The message is clear: What you have been doing is simply not good enough!

As chairperson I am now experiencing first-hand the monster of assessment at the university level. We have full time professionals on the campus hired to create new ways of assessing everything that goes on at the university. My academic unit actually earns points for changing our grading and outcome rubrics even if the outcomes are worse. It is change that is valued.

Aha! And now I see clearly: I need continue to write this column, at least for a time, and that as long as I do, it should remain the same. In 2004 my strategic plan for this column was to present to contemporary practitioners of the vocal art some of the important pedagogic principles that I have discovered in all-but-forgotten resources. I have offered original source material (often extended and complete) from writings by some of the great voice teachers of the past, such as Garcia, Stockhausen, Bassini, Root, Lamperti, Mancini, Tosi, and most recently Hermann Klein—in their own words, not how someone has misinterpreted them. Where else but here?

New ideas and teaching methods developed in the 20th century because teachers felt the need to do something novel, to change their strategic plan. It has now been so long, that many of us have never read or heard the wisdom of our ancient peers on the process of training a voice to excellence. That is not to say that contemporary theories and models have no validity, but "there is nothing true that is new."

So, in my own tradition, here are the preface and opening few chapters from Manuel Garcia's *Hints On Singing*. I recently acquired an original copy published in 1894 (very hard to find at an affordable price), and that is the source for the excerpts herein. The reader may recall that in an article called: "Hints on Singing . . . Hints Indeed!" (*Journal of Singing* 69, no. 2 [November/ December 2012]: 213), I presented Garcia's chapter on where and how to take a breath when the score does not seem to allow for it. I may just put the whole small but powerful book in this column over the next year. I cannot think of a more appropriate thing to do in 2014.

HINTS ON SINGING
by Manuel Garcia

PREFACE

Since the publication of "L'Art du Chant,"[§§] the invention of the laryngoscope and fifty years of additional experience have naturally enabled me to acquire many fresh ideas, and also to clear up all my pre-existing doubts. The result of this I now offer to the public in as concise and clear a form as I have found possible. The study of the physiology of the voice has been greatly facilitated by the use of the laryngoscope. This instrument, by laying bare the interior of the larynx, shows how the glottis proceeds to produce sounds and registers. It shows, also, the manner in which the ringing and veiled qualities are communicated to the voice. These qualities—produced by the glottis—are distinct from the characteristics of the voice called *timbres*, which are exterior to the vibratory organ and are originated in the pharynx by quite another mechanism. All this should dispel many false ideas afloat on the question of voice production.

I introduce a few anatomical figures to facilitate my explanations. The study of the anatomy and physiology of the vocal organs is not indispensable to the pupil, but might be most useful to the teacher. It will enable him, when a defect is to be amended, to detect the organ which is at fault, and to suggest the proper correction. For the pupil it is enough that, localizing his sensations through his master's explanations, he should learn to distinguish the various parts of his instrument and the manner of using them.

I have also introduced some exercises to give the pupil the opportunity of applying the precepts set forth. At the present day the acquirement of flexibility is not in great esteem, and were it not, perhaps, for the venerable Handel, declamatory music would reign alone. This is to be regretted, for not only must the art suffer, but also the young fresh voices, to which the brilliant florid style is the most congenial; the harder and more settled organs being best suited for declamation. It would not be difficult to trace the causes of the decline of the florid style. Let it suffice, however, to mention, as one of the most important, the disappearance of the race of great singers who, besides originating this art, carried it to its highest point on excellence. The impresario, influenced by the exigencies of the modern prima donna, has been constrained to offer less gifted and accomplished *virtuose* to the composer, who in turn has been compelled to simplify the *role* of the voice and to rely more and more upon orchestral effects. Thus, singing is becoming as much a lost art as the manufacture of Mandarin china or the varnish used by the old masters.

In adopting the form of question and answer, I have endeavored to foresee the difficulties likely to occur to an earnest student. I subjoin a sketch of the laryngoscope to satisfy the curiosity of any student who may be interested in the subject. The laryngoscope consists of two mirrors. One of them (very small) is attached to the end of a long wire and placed against the uvula at the top of the pharynx, the reflecting surface turned downwards. It must be moderately heated that it may not be tarnished by the breath. The other mirror is employed to throw rays of light on the first. The form and disposition of the mirrors will be shown more clearly by the following illustrations than by any attempt at explanation[***]:—[Figure 1]

[§§] "Traité Complet de l'Art du Chant," par Manuel Garcia. Paris: Brandus et Cie., 1840.

[***] Observations on the Human Voice, by Manuel Garcia. Proceedings of the Royal Society of London. Vol. VII. Meeting of May 24th, 1855. p. 399 to 410.

PREFACE.

Laryngoscopic mirrors, half size :—

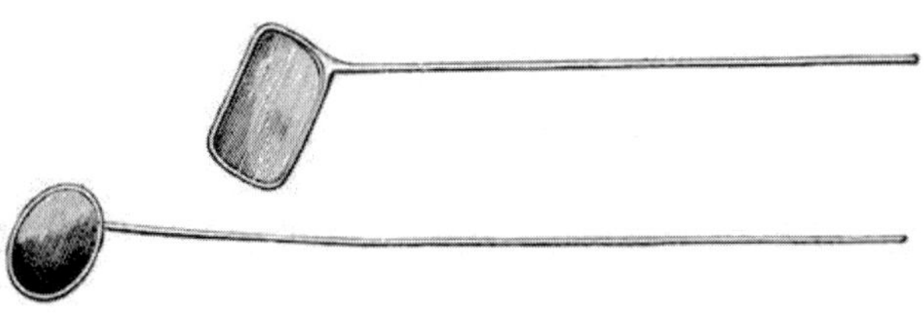

I wish to express my gratitude to DR. S. G. SHATTOCK for his great kindness in undertaking to make finished drawings from my rough sketches, and rectifying *con amore* any physiological or anatomical description that was not strictly technical. I have also to thank my old pupil, MR. HERMANN KLEIN, for his indefatigable patience and skill in preparing the MS. for the press and correcting the proofs.

MANUEL GARCIA.

CRICKLEWOOD,
LONDON, *October*, 1894.

Figure 1.

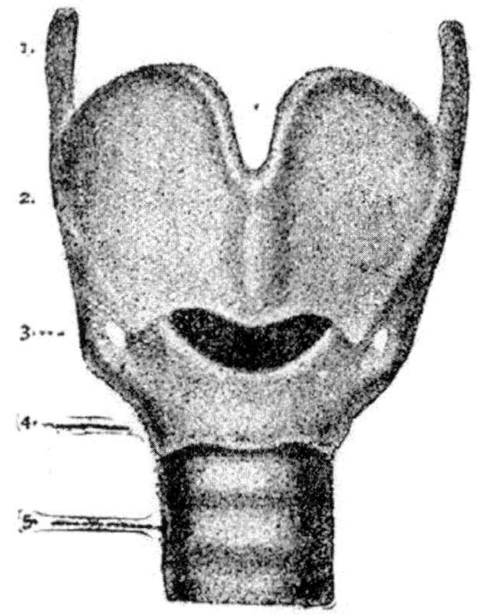

Fig. 1.
The Cartilages of the Larynx viewed from the front (*S. G. Shattock*).

1. Upper horn of the thyroid cartilage.
2. Thyroid cartilage, articulating by its inferior horn with the cricoid.
3. Lower horn of the thryoid cartilage, articulating with the cricoid.
4. Cricoid cartilage.
5. Upper end of the trachea.

The epiglottis is not represented.

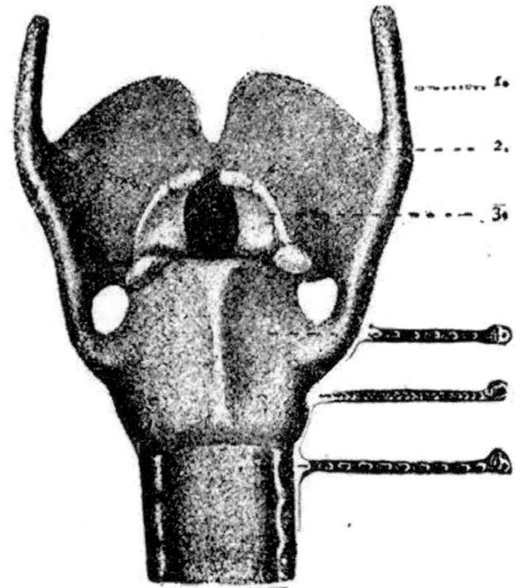

Fig. 2.
The Cartilages of the Larynx viewed from behind (*after Sappey*).

1. Upper horn of the thyroid cartilage.
2. Thyroid cartilage.
3. Arytenoid of the right side.
4. Cricoid cartilage.
5. Lower horn of the thyroid cartilage, articulating with the cricoid.
6. Upper end of the trachea.

The epiglottis is not represented.

Figure 2.

PART I.

OBJECTS OF VOCAL STUDY

Q. What is the object of vocal study?

A. To make the voice irreproachable in its intonation, firm, strong, flexible, extended, and to correct its faults.

Q. Is that all?

A. To teach the student the art of phrasing, to familiarize him with the different styles, and to develop his expression.

Q. Of what does the vocal instrument consist?

A. Of four distinct apparatus which combine their action; but with special functions, each being entirely independent of the rest. These apparatus are: -

The Bellows, *namely,* the *lungs.*

The Vibrator, *namely,* the glottis.

The Reflector, *namely,* the *pharynx,* and (when words are added)

The Articulator, *namely, organs of the mouth.*

[Figure 2]

Q. Give a concise description of the vocal instrument.

A. The *Lungs,* a spongy matter where the air is stored, are at the base of the instrument. Essential organs of the respiration, the lungs perform the function of an organ bellows, furnishing the air necessary for the sonorous waves. They are placed, one on each side of the chest, the expansion of which makes room for their inflation, and the contraction of which compels them to expel part of the air admitted. Above comes the *Larynx,* as sort of cartilaginous box; it is conspicuous in the front of the upper part of the neck, and forms that protection known as Adam's apple.

This box, in which every vocal sound is produced, is open at both ends, and communicates by its lower opening directly with the lungs through the *Trachea,* an elastic tube; the high opening communicates with the *Pharynx,* and when we swallow, is closed by a sort of cartilaginous leaf, called the *Epiglottis.* The larynx is surmounted by the pharynx, a large cavity which forms the back of the mouth; it is limited behind by a proper muscular wall, in front by the pillars of the *fauces.* The pharynx communicates with the *nasal fossae,* two cavities situated above the roof of the mouth, and extending from the pharynx to the nostril. The *palate* is the roof of the mouth; the anterior two-thirds are bony, the other third, called the *soft palate,* is a movable curtain continued backwards from the hard palate. The pharynx, on account of the numerous shapes it can assume, confers the colouring of *timbres* on sounds produced in the larynx, and contributes to the formation of vowels. [Figure 3]

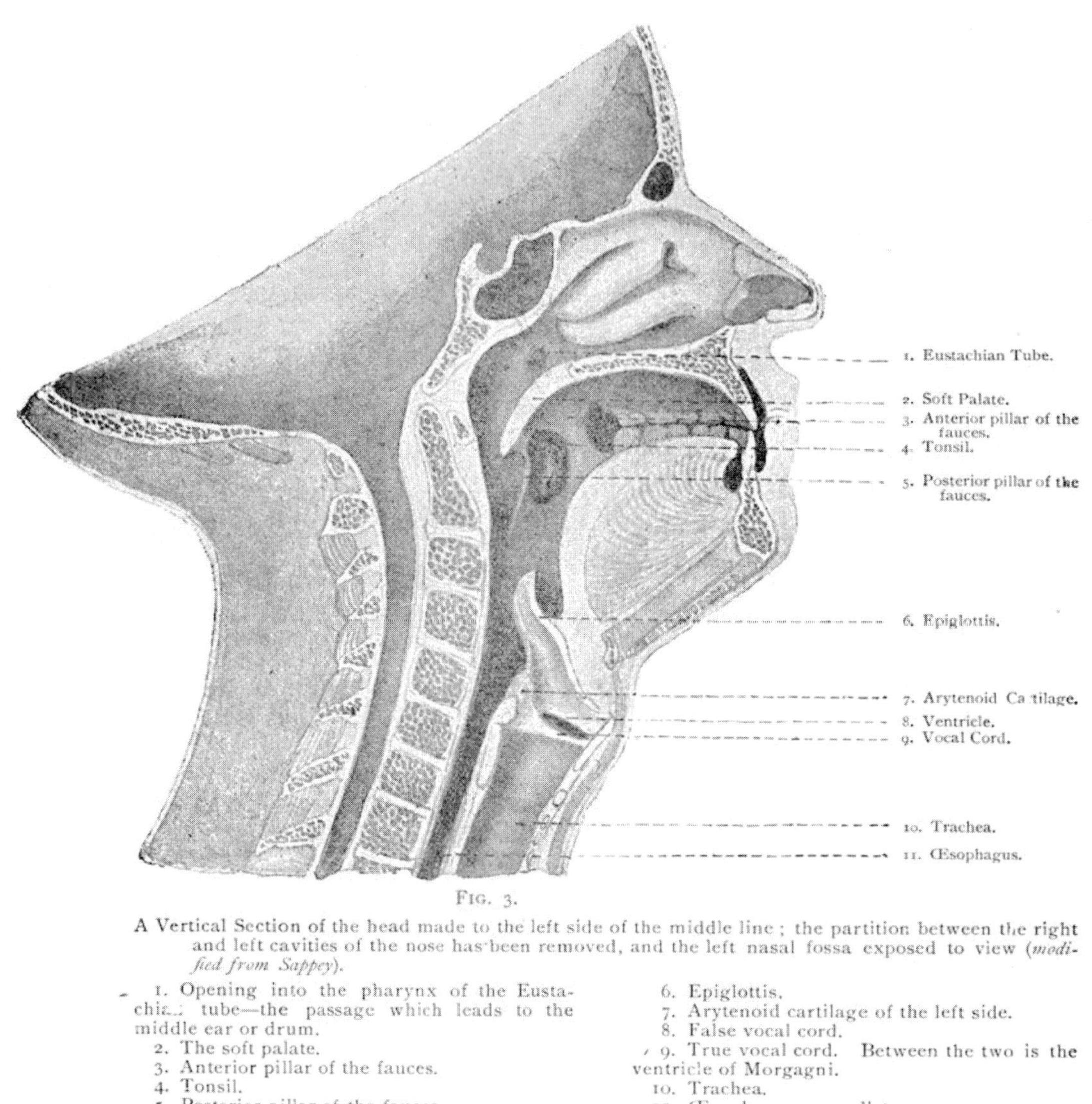

FIG. 3.

A Vertical Section of the head made to the left side of the middle line; the partition between the right and left cavities of the nose has been removed, and the left nasal fossa exposed to view (*modified from Sappey*).

1. Opening into the pharynx of the Eustachian tube—the passage which leads to the middle ear or drum.
2. The soft palate.
3. Anterior pillar of the fauces.
4. Tonsil.
5. Posterior pillar of the fauces.
6. Epiglottis.
7. Arytenoid cartilage of the left side.
8. False vocal cord.
9. True vocal cord. Between the two is the ventricle of Morgagni.
10. Trachea.
11. Œsophagus, or gullet.

Figure 3.

RESPIRATION

Q. What facts can you mention concerning the respiratory organs?

A. The *lungs*, as has been said, constitute the breathing apparatus, and contain the air, which is the substance of sound. To be admitted into and expelled from the lungs, the air must traverse the mouth or the nostrils, the pharynx, the glottis, and the trachea. The two acts of inhaling and of exhaling constitute respiration. The lungs are contained in the chest, a sort of cage formed by twenty-four ribs, together with the sternum, the vertical column, and the *Diaphragm*. This most important muscle (the diaphragm) forms the base of the cage; it is convex, and holds the act of respiration under its control. [Figure 4]

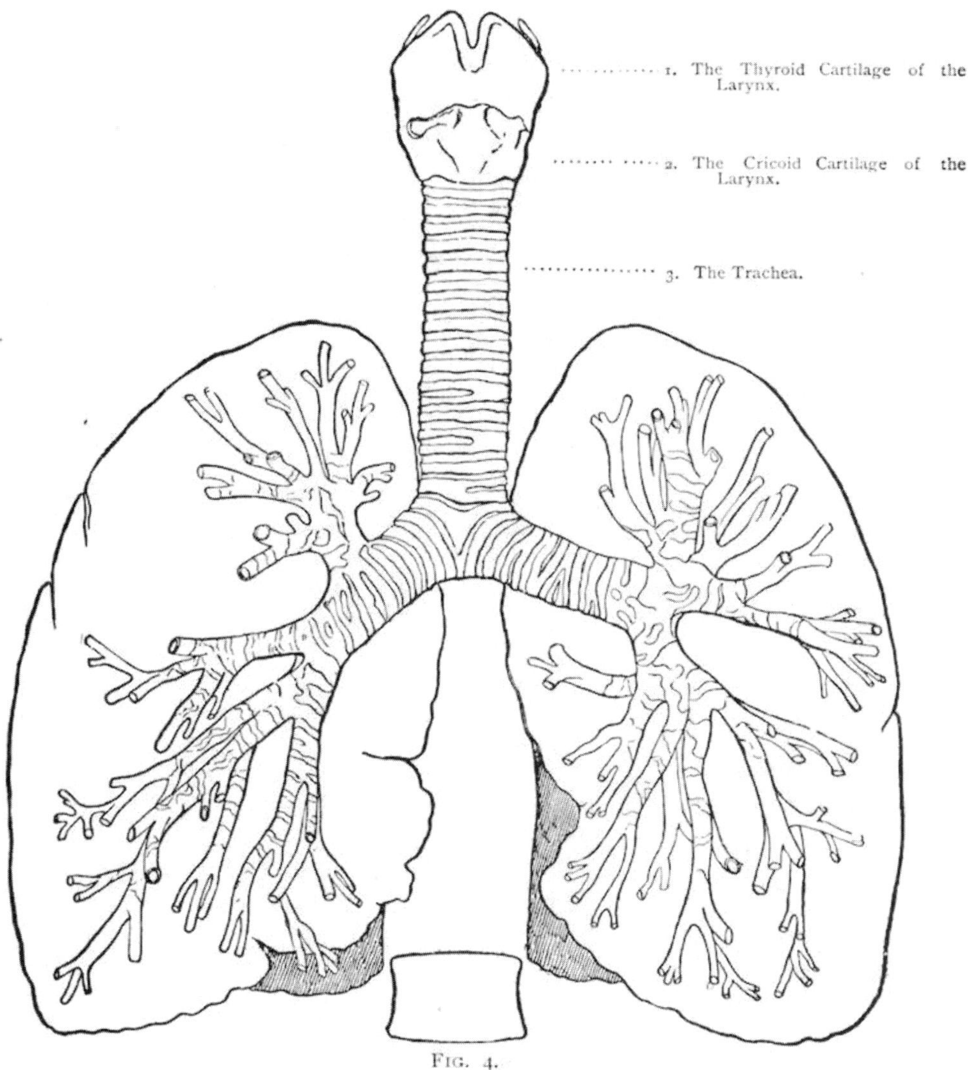

Fig. 4.

The Lungs, Trachea and Larynx, as viewed from the front.

1. The thyroid cartilage of the larynx.
2. The cricoid cartilage of the larynx.
3. Trachea, or windpipe, terminating in the bronchial tubes, which ramify through the lungs and end ultimately in the vesicles.

Figure 4.

Q. How does the diaphragm control respiration?

A. In the first attempt to emit a sound, the diaphragm flattens itself, the stomach slightly protrudes, and the breath is introduced at will by the nose, by the mouth, or by both simultaneously. During this partial inspiration, which is called *abdominal*, the ribs do not move, nor are the lungs filled to their full capacity, to obtain which the *diaphragm must and does contract completely*. Then, and only then are the ribs raised, while the stomach is drawn in. This inspiration—in which the lungs have their free action from side to side, from front to back, from top to bottom—is complete, and is called *thoracic* or *intercostal*. If by compression of any kind the lower ribs are prevented from expanding, the breathing becomes sternal or *clavicular*. [Figure 5]

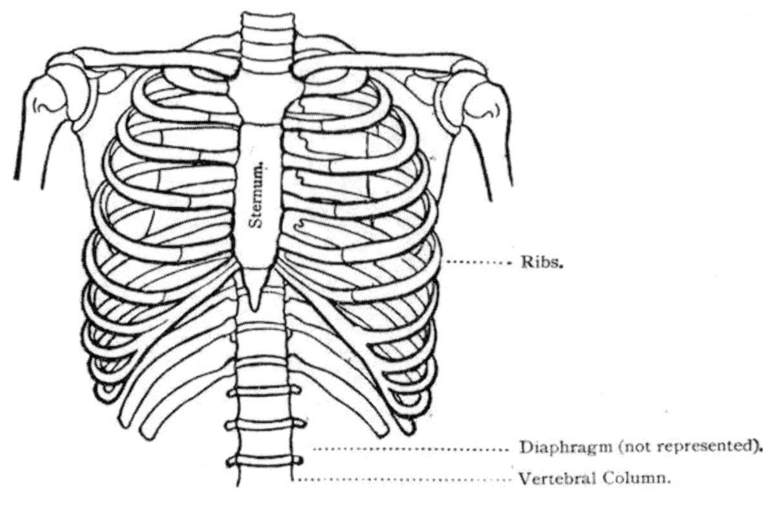

FIG. 5.

The chest, a conical cage which protects the lungs, is formed at the back by the vertebral column, in front by the sternum, and on the sides by twelve ribs. Seven of these are united to the sternum, three are attached to each other by a cartilaginous border, and two are floating. This cavity is closed at the base by a large thin muscle, slightly convexed, called the midriff or diaphragm. It separates the thorax from the abdomen, and plays a most important part in the expansion and contraction of the lungs.

Figure 5.

Q. Which do you approve?

A. The thoracic; and to obtain it the breath must be taken *slowly* and *deeply*.

Q. Can breathing be improved?

A. Yes, by proper exercises.

Q. How do you describe these exercises?

A. Dr. Roth teaches certain exercises suitable for strengthening the chest and regulating its movements. Being independent of sound, they have the advantage of not fatiguing the voice. To the exercises which he recommends I should propose to add the following:—

1. Draw a breath slowly through a very minute opening of the lips, then exhale freely.
2. Breathe freely and exhale slowly through the same small opening.
3. Breathe freely and retain the breath during ten seconds or more.

Q. Is it necessary always to regulate the pressure of the air from the lungs?

A. Undoubtedly. The glottis being under the direct influence of the lungs, any jerkiness or other irregularities in the action of these organs affects the sounds and impairs that continuous flow which is the charm of execution.

Q. What are the *faults of breathing?*

A. The greatest are that the breathing should be scanty, hurried, noisy, or drawn in by raising the shoulders. When the air is inhaled gradually and not by jerks, it does not rebound, and is retained by the lungs without fatigue.

Q. How are these faults to be remedied?

A. The first three by breathing slowly and deeply, and by opening wide the glottis. The noisy aspirations are cause by a semi-opened glottis.

Q. How can you obtain the sensation of the glottis action?

A. By coughing almost imperceptibly. The glottis then closes and opens; through these actions we feel it distinctly. [Figure 6]

* The importance of the larynx, as the producer of all vocal sounds, justifies us in studying it more minutely than other parts of the instrument.

The framework of the larynx includes the following cartilages :—the thyroid, the cricoid, the two arytenoids, surmounted by two nodules, called cartilages of Santorini, and the epiglottis. These cartilages are movable by means of appropriate muscles. The interior of the larynx narrows toward the center to a mere chink or fissure, called the *glottis*. This opening, which can be seen with the laryngoscope, is bounded by two edges, placed one on the right and the other on the left. These edges constitute the *lips* of the glottis. Posteriorly they are formed by the internal surface of the arytenoid cartilages, and in front by the vocal cords. The vocal cords are two deep folds of the mucous membrane. In each of them, immediately beneath the edge of the fold, lies a band of elastic tissue, known as the inferior thyro-arytenoid ligament or true cord; the outer side of this fold is filled by the internal thyro-arytenoid muscle.* At a little distance above these folds are placed two others called *false cords*, which are separated from the former by two cavities—the ventricles.

The lips of the glottis alone produce all vocal sounds, with their modifications of ringing and veiled quality, of piano and forte. The space between the lips, in the act of respiration, has nearly the form of a horizontal isosceles triangle, and becomes linear when preparing to produce a sound. The triangular is the form of silence, the linear of activity. The closing of the lips I call "pinching of the glottis" (Figs. 6, 7, 8.)

Glottis Opened.	Glottis Opened.	Glottis Shut and Vibrating.

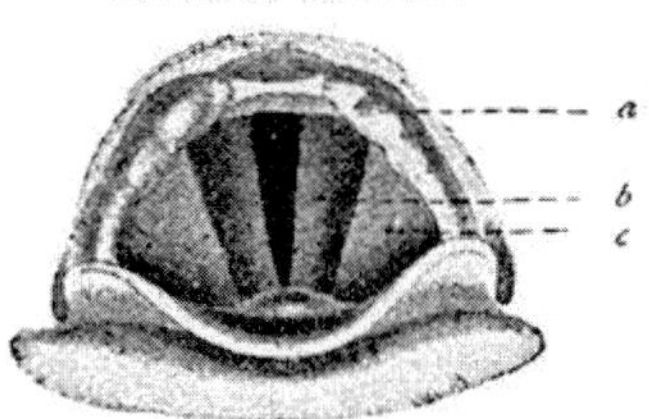

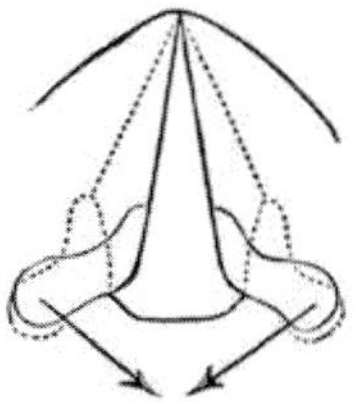

Fig. 6.

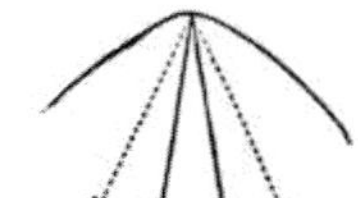

Fig. 7.

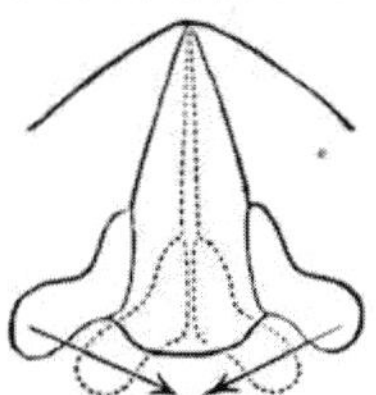

Fig. 8.

Fig. 6.—The *glottis*, as seen with laryngoscope during easy inspiration. *a*. Eminence formed by the cartilage of Santorini, which lies on the summit of the arytenoid cartilage. The epiglottis, *d*, is seen in bird's eye view ; the eminence close above the cords is its "cushion" (*Shattock*). *b*. The true vocal cord between this and its fellow is the chink of the glottis. *c*. The false vocal cords.

Fig. 7.—Diagram of the larynx in horizontal section, showing the chink of the glottis, bounded behind by the internal surfaces of the arytenoid and cricoid cartilages, and in front of these by the true vocal cords. The dotted lines show the position of the cricoid cartilage and vocal cords when the glottis is opened ; the direction of the contracting force (the crico-arytenoidous posterior muscle) is indicated by the arrows.

Fig. 8.—The same parts showing the position of the arytenoid cartilage and vocal cords of the

* Observations on the Human Voice, by Manuel Garcia. Proceedings of the Royal Society of London, Vol. VII., No. 13, 1855.

Figure 6.

SOUND

Q. What is *sound?*

A. The sensation made in the ear by vibrating air.

Q. How does the glottis produce sounds?

A. The two lips of the glottis, which are separated in the act of breathing, meet when preparing to produce a sound, and close that passage with the degree of energy demanded by the nature of the sound and the power with which it is to be emitted. Then, being pushed upwards by the air, they give way and allow a portion of air to escape, but immediately return to their original contact, and recommence the action. These intermittent emissions or explosions of air, when regular and rapid enough, form a sound. [Figure 7]

Q. Can you name any action which is an illustration of this?

A. The action of the lips of a horn player.

Q. Are the sound obtained always of the same character?

A. No. They may be bright and ringing or veiled.

Q. How do you obtain these bright and veiled sounds?

A. If after every explosion the glottis closes completely, each impinges sharply on the *tympanic membrane*, and the sound heard is bright or ringing. But if the glottis is imperfectly closed, and a slight escape of air unites the explosions, the impressions upon the tympanum are blunted, the sound being then veiled. The waste of air can be verified by placing a lighted match before the mouth. The brighter sound does not stir the flame, the veiled one will.

Q. Has this observation any importance?

A. Coupled with the theory of *timbres* and that of the breath, it puts the singer in possession of all the "tints" of the voice, and indeed initiates him into all the secrets of voice-production.

Q. What produces pitch?

A. The number of explosions that occur in a given time. The greater the number, the higher the pitch.

Q. What causes intensity of sound?

A. Intensity of sound is not due to the amplitude of movement of the glottis lips, but to the quantity of air which makes one vivid explosion. The resistance offered by the lips to the pressure of the lungs determines this quantity. The amplitude is therefore a result, not a cause. After each explosion the glottis must be reclosed; for if the air found a constant issue, the greater the expenditure of air the weaker the sound would be.

Q. How is volume of sound obtained?

A. The volume of sound depends on the expansion of the pharynx and of the vestibule of the larynx.

Q. What range of vibrations can the human ear perceive?

A. According to Helmholtz from 16 vibrations to 38,000 in a second.

Q. How is the rising scale formed?

A. By the gradual tension, shortening and thinning of the glottis lips.

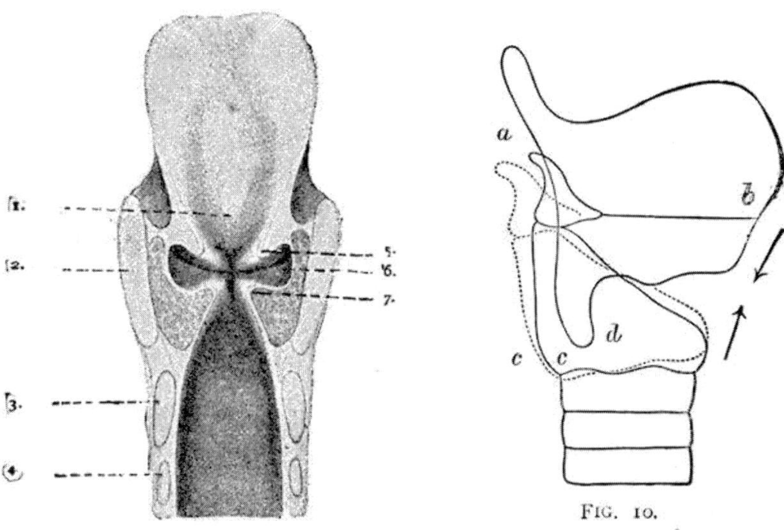

FIG. 10.

FIG. 9.

FIG. 9.—A vertical section of the Larynx carried from side to side, the anterior half of the Section being represented.

1. Cushion of the epiglottis.
2. Section of the thyroid cartilage.
3. Section of the cricoid.
4. Section of the first ring of the trachea.
5. The false cord in section.
6. The ventricle of Morgagni.
7. The true vocal cord in section, showing the internal portion of the thyro-arytenoid muscle lying in the fold of the mucous membrane. It is by the action of the true cords stopping and opening the air passage that the voice is produced.

FIG. 10.—An outline of the Larynx and upper side of the Trachea as viewed from its right side. Through the right ala of the thyroid cartilage are shown the arytenoid cartilage, *a*, and the vocal cord, *b*, forming together the right lip of the glottis. The dotted lines show the position taken by the arytenoid and cricoid cartilages, *a—c*, when the cricoid is drawn upwards by the contraction of the crico-thyroid muscle, acting as shown by the arrows. The dot, *d*, of the inferior horn of the thyroid marks the ideal center of movement. It will be seen that the result is to increase the distance between the vocal process of the arytenoid cartilage and the thyroid, and in this way to tighten the vocal cord.

* When a cord of a musical instrument oscillates it condenses the air on the side it approaches, leaving behind an amount of expanded air equal to that displaced ; these two portions of air, compressed and expanded, are inseparable, and form what is called a wave of sound. The waves of sound, in inverse order, are propagated on either side of the cord, and if the succession be regular or rhythmic, and sufficiently rapid, they form a musical sound. Any irregular succession of waves produces only noise. In reaching the ear the condensed portion of the air wave forces in the membrane which closes the bottom of the auditory meatus ; the rarefied portion draws it out again, and these oscillations transmit to the brain, by means of the auditory nerve, the vibrations which we appreciate as sound.

Figure 7.

[To be continued]

48. A Little "Vocal Wisdom"

Originally published in the *Journal of Singing*, volume 71, no. 1, 2014

Is there any teacher of singing of a certain age—or, for that matter, of any age—who does not have a copy of William Earl Brown's *Vocal Wisdom* sitting on the bookshelf? First published in 1931 and reissued by one of Brown's students in 1957, it is still published and easily available. The author was an assistant to Giovanni Battista Lamperti, son of Franceso Lamperti. The squabble between father and son is legendary, but Giovanni eventually took over his father's legacy when the elder Lamperti fell ill and could no longer teach.

Giovanni studied piano at the Royal Conservatory of Music in Milan into his early teenage years and accompanied for his father in his studio. His reputation as a coach led to his career as a teacher of singing. He wrote several books of vocalises throughout his career and published his method book, *The Technics of Bel Canto,* in 1905. The same year he moved his studio from Dresden to Berlin and hired one of his pupils, William Earl Brown, to help him manage the large studio.

Brown published his notes from his years of study with Giovanni Lamperti in his book *Vocal Wisdom: Maxims of Giovanni Battista Lamperti* in 1931.[1] I have a first edition of the book, which is inscribed to one of his pupils and includes a picture of him leaning against a tree, dated Nov. 2, 1935 (Figure 1). I am sure many of you can tell me more about Mr. Brown, but I have looked for information about his teaching career and can find nothing. Please share that with me!

At the very beginning of the book, Brown included an article that Lamperti wrote in 1893, and I present that article here. It is easy to consider this as just another voice teacher ranting about the decline of singing in his day (have not teachers been doing that since the very beginning?), but there are important principles to be taken. I hope you enjoy reading these words; there will be more discussion about Lamperti and Brown in future articles.

Figure 1.

PREVENTING THE DECADENCE OF THE ART OF SINGING[2]

By G. B. Lamperti

There has never been so much enthusiasm for the singing art, nor have there been so many students and teachers as of late years.

And it is precisely this period which reveals the deterioration of this divine art and the almost complete disappearance of genuine singers and worse, of good singing teachers.

What is the cause of this? How can it be prevented? By a return to the physiology of singing.

Just as the lack of good dramatic singers who can sing *Semiramis* or *Norma* becomes apparent, to a like degree do we find a lack of good singers who can sing *Donna Anna* or *Oberon*.

One part of the lay-world says that there are no longer real voices, and the other that there is no longer any talent. Neither is right. Voices still exist, and talent too, but the things which have changed are the study of the breath, of vocalization and of classic repertory, as cultivated by the singers of former times. They used to study for four or five years before they dared to be seen publicly in a small rôle.

Nowadays, after maltreating the larynx for a few months, a student considers himself an artist, and attempts the most difficult feats. Neither Verdi nor Wagner has ever said to singers: "in order to sing our music it is not necessary to study the art of singing; it is sufficient to have a strong voice and to be a good actor." On the contrary, when Verdi talked to the Congress at Naples on the decadence of music, he said that it was absolutely necessary to return to the serious study of former times.

But in Germany it is not only the true sopranos who have almost disappeared but also the tenors, because a German tenor who cannot sing Wagner cannot obtain an engagement or position of importance. Therefore the singers strain their voices; they force themselves in order to sing the Wagner repertory.

It would be much better, if tenors who did not possess the vocal resources for Wagnerian opera would refrain completely from singing that repertory. The Wagnerian operas demand powerful tenors who can sing the recitative with pompous voice; nevertheless, tenors who possess only pretty, fresh, agreeable but weak voices, insist on singing Wagner. They do this without a previous thorough *study of the breath, of solfeggio and vocalization,* and without any comprehension of *voice registers.*

A tenor possesses the most delicate type of voice; it demands a very earnest and carefully prepared course of study. But most tenors in Germany sing with the emission of a baritone because they then believe themselves to be Wagnerian tenors. They force the middle voice and do not realize that the maltreated voice will, with time, become old and tired.

I remember having heard a tenor named Pardini in Italy who at seventy-two years of age sang the *Otello* of Rossini. He still had the fresh voice of a young man. The tenor, Stagno, who I permitted to make his début in 1860 at Genoa, has been singing the last thirty-two years. "Cavalleria Rusticana" was written for him—he has sung the whole repertory of Wagner, Meyerbeer, Verdi, et al; yet he still maintains his fresh voice, as do others such as Negri, Companini and Tomagno.

Why are the voices of Patti and Madame Sembrich so well preserved?

Because they sing only the repertory which suits their voices.

In 1885 I was in Paris in order to assist Sembrich at her début in "Traviata" and "Lucia." One day she told me that she would like to sing "Faust." I protested energetically and urgently advised her to sing only the operas of her repertory. (She would have ruined her voice in "Faust" and in a short time would have become a singer like thousands of others.)

This period is swayed by a prejudice: everyone says the music of Verdi and Wagner spoils the voice. That is not true of perfected voice. And here we have the one cause of the deterioration of singing, which no one will grasp and which nevertheless is so simple. The insufficiently cultivated voice, which possesses neither the flexibility nor the art of the breath-supported legato, naturally quickly wears itself out.

Let us make a comparison: is a person who is strongly drawn to the piano necessarily a virtuoso? No, to the desire must be added serious study, in order to completely develop into artistry.

Therefore, how can one expect that the voice (which is the most beautiful, but at the same time the finest and most delicate instrument) will reveal all the passions of the soul without thorough study of its technique?

It is a pity that young singers, who are studying voice, immediately sing songs and arias, literally before they know how to open their mouths, instead of earnestly studying the real support of the voice (the mechanism of the breath) in order to develop the voice and to make it smooth and flexible.

Certain teachers are mainly at fault in that they take advantage of the inexperience of pupils, to the disadvantage of the art of song.

In my opinion, it is not absolutely necessary for a singer to have a big voice, nor even a pretty one: if one just acquires security of breath, purity of enunciation and legato, any voice will sound agreeable to the ear. Never more than of late, have the gymnastics of the breath and smoothness of tone (legato) been neglected by teachers of singing. And precisely these two things are the chief requirements of a singer and of those who wish to undertake the important position of a singing teacher.

In spite of the fact that modern music for light sopranos is devoid of the coloratura of the time of Mozart and Rossini, it is a necessary principle to again add the gymnastics of the breath, the larynx and the smoothness of tone (legato).

Without this study the art of good singing would in a short time become a chimera. Not until a singer knows how to control the breath and unite his tones is he equipped easily to convey every variety of expression which is demanded by the new composers; to hold the tone longer (as one can with a violin or violoncello) and to give to songs the *nuance* and color which dramatic art permits.

The foundation of all vocal study lies in the control of the breath.

The technical development of the voice is brought out by the double functioning of the lungs, which consist of: first, inhaling the breath noiselessly; and secondly, making use of the diaphragm to control the breath as economically as one pleases, in order to leave the vocal apparatus completely independent. (The diaphragm is a muscle on which the lungs rest and which is indispensable to singing.) Once one becomes master of the organs of breathing, one can begin the study of legato.

Legato means the carrying of the voice or the imperceptible merging of one tone into the other. Between one tone and the next the breath may not be interrupted, but must be held as though the tones were one. But in passing from low to high tones, the breath must take the opposite direction from the voice.

Without these precautions, one can neither sing legato nor achieve a pure coloratura, which would otherwise remain deficient or jumpy (*cavallina*). The control of the breath is the support of all vocalization.

It is possible to end phrases and cadenzas so that there will be a residue of air in the lungs. It is a great mistake to end a phrase with collapsed lungs.

The stroke of the glottis (violent attack) which many singing teachers advise, is absolutely harmful to the voice, and it is wrong to use it in order to begin a phrase well; one can easily in time develop a harmful or fatal inflammation of the larynx.

It is desirable for a student to follow certain hygienic principles.

Among other things he should talk little and not loudly, not sing immediately after meals, deny himself butter and other rich foods, practice with full voice, but reasonably and with rest periods. He should study before a mirror, in order to acquire a pleasant expression and never lift the shoulders, etc.

If the pupil has the weakness of holding his tongue high or keeping his teeth closed, the mirror is the only way to overcome it. I strongly advise refraining from the use of artificial devices, placing objects in the mouth, on the tongue or between the teeth, etc. These are playthings whose uselessness has been sufficiently proved by experience. In singing, one should not 'cock an ear' to listen any more than one does in speech. Through such efforts the muscles of the throat easily become rigid.

Beginners also often make the mistake of 'letting themselves go' while singing because they believe it achieves good results; that is untrue. The head must always be cool, only the heart should be warm.

The language best suited for the study of singing is Italian, because it is the only one without aspirate. The music which I prefer for vocalists is that of the masters Rossini, Mozart, Bellini, Weber, Donizetti, et al.

It is absolutely necessary for a pupil who wishes to devote himself to the study of singing, to choose a teacher from the very beginning who has made certain studies on the use of the voice and all aids of the breath. He must be absolute master of the legato, and be able to demonstrate it in order to carry over his knowledge to his pupils in all its branches and details.

Of course it is not necessary for the teacher to possess a splendid voice, but to the highest degree he must understand the art of imparting technical details to his pupils. In addition there must be a reciprocal magnetic attraction between pupil and teacher, which helps to convey ideas from teacher to pupil. The teacher must have a profound knowledge of the aids to a properly cultivated mechanism, and ability to impart this knowledge to his pupils. The teacher should hypnotize the pupil with his knowledge.

A great loss to the melodramatic art is the disappearance of *opera-buffa* and *'semi-seria'* (romantic opera), such as, for instance, "Don Pasquale," "The Marriage of Figaro," or "Linda di Chamounix," etc. In former days we developed true artists with such a repertory.

Those who were endowed with a robust voice and a truly dramatic talent discovered the truth of this after singing for several years in the comic or romantic operas, going through the "*tirocinio*." (*Tirocinio* means going through everything from the beginning thoroughly and practically.) Not until then could they offer their services in dramatic operas. These singers were then ripe (*provetti*) and thorough (*profondi*) artists of their medium.

The public tires of the "Barber," "Cosi Fan Tutte" or "Fra Diavolo" only if it is poorly done.

Now I ask, why do the modern composers not write good comic or romantic operas instead of imitating Wagner or Verdi? That would be a help to the renascence of the art of singing.

Often the cause of poor performances of art-operas is the conducting. When "Lohengrin," "Walküre," "Aida" or "Otello" is not being performed, no care is given to good color, good scenery or singing technique. No one bothers to see whether the singers are equal to their tasks. Finally in the small operas, the costumes are old and the whole performance of terrible frigidity. The effect of the opera is entirely lost. The critics blame the work. The director should honestly reply: "I, the conductor, have not used sufficient care. The singers are incapable of singing these melodies without support from the instrumentation, because we no longer possess the knowledge and ability of real singers. That is the reason why these performances actually arouse pity."

In spite of all this, it is my firm belief that we should not retrogress further. It is only necessary for the young composers to realize that they are not Wagners or Verdis who can write a "Tannhäuser" or "Aida" as a first creation. For their own good and the good of art, they should write operas of modest proportions. The success of Mascagni's "Cavalleria Rusticana" has proven this most decidedly.

It is wrong to believe that after studying the Italian method of singing (the one and only true method of good singing) it is impossible to interpret and sing dramatic music.

Were not Malibran, Pasta, Grisi, Sonntag, Cruvelli and Cattalani great dramatic and technically sublime singers, who excelled equally in *Norma, Otello, Semiramis*, and similar roles?

If these singers had been contemporaries of Verdi and Wagner, as they were of Bellini and Rossini, they would have been technically complete and at the same time truly dramatic singers, who could have sung "Norma" and "Die Walküre," "Aida" and "Semiramis" equally well.

One must not confuse the term "dramatic interpretation" with a vulgar demonstration or exaltation which forces the voice and exaggerates the gestures which accompany it. Unfortunately this is often seen even in artists of the present time, who do not consider them- selves dramatic singers.

Richard Wagner says in his writings on Madame Schröder-Devrient, "She had no 'voice', but she knew how to control her breath so perfectly, and to permit a truly womanly spirit to issue forth so wonderfully, that one thought neither of singing nor of voice, as one listened."

Only he who understands correct singing can obtain real power and expression in song, whether he sings Italian, French or German music. There are only seven tones in the scale, and it is equally difficult to sing them in any language, so that they will be agreeable to the listener, and conserve the voice.

In these times, when the demands of the singing art are growing vague, let us return to a study of physiology and the *older* Italian method!

These remarks are, of course, not a "method." They simply explain the causes of the decadence of singing as I have observed them in an experience of many years.

NOTES

1. William Earl Brown, *Vocal Wisdom: Maxims of Giovanni Battista Lamperti* (New York: William Earl Brown, 1931).
2. These thoughts of the master are so applicable to contemporary conditions that I am presenting this article in full. And Lamperti penned this article in 1893

49. More from Hints on Singing

Originally published in the *Journal of Singing*, volume 61, no. 2, 2014

In two previous articles, I have introduced significant portions of Garcia's *Hints on Singing.*[1] It has always been one of my goals in this column to present extended excerpts from important historical sources.

Garcia is as relevant today as he was during his lifetime, and the concepts that he espoused are still reflected in good teaching everywhere. This is not only due to his personal pedagogy, but because Garcia was at first a scribe, recording the common practice of voice teachers of his early years and from the time of his father, Manuel Garcia senior. After many years of teaching, he documents in his *Hints on Singing* the cumulative experience of a grand old man who had taught many of the world's elite singers for at least a half century.[2]

Garcia was the first to describe and use the word *timbre* with regard to the singing voice, an insightful observation based on his experience and knowledge of the vocal mechanism. It is particularly relevant to us who teach multiple vocal styles: his description of open and closed timbre accounts for most of the aesthetic differences between CCM and *bel canto* vocal qualities. I find the other principles presented here to be so helpful in my own teaching. I have had the privilege of working with singers from all over the country, and I often am amazed at what can be accomplished when I am teaching in front of others in an observed lesson or master class. These principles are so profound that a singer can experience remarkable improvement in a short amount of time. I am committed to the principles of posture, emittance, and onset which I learned right here, in his book! I use them in every lesson that I teach, and I encourage you to try them, even if like me, they are outside your own training experience. They are easy to learn and easy to implement. The application can be transformative.

8. TIMBRE

Q. What is meant by *Timbre?*

A. Every sound of the voice may assume an infinite variety of shades apart from intensity. Each of these is a *timbre*.

Q. What produces the variety of *timbres*?

A. They are due, first, to permanent causes that affect the voice of each individual, such as the constitution, age, health or disease of the vocal apparatus; secondly, to the action of the glottis; third, to the changes of form in the tube which the sounds traverse.

Q. Can you explain these changes?

A. The path of the sound, being formed of elastic and movable parts, varies its dimensions and forms in endless ways, and every modification—even the slightest—has a corresponding and definite influence on the voice.

Q. How is a student to select from among these intricacies of *timbre*?

A. The *timbres* may be divided into two classes, the clear (bright), or open, and the dark or closed. These two opposite qualities are obtained principally through the agency of the larynx and the soft palate. The movements of these two organs are always in a contrary direction. The larynx rises when the soft palate falls, and when the larynx falls, the soft palate rises. The high vault produces the dark *timbres*, the lower arch the clear ones. The arch rises when we are in the act of yawning, and falls when we are in the act of swallowing [Figures 1 and 2].

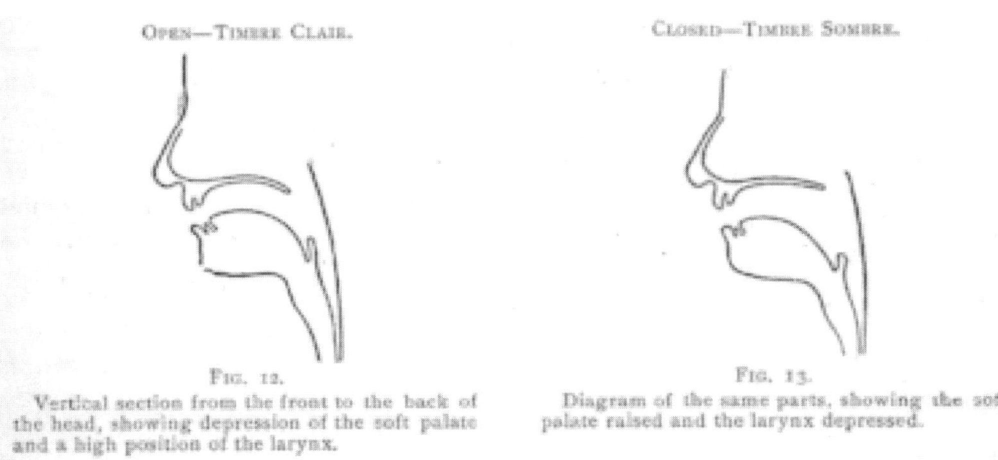

Fig. 12.
Vertical section from the front to the back of the head, showing depression of the soft palate and a high position of the larynx.

Fig. 13.
Diagram of the same parts, showing the soft palate raised and the larynx depressed.

Figure 1.

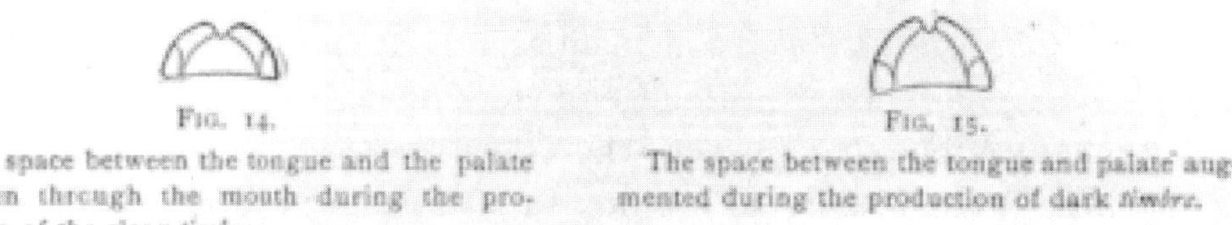

Fig. 14.
The space between the tongue and the palate as seen through the mouth during the production of the clear *timbre*.

Fig. 15.
The space between the tongue and palate augmented during the production of dark *timbre*.

Figure 2.

Q. What exercise will give command over the various *timbres?*

A. This: In the same breath, on the same note and on each of the vowels a, e, I, o, the student must pass through every shade of *timbre*, from the most open (or bright) to the most closed (or dark). The sounds must be maintained with an equal degree of force. The following table shows what change each vowel undergoes in passing from clear to dark; the process must also be inverted:

A approximates to o
E " to eu in French.
I " to u in French.
O " to u in Italian.

The Italian I and the French U in the head and high chest notes must be rounded rather more than in speaking, or their tint would be unpleasant. Carried to excess, these *timbres* would render the voice respectively hoarse and hollow, or harsh and trivial, like the quack of a duck.

The student should thoroughly understand that the ring or dulness of sound is in effect and mechanism, completely distinct from the open and closed *timbres*. The ringing and dulness are produced in the interior of the larynx, independently of the position, high or low, of this organ, while the open or closed qualities of the voice require the bodily movement of the larynx, and of its antagonist the soft palate. Hence, any *timbre* may be bright or dull. This observation is most important for the expressive qualities of the voice.[3]

9. PREPARATION FOR EMITTING THE VOICE.

Q. How do you prepare for emitting the voice?

A. By giving attention to the position of the body, the separation of the jaws, the shape of the throat, and the breathing.

Q. How would you describe the position of the body?

A. The body must be straight, well planted on the feet, and without any other support; the shoulders well back, the head erect, the expression of the face calm.

Q. Should the mouth be opened wide as a means of obtaining power and beauty of sound?

A. This is a common error. The mouth should be opened by the natural fall of the jaw. This movement, which separates the jaws by the thickness of a finger and leaves the lips alone, gives the mouth an easy and natural form. The tongue must be kept limp and motionless, neither raised at the point nor swollen at the root. Finally, the soft palate must be raised as in taking a full breath. The exaggerated opening favours neither low nor high notes. In the latter case it may help the vocalist to scream, but that is not singing; the face loses charm and the voice assumes a violent and vulgar tone. The real mouth of a singer ought to be considered the Pharynx.

Q. Why so?

A. Because it is in the pharynx that is found the causation of *timbres*. The facial mouth is but a door through which the voice passes. Still, if this door were not sufficiently open, sounds could not issue freely.

Q. How can you regulate the opening of the mouth?

A. Those who find it difficult either to diminish or increase the opening of the mouth will do well to place laterally between the jaws, from back to front, a small piece of wood not thicker than a pencil.

Q. Are there other defects of a similar kind?

A. Yes. Pushing the lips out like a funnel; protruding the jaws; separating the lips for the sake of showing fine teeth, and knitting the brows.

Q. What is the remedy?

A. The chin might be held back by a band of paper round the neck, and pinned through the ends in front of the chin. This band, which ought not to be wider than a finger, acts, of course, as a reminder. Any one afflicted with these or kindred habits should sing before a mirror.

Q. Have you anything to add to what has already been said about breathing?

A. It may be added that when the lungs are completely filled with air, the natural tendency is to be quickly rid of the super-abundance. Consequently the sounds at the start are strong and often unsteady; then they become weaker with the lessening of the breath. The majority of musical phrases demand the opposite method. On this account, the pupil should begin with a small amount of pressure, increasing it gradually as the supply of air diminishes. The even flow of a long phrase, a long passage of agility, the stability of a long note, all require a continuous and well-managed pressure of the diaphragm.

Q. Is not the size and sonority of the *locale* to be considered?

A. Certainly. The necessity for a steady pressure is especially felt in large halls and in places bad for sound. Air given out in jerks does not travel. A moderate and prolonged pressure, on the contrary, gradually puts in motion the whole mass of circumambient air; the faintest sound, given in this manner, if not drowned by the accompaniment, will reach the ears of the most distant auditor. *"Chi sa respirare sa cantare." (MariaCelloni.)*

10. THE ATTACK OF VOCAL SOUNDS.

Q. What follows after the preparation above noted?

A. The actual articulation or "stroke of the glottis."

Q. What do you mean by the stroke of the glottis?

A. The neat articulation of the glottis that gives a precise and clean start to a sound.
Q. How do you acquire that articulation?
A. By imitation, which is quickest of all; but in the absence of a model, let it be remembered that by slightly coughing we become conscious of the existence and position of the glottis, and also of its shutting and opening action. The stroke of the glottis is somewhat similar to the cough, though differing essentially in that it needs only the delicate action of the lips and not the impulse of the air. The lightness of the movement is considerably facilitated if it be tried with the mouth shut. Once understood, it may be used with the mouth open on any vowel. The object of this is that at the start sounds should be free from the defect of slurring up to a note or the noise of breathing.
Q. What are the principal qualities of a good tone?
A. Perfect intonation, absolute steadiness of sound, and beauty of *timbre*, these qualities—indispensable to good style—may be considered as the tripod of voice production.
Q. How are sounds to be attacked?
A. With the stroke of the glottis just described. The Italian vowels, a, e, as in the words *alma, sempre*, must be used. They will bring out all the ring of the voice. The notes must be kept full and equal in force. This is the best manner of developing the voice. At first the exercise must not exceed two or three minutes in duration.
Q. Why do you not use what is called the "messa di voce"?
A. The use of the "messa di voce" requires a singer to be expert in the control of the breath and of *timbres*. At this elementary stage it would cause only fatigue.

[to be continued]

NOTES

1. Stephen F. Austin, "Hints on Singing . . . Hints Indeed!" *Journal of Singing* 69, no. 2 (November/December 2012): 215; Stephen F. Austin, "Is It Time For A Change?" *Journal of Singing* 70, no. 5 (May/June 2014): 603.
2. Manuel Garcia, *Hints on Singing* (London: E. Ascherberg & Co., 1894).
3. From my reading of Garcia, particularly in the second volume of his *Complete Treatise on the Art of Singing* (1854), the use of both open and closed *timbre* within the operatic style (*bel canto*) was more common in Garcia's day than in the present.

50. Sterling is Gold!

Originally published in the *Journal of Singing*, volume 71, no. 3, 2015

Sterling MacKinlay (1876-1952) was the son of a famous singer by the name of Antoinette Sterling and a student of Manuel Garcia II. MacKinlay wrote the well-known biography of Garcia, *Garcia: The Centenarian and His Times*, in 1908, just two years after Garcia's death.[1] He wrote several other books, including *The Singing Voice and Its Training*, based on MacKinlay's understanding of the Garcia school based on his four years as a student.[2] In it are numerous references to Garcia and many direct quotes that I will share with you at a future time.

I have an original edition of the book in my library. The front piece of the book has MacKinlay's autograph, and it is signed to a student by the name of Audry Hancox "for good work in singing," dated March 30, 1922 (Figure 1). I treasure these old original volumes! There is much to appreciate in his technical approach to the singing voice; however, I want to share his whole chapter on the art of expression. It is important for us in this day to understand that the progressive methods that were common in the 19th century had only one goal: to give singers an instrument which would respond to their artistic inspirations. Here is pure gold from Sterling MacKinlay.

CHAPTER XI
THE ART OF EXPRESSION

All art is creation, idealisation, self-expression in a certain medium. The artist, as it were, absorbs certain impressions, passes them through his own mind and reproduces them in a fresh medium stamped with his own personality. When the landscape painter, for instance, gazes on a scene, his eyes note the form and colour, and his temperament adds something further of himself. He produces in the medium of paint a landscape showing us not merely those particular material things which we should at once recognise on visiting the spot, but also the personality of the artist, and in a certain degree his temperament at the time of painting it. The photographer imitates, the painter idealises.

It is the same with the writer, the actor, the sculptor. So, also, the singer absorbs certain material, the lines of the poet and the music of the composer. These he bathes in his own personality and translates the whole into another medium, his voice, the result being what is styled his interpretation of the song.

In all these cases, before the artist can accomplish his desire, he must be a perfect master of the technique of his art, and of the medium in which he works. Thus the singer, before he can become great in interpretation must be absolute master of his instrument. He must acquire firmness, power, flexibility, faultless intonation, extended compass, and pure emission. All these things, however, are but the preliminary studies of the singer, the necessary preparation for the proper interpretation of songs, which will require knowledge of the Art of Phrasing, insight into the different Styles, and development of the power of Expression. Of this wide field of study I am only here able to give a rough outline, but I hope to deal more fully with the Interpretative side of the singer's art upon some future occasion.

The singer must have a voice, and he must have it trained in all those things which contribute to the attainment of perfect breath control, the proper placing of the voice, the full development of its natural resources, and the acquirement of technique. But these are only preliminary to those finishing studies of the singer which are all important, and yet, alas! too often neglected—Phrasing, Style, Expression.

When one hears a vocalist with a fine voice trained to perfection but devoid of any expression, one can only lament the pity of it. The singing may be artistic, but it is cold and lifeless, and cannot appeal to us.

A vocalist, to attain real and lasting success, *must* master this stage of the art of singing. Without expression he cannot hope to hold the interest of the listener, for he is appealing neither to the intellect nor to the heart, but to the ear alone. Hence monotony will be the inevitable result.

How is the singer to avoid monotony? He needs no miracle, as did Pygmalion, for the answer to his question may be found in some degree by following a piece of advice which Sir Joseph Barnby once gave:—

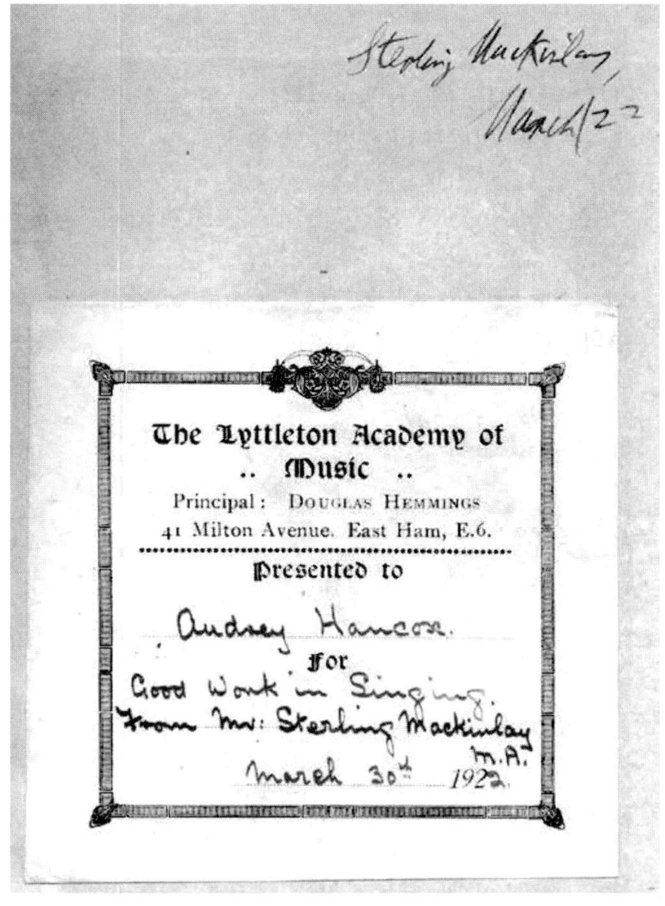

Sterling Mackinlay,
March/22

The Lyttleton Academy of
.. Music ..
Principal: Douglas Hemmings
41 Milton Avenue, East Ham, E.6.

Presented to
Audrey Hancox.
for
Good Work in Singing.
From Mr. Sterling Mackinlay M.A.
March 30th 1922.

Figure 1.

"Listen critically to vocalists whenever you can. You will find that there is no one from whom you cannot learn something. If the artist be good, analyse his success—find out what are his good points, and follow them. If he be bad, find out what are his bad qualities, and avoid them."

Take, then, the dull singer: lay him on the operating table, and dissect him carefully. What are the causes which are mostly responsible for producing apathy, almost antipathy, in the listener ~ Faults of "emission" and" execution" which have to do purely with the technical side of the art we will ignore, confining ourselves to those which deal, firstly, with the rendering of the music, secondly, with that of the words.

Of the first, perhaps the most common fault is that of the voice remaining *forte* throughout the composition. Another trial is the song in which uniform *tempo* is sustained from the first to the last note. Again, as regards the manner of rendering the music, a graceful *legato* is undoubtedly a consummation devoutly to be wished, being the foundation of all good singing, but, if adhered to without deviation from beginning to end, it is apt to become wearisome.

Of the second (the rendering of the words), perhaps the most trying of all faults is that of singing line after line without the accentuation of any syllables. The reason is this. In all human speech the emphasising of the most important words, and in a less degree those of secondary importance, is a universal characteristic. Without it speaking would lose half its significance, and singing without any accents sounds equally unnatural.

Scarcely less trying is it to hear verse after verse, sometimes song after song, rendered with exactly the same *timbre* or tone-colour. It is conducive to the most extreme monotony, and certainly conveys to the unhappy listener the idea that the vocalist is incapable of the smallest particle of feeling or expression.

Now, upon examining the above faults, one or more of which will be found in every dull singer, it does not take long to discover that one factor is present in all— "Sameness." There has been a sameness of quantity, *tempo,* manner, matter, or quality.

From this it would need no very daring reasoner to conclude that the "sameness" probably caused the dullness, and that consequently one might banish the dullness by removing the "sameness," introducing change and contrast in its place. As a matter of fact, this is the case. Variety of phrasing and of expression is absolutely necessary if the singer is to hold the attention of his audience. Having arrived, then, at the conclusion that if a vocalist is to hold the attention of the listener by appealing to the intellect instead of merely to the ear his singing must exhibit constant change and contrast, let us investigate the various ways in which this result may be obtained in Phrasing and Expression. Sir Charles Santley, whose name has been ever associated with what is highest and best in music, defines phrasing in the following terms: —

"It is the art of correctly distinguishing the outlines and periods which, so to speak, serve to represent the melody in relief. For the singer it consists in taking breath at the proper time and place, so that the phrase may appear executed as a single whole. This," he adds, "can only come from practice under the guidance of experienced masters."

Figure 2.

Certainly without good phrasing there can be no beauty of singing from an artistic point of view, and only those artists who have properly studied it can possibly expect to reveal the inmost meaning of the composer. A phrase is practically a musical sentence; there must be proper accentuation of certain notes which are meant to stand out, and there must be various degrees of force, otherwise the passage will be without meaning.

This brings us to a consideration of the methods by which variety may be obtained in singing.

(a) Changes in the volume of sound.—There are five alternatives—*fortissimo, forte, mezzoforte, piano, pianissimo,* and the choice of these must be subject to the feeling of the music and poetry. I have said that there are five, but the possible gradations of tone lying between the two limits, *pianissimo* and *fortissimo,* are more or less indefinite. To obtain full command over them it is necessary to practise the *messa di voce,* or, as it is usually termed, "swelled" note, though it would be more completely described as a "swelled-and-diminished" note. Whenever a long note occurs in a composition it should be treated in one of three ways: either it should increase from *piano* to *forte,* or commencing *forte* die away to *pianissimo,* or be sung as a *messa di voce.*

(b) Changes in tempo.—These must be made with the utmost discretion. To launch out into making perpetual little alterations in time throughout the piece, quickening here, slowing up there, without rhyme or reason, is the sign of a poor singer. The great artist is a great timist, and is found to interfere but little with the *tempo* of a piece. Consequently, when he does so, he produces a marked effect. It is necessary to make up the mind in advance where the words and music seem to demand a quickening or retarding of the time, or a pausing on some note. When one is satisfied that this alteration will be effective, and at the same time artistic—not a mere claptrap attempt to gain the vulgar applause of the ignorant—then let there be no half measures; make the change definite, steady, and pronounced. *Tempo rubato* does not properly come under this head, since the displacement of values occurs in the melody alone. The accompaniment is kept strictly to time throughout, the lengthening of certain syllables being equalized by the shortening of others. It is a style of singing principally useful for the interpretation of strong feeling, being governed by the accent which is given in ordinary speech. The subject will be referred to later under another heading.

(c) Changes in melody. —When a passage of notes occurs a second time during a song it is sometimes advisable to make changes by the introduction of turns, *appogiature,* or trills, or by absolute alterations in the melody. The latter alternative must, however, be adopted with the most irreproachable musical taste. It is but rarely resorted to, save in the old Italian music, where considerable latitude was not merely allowed to the singer, but almost expected of him. The accompanying examples will illustrate how the alterations may be made. They are typical of the many variants which the writer received from Senior Garcia during the four precious years spent under the *maestro's* tuition. One occurs in the famous *Aria di Chiesa* of Stradella, the other in the principal baritone air in the *Nozze di Figaro, Vedra, mentr' io sospiro* [Example 1].

So much for changes in melody. In addition to these there are certain possible

(d) Changes in the manner of executing passages.—(1) The *legato* is the most important of all, being the groundwork and dominant characteristic of all good vocalization. In it the notes are connected one to another with grace and smoothness, flowing with distinctness and evenness. The other four methods may be looked on as varieties of colouring:—(2) marcato, (3) portamento, (4) staccato, (5) aspirato. The mechanism by which these are produced is more suitably dealt with in a book containing exercises written for the acquirement of vocal technique.

(e) Changes in phrasing.—Alterations are often possible in breathing places, whereby the recurrence of a melody may receive fresh treatment. The choice of these, however, is subject to certain strict rules, which are accepted canons of artistic singing. Breath should not be taken in the middle of a word, between an adjective and its related noun, in the middle of a verb, or between any words which are intimately united by their grammatical sense. Consequently, the vocalist must replenish the breath only when the punctuation of words and music agrees. On the rare occasions when this is not possible, a half breath may be taken at a convenient place, but this must be done in such a way that it is not noticeable to the listener.

Perhaps the most artistic way of attaining this result is to take up the melody again with strongly-increased emphasis after breathing, since this suggests a natural reason for the pause. In ordinary conversation, and still more in acting or oratory, when it is intended to lay special stress upon a word, or to call particular attention to a phrase, it is often done by making a pause immediately before or after the word.

(f) Changes in accentuation of phrases.—Sims Reeves used to say, "A singer who does not recite or read the verses of a song aloud before attempting the music, will never become a great artist," and indeed it would be difficult to overestimate the importance of this preliminary. Manuel Garcia himself draws special attention to it when he refers to the preparation of a piece.

"The vocalist," he says, "should read the words of the piece again and again till each finest shadow of meaning has been mastered. He must next recite them with perfect simplicity and self-abandonment. The accent of truth apparent in the voice when speaking naturally is the basis of expression in singing. Light and shade, accent, sentiment, all become eloquent and persuasive. The imitation of instinctive impulse must, therefore, be the object of his special preparation."

Seeing that a composer seeks his inspiration from the lines of the poet, and attempts to bring out in his music the various feelings which these have conveyed to him, it should be unnecessary to insist on the importance of every word being uttered by the vocalist with irreproachable distinctness. The listener should not have to strain his ears to catch one single phrase. Such was the singing of Sims Reeves, Edward Lloyd, and Charles Santley, of Patti, Trebelli, and Antoinette Sterling, to mention but a few names taken at random. When listening to such artists as these there was never a moment's doubt as to what had been sung. Clearness of enunciation, therefore, should be the aim of all. A book of words should be as unnecessary in a concert-hall as a copy of the play at a theatre; or, at any rate, it should be necessary only for the giving of translations of German, French, or Italian songs for the assistance of members of the audience, who are unfamiliar with the languages.

In analysing the words of a song it must be borne in mind that nearly every sentence is susceptible of varying treatment as regards its accentuation. The principal stress may be laid on anyone of several words, each of which will give the sentence a different shade of meaning. This fact gives the singer a way of finding variety when a line or phrase appears several times in the song.

Let us take as an illustration the well-known line in Lord Tennyson's exquisite poem, *Crossing the Bar:* "I hope to see my Pilot face to face."

If the stress be laid on the first word, it might convey at least two meanings, suggesting either that "Others do not hope to see Him, but I do," or else that "I too hope, as others hope." Which of these two was implied would be determined by the tone of voice in which it was said. This question of tone or *timbre,* as conveying the different shades of expression, will be considered in the next and final section.

Now, by saying "I *hope* to see," we introduce an element of doubt. "I hope to *see*" suggests "I have always believed in His existence, but with death there will come the clearing up of all doubt." "I hope to see my *Pilot*" brings out the continuation of the metaphor drawn between dying and "putting out to sea," while the emphasis" on "face to face" gives still another meaning.

These, then, are the possible accents in this particular line, and other phrases are capable of variation in a lesser or a greater degree. For instance, the sentence, "I thought she loved me," would have five distinct shades of meaning through the stress being laid on each of the five words in turn, quite apart from the further changes which could be suggested by introducing variations in the tone of voice. When several alternatives of stress are possible (the composer will have already eliminated some by applying certain words to the strong beats of the bar, others to the weak) the artistic powers of the singer are brought out by the way in which he rejects some accentuations and retains others. The individuality of rendering finds perhaps most scope in the exercising of a wise choice over this and over the further question of tone-colour: that is to say, of—

(g) Changes of timbre.—It is well known that the speaking voice takes on a different "tone" and inflection according to our actual feelings at any particular time. Take, for instance, a single word such as "go." Whether the utterance is prompted by love or hate, joy or grief, anger, fear, or any other feeling, nature imparts to the voice a distinct difference of quality accordingly. One of the singer's principal aims must be the cultivation of the power to recognise the quality of tone which results from every possible individual feeling. Then he must set himself to acquire absolute command over these various changes, so that he may be able to reproduce them at will, for vocal expression depends upon this power to a large extent. With this means at his command he will be able to give artistic expression to his singing, conveying to the listener a tone-picture of his feelings. He will, of course, have previously studied the words, tried to penetrate the poet's inmost meaning, and decided what rendering he shall give, bearing in mind throughout that he must aim at variety of expression.

"Singing a song," Sims Reeves said, "is like painting a picture. The voice conveys to the mind the beauty and meaning of a song, as the eye conveys to the mind the beauty and meaning of a picture. But if the performer sings in one uniform colour of tone from beginning to end, the result is monotony and ineffectiveness. Light and shade in singing do not consist in making passages loud and soft alternately; they consist in using the various colours of the voice to suit the sentiment of the words. The *mezza-voce* is of great use in this respect."

To avoid monotony, then, one must analyse the poem, and if possible find some distinct change of feeling for each fresh group of ideas. It is not sufficient to ask oneself "what class of song is this? What is the primary feeling of the poet? Is it a note of love, of joy, of grief, of patriotism?" Having settled that a song primarily denotes, say, love, we must go further and consider what it connotes. What, then, are the feelings which anyone may experience when deeply in love? May he not be in turn wistful, gentle, tender, sympathetic, loving, passionate, hopeful that his love may be returned, fearful lest it be rejected? May he not grow anxious, jealous, angry, mocking; and may not this be followed by regret, pleading, happiness? There is, indeed, abundance of choice before one. Given the ability to reproduce the *timbre* or tone-colour suggesting the various feelings, there remains but the process of selecting and rejecting the various possibilities. The choice will depend on how far he is educated, refined, well-read, poetic, imaginative, and generally artistic. Here, then, we have the field of study which lies before every singer who wishes to appeal to the intellect and to the artistic feeling of the audience. The voice is the gift of nature; the rest may be acquired by study.

If he would appeal to the *heart* of the hearer, that is another matter. To make others feel deeply, one must feel deeply oneself. There must be an electric current of sympathy flowing out to the listener, and this can be generated only by the singer himself.

The truth of nature alone can awake an answer in the breasts of others. That indefinable something which grips, stirs, and moves to tears cannot be learned. It owes its origin to a power which is far beyond the control of man.

NOTES

1. M. Sterling MacKinlay, *Garcia: The Centenarian and His Times* (New York: D. Appleton and Co., 1908).
2. M. Sterling MacKinlay, *The Singing Voice and Its Training* (London: George Routledge & Sons, Limit, 1910).

51. Words! Words! Words! More from Garcia

Originally published in the *Journal of Singing*, volume 71, no. 4, 2015

I have written at least one previous column where I featured extended excerpts from the second of Manuel Garcia's *Complete Treatise on the Art of Singing* in two volumes.[1] The first volume was published in 1841 and the second appeared in 1847. Volume 1 is primarily the progressive method, and Volume 2 is a performance guide on how to interpret and sing the operatic literature being performed in the first half of the 19th century (much of which is still in the repertory). The only complete translation of both volumes in English was published by Donald V. Paschke in 1975.[2] Unfortunately, it is long out of print and very difficult to find. There were versions of the Garcia method published in English over the years, but they are edited and abridged and leave out some of the most interesting things that Garcia had to say, particularly in Volume 2. The following excerpt does not appear at all in the 1924 translation done by Albert Garcia, grandson of the author, and is only available in the Paschke translation. It presents very useful information on the form of Italian verse and guides the singer in how to deliver the text and the music most effectively. It is clear from Garcia's words that singers have much more leeway in how to make the score work for them than we are led to believe by contemporary coaches and conductors. I encourage you to study the excerpts carefully.

This is the seventh section of Chapter 1; the text is taken from the Paschke translation. The figures are scanned from my personal copy of an old parallel French and German edition which is undated, but I believe it to be the date of the second volume (1847). I have not attempted to translate the wording in the figures, but the text clarifies them sufficiently.

7. DISTRIBUTION OF THE WORDS UNDER THE NOTES

The simplest practical rule is that which shows how to apply one syllable to each isolated note, or to each group of slurred or beamed notes. This rule rests on this fact, that each syllable cannot be rendered by less than one note, whereas it can embrace an undetermined number of consecutive notes.[†††] When each syllable is sung to a group of notes, these notes are joined by one or several beams if their value will permit that method, or by a slur if that value excludes the use of beams; in this latter case, each group represents only one syllable.

But, as the connections between the syllables and the notes are not always exactly indicated in the written music, in order to correct the errors which are encountered, one will have recourse to the fundamental principle that we formulate thus: have the common accent of the line fall on the down-beat of the second, third or fourth bar, according to the length of the phrase or member of the phrase relative to the verse.[‡‡‡]

In fact, the composer himself, in the greatest number of cases, has the common accent of the line fall on the down-beat of the second, third or fourth bar; and the reason for this is that these down-beats mark the limit of the member of the phrase or of the melodic line. Only the meeting of this down-beat with the common accent can indicate the rhythmic cadence. Also one never sees a weak syllable corresponding with this down-beat. The adjustment with which it is concerned will thus consist of replacing that accent on the beat which corresponds to it, then to place the other *necessary accents* of the line on the other strong beats, more rarely on weak beats. Examples: [Example 1]

In the following aria of Handel, the translator has distributed the words badly. Handel: *Samson*, Aria.

---

††† This rule permits one exception more apparent than real in a case of which we will speak presently. It is that in which the vowels are joined to form only one group.

‡‡‡ In order to understand this paragraph, it is indispensable to have the formation of the phrase in mind.

[Example 2]

The observation of this precept assumes the profound knowledge of the prosody of the language in which one sings, as well as of its laws of versification.

Example 1.

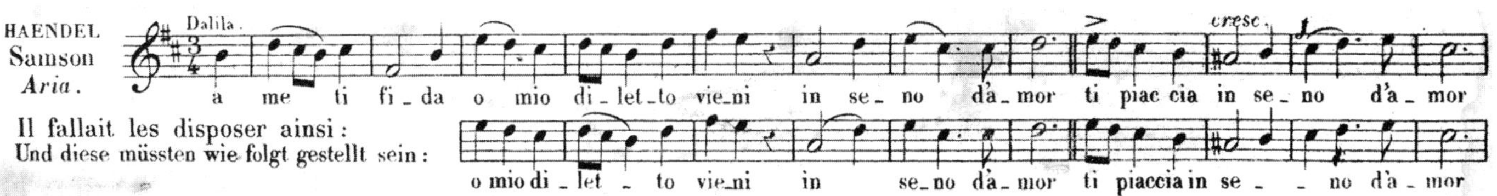

Example 2.

ITALIAN VERSE

Three principal laws preside over the formation of Italian Verse:

- The first determines the quantity of syllables which come into each kind of verse;
- The second fixes the number of long or accented syllables which must indispensably be found in each kind of 1ine, and the places which they occupy [*numero e luogo degli accenti*]. It is primarily to this condition that Italian verse owes its rhythm which is so favorable to melody;
- The third law distributes the rhymes. We will not have to concern ourselves with it.

The Italians count ten species of poetic lines; and as each line ends on a smooth, transitory, or imperfect word, each specie of poetic line can also have three types (*piano, sdrucciolo,* or *tronco*). These species are distinguished by the name which expresses the number of syllables in the smooth line. Thus the transitory line and the imperfect line, although containing one syllable more or less than the smooth line, are counted like the smooth line. Examples:

- Gia di monti le cime s'indorano (eleven syllables, transitory line.)
- E di perle di tremulo gielo (ten syllables, smooth line.)
- Ogni rosa conchiglia si fa (nine syllables, imperfect line.)

Before indicating the number and specific distribution of the accents, let us point out that in each line there is always one accent, namely, the final, which is subjected to an invariable rule. That accent consistently falls on the penultimate syllable of the *smooth* line, consequently on the third-to-the-last syllable of the *transitory* line, and on the final syllable of the *imperfect* line. Thus, for example, if the line is endecasyllabic (eleven syllables), the final accent will fall on the tenth syllable of the smooth line. This accent, because of its universality, has received the name of *common accent*. Let us pass to the rules which the other accents follow.

Endecasyllabic verse. In addition to the common accent on the tenth syllable, it takes another on the sixth. One may neglect this latter, but on the condition that two others be substituted for it, one on the fourth, and one on the eighth syllable. This variation of the rhythmic system is seen moreover in other species of lines. Apart from these indispensable accents, all occupy arbitrary places. We will content ourselves with giving a few examples of them, and for brevity, we will mark by numbers the various positions of the accents. [Example 3]

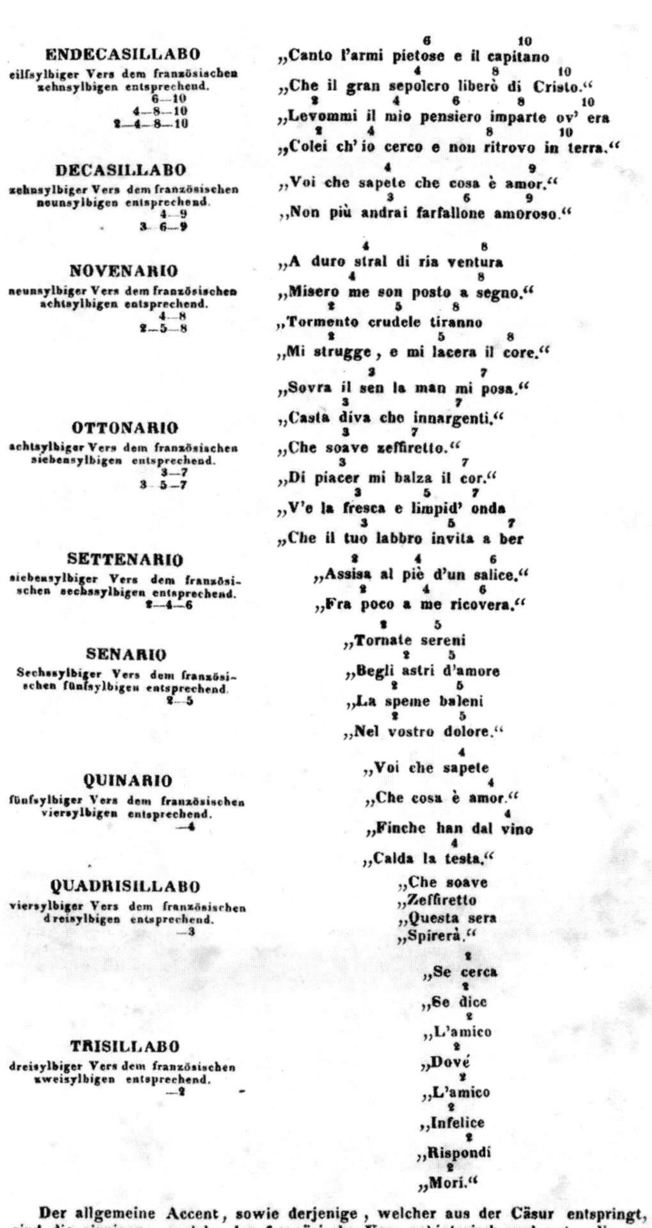

ENDECASILLABO
eilfsylbiger Vers dem französischen zehnsylbigen entsprechend.
6—10
4—8—10
2—4—8—10

6 10
„Canto l'armi pietose e il capitano
4 8 10
„Che il gran sepolcro liberò di Cristo."
2 4 6 8 10
„Levommi il mio pensiero imparte ov' era
2 4 8 10
„Colei ch' io cerco e non ritrovo in terra."

DECASILLABO
zehnsylbiger Vers dem französischen neunsylbigen entsprechend.
4—9
3—6—9

4 9
„Voi che sapete che cosa è amor."
3 6 9
„Non più andrai farfallone amoroso."

NOVENARIO
neunsylbiger Vers dem französischen achtsylbigen entsprechend.
4—8
2—5—8

4 8
„A duro stral di ria ventura
4 8
„Misero me son posto a segno."
2 5 8
„Tormento crudele tiranno
2 5 8
„Mi strugge, e mi lacera il core."

OTTONARIO
achtsylbiger Vers dem französischen siebensylbigen entsprechend.
3—7
3—5—7

3 7
„Sovra il sen la man mi posa."
3 7
„Casta diva che innargenti."
3 7
„Che soave zeffiretto."
3 7
„Di piacer mi balza il cor."
3 5 7
„V'e la fresca e limpid' onda
3 5 7
„Che il tuo labbro invita a ber

SETTENARIO
siebensylbiger Vers dem französischen sechssylbigen entsprechend.
2—4—6

2 4 6
„Assisa al piè d'un salice."
2 4 6
„Fra poco a me ricovera."

SENARIO
Sechssylbiger Vers dem französischen fünfsylbigen entsprechend.
2—5

2 5
„Tornate sereni
2 5
„Begli astri d'amore
2 5
„La speme baleni
2 5
„Nel vostro dolore."

QUINARIO
fünfsylbiger Vers dem französischen viersylbigen entsprechend.
—4

4
„Voi che sapete
4
„Che cosa è amor."
4
„Finche han dal vino
4
„Calda la testa."

QUADRISILLABO
viersylbiger Vers dem französischen dreisylbigen entsprechend.
—3

„Che soave
„Zeffiretto
„Questa sera
„Spirerà."

TRISILLABO
dreisylbiger Vers dem französischen zweisylbigen entsprechend.
—2

2
„Se cerca
2
„Se dice
2
„L'amico
2
„Dové
2
„L'amico
2
„Infelice
2
„Rispondi
2
„Mori."

Der allgemeine Accent, sowie derjenige, welcher aus der Cäsur entspringt, sind die einzigen, welche der französische Vers gebieterisch verlangt; die regelmässige Anwendung der übrigen Accente würde ihn aber ebenso melodisch als den italienischen machen.

Example 3.

It is known that the common accent and that which results from the caesura are the only ones imperiously required in French verse. The regular use of other accents would make it as melodious as Italian verse.

In stating that each syllable cannot be rendered by less than one note, we have not forgotten a particular case which seems to present a departure from that principle, but which one can easily reconcile to it.

In order to recognize in which cases one should run the vowels together, and in which cases to the contrary, one must isolate them, it is necessary to consider the place which the tonic accent occupies. If any group of vowels is without an accent, the voice should not fix itself on any of them; if there is an accent in the group, it is the accented vowel which dominates; as a consequence, the voice should glide equally over all the others, joining them into a single emission. That vowel can be found placed at the beginning, in the middle, or at the end of the group. Examples with two vowels: [Example 4]

Examples with three vowels: [Example 5]

Examples with four consecutive vowels: [Example 6]

Example 4.

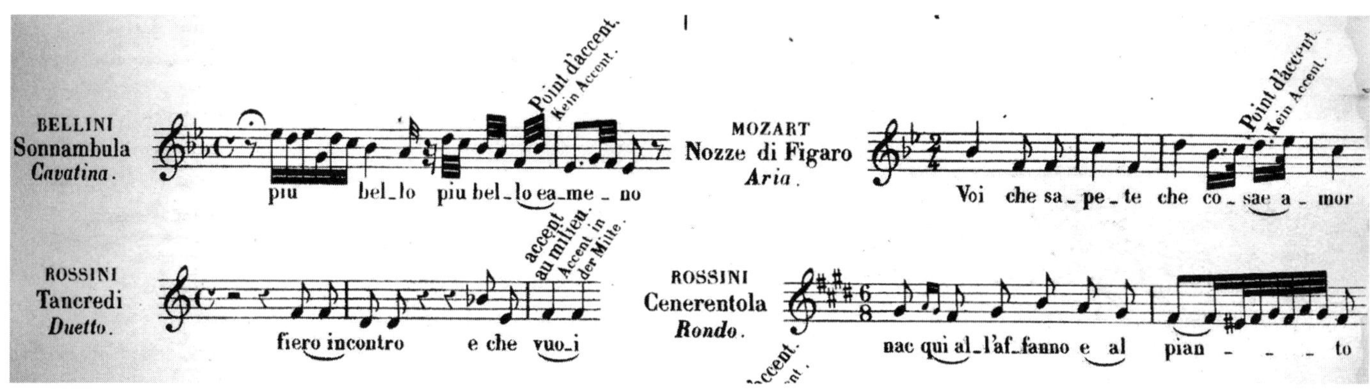

Example 5.

Example 6.

This contraction of several vowels into a single emission is one of the principal difficulties which hampers those to whom the singing of Italian is foreign.

When the tonic accent falls on the first vowel of the group, one separates it from the others. In the words: *IsA . . . ura, gemE . . . a,* we separate the A from the u, and the E from the a, because the tonic accent is placed on the first vowel. Now, in a similar case the accented vowel keeps its value as a syllable, and is distinguished from the vowel or vowels which follow. It would be the same if the accent fell on one of the middle vowels. The word *giOia* furnishes us an example of that: the voice stops on the vowel 0 of that word, and slides *with an equal movement* over all the others.

Sometimes one separates adjacent vowels of two words which follow each other in order to take a breath. [Example 7]

Each vowel should be formed distinctly, but not at all detached by a jerk. Only the mouth instantaneously modifies the tone which the larynx emits without the latter articulating a different note for each vowel, and also the linking of the vowels being accompanied by an effect like that of a yawn. It is necessary to assume that the note which carries the two or three vowels is divided into as many fractions which succeed each other without interval. In order to demonstrate this rule more clearly, we write the passages seen above thus: [Example 8]

The contraction takes place within the same word, or from one word to the following word, and allows one to avoid hiatus. See the examples:

Che faro senza Euridice,

Bel raggio lusinghiere.

Example 7.

Example 8.

Example 9.

In these examples, *senza Euridice* and *raggio lusinghiere,* the vowels AEU [aeu], IO [d ʒo], and IE [jɛ] have been contracted. In the first examples, as there is no accent, the voice glides over all the vowels. When the vowel is repeated, we have recourse to elision, which is only a kind of contraction.

As much as possible, the distribution of the syllables for the melody should be done in such a manner that they mark the measures with regularity. One will depart from this principle only when its application would present obvious inconveniences. [Example 9]

The need to facilitate the emission of the voice and the clarity of the vocalization forces one to break this rule and to choose among the words some words or syllables more favorable to the effect, and that one repeat without keeping strictly to a regular order.

Here are the various cases which may occur:

1. When one encounters a rather lengthy passage, one must choose, in order to perform it, the open vowels [a], [ɛ], [ɔ]. These vowels give the organ attractiveness and facility. Examples: [Example 10]
2. When multiple syllables too frequently cut a passage and tend to dull the voice, it is better to unite the entire passage into a single syllable. The variant of the passage below can serve as an example: [Example 11]
3. Sometimes one succeeds in freeing the performance only by omitting some words. [Example 12]

In the cavatina from the *Barber of Seville*, the disposition differs essentially from the written order. In the duet from *Andronico* the line is divided; this license seems permissible to us since it modifies the meaning only slightly. Moreover the line has already been heard in its entirely, and it is repeated only for the need of the music. The form that we propose offers a double advantage: it places the roulades on the vowels [o] and [a], and it avoids the need to articulate the syllable *tri* on the high B.

The following dispositions also permit the avoidance of articulations on high notes. [Examples 13 and 14]

Example 10.

Example 11.

Example 12.

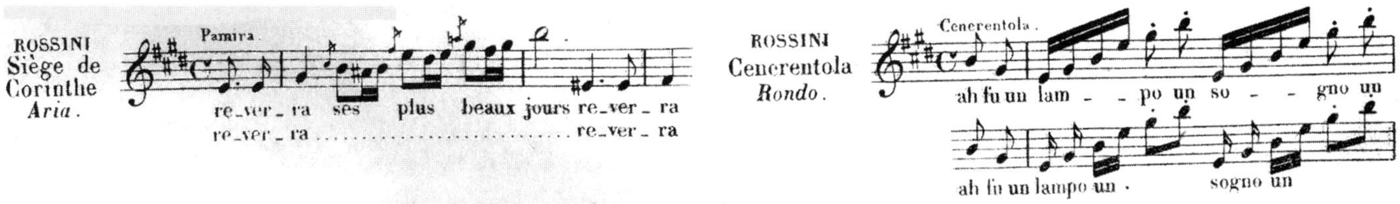

Example 13.

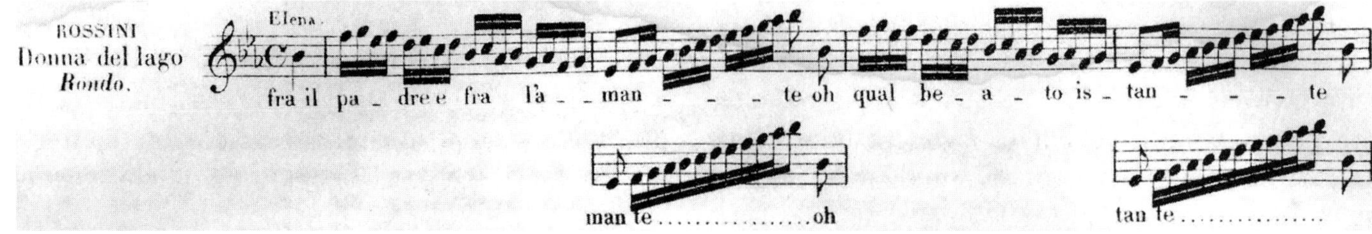

Example 14.

Except in cases of the same nature as these, one will avoid distributing the syllables in an unequal and irregular manner.

If the syllabication occurs on notes that are too high and one can do nothing to change the words, one will try to have the high tones preceded by an ascending portamento, but this portamento must be in accord with the musical sense. Examples: [Example 15]

Support would be useless if one would attack the B in falsetto register.

The voice thus placed on the high note by means of the portamento, one can change syllables more easily than if it were necessary to attack the syllable and the note at the same time.

In order to avoid syllabication on a high note, one can also have recourse to a lower grace note conveniently placed, on which one articulates the syllable in advance. Example: [Example 16]
The placement of the syllable on the lower grace note permits the organ to attain, by means of a light and rapid portamento, the high note, and on the first instant of that value.

In some cases one can again facilitate the attack of the high note if one takes advantage of the light internal sound which the preparation of certain consonants produces, that of the [m], the [n], the [d], the [b], etc., for example. This sound, preceding by an instant the explosion of the voice, permits one to attempt the tone accurately and with a firmness of the glottis, and removes the danger of producing what one calls a *couac* [squawk]. Examples: [Example 17]

The alteration of the vowel in certain syllables is a convenient resource. Example: [Example 18]
The I [j] has been changed into a U [ɥ].

Example 15.

Example 16.

Example 17.

Example 18.

Moreover, in whatever manner the voice takes it, the organ will always be able to approach these difficult notes with success, provided it is not caught off guard, but that at the moment of producing them, it is properly positioned; that is the only aim of the various procedures which we indicate.

NOTES

1. Stephen Austin, "'On Time' with Manuel Garcia," *Journal of Singing* 67, no. 2 (November/December 2010): 213–216.
2. Manuel Garcia, *Complete Treatise on the Art of Singing*, Part 1 and Part 2, translated and edited by Donald V. Paschke (New York: Da Capo Press, 1975).

52. Notes on Garcia's Memoir on the Human Voice

Originally published in the *Journal of Singing*, volume 71, no. 5, 2015

I have often written about Manuel Garcia in this column and have included extended excerpts from his two primary publications, *A Complete Treatise on the Art of Singing* two volumes, 1841 and 1847) and his *Hints on Singing* (1894). His first significant work however, was his *Memoire sur la voix humaine,*[1] which he presented to the Academy of Sciences in 1841. It is difficult to imagine that the complete *Memoire* has not been translated into English after all these years, but I cannot find where it has. An extended extract from it was published in English along with the official report of the Academy in an early Oliver Ditson publication, which I have in my own library, called *Garcias's Complete School of Singing, in which the art is clearly developed in a series of instructions and appropriate examples; to which are added numerous exercises, written and composed by Manuel Garcia.* This volume is undated, but looks to be from the 1860s, or so. The incomplete extract will be offered here in the future. For now, here is the report from the Academy for us pedagogy nerds who read this column.

Report of the Memoir on the Human Voice

Presented to the Academy of Sciences,
By M. Manuel Garcia.

(Commissioners, MM. Majendie, Savary, Dutrochet, reporting)
(Extracted from the minutes of the sessions of the Academy of Sciences,
meeting of April 12, 1841.)

The Academy has charged us, (MM. Majendie, Savary, and myself,) to make a report on the Memoir which has been presented by M. Manuel Garcia, and which is entitled "Memoir on the Human Voice." The state of M. Savary's health has not permitted him to make one of the Committee; another Fellow, M. Savart, whose recent loss we have to deplore, and to whom acoustics is indepted for so many original researches, was therefore joined to us; like ourselves, he has witnessed the fact which we now have the honor to lay before the Academy.

The theory of the formation and of the variation of tones by the human vocal organ is far from being complete; we are not even agreed as to what kind of instrument the human vocal organ should be compared. Almost all physicians have considered it as being of that kind of instruments in which the sound is engendered by the vibration of certain solid and elastic bodies; M. Savart, on the contrary, has compared the vocal organs to one of those instruments of which huntsmen make use to imitate the song of certain birds, and instruments of the flute-kind, and in which the sound is exclusively engendered by the vibrations of the air which strikes against the partitions of a cavity, or breaks itself against the edge of a pebble.
Despite the authority which our colleague necessarily had in matters of acoustics, it must be owned that his theory of the voice had met with but few partisans; he also told us himself, a few days before his death, that he was going to modify and complete it. Let us hope that amongst his papers there may be found some traces of this work, which cannot fail to be of great interest.

However, it may be, the vocal organ is so perfect, it gives rise to such marvelous and divers results, that one is tempted to believe that it is not a single instrument, but that it enjoys the admirable privilege of transforming itself incessantly into a number of different instruments. See it act, for example, in the chest-voice; observe it exercise itself in the falsetto voice; would it not be said that these two kinds of registers were produced by two instruments which were substituted one for the other? However, we have not yet arrived at determining what is the difference which exists, without doubt, in the mechanism of the production of these two sorts of voice, the qualities of which present so marked a difference; at the same time the certainty is acquired that they are perfectly distinct, and that they are not the immediate continuation of each other. Indeed, in the vicinity of the points of junction of these two voices or *registers,* where the deepest notes of the falsetto succeed the most elevated note of the full voice, there are many of those notes which can be equally produced by employing either of the two voices. This fact, known to artists, has only within the last few years been introduced into physiological science; it is found mentioned, for the first time, in the work of Dr. Rush, entitled "Philosophy of the Human Voice," a work of which a portion has been translated from the English into French by Dr. Bennati.

"It must not be imagined," says Rush, "that the particular step to this kind of voice *(the falsetto)* is comprised between the last note of the natural voice *(the chest voice),* and the most elevated that can be effected. Still a sort of falsetto may be formed a little above the point which binds the natural voice to this kind of intonation." The facts which have been submitted to us by M. Manuel Garcia have fully confirmed this assertion. This skilful professor of singing has formed pupils to whom he has taught the art of managing their vocal organs with sufficient facility to separate from each other, neatly and at will, the tones derived from the full voice, and those which are derived from the falsetto. Thus, we have heard male and female voices, after having pursued to their most elevated limit the diatonic notes which appertain to the full voice, take the falsetto voice, in order to rise higher, then descending diatonically, always retaining the falsetto, unto a certain distance below the limit at which the full voice had stopped; so that the same diatonic notes which have been produced in ascending by the full voice, are produced in descending by the falsetto voice. And more, we have heard the same singer produce at will and alternately the identical note with the full and with the falsetto voice; so that the tones produced by the two voices were thus rendered parallel. The extent of the portion common to the two voices or *registers* of the chest and of the falsetto is variable, according to the subjects and according to the habit which has rendered the facultative use of these two registers in the *medium* of the voice more or less easy. This extent is commonly from a sixth to an octave; but it sometimes reaches a tenth. According to M. Garcia, this portion, common to the two registers, is placed on the same notes in the male as in the female voices.

It can no longer be doubted, after these facts, that the full or chest voice, and the falsetto voice, are each produced by a particular and important modification in the mechanism of the vocal instrument. This conclusion is indeed confirmed by an observation of M. Garcia, an observation which greatly struck our colleague Savart, who, with ourselves, was a witness to it. The full and the falsetto voice, in order to produce the same note in the portion of the diatonic scale which is common to them, employs a quantity of air or breath which is far from being the same; M. Garcia demonstrates this by the following experiment. A singer, having his chest as completely filled with air as it could be, produced, with the full voice, a determined note, taken in the part com mon to the two registers, and prolongs this vocal tone until the exhaustion of the air contained in his lungs. The pendulum of a metronome, by its oscillations, served to indicate the time during which this vocal tone lasted: afterwards, having filled his lungs with air, the singer produced the same note with the falsetto voice, and sustained it as long as he was able. We then saw, by these two experiments, several times repeated, that the pendulum made from 24 to 26 oscillations whilst the tone of the full voice lasted, and but from 16 to 18 in the duration of the same tone in the falsetto voice.

This experiment proves that, in a given time, and for the production of the same diatonic note, the vocal instrument, in giving the falsetto voice, expends more air than in producing the full or chest voice.

According to the common opinion of artists, the falsetto voice forms a particular register, which differs at once from the register appertaining to the chest voice, which is inferior to it, and from the register of the *head voice,* which is superior. M. Garcia does not admit this opinion; he regards the falsetto and head voice as belonging to one and the same register, presenting, throughout its whole extent, the same mechanism for the production of tones. He supports his opinion on this point on the fact of the falsetto and the head voice presenting a perfect and constant continuity; there are no bordering tones which can be produced alternately by one or the other of these two voices, as we have represented relative to the transition of the chest and falsetto voices. This latter and the head voice appertain, therefore, to one and the same register, which M. Garcia designates by the name of the *falsetto head* register.

It is generally known that, when the human voice mounts from the grave to the acute, as well in the chest as in the falsetto head voice, the larynx gradually rises. This progressive ascent of the larynx has been considered to influence the gradual augmentation of the acuteness of the tones, since this ascent effects the progressive shortening of the vocal tube. Some physiologists have doubted whether this shortening of the vocal tube had the influence which has thus been attributed to it on the degree of acuteness of the vocal sounds. It is not our place here to occupy ourselves with these theoretical questions; our task is to establish facts, and here the art of song presents us with fresh ones. Here is what they consist in.

The full and the falsetto voices, each appearing to retain its own particular mode of production, presents two principal varieties in their quality, varieties which M. Garcia designates by the name of *clear quality* and *sombre quality*. These two qualities of voice are usually designated, by artists, the first by the name of *clear voice*, and the second by the name of *dull voice*. Besides, in the production of the chest and the *falsetto head* voices, whether with the clear or with the *sombre quality*, in the position of the larynx and in that of the veil of the palate, some very remarkable changes are manifest. We give the facts of which M. Garcia has rendered us witnesses.

In the diatonic production of the tones from the grave to the acute, equally with the full or chest voice as with the falsetto head voice, and with the *clear quality*, a continued and gradual ascent of the larynx is observed; the veil of the palate is then constantly depressed. It is not the same when the voice passes to the *sombre quality*.

In the full or chest-voice produced with this *sombre quality*, and in ascending from the gravest tones of this register to the most elevated notes appertaining to it, the larynx remains constantly fixed in its lowest position, and the veil of the palate is raised. It is the same in producing, in the *sombre quality*, the lowest part of the falsetto voice, or that of which the notes can be equally produced by the full voice; but when the singer passes, still in *sombre quality*, to the most elevated part of the falsetto voice, to that which is specially designated by artists under the name of *head voice*, then the larynx slightly ascends, but much less than it does when this same head voice is produced with the *clear quality*. In order to render this difference evident to your Commissioners, some pupils of M. Garcia, well practised in giving to their voices at will the *clear* and the *sombre* quality, allowed us to hear falsetto scales, in which each note was given alternately in falsetto *clear* quality, and in falsetto *sombre quality*. The difference between these two qualities, the one brilliant, the other somewhat deadened, was then perfectly distinguishable; and, although it was the same note of the falsetto voice which was produced, we beheld the larynx, fixed in an elevated position for the production of this note in clear quality, descend considerably in order to produce this same note in *sombre* quality; we could follow with the eye and the finger this alternate ascent and descent of the larynx.

These observations are not altogether new for the physiology of the voice.

In effect, there was presented to the Academy of Sciences, on the 1st of June, 1840, by MM. Diday and Petrequin, a Memoir having for its objects the physiological study of the *deadened-voice*, a peculiar voice, which had only been known in France for three years, it having been imported from Italy by a celebrated artist attached to our lyric stage. In this memoir is mentioned the physiological fact of the low and fixed position of the larynx in the diatonic production of all the notes of the *deadened* chest-voice; but these authors have not followed this same *sombre quality* in the phenomena which it presents when it invests the falsetto-voice with its particular character. They appear even to have thought that this *sombre quality* could only effect the chest-voice. M. Garcia may therefore lay claim to a share in the observation of the *deadened-voice.*[§§§] This mechanism shows that with the full or chest voice, as with the falsetto or head-voice, the human vocal organs can give the same scales with very different lengths of the vocal tube, which only gives rise to a change in the quality of the voice. Hence it results that the different elongations of this tube, necessarily have not all the influence which has been attributed to them on the determination of the tones, and that these same differences in the length of the vocal tube are constantly in relation to the existence either of the clear or the *sombre quality* of the voice.

In addition to these two principal qualities, designated by the names of *clear quality* and *sombre quality,* there are several other secondary qualities; such as, for example, the *guttural quality,* the *nasal quality,* etc. M. Garcia endeavors to determine the mechanical conditions of these qualities; on this head we shall say nothing, not having verified the assertions of M. Garcia.

There exists sometimes in the human voice an inferior register for the gravity of the tones in the lowest notes that can be given in the chest voice by ground-basses. This register, termed *counter-bass register* by M. Garcia, has never yet been observed in its full development, except amongst some singers employed in Russia for religious purposes. Dr. Bennati was the first to point this out to physiologists. The tones of this register belong indubitably to a vocal instrument *sui generis,* very different from that to which the tones of the chest-voice are due. In the gravest notes of this last voice, or of this last register, the larynx falls below its natural position; in the much graver tones of the counter-bass register, the larynx, on the contrary, is carried to its greatest possible elevation. In this register, M. Garcia could only present to us a very deep and very rough tone, which rather resembled the growling of an animal than the tone of a human voice. But one of us have been enabled to study, in the Russian singer Ivanoff, the counter-bass voice which this artist possesses, and which descends to the *sol* of the octave below ordinary ground-basses; although this note was infinitely superior in quality to the tone, or rather to the noise, which M. Garcia enabled us to hear, it would be difficult to comprehend it in singing.

After this examination, it will be easily understood, that one sole and identical mechanism cannot explain the formation of all the musical sounds which the human vocal organ can produce. This organ may truly be considered as being able, alone, to represent an assemblage of instruments differing from each other; mysterious modifications which arise and fix themselves with admirable celerity, according to the will of the practised singer. If hereafter, ceasing to consider the vocal organs as a musical instrument, we should enter upon the consideration of all the unmusical sounds which this organ can produce by the variety of tones of speech, by the imitation of certain noises, or the cries of different animals, etc., one could not be otherwise than profoundly astonished at the multiplicity of mechanical changes of which this organ, apparently so simple in its structure, is susceptible.

Finally, we think that M. Garcia, by his sagacity and judicious studies as a professor of singing, has observed and described in his Memoir many interesting facts, which will in future be included in the physical theory of the human voice. We have the honor of proposing to the Academy to make known to him its approbation.

The conclusions of this Report have been adopted.

NOTE

1. "Memoire sur la voix humaine," in: *Comptes-rendus des séances de l'Académie des sciences* (April 12, 1841)

[§§§] In a letter, read at the Academy of Sciences on the 19th April, 1841, M. Garcia proved that the lower fixedness of the larynx had been known to him for all the registers since 1832, and that, since that period, he had incessantly rendered it public by teaching.

53. More from Lamperti

Originally published in the *Journal of Singing*, volume 72, no. 1, 2015

In the introduction to an earlier article, "A Little 'Vocal Wisdom'," I referred to this little book with that title by Giovanni Battista Lamperti, son of Francesco Lamperti.[1] In the preface to *The Technics of Bel Canto*, Lamperti began by saying that he saw it superfluous to add yet another method book on singing to the pile, but it didn't stop him from writing it![2] It is indeed a vocal method book in the tradition of the 19th century: full of specific voice-building exercises and discussion about breath, resonance, articulations of various kinds, including portamento, staccato, and registers. He finishes his book with advice concerning other equally important things, and it is that part of *The Technics of Bel Canto* that I offer here.

THE TECHNICS OF SPEECH AND SONG

Language and Song rarely go hand in hand. The Italian language is the chief exception to this rule, being the one best adapted for artistic song on account of its wealth of vowels and lack of aspirates. Most Italians naturally pronounce the open vowel "a" (ah) correctly, whereas other nationalities have to make a special study of it; the English, for instance, often shade "ah" toward *a* or *o*. For us, however, the German language is the first in order. The vowels "i" (ee) and French "u" (ü) are hard to sing on the high notes. We shall take no singer to task for changing the position of such words, or for substituting others with more euphonious vowels—provided that he possess the technical ability to vocalize the above-named vowels on high tones. The pronunciation of the vowels having been sufficiently practised in the solfeggi and vocalises, we need dwell no longer on their quantity (as long or short); for a pure pronunciation, free from dialect and sharply articulated, is a prerequisite.

We proceed to the German diphthongs, pronounced as follows:

ai and ei	=	ah^{ĭ}
au and eu	=	ah^{ü}
au	=	ah^{oo}

The first vowel must be prolonged as much as possible, and the second sung short.

The pronunciation of the consonants presents greater difficulties than that of the vowels. Consonants are vocal or unvocal, the vocal nasal consonants (*m, n, ng*) require no special remark. Opinions differ concerning the correct pronunciation of *g* at the end of a word or syllable. In the words *König* and *heilig*, the soft sound of *g* (the German palatal *ch*) is preferable; on the other hand, we pronounce *weg* like *weck*, *sag* like *sak* (*zahk*), although we say *wech*-genommen (not *weck*genommen) because of the two successive *g*'s. The consonants *h* and *ch* are peculiar to the German language, and therefore familiar to all.[13] Far more unfavorable for vocal art are the numerous doubled consonants and combinations. The tone-accent always falls on the vowel; *e. g.*, pronounce *Hi-mmel*, not *Him-mel*. Where no ambiguity is created the final and initial consonants may be drawn together, *e. g.*, "im~milden Mondlicht" (English parallel: "in~noble hearts"); but make a distinction between "in Nacht" and "in Acht" (parallel: "a tall" and "at all"). Some sentences are so crowded with combinations of consonants as positively to hinder the freedom of delivery. The best way to over-

---

*For English-speaking students unacquainted with German, an explanation appears desirable: The hard, or guttural, *ch* is merely a rough breathing, as if one were trying gently to clear one's throat; the soft, or palatal, *ch* is obtained by setting the tongue as if to pronounce "ye," and then, *retaining the tongue in that position*, breathing (whispering) "he" through between tongue and hard palate. - TRANSLATOR'S NOTE.

come such difficult word-complexes is, to try to treat entire sentences like one word, to dwell on the vowels, and to glide lightly over the consonants, though without becoming indistinct. In extreme emotion the voice is sometimes intentionally modulated into a speaking tone, as when Fidelio exclaims, in the scene in the subterranean prison, "Töt' erst sein Weib!" (first kill his wife). The same likewise occurs in songs and ballads, or in any sharply and passionately declaimed passages.

SOME REMARKS ON MUSICAL STYLE

No one has as yet asserted his ability to teach the correct interpretation of music, although attempts have been made, especially of late years, to deduce rules of universal application from interpretations inspired by musical feeling and refined taste. As a noteworthy essay on this subject we would recommend Lussy's "Kunst des musikalischen Vortrags" (Art of Musical Interpretation), published by Leuckart, Leipzig—[**]a work which stimulates independent thinking about music which one hears. Innate talent, however, must be seconded by another gift—artistic taste, which is most clearly exhibited in the dynamics (tone-power) and correct tempo (instinct for time). Compositions of olden times are often played too fast; even as early as 1752 Quantz, in his "Essay on Playing the German Flute," makes the same observation. Especially in works by the old masters, with rare indications of the tempo, one should guard against a too-hurried *allegro*. Everything written about the embellishments of those days, has failed to settle the questions involved. Artistic taste is a greater help than interesting historical discussions. Many an old vocal grace, like certain forms of the trill, and the rapid repetition of one tone (compare Caccini, 1601), has become totally obsolete.

Correct musical accentuation depends, firstly, on the rhythmic phrasing, and secondly, on tone-accent and word-accent. Here the general theory of music steps in; the theory of the strong and weak beat, of consonance and dissonance, and of metrics. For a good style the art of correct phrasing is of the highest importance. Phrasing is simply musical punctuation, which frequently coincides with that of the words. The shading, or musical *nuances,* of a phrase will depend on tempo and general character of the composition. Although sentences should never be torn asunder by thoughtless breathing, there are times, nevertheless, when one is obliged to take breath before a new word. It is never permissible to separate the conjunction "and" from a following sentence which it joins to what precedes; breath must be taken beforehand.

In the Recitative (from *recitare,* to narrate), singing most nearly approaches ordinary speech. The chief requirement for this vocal style is, that the singer's imagination should be fired by the given situation. One of its forms, the so called *recitativo secco,* with a rather sketchy chord-accompaniment, was formerly employed to hasten the course of the dramatic action, and as a means of joining the principal numbers of the opera, or to put the epic (narrative) element in musical shape, more especially for narrating previous occurrences. It represents the light and easy conversational tone of everyday life. What an evolution, that of this simple musical form into the recitatives of a Verdi, and yet more into the recitative-style of Richard Wagner, in which tone-accent and word-accent coincide and blend in a manner unknown before! In the Wagner drama the vocal part is wrought into a symphonic tissue of tone, and only a singer with a perfectly trained voice can satisfy the demands of the musical declamation. Richard Wagner, himself, writes on vocal technics as follows: "It is certain that in no other study is such assiduous individual attention required, as in singing-lessons, It demands ever-vigilant supervision of the least details, and unwearying patience in most arduous practice, to acquire a really faultless development of the human voice, particularly in Germany under the influence of the German language. Whereas, in learning all in-

[**] The latest Paris edition (1904) is entitled "Traite de l'expression musicale."

struments the laws of their technics rest on a firm foundation, and may be taught the student, in accordance with fixed rules, by any thoroughly trained executant on a given instrument, the technics of vocal art are to this day an unsolved problem. Simply our observation of the fact, that the theory of singing has not been taught with genuine success in a single German Conservatory, is sufficient evidence of this difficulty."[14]

After finishing the most important vocal exercises, the student may begin the study of light Arias; for example:

For:	
Coloratura Soprano:	*La Sonnambula, Le Nozze di Figaro*
Dramatic Soprano:	*Otello* (Rossini), *Semiramide*
Mezzo-Soprano:	*La Favorita*
High Alto:	*Don Sebastiano* (Donizetti)
Low Alto:	*L'Italiana in Algeri*
Light Tenor:	*I Puritani* (Bellini)
Lyric Tenor:	*Lucia di Lammermoor*
Dramatic Tenor:	*Poliuto* (Donizetti), *Il Profeta*
Baritone:	*Maria di Rohan* (Donizetti) and *Il Barbiere di Siviglia*
High Bass:	*Semiramide* (Rossini)
Low Bass:	*Roberto il Diavolo*

Regarding them as studies, all arias are to be sung in Italian; the more difficult languages will be considered later. The first step is, to ascertain the prevailing mood to be interpreted, according to which the tempo and style can then be determined. The singer must clearly understand what the poem expresses, before undertaking serious study of the melody. What poet and composer felt while creating the composition, must be felt (or, better, *re-created*) by the singer. No interpretation can rightly be called perfect until the poetical and musical conception is exhaustively set forth; until the hearer, carried away by the artistic effect, forgets the artist in rapt contemplation of the art-work. —Breathing and phrasing must be settled, and all expression-marks carefully noted.

The Arioso and the Song make still higher demands on the artistic capacity. The modern German *Lied,* in particular, presupposes great technical skill and powers of interpretation to render it effective, not merely by potent characterization and fervor of style, but also from a purely musical viewpoint.[15] Powerful declamation cannot make up, in the long run, for defective tone production and ill-traced melodic lines. Were it otherwise, how sad for pure vocal art, which should find in the concert-hall, divorced from the actualities of the dramatic stage, a field for fresh triumphs!

Now, how should a Song ("Lied") be studied? Read through the poem carefully, and make mental note of its content. Then play the melody through slowly. Specially difficult intervals must be strongly impressed on the ear. It is a good plan to pass over gradually from the speaking-tone to the singing-tone. During this time the Song emerges in nebulous contours before the student's fancy. When the expression-marks are observed, its form grows clearer and clearer until, the accompaniment being added, it gains its true *coloris* and a well-defined shape. By dint of singing dubious passages over and over, with a decided inter-

---

[14] "Collected Writings," vol. viii, p. 199.

[15] We warn students against too much *Lied-singing* at first, the range being too limited and the numerous tone-repetitions calculated to tire the voice; coloratura sopranos, in particular, should take this warning to heart.

val between the repetitions, distinctness and confidence are obtained. And, finally, what we have learned has to be memorized. The singer is not invariably obliged to follow the composer's intimations exactly; take, for example, the passage in "Die beiden Grenadiere " by Schumann, "So will ich liegen und horchen still, wie eine Schildwach' im Grabe," for which *forte* is directed. But such cases are exceptional; as a rule the author's written instructions should be held by the pupil as most precious suggestions.

A WORD ON THE STUDY OF ROLES

The versatility demanded of our modern stage-singers excludes, to a certain extent, the possibility of their attaining real eminence in any one direction. What an amount of diligence and energy is required merely for mastering the repertory of a court theatre! Formerly it was different; the singer sang few roles, and those only for which he was adapted. Nowadays it may happen, that to-day a coloratura soprano has to sing Rosine, tomorrow Mignon, and the day after one of the Valkyries. This is not simply frivolous, but a sin against the spirit of art. Liberally endowed theatres should strictly define the various character-specialties, and spare the voices. There is no lack of vocal talent; but the conditions of modern art are unfavorable to orderly development. The singer does not study long enough, begins his stage-career unripe, and very seldom indeed grows up into the "great" roles. And besides, there is the fairly overwhelming crop of mediocrity, forced in music-schools of every degree, beleaguering the Director's door! Many a highly promising talent falls a victim to such competition, and prefers a private life to this hurry and worry.—But to return to our subject: How should one study an operatic role? Whoever would be an opera-singer, should early gain familiarity with the stage. After finishing, or even during, his vocal course, he must learn the elements of the mimic art, and take lessons in acting. While studying a role, the dramatic connection is important for correctly grasping its meaning. First of all, the climax of the action ought to be critically examined, for all secondary situations follow as a matter of course. Much practice tires the voice; it is therefore better merely to mark the tones lightly. In former times the singers were less lavish of their vocal material, than now; the less important passages were slighted, so that at critical moments they might be in full possession of their voices. Indeed, this style more nearly approaches nature; for no one, in everyday life, always speaks pathetically with a raised voice, however, singing *mezza voce* fatigues beginners in practising. It is more important to learn with the head, without using the voice. It is a great advantage to know how to study, that is, without tiring oneself. Whistling the melody makes the throat dry. It is not a good plan to hum the part an octave lower, or to transpose it for the sake of facility. Some modern conductors tire the singers out by keeping time too strictly. It is precisely in free delivery, in *"tempo rubato,"* that a great artist makes his effect, and more particularly in Italian music. Although the Pasta sang Norma according to Bellini's intentions, it was the Malibran who first made the well-known terzetto " Oh! di qual sei tu vittima" grandly effective, and this by following her own ideas quite regardless of the composer's. Frequent practice is of more use than long, wearisome rehearsals. The singer should become absorbed in the character of his role, and practice before a mirror: Keep the head cool, the heart warm! Through over-devotion to the comparatively mechanical" business" of the hands, the expression of the eyes, "the mirror of the soul," is often neglected. Distinct enunciation, pointed declamation, and a striking impersonation of the character enacted, are the chief requisites for the modern music-drama. Not merely seething blood and vulgar ranting, but, above all things, deep feeling![16] At this point, when the artist's entire individuality is taxed, there is no time left to repair defects of vocal technique; the singer must now learn to set forth, in the focus of the dramatic movement on the stage, what he has already acquired. A beautiful voice without emotional power is like a lovely woman without wit.

[16] Particularly for singing in Italian, "aspiration" is held to be a valuable technical device for increasing the intensity of emotional expression.

CARE OF THE VOICE. HYGIENE

If you would keep your voice fresh and vigorous, do not ask more of it than it can bear! A natural method strengthens the body and the vocal organ; the singer himself must now be careful to avoid everything which might affect his voice injuriously. A strong, thoroughly trained organ will by no means, as many erroneously think, be ruined by Wagner's music; the fatal mistake is rather, that unripe artists undertake the most difficult tasks before possessing the necessary ability. And even a singer with but a small voice, and obliged to limit himself to a narrow range, ought to make an intelligent selection from among these few roles. Too much song-singing, as we said before, is harmful. Besides, special hygienic directions should be followed. We would refer to the before-mentioned work by Professor Dr. Mandl (German title: "Gesundheitslehre der Stimme"), which gives most excellent advice, even for minor indispositions. Space forbids our entering into all details. We warn the singer against unnecessarily loud speaking, especially in the more important roles. One ought not to sing soon after eating; and it is injurious to eat much butter or fatty food in general. Practising with moderation, and with frequent interruptions, we have already advised. For the rest, one should lead a well-regulated life, and avoid whatever might affect the system injuriously. For the same reason, one should stop singing entirely during indisposition, and allow the vocal organ to rest. Avoid, above all, sudden changes of temperature, which may easily give rise to catarrh, whose unpleasant effects should not be underestimated by a vocal artist, of all persons. "Coddling," on the other hand, opens every avenue to disease; one should rather seek refuge in hardening the system. Breathing through the nose in the open air, and an avoidance of overheating sports and pleasures, are self-evidently wise precautions.

CONCLUSION

It has been our endeavor to set before the vocal student the fundamental principles of the technics of the *Bel Canto* in a concise form. In closing, a few general observations are to be made. What is the best age to begin study, and how long ought one to take lessons? Neither question can be answered off-hand, as all sorts of subordinate points also require consideration. A young man should begin when his voice is fully developed, after reaching, say, the age of twenty. As for the female voice, there is no reason (except a possible consideration of physical development) why training should not begin as early as possible, let us say in the seventeenth year. It was formerly the custom to study at least four or five years, even in Italy, the land of songful speech; nowadays, the shortest course is usually thought the best, with consequences everywhere in evidence. Perfect development alone should be the ideal. Then away with all high-flown schemes and foolish illusions, bringing bitter disappointment in their train! A good education—thorough mental training—will aid the artist everywhere in his future career, and prove of the greatest advantage. And all anemics, and persons with weak lungs or heart, should practise vocal gymnastics, at least, for from four to six months under the supervision of an instructor: for the exercises in deep breathing required by art vocalism not only expand the chest and strengthen the pectoral muscles and lung-tissue, but also promote in particular the general circulation of the blood, the heart-action, and the change of matter. (These last remarks are addressed especially to young women of weakly physique.) While speaking of vocal delivery, we emphasized the value of a knowledge of the general theory of music, including the intervals. Ability to play the piano is not absolutely essential, but is a great advantage to the singer, who will then not always be dependent upon the accompanist. But it would overtax his physical strength to add any considerable piano-practice to his strenuous vocal studies; either one study or the other! The human voice is the most precious of musical instruments, and more delicate than any other. Only a singer who can sing well is able to endow it with sustained force and expressiveness. It is a matter of but a short series of successive tones—yet what a difference in effect between the finished artist and a bungler! The singer who is once in possession of a perfectly trained voice, will preserve this inestimable treasure till an advanced age. How rich a reward for a few years of sensible and diligent study, reinforced by an orderly mode of life! So away with all artificialities and reckless theorizing; let us return to the simple, natural method!

NOTES

1. Stephen F. Austin, "A Little 'Vocal Wisdom'," *Journal of Singing* 71, no. 1 (September/October 2014): 89-93.
2. Giovanni Battista Lamperti, *The Technics of Bel Canto* (New York: G. Schirmer, 1905).

54. Read the Footnotes! Garcia on the Timbres

Originally published in the *Journal of Singing*, volume 72, no. 3, 2016

One of the many ways that Garcia helped us in our thinking about the voice was to differentiate timbre from the vowel. He allowed that there were two timbres: clear and somber, or bright and dark. The vowel sounds were separate from the timbres, the vowels being formed in the oral cavity with the tongue as the primary influence, and the timbres formed in the pharynx, primarily under the influence of the position of the larynx. Vowels can have a bright or dark character separate from the timbre. If the larynx was low it resulted in the somber timbre. A high larynx resulted in the clear timbre. This was the basis of a broad range of colors of the voice with which to express the emotion and thoughts of the character being portrayed.

In his second volume of the *Complete Treatise on the Art of Singing,*[1] Garcia provided many examples of coloring the voice to communicate the meaning of the text. Here is a section called "The Timbres" from Chapter 4 of Volume 2, entitled "Expression." There are extensive footnotes in the text that contain very interesting insight into his understanding of the influence of physiology upon tone quality. The figures are scanned from my ancient edition (undated), published by Schott's and Sons in Mayence (Mainz), Germany in parallel French and German.

THE TIMBRES (METALLI DELLA VOCE).

A few tries suffice to ascertain that each emotion, however slight the shade of it may be, will appropriately affect the vocal organ by modifying the capacity, the conformation, the rigidity, in short, all the physical conditions of it. The organ is therefore a mould which is constantly transformed under the action of the various emotions, and imparts their imprint to the sounds which it emits. Thanks to its admirable flexibility, this organ also aids, up to a certain point, in the description of exterior objects, as one can observe even in simple conversation. If it concerns, for example, representing a hollow, long [*étendu*] or thin object, the voice produces, by a mimicking movement, hollow, long or thin, etc., sounds.

The timbres are such an essential part of the discourse, they are so truly the condition of a sincere feeling, that one could not be negligent in the choice of it without falling infallibly into error. There are those which reveal the intimate feeling which the words do not always express sufficiently, and which they sometimes even tend to contradict. The pieces which portray indecision, troubled thought, irony, poorly restrained grief, require only the mixture and instability of the timbres; also it is necessary to express each of these feelings by the kind of disorder which is appropriate to it; wherever the idea is precise, the timbre maintains its unity.

We have said above (see Part One, chapter III); that the somber timbre (*metallo oscuro*, or *coperto*) was produced when the tube was deep and bent at a right angle by the lowering of the larynx; while on the contrary, the clear timbre (*metallo chiaro*, or *aperto*) is obtained when the buccal tube is slightly curved, the larynx is presented at the isthmus of the throat. At the point at which we have arrived, these notions do not suffice at all. It is necessary to know that the lips of the glottis can vibrate equally, either when the posterior extremities are put into contact (by the bringing together of the internal processes of the arytenoids), or when these extremities remain separated. In the first case, the sounds are emitted with all the brilliance possible; in the second, the voice takes a dull character.[1]

This brilliance or this dull color of the tones can indistinctly modify the clear timbre and the sombre timbre, and offer the student a throng of resources which permit him to appropriately vary the expression of the voice.[2]

The examples which follow will serve to illustrate the importance of this observation. The curse of Edgardo:

Maledetto sia l'istante
(Donizetti: *Lucia,* Finale.)

requires not only the clear timbre, but also all the brilliance of the voice.

On the contrary, the words:

Io credeva che alcuno
(Rossini: *Otello,* Recitative.)

should, because of the mental exhaustion which is overwhelming Desdemona, be pronounced with a clear, but smothered and colorless voice.

The arrogant challenge of Otello:

Or or vedrai qual chiudo
(Rossini: *Otello,* Duet.)

can be rendered only in a round and bursting voice; while the terror which takes possession of Assur at the sight of the shadow of Ninus:

Deh! ti ferma, ti placa, perdona
(Rossini: *Semiramide,* Aria.)

requires, in order to be truthful, the use of the sombre timbre and the muffled voice. If we should try to change in these examples the characters of the voice, the clear, the sombre, the brilliant and the dull, the effect of it would be detestable. This use made of the mistaken interpretation explains why the sounds which please in certain movements, displease elsewhere; why the unvarying singer recites only certain passages well. The clear and brilliant timbre, used out of its place, seems shrill; the clear and dull timbre, inane; the sombre and brilliant timbre seems grumbling; the sombre and dull timbre produces the effect of hoarseness.

The choice of the timbre will never depend on the literal meaning of the words, but on the movements of the soul which dictates them. The tender and languorous feelings, or even also the energetic, but concentrated feelings, do not go beyond the series of somber timbres. For example: in prayer, timidity, pity, the voice should be moving and slightly covered. Sometimes the noise of the breath is mixed with it in the feeling of tenderness. Examples: [Example 1]

Indignation, cursing, threatening and severe commands round the voice and make it abrupt, haughty. Examples: [Example 2]

Warlike or religious exhaltation round the voice while making it clear and brilliant. Examples: [Example 3]

Restrained threat, profound grief and repressed [*concentré*] despair take a hollow [*caverneux*] timbre. Examples: [Example 4]

Here the accents of grief are shaded, sometimes by a tint of melancholy, sometimes by bursts of sorrow, sometimes by a dark despair. Terror and mystery muffle the tones, and make them sombre and raucous. Examples: [Example 5]

In the depression which follows a strong disturbance, the voice is emitted dully, because the breath cannot be held back, and is mixed into the tones. Examples: [Example 6]
This dull character of the voice is the opposite of the brilliant, metallic timbre, which corresponds to vigorous feelings.

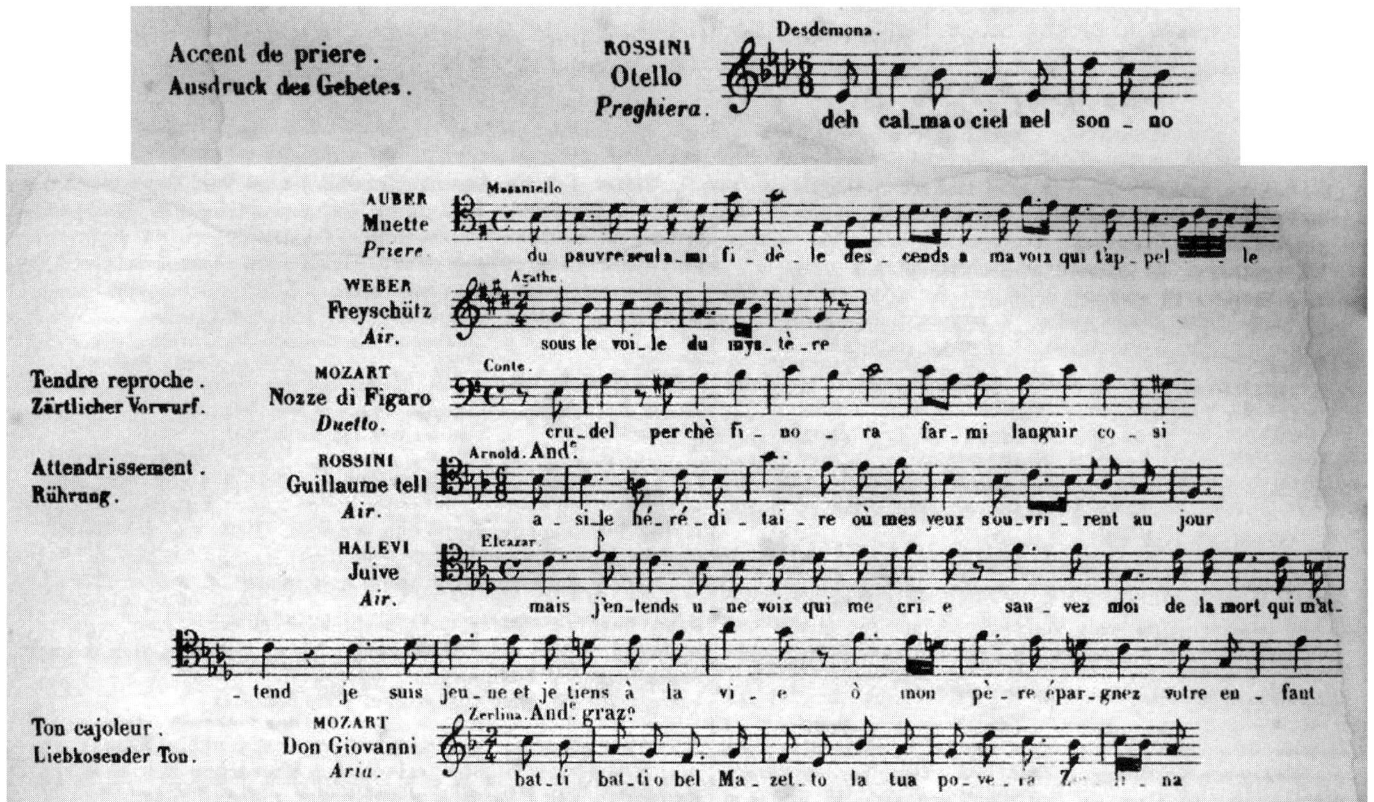

Example 1.

Example 2.

Example 3.

Example 4.

Example 5.

Example 6.

This first series of timbres forms a contrast with that which cheerful feelings produce, or also the frightful feelings, but which are given up without coercion.

The gentle and affectionate character which the vocal organ takes to express love partakes more of the clear timbre than of the somber timbre. Examples: [Example 7]

In joy, the timbre becomes vivid, brilliant and supple [*délié*]. Examples: [Example 8]

In laughter, the voice is shrill and yelping, interrupted, convulsive. Teasing makes the organ metallic, shrill. Example: [Example 9]

Threat, grief and despair which burst adopt the open and rending timbre. One sees some remarkable examples of it in the passages which follow: [Example 10]

The chest tones above f^1 are intolerable when one uses them in restrained songs; but here, for the very reason of their shrill effect, they adapt themselves to the accents of despair and rage. One could say much about it in the passage: [Example 11]

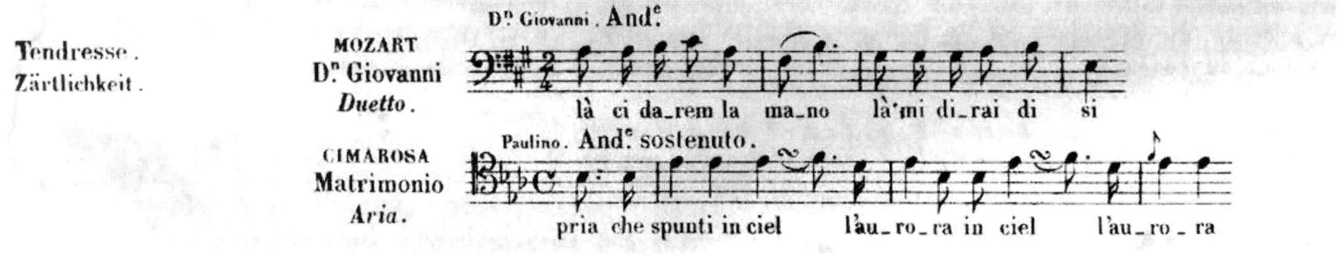

Example 7.

Example 8.

Example 9.

From the observations which precede there follow, it seems to us, several important consequences:

1. The tones lacking brilliance, used in a *just* measure and in a suitable timbre, should serve to express the feelings which disturb the soul and bring about the collapse of the vocal organs. These feelings are tenderness, timidity, fear, embarrassment, terror, etc. On the contrary, the sounds which have all their brilliance serve to express the feelings which excite the energy of the organs, vivid joy, anger, rage, arrogance, etc.
2. The two series of opposed timbres follow a course parallel to that of the emotions. The timbres set out from an intermediary point, where the expression of gentle feelings is placed, then they separate in opposite directions. The timbres arrive at their last exaggeration when the emotions themselves have attained their final limit; the lively emotions or the frightful ones which burst with violence take the open timbres. The serious feelings, openly voiced [*élevés*] or repressed [*concentrés*], take the covered timbres.[3]

Example 10.

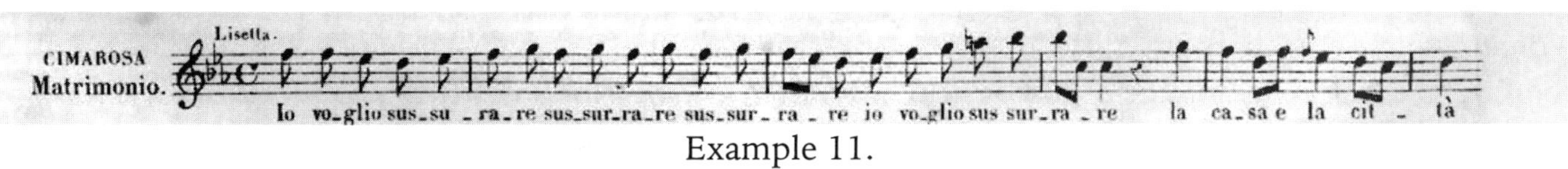

Example 11.

These first two series of facts, produced by the alteration of the breathing and by the use of the different timbres, form an inarticulate language, composed of tears, interjections, cries, sighs, etc., which one could properly name the language of the soul. These means can affect still more powerfully than the word, and take birth principally in the lungs and the pharynx. The exact knowledge of this last part of the vocal instrument in its relation to these kinds of products should be familiar to every dramatic singer, and will become the principal source of his success.[4]

FOOTNOTES

1. This important idea merits some developments. When one very vigorously pinches the arytenoids together, the glottis is represented only by a narrow or elliptical slit, through which the air driven out by the lungs must escape. Here each molecule of air is subjected to the laws of vibrations, and the voice takes on a very pronounced brilliance. If, on the contrary, the arytenoids are separated, the glottis assumes the shape of an isoceles triangle, the little side of which is formed between the arytenoids. One can then produce only extremely dull notes, and, in spite of the weakness of the resulting sounds, the air escapes in such abundance that the lungs are exhausted in a few moments. This enormous expenditure of air, which coincides with the production of veiled tones, indicates, according to us, that the glottis assumes the triangular form. One understands in fact that the air does not encounter any resistance toward the base of the triangle, and that it passes freely through the glottis almost without receiving any vibrations from it. It is only at the summit of the angle which parts from the thyroid cartilage that the condensations and rarefactions of the air are formed in a complete manner. Likewise, but in the opposite way, the brilliance of the sounds and the fourfold or fivefold duration of the breath indicate that the organ is offering no more than a linear or elliptical slit. Let us add that when we pinch the glottis strongly, we synergistically bring about a certain contraction, a kind of condensation of the tissues of the pharynx, most favorable states for the vitality [*nerf*] and the brilliance of the voice. On the contrary, the separation of the arytenoids brings about the softness of these same tissues, as a result of which, the sonorous waves, absorbed or poorly reflected, lose nearly all their brilliance. One sees, according to what precedes, that the timbre depends not only upon the modifications which the tube imparts to the sonorous waves, but also upon the place where these vibrations are born; that is to say that the voice receives its first character in the glottis, then from the numerous modifications of the pharyngeal and buccal cavities. One can summarize what precedes in this principle: *that each modification in the mode of production of the vibrations develops a different timbre, and each modification which the tube through which it passes undergoes modifies the original timbre.*

2. We are recalling here a rule stated above (see pages 7–8), and which is this: the modifications of timbre which the tones undergo depend upon the position which they occupy in the range. The range included between the notes e^{b1} c^2 in the chest with tenors will correspond to the open timbre of the lower tones, not with absolutely the same timbre, but with a clearer shade of the same timbre. [C] This observation is also applied to the head voice compared to the falsetto voice in women. The chest register should likewise receive on the notes e^{b1} to $f^{\#1}$ a more rounded shade than the lower notes.

3. The character of these timbres is necessarily related to the age and to the nature of the organ of each individual; let us even say that in young singers extreme freshness should be the dominant quality: it indicates an organ which is in all its virginity. When a voice has been experienced by the emotions, age and work, it is modified; the freshness and the brilliance of the timbre make way for solidity and volume. Some young people make the error of wanting to imitate the organs of artists matured by the stage and by years, and by means of obstinacy, they succeed in aging their voices before their time. Sometimes, by a contrary error, some singers, already aged, borrow, in order to rejuvenate themselves, a childish timbre. The voice, like everything else, should follow the progress of time.

4. We will terminate this chapter on the timbres by some important observations on the kind of voice incorrectly named the mixed voice, or *mezzo petto;* their rather technical nature advises us to put them into the form of a footnote.

In France, the highest part of the chest voice, including from f^1 to c^2, is given the name of mixed voice [*voix mixte*], whether the voice presents in this range the characters of the sombre timbre, or, on the contrary, the tones are excessively clear and sharp [*deliées*]. In Italy this same range is called, in the first case, *voce di petto,* and in the second, *voce di mezzo petto.* Whatever the character of these tones may be, they belong to the chest register, but with a modification of volume with which we are going to concern ourselves. The designations of *voix mixte* and *mezzo petto* are equally improper, for they would make us suppose that these clear and high pitched tones are produced by the two mechanisms of the chest and falsetto registers at the same time. Now, physiologically, the simultaneous conjunction of two different mechanisms serving to produce the same note, or two notes in unison, is an unacceptable idea. In fact, the production of any one sound places the organ into entirely different and irreconcilable conditions, according as it is formed by the mechanism of the chest voice or that of the falsetto. The conformity of position could be encountered only in the simultaneous emission of two notes of different pitch. But then one would have to ask oneself if it is possible for the larynx to simultaneously produce two distinct tones. This possibility would be admissible by supposing a larynx shaped in such a manner that the different registers remain independent of each other in their mechanism. The history of music furnishes several examples of this phenomenon (see Part One). The thin character of the high tones of the so-called [*prétendue*] mixed voice results only, according to us, *from the vibrations of the vocal cords,* without the cooperation of the pharynx to reinforce them. One knows in fact that the intensity of a tone depends in general upon the number of partials which vibrate concurrently to form it, and upon the amplitude [*étendue*] of the vibrations which these partials execute; as a consequence, by reducing the number of vibrating partials, one decreases the sound. Moreover, it is demonstrated that the glottis, by the gradual tension of its lips and the successive reduction of its dimensions, produces the entire series of chest tones; but the vibrations generated in the glottis acquire all their power only provided that they are extended into the ventricles, then into the pharynx. According to that, one understands that if it were possible to limit the vibrations to the glottis by reducing the ventricles and the pharynx to a purely passive role, one would have the thinnest tones possible. It is in fact this result that a capable singer knows how to obtain, when on one side he completely relaxes all the muscles of the pharynx, and on the other he narrows more and more the column of air. In these circumstances, the glottis, endowed with a complete liberty, can reach the final limits of its action. One is astonished to see tenors give, without any apparent effort, the notes a^1, b^1, c^2, $c^{\#2}$, d^2. For women, and especially for children, in whom the glottis is very narrow at the same time as the arytenoideous muscles are very delicate, one does not know how high that series of tones might rise: we presume, *a priori,* that it would go at least to the g^2. We always advise that it is well if these notes are replaced in practice by the falsetto tones, preferable in all respects. If, while the glottis alone vibrates and all other parts of the instrument are relaxed, one moderately increases the pressure of the air, one obtains an increase of brilliance and intensity, but never an increase of volume. One can conceive the immense advantage which the male voice can draw from these observations, completely new in theory and too rarely applied instinctively by same artists. They serve to clarify the relatively high notes ordinarily so thick in basses, baritones, and tenors. They indicate to these latter the mechanism to practice [*suivre*] to increase the range of the chest register; they permit the *piano* and *mezza voce* use of this register in the high tones and thus the dispensation of the excessive use of the falsetto tones; finally, they facilitate the union of the registers, etc.

The list of facts which we have just enumerated is completely modified when the contraction of the pharyngeal muscles is added to that of the glottis.

The instrument then forms a single whole which the excessively held column can no longer make vibrate, but which was sufficient to set the glottis alone into motion. A vigorous thrust here becomes indispensable to put the entire mass into action. The voice in this case has all its amplitude and power, but can no longer reach the extraordinary notes which concern us. The b^{b1}, b^{1}, and the c^{2} require energetic efforts which in the preceding hypothesis would not be appropriate. The glottis is pinched as much as the tone which one wants to produce requires, but the column of air, too powerful for its muscular strength, obliges it to enlarge and to lower the pitch. I am fully aware of it, a very strong thrust raises the pitch without the need of new contractions; but this procedure does not entirely remedy the weakness of the vocal cords. The reduction of size is already a fact in the clear timbre, where no infrahyoideous muscles came into action to counteract the action of the arytenoideous muscles; but it is especially striking, if we produce the sounds in the sombre timbre [*voix sombrée, voix mixte*]; the lips of the glottis must then, by their own contractive force, resist not only the column of air, but also the opposed and considerable force of the depressor muscles, which tend to open the thyroid cartilage and to separate these same lips. Some extraordinary efforts can momentarily overcome this resistance; but exhaustion and paralysis of the organ are the inevitable and unfortunately too frequent result of the use of this procedure.

NOTE

1. Manuel Garcia, *Complete Treatise on the Art of Singing, Part II,* translated and edited by Donald Paschke (New York: Da Capo Press, 1984), 151–163. Originally published as *Nouveau Traité Sommaire sur l'Art du Chant* (Genéve: Minkoff Éditeur, 1847).

55. Vibrato by the Seashore

Originally published in the *Journal of Singing*, volume 72, no. 4, 2016

I remember taking the Seashore Musical Aptitude Test as a freshman entering college. It was a listening task that was supposed to be predictive of success as a music major. I have no idea what my result was, but I finished the degree!

My next encounter with Dr. Carl E. Seashore happened many years later when I attended The University of Iowa to study Voice Science at the Department of Speech Pathology and Audiology. I remember taking a tour of Seashore Hall, which was the home of the Psychology Department that Dr. Seashore chaired for many years. He was an experimental psychologist during the dawn of the field. One of his many contributions was the development of a program to address speech and communication disorders. Out of this effort came the field of speech pathology and the foundation of the Department of Speech Pathology and Audiology at the university.

Seashore was responsible for the development of many interesting new tools and machines that were used to try to define in physical terms what humans perceived of the world that we live in and the effect those perceptions have upon our lives. Among his many interests were the arts, especially music.

Dr. Seashore along with several graduate students conducted experiments on the vibrato. Using new instruments that he developed in his laboratory, he could describe the characteristics of the vibrato in the human voice and in musical instruments. He provided us the definition of vibrato that we still understand today: a periodic fluctuation of pitch, amplitude, and timbre.

Then, as now, the vibrato was a topic of great interest to musicians, and he took to the task of defining, measuring, and understanding it. He did so because—as also now—there was a great deal of disagreement concerning the nature of the vibrato and whether it was a good thing or an abomination to good taste in music.

I offer here the introduction to *The Vibrato,* Volume 1 of a series titled *Studies in the Psychology of Music,* published in 1932.[1] This was the first volume of a number of reports that came out of Dr. Seashore's laboratory as a part of this series. Within this book are most of the initial studies on vibrato. It is a very interesting read—many of the articles have been published elsewhere.

Dr. Seashore's studies helped me understand some confusing statements by respected pedagogues from the past concerning the vibrato and its use in our profession. In *Hints on Singing,* we find Garcia answering his own question in his Socratic approach to the book.

> Q. How do you define steadiness of sound?
>
> A. A firm and continuous flow of sound, free from every sort of tremor or quavering. This definition holds good with words or without.[2]

Is it really possible that Garcia was against the use of vibrato? It is not likely. Seashore addressed this conundrum by saying that there are good and bad vibratos even in successful artists and that the bad ones create a false rejection of the good.

He and his students made the first measurements of vibrato in many of the professional singers of the day— often using recordings. Figure 1 is a sample graph from *Psychology of the Vibrato in the Voice and Instrument,* Volume 3 of the series.[3] Here we see a graph of the voice of Mr. Harold Stark, who is still remembered by many of us as a teacher of voice at the University of Iowa and who taught in San Antonio for many years after his retirement. In the graph we see a tracing of the pitch along with the constant presence of the vibrato while Mr. Stark sang the Bach-Gounod "Ave Maria." It is clear that every note included a regular variation in pitch of about 6 Hz around the center of the pitch being sung. There are many such examples in the collection of six volumes that make up the series. The details of the graph are described in the introduction.

The vibrato is still a topic that is likely to stimulate lively debate today: choral vs. solo singing, CCM styles vs. *bel canto* styles, and of course questions of how it was used in early music. Like everything else in voice, the arguments are never new—just the participants!

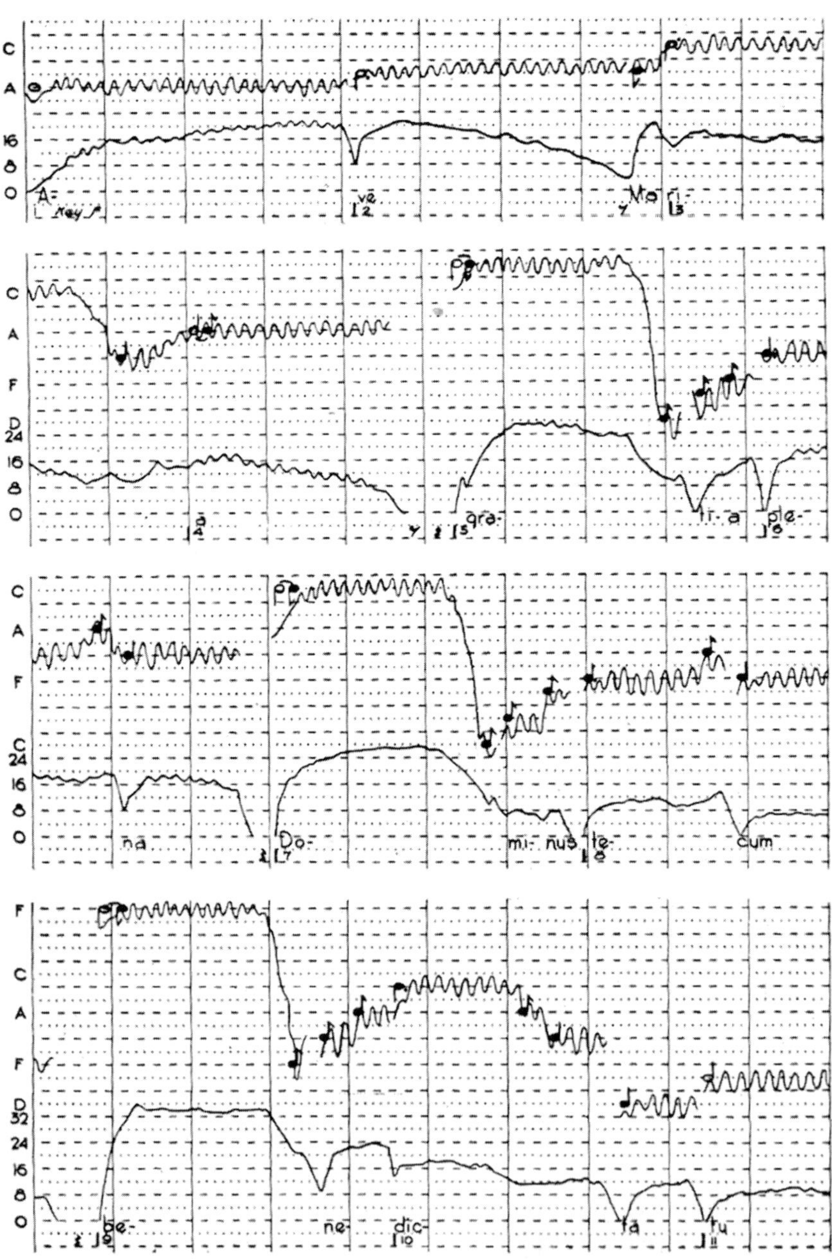

Figure 1. **The Bach-Gounod "Ave Maria" as sung by Herald Stark.**

INTRODUCTION
by
CARL E. SEASHORE

This volume is a digest up to date of the experimental studies made in the University of Iowa on the subject of the vibrato in music. A considerable amount of material appears in print here for the first time but earlier publications are reviewed and the findings are incorporated in a unified and comprehensive statement.

The subject is somewhat unique in the literature of psychology of music in that, although it is one of the central problems in music both in theory and in practice and is one of the most fascinating and profitable psychological approaches to the study of expression of emotion, the field had remained practically untouched by experiment until the problem was taken up in our laboratory. It is also a somewhat unique situation that for a decade or more we have been able to coordinate a continuous series of experiments within this field so as to cover it systematically, establishing adequate techniques for measurements, outlining a fundamental series of hypotheses, and progressively organizing data in a cumulative way.

One reason why this type of work has been held back until the present time is the fact that it really had to wait in large part for the opportunity of taking advantage of the marvelous recent developments in phonophotography and sound transmission associated with the development of electrical recording and transmission of sound. Developments in this field have come so fast that one of our special joys in the laboratory has been that of scrapping instruments; because we do not scrap fairly adequate instruments until we have better ones in sight. Within the last ten years, developments in phonophotography have gone by leaps and bounds to such an extent that at the present time we can record for scientific analysis not only the present musical performances, but what has been recorded on phonograph records and what is now recorded in sound movies on films, thus making it possible to compare musicians in all ranks and primitive music from all lands.

In the development of scientific instruments for work in this general field, we have had a threefold goal; namely, adequate precision, time-saving, and simultaneous records for tone analysis and tone recording. Precision and timesaving have been achieved in numerous ways and we are now equipped to record simultaneously the four characteristics of sound with synchronized cameras and, at the same time, make a durable phonograph record, all from the original rendition of music or speech in a single transmitter.

The vibrato is a part of the larger program pursued in this laboratory on the plan of recording adequately the musical performance. It has lent itself particularly well to the natural history method of collecting material, in this case actual performances, from every available source and classifying them in the manner the botanist classifies his plants.

The work has two aspects, the psychological and the musical. The psychological aspect presents in itself a somewhat radically new approach to the measurement of the expression of feeling in the creation or reproduction of a thing beautiful. This method of recording all forms of utterance through sound has a wide range of applicability in the study of behavior. Other psychologists must evaluate this approach; but it seems to the present writer that it is far more promising than any of the other techniques now in use in the measurement of the expression of emotion in that it provides for the adequate recording of expression in every detail under normal conditions of action. Therefore, while this volume is directed primarily to the musical constituency, it lays claim to recognition from the point of view of pure psychology.

For psychological technique, the studies on the vibrato have clarified our analysis of tonal hearing; have developed serviceable techniques for the measurement of the four factors, pitch, intensity, time, and timbre, in life situations applicable to all forms of behavior involving the production and hearing of sound; have thrown much light on the nature and extent of normal illusions in hearing; and have shown how the feeling of expressing a great variety of emotions such as fear, love, and anger, is largely subjective and does not correspond to objective facts, as when the same form of vibrato expresses both quiet and excited emotion. Indeed, the vibrato as a discrete phenomenon of expression has proved a most resourceful medium or instrument for control in the analysis of tonal performance and experience. Therefore, while there is in this volume a strict adherence to an aspect of applied psychology, much light is thrown on fundamental aspects of pure psychology.

Likewise in music, although this volume is restricted largely to the intensive treatment of one of the so-called ornaments in music, the vibrato, the acquisition and interpretation of this material makes large contribution to many other elements in musical expression, such as the fundamental issues in regard to intonation, rhythm, and tone quality, as well as the ornaments in each of these.

As to the vibrato itself, the volume deals in firm and bold strokes with musical history, theory, practice, pedagogy, and criticism in that it clears up the historical controversies as to what the vibrato is and should be by laying down objective and verifiable definitions, analyses, and principles. It lays a scientific foundation for esthetic theory in regard to this element of beauty in music, makes available exact measures in current practice, develops esthetic norms, and furnishes the means of remedial and artistic training in the art of control of the vibrato. It takes the problem from the realm of the hazy, misleading lingo of cults, which have prevailed in this musical field, and simplifies, clarifies, and places the phenomenon under control.

Musical esthetics falls naturally into four divisions; the musical medium, the musical form, the musical message, and the musical response. The medium is the physical sound which has musical values, the form is the structure built with the medium in the musical art of the composer and the interpreter, the message is that which the composer or the performer, in turn, feels and intends to convey, and the response is the effect that the musical medium produces in the listener. The present volume approaches the problem of musical esthetics primarily from the point of view of the musical medium, first, because that is what music, as music, in reality is; and, second, because musical form, message, and response can be treated scientifically in the best interests of the art from the point of view of this approach.

A study of this objective nature reveals the gaps in our knowledge and, in this case, the historical fallacies in musical criticism, practice, and education; but the musician cannot be blamed for not having laid these foundations before. It is a technical task which falls within the realm of psychology and could be accomplished only by psychological technique. Psychology applied to music has an opportunity to lay foundations for musical theory and practice, and it is the duty and privilege of the psychologist to do so. The responsibility cannot be thrown upon the musician.

It is interesting to note that the real ground for the confusion which exists in the musical world and even among scientific and critical listeners lies in the fact that in the hearing of the vibrato, the normal ear is subject to a series of gross normal illusions. Among these is the astonishing under-estimation of the magnitude of the vibrato in hearing which lies in the fact that the oscillation of pitch is heard as if it were only 1/4 to 1/2 of its actual extent, and a similar underestimate occurs for intensity. Another normal illusion consists in the persistent confusion of oscillations in pitch and intensity in listening so that a musician, or even a generation of musicians, will assert that it is oscillation in pitch, that it is oscillation in intensity, or, more frequently, that it is neither. A third normal illusion which makes the vibrato in its present gross form tolerable is the phenomenon of sonance, which lies in the fact that successive periodicities, when of sufficient rate, tend to fuse into a unified tone somewhat in the same manner that the simultaneous overtones in a violin clang fuse and are heard together as one tone. A fourth normal illusion which is a condition for making the vibrato tolerable is the fact that even with a pitch oscillation of a semi-tone the intonation is heard as of a particular tone which can easily be identified with standard pitch, the musical effect heard being that of a changing tone quality rather than specific changes in pitch, intensity, and timbre. Were it not for these four and numerous similar normal illusions which function in all musical hearing, the vibrato as it now exists would be utterly intolerable. It is this fact, that the vibrato is not heard even by the best musician as it really is, which lies at the bottom of the confusion which has prevailed on this subject.

It will be of interest to note what the effect of the established facts about the nature, role, and control of the vibrato herein described shall have upon musical theory and practice. To know exactly wherein a vibrato consists, how it develops, what its variants are, in what ways it is used in the present artistic performance, what may constitute improvements in present practice, how these improvements may be brought about, should be of profound interest to the musician. We are not over sanguine about the outcome because the present line of reasoning, fact-finding, and insistence upon practical application is not in harmony with the prevailing line of thought and action in music. Professor Ortmann says that the comments he received on his book of experimental studies in piano playing were characterized by such deliverances as, "The soul of the piano transcends all investigation," and "The records may all be true, but I do not believe them," from those who manifested interest in the subject.

In our work we have met with the most cordial cooperation and sympathetic interest on the part of leading musicians, yet we are quite prepared for responses of the type reported by Professor Ortmann. The experimenter, however, does not lose heart from such reactions, does not count on a universal and immediate acceptance, but takes comfort in the feeling that, in so far as his findings are scientifically sound, their promulgation, extension, and adoption will come in time. His life job is to discover and organize facts, not to sell things.

The work has not been completed. A series of projects are now in progress and it is hoped may continue for some years, particularly on the physiological side, determining the biological significance of the neuromuscular principles which operate in the phenomenon of vibrato. Since we know now that it is one of the fundamental biological periodicities this should furnish a fruitful approach to a general study of the basic periodicities in animal life. Among the other immediate projects are: the establishment of an organic series of aesthetic principles which determine what constitutes a beautiful vibrato, the functional relation of the vibrato to other media of musical flexibility, further studies on the illusions in the hearing of the vibrato, a more intensive study of the role of timbre in the vibrato, and a general reconstruction of our theory of auditory perception.

Some of the articles in this volume are fragmentary. They should not be judged by their length or the completeness of the solution of the problem, but rather by the fact that each opens up an approach to a difficult situation by the invention of instruments and the development of appropriate methods.

In preparing this volume, each contributor has been encouraged to present his findings from his own point of view in the light of the information available at the time that he writes and with such differences from the point of view of the group as he feels that he can defend. For this reason, the different articles vary in style, nomenclature, interpretation, and the aim and scope of the presentation. This giving of individuality and placing of full responsibility upon each contributor is the editor's apology for apparent editorial neglect and for presenting a series of separate articles instead of a coherent treatise.

We realize fully that the present volume makes rather heavy reading for those who are not interested in technical details. To remedy this situation, a small popular volume intended to serve as a textbook for students in music and general readers is in preparation. To supplement this student's edition, there will be phonograph records which will contain scales, by which the pupil may determine for himself the most pleasing form of vibrato in typical situations, and scales for the measurement of attainment in the control of the vibrato. This material will be prepared on the theory that in the early stages of training the student should have clear and concise knowledge of the nature of the vibrato, ready means for studying its variance, and standards in terms of which he can measure progress. This involves the psychological theory that, in the acquisition of a skill, the student should be profoundly conscious of each element involved in turn, so that in the later exercise of the skill the habituation will take care of these details automatically, unhampered by an analytical point of view and free for the artistic mood.

This psychological principle of separating the attitude at the study stage from the inspirational artistic mood in performance or in listening should give comfort to the musical reader of this volume. It is the firm conviction of all the contributors that the scientific analysis is necessary to progress in the refinement of musical skills; but there is equally strong conviction on the part of all of us to the effect that the singer may still sing without consciousness of the elements of the musical medium, and the listener may, and should, listen to the music in the artistic, rather than in the scientific mood.

Thus, the vibrato may rightly continue to be regarded as a quality of tone analogous to timbre and the general listener in music need not concern himself about its components any more than he is concerned about the relative presence and dominance of overtones. Both function musically as fusions giving character to the tone.

After all, perhaps the greatest significance of this volume lies in the demonstration that "it can be done": music as an expression of the human mind can be analyzed objectively in the laboratory. Each element can be studied and measured in its true functional musical situation. All factors in music as a message from the performer to the listener are now within reach of both qualitative and quantitative scientific approach so that we may take up any problem involved in this message for examination and "put questions to nature." There are hundreds of problems in music analogous to the problem involved in this message for examination now open to study by the means and methods here introduced; we adopt the natural history method of collecting all the available data on the particular problem and proceed to classify and explain.

The ultimate value of the whole procedure, of course, lies in the fact that this organization of knowledge in the field of music is and will become more and more essential to the pursuit and appreciation of the art.

A word of introduction for each of the present authors may be in place. Dr. Milton Metfessel, now Professor and Head of the Department of Psychology at the University of Southern California, took his degree in the University of Iowa and continued his post-doctorate researches in the laboratory for three years as National Research Council fellow, during which period he made several contributions to the psychology of music and speech. Dr. Joseph Tiffin, at present Assistant Professor of Psychology and Speech in the University of Iowa, took his degree here and continued in post-doctorate work for one year as a National Research Council fellow. Dr. Arnold Wagner took his Master's degree at Columbia University and wrote his Doctor's dissertation at the University of Iowa on training in the vibrato. He is Professor of Music at the University of Southern California and is continuing his studies in the vibrato both in research and in a professional way. Forrest Linder, Ray Miller, Donald Rothschild, Harold Seashore, Melvin Hattwick, and Scott Reger are now advanced graduate students in the department. The contributions of Eleanor Easley and M. T. Hollinshead were contained in their master's theses.

In conclusion, I desire to express my profound appreciation of the spirit of cooperation and continuity which has been demonstrated by the participants in this project. The work has been greatly favored by the opportunities afforded through the National Research Council fellowships and a series of fellowships maintained through the generosity of Mr. George Eastman.

NOTES

1. Carl E. Seashore, *The Vibrato* (Iowa City: University of Iowa Press, 1932).
2. Manuel Garcia, *Hints on Singing* (London: Lowe and Brydone Limited, 1894).
3. Carl E. Seashore, *Psychology of the Vibrato in Voice and Instrument* (Iowa City: University of Iowa Press. 1936).

56. Sound an Alarm!

Originally published in the *Journal of Singing*, volume 72, no. 5, 2016

In the 19th century it was clearly understood that the larynx needed to remain in a comfortably low position when singing, especially as a singer ascends into the higher part of the range. This is the subject of the sixth lesson from Volume II of *Esthetics of the Art of Singing* by Enrico Delle Sedie, published in 1895, and presented here in its entirety.[1]

Delle Sedie (1822–1907) was a baritone who notably sang the first performance of Renato in Verdi's *Un ballo in maschera* in 1860. After his singing career he taught voice in Paris and turned his creative energy to teaching and writing. He published multiple volumes on the art of singing. *Vocal Art* (1891) was published in English in three volumes by G. Schirmer.[2] The firm also published *Esthetics of the Art of Singing in English* in four volumes.

It is unfortunate that his books are not easily available, because they are very interesting and practical. He was influenced by the work of Helmholtz and developed a theory of vocal tract acoustics that points to the much later work of Berton Coffin and others almost a century later. He also introduced a system to help young performers train the importance of emotion in their singing. He created a table of abbreviations that would be written in the score to reflect the emotional and psychological state of the performer at that particular moment. I am reminded of the emotion cards that are in use today to develop this same skill.

In the last sentence of this article he says: "Having noticed the defects which result from the ascending of the larynx with respect to the high sounds, it is useless to insist any longer on this subject." I wish that we were in a place where we no longer had to insist on this any longer! But in my experience it is alarming how many young singers study for years with never being taught this important principle. There is no single technical issue that inhibits the natural growth and professional potential in young singers more than an unstable laryngeal posture, both in men and women. It is indeed a rare occasion when I meet a prospective student who realizes that his or her larynx is either habitually high or rises with ascending pitch; truthfully, I cannot recall a single one in 25 years of teaching. So many vocal faults and limitations disappear when the larynx is taught to remain calm in the neck so the mechanism can do its work freely. Thus, I continue to "Sound an alarm!"

SIXTH LESSON

Movements of the Larynx and of The Soft Palate

By

Enrico Delle Sedie

After having examined the vocal sound (the vowel), with regards to its sympathetic resonance in the mouth, we shall study in which homogeneous conditions sound may be emitted with regard to the movements of the larynx.

This cartilaginous tube being the main organ of the lungs, constitutes the basis of the vocal apparatus, and has been defined by eminent physiologists; therefore I do not think it necessary here to speak of the synthetical studies of this powerful organ of phonation; but I will add that the larynx with relation to the singing voice has two motions which we must bear in mind in connection with the timbres of the vocal sound. The first, called general motion, consists in raising the larynx; the second is called particular motion, and its object is to modify the state of the vocal chords [*sic*] by the constriction of the muscles which give action to the glottis. This second movement we have already examined in detail, and also the comparison which Dr. Fournié has made between the vocal chords [*sic*] and the lips of the mouth. Now we will analyze the effects of the general movement with regard to the phonic conditions of the vocal sounds. In my *Vocal Art* Dr. Mandl defined this phenomenon as follows:

> The rising or the falling of the larynx does not exercise any influence on the height of the sound. These variable positions depend on the motions executed by the tongue. As soon as this is drawn back, the larynx is forcibly lowered, whilst when the tongue is brought forward it rises. Such a displacement of the tongue affects the timbre but not the height of the sound.

Experience proves that the lowering the larynx facilitates the emission of high sounds with regard to the timbre, and that in a contrary direction an identical result will be obtained for the grave sounds.

If in this case we examine the emission of the sound with a laryngoscope, an opinion opposed to mine may arise. To see the vocal chords [*sic*] with this ingenious and useful apparatus, we must jut out the tongue, so as to allow a small mirror to be placed at the veil of the palate in order to reflect the vocal chords [*sic*]. We have noticed that the tongue when jutted out causes the rising of the larynx; thus this motion will give to it an invariable raised position.

When the larynx is so raised we may emit high sounds, but thin and shrill. It is true, that we are disposed to raise the larynx when we want to emit high sounds, but if we would closely observe the timbre, we would recognize that they are thin, contracted and shrill.

To sing correctly, it is necessary to give to the voice a flexible, homogeneous and full tone.

Therefore the ascension of the larynx in high notes cannot be favourable for this emission of the vocal sound. I will not extend myself too much on a subject so often disputed, but will limit myself to expose the practical use of my theory.

We admitted that the tongue when jut out determines the rising of the larynx, and if you execute this movement while emitting a high sound, you will acknowledge what we have already explained; viz: that the sound produced by the larynx so situated, has a timbre sharp, contracted, and hard. During the continuation of the same sound, retract the tongue by regular gradations, and the lowering of the larynx being effected in identical conditions to those of the tongue will make you appreciate a progressive change in the timbre of the voice, which will be rendered soft, flexible and full.

The same experience renewed without preparation by degrees, will produce two distinct vowels: the first one contracted and thin, the second full and soft.

The application of this theory in an opposite direction, with relation to the grave sounds, will give identical results; the sound emitted when the larynx is lowered will produce a tarnished and veiled tone, while the same tone produced with the larynx raised, will be resonant, large and flexible.

According to this experience, we conclude that the singer must apply himself to descend the larynx for the emission of high sounds and to raise it for the emission of the grave sounds.

The raising and lowering of the larynx must be affected by conjoined gradations corresponding to the degrees of the scale. Example: [Figure 1].

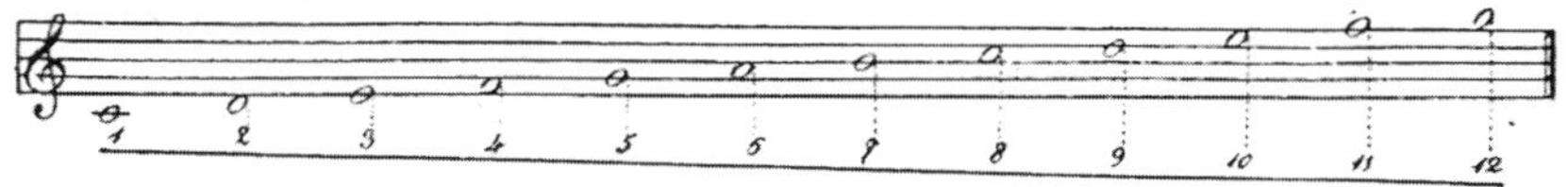

Figure 1.

The numbers placed under the notes serve to establish the gradations of the lowering of the larynx.

These motions of the larynx as shown by us cause analogous movements to the soft palate and both contribute strongly to an easy and flexible emission of the vocal sound.

The pharynx . . . constitutes the back part of the isthmus of the throat, and its front part is formed, below, by the root of the tongue, and above, by the veil of the palate and uvula. . . . On the two sides are the two pillars of the veil of the palate. All these parts are extremely movable, and under the influence of the muscular contraction, can either enlarge or contract the vocal tube; these motions act progressively according to the height of sound.

The soft palate plays a considerable part in these movements, and the sonorous column may pass through the nasal cavities or through the mouth, according to how it is lowered or raised.

When the soft palate is lowered, it approaches the root of the tongue and so narrows the sonorous tube; the tone resounds then equally in the nasal and oral cavities. If on the contrary the soft palate rises, the bucco-nasal orifice will be almost closed and the sound will escape from the mouth. This vocal tube does not contribute directly to the production of sound, but favours its formation by the dimensions it is susceptible of taking.

The following demonstrative table will serve as a practical study for the movements of the veil of the palate [Figure 2].

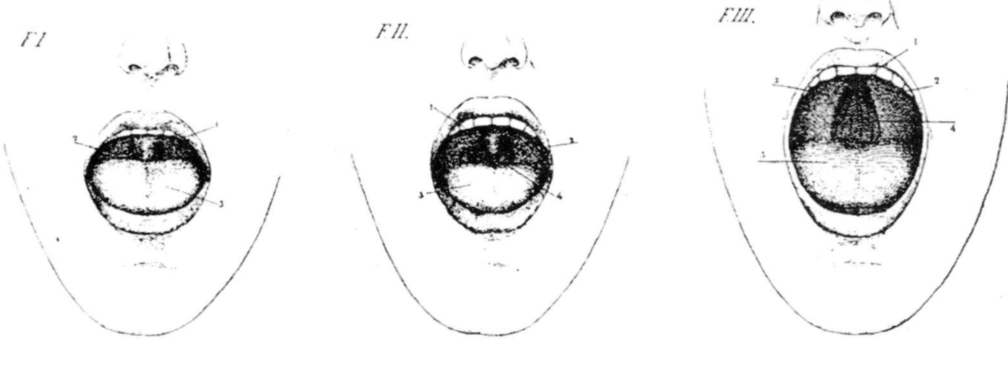

Figure 2.

In the examined table there are only the three main motions; on these depend all the corresponding gradations of the tones of the scale, and those of the movements of the larynx.

The fig. I. [*FI* of Figure 2] represents the grave sound. The soft palate lowered with the uvula (1) approaches the root of the tongue (3). The pillars of the soft palate (fig. III. 2,2) are lowered with the uvula and displaced from the middle part, so that the pharynx (fig. III. 4) is almost hidden.
This motion contracts the sonorous tube, and the tone resounds in the nasal cavities and in the pharyngobuccale-cavities; viz: in all the extension of the pharynx.

Between the position indicated in fig. I, and II, representing the type of the medium sound of the vocal scale, a series of ascending movements of the soft palate take place in direct relation to the height of the sound. The contraction of the isthmus of the throat being considerably less, the vocal sound finds its spontaneous resonance in the middle of the upper part of the pharynx as well as in the mouth.

The fig. III, presents the type of the high sound. Dr. Fournié says:

> The soft palate rises with the voice, and while the bucconasal orifice closes gradually it prevents the resounding of the voice more and more in the nasal cavities. In the last notes of the vocal scale the closing of this orifice is complete; and then we can see the pillars of the soft palate approaching each other on the middle line and forming a real wall before the wall of the pharynx.

The fig. III, presents almost identically the movements spoken of by Dr. Fournié.

By this configuration of the sonorous tube, the voice resounds in the upper part of the pharynx and in the mouth up to the fore sinus. These natural motions of the voice may be disturbed, delayed or neutralized by a too strong expiration of the air coming from the lungs; this exaggeration may give to the tongue an ascending motion.

The soft palate rises in a direction opposite to that of the larynx, following the same regular order of gradations; viz: it rises with the height of sound, whilst the larynx, for giving to the voice a homogeneous and easy tone, should descend in the same order.

Before finishing this demonstration it is well to warn the pupil against lowering the under jaw too much, particularly in high sounds.

The excessive lowering of the jaw contracts considerably the isthmus of the throat and the fullness of the vibrations of sound.

The mouth for the emission of high sounds is naturally open wider, but the separation of the jaws ought not be too great, for in this case disagreeable defects may arise; firstly, an imperfection in the timbre of the voice, and a forced and painful emission; secondly, a distorted face. We may easily understand that if the lower jaw falls in disproportion, the tongue and the larynx will rise relatively; and narrow the isthmus of the throat. Then the voice resounds in the back part of the mouth and comes out almost entirely by the nostrils; in this case the timbre becomes veiled, nasal, guttural, hard and contracted.
In order to obtain a vocal sound with ease, flexibility and fullness, it is necessary to second the natural movements of the larynx and those of the soft palate, which act simultaneously according to the height of the sound, so when we exaggerate the opening of the mouth we easily injure the easy emission of the vocal sound.

The following table shows us the practical effect of this abnormal position [Figure 3].

1. Lower jaw
2. Tongue
3. Soft palate
4. Isthmus of the throat
5. Larynx
6. Pharynx
7. Nostrils

The separation of the *lower jaw* (1) as seen here, is that which I disapprove of; by this excessive separation, the *tongue* (2) must rise and swell at its base; this muscular contraction makes it almost touch the *soft palate* (3).

The forced approaching of these two organs, narrows considerably the *Isthmus of the throat* (4), and the sound which comes from the *larynx* (5), not finding its natural egress, must necessarily stop in the *pharynx* (6), and escape greatly from the nostrils (7).

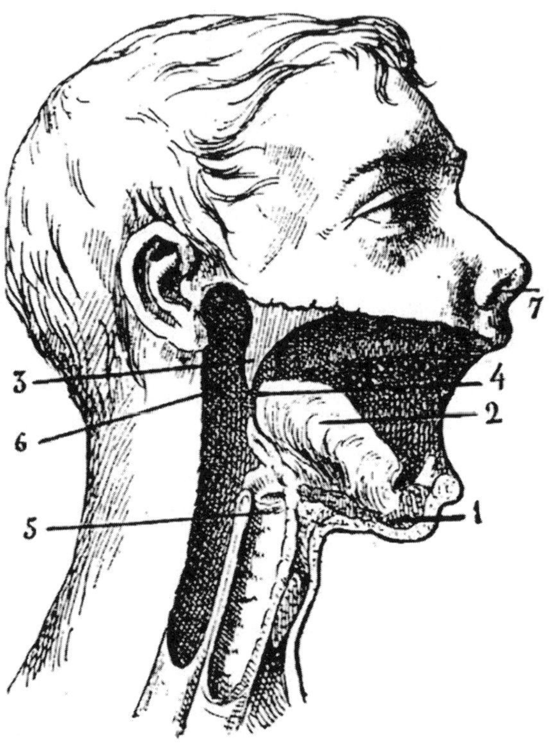

Figure 3.

This abnormal position of the mouth produces imperfection and disagreeableness in the timbre, the effects of which we have noticed above.

Similar defects could not be produced if the jaws were moderately separated.

The anatomical table on page 2 fig. I. [Figure 2] shows the natural and regular position of the opening of the mouth during the emission of the singing voice. In this table we see that the chin is jut out slightly, while in the figure examined, the chin is drawn back considerably.

The lower jaw when slightly jut out, leaves the larynx all freedom of action; but if it is drawn back, the larynx will assuredly make an ascending movement.

Having noticed the defects which result from the ascending of the larynx with respect to the high sounds, it is useless to insist any longer on this subject.

NOTES

1. Enrico Delle Sedie, *Esthetics of the Art of Singing* (New York: G. Schirmer, 1895), 21.
2. Enrico Delle Sedie, *Vocal Art* (New York: G. Schirmer, 1891).

57. Nasal Resonance—Fact or Fiction?

Originally published in the *Journal of Singing*, volume 57, no. 2, 2000

Publisher's note: While this article was not part of the *Provenance* series, it remains extremely relevant and merits inclusion in this volume. It originally appeared as a guest contribution to the column *From Speech to Song*, which was edited by Jean Westerman Gregg.

INTRODUCTION

I have come to realize as I have spoken to groups of voice teachers and students of singing that some of the most important physical and acoustic principles that could be guiding our teaching of voice are not widely understood. There is a proliferation of books currently available on the subject of vocal pedagogy and voice science, informative articles in our own professional singing voice journals, and of course, vocal pedagogy classes which are taught at most of our colleges and universities. These resources typically include discussions of acoustics, vocal tract resonance, articulation, vocal registers, laryngeal function, and of course, breath management. Still, this important body of knowledge remains underutilized in many vocal studios. The explanation is quite simple: people who have focused their energies on developing their singing voice and artistry have typically not studied anatomy, physiology, and acoustics. Most of us are simply too busy to take the time to learn the rigors of these disciplines. There are other important areas in which we must be experts in order to be successful singers and artists. After all, does a voice scientist need to know about the linguistic problems of performing fifteenth century French poetry? Yet, while knowing something about the pronunciation of the Middle French texts of Villon will not help a scientist in his or her work, I believe it is helpful to know something about what voice scientists understand about the voice, because it can help us tremendously as voice teachers!

SO, WHAT ABOUT NASAL RESONANCE?

One persistent idea is the value of the nasal passages as a resonator in good singing. It has often been asserted by singers and teachers of singing that resonance in the nasal passages and sinuses of the head make a significant and desirable contribution to the vocal production of good singers who have been trained in the Western tradition of operatic and art song performance practice. This idea persists in spite of several studies that indicate that well trained singers do not utilize the nasal cavity during singing and that the sinuses are not acoustically available to make a contribution to the sound that is heard from a singer. Wooldridge (1954) investigated this claim by filling the nasal passages of several singers with cotton. Acoustic analysis and perceptual judgments by a jury of professional singers failed to discriminate differences between tones sung with cotton occluding the nasal cavity and those with no occlusion. Vennard (1964) replicated this experiment and in addition filled the maxillary sinuses with water. Again, trained judges failed to discriminate the voice recordings made with occluded nasal passages from the unoccluded and the filled sinuses from the open ones. Yet in spite of these investigations, the notion that nasal resonance is a desirable thing persists. Reid (1950) stated that the practice of teaching nasal resonance can be traced to the methods of Curtis (1901), who claimed that nasal resonance could remove the strain from the vocal folds. Curtis was a physician who reportedly helped the tenor Jean de Reske regain his injured voice. The famous de Reske promoted their work together, and the rest is history. The use of nasalized syllables in vocal exercises such as "[ma], [me], [mi], [mo], [mu]" were not popular prior to Curtis's work.

Why does this notion endure? This author examines this issue by reviewing some of the anatomy and physiology of the head and neck and then describes some of the articulators that shape the vocal tract. Discussion follows regarding resonance in the vocal tract and specifically the effect on the acoustics of the vocal tract when the nasal cavity is coupled to it.

ANATOMY AND PHYSIOLOGY-ONCE OVER LIGHTLY

Figure 1 is a cross-section of the head showing the vocal tract and the primary articulators that control the shape of the air spaces. The vocal tract is the air space and the soft tissue surrounding it that begins at the larynx and extends to the lips. It is typically divided into three primary regions: the pharynx (which is further divided into the laryngopharynx, oropharynx, and nasopharynx), the oral cavity, and the nasal cavity. The pharyngeal space is the posterior air column that begins at the level of the larynx and extends into the nasal cavity. The oral cavity is the space of the mouth; defined by the walls of the cheeks and the lips, the hard palate, and the floor of the mouth and tongue. The nasal cavity is the air space above the hard palate. There is an external opening by way of the two nares of the nose and a posterior connection to the oropharynx by way of the velopharyngeal port. This passageway can be opened, closed, or in an intermediate posture, determined by the position of the velum (or soft palate).

The velum acts as a muscular valve and serves a very important function in speech production as well as other important non-speech roles. We typically breathe through the nose when we are at quiet rest. The velum is relaxed and low; the velopharyngeal port is open and air flows freely from the nares into the vocal tract and the lungs and back out again. The mucosal lining of the nasal cavity conditions the air we breathe; warming and humidifying it before going into the lungs. The nasal cavity also filters out small airborne particles of foreign matter that we don't want descending into the lungs.

The velum is lifted when we hold our breath (as when swimming underwater) by the muscles that insert into it (levator palatini, tensor palatini). The velopharyngeal port is closed, isolating the nasal cavity from the vocal tract, and water is prevented from making its way into the airway via the nose. Or we may close off the velopharyngeal port to avoid an unpleasant odor. This prevents air from moving through the nasal cavity as we breathe. Our sense of smell is centered in nerve endings that terminate high in the roof of the nasal cavity. In the absence of airflow, the molecular particles that carry the odor are not taken into the nose and our sense of smell is diminished, if not eliminated.

The activity of the velum is important for the production of speech. It is necessary that we lift the velum (closing off the velopharyngeal port) for the production of most consonant sounds in English. For example, to produce an [s], a high flow of air is emitted through a tiny opening between the tip of the tongue and the alveolar ridge (upper gum behind the teeth) producing what is classified as a lingua-alveolar fricative. A sudden release of pressure as we separate the lips produces the bilabial plosive consonant [pJ. Normal production of both of these consonants requires that the velum be high, closing off the velopharyngeal port, making it possible to build high air pressures in the vocal tract.

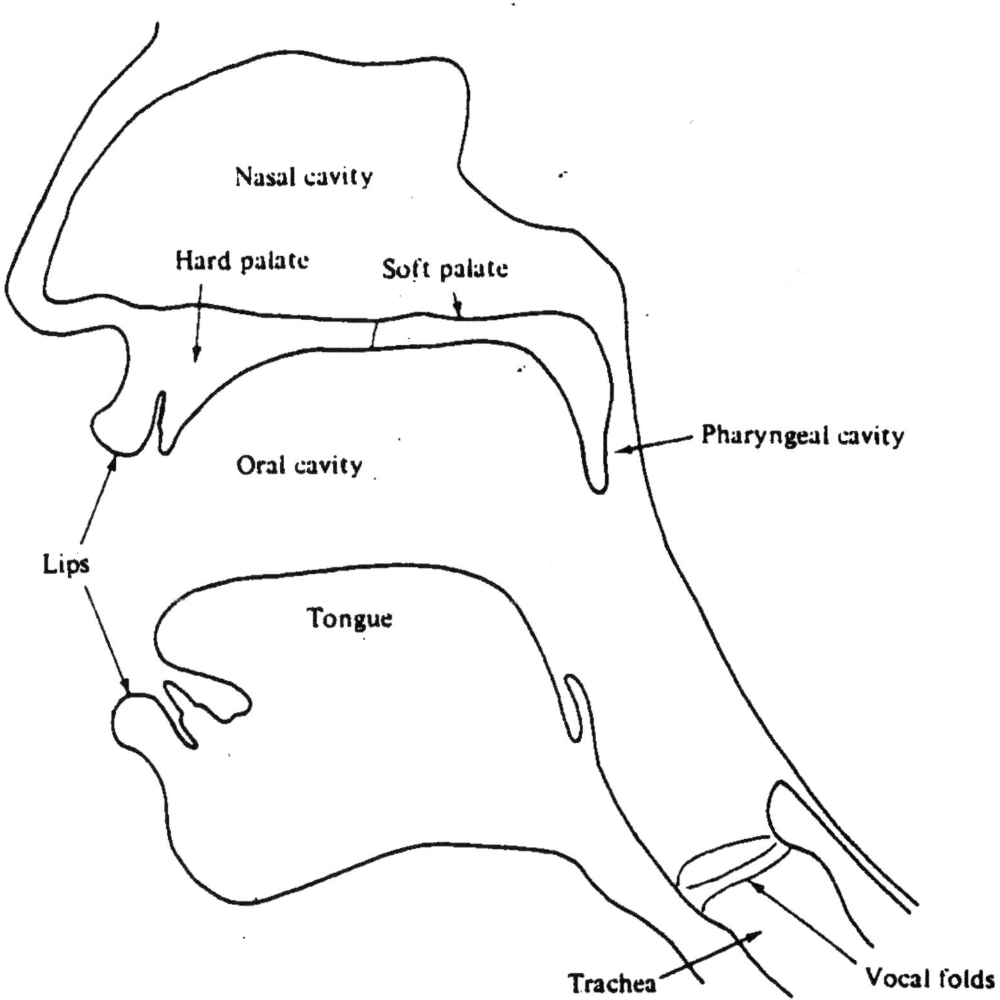

Figure 1. A cross section of the head showing the vocal tract and the main articulators that control the shape of the air spaces. (From "Normal Articulation Processes " by Raymond Daniloff in *Normal Aspects of Speech, Hearing and Language,* 1973. Englewood Cliffs, NJ: Prentice Hall, Inc. Used with Permission.)

Vowel sounds in spoken English are described as oral-resonant. That is, the velopharyngeal port is usually closed during production of vowels thereby eliminating or at least minimizing the possibility of resonance in the nasal cavity.

The importance of the velum in speech can be seen in persons without its normal function. Cleft palate is a congenital disorder that often makes it impossible for an individual to produce the closure necessary for normal consonant and vowel production. The coupling of the nasal cavity to the vocal tract gives the voice a noticeable nasal quality. It also results in the inability to impound air pressure in the vocal tract for consonant production. Fortunately, highly effective corrective surgery is available today, and normal speech is often restored.

In the English language there are three consonants that are defined as nasal semi vowels: [m], [n], and [ŋ]. They are produced with the intentional coupling of the nasal cavity to the rest of the vocal tract. The velum is relaxed and low, so the velopharyngeal port is open with the oral cavity closed by the lips or the back of the tongue. These are the only sounds in spoken English where a predominately nasal resonance is considered normal. Vowel sounds are sometimes nasalized when they occur before or after a nasal consonant. This is known as coarticulation and is a normal aspect of running speech, but is usually very brief in duration.

To summarize: the velum is a muscular valve that we use to control the coupling between the nasal cavity and the rest of the vocal tract during speech production and some other important nonspeech functions. Since we know that excessive coupling of the nasal cavity to the rest of the vocal tract is usually considered abnormal, we should question the notion that it is beneficial in singing. Let's begin by looking more closely at the acoustic implications of coupling the nasal cavity to the vocal tract.

A complete description of the sound production mechanism of the larynx and the resonances of the vocal tract are beyond the scope of this article. There are several thorough reviews of this information the interested reader is referred to Titze (1994) and Sundberg (1988).

SOURCE-FILTER THEORY OF VOWEL PRODUCTION

One theory concerning what we know about the voice and its function is summarized in the "source-filter theory of vowel production." Briefly stated, the vocal folds open and close as a result of airflow directed between them. They will go into oscillation when the vocal folds approximate and when there is sufficient airflow. The frequency of oscillation depends on a number of factors, but included among them is the amount of subglottal pressure (support) and the tension along the vibrating margin of the vocal folds (often referred to as the longitudinal tension). Longitudinal tension is primarily determined by the elongation of the vocal folds-the result of activity of the cricothyroid muscle within the larynx.

The oscillation of the vocal folds produces a buzzing sound that is the ignoble sound source for all voicing. The laryngeal buzz is much like that produced with the lips in vibration-like a brass player or as a child may do in imitating the sound of a motorboat. Acoustically it is a complex tone consisting of energy at the fundamental frequency (F_0) and at predictable frequencies above the F_0. The fundamental frequency is determined by the number of times in a second that the vocal folds open and close. If the vocal folds open and close 220 times a second the F_0 will be 220 Hz (Hertz). The series of overtones or partials occur at frequencies which are integer multiples of the F_0.If you multiply 220 (F_0) by the positive counting numbers (1, 2, 3, 4...) you will arrive at the frequency of each successive partial (220, 440, 660, 880 Hz, etc.). All these pitches occur simultaneously and make up the sound that is emitted from the larynx. We will hear this as the pitch A3 (A below C4 or middle C).

If we graph this information on a Cartesian plane with frequency on the x axis and intensity on the y axis, we get what is often called the source spectrum (Figure 2). The fundamental (first partial) is the strongest with each successively higher partial (overtone) being less intense. We usually say that the partials "fall off" at about 12 dB (decibels) per octave. Some perspective about decibels might be gained in knowing that a doubling of intensity is a 3 dB gain. If a brass section in an orchestra has four trumpets and you added four more there would be a 3 dB increase in intensity. A drop in intensity of 12 dB per octave means that the second partial will be 12 dB less intense than the fundamental; since the frequency distance between the first and second partial is one octave. A decrease of 12 dB is a significant drop in intensity.

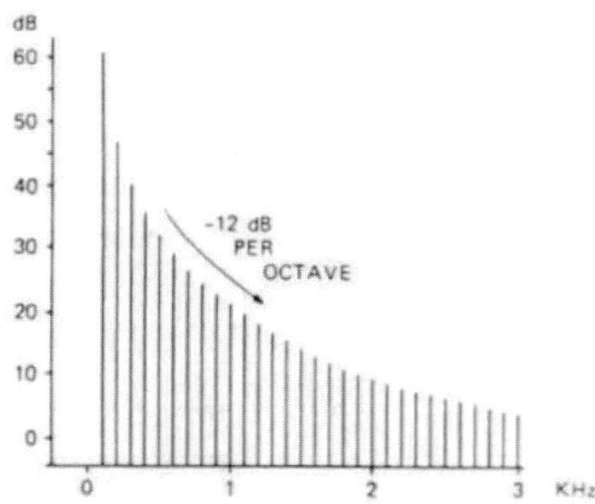

Figure 2. Source spectrum from the larynx. The intensity of the partials fall off at approximately 12 dB per octave. (From *The Sounds of Speech Communication* by J.M. Pickett. Austin, TX: PROED Inc., 1980. Used with Permission.)

What happens next to this rather unremarkable sound that comes from the larynx is really quite remarkable. The sound is treated or filtered by the vocal tract. The air within the vocal tract has all the physical properties necessary to be put into oscillation. Air has mass and elastic properties similar to the string of a guitar or a piano and it will oscillate if excited, or more accurately stated, it will produce a series of standing waves which are the source for resonance. The resonance frequencies (formants) are determined primarily by the shape of the vocal tract. This is defined by the position of the lips and the tongue and the length of the vocal tract as determined primarily by the position of the larynx in the neck.

A neutral or relaxed position of all the articulators of the vocal tract produces the vowel [ə]. Here the vocal tract is fairly uniform much like the shape of a straight tube (Figure 3). The fact that the tube is curved has little effect on its acoustic properties. This is a convenient model to consider because the formant frequencies are easily predicted. An average male vocal tract is about 17.5 cm in length. We can predict formant frequencies of 500, 1500, 2500, 3500 Hz (ad infinitum). A partial (the partial is produced by the larynx) that is near one of these formant frequencies will be amplified or resonated. The intensity of a partial may be boosted by as much as 30 dB if it happens to fall in the center of the formant. The formants drastically reshape the spectrum as it was produced by the larynx. Following is an analogy that this author uses with vocal pedagogy classes. It is rather simplistic, but simplicity often communicates!

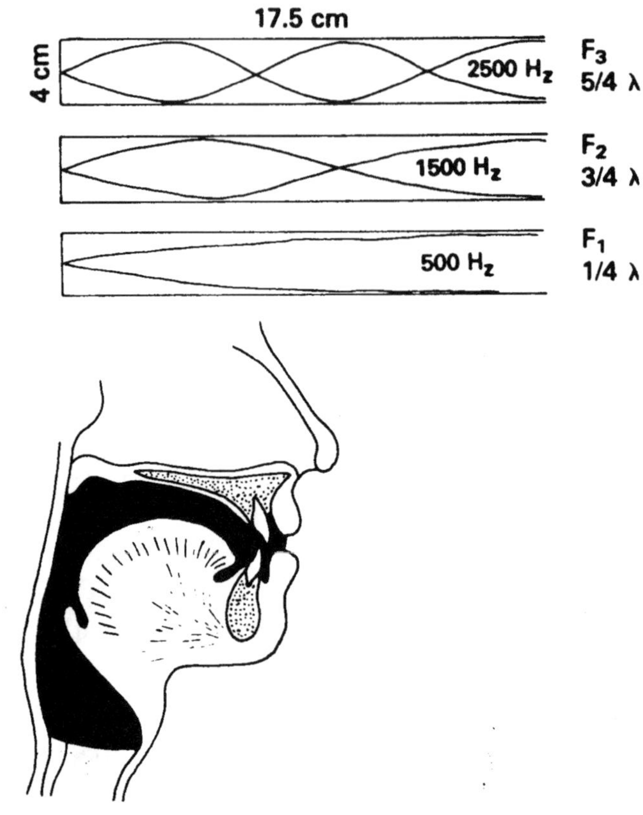

Figure 3. A diagram of the vocal tract in its most neutral position. The resonance frequencies are similar to that of a uniform closed open tube which is 17.5 cm in length. Formant frequencies are 500, 1500, and 2500 Hz. (From *Speech and Hearing Science Anatomy and Physiology*, 1988. Englewood Cliffs, NJ: Prentice Hall, Inc. Used with Permission.)

Think of the sound produced by the vocal folds as cookie dough and the shape of the vocal tract as a cookie cutter. We may have an assortment of cookie cutters to produce cookies of various shapes. Each cookie is shaped from the same dough; we have simply cut it into a different form. Each vowel that we use is a uniquely shaped cookie. The formants change frequency as we alter the shape of the vocal tract with the articulators, and with even a small formant frequency change we may perceive a different vowel quality. Just as the cookie dough and the cookie cutter are fundamentally different things, the series of partials produced by the vocal folds and the formants of the vocal tract are also different. Varying the shape of the vocal tract and producing different vowels does not change the frequency of the fundamental or the frequency of the partials, but because the relative intensity of the partials is being altered by the formants of the vocal tract, we hear different qualities or timbres that we associate with different vowel sounds. Figure 4 shows the formant envelope of the radiated spectrum (sound that comes out of the vocal tract) for the vowels [i] and [ɑ]. Formant frequencies of the vocal tract and the particular shape that produced them are indicated. The fundamental frequency is the same for both vowels, the partials are all at the same frequency, but the intensity of the partials relative to one another is quite different; it is this difference that explains our ability to perceive them as different vowels.

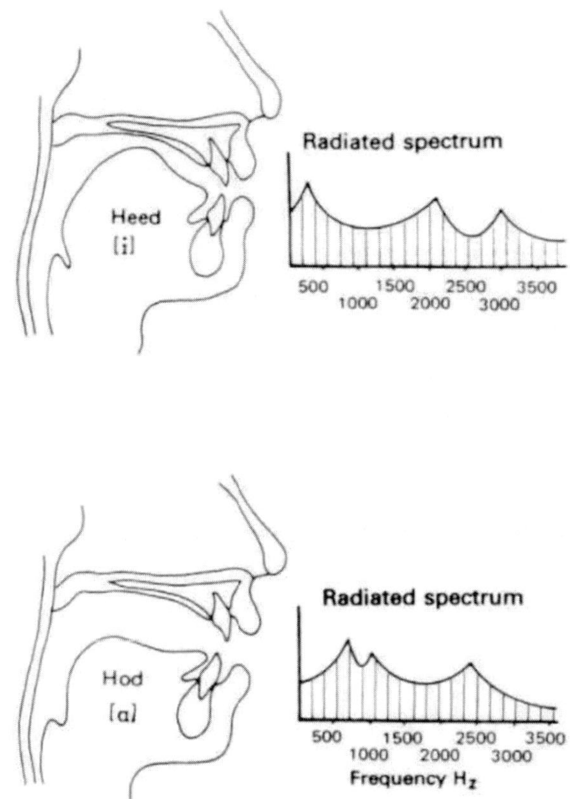

Figure 4. The formant envelope of the radiated vowel spectrum (the sound that comes out of the vocal tract) for the vowels [i] and [ɑ]. The fundamental frequency and the overtone series are represented by the vertical lines. (From *Speech and Hearing Science Anatomy and Physiology)*, 1988. Englewood Cliffs, NJ. Prentice Hall, Inc. Used with Permission.)

Absolute formant frequencies may differ considerably between individuals, allowing for variations in the shape and size of vocal tracts that go with bodies that are different shapes and sizes. Regional dialects and accents are responsible for some variation in formant frequencies of vowels. Certainly when considering a particular language which is spoken around the world (such as English) there are considerable differences in absolute formant frequencies, however, they are close enough that we are able to understand and communicate with little difficulty.

Although our ears will accept a broad range of formant frequencies for the identification of a vowel, it is very important to realize that our ears are very sensitive to even slight changes in formant frequencies. I believe this fact is important in classical singing where the range of what is an acceptably "pure" vowel is likely to be much more narrow than for speech.

NASAL PLACEMENT

What are the acoustic implications in this picture if we open the velopharyngeal passage? The top graph of Figure 5 shows the formant envelope of the [ɑ] vowel with the velopharyngeal passage closed. We see three pronounced formants, F1 at 800 Hz, F2 at around 115O Hz, and F3 at about 2600 Hz. These values fall within the average formant frequencies for the [ɑ] vowel. The bottom graph is the same speaker producing the same vowel but with the velum relaxed and open, coupling the nasal cavity to the rest of the vocal tract. This has some obvious and dramatic results. When coupled to the vocal tract (nasalization), the nasal cavity acts like a "side branch resonator." A common side branch resonator with which we are all familiar is the muffler on a car. The purpose of a muffler is to dampen the sound produced by the internal combustion engine. It does this by introducing anti-resonances or zeroes (z) into the system. Acoustically a zero removes any possibility of resonance occurring at that frequency. According to Pickett (1991) there are several predictable things that happen acoustically when nasalization occurs. Nasalization greatly reduces the intensity at and near the frequency of any of a number of anti-resonances. It is obvious in Figure 5 that there is an anti-resonance at about 600Hz. It can be seen that F1 is diminished in intensity and is shifted slightly higher in frequency. This can result in vowel distortion and a significant loss of carrying power for the voice. Two high frequency anti-resonances affect the spectrum between 2 and 3 kHz quite significantly. This is a crucial frequency range for the classical singer as it is the range in which the singer's formant occurs. The singer's formant is a unique clustering of acoustic energy that provides the voice much of its carrying power. It is the "ring" in the voice which is a prerequisite for all successful professional singing (especially for male voices and the mezzo-soprano) and usually occurs around 2800 Hz, right in the midst of this drastic reduction caused by the upper frequency zeros. This example is a highly nasalized condition. Less dramatically coupled conditions would be different and so would other vowels, but the general trend would be the same.

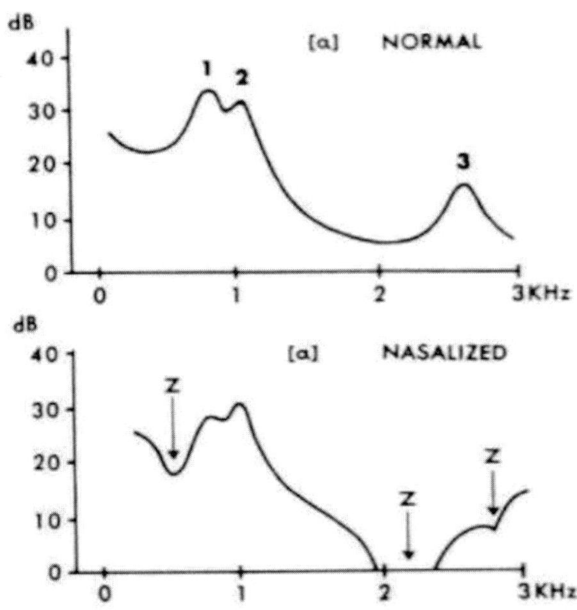

Figure 5. The top graph shows the formant envelope of the [ɑ] vowel with the velopharyngeal passage closed. There are three pronounced formants, F1 at 800 Hz, F2 at around 1150 Hz and F3 at about 2600 Hz. The bottom graph shows the effect of opening the nasal port. Spectral zeros reduce the overall intensity at about 500 Hz and in the region of the singer's formant between 2 and 3 kHz. (From *The Sounds of Speech Communication* by J. M. Pickett, Austin, TX: PROED Inc., 1980. Used with Permission.)

CONCLUSIONS

The information presented on the deleterious consequences on the acoustic spectrum of opening the nasal port, along with the fact that the practice of using intentional nasality as a pedagogical method is a twentieth century phenomenon, suggests that the principle of nasal resonance is of questionable benefit to the singer. The acoustic information says unequivocally that there are significant consequences to coupling the nasal cavity to the vocal tract that would not be beneficial for the *bel canto* singing voice (although in commercial styles it may be a desirable affect), resulting in formant shifts, zeros in the spectrum, and so forth. Experiments by Wooldridge (1956) and Vennard (1964) indicate that the professional singers used in their studies did not utilize the nasal cavity or the maxillary sinuses in good singing. In a recent study (Austin 1997) this author monitored the activity of the velum in four advanced female singers using a photodetector system that monitored the amount of light that was transmitted through the velopharyngeal port during normal speech and operatic singing. The assumption was that if light can be measured across the port then sound would also be transmitted. The singers were asked to speak and then sing the sentence "Connie came to Free Ontario for the firm's money." The subjects sang the sentence at a repeated pitch in a recitative style in their low, medium, and high range of their singing voice. Figure 6 is data from one of the singers in the study. In each graph the top trace is the acoustic signal from the microphone and the bottom trace is the output from the photodetector. Opening of the velopharyngeal port is indicated by a downward deflection in the photodetector trace and total closure can be seen in the flat plateaus. In the speech sample you can see the photodetector trace move down (indicating the port was opened) during the pronunciation of the [n] in "Connie" and then closed for the consonant [k] in "came." As you move from left to right you can see how the velopharyngeal port opens each time for nasal consonants and closes for the other consonants and vowels. There is normal coarticulation of the nasal quality in vowels immediately before and after the nasal consonant. Figure 7 is the data from the same singer in the low voice singing condition. It is obvious that the singer uses much less "port open" posture, even when singing words containing nasal consonants. The [n] in "Connie" and the [n] in "money" are the only times that the velopharyngeal port was opened at all. Figure 8 is the high voice condition for the same singer. The singer doesn't open the velopharyngeal port at all, not even to articulate the nasal consonants. The assumption must be made that this singer (a DMA student in vocal performance and a national semifinalist in the Metropolitan Opera Auditions) avoided any hint of nasality in her singing, especially as the pitch went up. Of the four subjects examined in this study all but one showed similar trends. It should be noted also that the one singer who did not show this habit was the least successful singer used in the study.

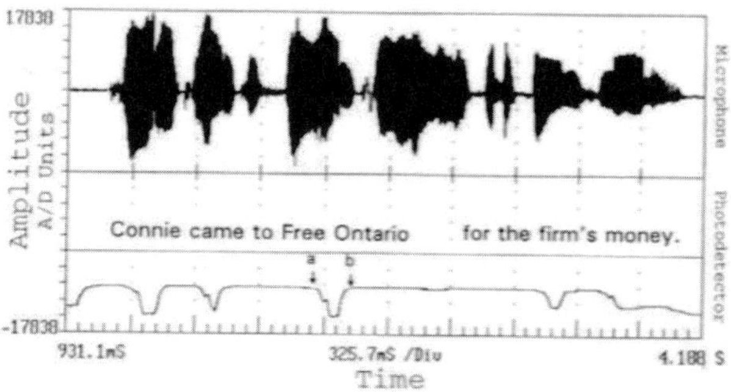

Figure 6. These signals are taken from a soprano speaking the phrase "Connie came to Free Ontario for the firm's money." The upper trace is the acoustic signal from a microphone. The lower trace is the output of a

photodetector system, designed to monitor the amount of opening of the velopharyngeal port by monitoring the amount of light transmitted through it. A negative deflection of the photodetector trace indicates opening of the velopharyngeal port for the production of a nasal consonant as in the [n] of "Connie" and the [m] of "came." The positive deflection and plateaus of the signal suggest full closure of the velopharyngeal port for the production of consonants as in the [k] of "Connie" and "came" and [f] in "free".

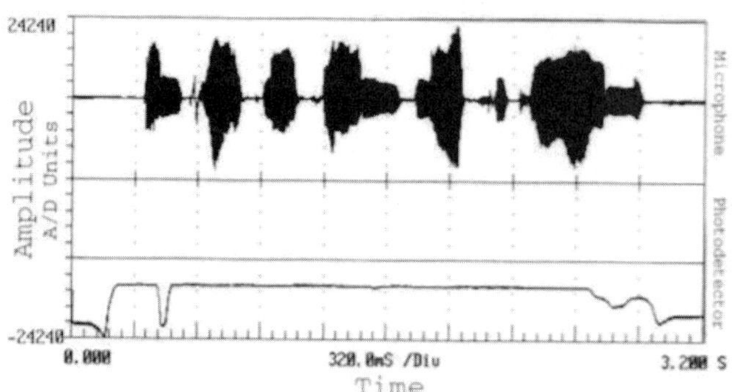

Figure 7. This is the same subject singing the phrase "Connie came to Free Ontario for the firm's money" at a low pitch in her singing voice. Note that the velopharyngeal port is open much less than in the speaking voice sample shown in Figure 6.

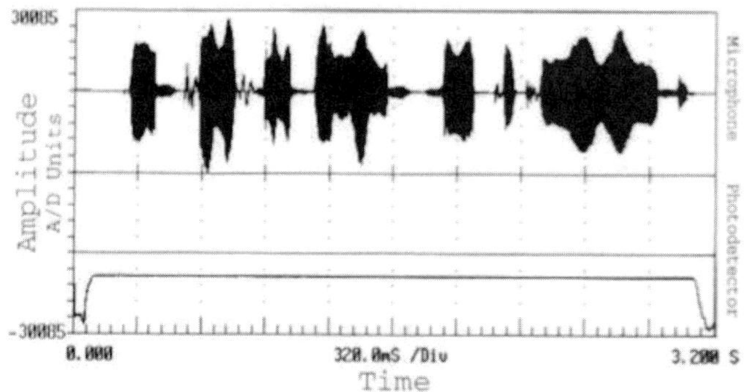

Figure 8. The same subject singing the phrase "Connie came to Free Ontario for the firm's money" at a high pitch in her singing voice. There is no opening of the velopharyngeal port. This suggests that no nasal consonants were sung.

The question remains: Why is the idea of nasal placement so persistent with some singers and teachers? The answer must lie in our sensation of what we do when we sing well.

There is a tremendous amount of energy that is created within the vocal tract when the voice is well produced. Only a part of the energy that is produced at the vocal folds and resonated by the vocal tract actually escapes the lips to be heard by our adoring fans. The rest remains inside and is bouncing and reflecting back and forth within the confines of the vocal tract. With all this energy in the vocal tract it is not surprising that many singers report sensations of vibrations in many parts of their body. Sensations may be localized on the chest wall, in the head; particularly in the front of the face or "the mask." It may be that strong sensations of secondary vibrations have led many to confuse it with nasalization. In fact, they are two very different things.

This is not to say that you don't hear real nasality in the singing of even some successful professional singers. We certainly do. It may also be more predominate in some voice types than others. High, light tenor voices seem to be able to use nasality as a part of their singing without dire professional consequences. It certainly influences the type of roles that he will sing (this particular voice type can also sing with a high larynx position but that is another article!). So, what do we do with a student who is singing with an undesirable nasal resonance? Well, a voice teacher shouldn't be without a strategy to fix a problem. One approach that has been very helpful to this author is based on what we know about consonant production. Earlier it was stated that one of the important functions of the velum was to close off the velopharyngeal port so that air could be impounded for the production of consonant sounds. We can simply ask the student to include an energetic plosive such as [b], [p], [t], or [k] or fricatives such as [f], [s], [v], or [z] prior to their vowel sounds that are nasalized. This will raise the soft palate, closing the velopharyngeal port. The student is then encouraged to maintain that high velar posture through the duration of the vowel. A sensory awareness of velum closure can be developed over time. Of course the idea of the yawn in the throat is tried and true and will also be helpful. As the larynx comes down, the velum goes up!

The point here is that we as teachers must be clear about what we want our students to do. If we are seeking the full and ringing sound of a mature well-produced voice and we think that it is produced by nasal resonance, then we may be wrong. The fullness, the intensity, the ring in the voice comes when the nasal cavity is separated from the vocal tract by lifting the soft palate. If we are interested in historic precedence for what we do in the studio (and we should be) then it is very enlightening to read that voice teachers have been decrying singing through the nose for centuries-from Tosi to Garcia . You will not find nasalized exercises in their methods. It seems that Reid (1950) was right, that we are indebted to H. Holbrook Curtis (who was a physician , not a singer) for the "mah, mei, mee, mow, moo" that is so often used as a caricature of the opera singer warming up!

In summary, this author believes that as teachers it is helpful to be familiar enough with the anatomy and physiology of the head and neck and the fundamentals of vocal tract acoustics that we can make useful, factual suggestions to our students. This is certainly not to say that every instruction should be crafted with anatomical terms and statements about physical law. However, it was said by a well-known voice teacher that he "encourages breathing through the nose because it lifts the soft-palate." A little familiarity with structure and function will tell us that this is not possible. Will this direction given to a student result in the desired response? Maybe. Maybe not. If not, it is here that informed teachers can be creative in communicating to their students with suggestions that will work. We must have an arsenal of instructions with which to achieve the desired response in a studio full of individuals, all of whom may respond differently to the same suggestion. We will be successful with a greater percentage of our charges if we base our suggestions on fact, not fiction.

Pier Francesco Tosi (1723), the great singer and voice teacher of the first half of the eighteenth century, warned:

> Let the master attend with great care to the voice of the scholar, which, whether it be *di petto* or *di testa* should always come forth neat anzd clear, without passing through the nose or being choked in the throat (which are the two most horrible defects in a singer, and past all remedy if once grown into a habit).

NOTES

1. Austin, S.F. 1997. "Movement of the velum during speech and singing in classically trained singers." *Journal of Voice 11, (1997)*
2. Curtis, H. H. 1901. *Voice Building and Tone Placing.* New York: D. Appleton and Co.
3. Pickett, J. M. 1991. "The Spectra of Vowels," found in *Readings in Clinical Spectrography of Speech.* Edited by Baken & Daniloff. Singular Press, San Diego.
4. Reid, C. 1950. *Bel Canto: Principles and Practices.* Coleman-Ross Co., Inc.
5. Sundberg, J. 1987. *The Science of the Singing Voice*. Dekalb, Ill: Northern Illinois University Press.
6. Titze, I. R. 1994. *Principles of Voice Production*. Englewood Cliffs, NJ: Prentice Hall.
7. Tosi, P. F. 1723. [1987]. *Observations on the Florid Song*. London: Stainer and Bell.
8. Vennard, W. "An experiment to evaluate the importance of nasal resonance in singing." *Folia Phoniatrica 16* (1964).
9. Woolridge, W. B "Is there nasal resonance?" *Bulletin of the National Association of Teachers of Singing* (Oct. 1956).

58. Treasure "Chest"—A Physiological and Pedagogical Review of the Low Mechanism[1]

Originally published in the *Journal of Singing*, volume 61, no. 3, 2005

Publisher's note: While this article was not part of the *Provenance* series, it remains extremely relevant and merits inclusion in this volume. It originally appeared as a feature article.

INTRODUCTION

I once had the privilege of sharing a number of students with a renowned soprano who had a significant career at the Metropolitan Opera and had sung all around the world. I was serving primarily as technical advisor and she as artistic coach. One of our mezzo sopranos was making wonderful strides in acquiring a new richness of tone and freedom in her singing, accessing a high voice that always had eluded her. When my teaching partner inquired as to the source of this development, she was surprised when I told her that we had been working very hard at building her chest voice and integrating its qualities into her whole range. My colleague stated that she never had been taught to use her low mechanism, and wasn't it after all, harmful to do so? I went to my recording of her singing the role of Leonora in Verdi's *Il Trovatore* where, in fact, she utilized her chest voice beautifully. Not only did she use it in an isolated fashion where appropriate, but the richness of her voice throughout her range convinced me that the low mechanism was indeed an integral part of her singing, even though she didn't recognize that it was.

Apparently, there are many who share this opinion about the chest voice. Is there a legitimate basis for concern? What do we know about the chest voice? Is there an historical precedence for its use in the studio? How does one go about training the chest voice, and why should we bother?

VOCAL REGISTER: A "MIXED BAG"

Chest register is but one of a number of unique, disparate qualities of sound that are found in the human voice. Most typically they are associated with different parts of the frequency range. By tradition we call them vocal registers. Their existence is most obvious when their boundaries are clearly marked by abrupt transitions. This condition is typically found in untrained singers and in singing styles that exploit their distinct qualities, as in yodeling, a singing style found throughout the world. A central tenet of singing in the Western tradition of opera and art song is that the boundaries between the vocal registers are not obvious, except when used for specific, intentional effect, such as the expression of deep emotion or for comedic effects.

Manuel Garcia II, renowned nineteenth century voice pedagogue, defines a register thus:

> By the word register we understand a series of consecutive and homogeneous tones going from low to high, produced by the development of the same mechanical principle, and whose nature differs essentially from another series of tones equally consecutive and homogeneous produced by another mechanical principle. All the tones belonging to the same register are consequently of the same nature, whatever may be the modification of timbre or of force to which one subjects them.[2]

This is the first formal definition of a vocal register. Garcia identifies the perceptual qualities associated with a vocal register with a particular vibrational mode of the vocal folds—exclusively a laryngeal event. It is interesting to note that Garia's definition predates by more than a decade his use of the laryngoscope to visualize the vocal folds during phonation in a living singer. His definition is so complete that he did not offer a correction after he was able to see what he previously imagined. Although Garcia's definition is still used by many, there never has been significant agreement among experts on this subject. Neither voice teachers nor voice scientists can agree either on how many registers there are or what they should be called. Various sources identify two, three, or more registers in the voice, while others do not even acknowledge their existence.[3]

Paul Oncley suggested that in addition to laryngeal registers, there are also acoustic registers that should be included in any complete definition. He offers that timbre shifts that result from the interaction of the partials from the sound source (the larynx) and the resonances of the vocal tract (formants) could describe a vocal register.

> Yet the review of literature shows that among the authorities in our profession there is not much agreement as to the number and dispositions of these registers, or even whether they exist at all. The discrepancy makes one wonder whether all these people are really talking about the same thing, or whether instead of Garcia's definition they are following that of Humpty-Dumpty in Lewis Carroll's "Through the Looking Glass," when he says: "When I use a word it means just what I choose it to mean; neither more or less."[4]

It should be no surprise that teaching methods vary widely on this issue. Some authors hardly mention registers of the voice at all, while for others they are central to the voice training process. The breadth of opinion can be exasperating if one attempts to review and understand the vast literature addressing vocal registers, and for that reason many don't try. And why should we? What difference does it make? Well, it can be stimulating to banter with colleagues about the various intellectual positions we might have on the subject, but ultimately it matters only if our students have something to gain from it.

There is a rich historical legacy from teachers of the past and present who utilize the registers of the voice in the teaching process. The physiology of the chest voice is fairly well understood, and it is now possible to offer an explanation for a long-standing pedagogical practice.

Nuts and Bolts

As has already been stated, an incredible amount of research on the registers of the voice has followed Garcia's first real observation of the vocal folds in action. In the past several decades, methods of measurement and observation have advanced to the point where a good deal of the mystery concerning the "hows" and "whys" of phonation and registration has been solved. A brief discussion of the physiology of the chest voice is a logical place to begin.

Figure 1 is taken from a series of electromyographic (EMG) studies conducted by Dr. Minoru Hirano and associates.[5] EMG is the technique of measuring the electrical activity of a muscle by inserting small wire electrodes into it. The theory is that the more a muscle is working, the larger the electrical signal that can be recorded by the electrode. This series of experiments, conducted on trained singers, was designed to study the activity of the intrinsic laryngeal musculature during various singing tasks.

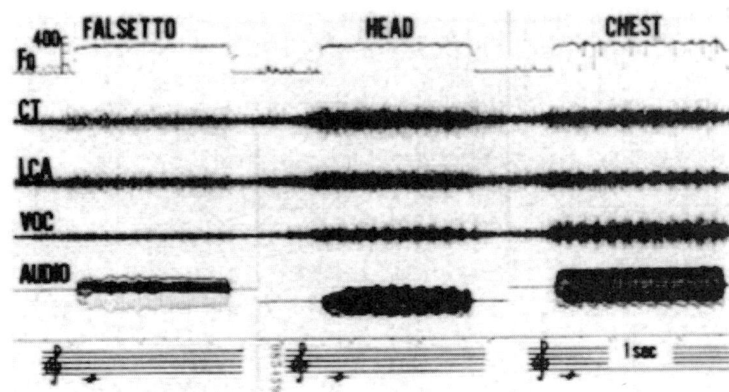

Figure 1. Electromyographic (EMG) signals from Hirano's study of the intrinsic laryngeal muscles. Signals from electrode placements in three muscles are shown: the cricothyroid (CT), lateral cricoarytenoid (LCA), and the vocalis (VOC). The subject sang the same pitch in three registers: falsetto, head, and chest voice. The only significant difference across the three conditions is found in the vocalis muscle.

The illustration displays EMG signals from three of the intrinsic laryngeal muscles in a bass subject: the cricothyroid (CT), lateral cricoarytenoid (LCA), and the vocalis (VOC). Again, the assumption is that the thicker signal trace indicates increased electrical activity in the muscle and suggests a more prominent role for that particular vocal task. There are three register conditions in Figure 1, falsetto, head voice, and chest voice, all sung at the same pitch. It can be seen in the signal traces that the vocalis muscle is the only one that changes significantly across the register conditions. A total of four subjects show similar trends in this study. Hirano defines the vocalis muscle as the "register agent" and suggests that the level of its activity defines the vocal register. He defines the CT as the "pitch agent." It is the activity of the CT that is the primary control mechanism for increasing pitch; its contraction results in the elongation of the vocal folds and an increase in tension along the vibrating margin, and results in an increase in frequency.

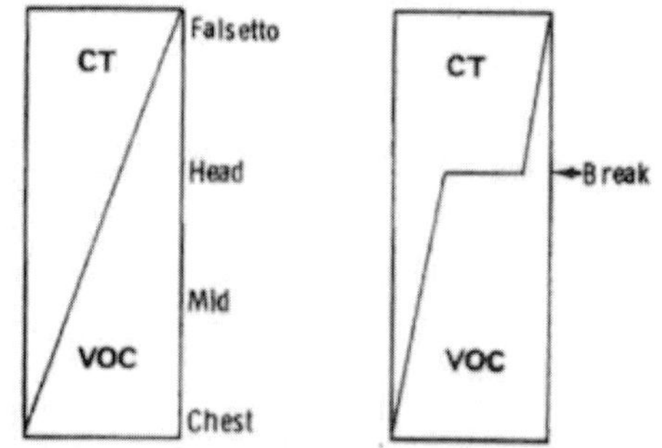

Figure 2. Hirano's two register model based upon his EMG data. The rectangle on the left is the idealized well-coordinated registration where the vocalis (VOC) and cricothyroid (CT) muscles balance their activity while going from chest to falsetto. The rectangle on the right is a model of a singer who has not learned to coordinate the two registers.

Hirano proposes a simple, useful model of the vocal registers for singing, seen in Figure 2.[6] The diagonal line in the rectangle on the left describes a seamless register transition from chest to falsetto on a sustained pitch. The chest voice is defined by the highly active vocalis, as suggested by the maximum width of the triangle labeled VOC at the bottom of the figure. Falsetto is defined by the absence, or minimal activity, of the vocalis muscle, as suggested by the diminishing width of the triangle labeled VOC toward the top of the figure. Intermediate activity of the VOC defines middle register and head voice. The activity of the CT must adjust for greater or lesser activity of the VOC in order to maintain constant pitch. The CT and VOC carefully balance their activity level and the result is a register transition without a change in pitch and without a noticeable break. This should be recognized as the *messa di voce* exercise as described in numerous texts, ancient and modern.

Hirano's model describes a well-coordinated transfer of power between these two muscles and would be found only in an accomplished singer. The rectangle on the right in Figure 2 suggests what might happen when the singer is not so skilled; a sudden break occurs in the transition from chest voice to a lighter mechanism. Leading up to the break (moving from the bottom to the top) the VOC remains too highly engaged. It does not diminish its activity gradually. The transition from the heavy mechanism to the lighter mechanism is cataclysmic rather than gradual. When the muscular balance changes abruptly, there is a sudden change of vibrational mode of the vocal folds—and a different mechanical principle takes over. We would probably perceive the voice as being too heavy leading up to the break and too falsetto-like after the break.

If we accept Hirano's evidence that the contraction of the vocalis muscle controls the register, we might wonder how the activity of this muscle could influence the quality of sound.

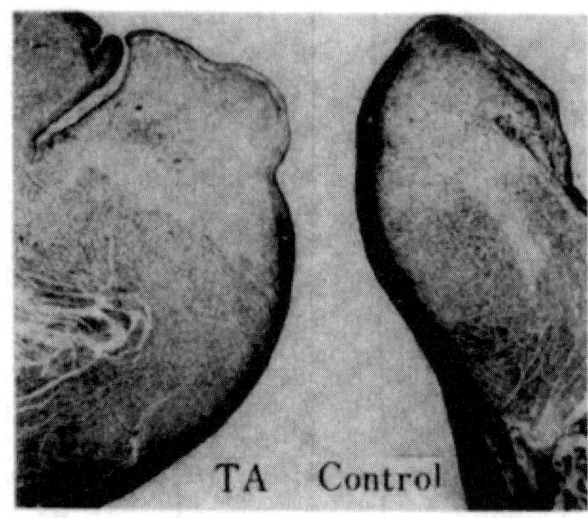

Figure 3. Cross sectional profiles of two excised vocal folds. The thyroarytenoid muscle (vocalis) on the left has been stimulated, increasing the thickness and depth of the vocal fold compared to the control on the right.

Figure 3 shows cross sections of two human vocal folds prepared by Hirano.[7] The vocalis muscle on the left was stimulated by a mild electric current simulating the activity of the nervous system. The effect upon the shape of the vocal fold can be seen when compared to the control on the right. The stimulated vocal fold is much more rounded and the depth of the fold is greatly increased. From this experiment we see that the contraction of the vocalis muscle affects the shape of the vocal fold dramatically. This is relevant in that it has been shown that a change in the cross sectional profile has profound implications for the way that the vocal folds vibrate and the resulting acoustic signal.

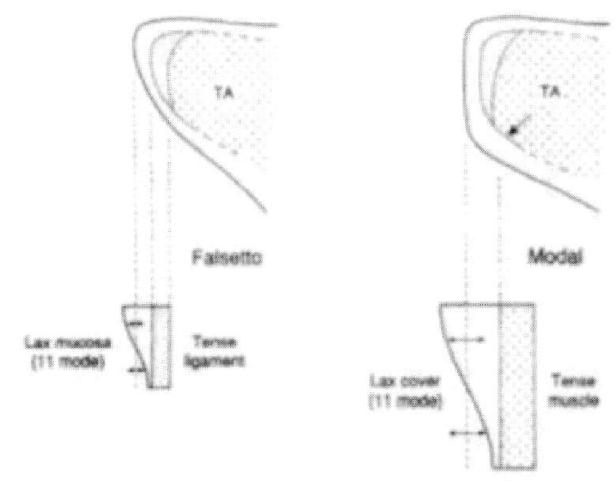

Figure 4. Cross sectional profiles of the vocal folds based upon Titze's description of the effect of contraction of the thyroarytenoid (TA) muscle. The profile on the right shows a rounded underside that goes into phonation at lower aerodynamic pressures and results in a richer harmonic spectrum.

Ingo Titze has described this relationship between the shape of the vocal folds and the acoustic signal that they produce during phonation. Figure 4 presents in cartoon form the cross sectional profiles of two vocal folds, one in falsetto and one in modal (or chest) register.[8] The difference in their profiles is obvious, and the similarity to the slide preparations by Hirano in Figure 3 should be obvious. According to Titze, when the VOC contracts; "[i]t bulges the vocal fold medially below the level of the vocal processes, creating a thicker and deeper vibrating structure."[9] This agrees with Hirano's example of the stimulated vocalis in Figure 3. When the VOC is stimulated, the vocal fold becomes thicker with a rounded underbelly. You can liken this to the bulging of the biceps that occurs when one "makes a muscle."

Further support for the effect of increasing the depth of the vocal fold on the quality of the tone can be seen in Titze's discussion of the changes in the vocal fold that occur during puberty. He suggests that it is the enlargement of the thyroarytenoid muscle (TA) that is responsible for the sudden change in the vocal quality.

> As the bottom of the vocal fold bulges out, the glottis becomes more rectangular than wedge-shaped (convergent). During vibration, then, glottal closure can be obtained over a greater portion of the vocal fold, and thereby over a greater portion of the cycle...The result is a voice of richer timbre, which we call *chest* or *modal* voice.[10]

Both of these examples explain the effect of the chest voice upon voice quality. The chest voice is defined by increased contraction of the vocalis muscle. This action increases the depth and thickness of the vocal folds and produces a rounding on the underbelly of the fold. When rounded, deep vocal folds are in phonation, the source spectrum is characterized by high levels of acoustic energy in the upper partials, giving it ring and a richer, fuller sound—qualities that have been ascribed to the chest voice. Titze explains that rounded vocal folds also have lower onset threshold pressures, therefore they go into phonation with less expiratory effort and require less airflow to maintain them in oscillation.[11]

Bridging the Gap

The physiology of the chest voice and its implications upon the sound quality have been described. What do we find in the pedagogical record of over 300 years of voice teaching? A written legacy left by eminent voice teachers, past and present, seems to suggest that these principles have been appreciated for many years. One of the first such references we find in a quote from Giambattista Mancini, a famous eighteenth century singer and voice teacher.

> This chest voice is not equally forceful and strong in everyone; but to the extent that one has a more robust or more feeble organ of the chest, he will have a more or less robust voice.[12]

The value of the chest voice was clearly appreciated by this early master. The term "feeble" is used here simple to describe a voice that is lighter or more lyric in quality with no value judgement implied. He goes on to say that a "sonorous body, or rather robustness of voice is ordinarily a gift from nature, but can also be acquired by study in art."[13]

Mancini describes a very common condition among singers. The voice is simply too "feeble" to show promise of professional success. It is clear that a "robust" voice was just as valued then at it is now. Mancini claims that a feeble voice could be made robust through study and art. He goes on to offer a specific solution.

> It remains for me now to speak of those voices which are slender and weak throughout their register...One observes that these voices are very weak in the chest notes, and the greater majority deprived of any low notes, but rich in high notes, or head voice...There is no method more sure to obtain this end, I believe, than to have such a little voice sing only in the chest voice for a time. The exercise should be done with a tranquil solfeggio; and as the voice enriches itself with greater body and range, one may blend it as much as possible with the low notes.[14]

Mancini recommends that the singer focus on the chest voice until it grows in strength. He prescribes consistent, diligent practice that would include slow-moving scale passages and sustained tones in the range of the chest mechanism.

We can see this same pedagogical principle in more contemporary teachers. A century later Garcia laments,

> As we have said, the chest register is generally denied or rejected by teachers, not that one could not draw from its application an immense advantage, nor that the suppression of the range which it embraces would not deprive the singer of the most beautiful dramatic effects or the more favorable contrasts.[15]

In the twentieth century there are many references to building to chest voice and blending the tones of the chest and the middle, or the chest and the falsetto. A wonderful example of this can be heard in William Vennard's *Developing Voices*, a series of sound recordings from his teaching studio. One of the featured students is a soprano called Mary Alice. Vennard says about their work together,

> During her studies she frequently asked for help with her high tones, which did improve during the work. More freedom and modification of the brighter vowels helped the top voice, but what she needed most was to develop the chest voice and blend it into her singing so that it would be usable.[16]

During the course of their work, which spanned several months, one hears the voice of Mary Alice take on much more depth and warmth as she first awakens the dormant chest resister and then integrates it into the rest of the range. It is fascinating to hear this voice transformed.

Many other teachers suggest that the chest voice can be strengthened with exercise. This is certainly true of the work of Cornelius Reid. In his pedagogical approach, the chest register is one of two fundamental qualities that must be identified, strengthened, and coordinated into a unified whole.[17] Reid has written extensively over the years on this subject, and would be identified as the "flag bearer" for this practice today. Finally, Richard Miller speaks of the importance of the chest mixture in the female voice when he says,

> Chest mixture will strengthen the soprano's lower-middle range. Almost every female can make some chest timbre sounds, no matter how insecure, in the lowest part of her range. These notes should be sung in short, intervallic patterns, transposing by half steps upward, as more sound emerges.[18]

PEDAGOGICAL APPLICATION

It has been suggested by a few respected voice teachers from the past and present that a feeble voice can be made robust. It seems that the mechanism for doing so lies in an ability to alter the cross sectional profile of the vocal fold by changing the shape of the vocalis muscle with appropriate exercise. If one wanted to build twenty-inch biceps, a good body trainer would know how to go about doing it. He would tell us to pick up a weight—light at first—and lift it. We would do ten to twelve repetitions in each of three or four sets. Before each set we would add a little weight. Given a little time, the inevitable result would be a larger muscle that would change the cross sectional profile of the upper arm and provide us with greater strength.

A singer may begin study with vocal folds that resemble the cross sectional profile on the left of Figure 4. The vocal fold is slender and lacking in depth along the vibrating margin. The voice quality is slender and weak throughout the singing range. It is suggested that by exercising the vocalis muscle the singer can transform the shape of his or her vocal fold to more closely resemble the profile on the right of Figure 4, increasing the squareness and depth of the vocal fold itself. This is at least a logical explanation of the underlying mechanism when we take a voice that is slender and weak and transform it into a voice that is robust and enriches itself with greater body.

The purpose of this work is not to develop the chest voice in order to gain low notes that a singer may never use in actual literature. This is a crucial point. The goal is to enhance the quality of the voice throughout its entire range, because we have built a more refined sound generator. The benefit of this work goes from bottom to top and without the loss of range that is in the mind of many. On the contrary, the high voice is often the real winner in this effort, gaining in richness, range, and ease. The ability to sing a greater range of dynamics is also improved. Reid states that "regardless of the intensity being sung, there should always be some amount of chest register participation."[19]

If we acknowledge that the fundamental quality of a voice can be changed over months and years of study, there must be some underlying mechanism to explain it. It does not seem likely that this can be accounted for only by more sophisticated coordination, breath support, or vowel modification. To summarize:

- Exercise can change the shape of a muscle.
- Square, deep vocal folds produce robust, full voice quality.
- The shape of the vocal folds is determined, at least in part, by the mass of the vocalis muscle.
- The chest register is the result of high levels of vocalis muscle contraction.
- Some well-known voice teachers throughout history have trained the chest voice to enrich the quality of voice.

What can we put together from these facts?

- The shape of the vocal fold can be enhanced by exercising the chest register.
- The quality of the whole voice is improved as a result of this effort.

Building the Chest Voice

What would an exercise to strengthen chest voice look like? Many teachers have offered excellent examples. The range of the chest voice is defined by Garcia as encompassing the octave between G_3 and G_4 for the typical female voice and from C_2 to C_5 for the typical male voice. Every voice will not have this compass in the chest voice, but it represents the range in which it will appear and can be trained to include.

When undertaking this work with a student, one must be aware of several conditions that can characterize the chest voice at the beginning among individual voices. Some women, for instance, who have never sung in chest voice will find that once it is discovered, there is considerable strength and presence there. In this case, nature has provided the optimum shape for the vocal folds. For such singers, discovery only means giving them permission to sing down there. Most good voices will have a significant chest mechanism, although they may have never consciously utilized it. The singer known as Mary Alice in the Vennard recordings is a perfect example. We hear Vennard leading her to a substantial chest voice quite easily. He does so by using her speaking voice quality, which is almost all chest voice. He then teaches her to integrate that quality into her singing voice for the first time, with astounding results.

The chest voice is common in the speaking voices of women and almost exclusively used by men. The speech voice can be an important first introduction to that quality that then can be brought into the singing voice. How often do we hear our beginning singer in possession of a loud, ringing speaking voice offer a breathy, insignificant singing voice? Speaking on pitch would begin with little short words or syllables such as an energetic greeting "Hi!" at about C_4 for women and C_3 for men. It could be helpful at this point to allow the singer to self-select the pitch but suggest that it be relatively low and loud in the speaking voice. A phlegmatic approach will not access the low mechanism, and the singer must be willing to sing with a full commitment and energy. Locate the student's selected pitch on the piano and then move up and down by half steps, all the while maintaining the speech voice quality.

Other voices might exhibit a robust nature and cannot manage to make a smooth transition into the lighter mechanism. This is often the case with lower male voices, especially the true bass and many who sing other vocal styles, including broadway belt and gospel. This is the voice represented on the right in Figure 2. In this case, the vocalis muscle must be taught how to turn off or decrease its activity gradually. Many of the exercises to be discussed will help this condition.

In many voices the chest voice will be very weak and insignificant. In those instances, the chest voice will have to be slowly and patiently built before it can contribute significantly to the rest of the instrument.

Garcia suggested that B_3 and C_4 is the place to start to begin the building process for the female voice. The tone is to be "attacked well" at *mezzo forte* or *forte*, as the chest register responds to high intensity levels. It is to be "held only a short time and repeated several times."[20] Even this may not achieve the desired results immediately. Garcia goes on to suggest that the vowel /i/ can be helpful in that it encourages the lips of the glottis to close more forcefully and "will facilitate the emission of the chest tones."[21] The next step is to move between two pitches at small intervals. The following tone comes from the one that is mastered and with a "vigorous portamento." Garcia states very clearly that this is the first step in training and that further success depends upon its mastery.

Reid states that since the chest register is seldom used in the female voice, the mechanism must be established. The register is "short ranged" and therefore single tones must be employed. He goes on to say that "since the chest register is known to respond only to high levels of intensity the tone selected must be sung *forte*."[22]

This is slow and laborious work and can take months or even years to see significant change. But, like any other muscle in the body, regular, consistent exercise will produce results. As it does, any previously acquired balance with the lighter mechanism will no longer be appropriate. The difference between the lower and higher mechanism will become exaggerated for awhile and a break may appear where before there was none. This has been described by Cornelius Reid and others as a "separation of the registers" and has brought him and other practitioners of this process considerable criticism over the year. However, it is an inevitable result of building the chest voice. The coordinative process is going to have to change as the strength of the vocalis muscles increases and the profile of the vocal folds is affected. You cannot improve the voice without changing it.

This condition is not gender specific. Men also can sing with an underdeveloped or underutilized chest voice. A common example is the *leggiero* tenor with a light, "fluty" voice. This voice has little chest resonance naturally, and it should be built with the same patience and care as the soprano. Greater depth and color of tone will result. Young baritones are often weak in the chest voice. This can sometimes lead to confusion related to voice classification. There are many hard to define young male voices that are wrongly trained as tenors, because there is no low voice and no depth in the tone. There is also no high voice, but the lack of color suggests that is cannot be a baritone. After years of study, the top never comes in and there is no next step available to him. Even if the voice is trained as a baritone, the voice remains feeble and unsatisfactory. Building the chest voice often will provide the evidence that we need to assign the best literature for this voice and in the right keys.

Integrating the Chest Voice

As the chest voice develops, integrating these new sounds into the rest of the mechanism is the critical challenge. The process of coordinating the chest and the lighter mechanism doesn't have to wait until some predefined goal for the isolated chest register is met. One of the methods for uniting the chest register and the lighter mechanism is register breaking, or singing sustained tones and intervals while "switching" or alternating the register. For the female voice, Garcia suggests singing each note between D_4 and F_4 first in chest and then changing to the lighter mechanism while sustaining the vowel. In Example 1 the singer begins in chest voice and then lets the voice break into falsetto or lighter mechanism without cessation of tone, and then back into chest voice. The frequency of this transition increases through the end of the exercise. This very likely will result in a register break. Garcia insists that the yodel is not to be avoided at first but is to be encouraged. Upon the next repetition the first pitch is to be sung in the lighter mechanism and then switched into the chest voice.[23] Additional exercises of this type include intervals up to a minor third, all the while shifting registers on the interval and with a very audible register break.

Example 5. Chest voice building exercise from Garcia's *Complete Treatise on the Art of Singing*. The singer is to alternate registers while sustaining the pitch, producing an audible register break.

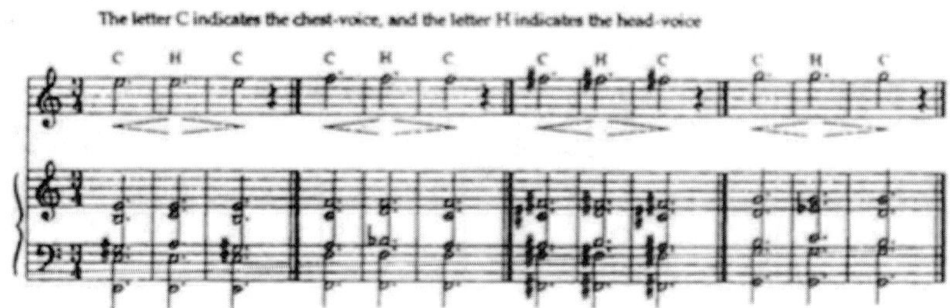

Example 6. From Bassini's *Art of Singing*. An exercise showing "register shifting" as a method of strengthening the chest voice. The pitches are repeated while alternating the register.

Example 7. From Lablache's *Complete Method of Singing*. An example of register shifting for the male voice.

Carlo Bassini's method *Art of Singing* follows a similar course. The very beginning exercises are those involving register shifting or breaking. Example 2 is very similar to Garcia's exercise in that the register is switched upon repetition of the pitch.[24] Bassini gives this work even more emphasis than Garcia in that he has several pages of exercises where he clearly marks above each note the register in which they are to be sung. Lest the male voice be forgotten, Example 3 is from Lablache's *Complete Method of Singing*.[25] Similar patterns of register shifting for the male voice are utilized throughout this work and that of Bassini, here involving the chest and head voice. Examples of register breaking from chest to falsetto in the male voice are also common. This register breaking is commonly found in pedagogy sources in one form or another in the middle to late nineteenth century but seems to be relatively uncommon in the twentieth and twenty-first centuries.

Other types of exercises dealing specifically with the chest voice are those that involve melodic or arpeggiated patterns where the register choice is varied. Bassini offers an exercise in which a series of ascending and descending tones are sung while varying the register choice (Example 4).[26] There are many examples of this type of study in methods both old and new.

Richard Miller suggests a similar series of exercises in which descending scales and arpeggios are sung with different register choices on each repetition. Example 5 illustrates a descending arpeggio 5-3-1 at F_4-D_4-B_3^b that is to be sung the first time with the pitches 5 and 3 in head and 1 in chest, the next time with pitch 5 in head and 3 and 1 in chest, and so on. Miller has several other similar examples in his book, *Structure of Singing*.[27] Exercises of this type are designed to strengthen the chest register and to help the singer develop a conscious and deliberate control of register choice.

Example 8. From Bassini's *Art of Singing*. Arpeggiated exercises designed to train the student's control over register choice.

(1) SING PITCHES 5 AND 3 IN *HEAD*, 1 IN *CHEST MIXTURE*. (2) SING PITCH 5 IN *HEAD*, 3 AND 1 IN *CHEST MIXTURE*. (3) SING PITCHES 5 AND 3 IN *HEAD*, 1 IN *CHEST MIXTURE*. (4) SING PITCHES 5, 3, AND 1 IN *HEAD*.

Example 9. From Miller's *Structure of Singing*. A modern example of register control designed to strengthen the chest voice.

Example 10. From Vennard's *Singing: The Mechanism and the Technic*. A wonderful example of a register coordination exercise. The combination of pitch and intensity help develop mastery of the relationship between the lower and higher mechanism.

The next step in this process is to begin to coordinate the activity of the vocalis and cricothyroid muscles so that the transition points begin to disappear; after all, the goal is to have a seamless, even scale from low to high. This level of coordination should not be undertaken too early in the process, only after the chest voice has developed a certain strength and presence throughout the range of the mechanism.

The premier exercise at this stage is the *messa di voce*. It has been the "gold standard" for hundreds of years for accomplishing this goal of even scale. Historically it has been used both as a vocal embellishment and as a pedagogical tool. As a means of coordinating the registers, it begins softly in the lighter mechanism, crescendos to full voice, and decrescendos to the lighter mechanism, all without an audible break. The involvement of the vocalis muscle is plainly seen in the EMG records by Hirano in Figure 5.[28] This is a swell tone on C_4 performed by a bass singer. He begins the exercise in a light head quality voice, increases intensity into a chest quality and back into head voice. The vocalis muscle can be seen to increase its activity as the intensity increases (as can be appreciated from the amplitude of the microphone record marked "audio"). It is important to recognize the increased vocalis activity as the source for the crescendo, not a result of it. Air flow and support issues also are involved with this coordinative process, but the registrational aspect of the exercise has been largely ignored in the twentieth century and should be considered when coordinating the chest voice and the lighter mechanism.

Other methods of coordination are of interest. The exercise in Example 6 is found in Vennard's, *Singing: the Mechanism and the Technic*.[29] The *messa di voce* in this pattern is significant in that as the singer descends into the range of the chest voice, the increasing intensity encourages the lover mechanism to participate. The singer then decreases intensity into the lighter mechanism as he or she ascends the scale and then invites an appropriate level of participation of chest voice during the crescendo on the penultimate note with the *fermata*. Example 7, from the same source, is also an excellent means of gradually engaging the chest mechanism and then tapering its activity for the octave ascent as the singer performs the dcrescendo.[30] The crescendo on the descending scale-wise passage will encourage the chest voice to speak.

It is important to remember that the chest mechanism responds to pitch, intensity, and vowel. Almost any pattern can be used to accomplish the coordination of chest voice with the lighter mechanism, if this is kept in mind. Example 8 can be used to engage the full chest voice and then to let it go gradually as the pitch ascends, lest the weight be taken up too high. The singer is firmly in chest voice at the beginning and in a lighter mechanism at the end. (All of the exercises shown should be freely transposed for the appropriate gender and voice type; they would also be used according to the needs of the particular voice.) Example 9 is used to engage the chest voice gradually as the pitch descends. During the exercise, the activity of the vocalis muscle would increase gradually as if it were an overhead light on a rheostat. Example 10 is a bit aggressive and should be done with care. The pitch range selected is very important here. For the female voice, the teacher would want to select a range that would be above the ability of the singer to carry the full chest to the top. The beginning point of A_3 would work for most women; A_4 is higher than most women can take the full chest voice. The octave leap is to be done with an energetic, legato connection. The tones are not to be separated, that is, not with a new attack at the top. The vowel should remain constant, and the throat should remain open. If the vowel space (shape of the vocal tract) is allowed to change on the top pitch, it will turn into a yell or a belt-like quality and is likely to be too heavy. This exercise can be very helpful as a first step in bringing a contribution of the chest voice higher than its isolated range. This can be very helpful in filling the "hole" that many female singers have in their middle range.

Example 11. This exercise, from Vennard's *Singing: the Mechanism and the Technic,* can be used to coordinate the registers.

Example 12. An exercise designed to train the vocalis muscle to gradually decrease its activity as the voice ascends.

Example 13. An exercise designed to train the vocalis muscle to gradually increase its activity as the voice descends.

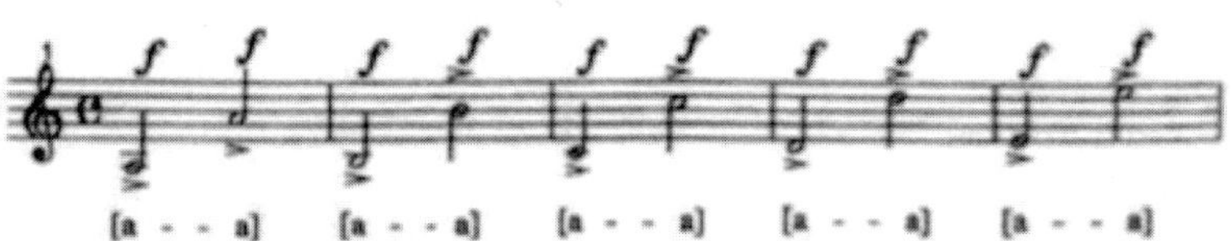

Example 14. This exercise is used to encourage the vocalis muscle to participate in the middle voice, outside of the range of the isolated chest mechanism.

Example 15. The ascending arpeggio marked *forte* is a difficult, advanced maneuver, because the muscular balance between the vocalis and the cricothyroid muscles must be very sophisticated as the top note maintains the influence of the lower mechanism but is not dominated by it.

Finally, Example 11 is designed to add some sophistication to what is begun in Example 10. There should be a register transition that is accomplished smoothly from the bottom to the top with a coordinated, full tone on the upper octave.

The operatic and art song literature is full of melodic examples that have similar shapes and those presented and can be very effectively used in lieu of any of the simple patterns presented. Familiarity with functional lessons from the past and present can open up a greater depth of expression that is available to the singer, as the voice is able to respond more freely to the meaning and emotion of the text and music.

CONCLUSION

There remains an intense prejudice against training the chest register, especially in the female voice. Perhaps it is simply as Garcia says:

> ...because one can approach the study of this register only with the help of profound knowledge, under the threat of ruining the student's voice, and because the blending of this register with that of the falsetto can be secured only by a long and ably directed labor. It has therefore been judged simpler and more natural to free oneself from the difficulty of studying it.[31]

The underlying principles as described in scientific reports and the pedagogical record can help guide the teacher through the difficulty that Garcia described. Voice teachers can choose to ignore chest voice, and many of our most gifted students will be successful anyway, but at least some pedagogical literature suggests that they would be depriving students of their full potential. Feeble voice quality is often accepted as an innate characteristic, and teachers are inclined to label voices as *leggiero* and assign them to the early music ensemble—not that anything is wrong with that! Recognizing limits as to what can be accomplished in any particular singer, it nevertheless is suggested that every voice would gain in body and size relative to the place where it begins.

Voice Science—"A Lamp to Guide Our Way"

Perhaps the most significant contribution of voice science to the art of voice teaching is that it offers a standard by which to evaluate pedagogical thought and practice. As one studies the science of voice production, some pedagogical principles seem to gain support while others are brought into question under the objective eye of scientific review. There are too many contradictory opinions contained in our pedagogical legacy written in the last 300 years for all to be right. Ultimately, of course, the value of any teaching method should be evaluated upon its effectiveness rather than its anatomical and physiological accuracy. However, some objective means of evaluation can be a valuable asset, especially when reviewing the wealth of information contained in our personal and academic libraries.

As the vocal mechanism is more completely understood, our thinking about the training process should be influenced accordingly. An analogous situation has occurred in the training of athletes during the last several decades. A greater knowledge of the mechanics of the human body has led to more effective training techniques. Human beings are running faster and jumping higher than could have been imagined only a few years ago. Like a coach-trained body of an athlete, the response of the vocal mechanism to the directives of a teacher will be defined by certain "rules of order" that are defined by the vocal mechanism and how it works—the physical laws involved. The results are therefore repeatable, predictable, and, for that reason, useful.

There are apparently two ways to acquire deep, rounded vocal folds: gift or training. Many singers are blessed with vocal folds that are ideal for singing. These are the *Wunderkinder* that grace our studios on occasion. Their voices are opulent and easily produced, even as youngsters. Clarity is in the tone from the outset. If they possess the musical talent and the desire to sing, they rise to the top rather easily.

Of course, it is also common for the chest voice to be too dominant in a singer. This condition creates its own problems and demands a different solution. It is likely that naturally large voices will have to subdue the chest voice, building the lighter mechanism and balancing it appropriately throughout the range. I believe that this explains the "top down" approach that helps many find ease, range extension, and flexibility. The work of Anthony Frisell[32] and Oren Brown[33] are among those whose methods focus more on bringing the unique qualities of the falsetto into the singing range.

A Personal Note

I have worked with many advanced, experienced singers who come to me with vocal issues standing in the way of further success. They typically over-support and ignore the relationship between their vocal problems and their vocal registers, often the underdeveloped chest register. When the chest voice is in this state of underdevelopment, singers tend to compensate for its absence. They attempt to make up for lack of depth and color in their tone by increasing adductory and expiratory forces. The result is often a voice that is inflexible, limited in range, and prone to fatigue. In my experience, an exercise regimen designed to strengthen the vocalis muscle and to train it to remain engaged appropriately throughout the range, while balancing the adductory forces and the expiratory drive, can improve the voice dramatically.

No pedagogical approach can focus only upon the chest voice and ignore the lighter mechanism and accomplish anything except the complete ruin of the voice. Every author cited in this review gives equal and sometimes more weight to the importance of the lighter mechanism—head voice, falsetto, high voice, whatever you want to call it. Most believe that the union of the chest and the lighter mechanism is the most important and difficult task of all.

To summarize, the goal for this review was to build a *passaggio* between what we know of the physiology of the chest voice and historical pedagogical practice associated with the chest register. A comprehensive pedagogical theory began with Garcia's definition of a register as having a mechanical source. Hirano's EMG evidence suggested that chest voice is defined by higher levels of activity in the vocalis muscle when compared to falsetto or head voice. Titze showed how increasing the bulge on the underside of the vocal folds can account for the unique, desirable qualities of the chest voice. Master voice teachers from the past three hundred years have suggested that much may be gained from building the chest voice and integrating its character into the whole range. When voice science confirms historical practice, it would appear worthy of consideration.

NOTES

1. This paper was presented in part to The First International Conference on the Physiology and Acoustics of Singing, Groningen, The Netherlands, October 5, 2002.
2. Manuel Garcia II, *Memoire on the Human Voice.* Found in *A Complete Treatise on the Art of Singing: Part One,* the editions of 1841 and 1872 collated, ed. and trans. Donald V. Paschke (New York: Da Capo Press, 1984), xli.
3. A thorough discussion of the various theories concerning vocal registers can be found in John Large, "Towards An Integrated Physiologic-Acoustic Theory of Vocal Registers," *The NATS Bulletin* 28, no. 3 (Feb/Mar 1972): 18-36.
4. Paul B. Oncley, "Dual Concept of Singing Registers," in *Vocal Registers in Singing: Proceedings of the Seventy-Eighth Meeting of the Acoustical Society of America Held in San Diego, California, 7 Novem-*

ber 1969 and Silver Jubilee Convention of the National Association of Singing Held in Cleveland, Ohio, 28 December 1969, ed. John W. Large (The Hague and Paris: Mouton, 1973), 35.

5. Minoru Hirano, William Vennard, and John Ohala, "Regulation of Register, Pitch and Intensity of Voice," *Folia Phoniatrica* 22 (1970): 1-20.
6. Minoru Hirano, "Vocal Mechanisms in Singing: Laryngological and Phoniatric Aspects," *Journal of Voice* 2, no 1 (1988): 51-60.
7. Ibid., 57.
8. Ingo Titze, *Principles of Voice Production* (Englewood Cliffs, NJ: Prentice hall, 1994), 262.
9. Ibid., 261.
10. Ibid., 182.
11. R. Chan, Ingo Titze, and M. Titze, "Further Studies of Phonation Threshold in a Physical Model of the Vocal Fold Mucosa," *Journal of the Acoustic Society of America* 101, no. 6 (1997): 3722-3727.
12. Giambattista Mancini, *Practical Reflections on Figured Singing*, the editions of 1774 and 1777 compared, ed., and trans. by Edward V. Foreman (Minneapolis: Pro Musica Press, 1967), 20.
13. Ibid., 34.
14. Ibid., 35.
15. Garcia, 50.
16. William Vennard, *Developing Voices* (New York: Carl Fischer, 1973).
17. Among C. Reid's many books and articles *Bel Canto, Principles and Practices* (New York: The Joseph Patelson Music House, 1971) and *The Free Voice* (New York: The Joseph Patelson Music House 1984) are recommended.
18. Richard Miller, *The Structure of Singing* (New York: Schirmer Books, 1986) 136-137.
19. Cornelius Reid, *The Free Voice*, 94.
20. Garcia, 43.
21. Ibid.
22. Reid, *The Free Voice*, 136.
23. Garcia, 50.
24. Carlo Bassini, *Art of Singing* (New York: Oliver Ditson & Co., 1856), 21.
25. Luigi Lablache, *Complete Method of Singing* (Boston: Oliver Ditson and Sons, 1852), 6.
26. Bassini, 20.
27. Miller, 137-140.
28. Hirano, *Vocal Mechanisms*, 64.
29. William Vennard, *Singing: The Mechanism and the Technic* (New York: Carl Fischer, Inc., 1967), 214.
30. Ibid., 155.
31. Garcia, 50.
32. Anthony Frisell, *Training Tenor Voices* (Boston: B. Humphries, 1964).
33. Oren Brown, *Discover Your Voice* (San Diego, Ca.: Singular Publishing Group, Inc. 1996).

59. L'ultimo Canzone!

Originally published in the *Journal of Singing*, volume 73, no. 1, 2016

It must have been sometime in 2003 that I wrote journal editor Dick Sjoerdsma with an idea for a column. I told him that I had "discovered" some ancient wisdom in the writings of voice teachers from the past that I thought deserved to be brought to our attention. I sent him a proposal (a first draft) for his review. He liked the idea, and now I have been doing this for 12 years!

When I look back over the long list of articles that have appeared in that time, I am reminded of how much I have learned from this opportunity. I have reviewed scores of pedagogy books from the 18th, 19th, and 20th centuries and attempted to derive from them a common theme in the method of teaching singing used over those years—an historical method, if you will. With the discernment afforded by a knowledge of the voice and how it functions and of the acoustics of the vocal tract, one can separate the wheat from the chaff; there are a lot of "fringe" methods and outright whacky ideas in voice culture! But, it is possible to derive the essence of a progressive method of effective teaching that has been practiced. I find that this information is all but lost to contemporary teachers, including myself.

Many have said that there is no "lost art of bel canto," and I believe that to be true; the principles are there to be discovered and utilized. As I find it, the bel canto method consisted of a process of building a vocal mechanism that had the strength, flexibility, and endurance to be able to sing expressively the literature intended for the voice. In almost 60 articles, I have presented the details of that process derived from historical sources, including original quotes, long excerpts, and some extended materials that encompassed several articles.

This has been a rewarding effort. The main benefit for me is that it has made me a much more effective teacher. The perspective of a progressive method makes the process more predictable and successful. Manuel Garcia II has been my most significant teacher. From him I learned the importance of teaching sostenuto, portamento, legato, staccato, marcatto, and aspirato. I learned about the difference between the two primary timbres of the voice (dark and bright) and vowel quality. Garcia offered many examples of how and when to use them for expressive purposes. I learned how the vocal registers could be exercised and strengthened to improve the basic nature of the voice. I learned about expressive things: how to move the text around in the score to make it easier to sing, how to vary time in a phrase to make it your own (rubato, for which his father was so well known), and where and how to take a breath in a long phrase. I learned about the breadth of his influence in the thinking and teaching around the world during his time and since. When I read Garcia's own words and description of his coup de la glotte and applied it as he intended, it transformed my teaching! I discovered that everyone had misrepresented this important idea and equated it with the "well coordinated onset"; it is not the same thing. You certainly can learn a lot about teaching from reading a good book on the subject.

I am taking my first sabbatical leave next spring. I plan to put these ideas and processes together in a larger work—a book. (Isn't that what everyone does on a sabbatical?) The plan is for a progressive method book in the tradition of those published in the 19th century. With the Association's permission, I also plan to put these articles from "Provenance" into a collection. I am giddy at the idea of a semester away from administration and teaching to accomplish—or at least begin—these projects.

I love demonstrating these ideas to teachers and singers around this country and other parts of the world. I find that the application of "tried and true" methods can be instantly observed and appreciated even within the context of a short master class. The concept of "open throat" and of clean onset, correct posture, and all the rest can make a huge difference in how the voice is able to deliver the goods artistically.

So, it's been fun, and a real privilege, actually. I had two significant mentors in my student days, John Large and Ingo Titze. Both have been regular contributors to this journal. I always dreamed of doing so myself. I would have never predicted that my contribution would focus on what others have said, but I do not believe that my efforts could have been better placed. Too often we start from scratch when we begin to teach. I hope that the information that I have resurrected to our contemporary awareness will shorten the learning curve that we all go through as teachers of this beautiful art form.

I have appreciated the kind words that I have received from so many of you whom I have the privilege to know and meet in person as I travel around the country doing workshops and master classes. I look forward to continuing to share these ideas that I have harvested from the literature in person. There is plenty left on the vine for others to glean.

Stephen F. Austin

About the Author

Stephen F. Austin, MM, PhD is Professor of Voice and Vocal Pedagogy at the University of North Texas. He serves as the Chair of the Division of Vocal Studies in the College of Music. Dr. Austin is a singer, voice teacher, and a trained voice scientist, having earned his Ph.D. in voice science under the direction of Dr. Ingo Titze at the Department of Communication Sciences and Disorders at the University of Iowa.

He has published original scientific investigations on articulation and acoustics of the singing voice in *Journal of Voice* and has published articles on pedagogy, voice science, and historical pedagogy in the *Journal of Singing, Australian Voice, The Choral Journal,* and *Classical Singer*. He was creator of the popular column, "Provenance" in the *Journal of Singing* from 2004 until 2016.

Dr. Austin is a popular lecturer and has given presentations and master classes around the world. Dr. Austin serves on the Editorial Board of the *Journal of Singing*. He is a successful studio teacher with current and former students singing throughout the United States and in Europe. He has mentored graduate students who hold university faculty appointments around the country and Australia. Dr. Austin conducts **The Vocal Pedagogy Workshop** around the country and every summer on the campus of the University of North Texas where he teaches the practical application of important scientific concepts and pedagogical tenets of the historical Italian School of singing.